Lecture Notes in Computer Science 4823

Commenced Publication in 1973
Founding and Former Series Editors:
Gerhard Goos, Juris Hartmanis, and Jan van Leeuwen

Howard Leung   Frederick Li   Rynson Lau
Qing Li (Eds.)

Advances in Web Based Learning – ICWL 2007

6th International Conference
Edinburgh, UK, August 15-17, 2007
Revised Papers

Springer

Volume Editors

Howard Leung
Qing Li
City University of Hong Kong
Department of Computer Science
83 Tat Chee Avenue, Kowloon Tong, Hong Kong, China
E-mail: {howard, itqli}@cityu.edu.hk

Frederick Li
Rynson Lau
University of Durham
Department of Computer Science
South Road, Durham DH1 3LE, UK
E-mail: {frederick.li, rynson.lau}@durham.ac.uk

Library of Congress Control Number: 2008923856

CR Subject Classification (1998): H.4, H.3, I.2.6, H.5, K.3, D.2, I.2

LNCS Sublibrary: SL 3 – Information Systems and Application, incl. Internet/Web
and HCI

ISSN   0302-9743
ISBN-10   3-540-78138-2 Springer Berlin Heidelberg New York
ISBN-13   978-3-540-78138-7 Springer Berlin Heidelberg New York

Springer is a part of Springer Science+Business Media

springer.com

© Springer-Verlag Berlin Heidelberg 2008
Printed in Germany

Typesetting: Camera-ready by author, data conversion by Scientific Publishing Services, Chennai, India
Printed on acid-free paper   SPIN: 12227808   06/3180   5 4 3 2 1 0

Preface

This year, we received a record high of about 180 submissions to ICWL 2007. From these, a total of 55 full papers plus one keynote paper were accepted for this LNCS proceedings volume, representing an acceptance rate of about 30%. The authors of these accepted papers were of a remarkable international diversity. We would like to thank all the reviewers for spending their precious time reviewing the papers and for providing valuable comments that aided significantly in the paper selection process. Authors of the best papers presented at this conference will be invited to submit extended versions of their papers for possible publication in 1) a special issue of *IEEE Trans. on Knowledge and Data Engineering*, for those papers relevant to knowledge and data engineering; and 2) a special issue of the *International Journal of Distance Education Technologies (JDET)*, for papers of other areas.

This was the first time that the ICWL conference was organized in Europe and 27 papers were from European researchers. We would like to thank our Organization Chair Dr. Taku Komura for spending an enormous amount of energy in coordinating the local arrangements. In fact, we would like to thank the entire conference organization committee for their hard work in putting together the conference. In particular, we would like to express our appreciation to our Registration Chair Dr. Jiying (Jean) Wang for her tremendous efforts in communicating with the authors regarding registration matters and keeping the registration and accommodation booking lists up-to-date. Our Workshop Co-chairs, Dr. Joseph Fong and Dr. Philips Wang, organized a Workshop on Blended Learning (WBL 2007), which was co-located with ICWL 2007. At this workshop, participants could share their ideas and experiences on supplementing e-learning with classroom learning.

We would also like to thank Prof. Nadia Magnenat-Thalmann, Prof. Myunghee Ju Kang and Prof. Won Kim for delivering keynote speeches and sharing their insightful views on web-based learning research issues. Finally, we would like to thank all the authors of the submitted papers, whether accepted or not, for their contribution to the high quality of this conference. We count on your continued support of the web-based learning community in the future.

December 2007

Howard Leung
Frederick Li
Rynson Lau
Qing Li

Organization

Organizing Committee

Conference Co-chairs	Rynson Lau, University of Durham, UK
	Qing Li, City University of Hong Kong
Program Co-chairs	Frederick Li, University of Durham, UK
	Howard Leung, City University of Hong Kong
Organization Chair	Taku Komura, University of Edinburgh, UK
Registration Chair	Jiying Wang, City University of Hong Kong
Tutorial Chair	Ling Feng, Tsinghua University, China
Poster Chair	Gary Tam, University of Durham, UK
Workshop Co-chairs	Joseph Fong, City University of Hong Kong
	Philips Wang, City University of Hong Kong
Publicity Co-chairs	Ling Feng, Tsinghua University, China
	Andrew Hatch, University of Durham, UK
	Gilliean Lee, Lander University, USA
	Marc Spaniol, RWTH Aachen University, Germany
Activity Co-chairs	Ming Cheung, City University of Hong Kong
	Philips Wang, City University of Hong Kong
Fund Raising Chair	Ioannis Ivrissimtzis, University of Durham, UK

Steering Committee

Chair	Qing Li, Hong Kong Web Society, Hong Kong
Members	Shi-Kuo Chang, University of Pittsburgh, USA
	Joseph Fong, Hong Kong Web Society, Hong Kong
	Horace Ip, City University of Hong Kong
	Rynson W.H. Lau, University of Durham, UK
	Xiaoming Li, Peking University, China
	Maria Orlowska, The University of Queensland, Australia
	Yuanchun Shi, Tsinghua University, China
	Timothy Shih, Tamkang University, Taiwan

International Program Committee

Howard Beck, University of Florida, USA
Stephane Bressan, National University of Singapore, Singapore
Liz Burd, University of Durham, UK
Shermann S. M. Chan, Florida International University, USA
Grainne Conole, The Open University, UK
Giuliana Dettori, ITD-CNR, Italy

Guozhu Dong, Wright State University, USA
Ling Feng, Tsinghua University, China
Baltasar Fernández-Manjón, Universidad Complutense de Madrid, Spain
Apple Fok, City University of Hong Kong, HK, China
Joseph Fong, City University of Hong Kong, HK, China
Andrzej Goscinski, Deakin University, Australia
Maria Grazia Ierardi, IMATI-CNR, Italy
Qun Jin, Waseda University, Japan
Myung Hee Kang, Ewha Women's University, Korea
Taku Komura, University of Edinburgh, UK
Rynson Lau, University of Durham, UK
Dik Lee, Hong Kong University of Science and Technology, HK, China
Gilliean Lee, Lander University, USA
Hong Va Leong, The Hong Kong Polytechnic University, HK, China
Clement Leung, Victoria University of Technology, Australia
Howard Leung, City University of Hong Kong, HK, China
Frederick Li, University of Durham, UK
Keqin Li, State University of New York at New Paltz, USA
Minglu Li, Shanghai Jiao Tong University, China
Qing Li, City University of Hong Kong, HK, China
Wenyin Liu, City University of Hong Kong, HK, China
Xiaofeng Meng, Renming University, China
John Murnane, Melbourne University, Australia
Chong Wah Ngo, City University of Hong Kong, HK, China
Sunsook Noh, Ewha Women's University, Korea
Philippos Pouyioutas, Intercollege, Cyprus
Geoff Romeo, Monash University, Australia
David Rossiter, Hong Kong University of Science and Technology, HK, China
Yuanchun Shi, Tsinghua University, China
Timothy Shih, Tamkang University, Taiwan, China
Marc Spaniol, Lehrstuhl Informatik 5, RWTH Aachen University, Germany
Chengzheng Sun, Nanyang Technological University, Singapore
Guoren Wang, Northeastern University, China
Hua Wang, University of Southern Queensland, Australia
Philips Wang, City University of Hong Kong, HK, China
Limin Xiang, Kyusan University, Japan
Simon Yip, Chinese University of Hong Kong, HK, China
Cha Zhang, Microsoft Research, USA
Kang Zhang, University of Texas at Dallas, USA
Si Qing Zheng, University of Texas at Dallas, USA

Table of Contents

Keynote

Personalized E-Learning

Learning Resource Organization and Management

Framework and Standards for E-Learning

Test Authoring, Question Generation and Assessment

Language Learning

Science Education

Visualization Technologies for Content Delivery and Learning Behavior

Practice and Experience Sharing

Security, Privacy and Mobile E-Learning

Blended Learning

Learning How to Dance Using a Web 3D Platform

Nadia Magnenat-Thalmann[1], Dimitrios Protopsaltou[1], and Evangelia Kavakli[2]

[1] MIRALab, University of Geneva
[2] CILab, University of the Aegean
{thalmann, protopsaltou}@miralab.unige.ch, kavakli@ct.aegean.gr

Abstract. In this paper we present the European project Open Dance and in particular our contribution to the 3D simulation of folk dances and their presentation on the web. Our aim is to provide a learning framework for folk dances. First we describe the conceptual and learning model that we apply, focusing on the requirements of dance education. Then we digitize folk dances, originating from several regions of Europe, using as a recording device an optical motion capture system. We allow dance teachers and students to use our web3D platform and interact with the animated dancers, aiming to the better understanding of dances. Students interact with the platform and observe how the virtual dance teachers perform. The evaluation of the system shows that the increased usability of our approach enhances the learning process. Our long term objective is to create an online dance learning community and allow dance teachers to create their own dance lessons online.

Keywords: Web3D, dance, motion capture, online learning.

1 Introduction

Dance has been characterised as an exciting and vibrant art that can be used in the educational setting to assist the growth of the student and to unify the physical, mental, and emotional aspects of the human being [1]. It is an art form characterised by the use of the human body as a vehicle of expression [2]. Others [3] suggest that dance is abstract in the sense that it is not an expression of an act but an expression of the feeling of an act. It is in this specific way that dance differs from creative dramatics and mime.

An educational dance programme is designed not only to give students experiences in expressive movement, but also to develop their ability to express themselves in movement. This is done through progressive experiences, which develop kinaesthetic and cognitive awareness of movement [3].

Dance education has experienced numerous changes in content and identity through its history [4]. Until recently dance was part of the physical education programme in many countries. It is now recognised as an art form comparable to music, drama, and visual arts and equally worthy of study. However, it is true that of all the art forms, dance receives the least attention.

It is interesting to note that the dance event constitutes part of our "intangible heritage" [5], because it, unlike other art forms, leaves few physical records behind. There

H. Leung et al. (Eds.): ICWL 2007, LNCS 4823, pp. 1–12, 2008.

are several limitations in the recording systems used by dance companies, organisations, folk clubs and bodies that perceive preservation of dances as part of their mission. For example, archival information in the form of documents and books offer rich information about dance as an agent of cultural meaning but fail to present the movement and stylistic aspects of dance genres. On the other hand, video addresses movement/audio aspects, but at the same time it lacks information about the wider context, meaning and cultural significance of the dance event recorded. Despite these limitations, video is currently the most efficient way of preserving dance of any kind. An example of systematic work in this direction is the LADD project [6] in the USA (LADD Dance Heritage Coalition). Furthermore, available information on the Web, relevant to dance, as part of the cultural education, is more or less unstructured (in the form of collections of HTML pages, PDF documents etc.). As such, it is hard to access and require additional processing before teachers and/or students can use it.

The objective of the Open-Dance project [7],[8] is the development of a web based platform that bypasses these problems and offers a structured set of learning tools based on a goal-driven learning framework. In the next section we review previous work that analysed the application of interactive technologies to dance. Following that, we describe the learning context that we adapt in our approach. We focus the main discussion on the description of our dance digitization pipeline using an optical motion capture system. The last part describes the web-based 3D visualization module and we give results from user evaluation sessions. For the sake of clarity, in the context of this paper as well as in the Open-Dance project we use the term "traditional dance" instead of "folk" as defined in [9] i.e. *"Dances that have evolved spontaneously from everyday activities and are informally passed from one generation to another"*.

2 Previous Work

Previous work [9] presented the progression of teaching or learning dance over the Internet. In [10] the authors suggested that in order to learn or teach dance over the Internet, there are several components that are required to makeup the entire system. In general such system involves the use of Networked Virtual Environment (NVE) systems. The required components consist of i) a platform or Virtual Environment that is required in order to represent an area to teach in ii) realistic looking virtual humans that are required in order for the real participants to be represented correctly in the virtual world and iii) a network, to link together the teacher and the students, and also a tracking system to accurately track the limbs of all participants.

The Cyber Dance [11] performance was the first real attempt for interactive dance using such a NVE System. This performance was shown many times and involved the interaction between many real and virtual humans. It was performed as a combination of real-time and autonomous virtual humans. VLNET [12] was the Virtual Environment System that was used. The performance was based on a dance sequence where Virtual Humans (Fig. 1) interacted with the real humans on stage. Obviously due to the complexity of having multiple Virtual and Real Humans it was not possible to track all the real dancers on the stage. The actual scenario involved a choreographed dance sequence from real dancers (Fig. 2).

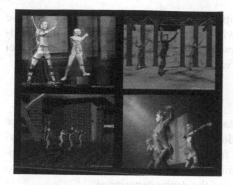 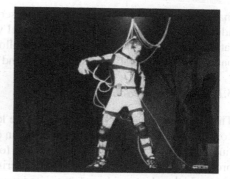

Fig. 1. Virtual humans interacting with real   **Fig. 2.** Real dancer on stage

Similarly [13] explored a variety of interfaces between the physical and virtual worlds. While taking the theme of "dance" and technology as a starting point, they supported a wider range of conceptions of the physical body or bodies. The focus was on the virtual space as a networked space that can function as a performance space, a shared, creative, social and playful space. Through exploring interference and mapping processes, the participants worked towards realising the transformative possibilities inherent in emerging technologies. Pfinder [14] is a real-time computer vision program, (i.e. "person finder"), a system for body tracking and interpretation of movement of a single performer. The model-building process is driven by the distribution of colour on the person's body, with blobs being added to account for each differently coloured region. DanceSpace was an interactive stage that took full advantage of Pfinder's ability to track the dancer's motion in real time. Finally on the commercial side, it is worth to mention Danceforms [15], 3D software devoted entirely on realistic character animation. The stand-alone animation tool offers an easy solution for motion capture editing or custom motion generation.

3 Traditional Dance Context

As we mentioned earlier the Open-Dance project aims to promote the use of interactive technologies in dance education and in particular (a) the use of interactive multimedia technologies (e.g., video, 2D and 3D graphics, interactive images and text) for representing information about traditional dances and (b) the use of the Internet as the learning medium.

From a methodological perspective, the design and development of the Open-Dance Learning Environment for assisting traditional dance education requires: (a) to identify the abstract concepts that define traditional dance together with the appropriate hypermedia forms for describing/visualizing each concept; (b) to organize the content and develop the teaching curriculum; (c) to design the structure and interactivity of the learning environment; (d) to implement the user interface; (e) to proceed in content production; (f) to develop E-Learning modules; (g) to incorporate the separate modules in the Open-Dance E-Learning environment and (h) to produce the accompanying material with explicit instructions for the users. In the following section we mainly focus our discussion in the description of the conceptual model that we adopted for traditional dances. This model will be our basis for the optimal documentation (recording) of the dance events. Following that, we describe the learning model based on that we evaluate our approach and validate our results.

3.1 Conceptual Model

The conceptual model of the Open-Dance learning environment is based on the dance conceptualization framework that has been developed within the Open-Dance Consortium [7]. This was motivated by the need to face the concept of dance in a holistic approach without following the usual discrimination between movement and context [16], which only provides a fragmented view of the dance experience.

In particular, the dance conceptual model consists of three types of dance concepts: concepts that focus either on the movement components of the dance, or the dance's context or both. We refer to these three categories as: Dance Activity, Dance Tradition and Dance Event, respectively. Each of these three categories is further divided into a number of sub-concepts and characterizes the entity of a Dance.

This conceptual model has been integrated in the Open-Dance Curriculum and the Learning Environment. Each sub-concept of the dance conceptual model forms a dance lesson in the Open-Dance curriculum, e.g. the subchapter of Dance Event consists of the following lessons for the music, the costumes and the roles of participants [16]. This relation of dance concepts and dance lessons is shown in Fig. 3.

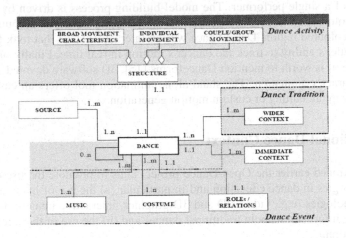

Fig. 3. Open-Dance Conceptual model

3.2 Learning Model

The Open-Dance learning model describes the educational philosophy adopted within the project and emphasises the need to identify the most appropriate uses of technology to support the overall learning experience. It is based on a three-stage process with the following steps (Fig. 4): i) the learners are asked to appreciate the new concepts they have to learn ii) specific activities drive them to fit new knowledge to their previous experience and knowledge (construction) and iii) extended activities allow them to reflect on the new concepts and issues [17]. Vital to this model are two learning approaches. The first approach is the goal–based approach [18] whereby the learning process is driven by the goal the learner aims to achieve (e.g., to present a certain dance in the school journal); this goal directs the learner's activities serving as a motivator for learning. The second is the learning-by-doing approach that focuses on acting rather than memorising facts and concepts. This is achieved by incorporating interactive components in the form of questions and answers, quizzes, and the use of extended activities.

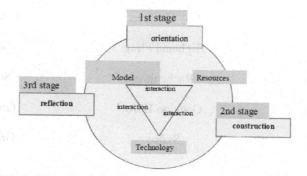

Fig. 4. Learning model

4 Dance 3D Digitisation

For the digitization of the dances we applied motion capture in order to recreate dances in three dimensions and represent them online in a 3D environment. We organized a dance recording session at MIRALab in the University of Geneva where we invited various dance groups from Greece, UK and Bulgaria. In the table below (Table 1) we provide the list of dances that we recorded, listing their particular performance characteristics in terms of interaction.

4.1 Motion Capture

Capturing motion is a long and difficult process, which requires a lot of heavy equipment and sophisticated software. There exists a plethora of technologies that enable one to record a motion. Among these, two classes of systems are more widespread than the others. The first one is optic based. An array of cameras (at least two and up to more than 20) can capture the trajectory of markers that are placed on the various locations that one wants to record (see Fig. 5). The cameras are calibrated so that their position in space and their internal configuration (focal length) are known in advance. Applying geometrical computation the system calculates the location of the markers with a fairly good accuracy (below one millimeter, depending on the quality of the calibration) and a high frame rate (up to 1 KHz).

Table 1. Motion capture session

Country	Dance Name	Description
UK	Landlord fill the flowing bowl	Set of six
UK	Shepherd's Hey	Pair clapping
UK	Pat-A-Cake	Couple dance
UK	Gay Gordons	Couple dance
UK	Highland Fling	Solo dance
Bulgaria	Rachenitza	Solo dance
Bulgaria	Gankino Horo	Group dance
Greece	Syrtos	Group dance

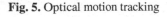

Fig. 5. Optical motion tracking   **Fig. 6.** Magnetic motion tracking

The second class of system is magnetic. A box emits an intense magnetic field which is analyzed by sensors attached to the body to track thus providing the position and orientation of each sensor (Fig. 6). Such system is more used for real-time applications due to its quick setup capabilities (no calibration is required for instance) and its transportability. The drawbacks, however, are a poor accuracy (around a centimetre), a small range of action (you mustn't get too far nor too close from the emitter), a huge sensitiveness to the surrounding environment (no metal allowed around the capture zone) and a lower frame rate (less than 200 Hz). Once the data was acquired, it presents itself under the form of a collection of trajectories of either points or rigid bodies.

In the context of Open-Dance we applied optical motion tracking using the VICON [19] system. We use trackers, strategically placed on each body. To calibrate the system, each body is calibrated before any motion is recorded. Due to the system performance, recording two bodies simultaneously is a difficult process if the dancers are close to each other. In this situation, the precision of our VICON system is not accurate enough and the workstation confuses some markers. To manage this kind of problem we made each couple dance three times. First, each dancer was recorded performing alone. Then we recorded the couples (Fig 7).

Fig. 7. Motion capture of couples dance

Needless to say that such data is quite useless if not linked to an object to animate (a body) and cleaned from all the artefacts that always occur during a capture session (occlusion of optical markers, perturbation of the magnetic field). The process of cleaning up the data is called post-processing.

4.1.1 Post-processing
There exists some powerful pieces of software for post-processing the data that use a lot of data estimation and smoothing techniques from the simplest one (e.g. linear interpolation) to the more complex (e.g. Vicon IQ uses a skeleton calibrated on the subject and error minimization for estimating it's pose at every frame and therefore the location of the markers), plus many others (Kalman filtering, a-priori knowledge about rigid bodies, spline interpolation and of course hand work).

4.1.2 Retargeting
Quite a lot of research has been conducted on the issue of motion retargeting (i.e. apply one motion to various skeletons) but so far it didn't achieve to be integrated into production software. Constraints based approaches aim at obtaining a visually plausible motion when the target model doesn't quite match the captured data. It formulates the problem of retargeting more or less as follows: the captured motion is the starting point for satisfying a set of constraints to be enforced (e.g. always at least one foot on the floor, no foot skating,) and the data is then optimized for satisfying the constraints while minimizing the change in the motion. However, this approach correct only what it is asked

for: if, say, the captured character was walking on a flat area and the animated one is walking uphill, then the final animation will dangerously bend downward, but the character will not fall. Further adaptation has to be done when such a case occurs, and Physics based approaches tend to address this issue. Physics based methods also aim at satisfying constraints without changing too much the original animation, but this time the constraints that are enforced are physical ones (ensure the right balance of the character,) either by non-linear optimization or more fancy methods like close-form [20].

Other problems may arise during the retargeting process. For instance parts of the body sometimes self-penetrate with others parts when the motion is mapped on another character [21] (this range of cases arise when e.g. the person that was captured was quite skinny, and the animated character is fat) or the recorded motion doesn't fit into the surrounding virtual environment. These issues are often edited by hand due to the large number of solutions that are available for one single case (e.g. when the hand of an animated virtual character penetrate the wall of a virtual house, how should he avoid that e.g. by bending his elbow or wrist, by moving himself etc.), and the research often focused on finding ways to make the editing by hand more easy [22] rather than doing it automatically.

4.1.3 Post processing in Open-Dance

The post-processing of motion sequences primarily involves the following two stages: trajectory reconstruction and labelling of markers/trajectories. Once those two steps have been completed, it is possible to visualize the technical skeleton (Fig. 8) obtained by drawing segments between the marker positions. From this information the subject skeleton and its animation are derived.

Fig. 8. Technical skeleton

It is relatively easy to construct the subject skeleton (or its approximation) from the markers. However, the problem becomes much more complex when considering the body meshes and its deformation parameters (Fig. 9). Skin deformation (or skinning) is based on three inter dependant ingredients. First the skeleton topology and geometry, second the mesh or surface of the body, and third the deformation's own parameters (very often consisting of vertex-level ratios describing the scope of deformation with relation to joints). Good skinning results are achieved by a careful design of these three components, where positions of joints inside the body surface envelope and attachments ratios are very important issues.

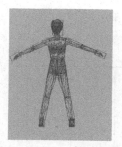

Fig. 9. Skeleton attachment

4.1.4 Music Synchronization

One of the main issues in this approach is to identify key frames where the element of time is evident in the performance of the dancer. (e.g. position of feet). The synchronization of frames generated from the dancer's motion with respect to the music frame, in such a way that it enables comparison, adds the element of rhythm in dance learning. Synchronizing the recording of the music with the motion sequence is a challenging and crucial task, especially for the evaluation the dance learning experience. A manual technique involving the dancers to indicate the starting frame of the audio and of the motion sequence can be used, which may later be evolved into an automatic system.

4.2 Web 3D Environment

The final step is the development of the web3D viewer [23] that allows the observation and manipulation of the 3D dancer online. The 3D viewer was developed with Adobe Director 8.5 Shockwave Studio and integrates several functionalities (e.g., start, stop, Zoom in / Zoom out, Focus, Change camera position, etc.) through the Lingo API [24]. The user is able to watch a dancing model, choosing the point of view and the zoom level, and finally control the speed of the 3D animation (Fig. 9).

Fig. 10. Open-dance web3D viewer

5 Evaluation

In this section we discuss our evaluation results [25] based on the learning model that we introduced previously. In our evaluation group we included internal experts from

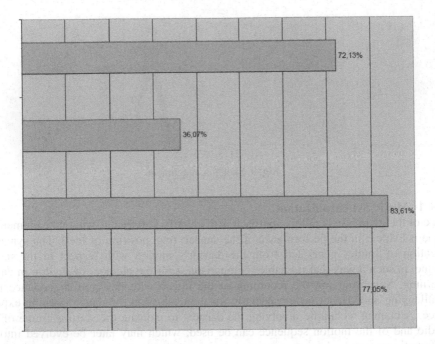

Fig. 11. Evaluation results of the 3D animation

the project's participating institutions, experts from the English Folk Dance & Song Society, teachers and students from the project's pilot schools and a high number of high school teachers and students as well as members of traditional dance related organizations. The evaluation criteria addressed the following aspects: (a) Quality of content (b) Presentation of content (c) Pedagogical quality (d) Use of the 3D animated dancer (interactivity and usability aspects). We provide an overview of the results (Fig. 11) obtained so far with relation to the 3D animated dances on the web.

The 3D animated dancer received very positive comments, regarding its effectiveness and usability. Most users found that it assisted them in learning the steps of the dance. They also made interesting suggestions regarding extra functionality they would like to be added. These included the ability to move the dancer in space; the ability to trace the dancer's movement; and the ability to use different costumes for different dances.

– Does the 3D animated figure look good? Do you find it enjoyable? Yes: 72.13%
– Are there any additional functions you would like to include in the 3D animation? Yes:36.07%
– Is it easy to use the 3D animated character? Yes: 83.61%
– Is the quality of the 3D animated character good? Yes: 77.05%

Open-Dance has shown that (a) the same conceptual model can be used to record different European traditional dances (b) web3D can be used to create dance resources for the web (c) there is a great interest from teachers in formal and informal educational settings that would like to use the Open-Dance platform and (d) there is a great interest from dance experts to use the platform in order to document traditional dances. Future projects will build upon the technological results and the experience gained through Open-Dance in order to (a) extend the usability of the web-learning environment (b) increase the teaching resources offered the (c) expand the number and type of users of the web platform. To this end, we are currently working on a new traditional dance E-Learning platform that will enable users to be part of an online community and create their own lessons.

Acknowledgements

The work presented in this paper has been supported by the Swiss State Secretariat for Education and Research (SER) Socrates-Minerva project (225471-CP-1-2005-1-GR-MIVERVA-M). The authors wish to acknowledge the Open Dance project partners for their collaboration. Special thanks are due to Etienne Lyard, Clementine Lo, Vincent Mugeot and Nedjma Cadi for their contribution in the motion capture session.

References

[1] Reston, V.A.: Dance Directions: 1990 and Beyond. National Dance Association (1988)
[2] Overby, L.Y.: Status of dance in education [Electronic version]. (Report No. EDO -SP-91-5). Washington, D.C. : Eric Clearinghouse on Teacher Education. (ERIC Document Reproduction Service No. ED348368) (1992)
[3] Siedentop, D., Herkowitz, J., Rink, J.: Elementary physical education methods. Prentice-Hall, Englewood Cliffs (1984)
[4] Bannon, F., Sanderson, P.: Experience every moment: aesthetically significant dance education. Research in Dance Education 1(1), 9–26 (2000)
[5] UNESCO: Recommendations on the Safeguarding of Traditional Culture and Folklore, adopted by the General Conference at its twenty fifth session, Paris, France (retrieved 10-04-01) (1989), http://www.unesco.org/culture/laws/paris/html_eng/page1.htm
[6] LADD Dance Heritage Coalition: LADD Project: Overview of LADD, http://www.danceheritage.org/ladd1.html
[7] Open-Dance (retrieved 15-06-2007), http://www.aegean.gr/culturaltec/opendance/
[8] Kavakli, E., Bakogianni, S. Damianakis, A., Loumou, M., Tsatsos, D.: Traditional Dance and E-Learning: The WebDance Learning Environment. In: Paper presented to the International Conference on Theory and Applications of Mathematics and Informatics, Thessaloniki, Greece (2004)
[9] Raftis, A.: Dance teaching, D.O.L.T, Athens (in Greek) (1993)
[10] Magnenat-Thalmann, N., Joslin, C.: Learning how to Dance on the Internet. In: Interface Conference, Hamburg (October 2000)
[11] Magnenat-Thalmann, N.: Cyberdance. In: Proc. of Virtuality and Interactivity, Firenze, Italia, pp. 72–73 (1999)
[12] Pandzic, I., Capin, T., Magnenat-Thalmann, N., Thalmann, D.: VLNET: A Body-Centered Networked Virtual Environment. Presence: Teleoperators and Virtual Environments 6(6), 676–686 (1997)
[13] Transdance (retrieved 15-06-2007), http://www.sdela.dds.nl/transdance/report/index.html

[14] Wren, C., Azarbayejani, A., Darrell, T., Pentland, A.: Pfinder: Real-time tracking of the human body. Photonics East, Bellingham, WA. SPIE 2615 (1995)

[15] DANCEFORMS (retrieved 15-06-2007), http://www.charactermotion.com/danceforms/

[16] Karkou, V., Sanderson, P.: Dance movement therapy (DMT) in the UK: issues of theory and assessment. The Arts in Psychotherapy 28, 197–204 (2001)

[17] Ferreira, M., MacKinnon, L., Demulliez, M., Foulk, P.: A multimedia Telematics Network for On-the-Job Training, Tutoring and Assessment. In: Conference proceedings ICEE 1998: International Conference on Engineering Education, Rio de Janeiro, Brazil (1998)

[18] Schank, R.C.: Goal-Based Scenarios (retrieved 15-06-2007) (1992), http://cogprints.org/624/00/V11ANSEK.html

[19] Vicon (retrieved 15-06-2007), http://www.vicon.com

[20] Shin, H.J., Kovar, L., Gleicher, M.: Physical Touch-Up of Human Motions. Pacific Graphics (2003)

[21] Jeong, K., Lee, S.: Motion adaptation with self-intersection avoidance. In: International Workshop on Human Modeling and Animation, Korea, pp. 77–85 (2000)

[22] Boulic, R., Le Callennec, B., Herren, M., Bay, H.: Experimenting Prioritized IK for Motion Editing. Eurographics (2003)

[23] Web3D viewer (retrieved 15-06-2007), http://www.vdu.lt/dancer/

[24] Adobe Director (retrieved 15-06-2007), http://www.adobe.com/support/director/

[25] Web-Dance Evaluation, Technical report, University of the Aegean (2005) (retrieved 15-06-2007), http://www.aegean.gr/culturaltec/webdance/reports/W5_UoA_01.pdf

Starting Directions for Personalized E-Learning

Won Kim

School of Information and Communication Engineering,
Sungkyunkwan University, Suwon, S. Korea
wonkim@skku.edu

Abstract. Personalized E-Learning is a research area with the grandiose goal of automatically or semi-automatically matching the learning contents with the needs and preferences of the learners. This paper proposes a modest goal of creating learning contents to help the learners engaged in self-paced E-Learning learn effectively at appropriate levels of difficulty and detail. It also proposes a goal of making it easier for the content creators to create new learning contents by reusing and adapting existing content fragments. More ambitious goals may be addressed by building on the results of these modest goals.

Keywords: Personalized E-Learning, self-paced E-Learning.

1 Introduction

E-Learning has become an important tool for augmenting the traditional classroom learning by making it possible for learners to learn something from anywhere at any time without having to be physically present in a classroom on a lecture schedule. It has been actively adopted by large corporations to train their employees and to inform their business partners and customers. It has also been adopted by cyber universities and, to a small extent thus far, by conventional universities. Although research on E-Learning is in its infancy, it has spawned a number of research areas with the view to making E-Learning more helpful to more learners. These include learning management, content creation and reuse, standardization, user interface, personalization, etc.

Personalized E-Learning has been a subject of research for the past several years [1-16]. Even some prototype personalized E-Learning systems have been developed [1][14][16]. The goal of personalized E-Learning includes automatically or semi-automatically identifying learning contents that match the needs and preferences of the learners. This requires obtaining, by some means, and managing learner profiles, and some means of matching the profiles with the learning contents. The goal of identifying learning contents in turn includes automatically or semi-automatically composing learning contents by reusing and adapting existing learning content fragments.

The goal of personalized E-Learning is grandiose indeed, as it requires a software-based system to perform what human instructors with domain expertise have done. There is a wide range of subjects (and levels and topics within the subjects) for learning, and there is also a wide range of needs, preferences, preparedness (in terms of knowledge of the topic) and circumstances for the learners. The goal of matching learning contents with the needs and preferences of the learners presumes the abundant existence

H. Leung et al. (Eds.): ICWL 2007, LNCS 4823, pp. 13–19, 2008.

of learning contents that satisfy a variety of needs and preferences of the learners from all walks of life. This is not a reasonable presumption. It also brushes aside the existence, and possible consequences, of various learning objectives. The related goal, sometimes mentioned, of creating new contents, semi-automatically, by reusing and adapting existing content fragments is no less grandiose. Today, one major challenge E-Learning faces is to significantly enhance its learning effectiveness in various situations, such as purely E-Learning-based courses in universities. It is unfortunate that without addressing such a serious challenge, the E-Learning research community just tries to move forward. In my view, if the academic research community is to deliver results that will have substantial near-term impact, it may be helpful for a segment of the community to establish and pursue much more feasible initial goals of personalized E-Learning.

I would like to propose, and address in this paper, two starting goals of research on personalized E-Learning. One is to help the learner achieve some degree of personalized learning, and also learn better. Another goal is to help the content creators create more effective learning contents, and create them more efficiently. Although there are different types of E-Learning, I will limit consideration to self-paced E-Learning. The discussions are applicable to other types of E-Learning (see [6]).

The remainder of this paper is organized as follows. In Section 2, I will outline how the first goal may be achieved. In Sections 3 and 4, I will discuss how the second goal may be achieved. I will conclude the paper in Section 5.

2   Making Self-paced E-Learning Personalized

An easy yet practical way to personalize learning contents is to provide links to additional contents. When the learner has studied a certain concept or topic, he may feel that the level of treatment may be too high (or low), and would like to study lessons that treat the same topic at a lower (or higher) level. Similarly, the learner may feel that, although the level of treatment is adequate, additional or different examples or illustrations would help clarify certain questions he may have. Further, the learner may feel that the exercises that come with the lesson may be too difficult (or easy), and would like to work with easier (or more difficult) exercises, or work with additional exercises. If there are desired additional contents (lessons, exercises), links may be provided to take the learner to such contents.

This is the most direct and sure way to make self E-Learning personal. Without contents at appropriate levels and details, it does not make sense to talk about "matching the contents to the needs and preferences of the learners".

Ultimately, if there are no lessons or exercises at desired levels, the learner has to find them on his own. In this case, the learner would find useful some facilities to organize the additional lessons or exercises he gathers, and fold them into the learning contents he is studying. It would be best if the additional lessons or exercises are treated as an integral part of the learning contents, such that such capabilities as topic indexing and future reuse, can be extended to them. Of course, the learner should be able to drop some of the learning contents from his view. These requirements will need to go into the design of a customizable learning framework. In my view, this is a major topic of research and development.

3 Creating Effective Contents for Self-paced E-Learning

In my view, there are two primary reasons learners have complained about the efficiency of E-Learning. One is the poorly designed and implemented contents. Content creators have not given sufficient consideration of how the contents would be accepted by the learners doing self-paced E-Learning without the in-person delivery of the contents by the instructor. Another reason for the low efficiency of E-Learning is the lack of learning-inducing stress for the students.

I will first summarize the objectives of creating contents for self-paced E-Learning as follows. These objectives will guide the selection of factors to consider when creating learning contents.

♦ Make it as easy as possible for the students to comprehend the lesson.
♦ Help the students to really learn.
♦ Anticipate and minimize potential confusion that will result in questions to the instructor or tutor that are not related to the concepts and applications of the concepts in the lesson.
♦ Minimize unusable course materials due to mismatch with the access capabilities of the learners. This means the computing power of the learners' PCs, operating system type and version, Web browser version, security setting, software tool, Internet access bandwidth, etc.

In the following subsections, I provide a list of considerations when creating the lesson part of the learning contents for self-paced E-Learning against each of the above four objectives.

3.1 Making It Easier to Comprehend

There are at least four major considerations that must go into the design of learning contents for easier comprehension.

♦ Sound structure. The entire lesson should be organized in a sound structure that will introduce elements of the lesson in logical grouping and progression.
♦ Stepwise progression. The entire lesson, and each part of the lesson, and each concept within each part, must be designed in logical and stepwise manner - from easy to difficult, and from simple to complex, from a single concept to a combination of concepts - so that the learners can gradually learn, without having to call on the instructor or tutor for clarification.
♦ Sufficient illustrations of key concepts. Each key concept and definition should be illustrated with appropriate examples and/or visual aids, such as figures, tables, images, graphs, etc. – again so that the learners can learn the lesson as much as possible on their own, without having to call on the instructor or tutor for help.

♦ Comfortable appearance. The learning contents should be comfortable to the students. A good layout, font styles and font sizes, colors, spacing, indentation, etc. should be selected. All visual aids and notations in them should be clearly legible. The uses of font styles and font sizes, spacing, indentation, upper case and lower case letters, acronyms, etc. should be consistent. Visual aids and the text that refers to them should be in close proximity.

3.2 Helping Students Learn Better

In traditional classroom learning, learners in general listen to lectures delivered by the instructor and ask questions. Learning does not stop there. The learners are given homework. To do the homework, the learners review what they learned in class, possibly study additional materials, try to apply what they learned, discuss with other learners, and even receive help from tutors. The learners also take exams; to do well, they again review what they learned in class. After the exams, they go over the problems they did not answer correctly. Homework comes with a deadline, and exams are given on specified dates and times. The following elements come into play to help the learners learn.

♦ Classroom lectures delivered by the instructor.
♦ Questions and answers with the instructor.
♦ Review and memorization of what is learned in class.
♦ Efforts to apply what is learned in class.
♦ The deadline pressure that forces focused thinking.
♦ The pressure to receive good grades.

If we are to significantly improve the learning efficiency of self-paced E-Learning, the learners should be made to review what they learn and should be given the same type of pressures that they receive from the classroom learning. I propose the following means.

➢ Lessons with a deadline. There may be a deadline associated with each part of the lesson. If the deadline passes, the learner may be prevented from proceeding to the next part, and instead a new deadline may be set for completing the part.
➢ Exercises with a deadline and a passing grade. There may be a deadline and a passing grade associated with the exercises at the end of each part of the lesson. If the deadline passes or the learner does not obtain the passing grade, the learner may be prevented from proceeding to the next part, and instead a new deadline may be set for rE-Learning and completing the part. If the learner does not obtain the passing grade, the learner may alternatively be forced to learn a lower-level lesson or more detailed lesson at the current level, and upon passing it, return to the current lesson.
➢ Testing with a time delay. In the classroom learning, the learners are not given exams at the end of every lecture. For example, in a university course, exams are typically given twice in a semester, after roughly about half of the course materials have been learned. During the period before each exam, the learners have time to digest, at their own pace, what they have learned and think about it from various perspectives. This process further solidifies what has been learned. It would be best to force a time delay between learning the lessons

and taking an exam. In other words, a learner should not be allowed to learn all the lessons in a very short period of time, and take the exam right away, while the undigested lessons are fresh in their memory.

➢ Designing the homework and exams. Homework and exam problems for self-paced E-Learning should be designed with the same care and consideration as for the classroom learning. The problems should test whether the learners understand the basic concepts, they are able to apply each of them, and they understand sufficiently to be able to apply some of them in combination. When designing exams, the content creators should take into account the "open book" nature of the E-Learning environment. Often, it is more appropriate to give closed-book exams than open-book exams.

3.3 Minimizing Confusion

There are a few important considerations prevent confusion on the part of the students when creating learning contents.

♦ Consistent terminology. Use of consistent terminology throughout the lesson would help avoid unnecessary confusion on the part of the learners. Further, it would make it easier for content creators to reuse content fragments.

♦ No undefined terms or acronyms in the text and the visual aids. This, too, would help avoid unnecessary confusion on the part of the learners. Further, it would make it easier for content creators to reuse content fragments.

♦ No ambiguous phrasing, typographical errors, misspelling, grammatical errors. This, too, would help avoid unnecessary confusion on the part of the learners. Further, it would make it easier for content creators to reuse content fragments.

3.4 Minimizing Unusable Learning Contents

There are a few considerations to prevent the creation of unusable learning contents.

♦ Taking into account the access capabilities of the learners. This would reduce the need for technical support for the learners, and also avoid making all or parts of the contents unusable to the learners.

♦ Use of standardized or interoperable content creation tools. This would make it easier for content creators to match the contents to the access capabilities of the learners, and also to derive new contents.

4 Making It Easier to Reuse Learning Contents

Once learning contents are created with considerations of personalization and learning efficiency for self-paced E-Learning, the remaining issue is how parts of the contents may be reused and adapted to derive new learning contents. Software-based facilities should be provided to allow the content creators to specify a group of content fragments as a unit of reuse. A group may ideally contain any combination of a lesson fragment, corresponding exercises, homework problems, and test problems. Verifying the "intra-consistency" of a group, however, is a difficult problem in general. For example, if a part of the original lesson is excluded from a group, corresponding exercise problems may need to be excluded also. Developing a guideline or automatic means of verifying the intra-consistency of a group of content fragments is a research issue, and initially it would be best to avoid such a problem when specifying a group.

Once a group of content fragments is selected for reuse and adaptation, the next step is to change the style (slide design, slide layout) and presentation details (e.g., font style, font size, color, indentation, etc.) of the content fragments in accordance with the layout and presentation details adopted for the new contents. Although such tools as Microsoft's PowerPoint offer some degree of automatic conversion, additional facilities are needed.

If the content creation tools support the automatic creation of a subject or keyword index, it should be extended to the group of content fragments brought into the new contents.

5 Concluding Remarks

The current goal of personalized E-Learning is too formidable, and this paper proposed two modest but significant starting points of research on personalized E-Learning. The context is self-paced E-Learning. One of the starting points of research this paper identified and addressed is how to design learning contents so that they can allow the learners to adjust to desired levels of difficulty and detail. In addressing this issue, it also addressed two accompanying issues: creating contents that take into account the circumstances of the learners, and increasing the efficiency of E-Learning by incorporating the learning-inducing stress that comes with the traditional classroom learning. A second starting point of research is to identify opportunities for making it easier to reuse and adapt existing content fragments when creating new learning contents.

There are some worthy research topics in pursuing the two starting points of research identified in this paper. One is the determination of a set of facilities that will make it as easy as possible for the content creators to fold a group of content fragments into new learning contents. It would include automatic verification of intra-consistency of the content fragments that form a unit of reuse. Another is to make such facilities as easy to use as possible.

Acknowledgments. This research was supported by the Korean Ministry of Information and Communication under the ITRC IITA-2006-(C1090-0603-0046) grant.

References

1. Banerjee, R.: An Innovative Methodology and Framework for Personalized E-Learning Using Conventional and Mobile Networking Technologies. In: Proceedings of the National Seminar on E-Learning and E-Learning Technologies: ELETECH-2001, pp. 1–4 (2001), http://www.cdac.in/HTML/pdf/Session6.2.pdf
2. Conlan, O., Dagger, D., Wade, V.: Towards a Standards-based Approach to E-Learning Personalization Using Reusable Learning Objects, E-Learn 2002. In: World Conference on E-Learning in Corporate, Government, Healthcare and Higher Education, Montreal (September 2002), https://www.cs.tcd.ie/Owen.Conlan/publications/eLearn2002_v1.24_Conlan.pdf

3. Dolog, P.: Knowledge Representation and Reasoning in Personalized Web-based E-Learning Applications, Znalosti 2006. Hradec Kralove. Czech Republic, Keynote speech (February 2006), http://www.cs.aau.dk/~dolog/pub/znalosti2006.pdf

4. Ilhami, G., Turker, A., Ozan, Y., Heller, J.: Learner Modeling to Facilitate Personalized E-Learning Experience. In: Kinshuk, D.G., Isaías, P.T. (eds.) CELDA 2005: Cognition and Exploratory Learning in Digital Age. International Association for Development of the Information Society (IADIS), pp. 231–237 (2005) http://wundt.unigraz.at/publicdocs/publications/file1170168718.pdf

5. Kim, W.: Directions for Web-Based Learning. In: Proceedings of the 5th International Conference on Web-Based Learning, Penang, Malaysia (July 2006)

6. Kim, W.: Towards a Definition and a Methodology for Blended Learning. In: Proceedings of the 1st International Workshop on Blended Learning, Edinburgh, Scotland (August 2007)

7. Kolas, L., Staupe, A.: A Personalized E-Learning Interface, http://www2.tisip.no/quis/public_files_final/PAPER-A-personalized-E-Learning-Interface.pdf

8. Li, X., Chang, S.-K.: A Personalized E-Learning System Based on User Profile Constructed Using Information Fusion. In: The Eleventh International Conference on Distributed Multimedia Systems (DMS 2005), Banff, Canada, September 5-7, 2005, pp. 109–114 (2005), http://www.cs.pitt.edu/~flying/File/DMS05-LC.pdf

9. Li, Y., Huang, R.: Dynamic Composition of Curriculum for Personalized E-Learning. In: Proceedings of the 14th International Conference on Computers in Education (ICCE2006), IOS Press, Amsterdam (2006), http://ksei.bnu.edu.cn/upload/paper/Dynamic%20composition%20of%20curriculum%20for%20personalized%20E-Learning.pdf

10. Mylonas, P., Karpouzis, K., Andreou, G., Kollias, S.: Towards an Integrated Personalized Interactive Video Environment. In: Proceedings of the 6th IEEE International Symposium on Multimedia Software Engineering, Miami, Florida, USA (December 2004)

11. Mylonas, P., Tzouveli, P., Kollias, S.: Intelligent Content Adaptation in the Framework of an Integrated E-Learning System. In: 16th ACM Conf. on Hypertext & Hypermedia - Workshop on Combining Intelligent & Adaptive Hypermedia Methods/Techniques in Web-Based Education Systems, Salzburg, Austria, 6-9/9/2005 (2005)

12. Otair, H., Al Hamad, A.: Expert Personalized E-Learning Recommender System, http://medforist.grenoble-em.com/Contenus/Conference%20Amman%20EBEL%2005/pdf/21.pdf

13. Rumetshofer, H., Woss, W.: Virtually Guided Personalized E-Learning. In: Pastor, Ó., Falcão e Cunha, J. (eds.) CAiSE 2005. LNCS, vol. 3520, Springer, Heidelberg (2005), http://www.faw.uni-linz.ac.at/PublicationFullText/2005caise/caise05_SWWL.pdf

14. Styliadis, A., Karamitsos, I., Zachariou, D.: Personalized E-Learning Implementation – The GIS Case. Intl. Journal of Computers, Communications & Control 1(1), 59–67 (2006), http://journal.univagora.ro/download/pdf/25.pdf

15. Turker, A., Gorgun, I., Conlan, O.: The Challenge of Content Creation to Facilitate Personalized E-Learning Experiences. Intl. Journal on E-Learning 1(1) (2006)

16. Tzouveli, P., Mylonas, P., Kollias, S.: SPERO - A Personalized Integrated E-Learning System. In: In Proceedings of the International Association for Development of the Information Society (IADIS) WWW/Internet 2004 International Conference, Madrid, Spain (October 2004), http://www.image.ntua.gr/php/savepaper.php?id=305

PLANT: A Distributed Architecture for Personalized E-Learning

Minglu Li[1], Hongzi Zhu[1], and Yanmin Zhu[2]

[1] Shanghai Jiao Tong University
[2] Hong Kong University of Science and Technology
{mlli, hongzi}@sjtu.edu.cn, zhuym@cse.ust.hk

Abstract. This paper presents PLANT, a distributed architecture for personalized E-Learning built upon the Edutella network which is a schema-based peer-to-peer system. The goal of PLANT is to facilitate individual learning on the Internet which abounds in a wide variety of educational resources and services. The distinctive features of PLANT are threefold. First, multifarious educational contents as well as individual learners can be evaluated by consensus in unified semantic contexts. This greatly encourages those educational resources with high quality. Second, individual learners can perform personalized search for educational contents and peer learners most relevant to their knowledge background and learning goals. Finally, a rich set of supportive services, such as real-time communications and personalized search, are integrated to provide end users with user-friendly interfaces.

Keywords: E-Learning, personalization, schema-based peer-to-peer systems.

1 Introduction

As the Internet is rapidly booming today, it has become the largest knowledge repository ever and abounds in a wide variety of educational resources. The Internet has brought unlimited flexibility for learning to the users having access to the Internet. The needs for personal learning environments (PLE) [13] have recently been recognized by both the E-Learning community and the software industry. A personalized E-Learning system built upon the Internet can be definitely appealing and useful. First, it enables so-called open learning which allows individual learners self-determined, independent and interest-guided learning. Second, it can realize the full utilization of valuable but scarce educational resources. Third, it provides a unique platform for users scattered widely around the globe to interact with each other. For example, in 2007, the number of students, who cannot enter colleges for higher education after graduate from their high schools, has already reached up to about 4.43 millions [12]. This large number is due to the great disparity between the rigorous demands for higher education and the quota limitations of colleges. The diversiform E-Learning systems including PLEs therefore have significant meaning as a complement approach to widely diffuse education in China.

Let's consider a motivating example. Bob, who is an advanced Java GUI programmer, wants to learn network programming using Java. With an adaptive E-Learning

H. Leung et al. (Eds.): ICWL 2007, LNCS 4823, pp. 20–30, 2008.

system, Bob can easily retrieve closely relevant educational resources focusing on knowledge of networking and skills of network programming in Java, other than irrelevant stuffs like the syntax of Java language. Furthermore, Bob can use the system to discuss with other users proficient in this area around the world. The users including Bob can also evaluate the quality of the educational resources according to their experience gained when using the resources. The system can therefore estimate the overall quality by taking the consensus of the users.

However, building such an E-Learning system has to face several grand challenges. First, the system needs to scale up with respect to the large number of potential users. Second, the system is in need of an effective infrastructure for describing, evaluating, distributing and retrieving educational resources which can be pretty heterogeneous. It is vital for the system to support complex queries compatible with standards like IEEE/IMS LOM [11] metadata. Third, identification and profile service for learners should be provided in a distributed environment. Security issues involved in such a system need to be resolved: access control for system membership control, key management for secure communication among members and trust management for reducing malicious attacks. Last, the system should allow owners of educational contents and services to have full control over their resources.

Modern E-Learning is mainly dominated by Web-based systems, such as so-called Learning Management Systems (LMS) [3, 4] and Adaptive Web-based Educational Systems (AWBES) [1, 8]. LMS effectively integrate the activities performed by teachers and students during the E-Learning process. As powerful as LMS are, they only serve users in a "one-size-fits-all" fashion. AWBES, which attempt to provide more personalized support, have demonstrated some impressive results. However, AWBES are mainly designed to serve domain-authorized users, such as students at schools and universities. None of them can satisfy the application challenges as described above.

During the recent years, Peer-to-Peer (P2P) systems, such as Gnutella and Kazaa, have become an important infrastructure for sharing music and other files over the Internet. Sophisticated P2P networks based on distributed hash tables (DHT) provide more efficient topologies than early P2P networks. Examples include Chord [9], CAN [16] and Pastry [2]. Schema-based P2P networks such as Edutella [17] have newly emerged, combining approaches from both P2P networking and data integration and semantic Web research areas. These schema-based P2P networks suggest a very impressive architecture as a cornerstone for building personalized E-Learning systems. There are several superior advantages with these systems.

- *Schema-based query.* These systems allow complex and extensible description of resources and provide more complex query capabilities than simple keyword-based search;
- *High flexibility.* Peers can join or leave the network dynamically;
- *Good scalability.* A hybrid solution with super peers [5] can scale well;
- *High autonomy.* Peers have the control over their resources; and
- *High resilience.* The system is resilient to peer failures.

Edutella adopts the hybrid P2P architecture which differentiates between super peers and normal peers. The super peers are organized in the hypercube topology, and normal peers connect to super peers in a star-like fashion. Super peers constitute the backbone network which is responsible for semantic message routing and integration/mediation of metadata. Edutella uses RDF schemas and RDF metadata for content description and uses RDF-QEL, a query language to access contents stored on the Edutella network. It provides five services: 1) Query Service for standardized query and retrieval of RFD metadata, 2) Replication Service for providing data persistence and workload balancing, 3) Mapping Service for translating between different metadata vocabularies to enable interoperability between different peers, 4) Mediation Service for defining views that join data from different metadata sources and reconciling conflicting and overlapping information and 5) Annotation Service for annotating materials stored in the network.

In this paper, we propose PLANT, a distributed architecture based on the Edutella network for individual personalized E-Learning. PLANT complements the Edutella network with a number of services to support personalized E-Learning. The goal of PLANT is to facilitate individual learning on the Internet where a wide variety of educational resources and services can be found. The distinctive features of PLANT are threefold. First, multifarious educational content as well as individual learners themselves can be evaluated by consensus in unified semantic contexts. This greatly encourages those educational resources with high quality. Second, individual learners can perform personalized search for educational contents and peer learners most relevant to their knowledge background and learning goals. Finally, a rich set of learning activity services, such as real-time communications and personalized search, are integrated to provide user-friendly interfaces to end users. In this paper, we will put emphasis on personalization support and don't care security issues.

The rest of this paper is structured as follows. In section II, we present the system architecture for the PLANT design. Section III describes the implementation of PLANT. Section IV compares PLANT with related work. Finally, we draw conclusions in Section V.

2   System Design

PLANT tries to build a personalized individual E-Learning environment leveraging the facilities of the Edutella network. Figure 1 shows the layered architecture of a peer node in PLANT, which consists of three layers: metadata representation, Edutella network, and E-Learner environment.

Metadata representation layer: To support personalized E-Learning, metadata schemas for describing educational resources are indispensable. The metadata representation layer consists of two metadata processors: schema transformation processor and metadata factory processor. Since these educational resources and content stem from a wide variety of domains and communities, existing metadata schemas can be pretty heterogeneous. The *schema transformation processor* transforms different schemas, such as XML schemas and relational schemas, into RDF schemas. Representing different metadata schemas with an identical one is necessary to facilitate the mediation between peers using different schemas. In order to maximize semantic interoperability, the *metadata factory processor* defines new metadata about resources, conforming to the IEEE/IMS LOM standard [11].

Edutella network layer: The Edutella network provides an RDF-based metadata infrastructure for P2P-networks based on the JXTA framework (*http://edutella.jxta. org*). A super peer implements at least four services: bind service, routing service, topology service and query service. The *bind service* handles peer registration. Peers establish the connection to a super peer with metadata generated by the metadata representation layer. The *routing service* routes queries to the appropriate super peers and normal peers, based on the routing indices created by the bind and topology service. The *topology service* is responsible for maintaining the super peer network topology and for keeping the routing indices up-to-date. The *query service* provides the interfaces for issuing new queries within the network.

E-Learner environment layer: This layer is built upon those two underlying layers, providing both personalization support and a wide spectrum of learning activity services to system users. It integrates four types of services: resource evaluation service, resource annotation service, communication service and learning assistant service. The *resource evaluation service* takes care of evaluating educational resources by allowing users to estimate these resources. Consequently, consensus building then becomes a natural part of metadata management. This eventually stimulates educational resources to evolve over time in the network. The *resource annotation service* allows users to annotate educational resources. The *communication service* provides both online real-time communication and off-line data sharing services to facilitate peer discussions and group-based study. The *learning assistant services* provide GUIs and serve end users by invoking underlying services.

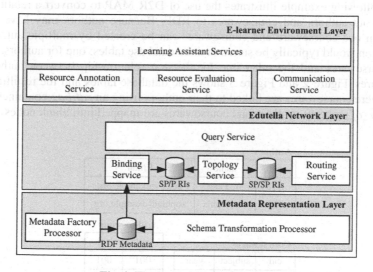

Fig. 1. The layered peer architecture

3 Implementation Details

The implementation specifications of Edutella protocols can be found at *http://edutella.jxta.org*. In this section, we focus on the implementation of primary services in the other two layers, namely, the metadata representation layer and the E-Learner environment layer.

3.1 Metadata Representation Layer

In the Semantic Web community, RDF and RDFS are used to annotate resources on the Web so that computer systems can exchange and comprehend data. RDF metadata have two important characteristics. First, they are very suitable for constructing distributed repositories. It removes the restriction that all annotations of a resource are stored on a single server. Furthermore, RDF schemas are very flexible to extend with additional properties. Recognizing these advantages of RDF and RDFS, the metadata representation layer aims to represent metadata about educational resources with RDF schemas.

3.1.1 Schema Transformation Processor

To map the relational database model to the graph-based RDF data model, we use D2R MAP mapping language [7]. The strength of D2R MAP is that flexible mappings of complex relational structures are allowed without having to change the existing database schema. SQL statements are directly employed in the mapping rules. This endows D2R MAP with the ability to handle complex relationships and conditions. For each record set selected from the database, records are grouped according to the *groupBy* columns of the specific *ClassMap*. Then the class instances are created and assigned a URI or a blank node identifier. Finally, property elements are created using datatype and object property bridges.

The following example illustrates the use of D2R MAP to convert a relational database about authors and coursewares to RDF. Because authors may have created more than one courseware and coursewares can be created by multiple authors, the information would typically be stored in three database tables: one for authors, one for their coursewares and the other one for the *m:n* relationship between authors and coursewares. Figure 2 and Figure 3 shows the database tables and the resulting RDF graph where coursewares are linked to their authors using an *rdf:bag* container for the *ex:author_of* property. Authors and coursewares are mapped into blank nodes.

Authors

aid	name	Email
001	W. Peter	peter@example.org
002	M. Sophia	sophia@example.org

Coursewares

cid	subject	year
001	s1	2005
002	s3	2006
003	s4	2006

Author_cour

aid	cid
001	001
001	003
002	002
002	003

Fig. 2. Tables in a relational database

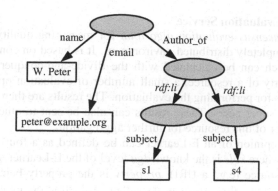

Fig. 3. One exported RDF graph

For XML schemas, we use the approach described in [10]. It is rather intuitive to convert complex elements into RDF classes and simple elements and attributes into RDF properties.

3.1.2 Metadata Factory Processor

In order to maximize semantic interoperability, we design our metadata schema for educational resources in compliance with the IEEE/IMS LOM standard. In PLANT, system users are also regarded as a class of educational resources. Therefore, PLANT provides a unified strategy to manage user profiles and education content metadata. The strength of this design is that system users can also be evaluated by those users in the same semantic contexts.

We extend the LOM standard with additional elements. For example, upon creating a new user, the new user should provide basic the information such as name (*1:General.Title*), gender (*1:General.Gender*), age (*1:General.Age*), affiliation (*1:General.Affiliation*) and interests (*1:General.Description*). When the user add a subject to study according to certain classification system (e.g., ACM-CCS, *http://www.acm. org/class/1998*), an instance of Classification category (*9:Classification*) is added. A new datatype *MeasurableInt* is also added which indicates a value should be interpreted as an integer and can be used for evaluation. A property defined as a *MeasurableInt* is called a measurable property. For example, each Classification category instance can contain a measurable property (*9:Classification.Description*) which describes the knowledge level of the user in that subject. When annotating a resource, an instance of Annotation category (*8:Annotation*) is added which may contain literal comments or measurable properties (*8:Annotation.Description*).

3.2 E-Learner Environment Layer

In PLANT, the quality of an educational resource is estimated based on consensus of system users in the network. The key point of this strategy is to let actual users of the educational resource evaluate and annotate it. This results in a global resource and metadata ecosystem where good resources and metadata can flourish and gain great popularity.

3.2.1 Resource Evaluation Service

We propose a *consensus evaluation algorithm* for measuring quality of educational resources in a completely distributed environment. It is based on consensus of all resource users, which can be calculated with the divide-and-conquer strategy. For a measurable property of a resource, a small number of evaluation opinions are gathered at super peers for performing the evaluation. The results are then updated into the routing indices at super peers. These results can also be sent to other super peers or the originating peer of this resource for further aggregation.

An evaluation opinion of an E-Learner can be defined as a four-tuple (*role*, *RId*, *property*, *score*), where *role* is the knowledge level of the E-Learner, *RId* is the identification of the resource (e.g., a URI), *property* is the property being evaluated and *score* is the evaluation value. Super peers gather evaluation opinions in their buffers for evaluation purpose. Note that an E-Learner might have had multidisciplinary knowledge and have different levels on each specific subject. Therefore, it makes more sense to let E-Learners who have qualification (e.g., by their knowledge levels) to evaluate certain educational resources within the same contexts.

More specifically, evaluation values from E-Learners are buffered and divided into different queues according to the knowledge levels of E-Learners. We differentiate the weight of each queue to the evaluation of this property and estimate the consensus by calculating the weighted mean of all queued values. This is based on the assumption that different groups of values might come from different probability distributions. Suppose the number of queues (i.e., the number of knowledge levels) is n. We denote q_i as the ith queue, $q_{i,j}$ as the jth element in q_i and $\overline{q_i}$ as the mean of q_i. Variable σ_i^2 and $\overline{s_i}$ are the overall variance and mean of all evaluation values by the ith-level E-Learners, respectively. Variable t_i is the total number of evaluation values of the ith-level E-Learners gathered on this super-peer. Denote w_i as the weight of the ith-level E-Learners.

Let $w_i = 1/\sigma_i^2$. Thus, the weighted mean of all evaluation values, denoted as $\overline{s}$, is,

$$\overline{s} = \frac{\sum_{i=1}^{n} \overline{s_i}/\sigma_i^2}{\sum_{i=1}^{n} 1/\sigma_i^2}. \tag{1}$$

The significance of this choice is that the weighted mean is the maximum likelihood estimator of the mean of the probability distributions of each queue under the assumption that evaluation values in different queues are independent and normally distributed with the same mean.

However, it is unlikely to gather all evaluation opinions from the ith-level E-Learners in the network before we can determine the explicit variance. The *law of total variance* suggests that the variance of the total group is equal to the mean of the variances of the subgroups plus the variance of the means of the subgroups. Thus, the variance σ_i^2 can be calculated in decomposition. If the queue length of each queue is m, then the variance of the ith queue $\sigma_{q_i}^2$ is,

$$\sigma_{q_i}^2 = \sum_{j=1}^{m} q_{i,j}^2 / m - (\sum_{j=1}^{m} q_{i,j} / m)^2. \qquad (2)$$

The number of evaluation values from the ith-level E-Learners is $t_i + m$, denoted as t_i'. The new variance and mean of all evaluation values by the E-Learners at the ith level, denoted as $\sigma_i'^2$ and $\overline{s_i}'$, are,

$$\sigma_i'^2 = (\sigma_i^2 + \sigma_{q_i}^2)/2 + (\overline{s_i} - \overline{q_i})^2/4,$$
$$\overline{s_i}' = t_i \cdot \overline{s_i} / t_i' + m \cdot \overline{q_i} / t_i'. \qquad (3)$$

Thus, the new weighted mean $\overline{s}'$ can be calculated with $\sigma_i'^2$ and $\overline{s_i}'$.

With the consensus evaluation algorithm, PLANT provides very flexible strategy for ranking resources according to various measurable properties. This can support distributed top-k queries for the best k resources satisfying certain complex constrains.

3.2.2 Resource Annotation Service

Educational resource creators are mainly responsible for defining contexts where all these resources are supposed to be used. However, these contexts may not be well known when the resource is created. Instead, they can arise over time. For example, a piece of music can have different meanings when used in an entertainment context and when used in a music composition context. Therefore, users should be allowed to annotate educational resources. New measurable properties can be created and added to the metadata. This can fertilizes the metadata in new and unanticipated contexts.

As described in the last section, an instance of Annotation category (*8:Annotation*) is added when annotating a resource. In addition, some properties of an E-Learner are automatically associated, such as the E-Learner's identification, the knowledge level of the E-Learner and the other possible contexts which this E-Learner is interested in. This information can be aggregated and further used to create recommendation links for this resource.

3.2.3 P2P Communication Service

In PLANT, E-Learners can communicate with each other via the versatile *P2P communication service*. There are many systems that can support users to send instant messages and share files with each other. Most of them (e.g., MSN Menssenger and Skype) also provide real-time voice or video communication. Peers can be found by either explicitly knowing their unique identities (e.g., E-mail address of a contact in Menssenger) or by searching randomly. In contrast, the P2P communication service in PLANT supports E-Learners to search for peers who have more experience and knowledge in the same semantic contexts.

This distinctive feature of the P2P communication service benefits from the fact that E-Learners are also treated as a class of education resources and therefore can be represented and evaluated using metadata. An E-Learner can instruct the search by specifying the knowledge levels and the classifications of the target peers. The E-Learner can also conduct a random search and hereby the system will take care of query rewriting based on the E-Learner's own profile.

3.2.4 Learning Assistant Services

The learning assistant services provide GUIs to end users. They utilize the services provided by the underlying layers and combine different services to support personalized individual E-Learning activities. For example, the *virtual course service* creates a learning space for an E-Learner when a subject is established by the E-Learner. In this learning space, the E-Learner can perform semantic search for educational contents. The results can be bookmarked for long-period learning. The E-Learner can evaluate and annotate any resource anytime during using this resource. For another example, *peer venue service* allows E-Learners to conduct search for learning peers. Communication patterns between peers can be very flexible. For instance, group or team learning, collaborative problem solving or task-based approaches can be realized by involving multiple participants in a conference using real-time video/audio communication services.

4 Related Work

As personal learning environments develop rapidly, many such systems have emerged using protocols like Peer-to-Peer and web services to connect a range of resources and systems within a personally-managed space. We summarize several similar and complementary research and development efforts in this area.

Colloquia [14] is considered as the first peer-to-peer learning system which provides support for a conversational and activity-based model of E-Learning. The system contains three main components: *people, resources* and *tasks*. Teachers can set up activities and assign people and resource to these activities. Learners can accept or reject received activities sent from teachers. They can also create sub-activities. However, personalization is only possible in a limited sense in that teachers and learners may add resources for an activity or sub-activity. Learners involved in an activity have to use the same resources. Furthermore, it does not provide means to evaluate and annotate resources.

Elgg system [6] which is a Web publishing application, uses social networks to offer blog, networking, community, collecting of news using feeds aggregation and file sharing features. It is based on FOAF which is a project for machine-readable modeling of profiles and social networks. Relationships between people and their various attributes are defined based on RDF using OWL. However, Elgg does not provide resource evaluation strategy either. In addition, it is initially described as an e-portfolio system and there is a lack of support for pedagogic approaches.

PLEX [15] has a basic structure which is very similar with that of Colloquia. The system has a resource manager, a people manager, and activities consisting of resources and people. People and resources are discoverable. It also provides assistant help for setting and realization of learner goals with the creation of learning opportunities and activities. However, PLEX provides limited metadata management. It has no support for resource evaluation and provides very simple literal annotation about resources.

5 Conclusion

This paper has proposed a distributed architecture for personalized individual E-Learning based on the Edutella network. Deploying RDF schema-based Edutella network, PLANT allow uses to conduct complex queries for best results according to their knowledge backgrounds and learning goals. With the distributed resource evaluation algorithm based on consensus, the quality of education resources can be precisely estimated, which stimulates resources to evolve in the network. By providing a rich set of learning assistant services, individual users can get good support to achieve their learning goals.

A prototype implementation of PLANT has been used in the Grid Computing Center of Shanghai Jiao Tong University for half a year. It combines the functionalities of LMS and flexibility of P2P systems into one unified platform. Two typical models have been recognized from the use experience of the prototype system. On one hand, teachers can set up virtual classrooms, assemble students and publish his educational material. Students can communicate with teachers or peer learners in either synchronous or asynchronous way. On the other hand, users consider the system just like a traditional P2P system but with more functionalities and are encouraged to create and share good-quality resources by stimulating their initiative during the learning process. These have demonstrated the efficacy of PLANT as a handy tool for communication and personalized E-Learning.

Acknowledgements

This work was supported by National Basic Research Program of China (973 Program) (No. 2006CB303000), National Natural Science Foundation of China (No. 60473092 and 90612018) and the grand project by Science and Technology Commission of Shanghai Municipality (No. 05DZ15005).

References

1. Rios, E.M., Trella, M., et al.: Internet Based Evaluation System. In: In Proc. of Artificial Intelligence in Education: Open Learning Environments (1999)
2. Rowstron, A., Druschel, P.: Pastry: Scalable, Decentralized Object Location and Routing for Large-Scale Peer-to-Peer Systems. In: Proc. of IFIP/ACM Int. Conf. Distributed Systems Platforms (2001)
3. Blackborad Inc. Blackborad Course Management System (2002), http://www.blackboard.com/
4. Blackboard Inc. WebCT Course Management System (2002), http://www.webct.com
5. Yang, B., Garcia-Molina, H.: Designing a Super-Peer Network. In: Proc. of Data Engineering (2003)
6. Werdmuller, B., Tosh, D.: Elgg - A Personal Learning Landscape. TESL-EJ vol 9, pp. 1–11 (2005)
7. Bizer, C.: D2R MAP - A Database to RDF Mapping Language. In: Proc. of WWW, Budapest, Hungary (2003)

8. Weber, G., Brusilovsky, P.: ELM-ART: An Adaptive Versatile System for Web-Based Instruction. Artificial Intelligence in Education 12, 351–384

9. Stoica, I., Morris, R., Karger, D., et al.: Chord: A Scalable Peer-to-Peer Lookup Service for Internet Applications. In: Proc. of ACM SIGCOMM (2001)

10. Cruz, I.F., Xiao, H., Hsu, F.: Peer-to-Peer Semantic Integration of XML and RDF Data Sources. In: Proc. of AP2PC (2004)

11. LOM: Draft Standard for Learning Object Metadata, (2004), http://ltsc.ieee.org/wg12/index.html

12. Ministry of Education of the People's Republic of China, The Total Enrollment of the Regular HEIs Bursts at the volume of 10 Millions This Year (2007), http://www.moe.edu.cn

13. van Harmelen, M.: Personal Learning Environments. In: Proc. of IEEE Advanced Learning Technologies (2006)

14. Liber, O.: Colloquia - A Conversation Manager. Campus-Wide Information Systems 17, 56–61 (2000)

15. Beauvoir, P.: PLEX Demonstration. In: Proc. of JISC-CETIS (2005)

16. Ratnasamy, S., Francis, P., Handley, M., et al.: A Scalable Content-addressable Network. In: Proc. of ACM SIGCOMM (2001)

17. Nejdl, W., Wolf, B., Qu, C., et al.: EDUTELLA:A P2P Networking Infrastructure Based on RDF. In: Proc. of WWW, Honolulu, Hawaii, USA (2002)

PeRES: A Personalized Recommendation Education System Based on Multi-agents & SCORM

Fan Zhu[1,2], Horace H.S. Ip[2], Apple W.P. Fok[2], and Jiaheng Cao[1]

[1] School of Computer, Wuhan University, PR China
whzhufan@yahoo.com.cn
jhcao@whu.edu.cn
[2] Department of Computer Science, City University of Hong Kong,
Hong Kong SAR, PR China
cship@cityu.edu.hk
applefok@cs.cityu.edu.hk

Abstract. Most E-Learning models proposed recently can offer personalized learning services for learners or make courseware reusable or portable. However, there are few models that can serve both purpose and none of them is designed to provide personalized services for both learners and instructors. This paper introduces an architecture of school-based personalized recommendation education system which can provide personalized services not only for diverse learners but also for instructors. In addition, it offers reusability and interoperability of courseware that is conformant with SCORM 2004 3rd Edition specifications. The architecture adopts multi-agents technology and consists of SIX software agents, which coordinate work hierarchy with each other to offer a range of primary functions that include static and dynamic users modeling, learning plan generation and adjustment, personalized content search, personalized recommendation, as well as real-time evaluation of learning progress. We provide the detail functional specification of these agents as well as a scenario walk-through of the architecture.

Keywords: Personalized Learning, Recommendation System, Multi-Agents, SCORM.

1 Introduction

With increasingly powerful hardware and advanced software technologies, it is possible for us to harness such technologies in education and, particularly, to cater to the diverse needs of learners as well as instructors. Riding on the successes of the deployment of web-based technologies in e-commerce, many researchers turn their focus to e-education. Kassim et al [15] has surveyed how the computer and Internet technology can play an important role in creating an effective web-based learning environment. While web-based applications in the two areas have very different goals and objectives, i.e. business vs. education, some of the core technologies in e-commerce make personalized e-education possible, particularly in areas such as personalized content search and recommendation, dynamic user modeling, learning plan generation and content annotation.

H. Leung et al. (Eds.): ICWL 2007, LNCS 4823, pp. 31–42, 2008.
© Springer-Verlag Berlin Heidelberg 2008

A few examples of Web-based intelligent learning environments have been illustrated in [17]. These previous works also highlight several problems in the Web-Based Educational Environments: (i) Lack of a mechanism to interoperate with other learning systems and interchange information such as educational material, learning pattern and learning sequence etc; (ii) Model of the users may often to be updated due to influence such as users' profile, users' interests, and users' activities; (iii) The key elements, which can be adopted to build and update the model of users from the view of designer of the learning systems, such as web pages visited by users and period of time of learning, is probably not reliable to achieve the perceived purposes during actual operation; and (iv) The most important problem that the designer of learning systems is facing is how to fuse technologies, methods and principles for the provision of personalized e-education to meet the requirement of most users.

In this paper, we concentrate our attention on the system design and development of PeRES that aims to encourage knowledge sharing and content re-use, personalized information delivery, more efficient personalized content recommendation and comprehensive service solution in school-based e-education. In Section 2, we introduce some related work in the personalized e-education area. Section 3 describes briefly the proposed architecture of PeRES. Section 4 presents each agent in the multi-agents platform in detail and a scenario walk through of the architecture to show the various communication/message paths among the agents. Finally, we draw a conclusion our work with a short summary.

2   Related Works

E-Learning models have evolved from classroom replication towards models that integrate information technology and pedagogical issues. While the first E-Learning models emphasized the role of the technology in providing content (information), delivery (access) and electronic services, recent models focus on pedagogical issues such as online instructional design and the creation of online learning communities. Three selected E-Learning models have been discussed in [8]: Content, service and technology model, Instructional design model and Learning communities. At the system framework aspect, Huang et al [7] introduces a smart E-Learning framework and develops a recommendation system, which applies the collaborative filtering approach that has an ability to predict the most suitable documents to the learner, and takes it as global web service so as to extend the E-Learning system from local learners to global learners. Chang et al [16] describes the design and implementation of multilayer educational services platforms that enable learners to establish their own online social learning communities and integrate their online social learning communities into a large public social learning portal site called EduCities. Multilayer educational services platforms were designed to integrate various individual online social learning communities, and to map these communities into physical social learning communities. Fok and Ip [4][3][2] study learning pedagogies in relation to personalization technologies and integration technologies for individual learning and integrate multiple Ontologies with personalized learning.

There are many approaches to applying personalization technologies in education. Hsu [11] develops an online personalized English learning recommender system capable of providing ESL students with reading lessons that suit their different interests and therefore increase the motivation to learn. Sun et al. [21] propose a method that helps instructors to form high-interaction E-Learning groups by applying rules based on data mining techniques. Dimitrova et al. [17] investigate the differences in the students' diverse learning styles and then proposes some measures to improve the E-Learning environment in a way that matches the students' learning styles more effectively. Brusilovsky and Nijhawan [5] present the KnowledgeTree, a framework for adaptive E-Learning based on distributed re-useable learning activities. Liao et al. [6] propose p-Learning grid, a service-oriented approach, based on a pervasive learning grid, for solving difficulties associated with the sharing of learning resources distributed on different E-Learning platforms.

The proliferation of E-Learning systems leads to the need to share and reuse learning materials developed in different formats in different E-Learning systems. Therefore, international organizations have proposed several standard formats including SCORM, IMS, LOM, AICC, etc. The current version of SCORM is SCORM 2004 3rd Edition, which has achieved the four high-level requirements set up initially by the ADL Initiative: reusability, accessibility, durability, and interoperability of E-Learning content. Recently, few researches [9] have been conducted on SCORM-conformant adaptive learning management systems. Kazi [20] raises a "Web-based Intelligent Learning Environments with Searchable and Reusable Learning Contents" by using SCORM 2004; however, it only includes three modules: communication module, expert module and pedagogical module. Therefore, the last two modules have heavy burden and it is short of functionality partition. Andreev et al. [19] introduce CMAPS framework which is an innovative framework for producing SCORM-conformant E-Learning content and describes a process model produced by the Learning Systems Architecture Lab (LSAL) at Carnegie Mellon University and used as a foundation to illustrate the sophisticated nature of the content creation/transformation process. It defines seven modules, which are according to the five stages of the content development process as seen by LSAL. Su et al. [14] & Yang et al. [13] introduce an object-based authoring tool that supports efficient construction of SCORM-conformant courseware according to some corresponding sequencing rules.

3   Overview of the Structure of PeRES

Considering extensibility and modularization of the learning system and the reusability and portability of courseware, here we introduce a school-based architecture of personalized E-Learning and recommendation system. We pay particular attention to the design and development of a system infrastructure, which can (i) provide flexible modularized functions in PeRES, (ii) take full advantage of existing SCORM-conformant courseware and interchangeability of learning resources, and (iii) support personalized services for learners and instructors. The architecture of PeRES illustrated in Fig. 1.

PeRES	Personalized Service	Planning		Recommendation		Evaluation	
		Searching		Monitoring		Communication	
	Multi-Agent Platform	Search	Plan	Monitor	Recommendation		Delivery
		Data					
	Data Storage	Principles	Profiles	Content	Activity	Communication	
	SCORM	Importer		Exporter		Editor	

Fig.1. Architecture of PeRES

As shown in Fig. 1, the PeRES consists of four layers: Personalized Services, Multi-Agents Platform, Data Storage and SCORM Interface. The lower layer provides data and service for the higher layer. The SCORM layer is the bridge to the other Learning Management System so as to exchange the learning resource conveniently and flexibly. The Data Storage layer is the system foundation. The Agents in the Multi-Agents Platform provide personalized service to the Personalized Service layer via collecting correlative information such as profiles, activities and communication record of users from the Data Storage layer and applying appropriate methods with certain learning pattern.

3.1 SCORM-Conformant

Based upon the SCORM formats, the learning materials in different learning management systems can be shared, reused and recombined. Nowadays, Sharable Content Object Reference Model (SCORM), which integrates specifications, standards and guidelines developed by IMS, LOM and AICC etc, has become the most popular international standard. SCORM seeks to knit together the contributions of disparate groups and interests in the distributed learning community. It is intend to coordinate emerging technologies and capabilities with commercial/public implementations.

PeRES adopts the latest SCORM specifications, SCORM 2004 3rd Edition, as the standard to organize the learning resources so that the system can interchange SCORM-conformant learning material in the form of Content Aggregation Package (CAP).

The proposed system includes three modules. The SCORM Editor can create SCORM components such as Asset, SCO (Share Content Object), Activities, Content Organizations, Content Aggregation manually systematically. Then it can build CAP by creating manifest file (imsmanifest.xml) and zipping all resources in the SCORM Exporter automatically. The SCORM Importer and Exporter can import and export learning resources, which are created in PeRES or others and conformant with SCORM 2004 3rd Edition specifications, into or from database. The SCORM layer meets the foundational functional requirements, which are accessibility, adaptability, affordability, durability, interoperability and reusability, for SCORM-based E-Learning environments.

3.2 Data Storage

The data in the system includes five main parts. (i) Principles data stores the learning rules for learners such as how to upgrade, how to re-learn and so on. (ii) Profiles data contains information of all the learners and instructors such as age, gender, grade and interest etc. (iii) Content data defines how the courseware is stored in the system. It should be convenient to transfer from or to SCORM format. Learning materials include compulsory courses, reading books, game, exercises, quiz and so on. Learning media include html, flash, audio, video etc. (iv) Communication data stores the communicating information among users and (v) Activities data records the learners' learning progress and the instructors' instruction activities.

The Profiles data can be used to produce the initial plan and recommendation for new learners via certain recommendation method and learning pattern. Then the PeRES can alter and fine-tune the plan and make recommendation along with the continuous learning activities that are recorded in the Activities Data and Communication Data. In the meantime, the learning patterns and styles will be analyzed and recorded in the Principles Data.

The Content data can be clustered via adopting certain classification algorithm according to the meta-data described in the CAP. The system can therefore deliver the appropriate recommendation or plan to learners systematically and personalizationally.

3.3 Multi-agents Platform Overview

After analyzing the requirement of PeRES, we propose SIX agents according to the criterion of mentioned in [13]. The conceptual framework of our multi-agents platform is shown in Fig. 2 that shows the relationship among these agents. The Data Agent in the benmost circle is the bridge linking the Database and the Searching Agent. They provide relevant data access service to the Searching Agent. Searching Agent provides search engine for the Recommendation Agent, Planning Agent, Monitor Agent and the Delivery Agent to search in the database or on the Internet. The kernels in the PeRES we proposed are Searching Agent, Recommendation Agent,

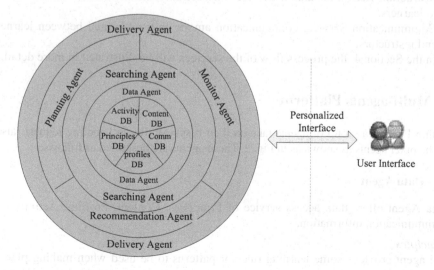

Fig. 2. Conceptual Framework of Multi-Agents Platform

Monitor Agent and Planning Agent. The various personalized services are offered by the four agents. We will discuss them in the Section 4. The Delivery Agent plays the role that communicates with GUI of the PeRES.

3.4 Personalized Service

The system provides different personalized services to cater to the diverse needs of learners.

The five most important learner behaviors on Web-based learning, which were described in [1], show the knowledge retrieval and learning progress of learners. The proposed PeRES offer pertinent services for learners.

1. Content Service: learning content representation and learning activity recording.
2. Planning Service: learning plan scheduling and incremental fine-tuning of the plan.
3. Searching Service: material searching in repositories and Internet.
4. Monitoring Service: learning progress monitoring and prompting at special time.
5. Communication Service: communication among students and between learners and instructors.
6. Recommendation Service: learning content recommendation in learning progress according to the learner's profile and activities.

In addition, PeRES adds personalized support that provides conventional and novel personalized services for instructors, these include:

1. Content Service: creating teaching material packages (CAP) and importing/exporting CAP.
2. Monitoring Service: monitoring learners' activities.
3. Searching Service: material searching in all repositories and Internet.
4. Evaluation Service: evaluating learners' learning progress and efficiency.
5. Instruction Recommendation Service: instruction recommendation for instructors to learners.
6. Communication Service: communication among instructors and between learners and instructors.

In the Section 4, the process flow of the services will be illustrated in more detail.

4   Multi-agents Platform

Within PeRES, a group of agents take on their responsibility in handling request raised by the outer agents as shown as in Fig. 2. These agents are described as follows:

4.1   Data Agent

Data Agent offers data access service of Principles, Content, Profiles, Activity and Communication information.

Principles
The agent provides some learning rules or patterns to be used when making plan or recommendation.

At the stage of system initialization, there are only few principles generated by the administrator manually. Along with increasing of learners and learning resources, the Recommendation Agent and the Planning Agent will form new principles and revise exist principles periodically. On the other hand, the instructors can also update learning rules to accommodate diversification of learning resource.

Content
The agent maintains all learning resources in the PeRES. Its main functions include creating, modifying, deleting, packaging, importing and exporting CAP material and maintaining consistency of learning resources in the PeRES.

The learning resources in the PeRES are compliant with SCORM RTE (Runtime Environment) specifications and all of them are labeled by clustering their meta-data. According to the Activity, Communication, Profiles data and direction of instructors, we can build up a set of learning principles and revise it dynamically and periodically. That has to recur to Recommendation Agent and Planning Agent.

Profiles
The agent maintains all users' information including learners, instructors, administer and so on.

Learners' profiles will identify their needs and expectations, as follows: (i) age, gender, culture and work experience; (ii) prior knowledge; (iii) prior experience with E-Learning; (iv) goals and motivation; (v) attitude towards E-Learning; (vi) learning patterns and styles; (vii) computer literacy; (viii) access to computers and the Internet;(ix) affordability of E-Learning etc.

In PeRES, the learners' profiles play an active role in the personalization process. All learners must have an active profile file for recording/tracking all current and previous behaviours so as to provide consolidate information for analyzing purposes. Learners' profiles will be treated as a key indicator for identifying learners' interests and needs. Therefore, the learner's profile should also be regularly updated in order to retain the desired accuracy in its exploitation.

Static profiles will be used as starting point and modified to fit the actual learners. Based on learners' behaviours, the system will give relevant responses with different technologies. For instance, dividing learners into segments based on rules, and then filtering learners' interests by using agent technologies or different filtering techniques. Finally modify learners' profiles and predict next action.

Activity & Communication
In the activity and communication aspect, the agent's responsibility is to record learners' and instructors' activities and communications, which can be use conveniently when making recommendation or plan.

4.2 Searching Agent

The agent can be called by Delivery Agent, Recommendation Agent and Planning Agent to search user's profile, learning contents, principles or some else which match certain combined condition. It has two tasks: (i) providing searching service in the database. The agent will search relevant information based on the query condition put forward by the three agents; and (ii) providing searching service on the Internet.

Similar with the existing search engines, personalized search collects user's interests and search goal and return back the results ranked by correlativity.

4.3 Planning Agent

The Planning Agent can make and adjust plan for every learner according to the learner's profile, learning activities and learning capabilities and so on. For the capable learners, the period will be planned shorter and learning content will be more abundant. For the less capable learners, the plan will be tuned to allow him/her to easily keep up with the learning progress. Learning capability is shaped in the learning progress, so the plan made at the initial phase can be tuned to fit the learner. This task will be accomplished by the Planning Agent periodically. Hidden Markov Model approach can be applied to achieve the requirement.

4.4 Monitor Agent

As an instructor, he should know the learning progress of learners. The Monitor Agent records learning information like as pages access, time rest on a page, functional modules use, learning time, learning rate of progress, quiz score and so on. It can inspect learners' activities in the light of certain learning sequence provided in the learning resources. If one is beyond the area or working for too long, the agent will remind him in time and inquire what he want to do afterward.

4.5 Recommendation Agent

The Recommendation Agent can make a recommendation for a learner what he/she should learn about next step after he/she has done in certain phase or what he/she should do at certain time. It can also be useful for instructors to suggest how an instructor to guide learners.

Learners' activities include page browsing, reading book, gaming, chatting and so on. Learners' activities imply the learning pattern of learner. Learning progress is individual activity, however, learning progress requires instruction of instructors and learner must accomplish tasks assigned by instructors. Therefore, recommendations to the learners depend not only on the learners' activities, communication and profiles but also direction of instructors. A balanced development on each lesson is the ultimate goal of learners in school. Hence, the content recommended by PeRES should be based on both learners' interests and instructors' guidance.

Traditional recommendation algorithms mentioned in [10] involve content-based approach, collaborative filtering approach and data mining technology. Collaborative filtering algorithms are used to recommend helpful content to the learners or instructors. Whereas, different from other recommendation system goal, the balanceable collaborative filtering algorithm is applied in the proposed PeRES on account of considering not only learner's interests but also learner's goal.

As an illustration of how these agents collaborate to achieve a task, Fig. 3 illustrates the message paths of the main services provided by the six agents. From the figure, we can observe the layered structure of the PeRES architecture such that the agent messages (or requests) pass from one layer to another layer from the outer agents to the inner agents and return the results in the opposite direction.

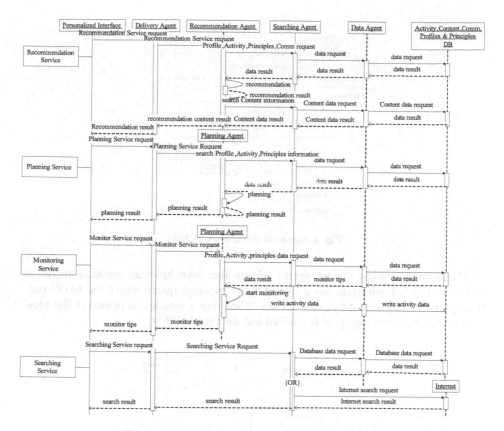

Fig. 3. Message Paths of the main Services in PeRES

5   Implementation of PeRES

There have several Multi-Agents Platforms like as Jade, Smart Platform. JADE is a software Framework fully implemented in Java language. It simplifies the implementation of multi-agent systems through a middle-ware that complies with the FIPA specifications and through a set of graphical tools that supports the debugging and deployment phases. The agent platform can be distributed across machines, which not even need to share the same OS, and the configuration can be controlled via a remote GUI [12]. So we adopt it to implement our multi-agents framework of PeRES.

The run-time framework of Jade is illustrated in Fig. 4. AMS is Agent Management System which provides naming services and represents the authority in the platform. DF (Directory Facilitator) provides a Yellow Pages service by means of which an agent can find other agents providing the services he requires in order to achieve his goals. The Platform consists of containers and Container can contain several agents and can be resident in several computers.

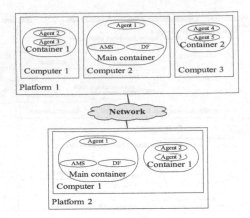

Fig. 4. Run-time framework of Jade

The communication among agents adopts the asynchronous message mode as shown in Fig 5. Each agent has a sort of agent message queue where the JADE run-time posts messages sent by other agents. Whenever a message is posted in the message queue the receiving agent is notified and then deal with it.

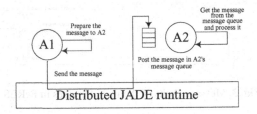

Fig. 5. The asynchronous message passing mode

The six Agents communicate with each other by send messages. Furthermore, we define message ontology to create the message passing mechanism. All the agents publish themselves and relevant functions on the DF and then wait for other agents sending requests. The run-time structure of PeRES is shown in Fig. 6.

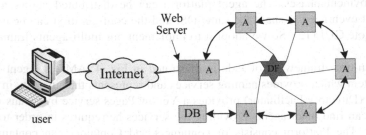

Fig. 6. The run-time structure of PeRES

6 Conclusions

In this paper, we have presented the functional models of a Personalized Recommendation Education System (PeRES). We have given a specific multi-agent-based design of PeRES and discussed each agent in detail. We have defined the functional services provided by the six core Personalized Education Agents (PEAs) used in PeRES. These agents related to each other hierarchically and collaborate with each other to provide the personalized study plan, search, recommendation and communication services for learners and instructors and achieve the system overall goal-Personalized Education and re-use of courseware.

The proposed PeRES can be applied to the school-based teaching environment. The architecture is hierarchical and represents the relationship between layers. Its function is modularized for adapting to various learning environments.

In our future work, we will research personalized recommendation methods such as collaborative filtering algorithm, data mining algorithm etc, learning progress evaluating and monitoring and learning activity sequencing based on SCORM and tag.

References

1. Fok, A.W.P., Xiao, X., Shi, Y., Ip, H.H.S.: A Personalized Agents Platform Design and Implementation for Personalized Education. In: International Conference on Computers in Education (ICCE2005) (2005)
2. Fok, A.W.P., Ip, H.H.S.: Ontology-driven Incremental Annotation of Educational Content for Instruction Planning. In: International Conference on Computers in Education (ICCE05), Singapore, November 28– December 02, (2005)
3. Fok, A.W.P., Ip, H.H.S.: Personalized Education – An Exploratory Study of Learning Pedagogies in Relation to Personalized Technologies. Advance in Web-based Learning, 407–415 (2004)
4. Fok, A.W.P., Ip, H.H.S.: Personalized Education – Technology Integration for Individual Learning. In: Third IASTED International Conference on Web-Based Education, Innsbruck, Austria, Feb. 16-18, 2004, pp. 48–53 (2004)
5. Brusilovsky, P., Nijhawan, H.: A Framework for Adaptive E-Learning Based on Distributed Re-usable Learning Activities. In: World Conference on E-Learning (2002)
6. Liao, C.-J., Ouyang, F.-C., Hsu, K.C.: A Service-Oriented Approach for the Pervasive Learning Grid. Journal of Information Science and Engineering 21, 959–971 (2005)
7. Huang, D.-S., Li, K., Irwin, G.W.: Smart E-Learning Using Recommender System. In: Huang, D.-S., Li, K., Irwin, G.W. (eds.) ICIC 2006. LNCS (LNAI), vol. 4114, pp. 518–523. Springer, Heidelberg (2006)
8. Engelbrecht, E.: A look at E-Learning models: investigating their value for developing an E-Learning strategy. Bureau for Learning Development, Unisa Progressio 25(2), 38–47 (2003)
9. Lin, F., Holt, P., Korba, L., Shih, T.K.: A Framework for Developing Online Learning Systems. In: International Conference Advances in Infrastructure for Electronic Business, Science, and Education on the Internet, L'Aquila, Italy (2001)
10. Guo, X., Zhang, G., et al.: A Hybrid Recommendation Approach for One-and-Only Items. In: Zhang, S., Jarvis, R. (eds.) AI 2005. LNCS (LNAI), vol. 3809, pp. 457–466. Springer, Heidelberg (2005)

11. Hsu, M.-H.: A personalized English learning recommender system for ESL students. Expert Systems with Applications (2006)
12. Java Agent DEvelopment Framework, http://jade.tilab.com/
13. Yang, J.T.D., Tsai, C.Y., Wu, T.H.: Visualized Online Simple Sequencing Authoring Tool for SCORM-compliant Content Package. In: 4th IEEE International Conference on Advanced Learning Technologies (ICALT 2004), Finland (August 2004)
14. Su, J.-M., Tseng, S.-S., Weng, J.-F., Liu, Y.-L., Tsai, Y.-T.: An Object based Authoring Tool for Creating SCORM Compliant Course. In: 19th International Conference on Advanced Information Networking and Applications (AINA 2005) (2005)
15. Kassim, A. A., Kazi, S. A., Ranganath, S.: A Web based Intelligent Approach to Tutoring. In: International Conference on Engineering Education, Oslo, Norway, pp. 8B4-25–8B4-30 (2001)
16. Chang, L.-J., Yang, J.-C., Deng, Y.-C., Chan, T.-W.: EduXs: multilayer educational services platforms. Computers & Education 41, 1–18 (2003)
17. Dimitrova, M., Sadler, C., Hatzipanagos, S., Murphy, A.: Addressing Learner Diversity by Promoting Flexibility in E-Learning Environments. In: Mařík, V., Štěpánková, O., Retschitzegger, W. (eds.) DEXA 2003. LNCS, vol. 2736, Springer, Heidelberg (2003)
18. Brusilovsky, P.: Adaptive and Intelligent Technologies for Web-based Education. Special Issue on Intelligent Systems and Teleteaching 4, 19–25 (1999)
19. Andreev, R., Ganchev, I., O'Droma, M.: Content Metadata Application and Packaging Service (CMAPS)–Innovative Framework for Producing SCORM-compliant E-Learning Content. In: IEEE International Conference on Advanced Learning Technologies (ICALT 2005) (2005)
20. Kazi, S.A.: A Conceptual Framework for Web-based Intelligent Learning Environments using SCORM-2004. In: IEEE International Conference on Advanced Learning Technologies (ICALT 2004) (2004)
21. Sun, P. -C. et al.: A design to promote group learning in E-Learning: Experiences from the field. Computers & Education (2006)

Personalising Learning through Prerequisite Structures Derived from Concept Maps

Christina M. Steiner and Dietrich Albert

University of Graz, Department of Psychology, Cognitive Science Section
Universitätsplatz 2, 8010 Graz, Austria
{chr.steiner, dietrich.albert}@uni-graz.at

Abstract. Current developments in Web-based learning are especially focusing on personalising learning by adapting the learning process to the student's prior knowledge, learning progress, learning goal, and possibly further characteristics. For creating personalised learning paths and efficiently uncovering the knowledge or competence level of a learner, prerequisite structures on learning objects and assessment problems, or on skills underlying those entities, are extremely useful. Knowledge Space Theory and its competence-based extensions provide a sound mathematical psychological framework that is based upon such prerequisite structures. Concept maps or semantic networks representing domain ontologies offer a valuable source of information for establishing prerequisite structures. This paper outlines approaches on the use of concept maps for deriving prerequisite relations and structures, which can subsequently serve as a basis for implementing personalisation and adaptivity in Web-based learning.

Keywords: Personalisation, Adaptivity, Knowledge Space Theory, Prerequisite Relation, Concept Map, Semantic Network.

1 Introduction

With the widespread use and infusion of the Internet, Web-based learning has emerged to be an important part of education. Research and development address the question how Web-based learning should function in order to assist teaching and learning processes. This issue is focused by the attempt of realising personalised, individualised learning experiences through intelligent and adaptive E-Learning systems. Personalised learning systems aim at adapting teaching and learning to the needs, interests, and aptitude of the individual learner – by diagnosing relevant learner characteristics and utilising the respective information during teaching. The learning system should tailor to the learner's prior knowledge, to the learning progress and growth in expertise, and of course to the desired learning outcome [1].

The mathematical psychological framework of Knowledge Space Theory [2] and its competence-based extensions (Competence-based Knowledge Space Theory; e.g. [3]) provide a sound basis for personalising learning. They utilise prerequisite relationships between learning objects and problems of a knowledge domain, or among skills characterising that domain, for structuring the learning and knowledge assessment process. For identifying those prerequisite relationships and subsequently creating a prerequisite

H. Leung et al. (Eds.): ICWL 2007, LNCS 4823, pp. 43–54, 2008.

structure on which intelligent Web-based learning technologies can be based, different methodologies have been proposed (e.g. [4], [5]).

After introducing the basic concepts of Competence-based Knowledge Space Theory (CbKST) and its application in Web-based learning, this paper presents a new methodology for building prerequisite structures. This methodology utilises information coming from concept maps or semantic networks in order to derive dependencies among learning objects, problems, or skills of a knowledge domain. Benefits and drawbacks of the discussed approaches are identified and an outlook on future research is provided.

2   Competence-Based Knowledge Space Theory

2.1   Knowledge Space Theory and Its Application in Web-Based Learning

Knowledge Space Theory [2] provides a set-theoretic framework for structuring knowledge domains and for representing the knowledge of learners. A domain of knowledge is represented by a set of typical assessment problems (subsequently denoted by Q). The knowledge state of an individual is identified with the subset of assessment problems the person is capable of solving. Among the problems of a domain most probably dependencies will exist and thus, not all potential knowledge states (i.e. subsets of problems) will be expected to be observable. Such dependencies are captured by a so-called prerequisite relation. Two problems a and b are in a prerequisite relation whenever a correct solution of problem a is a prerequisite for mastering problem b. Correspondingly, each knowledge will contain also a whenever it contains b. A prerequisite relation can be illustrated by a so-called Hasse diagram (see Figure 1(a) for an example), where ascending sequences of line segments indicate a prerequisite relationship. According to the prerequisite relation shown in Figure 1(a), the correct solution of problem b is a prerequisite for mastering problem d, while for solving problem c correct answers to problems a and b are prerequisites.

A prerequisite relation restricts the number of possible knowledge states and forms a quasi-order on the set of assessment problems. The collection of possible knowledge states of a given domain Q is called a knowledge structure, whenever it contains the empty set $\emptyset$ and the whole set Q. The knowledge structure K induced by the prerequisite relation depicted in Figure 1(a) is given by

$$K = \{ \ \emptyset, \ \{a\}, \ \{b\}, \ \{a, b\}, \ \{b, d\}, \ \{a, b, c\}, \ \{a, b, d\}, \ \{a, b, c, d\}, \ Q \} \ .$$

The knowledge states of a knowledge structure are naturally ordered by set inclusion, which results in the diagram shown in Figure 1(b).

Given a knowledge structure, there is a range of possible learning paths from the novice knowledge state $\{\emptyset\}$ to the expert knowledge state of full mastery $\{Q\}$. In Figure 1(b) one possible learning path is indicated by dashed arrows. This learning path suggests to initially present material related to problem a (or, equivalently, b), followed by material related to b, and so on. In this way, a knowledge structure can build the basis for creating a personalised learning path. Furthermore, a knowledge structure is at the core of an adaptive assessment procedure [2]. By exploiting the prerequisite relationships among the problems and presenting problems depending on

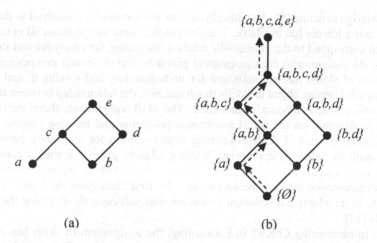

Fig. 1. Example of a Hasse diagram depicting a prerequisite relation (a) and the corresponding knowledge structure (b) with the dashed arrows representing a possible learning path

the learner's previous answers, the knowledge state of a learner can be determined by presenting him/her with only a subset of the problems. The result of such an assessment can be utilised as a starting point for realising individualised learning.

Knowledge Space Theory provides a powerful framework for domain and learner knowledge representation and supports significantly the implementation of intelligent E-Learning solutions. Knowledge Space Theory has, for instance, been successfully implemented in the RATH (Relational Adaptive Tutoring Hypertext, [6]) system. The commercial ALEKS (Adaptive Learning with Knowledge Spaces, [7]) system is the most prominent Web-based educational technology that grounds on Knowledge Space Theory and covers the assessment and teaching of mathematics. ALEKS exploits knowledge structures for adaptively assessing what the learner already knows, what he/she is ready to learn next, and which previously learned material should be addressed in case of repetition and review.

2.2 Competence-Based Knowledge Space Theory and Its Application in Web-Based Learning

Knowledge Space Theory in its original formalisation is rather behavioural, i.e. it focuses on the observable solution behaviour and does not refer to underlying cognitive constructs. To overcome this limitation, several competence-based extensions of Knowledge Space Theory have been devised incorporating underlying skills and competencies (e.g. [3], [8], [9], [10]) but also explicitly referring to learning objects for the first time [11]. Basic assumption of these approaches is the existence of a set of skills representing a knowledge domain and providing a fine-grained description of learners' capabilities. The relationship between skills and assessment problems or learning objects, respectively, is established through assigning those skills required or taught by the respective entity.

By establishing a prerequisite relation on the set of skills – capturing logical, psychological, or curricular dependencies – a competence structure can be built in analogy to a knowledge structure [9]. Accordingly, a competence state is conceived as the subset of skills that a learner has available. The competence structure includes all competence states that correspond to the prerequisite relation, including the empty set and the set of all skills. By assigning to each assessment problem one or several competence states (i.e. subsets of skills) that are sufficient for understanding and solving it, and equivalently, to each learning object the skills that it teaches, the relationship between the skills and the observable behaviour is modelled. The skill assignments therefore induce a knowledge structure on the set of assessment problems and learning objects, respectively. The assignment of skills to learning objects allows for realising a personalised learning path by selecting appropriate learning objects given a learner's competence state and learning goal [12]. Through the assignment of skills to assessment problems a learner's competence state can be uncovered – by first identifying the learner's knowledge state in an adaptive assessment procedure and subsequently mapping the respective skills [12].

When implementing CbKST in E-Learning, the assignment of skills has to be reflected in the metadata of the problems and learning objects. The consideration of skills facilitates adding learning content to the existing material or changing it, as the skill assignments to problems (or learning objects) are independent from each other. Modifying content in a problem-based system, however, is not a straightforward process, as the global prerequisite relation for all problems needs to be revised. Furthermore, CbKST is also able to model and integrate skill assignments coming from distributed resources [13].

CbKST has been successfully applied in the Web-based learning environment APeLS (Adaptive Personalised Learning Service, [11]). Moreover, CbKST builds a framework for domain and learner knowledge representation in iClass (Intelligent Distributed Cognitive-based Open Learning System for Schools), a current project funded by the European Commission aiming at the development of an intelligent cognitive-based open learning system allowing for personalisation and self-regulation by adapting to the learners' needs [14].

3 Building Prerequisite Structures by the Use of Concept Maps

To ensure the effective use of prerequisite structures (i.e. knowledge and competence structures) as a basis for personalising learning paths and adaptively assessing knowledge and competence, their well-founded creation is a critical precondition. A range of different methods has been proposed for identifying prerequisite relationships among assessment problems, learning objects, or skills – especially data analysis [5] and expert queries [4], but also systematic problem construction [10] and cognitive task or curriculum analysis [9]. These methods differ with respect to their underlying theoretical concepts and considerations, their implementation, and the conditions for their application. As an alternative to those methods we propose to utilise information coming from domain ontologies represented by semantic networks and concept maps ([12], [15]).

Concept maps and semantic networks constitute a natural way of representing the declarative knowledge of a domain. Both are essentially the same type of knowledge representation, but more or less common in different contexts. When using the term 'concept map' in the sequel, we refer to both. Typically, concept maps are depicted by graphical node-link representations (see Figure 3 for an example) with the nodes representing concepts and the links representing relationships among those concepts [16]. Two concepts of a concept map and the link relating them constitute a proposition, i.e. a statement forming an elementary unit of declarative knowledge [17]. Therefore, another way of representing a concept map is through a list of propositions.

The information provided by a concept map can be used for identifying prerequisite relationships among learning objects or assessment problems, as well as among skills, and may thus serve as a basis for establishing prerequisite structures [12]. In the sequel, different approaches are outlined that differ with respect to the entities they address and the level of granularity of the underlying concept map. Whereas the identification of prerequisite relationships among problems or learning objects often seems to be a quite straightforward procedure – as these entities are directly related to observable behaviour – determining dependencies among latent skills is more complicated and challenging. Therefore, and because of the overall benefits when considering underlying skills and their structure, we focus in the outlined techniques especially on competence structures. A general assumption in the context of all described approaches is the availability of a concept map that appropriately and validly represents the knowledge domain in question.

3.1 Establishing Knowledge Structures

The approach we suggest for establishing a knowledge structure among a given set of assessment problems (or learning objects) grounds on a concept map providing a fine-grained description of the knowledge domain in question, as it is for example necessary for a detailed description of learning content.

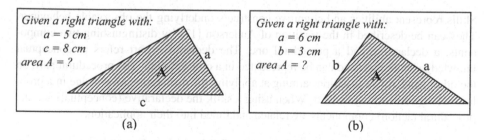

(a)   (b)

Fig. 2. Geometry exercises (a) and (b)

By determining the declarative knowledge required for solving the problems (or, equivalently, taught by the learning objects), each problem can be associated with the respective propositions of the concept map. In this way, each problem can be represented by a substructure of a concept map, i.e. a subset of its propositions [15]. Based on these representations, prerequisite relationships can be derived by set inclusion. This means, if the set of propositions representing a problem X is a subset of those propositions associated with a problem Y, then X constitutes a prerequisite for Y.

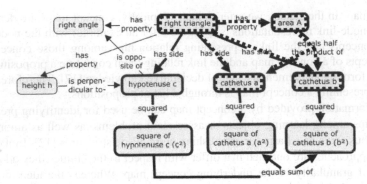

Fig. 3. Concept map with marked propositions corresponding to the geometry exercises (a) (continuous lines) and (b) (dashed lines)

Take for example the two geometry exercises presented in Figure 2. By comparing their representations on the concept map (see Figure 3) it can easily be recognised that the set of propositions associated with exercise (b) is a subset of that of exercise (a). Thus, it can be assumed that (b) is a prerequisite for (a).

Based on the prerequisite relationships identified in this way, a knowledge structure on the respective problems is induced. The established knowledge structure can then be utilised for personalising Web-based learning. For example, a learner having success-fully mastered geometry exercise (a) would be supposed to be also able to correctly solve (b) and therefore does not need to be presented with it. On the other hand, it would not be useful to present exercise (a) to a learner who failed in mastering (b).

3.2 Establishing Competence Structures

Skills represent abilities and cognitive constructs underlying the observable behaviour. They can be described in the tradition of Anderson [17] by distinguishing two compo-nents, a declarative and a procedural one. The declarative part refers to conceptual knowledge about facts and can be represented in a concept map. The procedural part, on the other hand, refers to actions aiming at applying the declarative knowledge in a prob-lem solving or learning context. When using a skill, the declarative (conceptual) and the procedural (action) components are related and tuned into their application.

Conceptual Skill Component: Substructure Set Inclusion. For deriving prerequisite relationships among a set of previously identified skills a similar approach as described above can be utilised [12]. Accordingly, this approach also builds upon a concept map providing a fine-grained description of the respective knowledge domain. Each skill is associated with those propositions of the concept map that correspond to the declarative component of the respective skill. Dependencies among skills can then be deduced by proceeding in the same way as described before, i.e. by applying the rule of set inclusion. This means, if the representation of a skill S on the concept map is a subset of that of skill T, then S can be understood as a prerequisite for T.

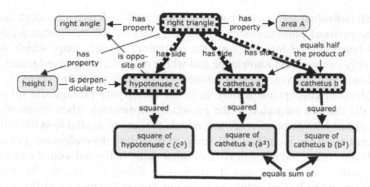

Fig. 4. Concept map with marked propositions corresponding to the skills 'state the sides of a right triangle' (dashed lines) and 'apply the Pythagorean Theorem' (continuous lines)

For a simple example consider the two skills 'state the sides of a right triangle' and 'apply the Pythagorean Theorem' from the knowledge domain of right triangles. As can be seen from Figure 4, the substructures of the concept map corresponding to these two skills are in a subset relation, such that the skill 'state the sides of a right triangle' can be interpreted as a prerequisite to the skill 'apply the Pythagorean Theorem'. Having determined prerequisite relationships among a set of skills in this way, a competence structure can be established which can serve for realising personalised Web-based learning. This means, for example, that first a learning object teaching the skill of stating the sides of a right triangle is presented, before providing the learner with learning objects that convey the skill of applying the Pythagorean Theorem.

Conceptual Skill Component: Analysing Individual Concept Maps. A second approach for identifying prerequisite relationships among pre-defined skills is again based on a concept map that provides a detailed picture of the knowledge domain in question. This concept map serves as a starting point for collecting concept maps from individuals with different knowledge level through a concept mapping task. The collected individual concept maps then provide information on the declarative component of persons' skills and are analysed in order to uncover existing prerequisite relationships among the skills.

For the concept mapping task the propositions of the concept map describing the knowledge domain are combined with incorrect statements (distractors) and are subsequently presented to individuals in form of a correct-incorrect discrimination task (see Table 1 for an example) – preferably including also confidence judgements in order to reduce the risk of guessing [16].

Table 1. Example of a correct-incorrect discrimination task

A right triangle has as side a hypotenuse c.	☐ correct	☐ incorrect
A right triangle has an obtuse angle.	☐ correct	☐ incorrect
The hypotenuse c is adjacent to the right angle.	☐ correct	☐ incorrect
The area A equals the product of cathetus a and cathetus b.	☐ correct	☐ incorrect

For each individual the answer patterns can be used to derive a concept map representing the personal understanding of this very person. All statements a person has judged as being correct together form the individual concept map, which will most probably only cover partial knowledge and which may of course also include misconceptions (whenever incorrect statements were erroneously judged as correct).

The individual concept maps may serve for identifying prerequisite relationships among skills that are subjected to the growth of proficiency when progressing from novice to expert knowledge. For all individuals the sets of available skills reflected in their concept maps are identified and analysed regarding dependencies. For example, if a skill U may occur independently from other skills in the individual concept maps, whereas a skill V contained only if skill U is available, too, this would indicate that U is a prerequisite to V. Grounding on prerequisite relationships identified in this way again a competence structure on the skills can be built.

Adding the Action Component: Using the Component-Attribute Approach. The third approach we suggest for building a competence structure incorporates both, the declarative as well as the procedural component of skills. The declarative component in this case is represented by a concept map on a higher level of abstraction, providing a more general description of the basic concepts of a knowledge domain as it may for example result from curriculum or content analysis. In case of such a more abstract concept map, a skill can usually be associated with one basic concept. The procedural component of skills is represented by an action related to and applying the respective concept. Correspondingly, a skill is defined as a pair consisting of an action and a concept [12]; the skill 'apply the Pythagorean Theorem' for instance consists of the concept 'Pythagorean Theorem' and the action 'apply'.

Both components are seen as separate dimensions of skills that can feature different attributes. This means, the declarative component of a skill can vary with respect to the concept it refers to, and the procedural component varies with respect to the involved action. A prerequisite relation on the skills can be established by the use of the so-called component-attribute approach ([10], [12]). For each component a structure is established by identifying dependencies among the set of attributes (concepts or actions) that these components can take on. Concerning the concepts, this structure is derived from the concept map. For instance, the concept map may reveal for the concepts 'Pythagorean Theorem' (c_1), 'Altitude Theorem' (c_2), and 'Euclidean Theorem' (c_3) that the first theorem is a prerequisite for the other ones, e.g. in accordance with the curriculum or the instructional sequence of text books (see Figure 5(a) for the respective structure). A structure on the set of actions may be introduced through a learning activity taxonomy such as for example Bloom's revised taxonomy [18] which defines cumulative levels of cognitive processing. The actions 'state' (a_1), 'explain' (a_2), and 'apply' (a_3), for example, can be associated with the categories 'Remember', 'Understand', and 'Apply' of Bloom's revised taxonomy, which – in this order – refer to gradual increasing levels of cognitive processes (see Figure 5(b) for the respective structure).

By forming the direct product of the two components all possible skills can be defined – e.g. 'state the Pythagorean Theorem' (a_1c_1), 'explain the Pythagorean Theorem' (a_2c_1), and so forth. The prerequisite relation on the set of skills is derived

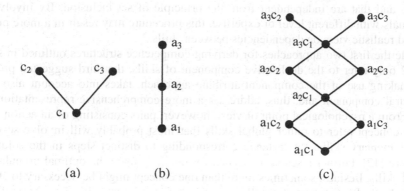

Fig. 5. Structures on the concepts (a) and the actions (b) and prerequisite relation on the skills (c) induced by those structures

from the orders defined on the attributes within each component. For an example see Figure 5(c), depicting the prerequisite relation induced by the structures given in Figure 5(a) and (b). As can be seen, for the skill 'state the Altitude Theorem' (a_1c_2) (or, equivalently, for a_1c_3), the skill 'state the Pythagorean Theorem' (a_1c_1) is a prerequisite, whereas for skill 'explain the Pythagorean Theorem' (a_2c_1) the skills of stating all three theorems, i.e. skills a_1c_1, a_1c_2, and a_1c_3, are prerequisites. The established prerequisite relation gives rise to the competence structure for those skills (i.e. combinations of actions and concepts) that can actually occur or are considered.

4 Discussion

The approach proposed for establishing a knowledge structure constitutes an easy and straightforward procedure. The identification of the declarative knowledge units corresponding to a problem or learning object can be carried out reliably and validly with sufficient expertise in the respective knowledge domain. This actually constitutes an in-depth consideration of the assessment problem or learning object and therefore provides a step towards CbKST, as each proposition could be considered as an atomic skill.

The outlined approaches that make use of set inclusion suffer from the weakness that these procedures may result in completely unrelated problems or skills, respectively. This means, it may be the case that the representations of several problems (or skills) on the concept map overlap, but are not in a subset relation. If so, either there may be actually no prerequisite relationships among the respective entities, or the procedure was not able to uncover them. Further research is needed for identifying other possible rules that could be used in this case. Potential approaches in this context would for example be to take into account the multiplicity of skills or knowledge elements occurring in the solution of a problem, or also their sequence. This could be captured by the principles of 'multiset inclusion' and 'sequence inclusion' [19].

The procedure based on the analysis of individual concept maps provides the opportunity of identifying prerequisite relationships among skills that exist in empirical practice and that are independent from the principle of set inclusion. By involving individuals with different level of expertise, this procedure may result in a more practical and realistic view on dependencies between skills.

While the first two approaches for deriving competence structures outlined in section 3.2 only refer to the declarative component of skills, the third suggested procedure, making use of the component-attribute approach, takes into account also the procedural component and, thus, addresses a more comprehensive representation of skills. From a psychological point of view, however, pairs consisting of an action and a basic concept refer to rather global skills that most probably will involve several more elementary skills, for instance corresponding to distinct steps in the solution procedure [12]. Further research is needed for deciding upon the optimal granularity level of skills. Besides, sometimes more than one concept might be necessary to characterise the declarative part of a skill.

In general, once prerequisite structures have been established, they need to be empirically validated in order to serve as a well-founded domain and learner knowledge representation and to ensure their successful implementation in Web-based learning and teaching solutions as a basis for realising personalisation and adaptivity.

5 Conclusion

Current developments in the context of Web-based learning especially focus on the creation of personalised and individualised learning experiences, by tailoring teaching to the needs and aptitudes of each learner. For efficiently and adaptively uncovering the knowledge or competence level of a learner and for creating personalised learning paths, prerequisite structures on learning objects, assessment problems, and skills are extremely useful. Prerequisite structures can be utilised for realising adaptive navigation support in Web-based learning [20], for instance by link hiding or by annotating learning content that suits a learner's current knowledge/competence. Knowledge Space Theory and its competence-based extensions provide a sound foundation for realising personalised learning on the basis of such prerequisite structures and have been successfully implemented in several Web-based E-Learning systems (for an overview see [21]).

This paper outlined a methodology of utilising concept maps as a valuable instrument for determining prerequisite relationships and establishing prerequisite structures on problems, learning objects, and skills. The suggested approaches constitute useful alternatives to existing methods for establishing knowledge and competence structures in the context of CbKST. Of course, there are still some open issues that have to be addressed by future research. The described approaches need to be applied in a practical context and directly compared to other methods to prove their significance and applicability and to identify opportunities for improvement.

A critical precondition for the application of the described procedures is the availability of a well-founded concept map of the knowledge domain in question. Suitable concept maps either have to be created especially for that purpose but probably also concept maps generated for other purposes can be reused. If a concept map has to be generated from scratch, this may be done by domain experts, through the use of textbooks, but also through automatic extraction from texts. In the context of Web-based learning, concept maps may already be available as a result of E-Learning design and instructional planning [22] and can subsequently be utilised for the purpose of building prerequisite structures. In this way, by reusing already available resources, a contribution towards shared or reduced efforts and costs and increased profitability in creating Web-based learning can be made. Conversely, concept maps that have been created for deriving prerequisite structures may be reused for visualisation purposes in Web-based learning environments, e.g. providing an overview and navigational interface for the learning content [23].

A future goal of applications of CbKST in E-Learning is to have at hand a set of (semi-)automatic procedures and tools (for identifying skills, building prerequisite structures, assigning skills to learning objects and assessment problems) that facilitate building the foundations of adaptivity and personalisation for Web-based learning.

Acknowledgments. The work presented in this paper is partially supported by the European Community (EC) under the Information Society Technologies (IST) program of the 6th FP for RTD-project iClass (contract no. 507922). The authors are solely responsible for the content of this paper. It does not represent the opinion of the EC, and the EC is not responsible for any use that might be made of data appearing therein.

References

1. Albert, D., Mori, T.: Contributions of Cognitive Psychology to the Future of E-Learning. Bulletin of the Graduate School of Education, Hiroshima University, Part 1 (Learning and Curriculum Development) 50, 25–34 (2001)
2. Doignon, J.-P., Falmagne, J.C.: Knowledge Spaces. Springer, Berlin (1999)
3. Doignon, J.-P.: Knowledge Spaces and Skill Assignments. In: Fischer, G.H., Laming, D. (eds.) Contributions to Mathematical Psychology, Psychometrics and Methodology, pp. 111–121. Springer, New York (1994)
4. Koppen, M., Doignon, J.-P.: How to Build a Knowledge Space by Querying an Expert. Journal of Mathematical Psychology 34, 311–331 (1990)
5. Schrepp, M.: Extracting Knowledge Structures from Observed Data. British Journal of Mathematical and Statistical Psychology 52, 213–224 (1999)
6. Hockemeyer, C., Held, T., Albert, D.: RATH – A Relational Adaptive Tutoring Hypertext WWW–Environment Based on Knowledge Space Theory. In: Alvegård, C. (ed.) CAL-ISCE 1998: Proceedings of the Fourth International Conference on Computer Aided Learning in Science and Engineering, Chalmers University of Technology, Göteborg, pp. 417–423 (1998)
7. Canfield, W.: ALEKS: A Web-Based Intelligent Tutoring System. Mathematics and Computer Education 35, 152–158 (2001)
8. Düntsch, I., Gediga, G.: Skills and Knowledge Structures. British Journal of Mathematical and Statistical Psychology 48, 9–27 (1995)
9. Korossy, K.: Extending the Theory of Knowledge Spaces: A Competence-Performance Approach. Zeitschrift für Psychologie 205, 53–82 (1997)
10. Albert, D., Held, T.: Component Based Knowledge Spaces in Problem Solving and Inductive Reasoning. In: Albert, D., Lukas, J. (eds.) Knowledge Spaces: Theories, Empirical Research, Applications, pp. 15–40. Lawrence Erlbaum, Mahwah (1999)

11. Hockemeyer, C., Conlan, O., Wade, V., Albert, D.: Applying Competence Prerequisite Structures for eLearning and Skill Management. Journal of Universal Computer Science 9, 1428–1436 (2003)
12. Heller, J., Steiner, C., Hockemeyer, C., Albert, D.: Competence-Based Knowledge Structures for Personalized Learning. International Journal on E-Learning 5, 75–88 (2006)
13. Heller, J., Repitsch, C.: Distributed Skill Functions and the Meshing of Knowledge Structures. Journal of Mathematical Psychology (in press)
14. Turker, A., Görgün, I., Conlan, O.: The Challenge of Content Creation to Facilitate Personalized E-Learning Experiences. International Journal on E-Learning 5, 11–17 (2006)
15. Albert, D., Steiner, C.M.: Representing Domain Knowledge by Concept Maps: How to Validate them? In: Okamoto, T., et al. (eds.) The 2nd Joint Workshop of Cognition and Learning through Media-Communication for Advanced E-Learning, Tokyo, pp. 169–174 (2005)
16. Steiner, C.M., Albert, D., Heller, J.: Concept Mapping as a Means to Build E-Learning. In: Buzzetto-More, N.A. (ed.) Advanced Principles of Effective E-Learning, pp. 59–111. Informing Science Press, Santa Rosa (2007)
17. Anderson, J.R.: Cognitive Psychology and its Implications. W.H. Freeman and Company, New York (1995)
18. Anderson, L.W., Krathwohl, D.R.: A Taxonomy for Learning, Teaching, and Assessing: A Revision of Bloom's Taxonomy of Educational Objectives. Longman, New York (2001)
19. Schrepp, M., Held, T., Albert, D.: Component-Based Construction of Surmise Relations for Chess Problems. In: Albert, D., Lukas, J. (eds.) Knowledge Spaces: Theories, Empirical Research, Applications, pp. 41–66. Lawrence Erlbaum, Mahwah (1999)
20. Brusilovsky, P.: Adaptive Navigation Support: From Adaptive Hypermedia to the Adaptive Web and Beyond. PsychNology Journal 2, 7–23 (2004)
21. Albert, D., Hockemeyer, C., Wesiak, G.: Current Trends in eLearning Based on Knowledge Space Theory and Cognitive Psychology. Psychologische Beiträge 44, 478–494 (2002)
22. Stoyanov, S.: Cognitive Mapping as a Learning Method in Hypermedia Design. Journal of Interactive Learning Research 8, 309–323 (1997)
23. Coffey, J.W., Cañas, A.J.: LEO: A Learning Environment Organizer to Support Computer-Mediated Instruction. Journal of Educational Technology Systems 31, 275–290 (2003)

A Pedagogy-Driven Personalization Framework to Support Automatic Construction of Adaptive Learning Experiences

Polyxeni Arapi, Nektarios Moumoutzis, Manolis Mylonakis,
George Theodorakis, and Stavros Christodoulakis

Laboratory of Distributed Multimedia Information Systems and Applications, Technical
University of Crete (TUC/MUSIC), 73100 Chania, Greece
{xenia, nektar, manolis, gtheodorakis, stavros}@ced.tuc.gr

Abstract. In order to effectively exploit the wealth of content in Learning Object Repositories several issues should be addressed including the "closed corpus" problem as identified in the field of Adaptive Hypermedia as well as the "one size fits all" problem. Both are related to personalization. The creation of personalized learning experiences is considered as a necessity to cope with the overwhelming amount of available learning material. This paper presents a personalization framework that allows for the automatic creation of pedagogically-sound learning experiences taking into account the variety of the Learners and their individual needs. This framework defines a model for the representation of abstract training scenarios (Learning Designs) encoded in an instructional ontology. This ontology clearly separates pedagogy from content allowing this way the construction of real personalized learning experiences where learning objects are bound to the learning scenario at run-time taking into account information encoded in Learner Profiles.

Keywords: Personalization, Instructional Design.

1 Introduction

It becomes more and more apparent that "one size fits all" solutions are no longer enough to satisfy the Learners' educational needs. Different Learners have different learning styles, educational levels, previous knowledge, technical and other preferences and all these are parameters that affect the learning function outcome. Learners expect from systems a "personal trainer" and not a "classroom" behavior, where their personality and needs are known and taken into account. Moreover, the proliferation of the Internet and the wealth of content in Learning Object Repositories call for flexible solutions where content is not strictly bound with the learning plan but could be retrieved at run-time and ideally from many sources according to the Learner needs. This is called in Adaptive Hypermedia "open corpus". Several research areas are related with the above challenges: Adaptive Hypermedia Systems, Intelligent Tutoring Systems, and Semantic Web [1]. Although each area treats adaptivity of learning experiences from a different point of

H. Leung et al. (Eds.): ICWL 2007, LNCS 4823, pp. 55–65, 2008.

view, there is a convergence in the research community that pedagogy is important and should be represented in a consistent way. Moreover, the pedagogical model should be reusable and separated from content allowing appropriate learning resources according to the Learner profile to be bound to the training scenario at run-time.

In order to effectively support pedagogically-sound adaptive learning experiences, several issues need to be addressed:

1. Appropriate formulation and description of learning objects giving special attention to elements related with educational context (e.g. Learning Objectives).
2. Consistent representation of pedagogy separated from content according to a model that allows for the binding of appropriate learning objects to the learning scenarios at run-time.
3. Appropriate representation of Learner Profiles giving special attention to elements representing the learning needs of Learners (e.g. learning goals, previous knowledge, learning style, educational level).
4. Specification of a personalization component that taking into account all the above constructs adaptive learning experiences that fit to the Learner's needs and preferences.

In this paper, we present a framework that addresses all the above issues exploiting existing eLearning standards. We use the IEEE LOM standard to describe learning objects and we make the necessary adaptation of this standard in order to be able to represent Learning Objectives in a structured way. Moreover, we propose a model for the representation of abstract training scenarios (Learning Designs) encoded in an instructional ontology. This model clearly separates content from pedagogy and defines reusable instructional units encapsulated in Learning Designs. This way the same Learning Designs can be applied in different instructional situations, by binding appropriate content to learning activities taking also into account the information represented in Learner Profiles. A Learner Profile usually includes information about demographic data, competencies, previous knowledge, interests, goals, technical and other preferences of the Learner. Here, we focus on the elements that should be present in order to support personalization in terms of the proposed framework. These elements could be mapped in appropriate elements of the IEEE Personal and Private Information (PAPI) and IMS Learner Information Package (LIP). Finally, we describe how the construction of adaptive learning experiences can be automated. The corresponding personalization component is able to select appropriate Learning Designs addressing the special instructional situations for each Learner and then create learning experiences by binding appropriate reusable learning objects according to the Learner Profile.

The structure of the rest of this paper is as follows: Section 2 presents a generic personalization architecture. Section 3 deals with aspects related with the formulation and description of learning objects. Section 4 presents a model for the representation of abstract training scenarios and a tool (Learning Designs Editor) that has been implemented for this purpose. Section 5 presents the important elements that should be included in a Learner Model to support the personalization framework presented in this paper. Section 6 presents the procedure of the construction of adaptive learning experiences by a personalization component. A review of the related literature is presented in Section 7 and the paper ends with some concluding remarks and future work.

2 Overall Architecture

In the architecture depicted in Fig. 1 one can see that in the proposed personalization framework personalized learning experiences are created in the form of SCORM packages using reusable learning objects residing at Learning Object Repositories in order to satisfy Learner needs and preferences expressed in Learner Profiles. To achieve this, the system consults Learning Designs (i.e. pedagogical templates) that describe how certain subjects should be taught.

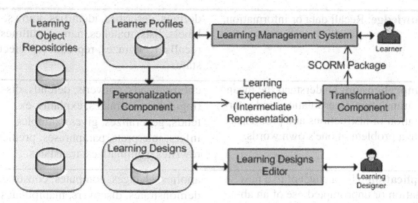

Fig. 1. Overall architecture for the automatic construction of pedagogy-sound personalized learning experiences

The main component of this architecture is the Personalization Component, which takes into account the Learner Profile and tries to find an appropriate Learning Design that will be thereafter applied to the construction of a learning experience. Then, based on the selected Learning Design, which is essentially a hierarchy of activities, the component is able to bind specific learning objects to each activity using information from the Learner's Profile and builds an intermediate representation of the learning experience. Finally, a Transformation Component creates a SCORM package from this intermediate representation. A special tool, called Learning Designs Editor has been also implemented for the creation of Learning Designs.

In order to be able to retrieve learning objects from learning object repositories these should be described in a consistent way. Without being restrictive, it is proposed to use the LOM standard for the description of learning objects. If this framework is applied on top of digital libraries, we propose to use the approach that we presented in [2] in order to support multiple context views of digital objects.

It is assumed that a SCORM compliant Learning Management System (LMS) is used to deliver the constructed personalized learning experience (i.e. the corresponding SCORM package) to the Learner. This LMS is also able to track Learner's behavior and progress in order to keep the Learner Profile up to date.

3   Formulation and Description of Learning Objects

Current developments in eLearning have promoted the concept of reusable learning objects. Traditionally, learning was organized in lessons and courses covering predefined objectives. In eLearning environments the material is broken into smaller independent pieces that can be used as they are or in combination with other material to form higher level objects covering the learning needs of the users on demand and at the right time.

Table 1. Bloom's Taxonomy descriptive verbs

Cognitive Category	Learning Objectives Verbs
Knowledge: Recall data or information.	defines, describes, identifies, knows, labels, lists, matches, names, outlines, recalls, recognizes, reproduces, selects, states.
Comprehension: Understand the meaning, translation, interpolation, and interpretation of instructions and problems. State a problem in one's own words.	comprehends, converts, defends, distinguishes, estimates, explains, extends, generalizes, gives examples, infers, interprets, paraphrases, predicts, rewrites, summarizes, translates.
Application: Use a concept in a new situation or unprompted use of an abstraction. Applies what was learned in the class-room into novel situations in the work place.	applies, changes, computes, constructs, demonstrates, discovers, manipulates, modifies, operates, predicts, prepares, produces, relates, shows, solves, uses.
Analysis: Separates material or concepts into component parts so that its organizational structure may be understood. Distinguishes between facts and inferences.	analyzes, breaks down, compares, contrasts, diagrams, deconstructs, differentiates, discriminates, distinguishes, identifies, illustrates, infers, outlines, relates, selects, separates.
Synthesis: Builds a structure or pattern from diverse elements. Put parts together to form a whole, with emphasis on creating a new meaning or structure.	categorizes, combines, compiles, composes, creates, devises, designs, explains, generates, modifies, organizes, plans, rearranges, reconstructs, relates, reorganizes, revises, rewrites, summarizes, tells, writes.

One important issue related to the concept of reusable learning objects is their description with metadata. The most popular metadata model used is the IEEE Learning Object

Metadata (LOM) standard. It is possible to represent some pedagogical properties that can be matched with corresponding properties of Learner Profiles in order to support an automated process for the construction of personalized learning experiences. However, one of the important aspects in personalization is the representation of Learning Objectives that capture the intended learning outcome of learning objects which is not directly addressed in LOM. Other elements of LOM, such as keywords or description are usually used to describe Learning Objectives. However, these simple text descriptions do not represent a formal way for defining learning objectives. Consequently, this approach presents a technical barrier because textual descriptions are not machine-readable and can not be exploited by personalization components.

```
<lom:classification>
    <lom:purpose>
        <lom:value>educational objective</lom:value>
        <!-- Each educational objective is defined as verb from Bloom's Taxonomy)+ Topic
(Ontology Concept/Individual) -->
    </lom:purpose>
    <lom:taxonPath>
        <lom:source>
            <lom:string language="en">http://somehost/bloomstaxonomy.owl</lom:string>
            <!-- The URL of the ontology containing the Bloom's Taxonomy Verbs-->
        </lom:source>
        <lom:taxon>
            <lom:entry>
                <lom:string language="en">explains</lom:string>
                <!-- The verb of the learning objective-->
            </lom:entry>
        </lom:taxon>
    </lom:taxonPath>
    <lom:taxonPath>
        <lom:source>
            <lom:string language="en">http://somehost/iconographyontology.owl</lom:string>
            <!-- The URL of the target ontology -->
        </lom:source>
        <lom:taxon>
            <lom:entry>
                <lom:string language="en">Iconographic Style</lom:string>
                <!-- The topic of the learning objective (a Concept of Iconography Ontology)-->
            </lom:entry>
        </lom:taxon>
    </lom:taxonPath>
</lom:classification>
```

Fig. 2. Use of *classification* element of LOM to represent Learning Objectives

To address the shortcoming described above we need to define a more formal and pedagogically-sound way of expressing Learning Objectives, as well as their representations based on appropriate adaptation of existing LOM elements. We have chosen to use Bloom's Taxonomy of educational objectives [3] and to define Learning Objectives pairs consisting of a verb taken from a Bloom's taxonomy and a topic referencing a concept or individual of a domain ontology. The taxonomy of educational objectives [3] is comprised of six levels, namely: knowledge, comprehension, application, analysis, synthesis, and evaluation. Each level as shown in Table 1 has a corresponding set of descriptive verbs that can be used to form Learning Objectives.

In LOM, Learning Objectives can be expressed following the above approach using its *classification* element. The *classification* element describes where a learning object falls within a particular classification system. To define multiple classifications, there may be multiple instances of this category. Fig. 2 shows how this element can be adapted in order to represent a specific Learning Objective.

4   Learning Designs

Learning Designs are abstract training scenarios that are constructed according to an instructional ontology coded in OWL (Fig. 3). This ontology has the important

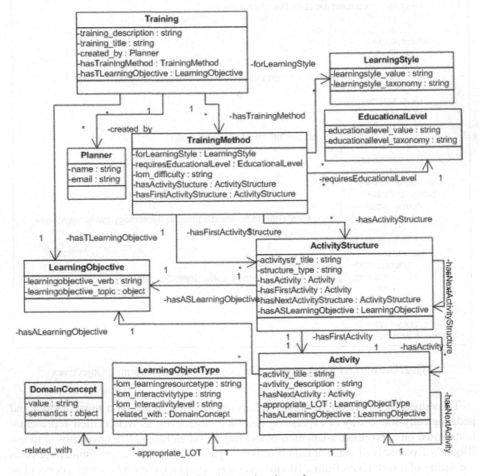

Fig. 3. The instructional ontology

characteristic that learning objects are not bound to the training scenarios at design time, as in current eLearning standards and specifications (e.g. IMS Learning Design-IMS LD and SCORM). Whereas, pedagogy is separated and independent from content achieving this way reusability of Learning Designs or parts of them that can be used from the systems for the construction of "real" personalized learning experiences, where appropriate learning objects according to the Learner Profile are bound to the learning experience at run-time taking into account several parameters of the Learner Profile. This is possible, since the model gives the opportunity to specify in each Activity the learning objects' requirements, instead of binding the learning objects themselves, as IMS LD and SCORM impose. This ontology exploits some elements and ideas from IMS LD and LOM.

A *Training* is a collection of *TrainingMethods* that refer to the different ways the same subject can be taught depending on the *LearningStyle*, the *EducationalLevel* of the Learner and the preferred *difficulty*. There are several categorizations of Learning Styles and Educational Levels, thus these elements are flexible so that being able to point to values of different taxonomies. A *TrainingMethod* consists of a hierarchy of reusable *ActivityStructures* built from reusable *Activities*. Each *Training*, *ActivityStructure* and *Activity* has a *LearningObjective*. Each *LearningObjective* is defined using the approach presented earlier. In particular it is composed of: (a) a *learningobjective_verb*, taken from a subset of Bloom's Taxonomy [3]) and (b) a *learningobjective_topic* that indicates the topic that the Learning Objective is about, referencing a concept or individual of a domain ontology. The *LearningObjectType* is used to describe the desired learning object characteristics without binding specific objects with Activities at design time. Via the *related_with* property we can further restrict the preferred learning objects according to their constituent parts (if they are semantically annotated) connecting them with *DomainConcepts* which refer to concepts or individuals from a domain ontology.

4.1 The Learning Designs Editor

The specification of Learning Designs is done using an editor that provides an intuitive GUI and is based on the above instructional ontology. The editor is able to create a Learning Design, open an existing one for further editing or reuse of a Learning Design or parts of it in the creation of other Learning Designs.

Each Learning Design is presented in a hierarchical structure with its underlying Training Methods, Activity Structures and Activities in the form of a tree. Each tree node can be edited in a special form that contains all the corresponding properties. After editing a Learning Design the user can save it. At this point a set of well-formed rules are applied to check the structure of the Learning Design and find any inconsistencies that may be present and the user is informed about these inconsistencies so that he can handle them.

Fig. 4 presents a screenshot of the Learning Designs Editor used to develop a Learning Design related to the teaching of Bulgarian Iconography. Four Training Methods are associated with this Learning Design forming alternative instructional paths for different combinations of learning style, educational level and difficulty. The screen shot also shows the editing form for a specific Activity inside the first

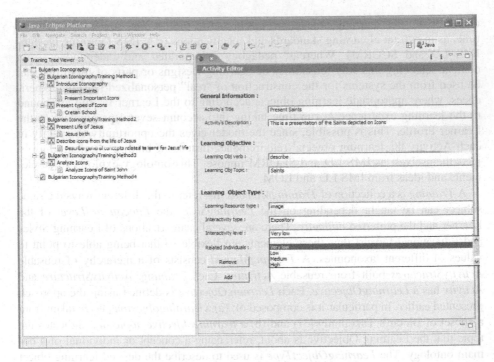

Fig. 4. The Learning Designs Editor user interface

Activity Structure of the first Training Method. The form contains fields for the editing of the title, the description, the Learning Objective and the Learning Object Type of the Activity.

5 Learner Profiles

Our intention here is to focus on the elements that should be included in a Learner Model in order to support personalization within the framework presented in this paper. These elements could be mapped in appropriate elements of the IEEE Personal and Private Information (PAPI) and IMS Learner Information Package (LIP) using extensions. We focus on the Learner's goals and preferences and we illustrate those elements and their relations in a Learner Ontology (Fig. 5).

A *LearnerGoal* is expressed in terms of *LearningObjectives* using the structure that was presented above in the instructional ontology. A Learner can have many *LearnerGoals*. A *LearnerGoal* has a *status* property (float in [0, 1]) indicating the satisfaction level of the goal (0 represents no satisfaction, 1 fully satisfied). Using this information one can also infer the previous knowledge of the Learner. The Learner can also define a *priority* for each *LearnerGoal*. The Learner can have several types of Preferences: *EducationalLevel* and *LearningStyle* matching with the corresponding elements of the instructional ontology, *Language*, *LearningProvider* (the author or organization making available the learning objects), *LearningPlanner* (the person that develops Learning Designs) and *Technical* preferences.

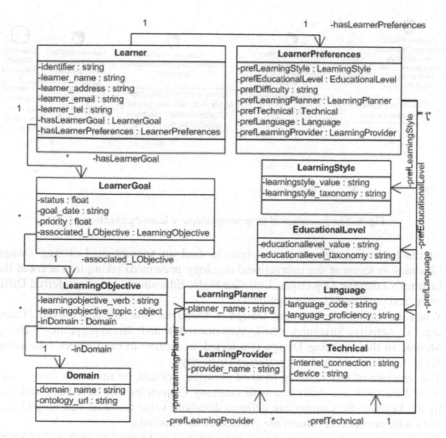

Fig. 5. The Learner ontology gathering important elements in order to apply the personalization framework presented in this paper

As it is described in the next section, these parameters affect both the construction of an appropriate learning path for a specific Learner according to existing Learning Designs and the selection of learning objects that are thereafter bound at run-time to the learning path to form the resulting learning experience.

6 The Personalization Component

The Personalization Component takes into account the knowledge provided by the Learning Designs and the Learner Profiles and constructs personalized learning experiences that are delivered next to eLearning applications in the form of SCORM packages. Specifically, the goal is to find an appropriate Learning Design that will be used thereafter to construct a learning experience adapted to the Learner's needs. As already mentioned, learning objects are bound to the learning scenario at run-time.

The procedure of constructing an adaptive learning experience is illustrated in Fig. 6. In each step several parameters of the Learner Profile (given in brackets in Fig. 6) are taken into account:

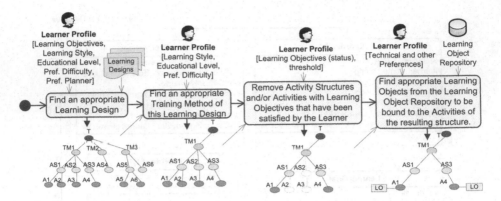

Fig. 6. The procedure of generating adaptive learning experiences

1. At the beginning, the component tries to find an appropriate Learning Design (Training in terms of the instructional ontology presented) taking into account the Learner's Learning Objectives, Learning Style, Educational Level, preferred Difficulty, and preferred Planner (optional).
2. When an appropriate Learning Design is found its structure is retrieved (Training(T), Activity Structures (AS), Activities(A)) and an appropriate Training Method of this Learning Design is selected, according to the Learner's Learning Style, Educational Level and preferred Difficulty.
3. The structure of this Training Method is further refined, by removing from it Activity Structures and Activities with Learning Objectives that have been satisfied by the Learner (the Learner can define a threshold value t, so that Learning Objectives with satisfaction value>t are considered as satisfied).
4. Finally, appropriate learning objects are retrieved and bound to each node (Activity) of this structure constructing the learning experience. Here, the Learning Object Type describing the characteristics of appropriate learning objects for each Activity is taken into account along with other learner's preferences (e.g. content provider, technical preferences). The resulted learning experience is transformed to SCORM (through a Transformation Component) and delivered to the Learner.

7 Related Work

In [4] a similar approach is followed to represent pedagogy in order to support run-time resource binding. Our approach differs in that it takes into account the learning style, the educational level and learning goals of the Learners, supporting the representation of different learning paths (Training Methods) for training in a specific subject. In [5], although the need for supporting different training methods for the same subject is recognized, these methods are not connected as in our approach with the learning styles and educational levels of the Learners. Moreover, description of appropriate learning objects characteristics beyond semantics is not supported. An alternative approach is presented in [6] regarding automatic course sequencing. In this work learning paths are not constructed based on pedagogical models, but are extracted from a directed acyclic graph that is the result of merging the knowledge space (domain model) and the media space (learning objects and their relation) using minimum learning time as an optimization criteria. However, since this approach is highly based on the domain model that does not necessarily imply an instructional model, and also on the relations of learning objects and their aggregation level, there is a risk that the result of the sequencing process may be not always "pedagogically-right" adapted to the Learners' various learning styles.

8 Conclusion and Future Work

We have presented a framework for supporting automatic construction of pedagogically-sound adaptive learning experiences using material in learning object repositories, taking into account the variety of learning needs of the Learners. Since pedagogy plays an important role to achieve this, a model for building abstract training scenarios (Learning Designs) has been also provided and an appropriate tool implemented, which guide the construction of pedagogically sound adaptive learning experiences and allow for the binding of appropriate learning resources at run-time according to the Learner Profiles. The framework has been initially implemented in a service-oriented architecture above an experimental digital library of audiovisual content [2]. Extensions are implemented and evaluation of the framework takes place within the LOGOS project.

Acknowledgments. The work presented in this paper is partially funded in the scope of the LOGOS STREP Project (IST-4-027451), named "Knowledge-on-Demand for Ubiquitous Learning".

References

1. Brusilovsky, P.: Adaptive and intelligent technologies for web-based education. Künstliche Intelligenz 4, 19–25 (1999)
2. Arapi, P., Moumoutzis, N., Christodoulakis, S.: ASIDE: An Architecture for Supporting Interoperability between Digital Libraries and ELearning Applications. In: 6th IEEE International Conference on Advanced Learning Technologies (ICALT2006), pp. 257–261. IEEE Computer Society Press, Kerkrade, The Netherlands (2006)
3. Bloom, B.S., Krathwohl, D.R.: Taxonomy of Educational Objectives: The Classification of Educational Goals. In: Handbook I. Cognitive Domain, Longman, New York (1965)
4. Capuano, N., Gaeta, M., Lannone, R., Orciuoli, F.: Learning Design and Run-Time Resource Binding in a Distributed E-Learning Environment. In: 1st International Kaleidoscope Learning Grid SIG Workshop on Distributed E-Learning Environments, British Computer Society, eWic, Naples, Italy (2005)
5. Meisel, H., Compatangelo, E., Hörfurter, A.: An ontology-based approach to intelligent Instructional Design support. In: Palade, V., Howlett, R.J., Jain, L. (eds.) KES 2003. LNCS, vol. 2773, Springer, Heidelberg (2003)
6. Karampiperis, P., Sampson, D.: Adaptive Instructional Planning Using Ontologies. In: 4th IEEE International Conference on Advanced Learning Technologies (ICALT2004), Joensuu, Finland, pp. 126–130. IEEE Computer Society Press, Joensuu, Finland (2004)

Authoring Learning Objects for Web-Based Intelligent Tutoring Systems

Ramón Zatarain-Cabada, Ma. Lucia Barrón-Estrada,
Leopoldo Zepeda-Sanchez, and Fernando Vega-Juárez

Instituto Tecnológico de Culiacán, Coordinación de Posgrado, Av. Juan de Dios Bátiz s/n,
Col. Guadalupe, C.P. 80220, Culiacán, Sin., México
{rzatarain, lbarron, lzepeda}@itculiacan.edu.mx

Abstract. This paper is about an author tool that can be used to produce learning objects for WEB-based intelligent tutoring systems. The learning objects are oriented to different competency-based courses that are taught in technical high schools in México under a norm of competency-based education. The norms have a defined structure which is convenient to plan, evaluate and organize the courses. The author tool has three main components: an editor of learning objects for rapid creation of web-classroom applications; a player for displaying learning objects in a convenient interface; and an intelligent tutoring module for adding adaptation features to learning objects. The author tool allows including different evaluations and later storing the learning objects under the SCORM standard. Right now the software has been used to produce basic courses for a high-school technical level and we are working in the implementation of the intelligent tutoring module.

Keywords: Web-based Teaching, Intelligent Tutoring System.

1 Introduction

In order to fulfill the educative policy that settles down in the National Plan of Development, the Main Board of Industrial and Technology Education in Mexico is modifying its curricula [2]. These modifications are based on the requirements of the industrial sector and on the norms of labor competition. In addition, it proposes flexible models of qualification towards the students, where priority to the job-related training activities occurs on the theoretical contents, and tries as well that the professors incorporate in the contents the advances of science and the technology, using, pedagogical and didactic innovations of the education based on the learning [10]. This new reform is called Competency Based Teaching (CBT) [2].

The characteristics that must have the students in this learning model are: to be able to work together (teamwork); to have ability to identify problems and to solve them; to suitably make decisions and to dominate several functions of work. The learning proposal has a constructivist approach.

H. Leung et al. (Eds.): ICWL 2007, LNCS 4823, pp. 66–77, 2008.

In order to work with this didactic proposal, we implemented an author tool where a non-programmer teacher can more easily produce Web classroom applications for competency-based teaching.

The arrangement of the paper is as follows: In Section 2, we present the author tool describing each one of the module components. In Section 3, we describe the software architecture of the tool. In Section 4, we discuss the implementation of the software tool, analysing first a compression algorithm for storing resource files, second the tool interfaces (an editor and a player), and third an implemented pre-compiler used to filter HTML files. Exporting files to SCORM is explained in Section 5. Some experimental results are shown in Section 6. Comparison to related work is given in 7 and conclusions are shown in Section 8.

2 The Author Tool

The proposed tool within this model is called CIBACO and derived its name from Intelligent Courses Based on Competitions (Cursos Inteligentes **Ba**sados en **Co**mpetencia). CIBACO is a multimedia tool that allows creating web-based courses, which will be provided to the students for their use in the presence of the instructor or in an independent way. Taking into consideration the importance that represents the availability of the teacher in the success of any system of distance learning; and taking into account the characteristics and background of a regular high school instructor, such as age and maximum level of instruction or preparation (where in Mexico is very common the rejection of using new technologies), it is necessary to think about tools that do not represent a drastic change in the accomplishment of their educational activities. CIBACO consists of three modules (Figure 1). The first one is an editor, and will be used by the teachers to create the courses. The contents of the courses are directly created from standard HTML files with other resources. The files which store the courses keep their own format called CBC. The second module is a player, which can be used by the students to view or run the courses. The courses are distributed with a tool used to visualize them. However, it is not possible to visualize the courses on the web unless we save the courses into a package using the standard format SCORM [14]. In this format, we can access and display the web pages of the courses from any learning Management System that uses the Standard SCORM.

The third module is the Intelligent Tutoring Module (ITM) which provides adaptation features to any course. The intelligent components added to the CBC course consist of three parts: the student adaptation class, the domain class and the pedagogical class. CIBACO builds a dynamic model class of the student by analyzing and recording individual participation for any course by the student. For example the time spent on each topic or the number of correct answers to topic questions. The domain model class is structured in three hierarchical levels of abstraction: the course, the units, and the subjects. Concepts in the knowledge base are stored in the subject level. Each subject consists of a SCORM learning object that explains a particular concept.

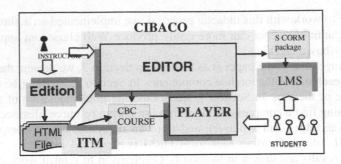

Fig. 1. Main components of CIBACO

Learning objects contain different media types such as text, image, audio and animation and they have been implemented using the principles of Multiple Intelligences [5]. The pedagogical model class defines several events (questions, awakenings, skip/repeat/ reinforce subjects, etc.) which accomplish a pedagogical activity or event used to improve student learning behaviors.

On the other hand, the structure of regular course is created from the training programs of the corresponding subject or course. A competency based course is structured according to the norm of labor competition to which they make reference. The course has a name, a set of units and contents. The contents of the course are equivalent to the elements of competition of the unit norm. The structure of a course is very similar to the structure of the norm and is equivalent to the one in the training program. The total of subjects of each unit is not a fixed number and varies depending on the contents specified in the course. It is important to mention that the proposed structure for the electronic courses only has three levels: course, units and subjects. According to the structure of training program, sub-subjects in a course are not considered.

2.1 The Evaluations

The courses created with CIBACO can have evaluations: One by each subject that contains the course. The format of the evaluation is one question and four possible answers. This format is originated from the standard that at this moment is used in the Mexican high school knowledge contest. In these contests a question always has an answer and three distracters. In CIBACO one question can have one, two, three or including four correct answers. The format is motivated from the CBT proposal where the evaluation process suggest not be rigid, but that causes a constant communication of instructors and students [2]. During this evaluation, the tool will not show the correct results. It will only inform which questions were answered correctly. This produces that the student consults the teacher or the teammate, which constitutes a collaborative activity; a learning methodology included within the constructivism [3, 9]. On the other hand, evaluations are an important part of the student model class because correct/incorrect answers establish the way or behavior of the course.

3   Cibaco Architecture

In order to develop this project we designed a three-layer architecture (see figure 2). The layer of the user interface is made up of the packages EDITOR and PLAYER. Package EDITOR generates the tool Editor, used by the instructor. Package PLAYER produces the tool Player used by the student.

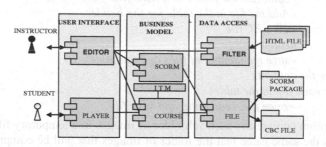

Fig. 2. CIBACO architecture

The BUSINESS layer consists of COURSE, which contains information of the courses, ITM which add the Intelligent Tutoring Module to the course and SCORM which keeps the structure of the courses in a specific format to produce a SCORM package. Finally, the data access layer has two packages: FILE that is in charge of handling the compacted file and exporting to SCORM; and FILTER, that is used to load the HTML files with the content of the courses. The complete project was implemented in Java version 1.5. For the interfaces classes of the package, javax.swing [7] was used. They have the information that will be saved in a file with the name arbol.cur. This file together with the HTML pages forms the compacted file CBC, as we have explained previously.

4   The Implementation

The content of the courses is stored in HTML files, one for each subject. These files contain labeled text and the images come separately. The editor uses a specific folder of work. The folder name comes from the name of the course. In this folder the pages of each subject are saved and if the page has images, a folder is created and those images are saved on it. The structure of the course along with the evaluations is stored in a file named arbol.cur. This file is generated using the method of serialization in Java.

File CBC is a compacted file from all the files that are written inside the folder of the course. Normal compressors like Tar, Zip or Arc were not used because these are highly formatted and have standard headers. These standards can be used to easily decompress the contents of the course; an unsafe situation because it is important to protect the access to the answers of the evaluations.

In order to compress files we used the algorithm that works as follow:

Compression Algorithm.

> *Create a Table*
> *   -Read the files from the folder*
> *For each element in the folder:*
> *   if the element is a fólder:*
> *   - compress the folder in a XBC file*
> *   - Add the file in the table for the header*
> *Create a new CBC file*
> *Save the header*
> *   - save the number of files and the table*
> *Save the contents*
> *For each file in the table:*
> *   - open file, read data, and save file*

The algorithm compresses each subfolder of images in a temporary file, call XBC. This file has the same name that the folder of images that will be compressed. A file for each folder of images is generated. The next step is to save the header of the compressed file that is made up of the number of files to save and a table of files. Finally, each byte from the files is saved into the compressed file.

The compressed file consists of three parts. First, it starts with an eight byte number, representing the amount of compressed files. Next, there is a table of file names, where each element of the table contains the name of each compressed file and its size. For each element of the table 108 bytes are required: 100 for the name of the file and 8 for its size. Last, the content of all the files. In this case the required space is variable depending of the file size.

The Editor: This tool has an interface that is shown in Figure 3. It divides the screen in two main areas: the structure and the content. The left section is used to define the structure of the course. The middle and right section are used to include the content of

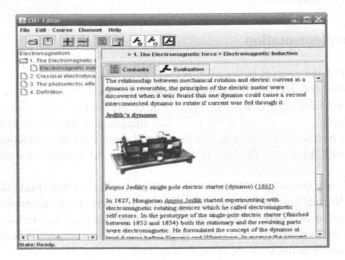

Fig. 3. Editor interface

such a course. The content is divided as well in three sections: the path, the contents, and the evaluations. These two last elements are handled with a Tabbed Panel.

The process of creation of a new course starts by assigning a name to it. Later the structure is created. The structure is made up of units which are numbered with a single consecutive digit; in subjects who are numbered with two digits, the first one indicates the unit and the second one the consecutive subject within the unit. The content is assigned by importing the corresponding HTML files: one for each subject.

The Player. This tool can open the files with the content of the courses and navigate through it. It allows also answering the examinations if that is the student wish. Its interface (Figure 4) is divided in two areas: the path and the content area.

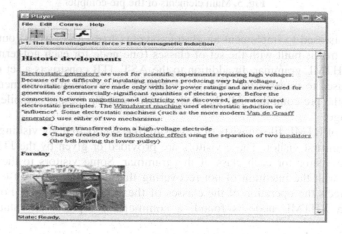

Fig. 4. Player interface

4.1 The Pre-compiler

HTML Java Components use the HTMLReader class to control the structuring of the document in the screen. This class implements a parser to read the documents. The parser ignores unknown labels and the text contained within them is shown in the screen. The purpose is not losing information. Nevertheless, the parser sometimes mark errors and it does not finish constructing the page in the screen or, causes that many HTML documents are shown with strange figures.

The parser can be modified by means of inheritance so we can extend the capacities of the HTML grammar. We can add more labels or attributes, but many documents are obtained using tools which use labels in XHTML format; however, the parser does not accept such a format yet. For this reason, a HTML pre-compiler was implemented. The main goal of the pre-compiler is to filter any HTML document that is read and displayed from CIBACO.

For implementing our Pre-compiler, we used two compiler construction tools: JavaCC [6] and JTB [8]. The first one is used to construct a scanner and a parser. The

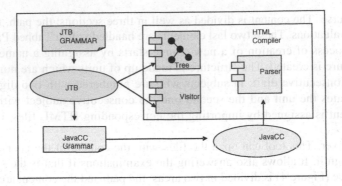

Fig. 5. Main elements of the pre-compiler

second one is used to implement an abstract syntax tree (AST) as the output of the parser. The tree is built with the set of classes (one node for each not-terminal symbol) of the HTML grammar. In addition to the AST, JTB constructs a set of visitors, which are used to traverse the AST [1]. Figure 5 shows the main elements used to implement the pre-compiler. All the classes produced by the pre-compiler form the Filter package.

Filtering of HTML file consists of traversing the syntax tree, by visiting the nodes using a depth first visitor. These visitors are provided or given by the JTB tool and there is one visitor for each class of the grammar. Some visitors to the nodes are cleared out with the intention of not recovering that information because this is the one that affects the operation of the classes of the JEditorKit de Java. For example, whenever a XHTML node is found, a commentary replaces the statements of the node:

```
public void visit(xmlt n) {
    //n.nodeChoice.accept(this);
}
```

In this way, all the nodes that are in the syntax tree and make reference to XHTML label will not be saved in the output file.

4.2 Linking CBT with Learning Objects

When users create a course, the editor produces a class instance for the course (see figure 6). This class instance generates three other classes for units, subjects and evaluations respectively. This tree structure (course, units and subjects) has compatibility with CBC and SCORM. As a result, there is a direct association between CI-BACO courses and SCORM learning objects. On the other hand, the evaluations are also class instance created from a new course. They are an important part for the student adaptation in the course. After a subject is covered by the student, the evaluation and others factors like time spent in the subject, define the sequence of the course.

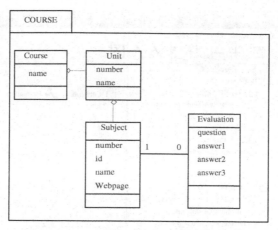

Fig. 6. Instances of classes created for a course

5 Exporting to Scorm

SCORM includes concepts of reusability, interoperability, durability and accessibility with the use of shared content objects (SCO) [14]. SCO Objects are made up of assets that are executed in the programs to show the contents of these objects.

In SCORM a package of contents is a set of related SCO object. This package of contents includes aggregations; aggregations have content objects; and they have assets. A course produced with CIBACO is a package of contents. These courses are structured by units and subjects. A unit makes the function of an aggregation, each subject is equivalent to a SCO object, and an asset is the web page of the subject besides the images that complement it. The package includes several aggregations, one for each unit of the course. In order to export a CIBACO course to the SCORM standard we made use of the classes contained in the package with the same name.

The process of exporting starts when a Java instance of the course is transformed into an instance of the SCORM class. At this point we visit the entire course and for each unit an Agg instance is created (with the corresponding unit). Inside the Agg instance, a similar process is completed and for each subject of a course, an SCO instance is created. Last, for each image found in a SCO instance, an asset instance is created. The reference to the Web page is kept in the SCO object.

6 Experimental Results

We conducted a user study in order to understand the user behavior when using CIBACO. First, we tested our tool with a group 24 college students. They developed different kinds of courses like Heat Transfer, Electromagnetic Theory, Digital Systems, and Mechanic Design. Each one of the courses had from 4 to 10 units of learning. They included evaluations on each unit. After the students ended the development of the courses, we applied a questionnaire or survey to the students in order to evaluate the effectiveness of CIBACO. For example we asked to list advantages

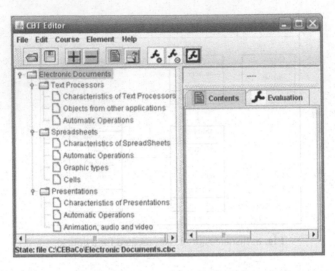

Fig. 7. Creating the index of a course

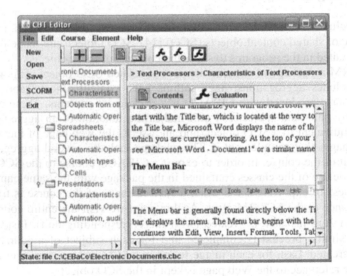

Fig. 8. Saving and exporting the course to SCORM

and disadvantages of CIBACO with respect to other tools like **eXe** [4] or **Reload** [12].
More than 90% of the students agree that CIBACO is easier to use than other tools.
This point is very important because CIBACO was developed to be used by regular
high school instructors. On the other hand, more than 70% of the students agree that
CIBACO needs more resources to be inserted into the produced courses.

Figures 8 to 11 show a running example of using CIBACO by producing the Electronic Documents course. The content of the electronic document program has three
units and 10 subjects. This program is based on the Mexican norm of labor competition CINF0376.01. Figure 7 illustrates how after launching CIBACO application, and

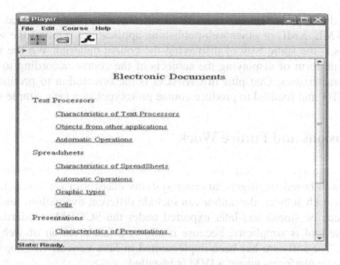

Fig. 9. Opening the last course

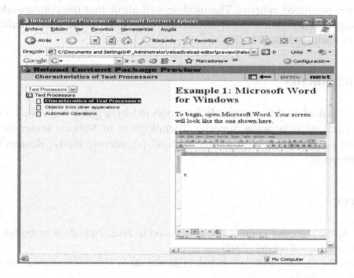

Fig. 10. Instances of classes created for a Course

by using icon plus (+), we create the index of the course. Figure 8 shows when we save the course and export it to SCORM format. Next, figure 9 demonstrates that the last course was created by opening it with CIBACO player. Last, the SCORM file is uploaded with the Reload Editor (figure 10).

7   Related Work

There are several author tools used to produce learning objects like Reload [12] and eXe [4]. Reload and eXe are web-based authoring environments designed to assist users in the development of web-based learning objects without the need to become expert in HTML, XML or other web-publishing applications. One of the weaknesses of both tools is the static way of displaying the course material. We are working to add a dynamic form of displaying the subjects of the course according to individual learning characteristics. One plus in CIBACO is the orientation to produce material focused in CBT and focused to produce course prototypes in a very simple way.

8 Conclusions and Future Work

CIBACO is an author tool that allows a High School instructor to produce learning objects for web-based intelligent tutoring systems classroom for competency-based teaching. For each subject, the author can include different evaluations and the whole application can be stored and later exported under the SCORM standard. The main feature of the tool is simplicity, because it allows a fast creation of web-classroom applications. The software has been implemented in Java version 1.5. So, we can use CIBACO in any platforms where a JVM is installed.

Right now we still are working with the addition of the intelligent tutoring module to each of the produced courses. The module will allow that the courses adapt to different strategies and contents from instruction according to the individuality and expectations of each student [11, 13].

Acknowledgments

The work described in this paper is fully supported by a grant from the DGEST (Dirección General de Educación Superior Tecnológica) in México under the program "support and development of academic bodies" [Academic Body: Research in Software Engineering].

References

1. Appel, A.W.: Modern Compiler Implementation in Java, 2nd edn. Cambridge University Press, Cambridge, England (2002)
2. Coordinación General EBC, Propuesta Didáctica de la Educación Basada en Competencias, DGETI (2002)
3. Leidner, D.E., Jarvenpaa, S.L.: The use of information technology to enhance management school education: A theoretical view, MISQuart (Septemper 1995)
4. eXe, eLearning XHTML Editor. (May 26, 2006), http://exelearning.com
5. Gardner, H.: Frames of Mind: The theory of multiple intelligences. New York Basic Books (1983)
6. Java Compiler Compiler. Build your own language with JavaCC (August 20, 2006), http://www.javaworld.com
7. Java Documentation. Java 2 Platform, Standard Edition 5.0 (2005)
8. Java Tree Builder (August 20, 2006), http://compilers.cs.ucla.edu
9. Nunes, J.M.B., Fowell, S.P.: Developing educational hypermedia applications: a methodological approach. Information Research News 7(1), 12–20 (1996)

10. Programa Nacional de Educación 2001-2006. SEP-México (2001)
11. Brusilovsky, P.: Adaptive Hypermedia. In: User Modeling and User-Adapted Instruction, vol. 11, Kluwer Academic Publishers, Dordrecht (2001)
12. RELOAD Editor, An IMS Metadata, Content Packaging and Learning Design Tool, (May 26, 2006), http://www.reload.ac.uk
13. Danielson, R.: Learning Styles, media preferences, and adaptive education. In: Sixth International Conference on User Modeling, UM (1997)
14. SCORM, The Sharable Content Object Reference Model. (May 26, 2006), http://www.adlnet.org

The ELEKTRA Ontology Model:
A Learner-Centered Approach to Resource Description

Michael D. Kickmeier-Rust and Dietrich Albert

Cognitive Science Section, Department of Psychology, University of Graz
Universitätsplatz 2 / III, 8010 Graz, Austria
{michael.kickmeier, dietrich.albert}@uni-graz.at

Abstract. There is little doubt that intelligent and adaptive educational technologies are capable of providing personalized learning experiences and improving learning success. Current challenges for research and development in this field concern, for example, the design of comprehensive data models for adaptive systems as well as the interoperability of systems and the re-usability of learning material across different systems. In the present work we introduce an ontology model, basically developed in the context of immersive digital games, which attempts to provide a solution to existing problems in resource description. On the one hand, comprehensive data models for adaptive systems are supported by separating static information from adaptive systems as far as possible. On the other hand, the ontology model offers a potential solution to precise and, above all, learner-centered resource description by separating latent competencies from observable performance (in learning objects or test items).

Keywords: Adaptive Tutoring, Game-based Learning, Resource Description, Ontology Model.

1 Introduction

In the past two decades learning technologies dramatically changed. Web-based solutions for educational purposes are widely accepted and commercially successful. Intelligent and adaptive educational technologies are a logical evolution, acknowledging the need for tailoring individual learning experiences. However, such intelligent and adaptive systems did not open up the market yet. Reasons are seen in the difficulty of designing comprehensive data models, interoperability, and re-usability of learning media as well as in a lack of a focus on the learner. At the same time, exciting new technologies for (web-based) learning are already dawning, for example game-based learning. The emergence of these new technologies is attended by further challenges and it is increasing the need for precise data models and resource description frameworks. In the present work we introduce an ontology model, developed in the context of game-based learning, that attempts to provide a solution to existing problems of adaptive systems as well as a potential solution to precise and, above all, learner-centered resource description.

H. Leung et al. (Eds.): ICWL 2007, LNCS 4823, pp. 78–89, 2008.

1.1 Intelligent and Adaptive Tutoring

The idea of using "intelligent" machines for educational purposes has a long tradition. It can be traced back to 1926 when Pressey [1] tried to build a machine that presented multiple choice questions and immediate feedback on the answers. Psychologists and educationists have since reported that carefully designed individualized tutoring produces the best learning for most people (e.g., [2]). First so-called intelligent tutoring systems (ITS) for web-based application were reported in the mid-nineties [3] and also research on adaptive hypermedia turned towards educational objectives, developing adaptive tutoring systems (ATS). Both use similar approaches and techniques to realize individualized tutoring.

Adaptive presentation refers to providing individual learners with personalized information, for example by conditional inclusion of information, re-ordering of information, or providing different media types [4]. Adaptive navigation support refers to guiding an individual learner through the learning material in the most suitable and successful way, for example by direct guidance, link sorting, or link hiding. Problem solving support is basically a concept of ITS that attempts to provide a learner not only with the final solution of a problem, for example when the learner is stuck, but to analyze how a solution was obtained and which knowledge might be missing, or which misconceptions might have been the cause for an error. An alternative terminology comes from [5], basically established in the context of educational games, macro and micro adaptivity. Essentially, macro adaptivity refers to traditional approaches of adaptive presentation and navigation on the level of LO or learning situations (LeS) whilst micro adaptivity refers to adaptive presentation and problem solving support within a LO/LeS. Although there is a strong need for personalized tutoring, such technologies are implemented sparsely in commercial E-Learning platforms. Reasons are for example:

- Adaptive features might still be a less important and visible factors in the market [6]
- ITS/ATS are often technology-driven and lack a plausible psychological and pedagogical background [6]
- Although there are significant efforts spent on providing suitable resource description [7], these are not commonly accepted and probably not sufficiently powerful to describe learning resources, especially in the context of ATS
- A number of authors [8] argue that it still is difficult to re-use and exchange learning material across different applications because of the often strong concatenation of LO, adaptive logic, and psycho-pedagogical background
- Most often the focus of resource description is -quite naturally- on LO, having the disadvantage of ambiguity of different learning methods and different learning objects covered by a single LO

The development of ITS/ATS is still facing major challenges and existing resource description approaches and standards are not commonly accepted yet and may be not complete enough. At the same time, the "very next big thing" (following the title of

Paul De Bra's article "The next big thing: Adaptive web-based systems" [9]) that is already dawning is using immersive digital games for educational purposes.

1.2 The Very Next Big Thing: Immersive Digital Educational Games

The majority of E-Learning systems and multimedia LO are based on traditional 2D user interfaces; provocatively speaking, they have all more or less the same unexciting look and feel. This perspective is compounded by the proliferation of appealing computer games. The idea of using such games for educational purposes was already born with the appearance of the first computer games. Ever since, scientists and developers have published numerous articles and books on the advantages of digital game-based learning as a promising approach to improve and facilitate learning, especially when fun, motivation, and immersion could be maintained [10]. In addition to single player games for educational purposes, multiplayer online games increasingly get in the focus of educational research [11]. Such games are interesting from a psycho-pedagogical perspective because they incorporate possibilities for collaborative peer-to-peer learning and social interactions.

However, educational games, and especially educational multiplayer games, bear further challenges to adaptive technologies, underlying data models, and resource description models:

- The complexity and scale of LO/LeS is substantially higher than in traditional LO. Moreover, LO/LeS are strongly integrated in a specific game's narrative and visual style
- The costs of developing LO/LeS for immersive, state-of-the-art educational games are extremely high and successful approaches to re-usability are even more important than in traditional E-Learning
- Adaptive technologies are facing new challenges in order to provide suitable adaptive interventions
- In multiplayer games learning may be independent from pre-described LO/LeS, for example through collaboration, peer-tutoring, and social interactions.

2   The ELEKTRA Project

The ELEKTRA project (www.elektra-project.org) has the ambitious goal to utilize the advantages of computer games and their design fundamentals for educational purposes and to address disadvantages of game-based learning as far as possible. Within the project a methodology for successful design of educational games shall be established and a game demonstrator is developed based on a state-of-the-art 3D adventure game teaching optics according to national curricula. ELEKTRA will also address important research questions concerning data model design as basis for adaptivity and resource description enabling interoperability of systems and re-using LO/LeS as well as the data model itself.

In view of the mentioned challenges to adaptive technologies, data models, and related resource description frameworks and also in view of the emerging challenges by (multiplayer) educational games, we propose a conceptual change towards a separation of competence (i.e., a set of skills) and performance.

2.1 Competence versus Performance

An early distinction between latent competence and observable performance was introduced by Chomsky [12] in the framework of linguistic theory. Today, this distinction has a much wider application, especially in knowledge and learning psychology. Still, in practice the concepts of latent competence and related observable performance often lack a thorough differentiation; operationalizations are often one-to-one mappings of underlying competencies and performance and often the same labels are used for both concepts. From a cognitive point of view, this approach is fraught with difficulty; for example, it does not acknowledge that performance (e.g., mastering a task) can be the result of various competencies. Thus, it is not only necessary to break down certain types of competencies to a certain level of granularity but also to separate competence from performance. Such separation enables establishing a sound basis to address existing challenges: (a) it offers a learner-centered and cognitively sound approach, (b) it enables resource description (and probably standards) without the focus on specific LO; it is not about which content is included in a LO, but what exactly a learner can gain from a LO, and (c) it enables a separation of LO, adaptive mechanism, and psycho-pedagogical principles and, therefore, serves the design of adequate data models underlying adaptive systems.

A method to realize such separation is ontologies. On such basis, a clear, precise, and probably standardized definitions of competencies in a given domain can be realized which, in turn, can be used as a data model for an adaptive system. The cognitive model underlying the data model of ELEKTRA is based on *Competence-based Knowledge Space Theory* (CbKST).

To address the challenges for research and development and to incorporate a separation of latent competence and observable performance, ELEKTRA utilizes the framework of CbKST to provide the game with a methodology for suitable adaptive interventions. It provides an internal cognition-based logic that is quite similar to the logic of ontologies: well-defined entities (the competencies or skills) are in a well-defined relationship (a so-called *prerequisite relation*).

CbKST is an extension of the originally behavioral *Knowledge Space Theory* [13] [14] where a knowledge domain Q is characterized by a set of problems. The knowledge state of an individual is identified on the subset of problems this person is capable of solving. Due to mutual dependencies between the problems captured by prerequisite relations, not all potential knowledge states will occur. The collection of all possible states is called a knowledge structure K. To account for the fact that a problem might have several prerequisites (i.e., and/or-type relations) the notion of a *prerequisite function* was introduced. The basic idea of CbKST is to assume a set E of abstract skills underlying the problems and LO of the domain. The relationships between the skills and problems (or LO) is established by a *skill function*. Such function assigns a collection of subsets of skills (i.e., *competence states*) to each problem, which are relevant for solving it and it assigns the skills to each LO taught. By associating skills to the problems of a domain, a knowledge structure on the set of problems

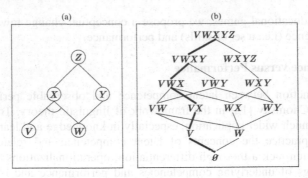

Fig. 1. The left panel illustrates a prerequisite function (the bended line below skill X indicates a logical or). The right panel shows the corresponding competence structure. The bolded line indicates one of several meaningful learning paths.

is induced. The skills, which are not directly observable, can be uncovered on the basis of a person's observable performance. A further extension is to assume prerequisite relationships between the skills, inducing a competence structure C on the set of skills [15]. To illustrate this approach, assume that a knowledge domain is represented by $Q=\{a, b, c, d\}$. Consider the *set* $E=\{V, W, X, Y, Z\}$ of skills that are relevant for solving them. A prerequisite function that might exist among these skills is demonstrated in Fig. 1a. For example, this function reads that if a student has skill X we can assume that this student also possesses either skill V or W, or both; the corresponding competence structure is shown in Fig. 1b. It includes only 13 possible competence states from a total of $2^5 = 32$ states.

The outlined approach entails several advantages. Given the performance, that is, the subset of problems a student could master, the latent skills underlying that problem solving performance can be identified. Due to the utilization of representation and interpretation functions no one-to-one mapping of performance to skills is required and meaningful learning paths can be identified.

3 The ELEKTRA Ontology Model

3.1 Ontology Web Language (OWL)

Originally, the term ontology was established in philosophy where it describes a discipline concerned with existence. The term was introduced to computer science by Gruber [16] where it describes "a formal, explicit specification of a shared conceptualization". An ontology provides a structured and semantically rich approach to model a certain domain; ontologies count classes, instances, inheritances, and relationships between classes as their major components. The entities of an ontology can be described with attributes, each having a name, a certain data type, and one or more values. In the context of E-Learning, ontologies serve as a means of achieving semantic precision between a domain of learning material and the learner's prior knowledge and learning goals. Ontologies bridge the semantic gap between humans and machines and, consequently, they facilitate the establishment of the semantic web and build the basis for the exchange and re-use of contents that reaches across people and applications. From a technical perspective, an ontology is a text-based reference of information, represented by an ontology representation language. Most of them are built upon XML and RDF. There is a variety of such representation languages (see [17] for a review). The primary benefit of using ontologies is their ability to reason over defined relationships and therefore to relate instances to their abstract types. Reasoning is used to derive new relations between individuals from an existing ontology by using and applying logical rules. Reasoning might refer to class memberships, to the equivalence of classes, to consistency, or to classifications. As an example, ontologies allow determining a complete list of skills required by a specific competence state or by a specific LO.

In 2004, W3C has officially released OWL (Web Ontology Language) as recommendation for representing ontologies. OWL is developed starting from description logic (DL) and DAML+OIL. The popularity of OWL, which is still increasing, might lead to its establishment as the standard ontology representation language on the semantic web. Basically, OWL is a set of XML entities and attributes with well-defined meaning that are used to identify concepts and relations between. OWL consists of three species, OWL Full, OWL DL, and OWL Lite [23]. OWL provides a set of constructors (e.g., *oneOf, intersectionOf, hasValue*) that allow deriving classes from other classes and a set of axioms (e.g., *subClassOf, disjointWith, sameAs, TransitiveProperty*) that allow asserting subsumption or equivalence in terms of classes, individuals, or properties, the disjointness of classes, or properties of properties.

3.2 Architecture

The ELEKTRA ontology model is supposed to address the requirements of providing adaptive interventions in the game in order to balance challenge and ability and therefore not only providing successful learning paths within the game's narrative but also to retain motivation and even flow experience. Thus, the ontology model incorporates the concepts related to adaptive interventions on a macro as well as on a micro-level, that is, it models problem solution spaces for problem solving tasks within the game environment. Although the re-usability of learning objects is more difficult in digital games for educational purposes because the learning objects are an integral part of the entire game which is not interchangeable between different games in most cases, the presented ontology model is supposed to serve the growing demands on standardization and semantically rich resource description in the context of educational technologies also. As mentioned before, some authors argue that currently a lack of commonly accepted resource description standards for learning objects exists. One reason might be a focus on learning objects in current approaches. In the presented ontology model we introduce a focus on the learner and, therefore, on latent skills. This approach might be a more comprehensive and easier to standardize method for describing and defining LO and learning objectives. While learning objects are most often strongly interlaced with instructional methods or events, the focus on underlying skills offers a cornerstone, which is not only directly related to human abilities and learning

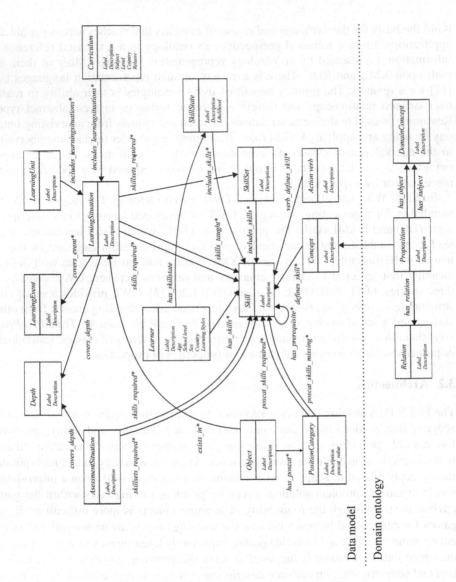

Fig. 2. The ELEKTRA ontology model architecture

objectives but which also allows a very precise description of LO. From a technical perspective the ELEKTRA ontology model builds upon OWL DL; due to its popularity it is the quasi-standard for ontology representation languages. All classes have the RDF-attributes label and description. The ontology model is illustrated in Fig. 2. Most relations between the classes' instances are non-functional (marked with an asterisk in Fig. 2), meaning that one or more instances of one class can be associated with the instances of a related class.

Learner. The ELEKTRA ontology model puts the human learner and, therefore, skills in the foreground. Consequently *Learner* is the center class of the ontology. Using attributes such as age, school level, sex, culture, country, or learning styles allows establishing distinct groups of learners. In turn, such well-defined groups of learners provide the adaptation engine of a learning environment, the game by the example of ELEKTRA, with a comprehensive learner model. The *Learner* class is (indirectly) associated with classes related to latent skills, LO (LeS in the terminology of ELEKTRA), problem solution states, and curriculum.

Skills. The most important component describing the learner is skills. The *Skill* class is defined by a factual concept (e.g., convex lenses) and related action verbs (e.g., recall or apply). This type of skill definition was introduced by [18] and is associated with Bloom's revised taxonomy of learning objectives [19]. There are six cumulative levels of cognitive processing, which can be thought of as degrees of difficulties which establish a hierarchical order; a more simple level of knowledge or ability must be given in order to reach a deeper one. The levels are (a) knowledge (the recall of factual information), (b) comprehension (understanding of the meaning, translation, interpolation, and interpretation of instructions and problems), (c) application (using of a concept in a new situation or unprompted use of an abstraction), (d) analysis (separating material or concepts into sub- components so that its organizational structure may be understood), (e) synthesis (building a structure or pattern from diverse elements, joining parts to form a whole, with emphasis on creating a new meaning or structure), and (f) evaluation (making of judgments about the value of ideas or materials). Action verbs are assigned to each category, describing recall methods or knowledge more detailed. For the category "knowledge" action verbs are, for example, "define", "describe", or "label"; for the category "analysis" "compare", "quantify", or "measure". The *Skill* class has a relational attribute *has_prerequisite*. This relation identifies skills that are prerequisites for a given skill as claimed by CbKST (see section 2.2) and, therefore, establishes a prerequisite relation between the skills. Fig. 3 shows the prerequisite relation for the physics course realized in the ELEKTRA game demonstrator. A related class is the *SkillSet* class. This class specifies a set of skills, which is in turn a prerequisite for other skills. This supplement is based on rather technical constraints when including and/or-type relations (i.e., prerequisite functions).

Learning Objects/Learning Situations. A further class defines LO or, in the context of game-based learning, LeS. The *LearningSituation* class has the relational attribute *skills_taught*, which refers to the skills that can be learned with certain LO or within a certain LeS. To acknowledge the fact that certain skills may be required to successfully apply such LO/LeS this class has the relational attributes *skills_required* and *skillsets_required*. The present ontology model includes both because the definition of skill sets is necessary when and/or-type prerequisite functions are required.

Although learning and assessment is often overlapping, in the present model we distinguish between LO/LeS and assessment objects/situations. Such objects are

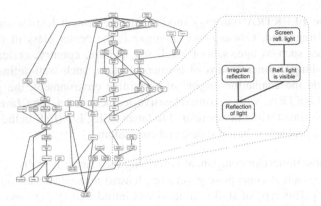

Fig. 3. Upward drawing for the prerequisite relation between skills realized in ELEKTRA

typical test items or learning situations primary aiming at assessing knowledge with which the current knowledge state is assessed. The separation facilitates the adaptive presentation of learning material and assessment of learning progress. The *Assessment Situation* class has the attributes *skills_required* and *skillsets_required*, specifying the skills that are necessary to successfully master such assessment. To account for pedagogical implications and strategies, two related classes concern the type of learning events and the depth of knowledge. Learning events (prototypically) refer to the *Eight Learning Events Model* [20], which is a pedagogical approach emphasizing that learning events are based on eight basic components. The eight learning events are (a) imitation / modeling, (b) reception / transmission, (c) exercising / guidance, (d) exploration / documentation, (e) experimentation / reactivity, (f) creation / confrontation, (g) self-reflection / co-reflection, and (h) debate / animation. The depth of knowledge refers to Bloom's taxonomy of learning objectives. To include these classes, the *LearningSituation* class has the attributes *covers_event* and *covers_depth* and the *AssessmentSituation* class has the attribute *covers_depth*.

Curricula and Units. An aim of ELEKTRA is to design a methodology for game-based learning that is close to school curricula. The game demonstrator, for example, will be relying on the curricula of France, Belgium, and Germany. To integrate such information, we used a *Curriculum* class. This class has the attributes *subject, level, country* and *release* (version or date) to identify the curriculum. To link the LO/LeS to the curricula, this class has also the relational attribute *includes_learningsituations*. A similar class is *LearningUnit*, which specifies larger learning units within the game or curriculum.

Problem Solution States. To provide a basis for micro adaptivity (as described in section 1.1), which attempts to analyze the states of a problem solution process in order to provide subtle adaptive interventions (e.g., giving hints), we included the *Object* class. This class is strongly related to the game-approach and identifies the manipulable objects that exist in different learning and assessment situations (e.g., books, tools, lenses, microscopes, etc.). These objects are linked to learning and assessment situations by the *exists_in* attribute. In order to allow the adaptive system to determine to progress in the problem solution process (and also possible misconceptions), this class is linked to the *Position_Category* class. The attributes *poscat_value, poscat_skills_missing,* and *poscat_skills_required* enable the assignment of some value of correctness, determined by a specific utility function, to each position category of each manipulable object and it allows determining available and missing skills. On the basis of the correctness value the probability distribution of the related skills states can be updated and interventions can be made on a skill-basis rather than on behavioral basis.

Domain Ontologies. As included in Fig. 2, in addition to the ontology structure that serves as a data model for the adaptive system, either on a macro or on a micro-level, also a domain ontology can be linked to the data model. Domain ontologies generally include propositions (two factual concepts which are connected by any type of relation) that describe a certain domain (e.g., the domain of optics). Such domain ontologies can be used to enable a manual or semi-automatic derivation of skills and the prerequisite relations between them [21].

4 Conclusion and Future Work

In the present work we introduced an ontology-based data model that essentially was developed in the context of game-based learning. This model is anchored in CbKST and supposed to enable suitable adaptive interventions on a macro and on a micro-level. In the framework of the ELEKTRA project, such adaptive intervention not only involves the learner's knowledge and learning progress, it involves pedagogical implications and strategies as well as motivational characteristics and immersion. Although developed in view of a specific application, the data model might serve as a role model for other adaptive systems and approaches to adaptive interventions.

The primary aim of the introduced ontology model is providing adaptive systems with a basis for suitable adaptive interventions and to separate static information from the adaptive system as far as possible. The architecture enables the realization of the initially described techniques of adaptivity (adaptive presentation, adaptive navigation, and adaptive problem solving support), on a macro as well as on a micro-level. In a context of probabilistic skill assessment and, particularly, in the context of evaluating the "correctness" of problem solutions states, which includes some characteristics of fuzzy logic, existing ontology representation languages have limitations. For example in OWL any sentence (e.g., reasoning results) must be either true or false. Consequently, ontologies cannot quantify the degree of the overlap or inclusion of concepts [22]. Future endeavors will incorporate existing approaches to probabilistic extensions to ontology representation languages (e.g., the Bayesian network approach of [22]).

In addition, we proposed a conceptual change towards a learner-centered focus on latent skills in resource description methods. Both data model and competence-performance separation may offer a promising approach to address the problems and challenges of adaptive educational technologies. First, the introduced approach to separate competence and performance and to include this separation in the data model offers a cognitive basis opening the doors for new development in knowledge construction and assessment. Furthermore, the data model acknowledges the need for pedagogical implications and strategies and for the integration of individual states and traits (e.g., motivational components). On the basis of this triad, LO/LeS and learning objectives can be defined very precisely. In view of resource description methods and their standards, the proposed separation of a learner's possessed and desired skills from LO and learning objectives establish similar to propositions of domain ontologies smallest - or at least sufficiently small - entities for describing the learner, LO/LeS, and learning objectives. At the same time, problems in tracking learning progress emerging from multi-learner environments (such as multi-player games), for example learning by social interactions and independent from specific LO, can be reduced by swerving from a focus on LO/LeS. Future endeavors will extent the present ontology model towards an increasing compatibility with existing attempts to provide metadata standards and to include ontologies for the definition of skills or competencies (e.g., the IMS information model specification for reusable definition of competency or educational objective). Moreover, the presented model offers a suitable supplement to attempts of combining learning design standards with ontology models, for example by providing a generalized taxonomy of pedagogical strategies and learning objectives or by acknowledge information for adaptive problem solving support.

Acknowledgements. The research and development introduced in this work is funded by the European Commission under the sixth framework programme in the IST research priority, contract number 027986.

References

1. Pressey, S.L.: A simple apparatus which gives tests and scores - and teaches. School and Society 23, 373–376 (1926)
2. Bloom, B.S.: The 2 sigma problem: The search for methods of group instruction as affective as one-to-one tutoring. Educational Researcher 13(6), 4–16 (1984)
3. Brusilovsky, P.: Intelligent tutoring systems for World-Wide-Web. In: 3rd International WWW Conference (1995)
4. Brusilovsky, P.: Adaptive and intelligent technologies for web-based education. In: Rollinger, C., Peylo, C. (eds.) Special Issue on Intelligent Systems and Teleteaching, Künstliche Intelligenz, vol. 4, pp. 19–25 (1999)
5. Kickmeier-Rust, M.D., Peirce, N., Conlan, O., Schwarz, D., Verpoorten, D., Albert, D.: Immersive digital games: The interfaces for next-generation E-Learning? In: Aykin, N. (ed.) HCII 2007. LNCS, vol. 4560, Springer, Heidelberg (2007)
6. Branko Neto, W.C., Gauthier, F.A.: Sharing and reusing information on web-based learning. In: Workshop on Applications of Semantic Web Technologies for E-Learning (2006)
7. Mizoguchi, R., Bourdeau, J.: Using ontological engineering to overcome common AI-ED problems. International Journal of AI in Education 11, 107–121 (2000)
8. Sampson, D., Karagiannidis, C., Cardinali, F.: An architecture for web-based E-Learning promoting re-usable adaptive educational e-content. Educational Technology & Society 5(4), 27–37 (2002)
9. De Bra, P., Aroyo, L., Chepegin, V.: The next big thing: Adaptive web-based systems. Journal of Digital Information 5 (2004)

10. Kickmeier-Rust, M.D., Schwarz, D., Albert, D., Verpoorten, D., Castaigne, J.-L., Bopp, M.: The ELEKTRA project: towards a new learning experience. In: Pohl, M., et al. (eds.) M3 – Interdisciplinary aspects on digital media & education, pp. 19–48 Österreichische Computer Gesellschaft, Vienna (2006)
11. Steinkuehler, C.A.: Massively multiplayer online videogaming as participation in a discourse. Mind, Culture, & Activity 13(1), 38–52 (2006)
12. Chomsky, N.: Aspects of the Theory of Syntax. MIT Press, Cambridge (1965)
13. Doignon, J.-P., Falmagne, J.-C.: Knowledge spaces. Springer, Heidelberg (1999)
14. Albert, D., Lukas, J.: Knowledge spaces: Theories, empirical research, and applications. Lawrence Erlbaum, Mahwah (1999)
15. Korossy, K.: Modelling knowledge as competence and performance. In: Albert, D., Lukas, J. (eds.) Knowledge Spaces: Theories, Empirical Research Applications, pp. 103–132. Lawrence Erlbaum, Mahwah (1999)
16. Gruber, T.A.: A translation approach to portable ontology specifications. Knowledge Acquisition 5, 199–220 (1993)
17. Gómez-Pérez, A., Corcho, O.: Ontology languages for the semantic web. IEEE Intelligent Systems 17, 54–60 (2002)
18. Heller, J., Steiner, C.M., Hockemeyer, C., Albert, D.: Competence-based knowledge structures for personalized learning. International Journal of E-Learning 5, 75–88 (2006)
19. Anderson, L.W., Krathwohl, D.R., et al.: A taxonomy for learning, teaching and assessing: A revision of Bloom's Taxonomy of educational objectives: Complete edition, Longman (2001)
20. Leclerq, D., Poumay, M.: The 8 Learning events model and its principles, http://www.labset.net/media/prod/8LEM.pdf
21. Mayer, B., Steiner, C.M., Heller, J., Albert, D.: Activity- and taxonomy-based knowledge representation framework. International Journal of Knowledge and Learning (in press)
22. Ding, Z., Peng, Y.: A probabilistic extension to ontology language OWL. In: 37th International Conference on System Sciences (2004)

Towards Fuzzy Domain Ontology Based Concept Map Generation for E-Learning

Raymond Y.K. Lau[1], Albert Y.K. Chung[1], Dawei Song[2], and Qiang Huang[2]

[1] Department of Information Systems
City University of Hong Kong
Tat Chee Avenue, Kowloon, Hong Kong
{raylau, ykchung}@cityu.edu.hk
[2] Knowledge Media Institute
The Open University
Walton Hall, Milton Keynes, MK7 6AA, United Kingdom
{d.song, q.huang}@open.ac.uk

Abstract. With the wide spread applications of E-Learning technologies to education at all levels, increasing number of online educational resources and messages are generated from these E-Learning environments. Accordingly, instructors are often overwhelmed by the huge number of messages created by students through online discussion boards. It is quite difficult, if not totally impossible, for instructors to read through and analyze these messages to understand the progress of their students on the fly. As a result, adaptive classroom teaching is handicapped. The main contribution of this paper is the illustration of a novel concept map generation mechanism which is underpinned by a fuzzy domain ontology discovery algorithm. The proposed mechanism can automatically construct a concept map based on the messages posted to an online discussion board. Our initial experimental results reveal that the accuracy and the quality of the automatically generated concept maps are promising. Our research work opens the door to the development and application of intelligent software tools to enhance E-Learning.

Keywords: Fuzzy Domain Ontology, Concept Map, Text Mining, E-Learning.

1 Introduction

E-Learning has proven to be an effective channel to enhance and enrich traditional classroom teaching and learning [14]. However, the increasing number of educational resources put online and the huge amount of information generated from interactive learning (e.g., on-line discussions) lead to the excessive information load on the learners and the teachers. For example, to promote reflexive and interactive learning, teachers often encourage their students to use online discussion boards or chat rooms to recall what they have learnt and to share their knowledge with other fellow students during or after normal class time. With the

H. Leung et al. (Eds.): ICWL 2007, LNCS 4823, pp. 90–101, 2008.

current practice, teachers need to read through all the messages in order to identify the current progress of their students. From the pedagogical point of view, such an analysis process is essential since teachers have to understand the learning states of their students before they can deliver the appropriate lessons in the following stage, that is the so-called *adaptive learning*. Nevertheless, manually browsing and analyzing the huge number of messages is very time-consuming, and it is extremely difficult, if not totally impossible, to do that in the middle of a lecture or a tutorial session.

To alleviate the above problem, we can introduce automated tools to assist teachers to analyze and visualize the contents embedded in the large number of messages posted to on-line discussion boards or chat rooms. According to assimilation theory [1], a concept map provides a good elicitation and representation of knowledge structure in an individual's memory. A context-sensitive text mining method [5] is applied to discover prominent concepts and their relationships from the on-line discussion board of an E-Learning platform. The resulting domain ontology [4] is used to develop a concept map reflecting the knowledge structure shared among a group of students. The main contribution of this paper is the illustration of our context-sensitive fuzzy domain ontology discovery algorithm and how it is applied to construct concept maps so that educators can conduct adaptive teaching, and the learners can realize their own learning performance as well as the perception shared among a group of peer learners.

Since the taxonomy relations discovered from a text mining method often involve uncertainty, an uncertainty management mechanism is required to address such an issue. The notions of Fuzzy set and Fuzzy Relation are effective to represent knowledge with uncertainty [17]. Therefore, a fuzzy ontology rather than a crisp ontology is discovered by the proposed text mining method.

Definition 1 (Fuzzy Set). *A fuzzy set $\mathcal{F}$ consists of a set of objects drawn from a domain X and the membership of each object x_i in $\mathcal{F}$ is defined by a membership function $\mu_{\mathcal{F}} : X \mapsto [0,1]$. If Y is a crisp set, $\varphi(Y)$ denotes a fuzzy set generated from the traditional set of items Y.*

Definition 2 (Fuzzy Relation). *A fuzzy relation is defined as the fuzzy set $\mathcal{G}$ on a domain $X \times Y$ where X and Y are two crisp sets.*

From the text mining perspective, a keyword is an object and it belongs to different concepts (a linguistic class) with various memberships. The subsumption relations among linguistic concepts are often uncertain and are characterized by the appropriate fuzzy relations.

Definition 3 (Fuzzy Ontology). *A fuzzy ontology is a quadruple $Ont = \ <X, C, R_{XC}, R_{CC}>$, where X is a set of objects and C is a set of concepts. The fuzzy relation $R_{XC} : X \times C \mapsto [0,1]$ maps the set of objects to the set of concepts by assigning the respective membership values, and the fuzzy relation $R_{CC} : C \times C \mapsto [0,1]$ denotes the fuzzy taxonomy relations among the set of concepts C.*

The remainder of the paper is organized as follows. Section 2 highlights previous research in the related area and compare these research work with ours. The computational details of the proposed ontology mining method are then illustrated in Section 3. Section 4 describe how the fuzzy domain ontology discovery method is applied to an E-Learning environment. Finally, we offer concluding remarks and describe future direction of our research work.

2   Related Research

Educational intermediaries store meta-data descriptions on each learning resource providing information on its characteristics [10]. In order to ensure the concise communications between the users and the learning resources, automatic discovery of taxonomies of learning resources is required. A data mining approach is proposed to discover the relations of the meta-data describing the various learning resources. Terms from the meta-data files are scanned and stop words are removed. Language engineering tools such as WordNet [8] are used for extracting the word roots (lemmatization) and the Brill tagger algorithm is used for part of speech tagging. As a result, a set of unique keywords is extracted. A data matrix with each column corresponding to a learning resource and each row corresponding to a keyword is developed. A graph-based clustering algorithm is then applied to the data matrix to discover meaningful concepts for the learning resources and to identify the relations among the concepts. Our work aims at discovering and visualizing the domain ontology from the on-line messages created by the learners rather than the map of educational resources. We employ a hybrid lexico-syntactic and statistical learning method rather than a computationally expensive graph-based approach for ontology extraction.

Cimiano et al. have presented an automatic taxonomy learning algorithm to extract concept hierarchies from a text corpus [3]. In particular, their taxonomy learning method is based on formal concept analysis [16]. Formal concept analysis is a systematic method for deriving implicit relationships among objects described by a set of attributes. Formal concept analysis can be seen as a conceptual clustering techniques at it provides intensional descriptions for the abstract concepts. Central to formal concept analysis is the notion of a context which is essentially the prominent attributes or features common to a set of objects of the same class. A formal context is a triple $K = (G, M, I)$ where G and M represent a set of objects and attributes respectively and I is a binary relation between G and M. Thereby, a formal concept (A, B) is defined by $A = \{g \in G | \forall_{m \in M}(g, m) \in I\}$ and $B = \{m \in M | \forall_{g \in G}(g, m) \in I\}$. In order to derive attributes from a certain corpus, part-of-speech tagging and linguistic analysis are performed to extract verb/prepositional phrase complement, verb/object and verb/subject dependencies. For each noun appearing as head of the extracted syntactic structures, the corresponding verbs are taken as the attributes for building the formal context. Their approach is evaluated by comparing the automatically generated concept hierarchies with hand-crafted taxonomies in a tourism and a finance domain. The fuzzy ontology discovery method illustrated in this paper employs a novel subsumption based mechanism rather than the formal concept analysis approach to generate concept lattice. Semantically richer context vectors are used to represent concepts in our approach as opposed to the simple verb-based features employed by formal concept analysis. In addition, our concept hierarchy represents a fuzzy taxonomy of relations rather than a crisp taxonomy as proposed in [3].

The FOGA framework for fuzzy ontology generation has been proposed [?]. The FOGA framework consists of fuzzy formal concept analysis, fuzzy conceptual clustering, fuzzy ontology generation, and semantic representation conversion. Essentially, the FOGA method extends the formal concept analysis approach, which has also been applied to ontology extraction, with the notions of fuzzy sets. The notions of formal context and formal concept have been fuzzified by introducing the respective membership functions. In addition, an approximate reasoning method is developed so that the automatically generated fuzzy ontology can be incrementally furnished with the arrival of new instances. The FOGA framework is evaluated in a small citation database. Our method discussed in this paper differs from the FOGA framework in that a more compact representation of fuzzy ontology is developed. The proposed method is based on previous work in computational linguistic and with the computational mechanism built on the concept of fuzzy relations. We believe that the proposed method is computationally more efficient and be able to scale up for huge textual databases which typically consists of millions of records and thousands of terms. Finally, our proposed method is validated in a standard benchmark textual database which is considerably larger than the citation database used in [15].

A fuzzy ontology which is an extension of the domain ontology with crisp concepts is utilized for news summarization purpose [6]. In this semi-automatic ontology discovery approach, the domain ontology with various events of news is pre-defined by domain experts. A document pre-processing mechanism will generate the meaningful terms based on the news corpus and a Chinese news dictionary pre-defined by the domain experts. The meaningful terms are classified according to the events of the news by a term classifier. Basically, every fuzzy concept has a set of membership degrees associated with the various events of the domain ontology. The main function of the fuzzy inference mechanism is to generate the membership degrees (classification) for each event with respect to the fuzzy concepts defined in the fuzzy ontology. The standard triangular membership function is used for the classification purpose. The method discussed in this paper is a fully automatic fuzzy domain ontology discovery approach. There is no pre-defined fuzzy concepts and taxonomy of concepts, instead our text mining method will automatically discover such concepts and generate the taxonomy relations. In addition, there is no need to set the artificial threshold values for the triangular membership function, instead our membership function can automatically derive the membership values based on the lexico-syntactic and statistical features of the terms observed in a textual database.

3   Text Mining for Fuzzy Ontology Discovery

It is believed that the main challenge in mining taxonomy relations from textual databases is to filter out the noisy relations[7]. Accordingly, our text mining method is specifically designed to deal with such an issue. After standard document pre-processing such as stop word removal, POS tagging, and word stemming [12], a *windowing process* is conducted over the collection of documents. The windowing process can help reduce the number of noisy term relationships. For each document (e.g., Net news, Web page, email, etc.), a *virtual window* of δ words is moved from left to right one word at a time until the end of a textual unit (e.g., a sentence) is reached. Within each window, the statistical information among tokens is collected to develop collocational expressions [13]. Such a windowing process has successfully been applied to text mining before [5].

The windowing process is repeated for each document until the entire collection has been processed. According to previous studies, a text window of 5 to 10 terms is effective [11], and so we adopt this range as the basis to perform our windowing process. To improve computational efficiency and filter noisy relations, only the specific linguistic pattern (e.g., Noun Noun, and Adjective Noun) defined by an ontology engineer will be analyzed. After parsing the whole corpus, the statistical data (by statistical token analysis) about the potential concepts can be collected. If a word has an association weight lower than a pre-defined threshold value, it will be discarded from the context vector of the concept. This is equivalent to the α-cut operation for fuzzy sets. For statistical token analysis, several information theoretic methods are employed. Mutual Information has been applied to collocational analysis [11] in previous research. Mutual Information is an information theoretic method to compute the dependency between two entities and is defined by:

$$MI(t_i, t_j) = \log_2 \frac{Pr(t_i, t_j)}{Pr(t_i)Pr(t_j)} \tag{1}$$

where $MI(t_i, t_j)$ is the mutual information between term t_i and term t_j. $Pr(t_i, t_j)$ is the joint probability that both terms appear in a text window, and $Pr(t_i)$ is the probability that a term t_i appears in a text window. The probability $Pr(t_i)$ is estimated based on $\frac{|w_t|}{|w|}$ where $|w_t|$ is the number of windows containing the term t and $|w|$ is the total number of windows constructed from a textual database (i.e., a collection). Similarly, $Pr(t_i, t_j)$ is the fraction of the number of windows containing both terms out of the total number of windows.

We develop *Balanced Mutual Information* (BMI) to compute the degree of association among tokens. This method considers both term presence and term absence as the evidence of the implicit term relationships.

$$\mu_{c_i}(t_j) \approx BMI(t_i, t_j)$$
$$= \beta(Pr(t_i, t_j) \log_2(\frac{Pr(t_i, t_j)}{Pr(t_i)Pr(t_j)}) +$$
$$Pr(\neg t_i, \neg t_j) \log_2(\frac{Pr(\neg t_i, \neg t_j)}{Pr(\neg t_i)Pr(\neg t_j)})) - \qquad (2)$$
$$(1 - \beta)(Pr(t_i, \neg t_j) \log_2(\frac{Pr(t_i, \neg t_j)}{Pr(t_i)Pr(\neg t_j)}) +$$
$$Pr(\neg t_i, t_j) \log_2(\frac{Pr(\neg t_i, t_j)}{Pr(\neg t_i)Pr(t_j)}))$$

where $\mu_{c_i}(t_j)$ is the membership function to estimate the degree of a term $t_j \in X$ belonging to a concept $c_i \in C$. $\mu_{c_i}(t_j)$ is the computational mechanism for the relation R_{XC} defined in the fuzzy ontology $Ont =< X, C, R_{XC}, R_{CC} >$. The membership function $\mu_{c_i}(t_j)$ is indeed approximated by the BMI score. $Pr(t_i, t_j)$ is the joint probability that both terms appear in a text window, and $Pr(\neg t_i, \neg t_j)$ is the joint probability that both terms are absent in a text window. The weight factor $\beta > 0.5$ is used to control the relative importance of two kinds of evidence (positive and negative). In Eq.(2), each MI value is then normalized by the corresponding joint probabilities. For the special case where $Pr(t_i, t_j) = 1$ is true, the joint probability value is replaced by a large positive integer because terms t_i, t_j have the strongest association. An α-cut is applied to discard terms from the potential concept if their membership values are below the threshold α. After computing all the BMI values in a collection, these values are subject to linear scaling such that each membership value is within the unit interval $\forall_{c_i \in C, t_j \in X} \mu_{c_i}(t_j) \in [0, 1]$. It should be noted that the constituent terms of a concept are always implicitly belonging to the concept with the maximal membership 1.

To further filter the noisy concept relations, only the relatively prominent concepts for a domain will be further explored. We adopt the TFIDF [12] like heuristic to filter non-relevant domain concepts. Similar approach has also been used in ontology learning [9]. For example, if a concept is significant for a particular domain, it will appear more frequently in that domain when compared with its appearance in other domains. The following measure is used to compute the relevance score of a concept:

$$Rel(c_i, D_j) = \frac{Dom(c_i, D_j)}{\sum_{k=1}^n Dom(c, D_k)} \qquad (3)$$

where $Rel(c_i, D_j)$ is the relevance score of a concept c_i in the domain D_j. The term $Dom(c_i, D_j)$ is the domain frequency of the concept c_i (i.e., number of documents containing the concept divided by the total number of documents in the corpus). The higher the value of $Rel(c_i, D_j)$, the more relevant the concept is for domain D_j. Based on empirical testing, we can estimate a threshold rel for a particular domain. Only the concepts with relevance score greater than the threshold will be selected. For each selected concept, its context vector will be expanded based on the synonymy relation defined in WordNet [8]. This is in fact a *smoothing* procedure [3]. The intuition is that some words that belong to a particular concept may not co-occur with the concept in a corpus. To make our ontology discovery method more robust, we need to consider these missing

Algorithm FuzzyOntoMine(D, *Para*, *Ont*)
Input: corpus D and vector of threshold values $Para$
Output: a fuzzy domain ontology Ont
Main Procedure:

1. $Ont = \{\}$
2. Foreach document $d \in D$ Do
   (a) Construct text windows $w \in d$
   (b) Remove stop words sw from w
   (c) Perform POS tagging for each term $t_i \in w$
   (d) Apply Porter stemming to each term t_i
   (e) Accumulate the frequency for $t_i \in w$ and the joint frequency for any pair $t_i, t_j \in w$
   (f) IF $lower \leq Feq(t_i) \leq upper$, $X = X \cup t_i$
3. End for
4. Foreach term $t_i \in X$ Do
   (a) compute its context vector c_i using BMI, MI, JA, CP, KL, or ECH, and perform an α-cut for c_i
   (b) $C = C \cup c_i$
5. End for
6. Foreach $c_i \in C$ Do /* Concept Pruning */
   (a) IF $\forall t_i \in c_i : \mu_{c_i}(t_i) < \sigma$
   (b) THEN $C = C - c_i$
7. End for
8. Foreach pair of concepts $c_i, c_j \in C$ Do
   (a) Compute the taxonomy relation $R(c_i, c_j)$ using $Spec(c_i, c_j)$
   (b) IF $\mu_{C \times C}(c_i, c_j) > \lambda$, $R = R \cup R(c_i, c_j)$
9. End For
10. Foreach $R(c_i, c_j) \in R$ Do /* Taxonomy Pruning */
    (a) IF $\mu_{C \times C}(c_i, c_j) < \mu_{C \times C}(c_j, c_i)$
    (b) THEN $R = R - R(c_i, c_j)$
    (c) IF $\exists P(c_i \to c_x, \ldots, c_y \to c_j)$
    (d) AND $\mu_{C \times C}(c_i, c_j) \leq \min(\{\mu_{C \times C}(c_i, c_x), \mu_{C \times C}(c_x, c_y), \ldots, \mu_{C \times C}(c_y, c_j)\})$
    (e) THEN $R = R - R(c_i, c_j)$
11. End For
12. Output Ont

Fig. 1. The Fuzzy Domain Ontology Discovery Algorithm

associations. For instance, our example context vector for "chief executive" will be expanded with the feature "presidency" based on the synonymy relation of WordNet, and a default membership value will be applied to such a term.

The final stage towards our ontology discovery method is fuzzy taxonomy generation based on subsumption relations among extracted concepts. Let

$Spec(c_x, c_y)$ denotes that concept c_x is a specialization (sub-class) of another concept c_y. The degree of such a specialization is derived by:

$$\mu_{C \times C}(c_x, c_y) \approx Spec(c_x, c_y)$$
$$= \frac{\sum_{t_x \in c_x, t_y \in c_y, t_x = t_y} \mu_{c_x}(t_x) \otimes \mu_{c_y}(t_y)}{\sum_{t_x \in c_x} \mu_{c_x}(t_x)} \qquad (4)$$

where $\otimes$ is a fuzzy conjunction operator which is equivalent to the min function. The above formula states that the degree of subsumption (specificity) of c_x to c_y is based on the ratio of the sum of the minimal membership values of the common terms belonging to the two concepts to the sum of the membership values of terms in the concept c_x. For instance, if every object of c_x is also an object of c_y, a high specificity value will be derived. The $Spec(c_x, c_y)$ function takes its values from the unit interval $[0, 1]$ and the subsumption relation is asymmetric. When the taxonomy is built, we only select the subsumption relations such that $Spec(c_x, c_y) > Spec(c_y, c_x)$ and $Spec(c_x, c_y) > \lambda$ where λ is a threshold to distinguish significant subsumption relations. The parameter λ is estimated based on empirical tests. If $Spec(c_x, c_y) = Spec(c_y, c_x)$ and $Spec(c_x, c_y) > \lambda$ is established, the *equivalent* relation between c_x and c_y will be extracted. In addition, a pruning step is introduced such that the redundant taxonomy relations are removed. If the membership of a relation $\mu_{C \times C}(c_1, c_2) \leq \min(\{\mu_{C \times C}(c_1, c_i), \ldots, \mu_{C \times C}(c_i, c_2)\})$, where $c_1, c_i, \ldots, c_2$ form a path P from c_1 to c_2, the relation $R_{(}c_1, c_2)$ is removed because it can be derived from other stronger taxonomy relations in the ontology. The fuzzy domain ontology mining algorithm is summarized and shown in Figure 1.

4   Application to E-Learning

In an E-Learning environment, learners are often encouraged to reflect what they have learned by writing on-line journals or sharing their ideas via an online discussion board. Figure 2 shows a sample of message entered by a student via the Blackboard E-Learning environment. Usually, teacher or other fellow students may reply and produce multiple threads of messages. If teachers want to know the current learning status of their students, they need to browse through all the threads of messages and make an analysis afterwards. This is a very time consuming process, and it is very unlikely that a teacher can do it when a lecture or tutorial is in progress. To alleviate this problem, we can apply the fuzzy domain ontology discovery algorithm to automatically discover and visual the concept map representing the collective knowledge of a specific subject among a group of students. Figure 3 highlights one of the interfaces of our prototype system. An instructor can click the "Discussion Board Ontology Analysis" button to activate the ontology discovery process and then click the "Launch Concept Map Viewer" button to display the related concept map. An example of an automatically generated concept map is shown in Figure 4. When a node at the second level is clicked, all the subclasses below the current node will be shown. Based on the concept map, the instructor can quickly identify the average progress of

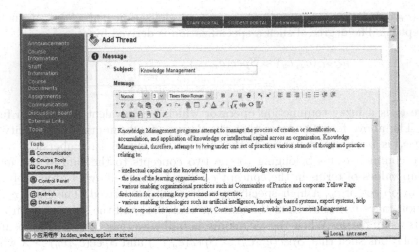

Fig. 2. A Message Entered via Online Discussion Board

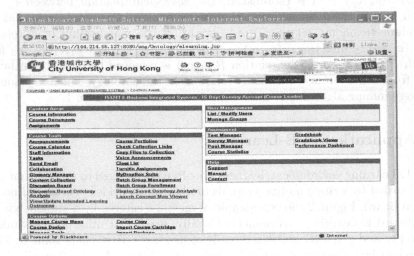

Fig. 3. The Concept Map Generation Tool on E-Learning Platform

a group of students (e.g., the important concepts and the relationships among these concepts which have been internalized by the students).

A small scale experiment of testing the functionality of the prototype system and the accuracy of the aforementioned fuzzy domain ontology discovery algorithm has been conducted. A group of ten undergraduate students were recruited to try the prototype system; all of these subjects have attended a course in knowledge management before. At the beginning of the experiment, they attended a briefing session of fifteen minutes to learn the objective of this experiment and were instructed to write the most important concepts in knowledge management using concise and precise statements on the discussion board. They were given thirty minutes to write their messages. After the message generation session, the coordinator of the experiment would execute the ontology discovery method to generate the concept map pertaining the group's perception about knowledge management. For this experiment, only the "Noun Noun" linguistic pattern was specified and the parameter $\alpha = 0.5$ was set. Each subject could then view the concept map on-line; the first level hierarchy of the resulting concept map is shown in Figure 4. Following the viewing session, a questionnaire was distributed to each subject to let them assess if the concept map could really reflect their understanding about the chosen topic. Our questionnaire was developed based on the instrument employed by [2]. It included the assessment of the following factors:

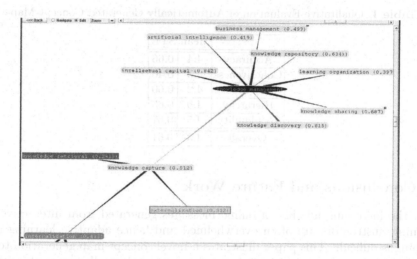

Fig. 4. An Automatically Generated Concept Map

- Accuracy - Whether the concepts and relationships shown at the taxonomy are correct;
- Cohesiveness - Whether each concept at the taxonomy is unique and not overlapped with one another;
- Isolation - Whether the concepts at the same level are distinguishable and not subsume one another;
- Hierarchy - Whether the taxonomy is traversed from broader concepts at the higher levels to narrow concepts at the lower level;
- Readability - Whether the concepts at all levels are easy to be comprehended by human;

A five point semantic differential scale from very good (5), good (4), average (3), bad (2), to very poor (1) is used to measure these variables. In general, a score close to 5 indicates that the automatically generated concept map is with good quality and it correctly reflects the mental state of the subjects. The average scores pertaining to various factors are shown in Table 1. The overall mean score is 4.3 with a standard deviation of 0.61; the overall mean score is close to the maximum 5. The time it takes to generate the concept map (including the underlying OWL statements) on a PC with a single Pentium 4 processor and 1 GB RAM is 1.3 seconds. There are 26 key concepts and 97 relationships spreading at 3 levels. From this initial experiment, it is shown that our fuzzy domain ontology discovery algorithm is promising for enhancing the effectiveness of E-Learning. In particular, it can assist instructors to quickly analyze and visualize the knowledge structure already acquired by a group of students. Thereby, adaptive teaching and learning is possible to further improve learning effectiveness.

Table 1. Qualitative Evaluation of Automatically Generated Concept Map

	Mean	STD
Accuracy	4.4	0.66
Cohesiveness	4.3	0.46
Isolation	4.2	0.60
Hierarchy	4.0	0.63
Readability	4.5	0.67
Overall	4.3	0.61

5   Conclusions and Future Work

With the increasing number of online messages generated from interactive E-Learning, instructors are often overwhelmed and hence adaptive learning and teaching is difficult. This paper illustrates a novel concept map generation technique which is underpinned by a fuzzy domain ontology discovery algorithm. The proposed mechanism can automatically construct a concept map based on the messages posted to an online discussion board. By providing such a tool on an E-Learning environment, instructors can quickly identify the learning status of their students, and hence more suitable pedagogy can be developed for the following teaching and learning stage. Our initial experimental results show that the accuracy and the quality of the automatically generated concept map is promising. Future work involves a large scale of evaluation work against our automated concept map generation mechanism. Other text mining method will also be explored to improve our fuzzy domain ontology discovery method. Moreover, more development work will be required to implement our prototype system on the production Blackboard E-Learning environment.

Acknowledgments. This work is funded in part by the UK's Engineering and Physical Sciences Research Council (EPSRC) grant number (EP/E002145/1), and the E-Learning project (Project No.: 6980081-680) of the City University of Hong Kong.

References

1. Ausubel, D.P., Novak, J.D., Hanesian, H.: Educational psychology: A cognitive view, Rinehart and Winston, New York (1978)
2. Chuang, S., Chien, L.: Taxonomy generation for text segments: A practical web-based approach. ACM Transactions on Information Systems 23(4), 363–396 (2005)
3. Cimiano, P., Hotho, A., Staab, S.: Learning concept hierarchies from text corpora using formal concept analysis. Journal of Artificial Intelligence Research 24, 305–339 (2005)
4. Gruber, T.R.: A translation approach to portable ontology specifications. Knowledge Acquisition 5(2), 199–220 (1993)
5. Lau, R.Y.K.: Context-Sensitive Text Mining and Belief Revision for Intelligent Information Retrieval on the Web. Web Intelligence and Agent Systems An International Journal 1(3-4), 1–22 (2003)
6. Lee, C.-S., Jian, Z.-W., Huang, L.-K.: A fuzzy ontology and its application to news summarization. IEEE Transactions on Systems, Man, and Cybernetics, Part B 35(5), 859–880 (2005)
7. Maedche, A., Pekar, V., Staab, S.: Ontology learning part oneon discovering taxonomic relations from the web. In: Zhong, N., Liu, J., Yao, Y. (eds.) Web Intelligence, pp. 3–24. Springer, Heidelberg (2003)
8. Miller, G.A., Beckwith, R., Fellbaum, C., Gross, D., Miller, K.J.: Introduction to wordnet: An on-line lexical database. Journal of Lexicography 3(4), 234–244 (1990)
9. Navigli, R., Velardi, P., Gangemi, A.: Ontology learning and its application to automated terminology translation. IEEE Intelligent Systems 18(1), 22–31 (2003)
10. Papatheodorou, C., Vassiliou, A., Simon, B.: Discovery of ontologies for learning resources using word-based clustering. In: Proceedings of the World Conference on Educational Multimedia, Hypermedia and Telecommunications (ED-MEDIA 2002), pp. 324–326 (2002)
11. Perrin, P., Petry, F.: Extraction and representation of contextual information for knowledge discovery in texts. Information Sciences 151, 125–152 (2003)
12. Salton, G., McGill, M.J.: Introduction to Modern Information Retrieval. McGraw-Hill, New York (1983)
13. Sekine, S., Carroll, J.J., Ananiadou, S., Tsujii, J.: Automatic learning for semantic collocation. In: Proceedings of the third Conference on Applied Natural Language Processing, Trento, Italy, March 31–April 3 1992, Association for Computational Linguistics, pp. 104–110 (1992)
14. Soong, M.H., Chan, H.C., Chua, B.C., Loh, K.F.: Critical succes factors for on-line course resources. Computers & Education 36(2), 101–120 (2001)
15. Tho, Q.T., Hui, S.C., Fong, A.C.M., Cao, T.H.: Automatic fuzzy ontology generation for semantic web. IEEE Transactions on Knowledge and Data Engineering 18(6), 842–856 (2006)
16. Wille, R.: Formal concept analysis as mathematical theory of concepts and concept hierarchies. In: Ganter, B., Stumme, G., Wille, R. (eds.) Formal Concept Analysis. LNCS (LNAI), vol. 3626, pp. 1–33. Springer, Heidelberg (2005)
17. Zadeh, L.A.: Fuzzy sets. Journal of Information and Control 8, 338–353 (1965)

Knowledge Element Extraction for Knowledge-Based Learning Resources Organization

Xiao Chang[1,2,3] and Qinghua Zheng[1,2,3]

[1] Dept. Computer Science and Engineering, Xi'an Jiaotong University
[2] Shaanxi Key Lab. of Satellite and Computer Network
[3] State Key Laboratory for Manufacturing Systems Engineering
No.28 Xianning West Road, Xi'an, Shaanxi, 710049, PR China
{changxiao, qhzheng}@mail.xjtu.edu.cn

Abstract. In this paper, we propose a machine learning method to knowledge element extraction from learning resources. First, we build a knowledge element taxonomy containing 25 semantic types. Second, we formalize the knowledge element extraction of single semantic type as binary classification. Finally, we construct the multi-class classification model which can predict the semantic type of knowledge element by merge the results of binary classifiers. We annotate three semantic types in corpus and use them as training data, train the machine learning models. In experiment, we compared three binary classification models: Decision Tree, SVM and Naïve Bayesian. The experimental results show that SVM has better average performance. We employ ECOC method to construct multi-class classification model and use SVM as base binary classifier in the model. Our approach outperforms the baseline in experiment. The experimental results indicate that our approach is effective.

Keywords: Learning Resource Organization, Knowledge Element Extraction, Machine Learning.

1 Introduction

Acquiring knowledge is the goal of learners using the E-Learning system. In most of E-Learning system, however, the learning resources are organized by the attributes of resource entity, but not by the content of resources in knowledge level.

Knowledge element is a relatively independent and integral knowledge module in a special discipline. Learning resources can be organized by knowledge elements. Extracting knowledge elements from learning resources is a key step to implement the knowledge element based learning resources organization. Knowledge elements are extracted from learning resources by manual in existing knowledge element based learning resources management systems. Knowledge element extraction by manual is inefficient and the results are inconsistent. Knowledge element extraction has become a bottleneck of knowledge element based learning resources organization.

We proposed a machine learning approach to extracting knowledge element from learning resources. We conduct the knowledge element extraction experiment to three

H. Leung et al. (Eds.): ICWL 2007, LNCS 4823, pp. 102–113, 2008.

semantic types of the knowledge element taxonomy. We employ three classification models to construct the classifier for every semantic type, include Decision Tree, SVM and Naive Bayesian.

In this paper, we investigate the following two problems.

1) Comparison between models: among the models above, which model performs best for single knowledge element type identifying;
2) Test the validity of the multi-class knowledge element extraction approach.

Experimental results indicate that our approach works well for knowledge extraction from learning resources. Our method can significantly outperform the baseline.

Our contributions in this paper are that we proposed an approach to extracting knowledge element from learning resources and conducted the experiment of knowledge element extraction. The experimental results show that this approach is effective.

The rest part of this paper is organized as follows. In section 2, we introduce related work, and in section 3, we explain the motivation and problem setting of our work. In section 4, we describe our method of knowledge element extraction. Section 5 shows our experimental results. We make concluding remarks in section 6.

2 Related Work

2.1 Knowledge Extraction

The research works on knowledge extraction are focus on ontology acquisition from text at present. The main task of ontology acquisition is to extract the (*concept1, concept2, relation*) triples. Concept extraction and concept relation extraction are two key tasks in ontology acquisition.

Likelihood ratio [1] is used for hypothesis testing in term extraction. MC-value [2] counting how independently the given compound noun is used in the given corpus. The statistic-base method showed higher performance in term extraction task. It also has disadvantages. In statistic-based method, statistic is computed only with the character of adjoined words in terms.

In recent years, machine learning based methods has been proposed. Naïve Bayesian, Maximum Entropy and SVM [3], three classifiers, for instance, have been proposed to extract Gene from MEDLINE corpus.

2.2 Answer Extraction

Answers in the QA system also can be looked as a kind of knowledge. So, answer extraction also can be look as knowledge extraction task. The proposed answer extraction approaches are focused on extracting single type answer, such as definition extraction.

The proposed methods fall into three categories: rule-based approach, statistic-based approach and the machine learning based approach.

Hovy et al. [4], for instance, use the rule-based approach to answer extraction. They first parse the question and text snippet, and then match answer in parse tree.

The rule-based approach can achieve higher performance. However, it also has disadvantages. It is less adaptive and robust when compared with other methods.

Therefore, some researchers introduced the statistic measures to answer extraction. Mutual Information Model [5] , has been used to estimate the relativity of Q&A (Question and Answer) pair in samples. Classification rules and information gain [6] are compound to mining answer. Linguistic features and linearly combined of statistic measures [7] is used to definition extraction.

In recent years, the machine learning attracted the attention of researchers for the higher adaptive and scalability. Perceptron model [8], for instance, has been used as a classifier to extract answer for open domain QA system. Maximum entropy model [9] has been proposed to construct the distribution model of matching question and answer. SVM [10] has been proposed to construct the answer extraction model, the features of Q&A pair are combined in model. HMM [11] has been introduced to extract fact answer. Logistic regression [12] has been proposed as learning model and Q&A pairs used as training data to extracting answer.

3 Motivation and Problem Setting

The most of existing E-Learning systems organize learning resources by metadata. This learning resources organization method will follow the educational resource metadata standards, such as IEEE LOM and DC-Education. These educational resource metadata standards are only defined by the attributes of resource entity, but not offer the help to organize the content of resources in knowledge level.

Knowledge-based learning resources organization method is proposed for make up for the shortcoming of educational resources metadata standards. Conceptual network model [13] was proposed for learning resources navigation in concept level. Knowledge elements [14] was used to build knowledge structures for online instructional/learning systems.

Knowledge element is a relatively independent and integral knowledge module in a special discipline. We can regard knowledge elements as the minimum knowledge modules, which can be integrated into any useful course according to the students' goals.

In different systems, the definition of knowledge element is evolved according to the characters of the system. The research object of us are text learning resources, include MS Office, HTML, PDF document, etc. Therefore, we define the knowledge element as the text snippet describing the locally integral knowledge unit. We formalize definition of the knowledge element as $KP= (T, ST, D)$. KP represents the knowledge element. T represents the core concept described in knowledge element. ST represents semantic type of the knowledge element. D represents the text snippet describing the knowledge element. In the field of automatic QA (Question Answering), most systems have their own question taxonomy. For example, 31 original question types are defined in [9] and 141 question types of the question taxonomy are also defined in [4].

Answers in QA system can be looked as a kind of knowledge. Therefore, we define a knowledge element taxonomy reference to question taxonomy. There are 25 semantic types in our knowledge element taxonomy, include definition, classification, property, relation, etc. As the limit of space, we only list the specifications of three types in Table 1.

Table 1. Semantic type specification

Type	Definition	Example
definition	Describe the definition of the concept.	*"Network protocol is a specification of transmitting and managing information in network."*
property	Describe the characters, attributes, advantages and disadvantages of thing.	*"The advantage of distance vector routing is simple and easy to be realized."*
classification	Describe the classification of a thing.	*"Undirected routing algorithm fall into two categories: centralized searching and nearest searching."*

A three tiers knowledge-based learning resources organization model is show in Fig. 1, in which the Knowledge element is used to organize the learning resources.

Conceptual Network is composed of concepts and the relations among them. Concept is basis unit to organize the knowledge. In layer of conceptual network in Fig. 1, a circle node represent a concept, the link between nodes represents the relation between concepts.

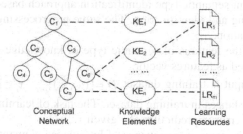

Conceptual Network   Knowledge Elements   Learning Resources

Fig. 1. Three tiers learning resources organization model

Knowledge Element is the integral knowledge unit used to teaching. We look it as knowledge object can exist independently and can't be divided again. Knowledge element contains the teaching information of the knowledge object.

Learning Resource describes the content of domain knowledge in detail. It is the carrier of teaching contents.

Analyzing the content of learning resources and extracting the knowledge element from them is a key step to implementing the knowledge-based learning resources organization in E-Learning. In existing knowledge-based learning resources management systems, the knowledge element is extracted by manual. Manually knowledge element extraction is inefficient and the results are inconsistent. Therefore, we proposed an approach to extracting knowledge element from learning resources automatically.

4 Knowledge Element Extraction Method

4.1 Outline

The goal of knowledge element extraction is to extract the (T, ST, D, KP) quaternion set, KP represents the position of knowledge element in learning resource.

First, we collect the knowledge element candidates using heuristic rules. Parse the knowledge element candidate and identify <*term*> in it. Label the position of the knowledge element candidate in learning resources. Second, we use knowledge element extraction model to identify the knowledge element from candidates. So, we can obtain the description text and the semantic type of knowledge element.

Both paragraphs and sentences can be considered as knowledge element description in our approach. Hereafter, we will only describe the case of using sentences. It is easy to extend it to the case of using paragraphs.

The first step can be omitted in principle. With the adoption of it, we can enhance the efficiency of both training and classification.

4.2 Single Semantic Type Extraction Model

Identify the knowledge element whether belong to a semantic type or not is a binary classification problem. We take a statistical machine learning approach to address the problem. We label candidates in advance, and use them for training.

Knowledge element semantic type identification approach based on machine learning consists of training and identification. The same preprocessing step occurs before training and identification.

In preprocessing, the features of semantic type of knowledge element will be extracted and represented as features vector.

In learning, the input is training dataset $D = \{(x_i, y_i)\}_{i=1}^{n} \cdot x_i \in \mathbb{R}^N$ and $y_i \in \{-1,1\}$. n is the number of instances in training dataset. The task of learning is to construct the model that minimize error in prediction of y given x.

In identification, the input is a sequence of knowledge element candidate. We employ trained model to identify whether a knowledge element candidate is an instance of a semantic type or not.

We employ Decision Tree, SVM and Naïve Bayesian models to construct the single semantic type classifier. We compare the performance of three models to single semantic type classification in experiment.

4.3 Features

In this paper, we only consider the knowledge element description is a sentence. We analyzed the sentences describing knowledge element in corpus, and defined the features as follows:

Length: This feature represents the number of characters or words contained in text snippet. Use the number of character will be simple to realize. Use the number of words will be complex to realize, but the number of words is more reasonable to represent the feature. We select the number of words in this paper.

Position: This feature represents the score of sentence position in the paragraph. We constructed a function to compute the score.

$$S_i = max(\frac{1}{i}, \frac{1}{n-i+1}) \tag{1}$$

S_i is the score of sentence position. i is the sequence number of the sentence in the paragraph. n is the total number of sentences contained in the paragraph.

Number of terms: This feature represents the number of terms included in the text snippet.

Single-Word: This is a binary feature set. We analyzed the sample text of every semantic type of knowledge element and build the Single-Words set for every semantic type. When the element of the Single-Words set occurs in the text snippet, we will set value of the feature as 1. Otherwise, we will set it as 0. The total number of Single-Words feature of every semantic type is equal to the number of elements in its cue words set. For example, "*definition*" will be useful for identifying the definition.

Bigram-Word: This is a binary feature set. Every semantic type has a Bigram-Word set, in which two continuous word sequences occurrence are contained. For example, combination of "*definition is*" will be useful for identifying the definition.

Word-And-POS: This is a binary feature set. Combination of word and POS (part of speech tag) of two continuous words are contained in it. For example, in sequence "definition/n is" the Word-And-Pos features are "*definition /v*" and "*/n is*". It will be related to "*definition/n is/v*" by feature "*definition /v*".

Before using machine learning models, each candidate snippet should be represented as an attribute vector consisting of the above elements.

4.4 Multi-class Extraction Model

To a knowledge element candidate, there are 25 possible semantic types. Therefore, the knowledge element candidate classification is a problem of multi-class classification.

The proposed multi-class classification methods fall into two categories: direct method and decompose method.

Direct method: such as KNN (K-Nearest Neighbor), K-classes SVM, etc. In this method, the classifier that can classify multi-classes is used directly. The principal of this method is simple. But it is difficult to realize the multi-class classifier. The performance of the multi-class classifier is poor too.

Decompose method: decompose a problem of multi-class classification into several binary classifications. The results of binary classifiers are synthesized to generate the result of multi-class classification. This method is more mature and simple to be realized. The base binary classifier in this method can be constructed by different binary classification model. The performance of this method also is better.

1-vs-rest, 1-vs-1(MaxMin [15], DAG [16]) and ECOC (Error-Correcting Output Codes) [17, 18] are more effective decompose methods. ECOC design the binary classifiers according to the principal of redundancy error correcting encoding. The 1-vs-rest, 1-vs-1 can be looked as the special case of ECOC.

Therefore, we employ the ECOC method to construct the knowledge extraction model. Coding matrix should be designed according to real problem when apply the ECOC. In ECOC method, the object class is look as a code. Every bit of code represents the result of a binary classifier. The coding matrix constructed in ECOC is showed in Table 2.

Table 2. Coding matrix

Class	Code						
	f_1	f_2	f_3	f_4	f_5	...	f_n
C_1	M_{11}	M_{12}	M_{13}	M_{14}	M_{15}		M_{1n}
C_2	M_{21}	M_{22}	M_{23}	M_{24}	M_{25}		M_{2n}
C_3	M_{31}	M_{32}	M_{33}	M_{34}	M_{35}		M_{3n}
...							
C_m	M_{m1}	M_{m2}	M_{m3}	M_{m4}	M_{m5}		M_{mn}

m represents the number of classes in multi-class classification. $C_i (i = 1, 2, \cdots, m)$ represents a object class. n represents the length of a code. $f_j (j = 1, 2, \cdots, n)$ represents a binary classifier.

$M_{ij} (i = 1, 2, \cdots, m; j = 1, 2, \cdots, n)$ represents a result of f_j . $M_{ij} \in [-1, +1]$. $M_i = M_{i1} M_{i2} \cdots M_{in}$ is the code of C_i class, and any two codes can't be equal.

5 Experiment Results

In knowledge element extraction experiment, we involve three semantic types to show the validity of our method. The three semantic types are definition, classification and property. Therefore the knowledge extraction model should be able to identify four classes, include the three semantic types and none knowledge element class. All knowledge element candidate that don't belong to the three semantic types will be look as none knowledge element class.

5.1 Data Set

First, we collected 500 learning resources in the domain of computer science from the learning resources base of our university's school of network education and 500 from internet respectively. These learning resources are Word and PowerPoint documents. Second, we manually extracted all (*term, sentence*) pairs, *term* is included in the *sentence*. We eliminated the duplicate pairs. Finally, we manually labeled semantic types for every pair. So, we obtained a (*term, sentence, semantic type*) triple set.

Our final data set contains 495 terms, 8061 candidates and 5000 none knowledge point sentences. We show the distribution of data set in Table 3.

Table 3. Semantic type distribution of knowledge element in data set

Semantic type	Number of sentences
Definition	3566
Classification	2557
Property	1938
None	5000
Total	13061

We randomly select 70% samples of every type as the training data and 30% samples of every type as test data.

5.2 Evaluation Measures

5.2.1 Binary Classification Evaluation Measures

In experiments, we conducted evaluations on knowledge cell extraction in terms of Precision (P), Recall (R), and F-measure. The evaluation measures are defined as follows:

$$P = \frac{a}{a+b}, \quad R = \frac{a}{a+c}$$

F-measure is the weighted harmonic mean of precision and recall. The formula of F-measure is as follows:

$$F\alpha = \frac{(1+\alpha) \times P \times R}{\alpha \times P + R}$$

$\alpha = 1$ is the common case. We use $F1$ in our evaluation.

Here, a, b, c and d are the number of the knowledge points as those defined in Table 4.

Table 4. Contingence table with regard to binary classification

		Expert Judgment	
		Definition	Non definition
Model Prediction	Definition	a	b
	Non definition	c	d

5.2.2 Multi-class Classification Evaluation Measures

The performance of Multi-class classifier also can be measured by Precision, Recall and $F1$. Two methods are used to generate the value of evaluation measures: Macro-average and Micro-average.

Assume a multi-class classification problem there are S object classes $\{OC_1, OC_2, ..., OC_S\}$. The evaluation measures of binary classification can be used to every object class. The value of Precision, Recall and $F1$ of OC_i class can be computed as follows:

$$P_i = \frac{a_i}{a_i + c_i}, \quad R_i = \frac{a_i}{a_i + b_i}, \quad F1_i = \frac{2 \times P_i \times R_i}{P_i + R_i}$$

Using Macro-average method, the formula of $MacroP$, $MacroR$ and $MacroF1$ of multi-class classification as follows:

$$MacroP = \frac{1}{S} \sum_{i=1}^{S} P_i, \quad MacroR = \frac{1}{S} \sum_{i=1}^{S} R_i, \quad MacroF1 = \frac{2 \times MacroP \times MacroR}{MacroP + MacroR}$$

Using Micro-average method, the formula of $MicroP$, $MicroR$ and $MicroF1$ of multi-class classification as follows:

$$MicroP = \frac{\sum_{i=1}^{S} a_i}{\sum_{i=1}^{S} (a_i + c_i)}, \quad MicroR = \frac{\sum_{i=1}^{S} a_i}{\sum_{i=1}^{S} (a_i + b_i)}, \quad MacroF1 = \frac{2 \times MicroP \times MicroR}{MicroP + MicroR}$$

5.3 Comparison Between Models

We employ the ECOC method to construct the knowledge extraction model. Therefore, we need to select the binary classification model to construct the base classifier. First, we employ three classification models to constructed the binary classifier and evaluate the performance of classifier in binary classification experiment. The three classification models are Decision Tree, SVM and Naive Bayesian model. Second, we compare the three classification models in multi-class classification experiment.

5.3.1 Comparison Between Models in Binary Classification

In our experiment, there are four object classes. Therefore, we constructed 7 binary classifiers for applying ECOC method. The experimental results of 7 binary classifiers constructed by every model are show in Table 5.

Table 5. Comparison between different learning models for knowledge element binary classification

Classifier	Decision Tree			SVM			Naive Bayesian		
	P	R	F1	P	R	F1	P	R	F1
f1	0.928	0.790	0.853	0.917	0.708	0.799	0.527	0.698	0.601
f2	0.928	0.613	0.738	0.944	0.739	0.829	0.485	0.691	0.570
f3	0.950	0.778	0.855	0.923	0.790	0.851	0.487	0.778	0.599
f4	0.936	0.579	0.715	0.924	0.820	0.869	0.457	0.781	0.577
f5	0.942	0.556	0.699	0.957	0.752	0.842	0.643	0.632	0.638
f6	0.912	0.596	0.721	0.892	0.635	0.742	0.579	0.423	0.489
f7	0.988	0.723	0.839	0.983	0.877	0.927	0.571	0.738	0.644
Average	0.957	0.829	0.879	0.956	0.878	0.912	0.754	0.807	0.771

$f1 \sim f7$ represent 7 binary classifiers. "Average" is the average result of all classifiers. The shadow parts in the table are the best results.

The experimental results show that SVM perform the best, followed by Decision Tree, and Naive Bayesian is the worst. Naive Bayesian hypothesize the features of model are independent to each other. We selected features are not independent to each other is a possible explain to the ill result of Naive Bayesian.

5.3.2 Comparison Between Models in Multi-class Classification

To compare the performance of different machine learning models in Multi-class Classification, we conducted another experiment. The experimental results of three models are showed in Table 6.

Table 6. Comparison between different learning models for knowledge element multi-class classification

Type	Decision Tree			SVM			Naive Bayesian		
	P	R	F1	P	R	F1	P	R	F1
None	0.939	0.997	0.967	0.955	0.993	0.973	0.944	0.912	0.928
Definition	0.953	0.567	0.711	0.937	0.747	0.831	0.471	0.815	0.597
Classification	0.912	0.596	0.721	0.882	0.577	0.698	0.700	0.135	0.226
Property	0.985	0.692	0.818	0.988	0.723	0.839	0.789	0.462	0.583
Macro-average	0.951	0.713	0.804	0.944	0.760	0.835	0.726	0.581	0.584
Micro-average	0.940	0.940	0.940	0.953	0.953	0.953	0.870	0.870	0.870

5.4 Comparison with Baseline

5.4.1 Baseline

We use matching word features method as baseline. We build the Single-Word or Bigram-Word features set for every semantic type of knowledge element in the step of analyzing features.

Strategy: If the knowledge element candidate contains a Single-Word or a Bigram-Word feature of certain semantic type, we will label it as the type.

5.4.2 Experimental Results

We conducted knowledge element extraction from the data set. As the binary model, we used SVM. In the evaluation, we use exact matching between the true knowledge

Table 7. Comparison between learning model and baseline for knowledge element extraction

Type	Baseline			Learning model		
	P	R	F1	P	R	F1
None	0.854	0.798	0.825	0.955	0.993	0.973
Definition	0.568	0.587	0.577	0.937	0.747	0.831
Classification	0.671	0.448	0.537	0.882	0.577	0.698
Property	0.694	0.768	0.729	0.985	0.723	0.839
Macro-average	0.697	0.650	0.673	0.944	0.760	0.835
Micro-average	0.642	0.642	0.712	0.953	0.953	0.953

elements annotated by humans and the extracted knowledge elements. Table 7 shows the results. The results indicate that classification method significantly outperforms the baseline.

6 Conclusions

In this paper, we have investigated the problem of knowledge element extraction from learning resources by machine. We employ the ECOC method to construct the multi-class classification model for knowledge element extraction. We compare our approach with baseline method in knowledge element extraction experiment. The experimental results show that the performance of our approach is better than baseline obviously. All the above investigations were not conducted in previous works. Through these investigations confirm the effectiveness of our method.

In future works, we will attack the problem of extracting knowledge element which is composed of multi-paragraphs or multi-sentences.

Acknowledgements. We thank the anonymous reviewers of ICWL'07 for their valuable comments on this paper. This paper is supported by the National Science Foundation of china (Grant No. 60473136, 60633020), the Doctoral Program Foundation of the China Ministry of Education (Grant No. 20040698028) and "11-5" National S&T Underlaid Plan of china (Grant No. 2006BAH02A2-4).

References

1. Moens, M.-F., Angheluta, R.: Concept extraction from legal cases- the use of a statistic of coincidence. In: 9th international conference on Artificial intelligence and law, pp. 142–146. ACM Press, New York (2003)
2. Nakagawa, H., Mori, T.: A Simple but Powerful Automatic Term Extraction Method. In: 2ed International Workshop on Computational Terminology (COMPUTERM 2002), pp. 29–35 (2002)
3. Chang, J.T.: Finding gene and protein names one word at a time. Bioinformatics 20(2), 216–225 (2004)
4. Hovy, E., Gerber, L., Hermjakob, U., Lin, C.-Y., Ravichandran, D.: Toward Semantics-Based Answer Pinpointing. In: Human Language Technology Conference (HLT2001), pp. 339–345 (2001)
5. Mann, G.S.: A statistic method to short answer extraction. In: Workshop on ARABIC language processing: status and prospects in Annual Meeting of the ACL, Association for Computational Linguistics, pp. 1–8, (2001)
6. Yamanishi, K., Li, H.: Mining Open Answers in Questionnaire Data. IEEE Intelligent System (2001)
7. Han, K.-S., Song, Y.-I., Kim, S.-B., Rim, H.-C.: Answer extraction and ranking strategies for definitional question answering using linguistic features and definition terminology. Information Processing and Management 43, 353–364 (2007)
8. Pasca, M., H.S.: Answer Mining from On-Line Documents. In: The ACL-2001 Workshop on Open-Domain Question Answering, pp. 38–45 (2001)

9. Ittycheriah, A., Franz, M., Zhu, W., Ratnaparkhi, A., Mammone, R.J.: IBM's Statistical Question Answering System. In: 9th Text REtrieval Conference (2000)
10. Suzuki, J., Sasaki, Y., Maeda, E.: SVM Answer Selection for Open-Domain Question Answering. In: 19th international conference on Computational linguistics, pp. 1–7 (2002)
11. Ng, H.T., Lai, J., Kwan, P., Xia, Y.: Question Answering Using a Large Text Database: A Machine Learning Approach. In: 2001 Conference on Empirical Methods in Natural Language Processing, pp. 67–73 (2001)
12. Ramakrishnan, G., Chakrabarti, S., Paranjpe, D., Bhattacharya, P.: Is Question Answering an Acquired Skill? In: 13th international conference on World Wide Web, pp. 111–120 (2004)
13. Luo, S., Sha, S., Shen, D., Jia, W.: Conceptual Network Based Courseware Navigation and Web Presentation Mechanisms. In: Fong, J., Cheung, C.T., Leong, H.V., Li, Q. (eds.) ICWL 2002. LNCS, vol. 2436, pp. 81–94. Springer, Heidelberg (2002)
14. Qing, Y., Yang, Y., Juan, C.: Goal-oriented platform based on knowledge-point: a new model of distance education system. In: 18th International Conference on Advanced Information Networking and Application (AINA 2004), pp. 528–531 (2004)
15. Kressel, U.: Pairwise classification and support vector machines. In: Advances in Kernel Methods —Support Vector Learning, pp. 255–268. MIT Press, Cambridge (1998)
16. Platt, J., Cristianini, N., Shawe-Taylor, J.: Large margin DAGs for multiclass classification. In: Advances in Neural Information Processing Systems, pp. 547–553 (2000)
17. Dietterich, T.G., Bakiri, G.: Solving multiclass learning problems via error-correcting output codes. Journal of Artificial Intelligence Research 2, 263–286 (1995)
18. Masulli, F., Valentini, G.: Effectiveness of error correcting output coding methods in ensemble and monolithic learning machines. Journal of Pattern Analysis and Applications, 285–300 (2004)

A Context-Based Framework and Method for Learning Object Description and Search

Xiaofeng Du, William Song, and Ming Zhang

Department of Computer Science, University of Durham, Durham, UK
{xiaofeng.du, w.w.song}@durham.ac.uk
School of Electronics Engineering and Computer Science Peking University, Beijing, China
mzhang@net.pku.edu.cn

Abstract. For the last decade, E-Learning has become an active research area. Many companies and organisations are now providing large amounts of online learning resources. These learning resources have covered most common education and learning areas and subjects and are always available so that the learners can access them from anywhere which has an Internet connection. Learners can flexibly choose the subjects they want and build up their own curriculum and study schedule. However, most of the online learning resources are poorly described and structured so causing huge problems in their use, search, organization, and management. To overcome the problems, we propose a novel and practical context-based semantic description framework which aims to describe information and knowledge about learning resources and their structures. Context-based semantic description is an effective way to extract knowledge from various aspects to depicting learning resources which are abstracted and termed as "Learning Objects". This framework consists of four parts: the definition of Learning Objects, a Context-based Semantic Description Model, an ontology, and learning concept dependency graphs. By using the Learning Object's attributes and their various semantic relationships addressed in the proposed framework, we attempt to search and match a learner's requirements against the description of Learning Objects provided by the framework with the help of knowledge from learning environments. A key step here is to compute semantic similarity using the modelled knowledge. The proposed work aims to support learners in using massive learning resources from the web to perform self-learning with or without the help of educators' advice and instruction.

1 Introduction

As the World Wide Web technologies have become mature, they have enabled people take conventional courses through the Internet without classrooms and instructors. Web-based training and distance learning have formed a new paradigm of education, known as E-Learning [11]. E-Learning has provided an easy way to access online learning resources at anytime and from anywhere and build up synchronous and asynchronous communication and collaboration channels between learners and between learners and instructors [1]. One of the most attractive features of E-Learning is that the learners can define their own learning goals and personalise their learning strategy.

H. Leung et al. (Eds.): ICWL 2007, LNCS 4823, pp. 114–125, 2008.

The individual learner's requirements can be satisfied by combinations of different online learning resources.

The Web can be described as an ocean of information and knowledge usable for learning. There are many E-Learning resources providers, each of whom have provided a large number of learning courses, such as MIT OpenCourseWare [1], eLearners.com[2], and GreatLearning[3]. These courses have covered most common education and learning areas and subjects. They are available all the time through out the year and can be accessed from anywhere which has an Internet connection. Learners can flexibly choose the subjects they want and build up their own curriculum and study schedule which suits their personal needs. However, most of the learning materials have not been described sufficiently. Therefore, it is hard for learners to locate and judge which courses are the right ones for them. This is one of the reasons why education that done through E-Learning is still less effective than through personal interaction in a classroom [7]. We summarise the problems that web course users encounter when using the online learning resources below:

o   Poor description of learning resources: The individual learning resources are poorly described and there lacks an effective description model for the relationships among different learning resources.

o   Little support for effective resource search: It is difficult to efficiently search the provided learning resources, especially when a learner is new to a subject area. Learners have great difficulty in specifying exactly what they want and therefore, their requirements are vague and incomplete. Furthermore, many search engines for the current learning resources require precise information and terminologies to locate the relevant learning resources.

o   Difficult matching adequate courses: It is more often than not that the chosen resources do not suit the learner's requirements. A learning resource may be too difficult to learn for a beginner whereas it may too easy for someone already educated in the domain. This is due to a lack of systematic organization of the learning resources on the web, and effective and formal description of the users' demands and background knowledge.

o   Poor internal structures for managing learning resources: Most of the online course providers use a rough subject category-based structure to organize their learning resources and primary metadata models to describe them. Such organization schemes and models do not offer a well-defined structure to store and manage learning resources.

o   Poor interoperability among the communities providing learning resources: This is an obvious consequence of the above-discussed problems.

In order to address the problems discussed, we need to make a clear and concise definition of the concept Learning Object. There are quite a number of different definitions for Learning Object, such as SCORM [12], LOM [9], and LOMD [13], but they lack a clear depiction of how a Learning Object is related to other Learning Objects. We believe this is crucial to making good use of learning resources from different learning communities. Taking Learning Object as the core concept to be defined,

---

[1] http://ocw.mit.edu/

[2] http://www.elearners.com/

[3] http://greatlearning.grids.cn/

we propose a Context-based Semantic Description framework, consisting of a Context-based Semantic Description model describing relative concepts of a Learning Object, an ontology to describe a conceptual taxonomy structure, and a set of learning concept dependency graphs to depict, e.g. what pre-requisites there are for a Learning Object. By having a clear definition of Learning Object, we can know what kind of contextual information is relevant to describing it, which should be addressed in the Context-based Semantic Description model. The contexts we focus on here are the information that can help a learner to understand a Learning Object and make an effective use of it and also can emphasise the relationships among Learning Objects. The ontology is used to define the concept of Learning Objects and it is created based on ACM/IEEE Computing Curriculum [16]. The learning concept dependency graphs give an overall and abstract description of the relationships among learning concepts. They are represented using Conceptual Graphs [14].

Based on our framework, we develop a two-step search mechanism. When a learner presents a learning query, it is first represented in the Conceptual Graph and then matched with the learning concept dependency graphs to locate the relevant concepts, i.e. the relevant Learning Objects because each learning concepts in the graph associated with a set of Learning Objects, and relations. In the second step, based on the learner's further detailed requirements we use the Context-based Semantic Description model and the ontology to refine the results from the first step and return the most relevant Learning Objects to the learner. Our proposed framework and search mechanism aim to support learners in using massive learning resources from the web to perform self-learning with or without the help of educators' advice and instruction.

The rest of this paper is organised as follow; section 2 gives a detailed discussion on the proposed framework whilst section 3 discusses the two-step search mechanism. In sections 4, we evaluate our work based on experimental result and, finally, a summary of the related work and conclusion are given in section 5 and 6.

2 Context-Based Semantic Description Framework

The proposed Context-based Semantic Description Framework (CbSDF) follows the belief that the identification of meaning of a concept mainly stems from its contexts [8], i.e. its relationships to other concepts. To fully express the meaning of a concept, simply using its dictionary definition is not sufficient. For example in a dictionary a hammer is defined as "a hand tool with a heavy rigid head and a handle; used to deliver an impulsive force by striking"[4]. If a person has never seen a hammer, she will not get much impression on what a hammer is from the definition because that definition is a type definition [14], i.e. the vertical relationships between the concept and its super/sub type concepts, which does not describe how the hammer can be used, i.e. the horizontal relationships between the concept and other types of concepts. If we say "a hammer is a tool that can strike a nail into wood", then the person will know at least one way of hammer's usage by understanding the relationships among "tool", "nail", and "wood", although she will know more ways to use a hammer after she really understands what a

---

[4] WordNet Search - 3.0,   http://wordnet.princeton.edu/perl/webwn

hammer is. Following this idea we propose the CbSDF that defines, describes, and organises Learning Objects in both vertical and horizontal relational manner in order to improve the efficiency and effectiveness of Learning Object search, usage, and management. In the following sections, we discuss each of the components of the framework in detail.

2.1 Learning Object Definition

The IEEE working group for Learning Object Metadata (LOM) [9] defines Learning Object as being *"any entity, digital or non-digital, that may be used for learning, education or training"*. In our work, we extend this definition based on the Learning Object's characteristics.

Definition 1. A Learning Object LO is a logical structure, defined as a 7-tuple:

$$LO =< id, C, A, \delta, P_r, P_o, R_s >$$

where,   *id*: an internal system identification number or a name of the Learning Object.

      C: the learning concept of LO. This concept is a leaf node in the Learning Object ontology which we will discuss in 2.3.

      A: a set of attributes that describe LO. Similar to the attributes in the Entity-Relationship Model, they will not describe relationships between this Learning Object with other Learning Objects.

      δ : an internal structure of LO. This structure is a set of learning concepts that make up LO's deliverable knowledge. It enables us to compose (and decompose) Learning Objects.

      P_r: a set of learning concepts that provides the pre-requisite knowledge for LO.

      P_o: a set of learning concepts that requires the pre-requisite knowledge from LO.

      R_s: a set of physical learning resources to implement LO.

It is of course allowed that the internal structure δ of a Learning Object to be empty. Consequently, we have two types of Learning Objects as follows.

Definition 2. A Learning Object is called an *atomic Learning Object*, denoted as LO_a, if δ is empty, i.e. $LO_a \rightarrow \delta = \varnothing$. A Learning Object is called a *composite Learning Object*, denoted as LO_c, if δ is not empty, i.e. $LO_c \rightarrow \delta = \{C_1, C_2...C_n\}$, $n \geq 1$.

Here we use an example, a composite Learning Object "Java Programming", to illustrate the definitions:

    LO(Java Programming): *id*: #0015

    C: "Java Programming".

    A: {"40 hours", "English", "Intermediate Level"}.

    δ : {"Classes and Objects", "Interface"}

    P_r: {"Basic Programming", "Object Oriented Theory"}.

    P_o: {"Java Swing"}.

    R_s: {ch1.avi, ch2.avi, …, Java programming.pdf}.

2.2 Context-Based Semantic Description Model

A Learning Object can be viewed as a carrier of knowledge which the learners hope to acquire. As known to us, knowledge is not isolated at all, and always related to other knowledge. Therefore, when we describe a knowledge carrier, i.e. a Learning Object, we cannot describe it independently. The inter-relationship among Learning Objects is an important issue that should be addressed in the Learning Object description. It intended to give learners the information about how the knowledge delivered by the Learning Object can fit into a general knowledge structure, i.e. the context of the knowledge, and helps them to choose the most suitable Learning Objects for them. To emphasise the contextual knowledge of Learning Objects, we propose a Context-based Semantic Description Model (CbSDM).

Definition 3. The CbSDM is defined as a triple denoted as:

$$M =< LO, R, L >$$

where,

LO: the described Learning Object.

$R = \{R_o, R_{pre}, R_{post}, R_{sub}\}$: a set of relations that contains four elements, which are explained as follows:

- R_o represents the relations between LO's learning concept and its super-concepts in the Learning Object ontology.
- R_{pre} represents the relations between LO and its pre-requisite LOs.
- R_{post} represents the relations between LO and its subsequence LOs.
- R_{sub} represents the relations between LO and its sub-Learning Objects.

$L = \{L_{Attr}, L_{Rec}\}$: a set of links that contains two elements, which are explained as follows.

- L_{Attr} represents the links from LO to its attributes, i.e. the metadata.
- L_{Rec} represents the links from LO to its physical learning resources.

A graphical illustration of the CbSDM is shown below, see Fig.1.

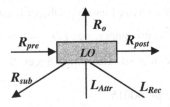

Fig. 1. A graphical representation of the CbSDM. It describes the direction of the relations from the LO to other LOs and the links to the LO's attributes and physical learning resources.

2.3 The Learning Objects Ontology

The Learning Objects ontology in this framework plays a critical role in conceptual description of Learning Objects and hence in semantic search. In our practice, we use the Computing Curriculum, a subject taxonomy for education systems, proposed by ACM/IEEE [16]. This taxonomy categorises the knowledge system of Information Technology into three levels: Area, Unit, and Topic. The Area represents a sub-domain of the knowledge system that is used to organise, categorise, and describe the top level knowledge structure of the knowledge system, the Unit represents a sub-direction in an Area, and the Topic represents a relatively independent content in a Unit. The Fig. 2 illustrates a part of the ontology created based on the taxonomy. This ontology has been applied to the *University Course Online* (*realcourse* in short) system [17] which is a Grid based video stream online education service. The leaf nodes of the ontology are the direct parents of Learning Object instances, i.e. the learning concepts in the Learning Object definition, which are normally the names of the courses that can be taken by the learners. A Learning Object instance of a leaf node concept can either represent the whole course or a part of the course.

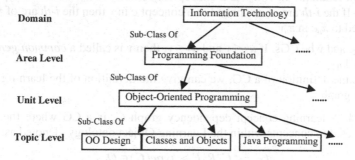

Fig. 2. Part of the Learning Object ontology. It gives the example nodes in different level of the Learning Object ontology.

2.4 The Dependency Graphs of Learning Concepts

In order to capture and represent conceptual dependency relations between Learning Objects, we propose a set of learning concept dependency graphs. As a part of the CbSDF, the dependency graphs are high level, abstract descriptions of the learning concepts and their relations. They can help the system in analyzing learner's query and locating relevant Learning Objects, especially when the learners are new to a subject area and cannot provide concrete queries to describe what they want. The dependency graphs also can help the learner in understanding the conceptual dependency relations between required Learning Objects and other Learning Objects. We propose using Conceptual Graphs (CGs) [14] to represent the dependency graphs. In the following, we introduce CG with some basic definitions.

A conceptual graph is a finite, connected, bipartite graph with nodes of one type called concepts and nodes of the other type called conceptual relations [15]. *Concepts* represent entities, actions, and attributes. The label of a concept node consists of two fields separated by a colon, [*type: referent*]. *Type* represents the class of a concept. *Referent* represents an instance of the class. The functions *type()* and *referent()* can be used to get a concept's type and referent. If the value of *referent(c)* is an individual marker (an identification of an instance, such as name or id), e.g. [Cat: Tom], then the concept c is an *individual concept*. If the value of *referent(c)* is "*", e.g. [Cat: *], then the concept c is a *generic concept*. A concept only with type label is equivalent to a generic concept, i.e. [Cat] = [Cat:*]. *Conceptual Relations* represent the relationships between concept nodes. *type(r)* is used to get the type of the relation r.

Suppose that u and v are two CGs. u is called a specialization of v (or v is called a generalization of u), denoted as $u \leq v$, if u is canonically derivable (derived by applying a sequence of generalization rules [14]) from v. In this case, there must exist a mapping $\pi: v \longrightarrow u$, where $\pi_u v$ is a subgraph of u called a *projection* of v in u. The projection operator π has the following properties:

- For each concept c in v, $\pi_u c$ is a concept in $\pi_u v$ such that $type(\pi_u c) \leq type(c)$, "$\leq$" here represents the sub-type relationship between concepts. If c is an individual concept, then $referent(\pi_u c) = referent(c)$.
- For each relation r in v, $\pi_u r$ is a conceptual relation in $\pi_u v$ such that $type(\pi_u r) = type(r)$. If the *i-th* arc of r is linked to a concept c in v then the *i-th* arc of $\pi_u r$ must be linked to $\pi_u c$ in $\pi_u v$.

Let u_1, u_2, and v be CGs. If $u_1 \leq v$ and $u_2 \leq v$, then v is called a *common generalization* of u_1 and u_2.

Based on the definition of a CG, we can give the definition of the learning concept dependency graph.

Definition 4. A learning concept dependency graph G_d is a CG where the concept type is restricted to concepts within the Learning Object ontology, denoted as:

$$G_d =< C, R, \overrightarrow{E} >, type(C) \in O$$

where, C: a set of learning concept nodes; *type(C)* returns a set of leaf node concepts in the Learning Object ontology.

  R: a set of relation nodes that represent the relations among learning concept nodes, including pre-requisite relation type and conceptual relation type etc.

  $\overrightarrow{E}$: a set of arcs that associate relation nodes with concept nodes.

  O: the Learning Object ontology.

An example Gd (Java Programming) is illustrated in Fig.3., where,

  C: {[Java Programming], [Java A-Z], [Object Oriented Theory], [Java Swing]}.

  R: {(require), (apply-to), (similar-to)}.

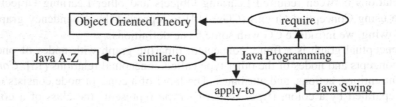

Fig. 3. A learning concept dependency graph example. It represents the relationships among different learning concepts.

3 Learning Object Semantic Search

As discussed previously, when a learner is not familiar to a subject area, it is unrealistic to expect her to provide a very detailed query. Therefore, a step-by-step process is required to lead the learner to gradually locate the suitable Learning Objects. Based on the CbSDF, we propose a two-step Learning Object search mechanism. The first step is preliminary learning concepts discovery step using CG matching technique. The proposed learning concept dependency graphs provide the information about learning concepts and their relations. When a learner submits a query, we first convert it into a CG and match it with the learning concept dependency graphs to obtain the query's relevant learning concepts and their relations. Because each learning concept corresponds to a set of Learning Objects, a series of Learning Objects related to learner's query are located. The second step, refining step, is to refine the results from the first step based on the learner's further query inputs which are captured using the CbSDM. At this step the learner can specify detailed requirements about a Learning Object, e.g. the metadata, because now she can browse through the returned Learning Objects from the first step and get some concrete information. Then the semantic similarity between the learner's requirements (i.e. the learner's queries) and the candidate Learning Objects is calculated and the matched Learning Objects are ranked according to their similarity degree to the learner's demands.

3.1 CG Similarity Calculation

After converting the learner's query into a CG, we turn the search in the learning concept dependency graphs for a match to the query into the computation of similarity of two CGs. According to Montes et al. [10], the similarity S between two CGs, G_1 and G_2, contains a concept similarity S_c and a relation similarity S_r. The concept similarity S_c is calculated using the Dice coefficient [6] similar expression:

$$S_c = 2\left(\sum_{c \in \bigcup O} (weight(c) \times \beta(\pi_{G_1}c, \pi_{G_2}c))\right) \Big/ \left(\sum_{c \in G_1} weight(c) + \sum_{c \in G_2} weight(c)\right)$$

where, $\bigcup O$ is the union of all of the common generalisation graphs of G_1 and G_2; O is a set of the common overlaps graphs of G_1 and G_2, $weight(c)$ is the importance factor of the concept type c. We take $weight(c) = 1$ as we assume that all the concept types are of the same importance. The $\beta(\pi_{G_1}c, \pi_{G_2}c)$ function is defined as follows to calculate the semantic similarity between two concepts:

$$\beta(\pi_{G_1}c, \pi_{G_2}c) = \begin{cases} 1 & \text{if } type(\pi_{G_1}c) = type(\pi_{G_2}c) \text{ and } referent(\pi_{G_1}c) = referent(\pi_{G_2}c) \\ depth/(depth+1) & \text{if } type(\pi_{G_1}c) = type(\pi_{G_2}c) \text{ and } referent(\pi_{G_1}c) \neq referent(\pi_{G_2}c) \\ 2d_c/(d_{\pi_{G_1}c} + d_{\pi_{G_2}c}) & \text{if } type(\pi_{G_1}c) \neq type(\pi_{G_2}c) \end{cases}$$

The first condition indicates that the two concepts are exactly the same. The second condition indicates that the two concepts have the same type but refer to different instances. The depth represents the number of levels in the Learning Object ontology. The third condition indicates that the two concepts have different types. The dc represents the distance from the least common super-type of $\pi_{G_1}c$ and $\pi_{G_2}c$ to the root of the ontology; $d_{\pi_{G_i}c}$ represent the distance from concept $\pi_{G_i}c$ to the root of the ontology. The relation similarity Sr is calculated using the following expression:

$$S_r = \frac{2m(G_c)}{m_{G_c}(G_1) + m_{G_c}(G_2)}$$

where, $m(G_c)$ is the number of the relation nodes in the common overlaps of G_1 and G_2; $m_{G_c}(G_i)$ is the number of the relation nodes of the common overlaps in G_i and the overlaps' adjacent relation nodes.

The overall similarity expression is shown below:

$$S = S_c \times (a + (1-a) \times S_r)$$

where, a is a value between 0 and 1 representing the impact factor of S_r. We use 0.9 for a to indicate that the concepts are overwhelmingly important over the relations.

3.2 Semantic Similarity Calculation Between Learning Object and Requirements

In the second step of the Learning Object search, in order to measure the semantic similarity between the learner requirements and the Learning Objects returned from the first step and rank the final results, we develop a semantic similarity measurement method, which is based on the CbSDM and the ontology, to measure semantic similarity between learner requirements and Learning Object, defined as:

$$sim(LO_r, LO) = \frac{\sum_{\forall \alpha \in \lambda} \omega \times dist(\alpha(LO_r), \alpha(LO))}{max(\lambda(LO_r), \lambda(LO))}$$

where, λ: a set of all the semantic characteristics functions;

$\lambda()$: a function that returns the number of semantic characteristics;

$\alpha()$: an element of λ that returns a semantic characteristic which can be, e.g. a element of the metadata;

$dist()$: a function that calculate the semantic distance between two semantic characteristic and its returned value is between 0 and 1;

ω: a weight factor that specifies how important a semantic characteristic to a learner is and its value is between 0 and 1.

$max()$: a function returns the greater of its two arguments values.

LO_r and LO: the required Learning Object and a candidate Learning Object.

Through this method, the similarity between learner requirements and each candidate Learning Object is calculated. Therefore, the result Learning Objects can be ranked according to their similarity degree to the learner's demands so that the learner can easily choose the best matched Learning Objects.

4 Evaluation

In order to evaluate the work proposed in this paper, we have implemented a web-based prototype system specifically designed for learners to search their required

Learning Objects. We collected approximately 2000 Learning Objects from different Learning Object repositories, including MIT OpenCourseWare and GreatLearning. We use descriptions based on CbSDF to describe collected Learning Objects and stored them in our local Learning Object database. Each Learning Object has hyperlinks to their physical resource locations so that the learners can search the Learning Objects locally and access the physical learning resources remotely. Our evaluation tries to compare two search methods: The first one is the advanced keyword-based search method that provides options for keywords matching, such as "with all of the words", "with the exact phrase", "with at least one of the words", and "without the words" and options for metadata matching, such as "Language", "Difficulty level", and "Typical learning time". The other one is our search method based on the CbSDF. Our method adopts the proposed two-step search mechanism. Through comparing and evaluating these two search methods, we aims to show our method can greatly improve the Learning Object search and discovery.

We choose two groups of users for evaluation. One group of users are computer science students who have strong computer background, thus they can create detailed concrete queries about computer learning courses. The other group of users know a little about computer, thus their queries about computer learning courses are general and vague. Therefore, we could observe how our method suits queries with different knowledge backgrounds from learners. The evaluation factors that we are interested in are the recall and precision rate from each group by using different search methods. The results represented using precision-recall curves are listed in Fig.4 (a).

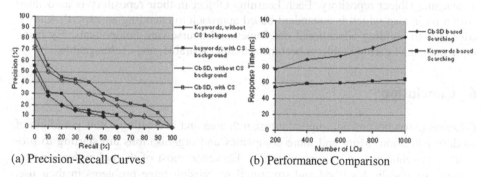

(a) Precision-Recall Curves   (b) Performance Comparison

Fig. 4. The experiment results including precision-recall curves and performance comparison

The Fig.4 (a) clearly shows that our method significantly improves the search results for both the user groups. During the experiment we observed that a large number of metadata fields provided in the keyword-based search method remained empty according to the users' query submissions no matter they have computer background knowledge or not. The graph, see Fig.4 (b), displayed that our method had a slight worse performance than the keyword-based search method because we adopted a complex algorithm for CG similarity calculation. However, our method provides high precise search results. So we consider our method offers a better general performance as the users have to spend longer time to retrieve the relevant results from the keyword-based search.

5 Related Work

Colucci et al. [3] propose a semantic framework and algorithms for automated composition of Learning Objects in order to achieve personalised E-Learning. They demonstrate in their work how a semantic specification, formatted in OWL-DL, of the Learning Objects can be used both to retrieve Learning Objects satisfying a user request from a repository and to compose such discovered Learning Objects in a courseware. The semantic description language used in their project is OWL-DL, the inference technique is based on Description Logic, and the framework can be integrated with other existing metadata specifications, such as LOM, SCORM, and Dublin Core [5].

Song [13] proposes a metadata framework for description of Learning Objects. The framework gives Learning Objects a structure- and metadata-based description. In this framework a Learning Object contains three types of components. The first is the resource type, which includes Learning Component, Learning Content, and Learning Carrier. The second is the reference type, which includes Learning Reference, Learning Neighbour, and Learning Link. The third is the attribute type, which has a Learning Intensity as its instance. Song also proposes a goal-driven Learning Object search method. This method pays attention to using synthetic representation of information from learning information consumers. It converts learning's requirements into goals and uses the goals matching with the Learning Object metadata model in the Learning Object repository to locate right learning materials.

Dichev et al. [4] discuss in their work how the topic map [2] can be used to manage a Learning Object repository. Each Learning Object in their repository is associated with a topic map which is a standard-based approach to encoding an expert's knowledge, i.e. to building educational ontologies and courseware components. By using topic map, the Learning Objects become reusable, sharable, and exchangeable.

6 Conclusion

E-Learning has become an important research area and is creating a new paradigm of modern education. More and more companies and organisations are starting to provide online courses and training materials. However, most of the online learning resources are poorly described and structured so causing huge problems in their use, search, organization, and management. To overcome the problems, in this paper we proposed a novel and practical Context-based Semantic Description Framework (CbSDF) to describe information and knowledge about learning resources and their structures. Based on our framework we developed a two-step search mechanism for searching learning resources by using the CG matching and the semantic similarity ranking techniques. The work proposed in this paper aims to support learners in using massive learning resources from the Web to perform self-learning with or without the help of educators' advice and instruction.

Our method was evaluated by a prototype using the learning resources from different Learning Object repositories. In next step, we will fully implement our framework

and develop more complete and suitable evaluation methods to assess the performance, scalability, and precision of the search methods, especially for large amounts of
learning resources.

References

[1] Andrews, K., Nedoumov, A., Scherbakov, N.: Embeding Courswere into Internet: Prob-
    lems and Solutions. In: Proceedings of ED-MEDIA 1995, Graz, Austria, June 1995, pp.
    69–74 (1995)
[2] Biezunski, M., Bryan, M., Newcomb, S.R.: ISO/IEC 13250:2000 Topic Maps, (December
    3, 1999), http://www.y12.doe.gov/sgml/sc34/document/0129.pdf
[3] Colucci, S., Noia1, T.D., Sciascio, E.D., Donini, F.M., Ragone, A.: Semantic-Based Auto-
    mated Composition of Distributed Learning Objects for Personalized E-Learning. In: Gómez-
    Pérez, A., Euzenat, J. (eds.) ESWC 2005. LNCS, vol. 3532, pp. 633–648. Springer, Heidel-
    berg (2005)
[4] Dichev, C., Dicheva1, D., Aroyo, L.: Using Topic Maps for E-Learning. In: Proceedings
    of The IASTED International Conference on Computers and Advanced Technology in
    Education (CATE 2003), Rhodes, Greece (2003)
[5] Dublin Core Metadata Element Set, Version 1.1: Reference Description.
    http://dublincore.org/documents/1999/07/02/dces/
[6] Frakes, W.B., Baeza-Yates, R.: Information Retrieval: Data Structures & Algorithms.
    Prentice-Hall, Englewood Cliffs (1992)
[7] Galusha, J.M. : Barriers to Learning in Distance Education. Interpersonal Computing and
    Technology, December, 1997, vol. 5(3–4), pp. 6–14 (1997)
[8] Guha, R., McCool, R., Fikes, R.: Contexts for the Semantic Web. In: McIlraith, S.A.,
    Plexousakis, D., van Harmelen, F. (eds.) ISWC 2004. LNCS, vol. 3298, pp. 32–46.
    Springer, Heidelberg (2004)
[9] IEEE Standard for Learning Object Metadata, STD 1484.12.1-2002 edition (2002)
[10] Montes-y-Gómez, M., Gelbukh, A., López-López, A., Baeza-Yates, R.: Flexible Com-
    parison of Conceptual Graphs. In: Mayr, H.C., Lazanský, J., Quirchmayr, G., Vogel, P.
    (eds.) DEXA 2001. LNCS, vol. 2113, pp. 102–111. Springer, Heidelberg (2001)
[11] Palmér, M., Naeve, A., Nilsson, M.: E-Learning in the Semantic Age. In: Proceedings of
    the 2nd European Web-based Learning Environments Conference (WBLE 2001), Lund,
    Sweden, October 24-26, 2001 (2001)
[12] Sharable Content Object Reference Model, http://www.adlnet.gov/scorm/
    index.cfm
[13] Song, W.: A Metadata Framework for Description of Learning Objects. In: Fong, J.,
    Cheung, C.T., Leong, H.V., Li, Q. (eds.) ICWL 2002. LNCS, vol. 2436, Springer, Hei-
    delberg (2002)
[14] Sowa, J.F.: Conceptual Structures: Information Processing in Mind and Machine. Addi-
    son-Wesley, Canada (1984)
[15] Sowa, J.F.: Conceptual Graphs for a Database Interface. IBM Journal of Research and
    Development 20(4), 336–357 (1976)
[16] The Writing Committee of CCIT, Computing Curricula 2005, Information Technology
    Volume, IEEE-CS/ACM, (April 2005)
[17] Zhang, J., Li, X.: The Model, Architecture and Mechanism Behind Realcourse. In: Cao,
    J., Yang, L.T., Guo, M., Lau, F. (eds.) ISPA 2004. LNCS, vol. 3358, Springer, Heidelberg
    (2004)

Knowledge Point Based Curriculum Developing and Learning Object Reusing

Xingwei Hao, Xiangxu Meng, and Xu Cui

School of Computer Science and Technology, Shandong University
250100 Jinan, China
{hxw,mxx}@sdu.edu.cn, cuixu20021981@163.com

Abstract. In an E-Learning environment, learning contents are usually organized through a series of courses, and the concrete learning contents are explained through various learning resources. With the development of E-Learning systems and the passing of time, courses and learning resources will update, develop, and change inevitably. Because, in a discipline, the knowledge body can be divided into a series of knowledge points, so we proposed and designed a discipline oriented common knowledge ontology base (KOB) to organize and store all the knowledge points and their relations in a discipline. On the basis of KOB, we proposed a knowledge point based course developing model and a learning object metadata model. Through KOB, the knowledge points can be reused in different courses, so to improve the efficiency in courses developing, course contents authoring and contents updating. Furthermore, when a new learning object is registered to an E-Learning system or a learning object updated, through knowledge points mapping between courses and learning objects, it will be automatically reflected in according courses that have the same knowledge points with the learning object. So, on the basis of KOB, the work of courses developing and learning resources management becomes easier and flexible.

Keywords: Knowledge Point, Ontology, Learning Object, Curriculum.

1 Introduction

In the application of E-Learning, with the increase of courses, many problems became more and more prominent, such as those in curriculum developing, update of contents, the using and management of learning resources, and the maintainability and extensibility of E-Learning systems. Although many international academic societies and standardization organizations have issued a series of educational technological standards and specifications, including courses metadata model, learning object metadata model, contents encapsulation specifications, etc., their main purpose is to achieve the resources sharing and systems interpretability among various systems. But as for the relationship among courses, overlapping of courses contents, and logical relations between course contents and learning objects, present E-Learning standards haven't involved them, and the related research is still a little.

H. Leung et al. (Eds.): ICWL 2007, LNCS 4823, pp. 126–137, 2008.

With the development of a discipline, new courses constantly emerge, and the contents of old courses might often change; all of these require the expression of courses to own flexibility. Course contents are explained via learning objects, thus learning objects are the carriers of knowledge. One learning object could explain one or more knowledge points, and one knowledge point may be explained by more than one learning objects. In the present educational technological standards, metadata models related to learning objects could not yet reflect this kind of knowledge layer relationship between learning objects and knowledge points. Thus, the increase and decrease of learning objects, the updates of learning objects themselves may all lead to the inconsistence between the curriculum contents and learning objects.

According to the above analysis, we can set up a discipline common knowledge ontology base (KOB) in a certain discipline, and all the knowledge points and their relations in the discipline can be organized and stored in the KOB. Within it, a knowledge point based network course metadata model is defined. On the basis of KOB, developing a new network course only need to define the course directory structure and to select knowledge points from KOB for every knowledge units (KUs) in the course directory. Because the knowledge points in a KU have been determined, so we can copy all the learning contents of knowledge points included in the KU from the KOB, then the learning contents might be reedited according to the learning objectives of the KU, thus the KU learning contents authoring work becomes easier. Additionally, the course updates can be done only through adjusting the course directory, and thus improving the flexibility of network courses.

2 Related Research

Curriculum and learning objects are important components of an E-Learning system, with the main research achievement reflected in a series of educational technological standards. The goals for setting network educational technological standards are to ensure the educational resource sharing, reusing and system interoperability, which are vital to the practicability and profitability of E-Learning systems [1].

2.1 Major International Educational Technological Standards and SCORM

In the field of educational technology, many international enterprises and academic organizations have conducted research work in the establishment of educational technological standards, and yielded a lot of achievements in standardization. These organizations include: Aviation Industry CBT Committee (AICC) [2], Instructional Management System Global Learning Consortium[3], Institute of Electrical and Electronics Engineers (IEEE) Learning Technology Standards Committee (LTSC) [4], Alliance of Remote Instructional Authoring & Distribution Networks for Europe (ARIADNE) [5], and the US Defense Ministry Advanced Distributed Learning Organization(ADL)[6] etc.

In all the standards that issued by the above mentioned organizations, the CMI(Computer Managed Instruction) specification (AGR-006), which is issued by AICC, and SCORM issued by ADL are relatively common standards. The core contents of the standards are the metadata model of all objects related to a network course, so to ensure that a standardizational course can be used in other E-Learning systems. But the standards only emphasize the standardization of a course, it does not take the contents reusing into account, so a new course developing is hard to use the contents that has already in other courses.

In the courses developing, researchers also made many researches on the learning contents organization, knowledge expression and courses modeling, the researches usually aimed at one course and not a series of courses [7,8,9]. But, in the knowledge body of a discipline, overlapping in contents of different courses, method of learning contents reusing among different courses etc., there is still a little research by now.

2.2 Learning Object

H.Wayne Hodins in Computer Education Management Association (CedMA) first raised the concept of "learning object" in his article "Learning architectures, API's, and Learning Objects" (1994). In 2000, the learning object data research group of IEEE defines "learning object" as "Learning objects refer to any digital or non-digital entity. This entity can be used, reused or referred to in the process of technology supporting learning" [10]. Due to almost all learning resources being digital or non-digital entities, in order to distinguish learning objects from other concepts, more concrete definition of learning objects emerged, among which David A.Wiley's is a typical one. He believes that the learning objects are any digital resources that can be reused to support learning [11].

By nature, learning objects are various types of data files. But, different from ordinary data files, they carry specific knowledge and learning contents; they are designed and organized according to different learning theories, and express the carried knowledge in specific forms and sequences, and hence realizes the explanation of knowledge, i.e. support the knowledge cognition of learners.

3 Knowledge Point Based Course Definition and Learning Object Metadata Model

Learning contents are usually organized in a series of courses, and the specific learning contents are explained through various types of learning resources. With the development of E-Learning systems and the passing of time, courses and learning resources will update, develop, and change inevitably. Because, in a discipline, the knowledge body can be divided into a series of knowledge points, so we proposed and designed a discipline oriented common knowledge ontology base (KOB) to organize and store all the knowledge points and their relations in a discipline. On the basis of KOB, we can define a knowledge point based course developing model and a learning object metadata model. Through KOB, the knowledge points can be reused in different courses, so to improve the efficiency in courses developing, course contents authoring and contents updating. Furthermore, when a new learning object is registered to the E-Learning system or a learning object updated, through knowledge points mapping between courses and learning objects, it will be automatically reflected in according courses that have the same knowledge points. Thus, we get a new method for learning resources using and management.

3.1 Knowledge Point and Knowledge Ontology

Knowledge points and knowledge units are the basic logical units to express a course. In order to describe the knowledge body of a course and the referred learning objects, we make two definitions as follows:

Definition 1. A Knowledge point refers to an independent, completely expressed, and independently usable declarative or procedural knowledge entity, such as a fact, a term ,a concept, a theorem, or an algorithm etc.

Definition 2. Knowledge ontology is defined to express the knowledge points and the relationships among them, each knowledge point corresponding to one knowledge ontology.

Knowledge ontology expresses the knowledge and the relationship among different knowledge points. The structure of knowledge ontology is illustrated in Fig.1.

In this figure, "name" refers to the name of a knowledge point, "description" is the description of the knowledge point, and "type" means the category of knowledge, which can often be divided into declarative and procedural knowledge [12]. Different categories of knowledge correspond to different cognitive structures and learning strategies. "alias" refers to the aliases of the knowledge point. "prevs" represents the set of its previous knowledge points, "succ" represents the set of its succeeding knowledge points, and "refs" is the set of its related knowledge points , which can be used for associative learning. The sets of previous, succeeding and related knowledge points form a knowledge network [13].

In a discipline, the body of knowledge is divided into a series of knowledge points, which is expressed via knowledge ontology and is organized in a common knowledge ontology base (KOB).

```
Name:
Description:
Type:
Alias: {     }
prevs: {     }
succs: {     }
refs:  {     }
```

Fig. 1. KP ontology

3.2 Knowledge Point Based Learning Object Metadata Model

The knowledge points are explained through learning objects. All educational technological standards have set up their metadata standards for learning objects, which is used for learners to retrieve, use, and assess learning objects, or to support the interoperability between learning objects and LMS. The main learning objects metadata standards include: IMS's learning source metadata (LRM), the learning object metadata (LOM) of IEEE/LTSC's and the SCORM which is virtually the E-Learning metadata standard of learning object. The metadata of SCORM mainly come from IEEE1484.12.1 (Learning Object Metadata, LOM) and the IEEE1484.12.3 (XML schema definition language binding), which is mainly used to describe the SCORM content model components.

On the basis of IEEE LOM, ADL SCORM and Dublin core metadata, we set up our knowledge points based learning objects metadata model, which is illustrated in Fig.2.

(1) "FileID" refers to the file identifier, including the file path and file name of a learning object.

(2) "MediaType" refers the file type of the learning resource, such as webpage file, pdf file, ppt file, doc file, image file, animation file, video file or audio file, etc.

(3) "kps" refers to a set of knowledge points, which is carried in the learning object; in others words, the set stores the knowledge points that the learning object will explain.

| FileID: |
| MediaType: |
| *kps:* { } |
| other metadata |

Fig. 2. LO metadata

In addition, other metadata of IEEE LOM, ADL SCORM or Dublin core can also be included in the above knowledge points based LO metadata model, so as to achieve the learning resource sharing with other systems.

The knowledge point based learning object metadata model owns two excellent features: (1) It expresses the semantic meaning of a learning object. The core metadata of the model are knowledge points, which come from the common knowledge ontology base in a discipline. (2) Through knowledge points, a logic relationship between a course and learning objects can be set up, which ensure the independence of the updates of courses and learning objects.

3.3 Knowledge Point and Reusable Learning Information Object

In the knowledge ontology definition (See Fig.1), because most declarative knowledge is relatively simple, it's difficult to set their learning objectives accordingly. So, in the organization of body of knowledge in a discipline, some relevant knowledge points are often combined into a knowledge unit (KU), each KU usually having a specific learning objective.

By reference to the contents packaging specification of SCORM, knowledge units are defined as different reusable learning information object (RLIO). A RLIO is an independent and reusable learning contents unit, including a set of knowledge points and a specific learning objective. RLIO can be divided into two types: (1) Basic RLIO, all members are knowledge points, excluding other RLIOs. (2) Complex RLIO, not only includes knowledge points, but also nests other RLIO members. The definition of RLIO is illustrated in Fig.3.

In Fig.3, "RLIO name" refers to the name of the knowledge unit, which will be displayed in the course directory tree and the KU webpage. "Learning Objective" refers

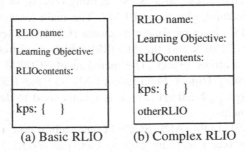

(a) Basic RLIO   (b) Complex RLIO

Fig. 3. Reusable learning information object definition

to the learning objective of the KU. "RLIO contents" refers to the contents of the KU (edited in XML), "kps" refers to a set of knowledge points included in the KU.

3.4 Knowledge Point Based Course Model

In a discipline, all knowledge points are organized into a series of courses under a certain curriculum. A course is the collection of selected learning contents for the achievement of a learning objective, which specifies learning objectives, learning contents, scale and learning process.

Through RLIO, knowledge points are encapsulated into KUs in different grains, which correspond to the chapter, section and subsection of the traditional paper books. As RLIOs, all chapters, sections and subsections have their specific learning objectives.The layering of knowledge points, RLIO (chapter, section or subsection knowledge unit) and courses is shown in Fig.4.

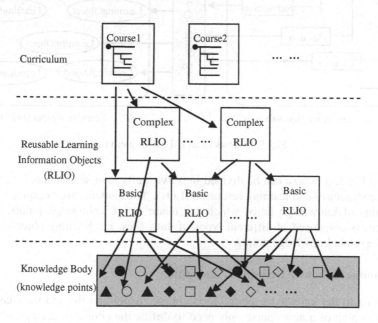

Fig. 4. Layers of knowledge points, RLIOs and courses

In order to describe the developing and maintenance of a course clearly, we make the formal definition of a course just as bellow:

First, the formal definition of a common knowledge ontology base is defined as:
$KOB = \{KP_i, \quad | i=1,2,...\}$
So, a course can be formally defined as:
$Course = \{Chapter_i | i=1,2,...\};$
$Chapter = \{Section_j , KP_i | j=1,2,..., KP_i \in KOB \}$
$Section = \{SubSection_k , KP_i | k=1,2,...,KP_i \in KOB\}$
$SubSection = \{ KP_i | k=1,2,...,KP_i \in KOB\}$

4 Courses Developing and Learning Object Reusing

According to the course formal definition and the learning object metadata model in Fig.2, a course in an E-Learning environment can be defined as in Fig.5.

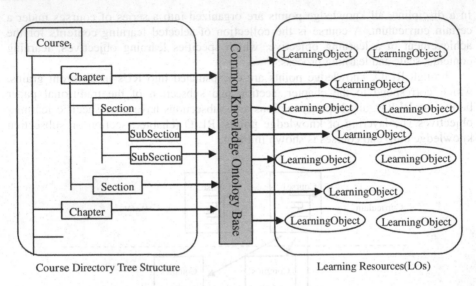

Course Directory Tree Structure   Learning Resources(LOs)

Fig. 5. Courses in an E-Learning environment

As in Fig.5, a course can be divided into two parts: course contents (course directory tree structure) and learning resources (LOs). The contents are organized in different grains of knowledge units, which are made up of knowledge points. Learning resources is composed of different types of data files, i.e. learning objects, which is used to explain knowledge points.

4.1 Course Structure Definition Algorithm

According to the knowledge point based course model and the LO metadata model, the developing of a new course only need to define the course directory and to select knowledge points for every knowledge unit in the course directory. The needed learning objects will be included automatically through the common knowledge ontology base. A course structure definition algorithm is as the following:

Algorithm CSD: Course Structure Definition Algorithm

Step1: According to the course learning objectives, add chapters accordingly, and finally get:

Course = {Chapter$_i$ | i=1,2,...m};

Step2: Define Chapter$_i$ = {Section$_j$ | j=1,2,...}

2.1 If Chapter$_i$ not further be divided into sections, go to Step 2 to define the next chapter;

2.2 Otherwise, add sections accordingly, and finally get:

Chapter$_i$ = { Section$_j$ | j=1,2,…, }

2.3 For all Section$_i$ (j=1,2,…,), add its all subsections accordingly, and finally get: Section$_i$ = { SubSection$_k$ | k=1,2,…, }

Step3: If i<m, go Step2 to define the next chapter; Otherwise ,go to Step 4.

Step4: Select knowledge points KPx from KOB for every KU (Chapters,Sections and SubSections).

Step5: End.

When the knowledge points that a knowledge unit will explain have been determined, then the work of KU learning contents authoring can be done through copying the metadata of the knowledge points from KOB, which will constitute primitive materials of the learning contents of the KU, and at last reedit the materials. So, the knowledge points data can be reused in different courses, thus the courses developing work becomes easier.

4.2 KU Bound to XML Page

According to the above definition of courses, in E-Learning systems, every KU will be bound with a XML file to express the KU structure and its contents. With xsl (eXtensible Style language), the XML file be styled and displayed in browser for learners to learn. In the bottom of web pages, there is a series of hyperlinks that point to corresponding learning objects, which are used to explain the knowledge points included in the KU.

The following is an example of a XML file for OSI knowledge unit in the course of "Computer Network".

An example of XML file of a KU (OSI model KU)

```
<?xml version="1.0" encoding="gb2312" ?>
<?xml-stylesheet type="text/xsl" href="RLIOpage.xsl" ?>
<RLIO>
<title>2.1 The OSI model</title>
<LearningObjectives>
<objectiveitem>
<goal>(1) Learn OSI model</goal>
</objectiveitem>
<objectiveitem>
<goal>(2) Master the concept of layering, the function of every layer
</goal>
</objectiveitem>
</LearningObjectives>
```

```
<content>
```
In the late 1980s and early 1990s, there was a significant increase in the number and overall size of network. The ISO researched many network schemes and recognized the need to create a network model that would help network builders implement networks that could communicate and work interoperability, therefore, released the OSI reference model in 1984.

....
```
</content>

<KPList>
<kpitem>
<kp>Layering </kp>
<los>
<loitem><url>../los/osilayers.gif</url></loitem>
<loitem><url>../los/osilayers.swf</url></loitem>
<loitem><url>../los/osilayers.ppt</url></loitem>
</los>
</kpitem>

<kpitem>
<kp>OSI model</kp>
<los>
<loitem><url>../los/osimodel.jpg</url></loitem>
<loitem><url>../los/osimodelfunction.swf</url></loitem>
<loitem><url>../los/osiencapsulation.ppt</url></loitem>
</los>
</kpitem>
</KPList>
</RLIO>
```

In the above XML document, the parameter "RLIO page.xsl" is a .xsl file, which is programmed in extensible style language and used to style and make layout of a xml document. The "RLIOpage.xsl" also need retrieving the common knowledge ontology base(KOB) and the learning objects base(LOB) for appending hyperlinks to corresponding learning objects in the bottom of the webpage.

By reference to the network courses of Cisco Networking Academy [14], an example of our learning web page of a KU is shown in Fig.6.

Each knowledge unit corresponds to a webpage, and the webpage is divided into five frames, which includes:

(1) Frame A, the frame for displaying a course logo.

(2) Frame B, the frame for displaying all learning objects. It is similar to the blackboard in traditional class teaching.

(3) Frame C, the frame for displaying the learning contents of a knowledge unit. At the bottom of the frame, there is a list of knowledge points included in the KU, following with some hyperlinks pointed to the learning objects that can explain the knowledge point.

Furthermore, according to the cognitive sequence relationship among knowledge points, for every knowledge point we can construct a group of hyperlinks links to its succeeding, previous and related knowledge points.

(4) Frame D, a portal of many learning tools, such as instant message tool, online discussion tool, BBS, teacher's blogs, Q/A tool and message board etc. In this area, the run time status of the E-Learning system can also be displayed.

(5) Frame E, the integration of a group of navigation buttons, including "Index" button, "Next" button , "Back" button, etc. The "Index" button corresponds to the directory of a courseware, where the learners can navigate their learning page among the knowledge units. The "Next" and "Back" buttons can navigate to the next or previous knowledge units.

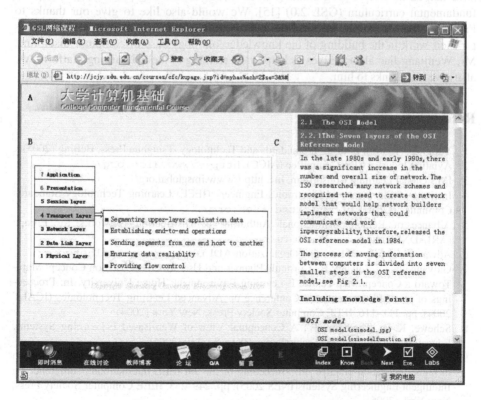

Fig. 6. An example of KU learning web page

5 Conclusions

Through knowledge points, a logic relationship between course contents and learning objects can be set up, which enhance the flexibility of curriculum development, updates and maintenance and ensure the independence of the updates of courses and learning objects.

Building up a common knowledge ontology base for a discipline is a key and very hard work. Based upon the above research, we, a group of teachers and experts in computer science discipline, have already completed most ontology definitions in the discipline of computer fundamental courses. And a lot of learning objects have been developed by another group of media developers.

On this basis, through our E-Learning platform of computer fundamental curriculum, many teachers have developed their own specific network courses for their non-computer-major students. The selection of contents of a course is usually based on the requirements of students of different disciplines.

Acknowledgments. We would like to express our thanks to the author's graduates, Yaofeng Chang, Xue Su and many other undergraduate students like Yan Zhu, who have helped do lots of programming work in our E-Learning platform of computer fundamental curriculum (GSL 2.0) [15]. We would also like to give our thanks to Professor Jun Ma, Professor Yuwei Gong, and many other colleagues of the authors for their work in the building of the knowledge ontology base of computer discipline. Mr. Wenjiang Jiao always gives us help in the running of the E-Learning platform, we also give our thanks to him.

References

1. Yang, Z.: Network Education Standards and Technology. Tsinghua Press, Beijing (2003)
2. Aviation Industry CBT Committee (AICC). http://www.aicc.org/
3. IMS Global Learning Consortium, Inc. http://www.imsglobal.org/
4. Institute of Electrical and Electronics Engineers (IEEE) Learning Technology Standards Committee (LTSC). http://ltsc.ieee.org/
5. Alliance of Remote Instructional Authoring & Distribution Networks for Europe (ARIADNE), http://www.ariadne-eu.org/
6. Advanced Distributed Learning Organization(ADL), http://www.adlnet.org/
7. Giovannella, C., Selva, P.E.: Curricula Planner and User Modeler based on Concept Map - Toward a Concept Map-centric E-Learning Environment: Home University. In: Proceedings of the IEEE International Conference on Advanced Learning Technologies (ICALT 2004), pp. 111–116. IEEE Computer Society Press, New York (2004)
8. Schewe, K.-D., Thalheim, B.: A Conceptual View of Web-Based E-Learning Systems. Education and Information Technologies 10(1), 83–110 (2005)
9. Gati, J., Kartyas, G.: Evaluation of course model for implementation of virtual classroom in higher education practice. In: Proceeding of the 9th IEEE International Conference on Intelligent Engineering Systems(INES 2005), pp. 249–253. IEEE Computer Society Press, New York (2005)
10. Hu, X., Zhu, Z.: Learning object—New concept in network instructional technology. [J] Research In Electronic Education 4, 22 (2002)

11. Wiley, D.A.: Connecting learning objects to instructional design theory: A definition a metaphor, and a taxonomy (2004), http://reusability.org/read/chapters/wiley.doc
12. Woolfolk, A., Chen, H., Zhang, C.: Translation Education Psychology (8th Edition, Simplified Chinese Edition). Pearson Education North Asia Limited and Jangsu Education Publishing House (2005)
13. Hao, X., Meng, X.: Research on a Kind of Knowledge Network for Self-learning. In: Pan, Z., Aylett, R.S., Diener, H., Jin, X., Göbel, S., Li, L. (eds.) Edutainment 2006. LNCS, vol. 3942, pp. 116–123. Springer, Heidelberg (2006)
14. Cisco Networking Academy. http://www.cisco.com/web/learning/netacad/index.html
15. Generalized Self-learning Platform (GSL), http://jcjy.sdu.edu.cn/

An Informatic Model for Open Contents Management

Leonel Iriarte[1], Manuel Marco[2], and Pedro Pernías[2]

[1] Department of Computer Science, Agrarian University of Havana
San Jose de las Lajas , Prov. Habana, Cuba
lin@infomed.sld.cu
[2] Department of Languages and Computer Science, University of Alicante
San Vicente del Raspeig, Alicante, Spain
{marco.such, p.pernias}@ua.es

Abstract: There is a tendency towards developing initiatives and projects to promote the development of open contents to attain reusability of educative resources integrating technological, pedagogical and legal components as a basis. Despite projects have developed to support this new method of approaching contents, specifications and designs that can be the basis for its implementation and practical use are not enough. This article proposes an informatic model for managing open contents which specifications can be the basis for developing applications oriented at this aim. An application called CMS4ROCKL is presented. It is based on the proposed model and it is a simple and practical content manager for professors and institutions that deal with open contents.

Keywords: Open Content, CMS, elearning, Learning Objects, Opencourseware.

1 Introduction

The current tendency for content management is very well defined. It integrates data, information and knowledge, all recorded in the socio-institutional context of society; to share them through tools, software systems, services, methods and other resources that may allow their availability and use from different parts at the same time, from a fast and reliable connectivity infrastructure. All these, to do as the Homo sapiens used to do when hunting the mammon, coordinating the actions of the community efficiently and effectively to reach goals to be shared by all [1] .

In the last few years, institutions have considered the need to use informatic tools to organize and manage efficiently the contents generated internally, as well as those that are in the web. These tools are called Content Management Systems (CMS).

Sharing educative contents is as old as the internet. The appearance of the World Wide Web made it simpler and there are uncountable web pages of professors who offer their resources freely. In the last few years there have developed Learning Management Systems that combine the contents with other facilities necessary to make a virtual teaching process. As a result, collections of educative materials have been created to increase the quality of teaching processes that use informatic technologies.

H. Leung et al. (Eds.): ICWL 2007, LNCS 4823, pp. 138–147, 2008.
© Springer-Verlag Berlin Heidelberg 2008

With the development of standards as IMS, Learning Objects Repositories (LOR) have emerged. They contain the educative materials and the metadata that describe them according to a standard. Besides, many institutions have developed initiatives to attain reusability from a legal and pedagogical viewpoint, so that contents may be reused. As a result, a new quality in the contents has appeared. It is known as Open content or Open Educational Resources (OpenER).

Open Educational Resources are materials, documents and especially learning resources that are free and can be reused by the educative community. They are those resources that may be used by anyone who may want to use them. They are copyright as the "closed" contents. What makes them different is their economical utilization [2].

The OpenCourseware project, developed by the MIT [3] has opened a number of conceptual, pedagogical and technological possibilities as it has systematized the content production to be published in the web , trying to find a solution for some difficulties related to technological formats and copyright, which any academic pro- duction may have.

There are other projects that have developed more integrated applications as is case of Educommons [4] that is trying to be an authentic LMS. It manages contents in an open way and includes the necessary communication tools between professors and students to realize this function.It is evident that the philosophy of open contents that we have referenced is the real solution to make a rational use of the contents existing in the network, as the access is easier and the processes of selection, control and utili- zation of the existing resources are simplified.

Despite the results obtained in contents management, there are still some techno- logical barriers that hinder the open treatment of those existing contents as described above and therefore, not allowing a generalization of such experiences in accordance with the demands of the new university. There are lots of management systems, as we have stated, each in accordance with the interests and philosophy of independent insti- tutions or people. When analyzing them separately they function correctly, but as each has a different data design, it provokes difficulties to manage contents in a dis- tributed way and incapability to communicate with other management systems or repositories which contents are useful. They do not offer any alternatives for manag- ing the great diversity of standards and initiatives as for cataloguing, packaging, dis- tributing contents and designing complex learning units to adapt them to the different pedagogical situations of the present time. It is necessary that content managers in- crease the facilities so that users may manage easily and clearly the legal elements of the resources that they use and publish.

Taking into account the aspects stated above, we have designed an informatic model for managing open contents as a basis to design applications aimed at it. This model takes into account the general characteristics of a CMS but it has the elements and resources necessary to manage contents in an open way. It is based on a distrib- uted data model and has a set of elements and services that guarantee the design, management and reusability of contents in different pedagogical contexts and in a legal manner. The model provides alternatives for connecting with other CMS and LMS.

2 An Informatic Model for Open Contents Management

The model created is based on the most well known CMS but it has some characteristics that make it different; it offers more orientation towards managing open contents.

- ❖ It is based on a data and distributed services model which provides more efficiency when managing and reusing contents.
- ❖ It offers secure and efficient alternatives to reuse contents organized in different data sources, including files organized in the computer of a professor and those organized in complex CMS and digital libraries.
- ❖ It has its own metadata model that we have called VirtuaMetadata (VMD) that groups the existing models. It is flexible enough as to incorporate those elements that emerge from new initiatives and standards or from specific needs of research groups or educative institutions.
- ❖ It permits to characterize learning objects from the viewpoint of content and usefulness, from the simplest as an image or a file, up to complex learning structures created through IMS LD and other similar initiatives.
- ❖ It takes into account not only educative resources, but also their interrelation with learning processes, pedagogical models and the management of those who get involved in these processes.

For a better understanding, we have divided the model in three layers that allow us to offer a logical view of the system proposed (Figure 1).

Source Layer: It contains a set of services that allow both the incorporation of isolated contents or those of recent creation and the usage of the existing ones in other CMS and digital libraries.

The main component of this layer is the Publication Manager (Figure 2) which analyzes, catalogues and puts into the data base of a specific repository the contents and/or metadata coming from different data sources like independent files, images, videos or those that come from more complex storing means.

The Analyzer Service allows extracting from files, the characteristics and useful properties in the process of cataloguing we will see later; so that users do not have to

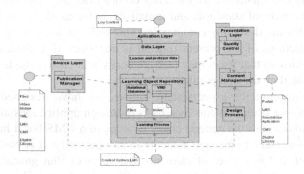

Fig. 1. View of implementation in UML

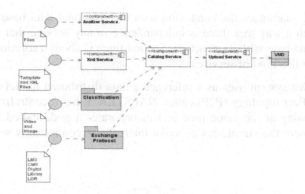

Fig. 2. View of Publication Manager implementation in UML

introduce them manually. Besides, it identifies those files that have been packaged through well known standards or initiatives as IMS, for using the previous classification as well as the information present in learning structures modelled through initiatives as IMSLD which can be useful later on.

XML Service is oriented towards processing those documents which format is XML and that are obtained through templates designed previously or through applications as OpenOffice that can generate files compatible with OpenDocument standard [5].

Images and videos have a special treatment in our model, because if we consider them as a simple file we could lose some important information that is in some parts of the image or in the intervals of time in the streaming of video. We are considering a special classification for these resources taking into account the relationship among these zones or intervals with other learning resources.

The reutilization of contents classified and organized using other environments is very important in a management system for educative contents, as one can take advantage of other elaborated resources in designing and creating a new content. Libraries and repositories have incorporated protocols and other alternatives for the collection, interchange and syndication of contents. Making good use of the facilities that these techniques offer, this process establishes communication with other systems that have a stable functioning and can provide us with contents. We have conceived the use of OAI-PMH[6] ,RSS [7] and Open Search [8].

The processes we have explained are the basis for cataloguing, that is the process through which the classification of resources that enter the data base finishes. It is obtained a file with a format called VirtuaMetadata (VMD) that constitutes the model of metadata we use in our system. Cataloguing can be automatic in those cases where there is a previous classification and only the conversion to VMD is required; or it can be manual in those cases where it is necessary to complete it.

The resource is introduced in the data base together with its Metadata in VMD format through a process that we have called Upload Service that also updates the tables in the corresponding repository.

Service Layer: It contains a set of processes that guarantee the interface with the data layer and the presentation layer. Within these services there is one for managing persistence that guarantees the connexion with the relational data base that has a repository, in such a way that there is independence in any service that needs to have access to the data base with its structure. Section three is about a solution we have put into practice for this kind of services.

Data Layer: Our system uses as a reference a data distributed model that combines with a Peer-to-Peer topology (P2P) called NAPSTER. It has a centralized and decentralized functioning at the same time and incorporates a node called NAPSTER or super server where the simple nodes make intermittent connections searching information. [9]

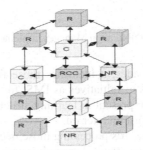

Fig. 3. Data Model

An R repository may belong to one or some C collections that allow to group repositories of the same theme or according to a specific logical grouping. The collection may or may not have the metadata of the repositories that belong to it. At the same time, the collection may belong to a central register of collections (RCC). It has information about the collections and can be used as Gateways to searchers or meta searchers in order to get a more effective search in the distributed network of learning objects repositories.

Each repository has a relational data base that has the description of its resources and the metadata associated, as well as some information about users, collections and other necessary aspects for managing the repository.

Apart from the data base, the repository has resources that, as we just stated, may or may not be physically present in our repositories. They can be as simple as a text file or a PDF, or as complex as zipped files or packages compatible with different standards oriented towards packaging contents.

As it can be seen in figure 1, we have included as part of the information of repositories, the data that permits to characterize the learning processes and their protagonists such as curricular structures, information of subjects, syllabuses, competence, users and professors, etc. The structure and nomenclature of these elements depend on the country or organization and play an important role in the processes of content management, as when combining it with the semantic information of the repositories it allows us to increase the usefulness of a resource in a specific context. These data can be filed up through a relational data base or through XML structures and some software pieces that permit an independent access to the structure. It could be a good practice to use the standards and initiatives to classify and model educative processes as RCDEO of IMS [10] for competence management, or Learner Information Package (LIP) [11],for information management about students.

To file up the metadata , it has been defined a model called VirtuaMetadata (VMD) that groups different existing standards and it is flexible at changes and to the needs of research groups or institutions. To convert from and to our metadata model, it can be used converters that transform from one structure to another.

Presentation Layer: This layer is the interface to other CMS, LMS, applications or users. It includes the classical processes that a CMS has, which will not be detailed now. We will describe the three processes we consider most important, the one to control quality, the design and the search ones.

The process to control the quality of a resource is essential to accomplish its real reusability as it offers the necessary information concerning its authentic potentiality; that is, its capacity to achieve its objective. We have to take into account what pedagogical value of a resource depends on its usage or on its external context, as stated by David Wiley [12] more than on its composition or structure (internal context). Obviously, the evaluation made by others might help us to determine its quality. Our model takes into consideration the previous elements and proposes some indicators that define the quality of an educative resource. These indicators are based on the elements that make up the data base and the relationship between them.

We are only studying some indicators as the frequency of usage of a resource, number of times it is solicited in a specific period of time and other more complex indexes, as the use of the resource to solve competence, objectives and other elements of the learning process and the protagonists that appear in a repository data base. These indicators, in combination with popularity related elements similar to those used by social networks based on 2.0 web, offer more precision in the quality of resources.

The design process is oriented towards the creation of content structures that adapt to the characteristics of learning scenarios for which the resources and data registered in the repositories can be the basis. As seen in figure 1, this process uses the quality and management control components to select the most adequate resources to a specific design through the alternatives of standards related to content packaging. The new resources obtained are put into the data base through the Publication Manager. We have designed some applications like CMS4ROCKL, that will be dealt with in the next epigraph which uses IMS Content Packaging to create new learning structures. Nevertheless, other alternatives like Exelearning [13]can be studied. They have GNU license and introducing some changes they could reuse the components of our model to manage contents form these applications, so that the design capacity of this model and those to manage resources of our model can be combined. Similar experiences in some LMS as Moodle [14] can be used. It offers many possibilities for the interaction with other systems as the one we are proposing.

Management services are composed of classical processes of a CMS to guarantee the interface with the user and applications such as: searching, notifying, controlling users, visualizing, etc. This paper makes emphasis on the copyright control service and the search one that are the most remarkable in our model.

The copyright control service facilitates users the search for licences of both resources as such and of materials that complement them in sets of contents where more than one resource is used. In this way, users or applications may have a list of authors and institutions where the material was produced. This service starts when filing each licence in the metadata. In most metadata models, it is possible to include licences like CreativeCoomon [15] that are well known in the intellectual production context.

Searching is one of the main resources in content management. We use the general principles that modern searchers have, but we adapt them to the structure of our distributed data model and also to the requirements of open contents management, where it is necessary the combination of elements related with the content, semantics, pedagogical usefulness and the resource copyright. Both contents and metadata are indexed. The searching engine has a distributed functioning through the nodes that make up a collection of repositories, as already explained; and the parameters necessary for the search as range, words or phrases and their relationships reach the searcher through an input message formatted in XML.(figure 4)

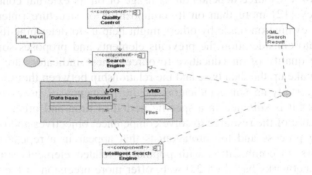

Fig. 4. View of Search Implementation in UML

We are looking for alternatives that permit to model complex relations that exist among the elements that make up the data base to get a higher level of intelligence in the search. In this sense, the system proposes the user the most adequate educative resources or combinations to solve a specific learning situation.

3   Results

As we have advanced in designing the model, we have noticed the need to create a tool that based on the specifications stated, it might allow professors to manage, in a simple way, the learning resources distributed all through the web so that they might create more complex and useful resources. These aspects were the basis to create CMS4ROCKL, a simple contents manager oriented towards managing open contents for learning and knowledge. Then, it was needed to implement data structures and processes necessary to put the model into practice.

CMS4ROCKL is a web application structured in three layers that we detail below (Fig 5)

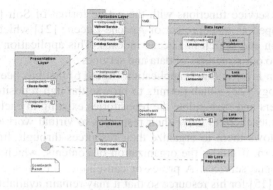

Fig. 5. View CMS4ROCKL Implementation

Data layer: It is formed by a network of learning objects repositories that we call LORA type repository. Its persistence has the structure explained in item 2. Such persistence can be accessible through a web service we have called LORASERVER which permits to make the operations necessary to manage the repository data. The access to the relational data base of each repository is based on Hibernate [16] a powerful library with GNU license that allows us the access to the relational data base of each repository despite the relational data base manager used. In this way, a LORA repository can use any available manager without making any changes in LORASERVER.

LORASERVER is a web service implemented on Axis [17], so it can be reused by any application that requires the access to a LORA repository. It offers services to manage resources, files, users and other services to use OAI-PMH through the library OAI-CAT [18] as well as services to manage the syndication of contents through RSS and other standards. It allows the interchange of metadata with other repositories or libraries we have called No LORA. (Figure 4)

In the application layer we have implemented the services of cataloguing, Lora collection and that for searching that we explain below.

The catalogue service allows users to classify a simple or complex model according to the VMD metadata model that as we have said, groups different standards. The capture screen is generated through an XML structure that has the fields to capture and other specifications necessary for the processes of validation, managing of vocabulary and the language of screen. This XML structure can be edited and adapted to the requirements of each institution in combination with some converters we have created to obtain metadata in a specific standard.

LORACOLLECTION service provides a set of facilities to manage groups of Lora repositories that have access through our CMS4ROCK application. This service is used by LORASEARCH for distributed search in parallel with the repositories that make up a collection, which presents the results formatted in OpenASearch standard [8]. Through a file called Opensearch description it obtains parameters necessary to search in the repositories. The results are returned in atom 1.0 format [19] extended with Open Search.

The indexation service functions with the native format of Solr [20] . It is a web application developed as a subproject of Apache-Lucene [21] which gives possibilities for the creation and search in Lucene indexes. This application has been configured and adapted to our structures of data and services.

The presentation layer is a web application (figure 6) that has been constructed using GWT technology [22] which permits to browse through repositories of a collection, to control users and manipulate the repositories existing in each repository. This application allows teachers to move their resources to virtual work shelves that, as a remote desk; it allows them to organize their resources through different templates. As a didactic pattern, it guides the organization of contents, which can be described through the catalogue services. A professor can choose the most adequate Creative Commons license [15] for his resource so that it may remain available for other users. At the same time, he can create more complex elaborations from the resources filed in the collections of repositories.

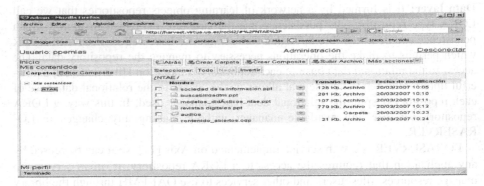

Fig. 6. Application CMS4ROCKL

This application is used by different professors to manage repositories based on our model. Conditions are being created to form a network of repositories to evaluate rigorously the model proposed.

4   Conclusions and Recommendations

The model we have presented is the basis for developing informatic tools to manage open contents, as it offers alternatives for reusing educative resources. It constitutes the main difference with commercial CMS, which are unable to integrate technology and pedagogy in a legal framework according to the requirements of modern Education.

We have taken into account the elements and structures that conform the pedagogical processes and we combine them with educative resources and their metadata, to achieve a higher level of efficiency and precision in the management of contents for learning and knowledge.

As a result, it has been obtained a library of services and applications that allows implementing the model in a practical and open way. It can be done by reusing Open

Source projects as Lucene, using architectures for programming like SOA and initiatives and standards like Open Search. They are efficient and offer possibilities for reusing these applications through which we have developed CMS4ROCKL application, still in development. It will help us to prove the efficiency of our model.

It is necessary to continue developing some services stated in the model, such as that to control quality and design, to improve the model documentation and the informatic applications, so as to increase the number of applications that use this alternative to manage open contents.

References

[1] Arango, H.: Gestión de contenidos: el homo sapiens desde la antigüedad hasta la era digital (2003), http://bvs.sld.cu/revistas/aci/vol11_5_03/aci09503.htm

[2] Alicante, U.d.: El proyecto de contenidos Abiertos (2006), http://www.contenidos-abiertos.org

[3] MIT. MIT's OpenCourseWare (2005), http://ocw.mit.edu/index.html

[4] COSL. The Educommons Project (2005), http://cosl.usu.edu/projects/educommons

[5] OASIS. OASIS Open Document Format for Office Applications (2006), http://www.oasis-open.org/committees/tc_home.php?wg_abbrev=office

[6] OAI-PMH. The Open Archives Initiative Protocol for Metadata Harvesting (2002), http://www.openarchives.org/OAI/openarchivesprotocol.html

[7] RSS: RSS 2.0 specification, http://www.rssboard.org/rss-specification

[8] Open Search. OpenSearch, http://www.opensearch.org/Home

[9] Hatala, M., Richards, G.: POOL, POND and SPLASH: A Canadian Infrastructure for Learning Object Repositories (2002), http://www.sfu.ca/~mhatala/pubs/CATE2002-hatala-richards.pdf

[10] IMS Global Learning Consortium, Inc., IMS Reusable Definition of Competency or Educational Objective - Information Model. Version 1.0. Final Specification (2002)

[11] IMS Global Learning Consortium, Inc., IMS LIP Specification (2001)

[12] David, W.: Getting axiomatic about learning objects (2005), http://www.reusability.org/axiomatic.pdf

[13] Exelearning. Web sobre el exelearning en español. http://www.exe-spain.es

[14] Moodle. Moodle (2007), http://www.moodle.org

[15] Creative Commons: Creative Commons España (2007), http://es.creativecommons.org/

[16] Hibernate. Hibernate (2007), http://www.hibernate.org/

[17] Apache Axis: Taller de Web Service con Apache AXIS (2005), http://www.acis.org.co/index.php?id=519

[18] OAI-CAT. Fundamentos tecnológicos del acceso abierto. http://eprints.rclis.org/archive/00005887/01/EPITSilio.pdf

[19] Internet Engineering Task Force (IETF). Atom. 1.0, http://tools.ietf.org/html/rfc4287

[20] Apache Lucene: Open Source Aplication Solr (2006), http://lucene.apache.org/Solr

[21] Lucene Project: Apache Lucene Project (2006), http://jakarta.apache.org/lucene

[22] Google. Google Web Toolkit (2005), http://code.google.com/webtoolkit/

On Line Course Organization

Ming Zhang[1], Weichun Wang[1], Yi Zhou[1], Yu Yang[1], Yuhong Xiong[2],
and Xiaoming Li[1]

[1] School of Electronics Engineering and Computer Science
Peking University, Beijing, 100871, China
{mzhang, wangwch, zhouyi, yyang, lxm}@net.pku.edu.cn
[2] HP Labs China, Beijing
yuhong.xiong@hp.com

Abstract. In order to help users access on-line materials with more specific questions, we build a learning portal named Fusion[1]. First we develop Fusion-Crawler, a link classification focused crawler, to download potential course pages. We then use a binary classifier to pick out the course pages. After the course pages are identified, we use FusionExtractor, a DOM tree based regular expression wrapper, to extract metadata. The metadata include Course Name, Instructor Information, Course Outline, and other relevant information, and they are stored in a database behind the portal. Experimental results show that our approach to organize on-line courses based on focused crawling and metadata extraction approach is effective. The FusionCrawler got average 40-50% more on-topic learning materials than normal focused crawler, while the average F1 in FusionExtractor is 85%. With metadata of more than 1,400 MIT OCW, 3000 UIUC and 1000 WISC courses; 300 courses from GreatLearning with 3000 Chinese course videos; and nearly 1000 videos from Internet Achieve; the Fusion portal provides several kinds of searching function, like quick search, advanced search and semantic navigation browsing.

Keywords: Focused Crawling, Metadata Extraction, Learning Object Management, Ontology.

1 Introduction

The World Wide Web contains a huge amount of learning information and it is continuing to grow. More and more universities put up course materials on the web, e.g., there are 20,000 courses under http://www.cuinfo.cornell.edu/Academic/Courses/, 7,200 courses under http://schedule.berkeley.edu/. Some permanent course archives like GreatLearning [1] and MIT's Open Courseware [2], maintain course videos, course syllabus, course notes, etc. Many companies, such as HP, also have a large amount of online training materials. Some Popular commercial like BlackBoard [3], WebCT [4], and Desire2Learn [5],

---

[1] This work is supported by the National Natural Science Foundation of China under Grant No. 90412010 and 60573166, the Ph.D Programs Foundation of the Ministry of Education of China under Grant No. 2007108, HP Labs China under "On line course organization", as well as Network Key Lab Grant of Guang Dong Province.

H. Leung et al. (Eds.): ICWL 2007, LNCS 4823, pp. 148–159, 2008.

contain spaces for the incorporation of granular objects. SCORM (Sharable Content Object Reference Model) adopted a subset of LOM elements, integrated with a runtime environment and aggregation model for learning content and provides a "conformance testing tool" that validates XML bindings and inclusion of mandatory elements [6].

But it is still difficult to find precise and complete answers for more specific questions with a general purpose search engine like Google. For example, if we want to know which universities in the US and China offer "Computer Architecture" courses, a general purpose search engine usually does not give a good answer. Therefore, we work on a project named Fusion (http://fusion.grids.cn:8080/ocos) to construct a web portal that effectively and efficiently collects, indexes, ranks, and organizes the online course materials, as shown in Fig. 1.

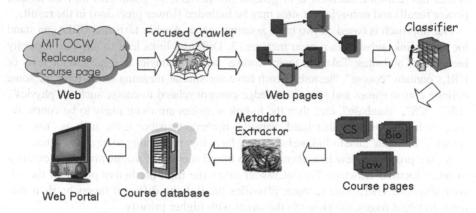

Fig. 1. System architecture for an online course portal

In this project, there are several research problems and development tasks which will be discussed in the remainder of this paper. Section 2 introduces the focused crawling strategy. Section 3 explains the automated metadata extraction. Section 4 describes the Learning Object Management and Search module. Section 5 shows the experiments of related algorithms. We summarize our works in section 6.

2 Focused Crawling

Since most of the courses are within university websites, we concentrate our crawling to those sites. After trying a few crawlers including JSpider, Wget and Nutch, we decided to use Nutch [7] for its rich features and extensibility. At the beginning of the crawling effort, we tried to download the complete website of some major US universities, such as www.berkeley.edu and www.stanford.edu. However, we later found out that the size of those sites is quite large. Using queries like "site:berkeley.edu" or "site:mit.edu" on Google, we estimate that the number of web pages on these sites can be over 20 million. If we run Nutch on a single server, it will take a few weeks before we finish downloading a complete website, even if we run multiple crawling threads in parallel. To shorten the crawl time, we need to selectively prune out some portion of the web sites to reduce the download burden.

Focused Crawler was introduced by Chakrabarti et. al. in 1999 [8]. There are also other crawlers, such as Intelligent Crawling with keywords [9], OPIC algorithm computing the importance value of websites [10], Learnable Crawler using URL seeds, topic keywords and URL prediction [11], Decision Tree method [12], distance to topic website based on contents [13], etc. Most focused crawlers considered the content of websites as main factors. But in our daily lives, we browse websites mainly by use of their URLs or anchor texts in other pages.

The focused crawler makes real-time decisions on which site to crawl, and aggressively discards websites that it deems not relevant. The disadvantage of this approach is that the real-time decision is in general not perfect, so good sites may be missed (lower recall) and non-relevant sites may be included (lower precision) in the result.

Our approach is based on two basic assumptions: 1. Anchor texts and URLs can stand for the to-link websites in a great measure. 2. Different links lead to different topically hierarchical websites. Take the topic "course" as an example, if some anchor texts or URLs contain "course", "lecture" which have the similar meaning to the topic, or some definite course names and some knowledge concept related to course such as "physics", "EE", "CS", "database", etc., then the to-link websites are more likely to be course related websites. On the other hand, with the irrelevant anchor texts, such as "library", "news", "calendar", the to-link websites may have low probability to be course sites.

So we propose a new link classification based method, FusionCrawler. In contrast to other focused crawlers, FusionCrawler takes the high predictive power of the anchor texts and URLs into account: classifies the links to different layers by their distance to target pages, the closer to the target with higher priority.

FusionCrawler consists of three main components: a training set which provides enough data to conduct classification, a link classifier which determines a measure of centrality of to-link pages to determine visit priorities, and a crawler providing priority queue based crawling.

Training set: In fig. 2, black circles stand for topic related pages, while the white ones stand for non-related pages. The training set is generated from anchor texts of real websites. We denote the interlinked websites as a graph G(V,E,L), in which V stands for the set of all websites, E stands for the set of all links and L is the set of all possible link path from one website to another. If v_2 is a topic related site,

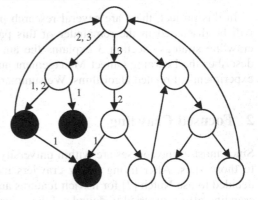

Fig. 2. Link classification tree

and the path $l=v_1e_ne_{n-1}...e_2e_1v_2$ ($l \in L$) exists, then e_i in the path L should be assigned to class i (we only denote links belonging to class 1-3 in fig. 2). One link can be assigned to different classes. The smaller the class number is, the higher crawling

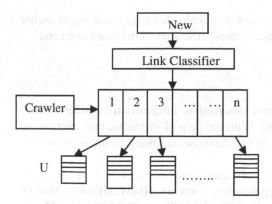

Fig. 3. The priority queue of FusionCrawler

priority the link is given. We built the training set from all the pages under www.caltech.edu and limited the class number to be 9.

Link Classification: The task of this step is to calculate the crawling priority of every link which is extracted from download pages. We consider each class as a set of terms S_i, and every extracted link (anchor text and URL) also as a set of terms A_j. We assume that there is no dependency between each two words. So like Naïve Bayes classification, for each class, we can formulate the prediction value $P(A_j \mid S_i)$ as follows:

$$P(A_j \mid S_i) = \prod_{w_k \in A_j} P(w_k \mid S_i) \tag{1}$$

w_k stands for appearance of the word in a link and $P(w_k \mid S_i)$ stands for its prediction value in class i. If the word w_k appears in S_i, we can calculate $P(w_k \mid S_i)$ as follows:

$$P(w_k \mid S_i) = n_{w_k,i} / N_i \tag{2}$$

$n_{w_k,i}$ is the frequency w_k appears in class i, and N_i is the total word number of class i.

If the word does not appear in any class, we simply not calculate $P(w_k \mid S_i)$ and bypass to the next word. If the word appears in some class, but does not appear in S_i, then we can estimate its value to be the average appearance probability in all classes:

$$P(w_k \mid S_i) = \sum_i n_{w_k,i} / \sum_i N_i \tag{3}$$

Finally, we choose the largest prediction value $P(A_j \mid S_m)$, and assign the to-link URL to the crawling queue m (as shown in fig. 3).

Crawling: This step does the exact crawling procedure. First, the crawler exams the crawling queues in the sequence from small numbers to big numbers. If small number queue (high priority in contrast) is not empty, the crawler crawls all the URLs contained in it. Otherwise, the crawler goes to next queue and start examine in the same way. Second, when the job of crawling one queue has been done, FusionCrawler extracts the anchor texts and URLs from newly downloaded pages, and begin anchor Linkage Classification step. If all queues are empty, the algorithm comes to an end.

3 Metadata Extraction

Metadata plays a key role for information description, information discovery, information retrieval, and information sharing. With the help of metadata, user queries can be processed using the structured data in the database, resulting in more precise response than full-text keyword search.

Besides Many DOM-tree and rule based approaches referred in [14], there are some statistics metadata extraction approaches such as HMM (Hidden Markov Model) [15] [16], CRF (Conditional Random Fields) [17] and SVM (Support Vector Machine) [18], which apply probability, statistics, rough reasoning, or random procedure to form suitable models.

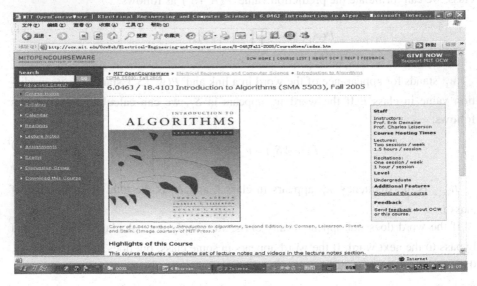

Fig. 4. The layout of OCW course "6.046J / 18.410J Introduction to Algorithms (SMA 5503), Fall 2005"

Fig. 4 shows a page of the course "6.046J / 18.410J Introduction to Algorithms (SMA 5503), Fall 2005" presented in OCW. Observing the fact that the materials in OCW obey the same structure or schema, we choose rule-based extraction method.

Several basic information extraction fields we need are placed in a stable sequence and web layout, such as Course ID, Course Name, Instructor Name and Lecture Time. But some elements are not stable, e.g. Lecture Notes, Course Outlines, Reading Lists, and Assignments. It means that the MIT OCW website is coherent in design but flexible enough to accommodate many different types of courses, lectures, seminars, etc.

This makes the rule-based process confused some time with poor performance. So we have to offer a procedure to first separate the target area in one page and eliminating other noisy information.

First, we integrate an open source tool "NekoHTML" (http://www.apache.org/~andyc/neko/), which is a simple HTML scanner and tag balancer that enables application programmers to parse HTML documents and access the information using standard XML interfaces. The parser can scan HTML files and "fix up" many common mistakes made by human (and computer) authors while writing HTML documents. NekoHTML adds missing parent elements; automatically closes elements with optional end tags; and can handle mismatched inline element tags. This tool can help us convert html page files into xml format and generate a DOM tree as we need. After that, the DOM tree is delivered to XSLT processor "Xalan" (http://xml.apache.org/xalan-j/), an open source package provided by Apache.

We pre-extract the target area mentioned above. For example, we figure out the solid XPath expression for the Course Outline, then pass it to the Xalan tool and also pass the web page which may contain the outline information. The Xalan tool will find the subset of the web page, according to the XPath, which just contains certain kind of education material we are interested in, as well as the structure information, and then we can decide to extract the outline part further or just skip to the next extraction field.

Through the whole pre-process work, we finally focus on the target part of given page that contains information we want, with certain stable schema or structure follow which we can extract metadata of the course.

So we make some rules to parse the piece of page content, and extract step by step. To implement this part of procedure, we need to choose a format to describe rules, and in the end we settled with java.util.regex, a java regular expression package. We first design a regular expression created as an instance of the Pattern Class, then generate an instance of the Matcher Class to match text content with given patterns, and then we easily extract contents from the pre-processed parts and receive valuable metadata.

The information may be placed in a different layout with other pages, which means the information is under some other node in the DOM tree. Therefore, we provide an optimization by designing several kinds of XPath and regular expression to avoid incorrect extraction caused by structure flexibility, and organizing them into a tree structure followed by ranking number assigned to each XPath and each regular expression. When the first one failed (return null), then the consequent one should be considered next, and so on, until we find needed metadata or run out of all the XPath or regular expression.

Our method is also combined with information refinement technology to make sure the final extraction result is as accurate as possible. In the following segment,

The 1st part is in (chapters 3, 4 and 5 of) Deen, W. M. Analysis of Transport Phenomena. The book: New York: Oxford University Press, 1998. ISBN: 0195084942.

Both "The 1st part is in (chapters 3, 4 and 5 of)" and "The book:" are redundant. Fusion Extractor learns the rules as "chapter", pure number "121143" etc. as stop words to be expunged. Following is the framework of extraction algorithm.

FusionExtractor ： the algorithm extracts course metadata
Input ： the web pages and regular expression rule set S
Output ： the metadata
Procedure ：
1. Choose the appropriate rule Si in set S
   (1) Extract the data which fit the specific keywords or tags;
   (2) If the extracted data match rule Si, then choose Si.
2. Apply rule Si to delimit the XML tags in parsed DOM tree and got data blocks.
3. Refine the data by eliminating noisy data.
4. output the extracted fields.

4 Learning Object Management and Search Module

The present recommended metadata standard is IEEE-LTSC LOM (Learning Object
Metadata), which is developed upon IMS metadata [19]. Many metadata standards
adopt subset of LOM elements. For example SCORM (Sharable Content Object Reference Model): A subset of LOM elements, integrated with a runtime environment
and aggregation model for learning content. SCORM provides a "conformance testing
tool" that validates XML bindings, and inclusion of mandatory elements [20].

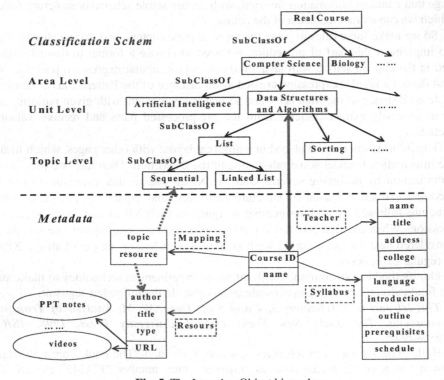

Fig. 5. The Learning Object hierarchy

To ensure simplicity and understandability, meanwhile keeping the consistency with GreatLearning, Fusion establishes a combination of classification taxonomy and metadata schema. We adopted the three level hierarchy of IEEE/ACM CC2005 to organize the knowledge body of "Discipline Classification and Code" issued by the China's Ministry of Education [21]. According to IEEE/ACM CC2005, the CS body of knowledge is organized hierarchically into three levels: area, unit, and topic. The highest level of the hierarchy is the area, which represents a particular disciplinary subfield. The areas are broken down into smaller divisions called units, which represent individual thematic modules within an area. Each unit is further subdivided into a set of topics, which are the lowest level of the hierarchy.

The Learning Object Organization is shown in fig. 5, where the metadata is organized under the classification schema of MOE. The classification and metadata structure of Fusion. Course, Resource and Teacher are the three major metadata categories for the learning information. Course: Course ID, Course name, Language, Course Introduction, Course Outline, Prerequisite, Schedule, etc.; Resource: Author, Title, Type (e.g. PPT notes, video), Link URL, etc; Teacher: Teacher Name, Title.

Address (e.g. email), etc; There are two kinds of relation between the knowledge body and course metadata, one is between the Knowledge Unit and Course ID, the other is between the Knowledge Topic and the Course Resource.

We use OWL to describe the area, unit, topic and related learning information. To design a course on the ontology, e.g. "Data Structures and Algorithms", first define a concept class "COURSE", and then define an instance "C_DataStructures_Algorithms", shown as following,

<COURSE
rdf:about=""http://fusion.pku.edu.cn:8080/ocos/searching/#C_DataStructures_Algorit hms"/>

Base on the ontology schema and learning metadata, we built a bilingual (Chinese-English) prototype portal (http://fusion.grids.cn:8080/ocos) shown in figure 1 previously, with metadata of more than 1,400 MIT OCW, 3000 UIUC and 1000 WISC courses; 300 courses from GreatLearning with 3000 Chinese course videos; and nearly 1000 videos from Internet Achieve.

The searching part is an important function part of learning object repository. Fusion provides several kinds of searching function, like quick search, advanced search and navigation browsing.

First of all, the quick searching part is a normal option, a user can quick search by giving Course Code, Course Name, College Name, or Teacher Name. And the user just need to give some key words, and set the searching field as Course introduction, Course Outline or, and All Field, then Fusion will find out all relevant candidate courses.

Actually the course introduction should include all those most typical words to describe what the course is about; meanwhile the course outline is about the detailed topics to be discussed.

After that, if the user can not find what he wants by quick searching, or there are too many candidate materials returned, then he can try the advanced searching function provided in page http://fusion.grids.cn:8080/ocos/AdvSearch_en.jsp. The query syntax is shown as following:

```
Query ::= ( Clause )*
Clause ::= ["+", "-"] [Field ":"] ( TERM | "(" Query ")")
Field ::= "CID" | "CN" | "CI" | "CO" | "CC" | "TN" | "CR"
```

A user can simply fill in certain fields with key words and combine them through the operators AND, OR and NOT and form an advance query in the text area. Through this way, anyone can create an accurate query without training, and it makes our advanced searching easy to user and more efficient.

Besides the quick searching and advanced searching function, we actually serve another one called Subject Navigation Searching. If the user clicks on a certain item in the Discipline hierarchy (http://fusion.grids.cn:8080/ocos/Navigation_en.jsp), the matched courses will be displayed on the result page.

Another Navigation Searching is "Teacher Name" navigation list, all the teachers' name is put into categories of alphabet and stored in order, so the users can get a whole picture of all the instructors and find any teacher at the category and all the courses the instructor provided.

We also implement a semantic query function using Jena [22], a rule-based inference engine supports RDQL [23]. An RDQL consists of a graph pattern, expressed as a list of triple patterns. Each triple pattern is comprised of named variables and RDF values (URIs and literals). An RDQL query can additionally have a set of constraints on the values of those variables, and a list of the variables required in the answer set. Giving the teacher's name, following RDQL statements return all the courses the teacher taught.

SELECT ?x

WHERE (?resource, <"http://fusion.pku.edu.cn:8080/ocos/searching/#NAME>, teacher)

(?resource, <"http://fusion.pku.edu.cn:8080/ocos/searching/#TEACH>, ?y)

(?y, <"http://fusion.pku.edu.cn:8080/ocos/searching/#NAME>, ?x)

We are planning to pre-build other similar semantic search functions, furthermore even parse the on-the-fly RDQL queries submitted by the professional users.

5 Experiment

5.1 The Performance of FusionCrawler

In the experiment, we built the training set with only anchor texts extracted from some pages under www.caltech.edu and limited the layer number to 9, in order to make implementation easier. To build the training set, we first labeled 1543 course pages from www.caltech.edu and recorded their URLs manually. We then used Nutch [7] to crawl all pages under www.caltech.edu, retrieving a total of 300,000 pages. We produced all layers by back tracing from the labeled course pages.

We use SVM classifier which was trained by two classes: course and non-course, and get average recall and precision over 85% respectively using 10 folders cross validation. To evaluate our algorithm, we use the fraction of pages that are on-topic. The results are shown in the fig. 6 where the percentage of crawled relevant pages (Y-axis) is plotted against the number of all crawled pages (X-axis). There are three crawlers compared: (1) FusionCrawler, Link Classification Method; (2) a traditional high-performance focused crawler, which makes use of the contents of crawled pages described in [13]; (3) breadth first crawler without filtering. Because Fusion processes pages from the home page of universities, the course relevant pages are not rare. But we can still see that the focused crawlers outperform the standard breadth-first crawler more or less. The proportion of relevant pages of Fusion-Crawler is about 41% on average. But the propor-

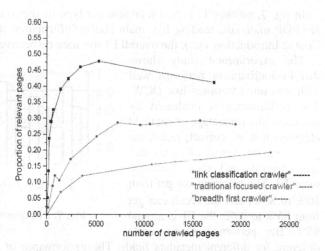

Fig. 6. Crawling performance on CalTech

tion of traditional high-performance focused crawler is only 28% on average, and the proportion of breadth first crawler is 19% on average. So our method found on average 40-50% more on-topic documents than the focused crawler based on content distance to topic website described in [13].

While crawling on WSU dataset, the proportion of course relevant pages is much lower, the difference is more obvious. The proportion of relevant pages: Fusion-Crawler is about 21% on average, traditional focused crawler 12% and breadth first crawler (BFS crawler) is only 7%. So, FusionCrawler outperforms about 77% than the BFS crawler.

To compare with other algorithms which related to focused crawling, Fusion-Crawler has such advantages: (1) It confirms to the real situation of internet. We have considered this situation: the from-link pages and the to-link ones are not in the same topic. Many other focused crawlers [8] [13] predict priorities of to-link pages based on from-link pages. That is, if the from-link pages are more irrelevant, the to-link pages should be crawled after a longer time. Otherwise, the to-link pages should be crawled sooner. It is a prejudice because there are many examples showing that irrelevant topical pages are linking together. In our method, if an irrelevant page links to a relevant page, or a relevant page links to an irrelevant page, the crawler can find the right pages to download intelligently. (2) We only need the set of anchor texts to build training set. Compared to methods using information about contents, our training set is small. As a result, it brings a faster crawling speed.

In FusionCrawler, we greatly reduce the amount of real-time processing in the crawler, and only discard pages that may not lead to learning object pages. This ensures high recall during crawling.

5.2 The Evaluation of FusionExtractor

We have successfully extracted metadata from more than 1400 OCW courses. The information we extract includes course title, course number, teacher name(s) and email(s), course introduction, syllabus, instruction hours, lecture notes, and reading materials.

In fig. 7, number 1, 2, 3, 4 represent the type of metadata items, which are which are PDF materials, reading list, main course information (Course Name, Course ID, Course Introduction, etc.), the overall F1 mesuare respectively.

The experimental study shows that FusionExtractor performs well with structured websites like OCW. The performance is evaluated by precision, the percentage of returned elements that are correct; recall, the percentage of correct elements that are returned; and their harmonic mean F1. The precision can get from 80% to 85%; and the recall can get from 85% to 90%; the F1 is around 85%. But performances are quite

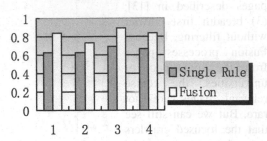

Fig. 7. F1 performance of metadata

different for different metadata fields. The performance of stable course id or course name is quite satisfied, but the free structured lecture note or course outline only got with 80% F1 value. Most of the remaining errors occur in the course readings section, because that part of the course page was not written in a regular way.

In general, the multi-rule model made the whole system act more precisely and the progress is quite obvious.

6 Conclusion

In this paper, we introduced Fusion, a bilingual on-line learning portal based on focused crawling and metadata extraction technology. The FusionCrawler got average 40-50% more on-topic learning materials than normal focused crawler, while the average F1 in FusionExtractor is 85%.

Besides further algorithm study and development for various components of this project - the focused crawler, the classifier, and the metadata extractor, we will apply these components to more universities and provide more structured learning materials and objects.

Along with the semantic issues, we will further develop the online course portal to support eLearning 2.0 features, for example, personal learning space, user contributions, user feedbacks, user tags, user comments, etc.

References

1. ChinaGrid GreatLearning project, http://greatlearning.grids.cn
2. MIT's Open Courseware (OCW), http://ocw.mit.edu/index.html
3. BlackBoard, http://www.blackboard.com/
4. WebCT, http://www.webct.com/
5. Desire2Learn, http://www.desire2learn.com/
6. Kazi, S.: A conceptual framework for Web-based intelligent learning environments using SCORM-2004. Proceedings of the IEEE International Conference on Advanced Learning Technologies (ICALT 2004). pp. 12–15 (2004)

7. Nutch, http://lucene.apache.org/nutch/
8. Chakrabarti, S., van den Berg, S.M., Dom, B.: Focused Crawling: a new approach to topic-specific Web resource discovery. In: Proceedings of the 8th World Wide Web Conference (www 1999), Toronto, Canada, 1999, pp. 1623–1640. Elsevier North-Holland, New York (1999)
9. Aggarwal, C., Al-Garawi, F., Yu, P.: Intelligent crawling on the World Wide Web with arbitrary predicates. In: Proceedings of the 10th international conference on World Wide Web (WWW 2001), Hong Kong, China, 2001, pp. 96–105. ACM Press, New York (2001)
10. Abiteboul, S., Preda, M., Cobena, G.: Adaptive On-Line Page Importance Computation. In: Proceedings of the 12th international World Wild Web Conference (WWW 2003), Budapest, Hungary, 2003, pp. 280–290. ACM Press, New York (2003)
11. Angkawattanawit, N., Rungsawang, A.: Learnable Crawling: An Efficient Approach to Topic-Specific web Resource Discovery. In: Proceedings of the 2nd international Symposium on communications and Information Technology (ISCIT' 02), Bangkok, Thailand, 2002, pp. 97–114. Academic Press, London (2005)
12. Li, J., Furuse, K., Yamaguchi, K.: Focused Crawling by Exploiting Anchor Text Using Decision Tree. In: Proceedings of the 14th international World Wild Web Conference (WWW 2005), Chiba, Japan, 2005, pp. 1190–1191. ACM Press, New York (2005)
13. Diligenti, M., Coctzee, F., Lawrence, S., Giles, C.L., Gori, M.: Focused Crawling Using Context Graphs. In: Proceedings of the 26th International Conference on Very Large Data Bases (VLDB 2000), Cairo, Egypt, 2000, pp. 527–534. Morgan Kaufmann Publishers Inc, San Francisco (2000)
14. Kayed, M., Shaalan, K.F., Chang, C.H., Girgis, M.R.: A Survey of Web Information Extraction Systems. In: IEEE Transactions on Knowledge and Data Engineering, IEEE Educational Activities Department, Piscataway, NJ, USA, October 2006, vol. 18(10), pp. 1411–1428 (2006)
15. Seymore, K., McCallum, A., Rosenreid, R.: Learning Hidden Markov Model Structure for Information Extraction. In: Proceedings of AAAI-1999 Workshop on Machine Learning for Information Extraction, Orlando, Florida, 1999, pp. 37–42. AAAI Press/The MIT Press (1999)
16. Yin, P., Zhang, M., Deng, Z.H., Yang, D.Q.: Metadata Extraction from Bibliographies Using Bigram HMM. In: Chen, Z., Chen, H., Miao, Q., Fu, Y., Fox, E., Lim, E.-p. (eds.) ICADL 2004. LNCS, vol. 3334, pp. 310–319. Springer, Heidelberg (2004)
17. Lafferty, J., McCallum, A., Pereira, F.: Conditional Random Fields: Probabilistic Models for Segmenting and Labeling Sequence Data. In: Proceedings of International Conf. Management on Machine Learning (ICML 2001), Massachusetts, USA, pp. 282–289. Morgan Kaufmann, San Francisco (2001)
18. Han, H., Giles, C.L., Mnavoglu, E., Zha, H.Y.: Automatic Document Metadata Extraction Using Support Vector Machine. In: Proceedings of the Joint conference of Digital Libraries (JCDL 2003), Houston, Texas, 2003, pp. 37–48. IEEE Computer Society, Washington (2003)
19. LOM, WG12: Learning Object Metadata, http://ltsc.ieee.org/wg12/
20. SCRORM, http://www.adlnet.org/index.cfm?fuseaction=scormabt
21. China's Ministry of Education, Discipline Classification and Code, http://fusion.grids.cn:8080/ocos/Navigation_en.jsp
22. http://jena.sourceforge.net/
23. Seaborne, A.: RDQL - A Query Language for RDF, W3C Member Submission, (January 9, 2004)

Learning as a Service: A Web-Based Learning Framework for Communities of Professionals on the Web 2.0

Marc Spaniol, Ralf Klamma, and Yiwei Cao

RWTH Aachen University, Informatik 5, Ahornstr. 55, D-52056 Aachen, Germany
{mspaniol,klamma,cao}@cs.rwth-aachen.de

Abstract. With the advent of the Web 2.0 technologies, web-based learning is shifting to new learning community driven requirements. While the success of web-based learning (still) requires a careful selection of appropriate communication/collaboration tools, the underlying software methodology is shifting from (passive) content consumption towards (active) content creation. Even more, the professionals' socio-cultural background influences the attitude towards the collaboratively created learning contents. Thus, successful web-based learning community hosting for professionals depends on a comprehensive cross-media support such as capabilities to share drawings, animations, pictures, digital videos, texts etc. among users. In this paper, we present the "Learning As a Service" (*LAS*) framework. *LAS* is an approach supporting web-based learning for professionals on the Web 2.0. It employs advanced multimedia technologies in order to promote a wide range of web-based learning community information systems for interdisciplinary, intercultural as well as intergenerational learning. We present a set of services on the basis of *LAS* showing best practices for various application scenarios.

Keywords: Technology Enhanced Learning, Web 2.0, Multimedia, Metadata, Web Services, SOA.

1 Introduction

Providing learners with the most suitable contents at any time and in any context is one of the most critical aspects in technology enhanced learning. In particular, the design of web-based learning applications for communities of professionals is a challenging issue. This problem becomes even more visible when the applications aim at supporting interdisciplinary, intercultural, and intergenerational learning communities. Furthermore, problems arise if the heterogeneous needs of professionals have to be satisfied. While "classical" E-Learning systems try to overcome these problems by applying learner modeling strategies like IMS Learning Design in order to select and customize the content delivery within a single application, "Learning As a Service" (*LAS*) aims at the flexible orchestration of social software within a web-based learning framework according to the professionals' needs.

H. Leung et al. (Eds.): ICWL 2007, LNCS 4823, pp. 160–173, 2008.

In addition, multimedia technologies, social software and new Web 2.0 business models are rapidly developing and giving rise to new hardware and software requirements. Combined with a trend for multidisciplinary work and research, novel approaches for flexible, evolving, adaptable, and interoperable community engines are required. The success of social software and Web 2.0 depends greatly on user-generated content, since one of the Web 2.0 business models is "Data is the next Intel Inside". But available social software solutions often neglect requirements of user communities. Therefore, social software and Web 2.0 need to reflect the nature of the underlying community processes and their discourses for technology enhanced learning. Consequently, the first research question is how to exploit the features of the Web 2.0 in order to design flexible, constructable web-based learning frameworks?

The design of applications for web-based learning for interdisciplinary professional communities of practice (in general) and for web-based learning frameworks (in particular) is a challenging issue [23,27,35]. Principles like legitimate peripheral participation, group knowledge, situated learning, informality, and co-location have to be taken seriously during the design of the learning framework. For that reason, the web-based learning framework has to reflect the social learning processes which are very community-specific. Even more, (some) non-technical communities of professionals are usually not able to express their needs in the very beginning of technology enhanced learning application usage. Thus, the communities have to gain experiences on their own learning processes while using the systems. Additionally, the multimedia technologies are being developed so rapidly that great hardware and network capabilities are required. Consequently, the second research question is how to bring system developers and user communities together in order to jointly develop technology enhanced learning solutions?

In this paper we present a novel approach to realization of freely constructible web-based learning applications in the Web 2.0 era based on our "Learning As a Service" (LAS) framework. In order to meet these requirements we combine approaches from various disciplines such as software engineering, sociology and cultural sciences, led by the transcriptivity idea as a design principle in computer science [17,19]. The development process of community information systems is based on ideas of joining usability and sociability [29] by constantly assessing and supporting community needs in a socio-technical information system development process. From the technical point of view, the server architecture of the LAS framework allows communities to add, remove and exchange services in their community information system from anywhere at runtime. On top of it, we design and implement a Web 2.0 community platform, the Virtual Campfire, a technology enhanced learning environment for communities of professionals e.g. in cultural heritage management.

The rest of the paper is organized as follows. In Section 2 we give an overview of recent trends on the Web 2.0 with a focus on courseware management systems. Particularly, we discuss how far web-based learning specific courseware management systems are capable of community support in a Web 2.0 fashion. We will point out, that the desired solution requires bridging the gap between (passive) content consumption in the Web 1.0 and (active) content creation in the Web 2.0. In Section 3 we introduce *LAS* as a framework to comply with these tasks. Even more, we explain its technical features for the modular composition of services. After that, we present *Virtual Campfire* and its core modules in a scenario of non-linear multimedia storytelling for professionals in the application area of cultural heritage management in Section 4. The paper closes with a summary and an outlook on further research.

2   Recent Trends on the Web 2.0 - CMS Reviewed

In a rapidly changing world of Web applications, web-based learning has got in place recently. Nowadays, the Web 1.0 is shaken by the fundamental changes brought by the emergence of a new understanding of the Web itself. The term "Web 2.0" is therewith coined. In the Web 2.0 era the attitude towards software has changed dramatically. Projects like Wikipedia create knowledge prosumers, which unify consumers and producers, and participation becomes essential for wikis. They are replacing those now old-fashioned content management systems in organizations. Interoperability between content and services is realized by syndications tools such as the RSS. In a similar fashion, this also holds for courseware management systems. In order to highlight these differences between the "new" and the "old" Web paradigms, we introduce the core Web 2.0 business processes presented in O'Reilly's seminal article [28]. We will not repeat all features of the Web 2.0 here, but put forward the impact of Web 2.0 technologies on web-based learning. In addition, we discuss whether and how far the most prominent courseware management systems (CMS) such as *Blackboard Academic Suite^{TM}* [8], *CLIX* [15] or *Moodle* [25] "comply" with the Web 2.0 concepts.

2.1   Folksonomies

Tags are user-generated keywords (metadata) describing content (data). Web 2.0 uses tagging technologies for the categorization of multimedia content, usable for search and retrieval of very large collections. So far, the use of content-based retrieval techniques was limited for multimedia content, since they only work efficiently enough on a limited amount of material. Even more, in some larger collections, only a limited amount of retrieved multimedia content has a high ratio in terms of precision and recall. However, a "semantic gap" between the technical extraction of metadata and the semantically correct interpretation of content can be recognized [6]. In this aspect, tagging systems have the shortcoming that they only offer plain keywords, where tags carry their semantics implicitly only. Despite their potential in improving search and retrieval of multimedia contents, tagging systems face the problem inherent in the implicit semantics of the vocabulary used for tagging [7,24]. Particularly, the semantics are not accessible for further machine processing. Current trends and evolving standards in multimedia technologies are intended for enriching multimedia content with semantic metadata leading to more advanced multimedia management and retrieval methods in order to handle the dramatically increasing amount of publicly available multimedia content on the web [5]. Consequently, the tags themselves should carry their semantics explicitly in order to make this additional information machine-accessible.

For web-based technology enhanced learning applications, multimedia and Web 2.0 technologies have to converge on multimedia management. Tagging technologies are needed to retrieve interesting multimedia content, but we also need some kind of emergent semantics for multimedia using well-established content-based retrieval techniques. In "classical" CMS the concept of folksonomies is unknown. In contrast to the bottom up approach of folksonomies, they mostly stick to a predefined categorization scheme. Nevertheless, CMS like *Blackboard Academic Suite*^{TM}, *CLIX* or *Moodle* provide other means to access the contents. While Web 2.0 software allows the exploration of all kinds of multimedia, CMS currently only cover learning contents. In the future there will be a clear need to cross-walk between multimedia description standards like Dublin Core [2,12] and MPEG-7 [16,21] on the one hand and Learning Objects Metadata (LOM) [14], SCORM [1] and IMS LD [22] on the other hand.

2.2 Syndication

Lately, Web 2.0 is also featured as a kind of attitude with which people handle interactions on the web. More and more web sites support services like RSS, social bookmarking, and Web site personalization instead of placing a button labeled with "Set this page as your home page". It has become natural and a kind of fashion to integrate third-party web services like Google, Yahoo and del.icio.us etc. Web services and syndication will be even more important in ubiquitous learning contexts when learners need support based on their location, their schedule, their connectivity, their device capabilities and their usage context. Content has to be adapted to the various unreliable or hardly predictable contexts of the learners instead of delivering the same content to every learner in every situation.

Syndication is somewhat a "new" concept to CMS. However, CMS focus on interoperability of learning contents. While systems like *Blackboard Academic Suite*^{TM}, *CLIX* or *Moodle* "syndicate" their contents in interoperable metadata standards, they have not yet discovered the multimedia description standards or even other standards from entertainment, library sciences, science and so on. Nevertheless, with the advent of Web Services *Blackboard Academic Suite*^{TM}, *CLIX* or *Moodle* have got more and more openness and become "service-oriented".

2.3 Participation

"Everybody's invited!" is the slogan of social software ranging from the social bookmarking pioneer del.icio.us to Wikipedia. Users can subscribe to communities in order to make their contributions to a dedicated topic regardless of social background, age or ethnicity. Thus, social networks are facilitated up to get a broader perspective on available information (opinion network) instead of a narrowed-by-personalization piece of information. In the present information world, one can get whatever information he wants by finding the right community. Social navigation, social recommendation and social filtering techniques are even more important in a multimedia Web, while classical information retrieval techniques only provide limited support for communities' participation. For example, merging and recombination of content is a technique which can be easily applied on existing Web 2.0 multimedia repositories. Nevertheless, participation sets new challenges for content retrieval techniques. It is questionable, what information quality can be retrieved from Wikipedia (cf. http://en.wikipedia.org) and Wikimedia Commons (cf. http://commons.wikimedia.org) e.g. related to the two different architectural styles of Florence Duomo's cathedral.

Referred to "classical" CMS, *Blackboard Academic Suite*^{TM}, *CLIX* or *Moodle* are based on participation, too. However, participation of contents is usually based on a learner model and sophisticated roles. While *Moodle* is the pioneer in being more or less the "Wikipedia" of E-Learning, also *Blackboard Academic Suite*^{TM} and *CLIX* have just discovered the power of bottom up activities. Thus, the trend in CMS goes to collaborative authoring by shifting from consumption to prosumption. Thus, wikis are providing an approach to contextualization of learning content as much as possible. However, the wiki approach is different as it tells the story behind the content.

2.4 Sharing Knowledge and Control

Control freaks are worrying about the principal openness of the new social software applications like diverse wikis, but it turnes out that participation increases just by those low barriers. Even if inappropriate content is uploaded or created, or existing content is modified or even vandalized, the communities have some self-repair strategies and developing social norms in place which are more flexible than any technological approach protecting content. But when these repair strategies do not work anymore, the community may have problems by itself and will disappear eventually. This openness accepts various types of multimedia. It is possible to reuse multimedia, which takes advantage of well-rated community media. Rip, mix, and burn as classical multimedia sharing models have to be re-invented for learning communities. While it is relatively easy to forward a YouTube video, it is still a professional task to edit new videos out of existing materials for learning purposes, which is not yet well supported by either social software or CMS.

Digital media allows fast creation, sharing and consumption of interactive content. "Classical" CMS like *Blackboard Academic Suite*^{TM}, *CLIX* or *Moodle* aim at delivering learning objects. Their contents are "valid only" in certain conditions such as a particular status of the learner model. To the best of our knowledge there is no way in the moment to allow learning designers or learners to create, share or consume re-contextualized multimedia contents in a Web 2.0 manner.

2.5   Summary

There is a gap between (passive) content consumption in "classical" CMS and (active) content creation in Web 2.0. However, the gap is not such big as it might appear at first sight. It can be recognized that there is an increasing alignment of CMS like *Blackboard Academic Suite*^{TM}, *CLIX* or *Moodle* move towards the Web Services and Web 2.0 (c.f. Table 1). In this aspect, particularly *CLIX* has introduced sophisticated features towards Web 2.0 functionalities in its recent version.

Table 1. Differences between Technologies for CMS and Social Software

Web 2.0 Paradigm	Technologies in Social Software	Technologies in CMS
Folksonomies	Tagging	Categorization
Syndication	Web-Services, RSS, MPEG-7	SCORM, SOA
Participation	Community	Based on Learner Models
Knowledge Sharing	Multimedia, Stories	Learning Objects

Correspondingly, we'll present an approach that might help developers as well as learning communities narrow or even close the gap between "classical" courseware management systems and freely adjustable Web 2.0 technologies. The "Learning As a Service" (*LAS*) Framework uses Web 2.0 technologies and provides services for:

- Exploration of multimedia contents (Folksonomies & Participation)
- Collaborative authoring of multimedia contents (Syndication & Participation)
- Re-contextualization of episodic knowledge (Knowledge Sharing & Participation)

3   The "Learning as a Service" Framework - *LAS*

With both aforementioned research questions, our research starts from media theoretical starting point. Empirical studies have shown that there are considerable differences in the perception process of learners depending on the medium through which the content has been communicated [11,13]. Even more, dedicated studies on the efficiency of computer mediated communication indicate that not a single medium might be considered most suitable, but an almost freely configurable media mix is the solution of choice [26,30]. That means a singular artifact lacks its context. Thus, it is impossible to create knowledge separately from the media through which it is communicated. Similarly, media play a crucial role

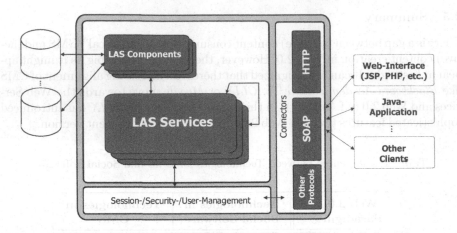

Fig. 1. Simplified *LAS* Architecture

in technology enhanced learning. Especially, multimedia processing features are required within the community's collaboration platform because of the variety of end user devices, network capabilities, and other factors in the learning context.

In order to encourage and enable communities to decide about the features and adjust the functionalities of their learning community information systems, a constant self-monitoring and self-reflection process is required. Correspondingly, the orchestration of services within the web-based learning framework is part of the professional communities' learning process itself. In addition, the interoperability of multimedia contents is an indispensable prerequisite.

For that purpose, "Learning As a Service" (*LAS*) is a framework to simplify the development of web-based applications in order to support technology enhanced learning for professionals. It offers an open architecture that helps professionals to create community information systems in versatile application domains. It employs advanced multimedia standards and database technologies that support the realization of the state-of-the-art community information systems for web-based technology enhanced learning. As a result, *LAS* bridges the gap between classical web-based learning specific courseware management systems and freely adjustable but not web-based learning specific community engines.

In addition, advanced multimedia technologies are employed to support a wide range of communities for interdisciplinary, intercultural and intergenerational learning. The highlights are the incorporation of multimedia content adaptation to the learning communities and a framework of learning services that help professionals create information systems in order to foster knowledge sharing in communities. Its architecture is based on a lightweight application server as a community engine that supports various services such as user management services, MPEG-7 services, database connection services etc. (cf. [20] for details).

In technical details, *LAS* is a platform-independent lightweight middleware platform implemented in Java. It employs principles of service oriented architectures (SOA) to provide web-based learning services. The learning services can be shared among various tools to support the work of professionals in communities of practice. The *LAS* API and its concepts are used to build the server's functionality and thus allow open and user-defined server extensions by three basic element types: connectors, components and services. Figure 1 shows a simplified diagram of the *LAS* architecture and the interrelations among server elements (cf. [32] for details).

What makes the "Learning as a Service" Framework *LAS* unique is its capability of hosting a large number of overlapping web-based learning communities at once. Agents grant a variety of rights for different learning communities. Furthermore, the architecture of the server software is able to run either a heavyweight XML based community engine or a very thin and hardware saving offline server on mobile devices for later synchronization in the ongoing development. The main task of *LAS* is to maintain the clean and orderly service oriented architecture by keeping all learning infrastructure logic on the server side. The main focus of *LAS* is rather server-side development than front-end user interface or related functionality like JSP containers, Servlet engines or HTML templates. Through a performance evaluation, *LAS* is much easier to use and configure than application servers like Tomcat [3], other J2EE application servers [18] or ZOPE/PLONE [36,37] to support web-based solutions. The main difference to such frameworks is that *LAS* tries to offer service programmers as much flexibility as possible. Developers are supported to concentrate on the middleware level of the overall architecture through a very flexible and fine grained user, group and rights management. In addition, a *LAS* environment allows hot deployment, i.e. dynamic reloading of services and components at runtime.

4   *Virtual Campfire*: Learning as a Service Applied

In this section, we demonstrate a web-based learning approach based on the *LAS* framework, so-called *Virtual Campfire*. The starting point is to use storytelling for technology enhanced learning in user communities who share knowledge about cultural heritage management. While corporate learning has been incorporating storytelling approaches for many years [9], the general technology enhanced learning is not advanced in using stories very much for educational purposes on the web. To explore the potentials of social software, *Virtual Campfire* employs a set of community tools including *Semantic Zapping Services*, *Collaboration Services* and *Storytelling Services* all based on *LAS* to inspire communities for storytelling and cultural knowledge sharing.

4.1   Semantic Zapping Services: Metadata Standard Driven Exploration of Multimedia Contents

Semantic Zapping Services in *Virtual Campfire* try to bridge the gap between folksonomy-style high-level semantic knowledge about multimedia and purely technical low-level content descriptions. These services are intended to support collaboration in communities by the exchange of multimedia contents and their low-level and high-level semantic descriptions. In order to ensure interoperability among the contents description multimedia metadata standards are being incorporated. In this aspect, the Dublin Core (DC) metadata standard [2,12] has its advantages, since it is an easy to understand and a concise method for media annotations in many domains. Nevertheless, DC still has the limitations e.g. not suitable for temporal and media specific annotations of multimedia contents. For that reason, we try to surmount these limitations by combining the loose classifications in DC with more sophisticated description elements for time based media in MPEG-7. Thus, our semantic zapping services are based on an excerpt of the extensive MPEG-7 multimedia metadata standard. Even more, we provide services for a semi-automatic conversion from DC to MPEG-7 [34] while an affiliated FTP server is used for an automated upload and download of multimedia artifacts by the community to the common repository. Consequently, the semantic zapping services of *Virtual Campfire* allow the community members to search and browse multimedia contents described by MPEG-7 for professional learning purposes.

4.2 Collaboration Services: Collaborative Authoring of Multimedia Contents

Knowledge sharing in *Virtual Campfire* is supported by annotating, tagging and sharing multimedia contents within the learning community. In contrast to a conventional categorization system, multiple concepts are used for one piece of information. All metadata generated in *Virtual Campfire* is MPEG-7 compliant by using MPEG-7 *LAS* service methods. For that purpose, *Virtual Campfire* offers two types of tagging: keyword tagging and semantic tagging (cf. Figure 2).

Keyword tagging enables users to assign a set of plain keywords to an image, as it can be done in Flickr (cf. www.flickr.com). However, one prominent problem of plain keyword tagging is the potential risk of semantic ambiguities. For example, consider the word "Portrait" being a polysemy of different meanings: A certain kind of painting or a dedicated camera angle. While plain keyword tagging users would assign the identical keyword tag to both media, semantic tagging reflects this difference in semantic meanings by assigning two different semantic tags. Therefore, semantic tagging goes a step further by allowing the users to define semantic entities and to assign semantic entity references to an image or a video. Different from plain keyword tags that are represented by their name exclusively, semantic tags consist of a name, an optional definition, a mandatory type and optional type specific information. Following the MPEG-7 standard, semantic tags are classified into the seven semantic tag types `Agent`, `Object`, `Place`, `Time`, `Event`, `Concept` and `State`. Each of these seven types allows the specification of additional type-specific information of learning contents such as geographic coordinates for locations, time stamps resp. intervals for time, parameter name/value pairs for states, etc. For example, one could not derive from a plaintext keyword `Buddha`, that it describes an agent, while for semantic tagging, `Buddha` has been modeled as a semantic entity of type agent. Semantic entities are defined based on the methods provided by the

Fig. 2. Keyword and Semantic Tagging of Multimedia Contents

`SemanticBasetypeService`. Semantic references are assigned to images using methods of `MultimediaContentService`. All these high-level content descriptions can be cross-walked with any learning standard by fixed mappings or even dynamically by mapping services [10].

Similarly, retrieval is based on the multimedia descriptions. For multimedia retrieval by plain keyword tags users can formulate keyword search expressions in propositional logic formulae using keywords as atomic propositions. For example, the keyword search expression "`Buddha` ∧ `Bamiyan` ∧ ¬(`Destroyed` ∨ `Taliban`)" would retrieve all images and videos having been assigned with the keywords Buddha and Bamiyan, but none of the two keywords Destroyed or Taliban. The concepts above are transferable to the more expressive semantic tagging, which can be easily realized on the basis of the MPEG-7 services.

4.3 Storytelling Services: Re-contextualization of Episodic Knowledge

Re-contextualization of episodic knowledge *Virtual Campfire* provides dedicated non-linear storytelling services. In order to help learning designers or learners at creating useful stories (from a structural point of view), the MOD paradigm [31] is being applied as a theoretical basis. For the sake of brevity, we only briefly discuss the major principles of this service. A detailed description can be found in [33].

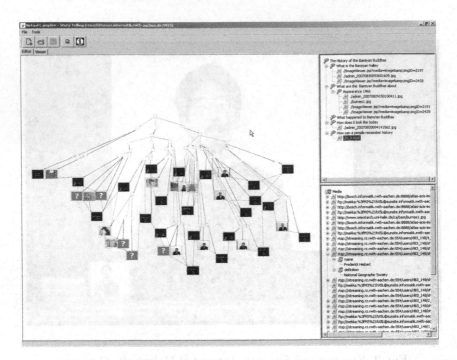

Fig. 3. A non-linear Story created in the MIST [33] Service of *Virtual Campfire*

Two dedicated user interfaces are available for the storytelling services, an editor and a player. The editor allows users to edit already existing non-linear multimedia stories or to create a new one. The player is used to consume and interact with existing non-linear multimedia stories. Besides the explicit knowledge contained in the multimedia contents the high-level semantic tags are also accessible here. These contents can be thereafter temporally arranged in the way that they depend on a certain context. At creating a story authors can create paths covering different problematic aspects along the contents. Thus, the problems addressed depend on the path selected and lead consequently to different results in a story. Figure 3 shows the editor consisting of three main elements: storyboard (left-hand side), plot (upper right-hand side), and semantic annotations (lower right-hand side). The plot in upper right panel represents the declarative knowledge captured in a story. It is rendered by a tree hierarchy which allows the further decomposition into sub-problems. In addition, problems addressed in a multimedia story can be linked to related multimedia contents. The storyboard in the left panel illustrates a visualization of episodic knowledge as paths between content elements. In addition, the decomposition of stories according to MOD paradigm into begin (B), middle (M), and end (E) is depicted. Finally, in the lower right panel additional semantic annotations can be added to any multimedia element. Thus, users may express verbal-knowledge being associated with non-verbal knowledge.

5   Conclusions and Outlook

The rapid growth of Social Software and Web 2.0 has raised new challenges to design and develop web-based learning applications. Starting from a survey of the employment of Web 2.0 technologies in the courseware management systems, we have presented *LAS* as a framework for web-based learning services in professional learning communities. As creation of new knowledge in learning processes is a discursive and multistage process, the user requirements are rapidly changing and several new features need to be integrated into web-based learning environments. In contrast to existing implementations the methodology and architecture *Virtual Campfire* is more flexible to assess the community needs over time and to integrate the community members in the community development process. Even more, the semantic zapping services of *Virtual Campfire* based on MPEG-7 provide interoperability and exchangeability of learning contents. Thus, *LAS* simplifies the support process for communities of practice drastically and offers at the same time much more flexibility in the development process.

Based on the *LAS* framework we can now easily create and deploy MPEG-7 services. With the power of the MPEG-7 services realized on top of the unique community engine *LAS* we can create web-based learning environments like *Virtual Campfire* in a systematic way. A possibly thin client is the main advantage of our approach against the-state-of-art frameworks such as AJAX [5]. With the growing importance of mobile and ubiquitous applications the server still should handle the computational complexity while clients may be able to reduce computational load with limited computational power. We will also develop a mobile *Virtual Campfire* demonstrator for the *LAS* framework, based on the different connectors available.

In our ongoing research work we are going to investigate unsupervised learning algorithms to unleash fully the power combining low-level and high-level semantics of multimedia materials in social software applications. *LAS* simplifies the learning community support process. However, the direct support of computer programmers and learning designers is still needed. In future, graphical editing support for community web sites could leave even more development responsibilities to communities.

Acknowledgements

This work was supported by German National Science Foundation (DFG) within the collaborative research centers SFB/FK 427 "Media and Cultural Communication", within the research cluster established under the excellence initiative of the German government "Ultra High-Speed Mobile Information and Communication (UMIC)" and by the 6th Framework IST programme of the EC through the Network of Excellence in Professional Learning (PROLEARN) IST-2003-507310. We thank our colleagues Nalin Sharda and Georgios Toubekis for the inspiring discussions. In addition, we thank our students D. Renzel, H. Janßen, M. Pienkos, P. M. Cuong, D. Andrikopoulos and A. Hahne for the implementation of the *Virtual Campfire* services.

References

1. ADL Technical Team. SCORM 2004 Conformance Requirements Version 1.2. September 16, 2004 (17.3.2007), http://www.adlnet.gov/downloads/files/67.cfm
2. ANSI/NISO Z39.85-2001. The Dublin Core Metadata Element Set. September 10, 2001 (19.3.2007), http://www.niso.org/standards/resources/Z39-85.pdf
3. Apache. Apache Tomcat. 2006 (17.3.2007), http://tomcat.apache.org/
4. Asleson, R., Schutta, N.T.: Foundations of Ajax (Foundation). Apress, Berkley, CA, USA (2005)
5. Benitez, A.B., Rising, H., Jörgenson, C., Leonardi, R., Bugatti, A., Hasida, K., Mehrotra, R., Murat Tekalp, A., Ekin, A., Walker, T.: Semantics of Multimedia in MPEG-7. In: Proceedings of 2002 IEEE Conference on Image Processing (ICIP 2002), Rochester, New York, USA, pp. 22–25 (Sep. 2002)
6. Del Bimbo, A.: Visual Information Retrieval. Morgan Kaufmann, San Francisco (1999)
7. Furnas, G.W., Landauer, T.K., Gomez, L.M., Dumais, S.T.: The vocabulary problem in human-system communication. Communications of the ACM 30(11), 964–971 (1987)
8. Blackboard Inc. Blackboard Academic Suite™(2007), www.blackboard.com/clientcollateral/Academic_Suite_Brochure_New.pdf
9. Brown, J.S., Duguid, P.: The Social Life of Information. Harvard Business School Press, Cambridge (2000)
10. Chatti, M.A., Klamma, R., Quix, C., Kensche, D.: LM-DTM: An Environment for XML-Based, LIP/PAPI-Compliant Deployment. In: Transformation and Matching of Learner Models. In: Goodyear, P., et al. (eds.) Proc. of the 5th Intl. Conf. on Advanced Learning Technologies (ICALT 2005), Kaohsiung, Taiwan, July 5-8, 2005, pp. 567–569 (2005),
11. Daft, R., Lengel, R.: Organizational Informations Requirements, Media Richness and Structural Design. Management Science 32(5), 554–571 (1986)
12. Dublin Core Metadata Initiative. Dublin core metadata element set, version 1.1: Reference description. Technical report, Dublin Core Metadata Initiative (1999) (19.3.2007), http://dublincore.org/documents/dces/
13. Grote, K., Klamma, R.: Media and Semantic Relations: Comparison of Individual and Organizational Knowledge Stuctures. Talk at Seminar Knowledge Management: An Interdisciplinary Approach, Schloss Dagstuhl, Germany, (July 9-14, 2000)
14. IEEE. IEEE Draft Standard for Learning Object Metadata (LOM). IEEE 1484.12.1-2002, (2002) [23.3.1997], http://ltsc.ieee.org/wg12/files/LOM_1484_12_1_v1_Final_Draft.pdf
15. imc. Advanced Learning Solutions. (2007) [19.3.2007], http://www.imc.de/
16. ISO/IEC. Information technology – Multimedia content description interface - - Part 5: Multimedia description schemes. Intl. Organization for Standardization (2003)
17. Jarke, M., Klamma, R.: Transkriptivität als informatisches Designprinzip. Mediale Spuren in rechnergestützten Entwicklungsprozessen. In: Fehrmann, G., Linz, E., Epping-Jäger, C. (eds.) Spuren Lektüren. Praktiken des Symbolischen, Festschrift für Ludwig Jäger zum 60. Geburtstag, München: Fink, (in German) pp. 105–120 (2005)
18. Java. J2EE Java Platform Enterprise Edition Specification 2006 (19.3.2007), http://jcp.org/aboutJava/communityprocess/pfd/jsr244

19. Jäger, L.: Transkriptivität. In: Jäger, L., Stanitzek, G. (eds.) Transkribieren – Medien/Lektüre, Wilhelm Fink Verlag, Munich (in German) (2002)
20. Klamma, R., Spaniol, M., Cao, Y.: MPEG-7 Compliant Community Hosting. In: Lux, M., et al. (eds.) MPEG and Multimedia Metadata Community Workshop Results 2005, J.UKM Special Issue (Journal of Universal Knowledge Management), vol. 1(1), pp. 36–44 (2006)
21. Kosch, H.: Distributed Multimedia Database Technologies Supported by MPEG-7 and MPEG-21. CRC Press, Boca Raton (2003)
22. Koper, R., Tattersall, C.: Learning Design: A Handbook on Modelling and Delivering Networked Education and Training. Springer, Heidelberg (2005)
23. Lave, J., Wenger, E.: Situated Learning: Legitimate Peripheral Participation. Cambridge University Press, Cambridge (1991)
24. Marlow, C., Naaman, M., Boyd, D., Davis, M.: HT06, Tagging Paper, Taxonomy, Flickr, Academic Article, To Read. In: HYPERTEXT 2006: Proceedings of the seventeenth conference on Hypertext and hypermedia, pp. 31–40 (2006),
25. Moodle Docs. The documentation for Moodle (2006) [19.3.2007]. http://docs.moodle.org/
26. Nohr, H.: Elektronisch vermittelte Wissenskommunikation und Medienwahl. Information – Wissenschaft und Praxis (in German) 53(3), 141–148 (2002)
27. Nonaka, I., Takeuchi, H.: The Knowledge-creating Company. Oxford University Press, Oxford (1995)
28. O'Reilly, T.: What Is Web 2.0 – Design Patterns and Business Models for the Next Generation of Software (2005) [19.3.2007]. www.oreilly.com, http://www.oreillynet.com/pub/a/oreilly/tim/news/2005/09/30/what-is-web-20.html
29. Preece, J.: Online Communities: Designing Usability, Supporting Sociability. John Wiley & Sons, Chichester (2000)
30. Schwabe, G.: Mediensynchronizität – Theorie und Anwendung bei Gruppenarbeit und Lernen. In: Hesse, F., Friedrich, H. (eds.) Partizipation und Interaktion im virtuellen Seminar. Waxmann, Münster, pp. 111–134 (2001)
31. Sharda, N.: Movement Oriented Design: A New Paradigm for Multimedia Design. International Journal of Lateral Computing (IJLC) 1(1), 7–14 (2005)
32. Spaniol, M., Klamma, R., Janßen, H., Renzel, D.: LAS: A Lightweight Application Server for MPEG-7 Services in Community Engines. In:Tochtermann, K., Maurer, H. (eds.) Proceedings of I-KNOW2006, 6th International Conference on Knowledge Management, Graz, Austria, J.UCS (Journal of Universal Computer Science) Proceedings, September 6-8, 2006, pp. 592–599 (2006)
33. Spaniol, M., Klamma, R., Sharda, N., Jarke, M.: Web-Based Learning with Nonlinear Multimedia Stories. In: Liu, W., Li, Q., Lau, R.W.H. (eds.) ICWL 2006. LNCS, vol. 4181, pp. 249–263. Springer, Heidelberg (2006)
34. Spaniol, M., Klamma, R.: MEDINA: A Semi-Automatic Dublin Core to MPEG-7 Converter for Collaboration and Knowledge Management in Multimedia Repositories. In: Tochtermann, K., Maurer, H. (eds.) Proceedings of I-KNOW 2005, 5th Intl. Conf. on Knowledge Management, Graz, Austria, J.UCS (Journal of Universal Computer Science), June 29 - July 1, 2005, pp. 136–144 (2005)
35. Wenger, E.: Communities of Practice: Learning, Meaning, and Identity. Cambridge University Press, Cambridge (1998)
36. Zope, Plone, CMS. Plone Content Management System (2006) (19.3.2007), http://www.plone.org
37. Zope, Python, Web-Applications. Zope Web Application Framework (2006) (19.3.2007), http://www.zope.org

Addressing Context-Awareness and Standards Interoperability in E-Learning: A Service-Oriented Framework Based on IRS III

Stefan Dietze, Alessio Gugliotta, and John Domingue

Knowledge Media Institute, The Open University, Walton Hall,
MK7 6AA Milton Keynes, UK
{s.dietze, a.gugliotta, j.b.domingue}@open.ac.uk

Abstract. Current technologies aimed at supporting learning goals primarily follow a data and metadata-centric paradigm. They provide the learner with appropriate learning content packages containing the learning process description as well as the learning resources. Whereas process metadata is usually based on a certain standard specification – such as ADL SCORM or the IMS Learning Design – the used learning resources – data or services - are specific to predefined learning contexts, and they are allocated manually at design-time. Therefore, a content package cannot consider the actual learning context, since this is only known at runtime of a learning process. These facts limit the reusability of a content package across different standards and contexts. To overcome these issues, this paper proposes an innovative Semantic Web Service-based approach that changes this data- and metadata-based paradigm to a context-adaptive service-oriented approach. In this approach, the learning process is semantically described as a standard-independent process model decomposed into several learning goals. These goals are accomplished at runtime, based on the automatic allocation of the most appropriate service. As a result, we address the dynamic adaptation to specific context and - providing the appropriate mappings to established metadata standards - we enable the reuse of the defined semantic learning process model across different standards. To illustrate the application of our approach and to prove its feasibility, a prototypical application based on an initial use case scenario is proposed.

Keywords: E-Learning, Semantic Web Services, Ontologies, Learning Process, Context Adaptibility, Standards Interoperability.

1 Introduction

E-Learning is aimed at supporting individuals in fulfilling a specific learning need within a specific situation through the use of information and communications technology. The current state of the art is mainly represented by approaches based on software systems – e. g. learning content management systems (LCMS) – which provide a learner with composite learning contents – the so called Learning Objects (LO). Several metadata standards are available for supporting the interoperability

H. Leung et al. (Eds.): ICWL 2007, LNCS 4823, pp. 174–183, 2008.
© Springer-Verlag Berlin Heidelberg 2008

between different learning software platforms; they aim to provide a common specification for describing complex learning objects as well as the sequencing which has to be followed by the learner to fulfil his current learning need. Widely established E-Learning standards are IEEE LOM [6], ADL SCORM [1] – based on IMS Simple Sequencing - or IMS Learning Design (IMS LD) [7]. Complex learning objects are composite content packages containing the learning resources as well as its metadata. Thus, learning support usually follows the following practices:

- Use of specific metadata and learning resources – whether data or services - to support a specific learning objective
- Resources are manually associated with specific learning objectives based on the subjective appraisals of an individual learning designer
- Learning resources are allocated at design-time, i. e. when the actual learning context is not known

Due to these facts, the following limitations have been identified (cf. [2], [8], [4]):

L1. Limited appropriateness and dynamic adaptability to actual learning contexts. It is assumed that every learning objective occurs in a specific context which, for instance, is defined by the preferences of the actual learner – e. g. his native language or his technical platform. Learning data is allocated at design-time of a learning process – i.e. when the composite content package is developed. This limits the appropriateness of the data to the actual learning context, since the actual learning context can only be considered at runtime of a learning process. Moreover, the use of data excludes the dynamic adaptability a priori. In parallel to data-centric approaches, analogous issues can also be observed with service-oriented approaches. However, in that case, these issues are related to the allocation of services only.

L2. Limited reusability across different learning contexts and metadata standards. Due to L1, for every different learning context or specific learner requirement a new learning content package has to be developed. For example, a learning package suiting the needs of a learner with specific preferences – e. g. his native language – cannot be used for other contexts or learners having distinct requirements. Since metadata is described based on standard-specific specifications, an individual content package cannot be reused across different standards.

L3. High development costs. Due to L1 and L2, high development costs have to be taken into account when developing standard-compliant E-Learning packages.

To overcome these issues, the approach described in this paper changes the current data- and metadata-based paradigm to a dynamic service-oriented approach based on Semantic Web Services (SWS) technology.

SWS enable the automatic discovery, composition and invocation of available Web services. Based on the semantic descriptions of functional capabilities of available Web services, a SWS broker automatically selects and invokes Web services appropriate to achieve a given user goal.

IRS-III [3], the Internet Reasoning Service, is an implementation of a SWS broker environment. It provides the representational and reasoning mechanisms, which enable the dynamic interoperability and orchestration between services as well as the mediation between their semantic concepts. IRS-III utilizes a SWS library based on the reference ontology Web Service Modelling Ontology (WSMO) [12] and the OCML representation language [5] to store semantic descriptions of Web services and knowledge domains.

WSMO is a formal ontology for describing the various aspects of Web services, in order to enable the automation of their discovery, composition, mediation and invocation. The meta-model of WSMO defines four top level elements: *Ontologies*, *Goals*, *Web Services* and *Mediators*. Whereas *Ontologies* describe the terminology and its semantics used by the other WSMO elements, *Web Service* describes the capabilities and interfaces of a particular service; *Goal* describes a task from the user perspective; and *Mediator* solves data and process interoperability issues that arise when handling heterogeneous systems.

In our approach, we abstract from learning data as well as existing learning process models. We semantically describe a learning process as a composition of learning goals. Learning goals are mapped to WSMO goals; in this fashion, we exploit the benefits of SWS in our framework. Moreover, our semantic model of learning processes is independent from any metadata standard; to achieve compliancy with them, we can be link to multiple metadata standards by providing the appropriate mappings.

2   Semantic Web Service Based E-Learning Applications: Vision and Approach

This section describes our vision as well as the approach to support context-adaptive learning designs. Moreover, we use the formalization introduced in the previous section to highlights the benefits of our approach.

2.1   Vision: Context-Adaptation Through Automatic Service Selection and Invocation

To overcome the limitations L1 – L3 described in Section 1, we consider the automatic allocation and invocation of functionalities at runtime. A typical learning related service functionality provides the learner with, for instance, appropriate learning content or topic-specific discussion facilities. Learning processes are described semantically in terms of composition of user objectives (goals) and abstract from specific data and metadata standards. The most adequate functionality is selected and invoked dynamically regarding the demands and requirements of the actual specific context. This enables a highly dynamic adaptation to different learning contexts and learner needs.

This vision is radically distinctive to the current state of the art in this area, since it shifts from a data- and metadata-centric paradigm to a context-adaptive service-oriented approach. Moreover, using adequate mappings, our standard-independent process models can be translated into existing metadata standards in order to enable a reuse within existing standard-compliant runtime environments.

Addressing limitations L1 and L2, we consequently reduce the efforts of creating learning process models (L3): one unique learning process model can adapt dynamically to different process contexts and can be translated into different process metadata standards.

2.2 Approach: Semantic Abstraction from Process Metadata, Functionalities and Data

Our approach is fundamentally based on utilizing SWS technologies to realize the following principles:

P1. Abstraction from learning data and learning functionalities
P2. Abstraction from learning process metadata standards

To support these principles, we introduce several layers as well as a mapping between them in order to achieve a gradual abstraction (Figure 1):

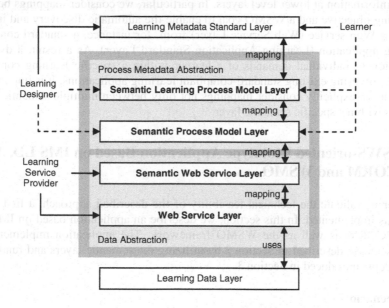

Fig. 1. Semantic layer architecture for supporting context-adaptive learning designs

Abstraction from Learning Data and Functionalities. To abstract from existing learning data and content we consider a Web Service Layer. It operates on top of the data and exposes the functionalities appropriate to fulfill specific learning objectives. This first step enables a dynamic supply of appropriate learning data to suit a specific context and objective. Services exposed at this layer may make use of semantic descriptions of available learning data to accomplish their functionalities.

In order to abstract from these functionalities (Web services), we introduce an additional layer – the Semantic Web Service Layer. This layer enables the dynamic selection, composition and invocation of appropriate Web services for a specific learning context. This is achieved on the basis of formal semantic; i.e. declarative descriptions of available services that enable the dynamic matching of service capabilities to specific user goals.

Abstraction from Learning Process Metadata. A first layer concerned with the abstraction from current learning process metadata standards is the Semantic Learning Process Model Layer. It allows the description of processes within the domain of E-Learning in terms of higher level domain concepts - e. g. learning goals, learners or learning contexts. This layer is mapped to semantic representations of current learning metadata standards in order to enable the interoperability between different standards. To achieve a further abstraction from domain specific process models – whether it is e. g. a learning process, a business process or a communication process – we consider an upper level process model layer – Semantic Process Model Layer. This layer introduces for instance the mapping between learning objectives and business objectives to support all kind of organizational processes.

Mappings. Based on mappings between the described layers, upper level layers can utilize information at lower level layers. In particular, we consider mappings between a learning objective and a WSMO goal to enable the automatic discovery and invocation of a Web service (Web Service Layer) from, for instance, a standard-compliant learning application (Learning Application Standard Layer). As a result, a dynamic adaptation to individual demands of a learner within a specific learning context is achieved by using existing standard-compliant learning applications. It is important to note that we explicitly consider mappings not only between multiple semantic layers but also within a specific semantic layer.

3   A SWS-oriented Prototype Application Based on IMS LD, ADL SCORM and WSMO

In order to validate the technical feasibility of the described approach, a first prototype was implemented. In this section, we describe an application based on IMS LD, ADL SCORM as well as the WSMO framework. The application implements the initial scenario described in Section 2 by utilizing the semantic layers and fundamental concepts introduced in Section 3.

3.1   Scenario

To report a simple - but concrete - scenario, we consider several learners that request to learn different languages: English, German and Italian. It is assumed, that all learners have different preferences – e.g. their spoken native language – which have to be considered. For example a German native speaker requiring to learn the language "English" should be provided with German learning resources to teach the English language. Furthermore, we are going to support two different metadata standards – ADL SCORM and IMS LD. Following the current approach of creating a standard-compliant learning content package, for every individual learner a specific package would have to be created in order to achieve a high level of appropriateness.

In addition, for every metadata standard which has to be supported, a new standard-compliant process model has to be created. Applying our SWS-based approach, we enable all learners to utilize the same standard-compliant learning package – respectively learning process model – which dynamically adapts to the actual learning context and learning need.

3.2 SWS-oriented Architecture

Our current implementation makes use of standard runtime environments: IRS III [3] is used as SWS broker as well as development environment for WSMO descriptions; the Reload software suite [11] is used for editing and runtime processing of IMS LD and ADL SCORM content. Figure 2 outlines the Semantic Web Service Oriented Architecture (SWSOA) used in the current prototype. The defined architecture realizes all of the principles described in Section 3.

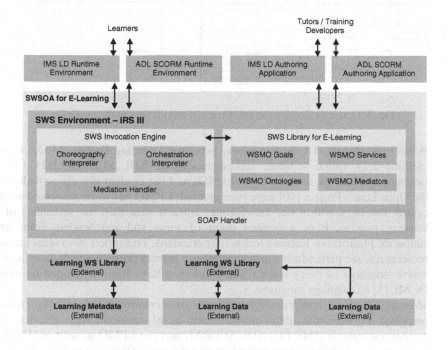

Fig. 2. SWS-based software architecture as utilized in the prototype application

To support the scenario described in Section 2, the following elements had to be provided within the architecture presented above:

1. *Learning Web services libraries.* Web services were provided to support the authentication of the learner, the retrieval of semantic learner profiles, learning metadata and learning contents. Web services utilized in this demonstrator were partly developed within the LUISA project [9].

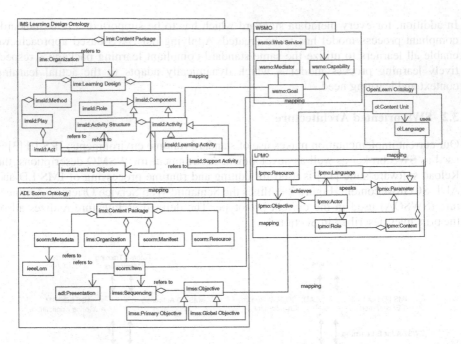

Fig. 3. Ontological mappings implemented and utilized in the prototype

2. *WSMO Ontologies.* To implement the Semantic Learning Process Model Layer (Section 2.2), initial semantic representations of ADL SCORM, IMS LD, a Learning Process Model Ontology (LPMO) and the content objects provided by the Open Learn Project [10] have been created. LPMO has to be perceived as the central ontology within our architecture, since it describes the semantics of a learning process from a general point of view and independent from any supported platform or learning technology standard. To support individual learner preferences, we particularly consider semantic learner profiles which describe the native language of every learner. All ontologies have been developed by using OCML [5] as ontology language.

3. *Mappings between semantic layers as well as metadata standards.* We created mappings between the initial implementations of semantic representations of metadata standards (IMS LD, ADL SCORM) and the LPMO as well as WSMO. For instance, we defined a mapping between the *lpmo:Objective* and the objective description used within the IMS LD metadata (*imsld:Objective*). Moreover, semantic learning object descriptions based on the LPMO were mapped to OpenLearn content units (*ol:Content Unit*), whereas the language of a content unit (*ol:Language*) was mapped to the native language of a learner (*lpmo:Language*). Since the Semantic Process Model Layer (Section 2.2) is not currently fully implemented, the LPMO objective is directly mapped to a WSMO goal. Figure 3 depicts the main ontological mappings as defined in our prototype. The defined mappings are performed at runtime as specific functionalities. These functionalities are exposed as Web services, which are part of an external learning Web services Library.

4. *WSMO Goal, Web Service, and Mediator descriptions* of the available Web services, based on the concepts defined in the WSMO ontologies.
5. *Standard-compliant content packages describing the learning activities.* IMS LD and ADL SCORM compliant learning processes were provided and included into IMS content packages. Instead of grounding the learning activities to static learning data, we link to the respective WSMO goal descriptions. This mapping is achieved by associating a learning activity within the learning metadata with HTTP references to a Web applet enabling to request the achievement of a specific WSMO goal from the SWS broker (Figure 2).

3.3 Dynamic Adaptation at Runtime

At runtime, an end-user (learner) accesses a standard-compliant player. He/she loads the content packages compliant with IMS LD and ADL SCORM that were developed as described in bullet 5 of the previous section. The learning application then sequentially presents all of the learning activities that would have to be performed. The WSMO goal associated with such an activity is invoked, and the SWS broker dynamically selects and invokes the Web service exposing the appropriate capabilities to achieve the specified goal.

First, an initial activity authenticates the learner and retrieves the semantic learner profile description. At this point, the learner preferences are set within the player environment. In the same way, when the learner selects an individual objective within the standard content package, our infrastructure dynamically selects and invokes semantic Web services according to his/her preferences and stated objectives. For instance, if a learner is authenticated as an English-speaking person (*lpmo:Language=English*) and uses an ADL SCORM-based package to learn the language German, a *scorm:Item* with the *imss:Objective=Learn German* is mapped to a WSMO *Learn-German-Goal*. The accomplishment of such a goal involves the selection, orchestration and invocation of different Web services, which perform the described mappings and retrieve appropriate learning content. The following OCML code listing shows a portion of the capability description of a Web service, which is able to provide learning content to teach German. Specifically, the capability assumes that the objective provided by the ADL SCORM package has to be "Learn German".

```
(DEF-CLASS ACHIEVE-OBJECTIVE-GERMAN-WS-CAPABILITY
   (CAPABILITY)
   ?CAPABILITY
     ((USED-MEDIATOR :VALUE ACHIEVE OBJECTIVE-GERMAN-MED)

        (HAS-ASSUMPTION
           :VALUE
           (KAPPA
              (?WEB-SERVICE) (= (WSMO-ROLE-VALUE ?WEB-
              SERVICE 'HAS-IMSS-OBJECTIVE)"Learn German")))
```

Listing 1. Partial source code of a Web service capability description

Such a Web service orchestrates the following WSMO Web services: (i) the *imss:Objective* is mapped to the *lpmo:Objective* concept; (ii) the *lpmo:Objective* is used to retrieve the semantic metadata of an appropriate learning object; (iii) the retrieved learning object identifier is used to obtain an Open Learn learning unit appropriate to the individual language of the learner and its current objective. Each of these goals is accomplished by a distinct Web service dynamically selected at runtime. The retrieved learning object is finally presented in the ADL SCORM runtime environment.

Fig. 4. Reload ADL SCORM 2004 Viewer while dynamically invoking SWS to retrieve appropriate learning content

Figure 4 depicts a screenshot of the Reload ADL SCORM 2004 Package Viewer while presenting a standard-compliant ADL SCORM 2004 content package and dynamically invoking SWS appropriate to fulfil the given learning objective "Learn German". Besides several limitations, our current prototype implements the basic approach of a standard-compliant SWSOA for E-Learning, as described in this paper.

4   Conclusion

Our approach - the support of learning objectives based on a dynamic invocation of SWS at runtime of a learning process model - follows an innovative approach and is distinctive to the current state of the art in this area. By using SWS technology, we overcome the limitations described in section 1 and support a high level of standard-compliancy and reusability within existing runtime environments, since it is fundamentally based on compliancy with current E-Learning metadata standards. In particular, the following contributions should be taken into account:

- Dynamic adaptation to specific learning contexts at runtime
- Automatic allocation of learning resources based on comprehensive semantics
- High reusability across learning contexts

- Platform- and standard-independence
- Reuse and integration of available learning resources
- Decrease of development costs

Since our framework is currently developed to some extent only, next steps have to be concerned with the implementation of complete ontological representations of the introduced semantic layers as well as of current E-Learning metadata standards and their mappings. For example, currently the Semantic Process Model Layer is not fully implemented and semantic mappings between the Learning Process Model Ontology and available process metadata standards are only developed in extracts. Nevertheless, the availability of appropriate Web services aimed at supporting specific process objectives has to be perceived as an important prerequisite for developing SWS based applications. To provide more valid quantifications of the expected benefits, further case studies are needed to illustrate the formalized measurements introduced in the sections above. Besides that, future work could also be concerned with the mapping of semantic process models across different process dimensions – e. g. business processes or learning processes to enable a complete integration of a SWSOA in an organizational process environment.

References

1. Advanced Distributed Learning (ADL) SCORM 2004 Specification, http://www.adlnet.org
2. Amorim, R.R., Lama, M., Sánchez, E., Riera, A., Vila, X.A.: A Learning Design Ontology based on the IMS Specification. Journal of Educational Technology & Society 9(1), 38–57 (2006)
3. Cabral, L., Domingue, J., Galizia, S., Gugliotta, A., Norton, B., Tanasescu, V., Pedrinaci, C.: IRS-III: A Broker for Semantic Web Services based Applications. In: Cruz, I., Decker, S., Allemang, D., Preist, C., Schwabe, D., Mika, P., Uschold, M., Aroyo, L.M. (eds.) ISWC 2006. LNCS, vol. 4273, Springer, Heidelberg (2006)
4. Collis, B., Strijker, A.: Technology and Human Issues in Reusing Learning Objects. Journal of Interactive Media in Education, 2004 (4). Special Issue on the Educational Semantic Web (2004), http://www-jime.open.ac.uk/2004/4
5. Domingue, J., Motta, E., Corcho Garcia, O.: Knowledge Modelling in WebOnto and OCML: A User Guide (1999), http://kmi.open.ac.uk/projects/webonto/user_guide.2.4.pdf
6. Duval, E.: 1484.12.1 IEEE Standard for learning Object Metadata, IEEE Learning Technology Standards Committee (2002), http://ltsc.ieee.org/wg12/
7. IMS Learning Design Specification, http://www.imsglobal.org
8. Knight, C., Gašević, D., Richards, G.: An Ontology-Based Framework for Bridging Learning Design and Learning Content. Journal of Educational Technology & Society 9(1), 23–37 (2006)
9. LUISA Project - Learning Content Management System Using Innovative Semantic Web Services Architecture, http://www.luisa-project.eu/www/
10. Open Learn Project: Online Educational Resources, http://openlearn.open.ac.uk/
11. Reload Project, http://www.reload.ac.uk/
12. WSMO Working Group, D2v1.0: Web Service Modeling Ontology (WSMO). WSMO Working Draft (2004), http://www.wsmo.org/2004/d2/v1.0/

Extending CORDRA for Systematic Reuse

Timothy K. Shih[1], Freya H. Lin[2], Yue-Lin Du[1], Louis R. Chao[1], and Won Kim[3]

[1] Dept. of Computer Science and Information Eng., Tamkang University, Taiwan
[2] Dept of Information Management, Chihlee Institute of Technology, Taiwan
[3] School of Information and Communication Eng., Sungkyunkwan University, Korea
FreyaH.Lin@gmail.com

Abstract. The SCORM (Sharable Content Object Reference Model) specification defines metadata of learning objects, which are used as the elementary reusable components in distance learning. The CORDRA (Content Object Repository Discovery and Registration/Resolution Architecture) specification provides a common architecture for the resolution, discovery, and sharing of these learning objects. They define standardized ways in which learning objects can be discovered and reused by content designers. However, the current CORDRA and the definition of objects in SCORM only allow an object to be copied, updated, and re-organized in a new content aggregation, which is used as a delivery package to end users. This paper proposes a revised CORDRA architecture and a reusability mechanism to make instruction design easier. We propose a structure called a reusability tree for tracking the history of reuse of learning objects in CORDRA. This paper also defines the notions of similarity and diversity of learning objects to make easier for users to precisely search for reusable learning objects, with additional meaningful information to support instruction designs.

Keywords: SCORM, CORDRA, Reusability, Learning Object Metadata, Distributed System, Distance Learning.

1 Introduction

The Sharable Content Object Reference Model (SCORM) [2] has become a de facto international standard adopted by the distance learning community. Although one of the most significant contributions of SCORM is the definition of Learning Object Metadata (i.e., IEEE LOM) for object search, very few reusable learning objects (LOs) follow the requirements of IEEE LOM [6] due to the complexity of metadata definitions. Authoring tools always suggest users to fill in appropriate metadata items one-by-one after creating an LO. However, such tedious and complicated demands on the users have led most course creators to abandon this important standard. This explains why to date LOs have not been widely shared and reused. In our earlier work, we proposed a Metadata Wizard framework [5] based on a deduction engine to fill in metadata automatically. The framework simultaneously lessens the creators' work and increases the completeness degree of metadata, which in turn can potentially increase searchability. As a significant extension of this work, in this paper we address systematic reusability.

H. Leung et al. (Eds.): ICWL 2007, LNCS 4823, pp. 184–195, 2008.
© Springer-Verlag Berlin Heidelberg 2008

For an LO to be reusable, not only the LO must contain sufficient descriptions of metadata but the repository must store the LO in a searchable and accessible manner. However, various platforms, schemas and frameworks [7, 9, 11] are not interoperable, resulting in low sharability and reusability of course contents. The user needs to find out who else has useful LOs (with metadata to facilitate search). When someone creates a new LO, it must be made known to others. The Content Object Repository Discovery and Registration/Resolution Architecture (CORDRA) [1] addresses such issues.

CORDRA is described as "an open, standards-based model for how to design and implement software systems for the purposes of discovery, sharing and reuse of learning content through the establishment of interoperable federations of learning content repositories". The CORDRA specification is a joint work among ADL, CNRI (Corporation for National Research Initiatives, USA) and LSAL (Learning Systems Architecture Lab, CMU, USA). Its architecture aims to provide a way to resolve the conflict of name space by means of a unique handler for each LO. It also provides a way to allow discovery and sharing of LOs. However, CORDRA only suggests the discovery and resolution solutions. Relations among reusable objects and the history of using these objects are not maintained. As a consequence, if a user obtains a large number of reference objects in a particular search, the user needs to look at these references one by one to find their relations and the usage history. This discourages reuse. A similar situation occurs when one uses an Internet search engine.

In this paper, we systematically reconsider reusability in CORDRA by examining various potential reuse situations. An LO can be reused in several stages by different users via different topology. Thus, the evolution of reuse of a particular LO in CORDRA can be organized in a data structure that we call the reusability tree. In general, a reusability tree is distributed; it exists in several repositories, which constitute a federated CORDRA.

This paper makes the following contributions:

1. We propose the reusability tree for maintaining relationships among LOs, so that the usage history, copyright, etc. of LOs can be tracked.
2. Two primary subsystems of the CORDRA framework have been implemented, allowing registration and discovering of LOs.
3. We develop notions of the similarity function and diversity function as a basis for an evaluation mechanism for usability.

The organization of this paper is as follows. Section 2 proposes a revised CORDRA architecture and the reusability tree. An implementation of the architecture as a distributed system is described in Section 3. Section 3 proposes a number of evaluation functions to support search, including such notions as similarity and diversity of LOs. Section 4 concludes the paper.

2   Extending CORDRA with a Reuse Model

An LO may be regarded as an object similar to a class object that is used in software development. When an LO is reused, a link (edge) and a node are created in the reusability tree to incorporate changes. (We note that the reusability tree is strictly speaking a directed acyclic graph.) There are several possible types of changes, including metadata changes, structure changes, sequencing changes and multiple type changes. In this paper, we only focus on the metadata and structure changes.

As an illustration of the reusability tree, Figure 1 shows the history of evolution of a learning object LO_1. The LO is retrieved and used by three different authors, with changed LOs (i.e., LO_2, LO_3, and LO_4) inserted into the repository. The reusability tree keeps track of the association among these objects. When a new user issues a query (i.e., LO_q), this query is compared with all LOs in the repository. Since LO_q has three descendants (i.e., CPU History, CPU Category, and CPU Structure), it is likely that LO_q matches only LO_1 and LO_2. In a practical implementation, since the similarity between LO_q and LO_3 is below a threshold[1], LO_3 is disregarded. Similarly, LO_4 is not recommended. Therefore, the new user only finds LO_1 and LO_2. However, when a user searches for an LO, additional information related to the query plays an important role. That is, information such as "CPU Market" and "Microprogrammed Control" could be meaningful to the user. With the reusability tree, we introduce a set of measurement methods, along with their implementation methods, to help the user discover such additional information.

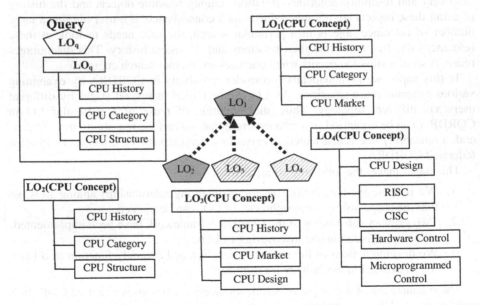

Fig. 1. An Illustration of the Reusability Tree

In practice, the reusability tree is a distributed structure since different LOs are stored in different repositories. When the user updates an LO, the distributed structure is maintained. After the user completes the modification and registers a new LO in the CORDRA repository, a link is built with the updated property identified. The relations and links are revealed when the user searches for an LO. We will elaborate on the advantages of the reusability tree in section 3.

---

[1] A practical system needs to set a threshold to screen out mismatched items. Thus, a threshold is used to measure similarity.

3   The MINE Registry – An Instance of CORDRA

The federated CORDRA is a two-level hierarchy. The first level describes a federated common infrastructure, and the second level describes the interconnection of local repositories. This two-level hierarchy is a minimal but sufficient design to build a universal common repository to store all LOs defined in SCORM.

However, the CORDRA architecture should be enhanced to address the complex LO discovery process. Additional servers to support advanced search should be considered. Techniques in distributed computing should be incorporated in the design of the architecture. Thus, we have developed an instance of CORDRA (a practical implementation as a test bed of our proposed mechanisms). We call the system the Registry that consists of two primary subsystems: Registration Subsystem, Discovery Subsystem.

3.1   Registration Subsystem

The first subsystem allows users to add an LO to the repository. Components of this subsystem are illustrated in Figure 2. The process of adding object is called registration in CORDRA. Our architecture is based on [12], with additional functions such as maintaining the reusability tree. However, LOs created may not be entirely new, as LOs may adopt properties from others with updates. Thus, the subsystem for adding LOs is somewhat complex. The association among LOs must be maintained in a reusability tree. In Registry, the subsystem for registering an LO, consists of 8 key steps, as illustrated by the numbers in Figure 2.

1. The Client Computer uploads LO(s) to Content Object Registry.
2. The Content Object Registry extracts metadata from the uploaded LO(s).
3. The Content Object Registry requests the Local Handle Service to generate handle(s) for the LO(s).
   a. If the LO is a newly created object, a new Object ID is generated (by using GUID function).
   b. If the LO is an updated object, a concatenated Object ID is used (i.e., 2096/123-235 is an object updated from 2096/123, where 2096 is a Local handle assigned by CNRI).
4. The Local Handle Service returns the handle(s) of LO(s) to the Content Object Registry.
5. The association between Object ID and Metadata ID is stored in the Content Object Registry.
6. The Content Object Registry stores the physical multimedia objects of the LOs in the Content Server and stores the metadata in the Master Content Catalog.
7. The Master Content Catalog creates or updates a reusability tree. Different properties should be addressed in the reusability tree. The Master Content Catalog has centralized control of the reusability tree.
8. The Content Object Registry modifies the URL(s) of handle(s) previously created by the Local Handel Service. The URL(s) is incorporated in the address of the Content Server.

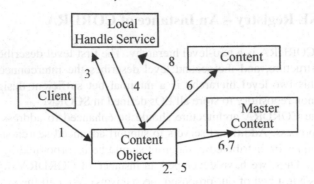

Fig. 2. Components of the Subsystem for Learning Object Registration

Interested readers are welcome to visit our demo website at http://www.mine. tku.edu.tw

3.2 Discovery Subsystem

The second subsystem allows users to search and retrieve LOs from the repository. The discovery subsystem is also distributed. Figure 3 illustrates the subsystem. A Global Handle Proxy Server is included and multiple instances of Local Handle Service can be used. Similar to registering an LO, the search for existing objects takes several steps.

1. The Client computer sends search criteria to the Learning Object Search Engine. The search process can be incremental (i.e., criteria is rewritable) to include sufficient metadata.
2. The Learning Object Search Engine finds proper LOs (or reusability trees) by pooling the Master Content Catalog and keeps the retrieved Metadata IDs.
3. The Learning Object Search Engine and the Content Object Registry finds the associated Object IDs for each Metadata IDs.
4. The Learning Object Search Engine passes the Object IDs (or reusability trees) and Metadata IDs back to the Client Computer.
5. The Client Computer selects the LOs to be downloaded by providing the Object IDs to the Global Handle Proxy Server.
6. The Global Handle Proxy Server uses the Handle IDs and uses a naming authority (provided by the CNRI) to find the Local Handle Service.
7. The Local Handle Service finds the physical URLs of the LOs (or reusability trees) and passes them to the Client Computer.
8. The Client computer downloads the physical multimedia files of the LOs (or reusability trees) from the Content Server according to the URLs.

The search criteria are the most important factor in discovering desired LOs. However, due to the number of IEEE LOM metadata items, it is still inconvenient for general users to precisely provide or select metadata. We introduce a concept called *rewritable metadata template*. Since metadata in SCORM is used as a search specification,

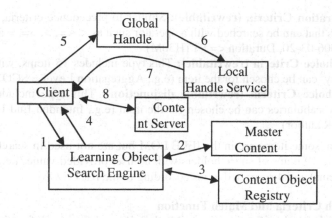

Fig. 3. Components of the Subsystem for Learning Object Discovery and Reuse

the specification should be flexible so that the recall ratio of search is reasonable. Users can narrow down the search range to achieve a higher precision ratio by incrementally adding/increasing constraints to the rewritable metadata template.

Metadata items defined in SCORM may be mandatory or optional. However, for the search process, metadata items can be defined in a different manner as follows:

- **Mandatory Search Criteria:** The mandatory search criteria as the minimal requirement for guaranteeing a certain recall ratio for a search. For instance, in a particular implementation, only "Title" is included in the mandatory search criteria.
- **Rewritable Search Criteria:** Other metadata items can be defined as rewritable search criteria. These criteria can be applied to sharpen a search specification such that the precision ratio is increased. For instance, additional keywords are added to a conjunctive logical expression. Also, the minimal version of the Web browser for delivering the LOs can be increased to narrow down the search result.

The use of the rewritable metadata template as an incremental search interface is based on a careful analysis of the fundamental characteristics of metadata items. IEEE LOM (part of SCORM) defines 77 metadata items. In order to bring some sense of order to this, we classify them into the following six types:

1. **Precise Criteria (mandatory):** There are 14 items that must be precisely described (e.g., Title = "Photoshop Tutorial", Language = "en"). According to the IEEE LOM, each element appears at most once in an LO.
2. **Incremental Criteria (rewritable):** There are 12 items that can be incrementally revised to constraint a search specification. For instance, one can issue Keyword = "Tamkang University", Keyword = "Tamkang University AND Multimedia Lab", or Keyword = "Tamkang University AND Multimedia Lab AND Freya Lin"), with additional constraints added one-by-one. In the IEEE LOM, each element can appear many times.
3. **Precedence Criteria (rewritable):** There are 4 items that can be searched with a operator, $<$, $<=$, $>$, $>=$, $=$ and $!=$, or the combination (e.g., $512 < Size <= 1024$).

4. **Time/Duration Criteria (rewritable):** Similar to precedence criteria, there are 5
   time items that can be searched with a operator such as $<$, $<=$, $>$, $>=$, $=$ and $!=$ (e.g.,
   Date $>$ 2006-03-20, Duration $<=$ PT1H30M).
5. **Single Choice Criteria (rewritable):** This type includes 15 items, with only one
   vocabulary[2] can be chosen for the item (e.g., Aggregation Level = SCO).
6. **Many Choice Criteria (rewritable disjunction):** This type includes 4 items,
   multiple vocabularies can be chosen for the item (e.g., Intended End User Role =
   teacher OR author).

In addition, some items are in the IEEE LOM but are not used in search specification. These are 19 items of space holders with no user provided value (i.e., the root of
a group of items) and 4 restricted items according to the IEEE LOM.

3.2.1 Search Criteria and Match Function

Based on the above classification, a possible definition of the match function follows.

$match(O_a, O_b) = \Sigma(\forall M_i \in O_a \; \exists! \; M_j \in O_b \bullet e(M_i, M_j)) / m$

$where\ e(M_i, M_j) =$

$\begin{cases} V_1 = 1.0, \text{ if } M_i \text{ and } M_j \text{ are the same Precise or Single Choice Criteria;} \\ \quad = 0.0, \text{ otherwise} \\ V_2 = f(M_i, M_j), \text{ if } M_i \text{ and } M_j \text{ are Incremental Criteria} \\ V_3 = c(M_i, M_j), \text{ if } M_i \text{ and } M_j \text{ are Precedence or Time /Duration Criteria} \\ V_4 = d(M_i, M_j), \text{ if } M_i \text{ and } M_j \text{ are Many Choice Criteria} \end{cases}$

The function $f(M_i, M_j)$ takes two incremental criteria and performs a fuzzy match
using an ordinary keyword search mechanism, and returns a real number between 0.0
and 1.0 to indicate the strength of match. Similarly, the function $c(M_i, M_j)$ evaluates the
precedence order or compares the order of time point/duration slot, and returns 1.0 if
the condition is satisfied; 0.0 otherwise. The function $d(M_i, M_j)$ reviews the alternatives
provided in a disjunctive expression (logical OR expression), and returns 1.0 if the
condition is satisfied; 0.0 otherwise. In a practical system, the user may optionally
select a weight for the values V_1, V_2, V_3, and V_4, to emphasize a particular type of
search preference. The accumulated values from each type of comparison are divided
by the number of effective metadata entries, m. Missing metadata items are not counted
in the match function. The match function is used in the evaluation of similarities of
LOs, as we should discuss in the following section.

The match function, when implemented with the interface, allows the users to use
precedence operators to provide a range of search. At this moment, our system uses
exact match for keywords and titles. However, it is also possible to extend the match
function to incorporate fuzzy match. Also, we use a fixed weight for each metadata
item now. Future implementation will remove these limitations. The match function is
used in the next section to define the similarity function.

3.2.2 Similarity and Diversity of Learning Objects

Similarity between two LOs (one for the query and another as the search target) can be
measured from two perspectives: how much they match and how much they do not

---

[2] The SCORM 2004 specification defines a set of "vocabularies" for some metadata items. For
instance, if Aggregation Level = SCO, "SCO" is the vocabulary for metadata item "Aggregation Level."

match. The evaluation is taken from the perspective of the query LO_q. We present several functions in this section which can be used as a basis for designing a search mechanism.

An LO is used in a query. In a practical implementation, the metadata items of an LO are used in the match function. An LO can contains a number of descendant objects (DOs), such as SCOs or assets. Therefore, a decomposition of a query LO and target LOs is necessary. We use first order logic to define functions. In the implementation, a recursive function can be used to search for descendant objects.

The *similarity of learning objects* is defined as follows. The function Similarity(LO_q, LO_t) is a subjective evaluation based on the query LO_q:

$$Similarity(LO_q, LO_t) = \Sigma(\ \forall DO_i \in LO_q\ \exists!\ DO_j \in LO_t \bullet match(DO_i, DO_j) \geq \alpha)\ /\ |LO_q|$$

The similarity function is taken from the perspective of the query. Hence, the function is non-symmetric in general (i.e., Similarity(LO_x, LO_y) $\neq$ Similarity(LO_y, LO_x)).In order to make the search results useful, a *similarity threshold*, α, is introduced. This threshold can be set by the manager in a community, where a common repository is used for exchanging Los.

The evaluation of the similarity function uses the match function discussed in the previous section. Figure 4 gives an example of a query LO_q with 6 additional LOs as targets (LO_1 to LO_6). In Table 1, the values of the match function applied to descendant objects in Figure 4 are given. Assuming that the similarity threshold, α, is 0.5, similarity values are computed. In Table 2, a complete set of similarity values is provided.

Similarity of LOs can be used in a search process. However, in addition to find out how much a target LO is similar to a query LO, we also want to find out how much additional information that can be used in the target LO. This concept of search is important since additional course materials in the object could be the content we want to reuse in an instruction design. We introduce a new concept in the reusability tree. The *diversity* of a search process w.r.t. a query LO may represent the degree of additional useful descendant objects irrelevant to the search criteria but meaningful. Conceptually, diversity represents the hidden information in the search targets, w.r.t. a given search criteria. If we instinctively consider diversity as a dual complement of similarity, diversity is just the negation of similarity and also non-symmetric. However, dual complement of similarity, may not reflect the essential meaning of "additional information." For examples, assuming that LO_3 in Figure 4 is the query LO this time, the similarity values between LO_3 and LO_1, LO_2, LO_4, and LO_6 are all 0.5 (highlighted in Table 2). The real phenomenon is, based on LO_3, LO_1 has two additional descendant objects A_2 and B_2; and, LO_2 also has two additional descendant objects A_2 and D_2. Both LO_4 and LO_6 have one extra descendant object to LO_3. However, the diversity values deduced from dual complement of similarity concept do not reflect the degree of differences. Furthermore, even with the same diversity values deduced from dual complement of similarity concept (e.g., Diversity(LO_1, LO_4) = Diversity(LO_1, LO_5)), the meaning of "additional information" can be misleading.

Table 1. Values of the match function applied to descendant objects

	A	B	C	A_2	B_2	C_2	D_2	E_2	F_2
A	1.0	0.1	0.2	1.0	0.1	0.2	0.2	0.1	0.1
B	0.1	1.0	0.1	0.3	0.9	0.1	0.1	0.1	0.2
C	0.2	0.1	1.0	0.0	0.1	0.8	0.2	0.1	0.3
A_2	1.0	0.3	0.0	1.0	0.0	0.0	0.4	0.0	0.3
B_2	0.1	0.9	0.1	0.0	1.0	0.1	0.0	0.0	0.1
C_2	0.2	0.1	0.8	0.0	0.1	1.0	0.1	0.0	0.4
D_2	0.2	0.1	0.2	0.4	0.0	0.1	1.0	0.2	0.0
E_2	0.1	0.1	0.1	0.0	0.0	0.0	0.2	1.0	0.2
F_2	0.1	0.2	0.3	0.3	0.1	0.4	0.0	0.2	1.0

Table 2. Similarity Values among LOs in Figure 4

LO_q \ LO_t	LO_q	LO_1	LO_2	LO_3	LO_4	LO_5	LO_6
LO_q	–	0.9	0.6	0.3	0.0	0.9	0.6
LO_1	0.9	–	0.7	0.3	0.0	1.0	0.7
LO_2	0.6	0.7	–	0.3	0.0	0.7	0.7
LO_3	0.4	**0.5**	**0.5**	–	**0.5**	1.0	**0.5**
LO_4	0.0	0.0	0.0	0.5	–	1.0	0.0
LO_5	0.5	0.6	0.4	0.4	0.4	–	0.4
LO_6	0.9	1.0	1.0	0.5	0.0	1.0	–

Therefore, the concept of dual complement may not lead to the solution. We define the diversity function according to the similarity function as well, but in a different manner:

$$Diversity \ (LO_q, LO_t) = \frac{1}{2} (\log \frac{1}{Similarity \ (LO_q, LO_t)} + \log \frac{1}{Similarity \ (LO_t, LO_q)})$$

$$= \frac{1}{2} (-\log Similarity \ (LO_q, LO_t) - \log Similarity \ (LO_t, LO_q))$$

The diversity function is symmetric. A complete evaluation of diversity values of the examples given in Figure 4 is provided in Table 3. The diversity function, in a practical implementation, is computed at the same time when the function Similarity is evaluated.

Based on the examples of LO_3 as the query LO and the computation of diversity values between LO_3 and LO_1, LO_2, LO_4, and LO_6, we have Diversity(LO_3, LO_1) = Diversity(LO_3, LO_2) =0.949 and Diversity(LO_3, LO_4) = Diversity(LO_3, LO_6) =0.693. The result reflects the situation better since A_2 and B_2 of LO_1 may provide the same amount of additional information to LO_3, as compared to A_2 and D_2 of LO_2. However, the diversity function can have a "null" value if the corresponding similarity function is evaluated to 0.0. The null values are acceptable since there is no need to look at the additional information in the target if there is no match of the query and a target. In addition, when similarity function is evaluated to 1.0 (i.e., the same object), the diversity value is equals to 0.0 (i.e., no additional information from the same object).

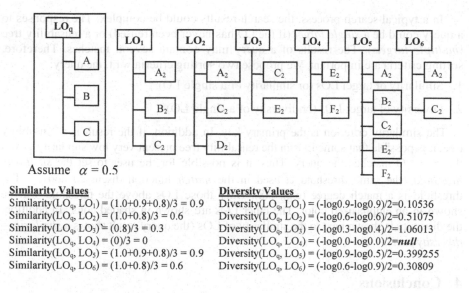

Assume $\alpha = 0.5$

Similarity Values

Similarity(LO_q, LO_1) = (1.0+0.9+0.8)/3 = 0.9
Similarity(LO_q, LO_2) = (1.0+0.8)/3 = 0.6
Similarity(LO_q, LO_3) = (0.8)/3 = 0.3
Similarity(LO_q, LO_4) = (0)/3 = 0
Similarity(LO_q, LO_5) = (1.0+0.9+0.8)/3 = 0.9
Similarity(LO_q, LO_6) = (1.0+0.8)/3 = 0.6

Diversity Values

Diversity(LO_q, LO_1) = (-log0.9-log0.9)/2=0.10536
Diversity(LO_q, LO_2) = (-log0.6-log0.6)/2=0.51075
Diversity(LO_q, LO_3) = (-log0.3-log0.4)/2=1.06013
Diversity(LO_q, LO_4) = (-log0.0-log0.0)/2=**null**
Diversity(LO_q, LO_5) = (-log0.9-log0.5)/2=0.399255
Diversity(LO_q, LO_6) = (-log0.6-log0.9)/2=0.30809

Fig. 4. Examples of Similarity and Diversity Values

In summary, the evaluation of the match function, the similarity and diversity values are computed. Diversity indicates the additional useful information w.r.t. a search while similarity of LOs indicates the degree of a match. Our motivation is as follows. *Given a search query (metadata of LO), find a single target (another LO) or multiple targets (some LOs in a reusability tree) which has the highest **similarity** w.r.t. the query. The target(s) found should also show the highest **diversity** w.r.t. the query when applicable.*

With the definitions of the above functions, we have implemented the search subsystem of the revised CORDRA architecture. The query given by the user is an LO. There are a couple of alternatives for the interface design. One allows the user to drag and drop a portion of SCORM content, such as an SCO (including the metadata) as the query. Another is to allow the user to specify the metadata items. In both alternatives, metadata items are used in the evaluation of similarity and diversity.

Table 3. (Symmetric) Diversity Values According to the New Definition

	LO_q	LO_1	LO_2	LO_3	LO_4	LO_5	LO_6
LO_q	–	**0.105**	0.511	1.060	null	**0.399**	0.308
LO_1		–	0.357	0.949	null	0.256	0.179
LO_2			–	0.949	null	0.637	0.179
LO_3				–	0.693	0.458	0.693
LO_4					–	0.458	null
LO_5						–	0.458
LO_6							–

In a typical search process, the search results could be complex. The responses to a query could be a *single target* (if the LO has never been reused) or a reusability tree (*multiple targets*). The results of a query may contain several matches. Therefore, sorting criteria are important. We propose two sorting criteria w.r.t. the query:

1. Similarity of target LOs (or similarity of a single LO)

2. Diversity of target LOs (or diversity of a single LO)

The similarity criterion is the primary key. In addition, if the result is a reusability tree, it is possible that some LOs in the reusability tree present very low similarity[3], even the root LO matches the query. Thus, it is possible for the user to set the *similarity threshold* (the same threshold α used in the *match* function discussed above). The threshold is a match degree (e.g., 0.8). Only those LOs above the threshold will be shown in an emphasized color. The other LOs are shown in shaded color. In addition, the diversity is shown next to the similarity of LOs (the query result shows a *similarity – diversity pair*).

4 Conclusions

Reusability is one of the most important issues in object-oriented computing and database systems. An essential strategy is to provide a mechanism that will help any end users to find objects which can be reused. Thus, the construction of a federated search and sharing architecture is particularly important for distance learning. This paper provided some considerations for reusability in the context of SCORM and CORDRA. First, we analyzed the relationship of LOs. Our reusability tree is built in the Master Content Catalog of a CORDRA environment. We then discussed a distributed architecture as well as its subsystems for registering and discovering LOs. These subsystems are implemented as an instance of CORDRA, called the Registry. The Registry provides a way for users to search for LOs via a common infrastructure and a generic naming space. Such a federated repository provides a solution for LO reuse. We also provided a set of evaluation mechanisms to estimate the similarity and diversity among LOs.

At this moment, the similarity function is not incorporated into the system. So far, we have only addressed similarity among LOs from the perspective of metadata. On the other hand, due to the use cases of rewritable metadata templates, user behaviors can be recorded for analysis. Guided search can be investigated based on machine learning mechanisms. Therefore, new users of the Registry system can follow suggestions from the search subsystem to quickly find reusable LOs. In addition, we will test our Registry with another instance of CORDRA – the ADL Registry developed by the technical group of ADL. We believe that, with the proposed mechanisms and the standard metadata (i.e., IEEE LOM), LOs can be searched and reused in a systematic manner, which will help the promotion of SCORM and CORDRA specifications in the international community of distance learning technologies.

---

[3] If the history of an LO is long, the reusability tree will grow very deep. A leaf LO may have low similarity to the root LO.

Acknowledgments

The research for this paper is partially supported by the National Research Council, Taiwan, under the grant number 93-2524-S-032-001.

For the final author of this paper, the research was supported by the Korean Ministry of Information and Communication under the ITRC IITA-2006-(C1090-0603-0046) grant.

References

1. ADL Technical Team, Content Object Repository Discovery and Registration/Resolution Architecture (CORDRA), ADL 1'st International Plugfest, (June 07, 2004)
2. ADL Technical Team, Sharable Content Object Reference Model (SCORM) 2004 Documentation 1st Edition, Advanced Distributed Learning (ADL), (January 30, 2004)
3. Alliance of Remote Instructional Authoring and Distribution Networks for Europe (ARIADNE) Project (accessed January 2005), http://ariadne.unil.ch
4. Dubline Core Metadata for Resource Discovery. Internet RFC 2413, (accessed October 2005), http://www.ietf.org/rfc/rfc2413.txt
5. Lin, H.W., Tzou, M.-T., Shih, T.K., Wang, C.-C., Li-Chieh, L.: Metadata Wizard Design for Searchable and Reusable Repository. In: Proceedings of the 2006 International Conference on SCORM (ICSCORM 2006), Taipei, Taiwan, January 17–19 (2006)
6. IEEE Draft Standard for Learning Object Metadata, IEEE P1484.12.1/d6.4 (2002)
7. Vassiliadis, N., Kokoras, F., Vlahavas, I., Sampson, D.: An Intelligent Educational Metadata Repository. In: Leondes, C. (ed.) Intelligent Systems: Technology and Applications. Databases and Learning Systems, vol. 4, CRC Press, Boca Raton (2003)
8. Karampiperis, P., Kastradas, K., Sampson, D.: A Schema-Mapping Algorithm for Educational Metadata Interoperability. In: Proc. of the 15th World Conference on Educational Multimedia, Hypermedia and Telecommunications, USA, June 2003, pp. 1359–1366 (2003)
9. Pasini, N., Rehak, D.: A Process Model for Applying Standards in Content Development. World Conference on Educational Multimedia, Hypermedia and Telecommunications 2003(1), 542–544 (2003)
10. Karampiperis, P., Sampson, D.G.: Enhancing Educational Metadata Management Systems to Support Interoperable Learning Object Repositories. In: Proceedings of the 3rd IEEE International Conference on Advanced Learning Technologies, Athens, Greece, July 2003, pp. 214–218 (2003)
11. Hasegawa, S., Kashihara, A., Toyoca, J.: An E-Learning Library on the Web. In: Proceeding of the ICCE 2002, vol. 2, pp. 1281–1282 (2002)
12. Shih, T.K., Chang, C.-C., Lin, H.W.: Reusability on Learning Object Repository. In: Liu, W., Li, Q., Lau, R.W.H. (eds.) ICWL 2006. LNCS, vol. 4181, pp. 203–214. Springer, Heidelberg (2006)

Adaptivity in a SCORM Compliant Adaptive Educational Hypermedia System

Ioannis Kazanidis and Maya Satratzemi

Department of Applied Informatics, University of Macedonia,
54006, Thessaloniki, Greece
{kazanidis, maya}@uom.gr

Abstract. This paper presents a Learning Management System (LMS) that provides adaptive hypermedia courses adopting SCORM standard and its specifications. Its main aim is to manage and deliver SCORM compliant courses, adapt those courses accordingly to the learner knowledge and individual characteristics and monitor user's progress and course effectiveness providing feedback to the tutors. It is going to be used for the distribution of an adaptive Java programming course which will provide useful statistical feedback to the tutors. The focus of the paper is on the system's architecture and in adaptation technologies that were used.

Keywords: Educational Hypermedia Systems, AEHS, SCORM, LMS.

1 Introduction

Internet and WWW have brought revolutionary changes in the open and distance learning. Learning environments and web based courses have become popular ways to distribute learning content to learners. They can be used either to support traditional direct-communicated education (complementing books and direct-teaching process) or autonomous as integrated asynchronous education solution, for self and distant learning. One of the main advantages of web based courses is that they are available to a big number of learners regardless their lodging, age or study time constraints. Therefore web based courses could be accessible by many users with different characteristics, needs and previous knowledge of the domain. However this could simultaneously be a weakness of those courses since they cannot be descended to any particular learner. Moreover some major problems of web-based courses such as *Cognitive Overload, Disorientation, Narrative flow* and *Content readiness* [1] could reduce teaching attitude to the learner. Consequently educational web based systems, in order to increase their performance, should provide interactivity and adaptability to individual user needs and characteristics.

Since middle nineties various techniques were used in several educational systems in order to adapt to individual user needs and characteristics. Those *Adaptive Educational Hypermedia Systems* (AEHS) integrate several technologies from both hypermedia and *Intelligent Tutoring Systems* (ITS). Thus combine the tutor-driven learning

H. Leung et al. (Eds.): ICWL 2007, LNCS 4823, pp. 196–206, 2008.

process of ITS and the flexibility of a student centered Hypermedia System [2]. AEHS personalize dynamically the navigation process, the educational content and its presentation to particular user, according his individual needs characteristics and current progress. Therefore with these systems every single user can has an individual view and individual navigation through the educational content of hypermedia systems.

One of the most used ways to distribute learning content to the end-user is via a *Learning Management System* (LMS). However a course that is distributed by a LMS most times cannot be used by another due to incompatibility issues. Some standards were applied such as *Shareable Content Object Reference Model* (SCORM) so that courses can be interoperable and educational content reusable to different courses. Consequently a SCORM compliant course can be distributed by any SCORM compliant LMS.

In this paper we present a system which is a combination of a SCORM compliant LMS and an AEHS. Thus system provides adaptive web courses to learners adopting SCORM and its specifications. The system is intended to support the distribution of an adaptive Java Programming course, returning useful feedback to the tutors.

First available adaptive technologies and techniques are described. The prototype's architecture and its provided functionality, focused on technology manner, follow. Finally we present system's implementation and conclude with discussion about system technology issues.

2 Introduction

All adaptive hypermedia systems adopt a general structure, composed by three main components. These are the *domain model* (DM), the *user model* (UM) and the *adaptation module* (AM).

- The domain model represents the teaching domain of the system.
- The user model represents the learner's knowledge of the domain and his individual characteristics.
- The adaptation module defines the adaptation rules plus which items are going to be adapted [3].

2.1 Domain Model

The role of the DM is to represent the knowledge about teaching domain [5]. Although many types of domain models have been applied, a typical DM could be divided into three layers.

The *first layer* consists of concepts. Concepts are elementary pieces of knowledge. The amount of domain knowledge that every concept represents can differ between systems, depending on the domain size, the application area and the designer's choice [4]. Each concept can be corresponded to one ore more web pages where comprise the *second layer*. A web page is consisted by smaller fragments such as text, images, animation etc [6]. Those small fragments constitute the *third layer* of the domain model.

The simplest form of domain model is when concepts are independent. On the other hand sometimes domain model is more complex and concepts can have relationships between each-other and constitute a conceptual network which represents the domain's structure [4]. The most popular relationship between concepts is the hypertext link when a concept links to another [7].

The "prerequisite" relationship is also used by many systems. A concept considered prerequisite of another when learner has to know the first concept before he starts studying the related second concept.

Other relations are the "part of" when some concepts are part of another concept and the "is a" relation which links a concept to others that are its typical instances [6].

2.2 User Model

In order an AHS to be able to adapt to any user, has to be aware of user's initial and current knowledge of the domain, and his individual characteristics. All this information about the user can be separated into two main categories [8].

The category that contains the info about user knowledge of the domain and the category witch contains all the domain independent info such as user individual characteristics, preferences, learning style etc. That data can be either static, when is gathered during the initialization of the user model and does not change during the educational process (user individual characteristics, preferences, capabilities etc) or dynamic when is collected during the learning process (user progress, current knowledge, actions etc) [8][9]. Usually student personal characteristics are static data while his knowledge is dynamic. Sometimes user has the right to change in the middle of a course data such as user goals, previous knowledge, preferences etc. Although the user model can store a lot of information, should not contain more than the necessary info so as system not to be surcharged with useless interactions [10].

In order to build the user model several techniques have been figured. The most widely used is the *overlay model*, where the user's knowledge of the subject considered as a part of an expert's knowledge in the particular subject [9]. User model stores a value (binary, qualitative or integer quantitative) for every domain model concept that represents user's knowledge on this concept [4]. One simpler technique is the *stereotype model* [9]. Stereotypes define specific classes of users with common characteristics. When a user adopts a stereotype is categorized into those classes inheriting their properties. The stereotype and overlay models can be combined by categorize users initially using stereotypes and then gradually redefine this model as an overlay model from user's progress [11]. Other techniques of user knowledge representation are the *perturbation* or *buggy model* [3], where a part of the domain model and some misconceptions of the user are joined as a group in order to represent the user knowledge, and models based to uncertainty [6].

2.3 Adaptation Module

Adaptation module, through a set of rules, applies various adaptation technologies in order to adapt courses to the user.

AEHS have inherited adaptation technologies both from ITS and AHS. The main ITS adaptation technologies are the *curriculum sequencing* which provide user with the most suitable path of learning units in order to achieve his goals (ELM-ART, KBS-Hyperbook, Interbook) [12], and the *problem solving support* where provides intelligent support while a user solving a problem (ELM-ART [13]).

According to Brusilovsky there are two main groups of adaptation hypermedia technologies in AEHS: the *adaptive presentation* which provides content-level adaptation and the *adaptive navigation* which reside to the link-level adaptation of the system [11][12].

Adaptive presentation can be applied via text and multimedia adaptation technologies. According to this technology, a hypermedia page is dynamically generated by a number of educational content elements (texts, images, audio, video, animation), proper selected so that suit to the knowledge, goals and other characteristics of the particular user [5]. Many systems provide full or a kind of adaptive presentation such as AHA! [14] and INSPIRE [15].

Adaptive navigation support is divided into [11] *link hiding* when system hides a link to an inappropriate concept for study, *link sorting* when the sequence of links can be changed, *link annotation* when links annotated corresponding to the user model, direct guidance where system propose the next best concept for study and finally hypertext map adaptation when system provides and changes properly a graphical representation of the link structure like AHA! does [14]. Almost every AEHS uses one or more of the adaptive navigation support technologies.

3 System Architecture

System's architecture is a combined architecture of SCORM LMS and AEHS. As shown in simplified form, in figure 1, we adopt the typical SCORM *Run Time Environment* (RTE) structure adding an adaptation module and extending the preexistent Domain and User Models. Thus prototype involves four main modules.

- The *Domain Model* that represents the domain knowledge of the system.
- The *User Model* that represents the particular user's knowledge of the domain as well as his individual characteristics; both these models comprise the Data Model of the system.
- Furthermore system involves the *Adaptation Module* (AM) which interacts with DM and UM in order to provide adaptive navigation to the course
- and the RTE Sequencer that is triggered by course navigating controls, interacts with DM and delivers the appropriate educational content to the learner.

The educational content can be delivered either *as Sharable Content Objects* (SCOs) or Assets. SCOs can interact with DM and UM via a specific SCORM specified API Instance and provide some kind of adaptation. On the other hand Assets are static hypermedia content (text, images etc.). Finally for data storage we use both Database and File server.

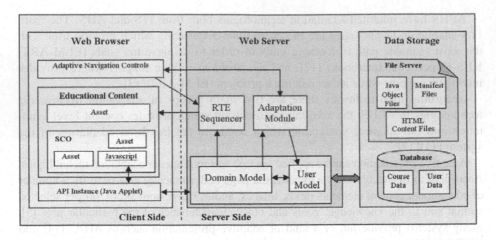

Fig. 1. System architecture

3.1 Domain Model

The domain model represents the domain knowledge of the system. It provides the essential educational content, in forms of concepts with specific properties and relationships between them. Prototype's DM contains the entire mandatory from SCORM Content Aggregation Model and SCORM RTE Data Model [16] data, for every single concept of the course. Moreover involves additional data required for the adaptation process. The DM of every course is originated by a course manifest file - which is comprised by course structure and concepts' properties (like concepts' relationship data, concept weight etc.) - course educational content and tutor preferences for each unit of the course. Each concept (SCO) is structured by one or more topics (web pages) and each topic contain some elementary pieces of knowledge (text, images etc.).

As mentioned above DM can contain additional data such as in which units the learner has the option to define manually if he has learned the correspondent concept or not. In addition DM contains FAQ questions for every unit with their answers.

3.2 User Model

Our system provides adaptation according to user model information. User model is comprised by three main categories of data. Data about user knowledge of the domain, data about user actions and goals (time spent studying a concept, number of visits, goals) and domain independent data (like user name, password, mail, language and privileges).

User personal data retrieved through the registration of the user and is static. For user knowledge representation we use as the majority of AEHS a multilayered overlay model which consequently follows the domain structure. The first layer stores the navigation history, data that present if the learner has study a particular concept and actually if he has visited the corresponded web page. The second layer contains learner's estimated knowledge, which has been derived by study of a concept, representing as a percentage score. The third layer describes the previous learner's knowledge of the domain and can be declared initially or during the course study. Consequently being that data stored into different layers, allows independent update. Thus user knowledge data from one layer does not overwrite identical data from another layer. The third category of data stores the time a learner spends to a specific concept, the number of times that he has visited the correspondent web page, draft notes of user on the specific concept and whether a concept considered as one of his goals or not. The user goals' model is a combination of overlay and stereotype model since user can manually define his goals (overlay model) or select a group of goals according a category i.e. novice – expert (stereotype model).

3.3 Adaptation Module

Adaptation Module (AM) is responsible for the system's adaptation. The adaptation model interacts both with UM and DM and provides link annotation (see bellow) and direct guidance through a set of adaptation rules. For example, a concept is considered known by study in case that learner's score (retrieved by UM) is bigger than the required by the author minimum concept's score (retrieved by DM). It is also consider known if the user already knew that concept (UM). In both cases a "✓" symbol is appeared on the title icon of the correspondent link at the table of contents (adaptive navigation-link annotation). Additional adaptation rules applied by the SCORM Sequencing and Navigation Model [16], providing link hiding, link disabling and random link order to the links in the table of contents.

3.4 RTE Sequencer

The RTE Sequencer is triggered by course navigating controls, interacts with DM and delivers the appropriate educational content to the learner. Educational content can be either SCO or Asset. SCORM can provide some kind of adaptivity in case author takes advantage of its functionality, during the course authoring. Thus SCOs is possible under specific conditions, to support adaptive presentation of their contents in forms that SCORM specification and course authoring allows it.

4 System Adaptive Functionality

Our prototype is a LMS that provides adaptive hypermedia courses adopting SCORM standard and its specifications. The adaptive functionality can be provided by two ways. Using the Adaptation Module of the system or taking advantage of SCORM functionality at the course authoring phase, designing a course in that way so as to provide a kind of adaptation.

Adaptive Navigation: System can provide adaptive navigation by two ways. First way is using the AM. Using that way direct guidance and link annotation can be provided. The direct guidance is provided with a "Next" button on the screen that "opens" the most appropriate concept for study according to current UM. On the other hand with the link annotation all links at the provided table of contents are annotated properly according to UM. Links are annotated for five instances : already visited links, links that their correspondent concepts is considered as known, links that constitute learner's goals, link of the current opened web page and finally the proposed next link for study. Moreover system annotates respectively in course and main units level, whether they considered as known and whether the user goals on them have been accomplished.

Another two adaptive navigation techniques can be applied with appropriate design of the course, the link hiding and link disabling. Those techniques plus random link order can be applied with specific conditions into the DM of the course.

Adaptive presentation: System is possible to provide adaptive presentation only utilizing SCORM functionality. In SCORM a course can involve a number of objectives. Author can write conditions that let system present content with specific way, counting objectives' completion. That means course structure and HTML files which correspond to the educational content have to be designed with appropriate way. That way author can apply a lot of more or less intelligent course build-in functionality, such as adaptive presentation displaying appropriate selected content of the SCO, providing or not "Back" and "Next" buttons, specify cases to hide table of contents, appearance of personal messages, define prerequisite concepts, change the design of the presentation etc.

Additional adaptive functionality: System provides tutor functionality to adapt any SCORM compliant course to his preferences modifying specific attributes of the DM. First he can apply FAQ and their answers for every concept of the course. Second he can let learner or not to have the option to specify by self if he learn a concept or not. We recommend all units of the course provide that functionality except the units which estimate user knowledge with questionnaires or tests. Third tutor can provide set of goals for specific class of learners, or for different levels of desired acquisition knowledge. This helps especially novice learners that might have difficulties in estimating alone their educational targets. Finally system provides in real time the learner with his total estimated score of the course plus with the coverage percentage of his goals.

5 System Implementation

Our system derives from SCORM 2004 Sample RTE Version 1.3.3 that is based on SCORM 2004 specification. Thus its architecture is a typical of a SCORM compliant LMS (Fig. 1). We use Apache Tomcat 5.5 as web and application server and MySQL 5 as database server. Our prototype resides on a Windows XP operating system. System retrieve course files initially from a zip file, which contains a manifest xml file and all the html and media required files. The DM structure is exported by the manifest file and is stored into Java Object Files. However additional data about the course is stored into the database. Moreover domain independent data of UM is stored into the database while at the same time, data about user knowledge is stored into Java Object Files.

Educational content is delivered from the server, in form of HTML files, into the "Educational Content frame" (Fig. 2) of the web browser. HTML files can include appropriate Javascript that let them communicate with the DM of the system. In that operation an API instance is involved, that is an applet on the top frame of the browser, "Functionality Toolbar and API Instance frame" which mediates between Javascript and

DM. The table of contents is delivered into the "Table of Contents frame" of web browser, while adaptative navigation techniques have been applied to it via Java servlets and *Java Server Pages* (JSP). Current user score, direct guidance button and buttons to declare user if he learned a concept are appeared on"Extra Features frame". All the runtime data about user actions and performance is stored into Java Object Files via JSP and Java servlets. All other supportive functions of the LMS are applied via JSP and the required data is stored into the database of the system.

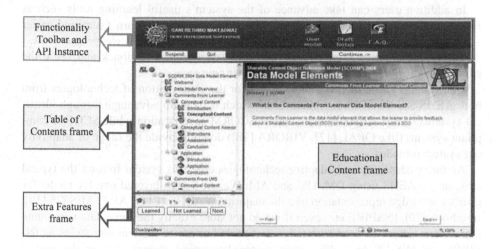

Fig. 2. System interface

6 Conclusion and Future Work

In this paper, we analyzed the special features of an AEHS system developed at the department of Applied Informatics in University of Macedonia. Our prototype is a LMS that provides adaptive hypermedia courses adopting SCORM standard and its specifications. The main aim of our system is to be able to manage and deliver SCORM compliant courses, adapt those courses accordingly to the UM and monitor user progress and course effectiveness providing feedback to the tutors. System provides adaptive navigation and under specific conditions, adaptive presentation of its educational content.

We estimate that studying with the proposed adaptive educational system is going to help users to avoid major problems of web courses [1].

- *Disorientation problem* is addressed by the *adaptive link annotation* that system provides. As mentioned above, all the links in the TOC are annotated dynamically according to the user's knowledge, goals and navigation history. Thus the user has precise information about where he was, where he is now and which is his current "status" into the course.
- *Adaptive presentation* addresses the issue of *Cognitive Overload* (CO). Two main sources of CO are the *Intrinsic Cognitive Overload* (ICO) and the *Extraneous Cognitive Overload* (ECO) [23]. The system using SCORM functionality, can adapt educational content and the design of content presentation according to

user's current knowledge, age, preferences, specific user classes etc, so as to reduce the ICO and ECO respectively.

• *Content Readiness* and *Narrative Flow* can be addressed by *adaptive annotation* techniques like *link hiding* and *link disabling* and *link annotation* of inappropriate content for current user's knowledge, as well as by *adaptive presentation* displaying appropriate content and/or personal messages for the current user's knowledge and course "status".

In addition users can take advance of the system's useful learning tools such as Java compiler, FAQ, user remarks etc. Novices are going to learn faster and easier and experts can focus on specialized content according to their knowledge and goals.

Tutors can improve their courses according to system's feedback and reuse the educational SCORM compliant content to other courses.

Our system can be mainly characterized for the combination of technologies from both AEHS and SCORM compliant LMS which is its main advantage through identical systems. Most AEHS do not support SCORM specification while SCORM compliant systems (like OPAL [17], VIBORA [18]) do not provide the range of adaptivity our system provides.

As far as adaptivity and adaptive technologies concerns system follows the typical structure of AEHS using DM, UM and AM. We use a multilayered overlay model for user's knowledge representation like the majority of AEHS (ELM-ART, AES-CS [19], Interbook [20], INSPIRE etc) even if we do not store exactly the same data with them. Our system adapts to user knowledge and goals but not to his learning styles as INSPIRE and AES-CS do. Unlike others, system lets author, change specific elements of DM via web, any time after uploading course to the server. In addition user can change his UM during course study unlike Interbook and AES-CS. System provides adaptive navigation like most of AEHS. However we disagree with the link hiding technique that some adaptive systems use (AHA!, Anes [5]), even if authors can apply that in our system with course build-in SCORM functionality. System can additional provide adaptive presentation, like many AEHS (AHA!, INSPIRE, AES-CS, ALICE [21], TANGOW [22]) do, but this can be done indirectly by the author at the authoring phase of the course, using SCORM functionality. By the same way course can include pretests or tests as ELM-ART, Interbook and AES-CS do.

Prototype is based on SCORM 2004 specification. However, we intend to keep it up to date making it compliant with the latest SCORM 2004 second edition.

One of the goals of our system is to support an adaptive Java programming course. For that reason we develop an extra feature that will let learners write and compile Java programs, returning useful feedback. User model is going to change respectively. When Java code editor development completed, we are going to design an adaptive Java programming SCORM compliant course. The course will be designed that way in order to make use of all the provided by the system adaptive functionality. Pilot operation and evaluation of course and system effectiveness is going to follow in order to discover system weaknesses and check for possible improvements of either prototype or Java course. Assessment of the prototype is going to be based on thecomparison between users' acquired abilities when they study from a simple web-based course and when they study the same educational content, incorporated into our prototype.

References

1. Murray, T., Shen, T., Piemonte, J., Condit, C., Tibedau, J.: Adaptivity for conceptual and narrative flow in hyperbooks: The Metalink system. In: Brusilovsky, P., Stock, O., Strapparava, C. (eds.) AH 2000. LNCS, vol. 1892, pp. 155–166. Springer, Heidelberg (2000)
2. Eklund, J., Zeilenger, R.: Navigating the Web: Possibilities and Practicalities for Adaptive Navigation Support. In: Proceedings of AusWeb96: The Second Australian World-Wide Web Conference, pp. 73–80. Southern Cross University Press (1996)
3. Surjono, H., Maltby, J.: Adaptive Educational Hypermedia Based on Multiple Student Characteristics. In: Zhou, W., Nicholson, P., Corbitt, B., Fong, J. (eds.) ICWL 2003. LNCS, vol. 2783, pp. 442–449. Springer, Heidelberg (2003)
4. Brusilovsky, P.: Developing Adaptive Educational Hypermedia Systems: From Design Models to Authoring Tools. In: Murray, T., Blessing, S., Ainsworth, S. (eds.) Authoring Tools for Advanced Technology Learning Environments: Toward cost-effective adaptive, interactive, and intelligent educational software, Norwood, Ablex, pp. 337–409 (2003)
5. Kavcic, A.: Adaptation Techniques in Adaptive Hypermedia Systems. In: 22nd International Convention MIPRO 1999, Conference on Multimedia and Hypermedia Systems, Hrvaska, vol. 1 (1999)
6. Prentzas, D., Hatziligeroudis, I.: Adaptive Educational Hypermedia: Principles and Services. In: 1st Panhellenic Conference in Open and Distance Learning, Patra, Greece (in Greek) (2001)
7. Wu, H., De Bra, P., Aerts, A., Houben, G.J.: Adaptation Control in Adaptive Hypermedia Systems. In: Brusilovsky, P., Stock, O., Strapparava, C. (eds.) AH 2000. LNCS, vol. 1892, pp. 250–259. Springer, Heidelberg (2000)
8. Kavcic, A.: The Role of User Models in Adaptive Hypermedia Systems. In: Proc. of the 10th Mediterranean Electrotechnical Conference MEleCon 2000, Lemesos, Cyprus (2000)
9. Carmona, C., Cionejo, R.: A Learner Model in a Distributed Environment. In: De Bra, P.M.E., Nejdl, W. (eds.) AH 2004. LNCS, vol. 3137, pp. 353–359. Springer, Heidelberg (2004)
10. Prentzas, D., et al.: The architecture of a Web-based Intelligent Tutoring System for the Instruction of New Informatic's Technologies. In: Proc. of 1st Panhellenic Conference in Open and Distance Learning, Patra, Greece (in Greek) (2001)
11. Brusilovsky, P.: Methods and Techniques of Adaptive Hypermedia. In: Brusilovsky, P., Kobsa, A., Vassileva, J. (eds.) Journal of User Modeling and User-Adapted Interaction. Special Issue on Adaptive Hypertext and Hypermedia, 6 (2-3), 87–129 (1998)
12. Brusilovsky, P.: Adaptive and Intelligent Technologies for Web-based Education. In: Rollinger, C., Peylo, C. (eds.) Künstliche Intelligenz, Special Issue on Intelligent Systems and Tele-teaching, vol. 4, pp. 19–25 (1999)
13. Brusilovsky, P., Schwarz, E., Weber, G.: ELM-ART: An intelligent tutoring system on World Wide Web. In: Lesgold, A., Frasson, C., Gauthier, G. (eds.) ITS 1996. LNCS, vol. 1086, pp. 261–269. Springer, Heidelberg (1996)
14. De Bra, P., Calvi, L.: AHA! An open Adaptive Hypermedia Architecture. The New Review of Hypermedia and Multimedia, pp. 115–139 (1998)
15. Papanikolaou, K.A., Grigoriadou, M., Kornilakis, H., Magoulas, G.D.: Personalizing the Interaction in a Web-based Educational Hypermedia System: the case of INSPIRE. In: User Modeling and User-Adapted Interaction, pp. 213–267. Kluwer Academic Publishers, Netherlands (2003)
16. SCORM, Sharable Content Object Reference Model, Advanced Distributed Learning, http://www.adlnet.gov/scorm/index.cfm

17. Conlan, O., Dagger, D., Wade, V.: Towards a Standards-based Approach to E-Learning Personalization using Reusable Learning Objects. In: Procceedings of ELearn 2002, World Conference on E-Learning in Corporate, Government, Healthcare & Higher Education (2002)
18. Morales, R.: The VIBORA project. In: Richards, G. (ed.) World Conference on E-Learning in Corporate, Government, Healthcare, and Higher Education, pp. 2341–2344 (2003)
19. Triantafillou, E., Pomportsis, A., Georgiadou, E.: AES-CS: Adaptive Educational System based on Cognitive Styles. In: The Workshop on Adaptive System for Web-based Education, held in conjunction with AH 2002, Malaga, Spain (2002)
20. Brusilovsky, P., Schwarz, E., Weber, G.: A tool for developing adaptive electronic textbooks on WWW. In: WebNet 1996, World Conference of the Web Society, San Francisco, pp. 64–69 (1996)
21. Kavcic, A. Privosnik, M., Marolt, M., Divjak, S.: Educational hypermedia system ALICE: an evaluation of adaptive features. In: Advances in multimedia, video and signal processing systems (Electrical and computer engineering series), WSEAS, cop. pp. 71–76 (2002)
22. Carro, R.M., Pulido, E., Rodríguez, P.: Dynamic generation of adaptive Internet-based courses. Journal of Network and Computer Applications 22, 249–257 (1999)
23. van Merriënboer, J.J.G., Sweller, J.: Cognitive Load Theory and Complex Learning: Recent Developments and Future Directions. Educational Psychology Review 17(2), 147–177 (2005)

Synergistic Learning for Knowledge Age: Theoretical Model, Enabling Technology and Analytical Framework

Zhiting Zhu[1], Youmei Wang[2], and Hongwei Luo[3]

[1] East China Normal University,Shanghai,China
ztzhu@dec.ecnu.edu.cn
[2] Wenzhou University, Wenzhou,Zhejiang,China
wangyoumei@126.com
[3] Nanhai Radio & Televison University, Nanhai,Guangzhou,China
angelahong835@163.com

Abstract. The existing learning theories and learning technology systems are faced with quite many problems in meeting educational challenges of the knowledge age. Based on the vast study of the learning models and technology systems, we put forward a theoretical framework of synergistic learning and develop a set of tools, such as synergistic building technology (ClassKC) and synergistic annotation technology (ClassCT), to facilitate synergistic learning activities and synergistic thinking, building and internalizing of knowledge and to promote high-level leaning in the learning context. At the same time, this study assesses the particularity of synergistic learning technology system with the collaborative innovation networks mapping model and the discourse analysis method. The findings indicate there is a considerable actual effect on learning and teaching in interactivity, connection and sharing.

Keywords: synergistic learning, theoretical model, support toolkit, analytical framework.

1 Introduction

Rapid globalization, far-reaching impact of information and communication technology and strong appeals of social development under intense international competitions have given an impetus to educational reforms and learning transformations. In order to provide sufficient theoretical support to these changes in knowledge age, a great number of researchers have done quite a lot of work: they study learning from multi-dimensional perspectives and make attempts to construct new multi-layer learning theory system. Peter Javirs proposes a comprehensive learning theory to support life-long learning in the information age [1]. The comprehensive learning theory ascertains that learning subject is the human being himself. The human learning is a combination of serial processes, including bodily, psychological and experienced processes. The theory now is used in the development of online learning materials. Focusing the research on schooling performance, Cheng brings forward the theory of Contextualized Multiple Thinking (CMT) and Creativity [2]. CMT presents a five- dimension model

H. Leung et al. (Eds.): ICWL 2007, LNCS 4823, pp. 207–217, 2008.

of Intelligence, which provides a new systematic framework for guiding educational reforms in the new century.

Garrison, Anderson & Archer develop the theory of presence under the technological context [3], which explores the implications of presence in the context of online learning from three dimensions of learning: cognitive presence, teaching presence and social presence. Recently, Campbell & Cleveland extend the study on presence to the emotional presence, which is one of the most important factors in learning process [4]. Clark Quinn considers emotion as the most important element in the design of educational simulation games [5]. However, the above mentioned learning theories expatiate differently on learning strategical frameworks from various perspectives and demands. It seems that a general framework is in need. The new framework should take the mechanism of learning occurrence and knowledge construction into account under the technological condition and integrate with traditional learning theory as well. Therefore, it is necessary to conduct a more thorough thinking on the existing frameworks of the learning technology system.

2 Synergistic Learning Technology System Frameworks

As far as learning technology is concerned, learning theories are interrelated with technology evolution. In the recent several decades, technological innovation has transformed greatly our living styles. However, in the field of education, technology functions less efficiently than in other domains. The reason is that the existing learning technology system designed on the basis of traditional learning theories cannot meet the demands of fostering intellectuals who adapt to the society. The complexity and ecological evolution of knowledge and lasting technological innovation have brought about more intense appeals for the alteration of instruction and learning. Meanwhile, individual and collective knowledge management has formed a new view. All this indicates the new era requires those who take possession of multi-literacy and are capable of problem-solving and critical thinking. In the paper, we propose the concept of synergistic learning as a new framework of learning technology system toward knowledge age. Synergistic learning, based on systemic synergistic ideas and knowledge creation, develops traditional learning theories. The synergistic learning technology system will have become a new framework which acclimatizes itself to the social structure and technological requirements and adapts itself to social reform and learning innovation.

Since technology has become an important factor in the learning system, the term of technology-based learning system must be replaced by the learning technology system. The traditional learning system cannot provide sufficient supports for creative learning through taking advantage of technology-pedagogy integration while the existing learning technology system actually represents a kind of discrete thinking for lack of an all-around theoretical framework. In this schismatic instructional architecture, educators and learners act and abide by some isolated instructional concepts which cannot acclimatize itself to the society. To be more concrete, this kind of "isolation" is explained by five aspects [6]: firstly, on the interactive level, no deep interaction happened between the learners and content;   secondly, on the level of communicative structure, no information aggregative mechanism presents; thirdly, on the level of information processing, no collective thinking involved ; fourthly, on the level of knowledge construction, no cooperative and integrative tools available; fifthly, on the pragmatic level, no organic connections among information, knowledge, action, emotion and value are demonstrated. The isolated aspects have a serious influence upon instruction. Accordingly, we are in need of a new learning technology system framework to meet the requirements of the knowledge age.

In fact, it is a general understanding to focus on the multi-dimensional features of learning. Viewing whether from the nature of education and learning or from instructional objectives and learning outcomes, the educators and researchers hold that knowledge, emotion, attitude and value are the basic dimensionalities of learning. However, few researches are concerned about the technological factors and knowledge creation in the learning context, particularly about the ontology of the learner. Based on the above analyses, we introduce multiple elements of learning into the field of dynamics, and puts forward the concept "synergistic learning". As a new framework of learning technology system for the knowledge age, synergistic learning, which is based on theories of system synergy [7] and knowledge creation[8], enlarges traditional framework of learning theories as to imbibe principles of epistemology, ontology and cognition processing so that both the requirements of individual development and knowledge building could be met. Simultaneously, this new paradigm can become a creative framework to support the development of learning technology in the age of connectivity so as to adapt itself to the social structure and technological demands of network times and to satisfy the needs of social transformation and learning innovation.

The synergistic learning framework is based on the idea of system synergy and knowledge creation. The phrase "synergistic learning" here indicates a kind of instructional relationship construction and instructional structure reform from the perspective of synergism. Synergistic learning makes a breakthrough at the existing learning technology system: it establishes an organic and coordinative relationship among information, knowledge, action, emotion and value; it enables a deep interaction between content and learners; it supplies information aggregative mechanism on the level of communicative structure; it provides a system of group brainstorm and cooperative construction on the level of information processing. In a word, we can conclude the basic principles of synergistic learning as "Deep Interaction between the learners and contents, information aggregation into GSTM for sharing, collective thinking operated on GSTM, collaborative creating of knowledge artifacts, Coordinating between multiple fields" [9].

3   Theoretical Model of Synergistic Learning

3.1   Meta-model of Synergistic Learning

A meta-model of synergistic learning is presented in fig.1. In this synergistic learning framework, learning is a synergistic process of information processing and knowledge creating, in which there is a synergistic relationship between information processing and knowledge creating and between individuals and collective as well. The micro-level, meso-level and macro-level of learning are connected organically together in

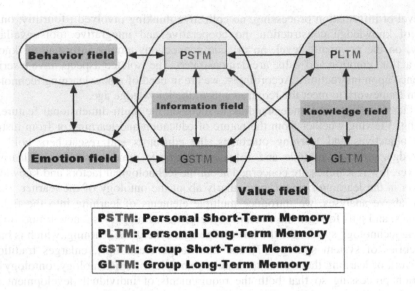

Fig. 1. Meta-model of Synergistic Learning

this framework. Hereby, this is a new comprehensive paradigm combining ideas, context, technology, models to obtain synergistic learning efficiency. At the same time, it can be considered as meta-model of learning systems, from which, a lot of specific models can be derived.

"Field", a concept borrowed from dynamics [10], is introduced into the synergistic learning system. It is an existence which takes a specific cognitive space as its reference and regards the cognitively interactive relationship between cognitive subject and learning environments as its core. That is to say, in the cognitive relationship between subject and object, there exists a grand system——"learning field", associated organically with human cognition and practical activities. Learning field is an entitative space which supports generation and development of the structure and function of synergistic learning system. And learning field is formed due to the collaborative interplay of multi-fields. In our synergistic learning frameworks, information field, knowledge field, behavior field, emotion field and value field interact and construct a functionary space of synergistic learning.

Five fields, which constitute the learning field, including information field (I-field), knowledge field (K-field), behavior field (B-field), emotion field (E-field) and value field (V-field), partly originate from the classical classification of instructional targets, that is, cognition, action and emotion. The first four fields are derived from the foregoing three objects while the value field is regarded as the pragmatic orientation and the terminal pursuit of a desirable learning system. These five fields are both learning objectives and means to realize these objectives. Through the systematic driving power and the reciprocal function mechanism, self-organization, connection and coordination happen between each field and between the elements of the fields.

3.2 Synergistic Learning Mechanism

In the framework of synergistic learning, coordinating between multiple fields and information processing between individuals and collective and knowledge construction compose the mechanism of learning. The emphasis of the metal model of synergistic learning, based on interactive coordination between multiple fields, is laid on information processing between individuals and collective and knowledge construction. By way of collaborative internalization, collaborative thinking and collaborative construction, the learners accomplish their individual knowledge construction and development.

Teaching is a process in which knowledge, emotion and action interplay reciprocally. Although teaching activities are developed by transmitting cognitive information, they cannot be separated anytime from inborn emotion and action of human beings. Instruction is thought as "a dynamic interpersonal process involving teachers and students rationally and emotionally", on the one hand, as "a dynamic process in which emotion, which is connected with personality and social psychological phenomena, and cognition interplay" on the other hand [11]. As for the behavior field which is the externalization of action and activities, it plays multiple roles in the learning course likewise. Performance and activities of mankind constitute various fields of the human society, even "A subject is equal to its course of action" [12]. In learning, individual activities and collective activities are closely connected in order to sustain the occurring of learning activities and the development of practice. As far as the relationship of actions with learning is concerned, Revans lays bare the truth with one remark: "There is neither learning without action nor (sober and prudent) action without learning" [13]. The contemporary context-cognitive theory also indicates that knowledge and action are interactive. Knowledge is contextualized and advances continuously forward through activities, at the same time it contributes to learning and understanding after its integration with practice. J. Lave & E. Wenger stress that active performers, activities and world can be taken as an interrelated whole, learning is no longer assumed only to accept knowledge and information [14].

The mechanism of the synergistic learning rests on the meaning construction process which takes multiple-fields-synergy-based information processing between individual-collective and knowledge construction as its core. Different technologies offer the possibility for high convergence of information & knowledge and synergy. The information field and the knowledge field provide space for knowledge creation; the emotion field which supplies the essential source of driving power to learning reconciles the whole learning progress as a power of knowledge synergistic processing while the behavior field providing room for behavior presentation, behavior development and wisdom generation is the extension and transference of learning. The value field, concerned about collective and individual value, rules and moral system, is the basis on which subject responds to object, including learning culture, social culture, viewpoints of value, etc. The v-field represents the basic orientation and pursuit of individuals and collective. From the practical perspective, synergy between multiple fields establishes a brand new framework for the learning technology system. After we integrate multi-resources and information architecture, technology synergistic mechanism is constructed to promote content-media deep interaction. Utilize different technologies to contribute to transference, generation and collaboration of synergistic learning fields so as to realize the organic collaboration of information, knowledge, emotion, action and value; reorganize classroom ontology to put knowledge convergence of informational technology into full play and implement the collaboration of thinking process between individuals and collective.

4 Synergistic Learning Toolkits

The synergistic learning technology system is a practical innovative model. The study, adopting the design-based research method (DBR) of learning science [15], intends to construct a creative new learning framework for the knowledge age in the interaction of theory-technology-practice. We have developed synergistic learning toolkits to support synergistic learning activities, including such sub-tools as synergistic knowledge annotation tools and synergistic knowledge construction tools. The function of annotation tools is to externalize thinking as symbols while that of construction tools is to facilitate instructors to describe collective thinking with diagrams. The synergistic learning toolkits are used to visualize class information by making information from the mental activities of the students visible to facilitate information sharing for learners and decision-making for teachers. Class information includes mind artifacts such as questions, concepts, rules, memories of past experience and emotional experiences produced in the learning course.

4.1 Synergistic Knowledge Annotation Tool: ClassCT

The principle of the synergistic annotation tool is to symbolize the information of students' minds first, then to aggregate the symbols, finally to generate logic views adaptable to different situations with algorithms. ClassCT resembles CT (computed tomography) used by doctors during diagnosis so as to collect stratum scanning diagrams. Here, ClassCT is like a CT utilized by teachers. Symbolization is the crucial stage at which inner information is transmitted as symbols and recorded on media through actions and performances. In practice, the teacher delivers an electronic file to all the students and then they add annotations to the file. Once the information

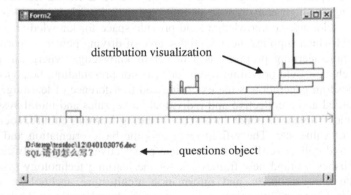

Fig. 2. Questions distribution visualization with knowledge annotation

is symbolized, the symbol machine, that is, the computer is used to aggregate and process these symbols rapidly. After that, various logic diagrams are drawn in accordance with the requirement, such as students' questions-distributed diagram (Fig.2).

4.2 Synergistic Knowledge Construction Tool: ClassKC

The synergistic construction tool realizes the diagrammatic presentation of collective construction and memory of knowledge. Understanding many solutions to a single problem is of great help to enlighten students' thinking, especially the peers' methods of working out the problem and meanwhile can arouse more interest of other students, for example, after the teacher hands out the homework exercise books to the students, some students are anxious to know how the others answer the questions which they have done wrong. In addition to providing answers for reference, the teacher should present other correct solutions to the students. However, after class, these short collective memories disappear. If individual memory is aggregated into collective memories and stored, it is helpful to remind the students of previous class discussion during the terminal review and of avoiding making the same mistakes. Therefore, the construction tool can be used to converge, process and store collective memories. Seen from the mechanism, ClassKC is a collaborative knowledge construction tool with co-authoring concept mapping (see Fig.3).

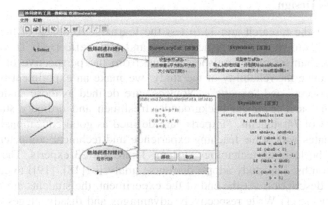

Fig. 3. Synergistic Knowledge Construction

5   Analytical Framework and Research Design

5.1   Three-Dimension Analytical Model of the CoINs

In view of the target and the situation of synergistic learning technology system, we can take the learning technology system as a "collaborative knowledge network" [16]. The study initiates evaluation and research on the system from an analytical model of CoIN. Collaborative Innovation Networks(CoIN) [17] is a new team management ideology and a practical framework while collaborative knowledge networks is a new management method of the innovation group whose aim is at establishing a more smooth, collaborative and innovative organization, with CoIN as its core. A group of self-motivated people with collective visions hope to share thoughts, information and work in order to realize their common objectives. Peter Gloor with his team develops a tool adaptable to CoINs and proposes a basic analytical dimension of CoINs, including connectivity, share and interaction. After coding the original discourse materials in accordance with three analytical dimensions of CoINs, we obtain the following coding system in Table 1.

Table 1. CoINS-based Analytical Dimension Coding

Dimensions	Coded keywords description	Positive discourse	Negative discourse
Connectivity(C)	Technology, connectivity, connecting points, connection between individuals, communication between individuals and machines	yes	no
Interactivity(I)	individual interactive degree, interactivity, content interaction	yes	no
Sharing(S)	Communities, group function, knowledge sharing	yes	no

5.2 Research Design

The focuses of the research are: 1) to test the learners' feedback of the synergistic learning tool; (2) to study synergistic learning and tool's effect. (3) To validate principles and mechanism of synergistic learning from the perspective of learners. In order to guarantee the reliability of the study, we make an experiment by observing two roles, "novices" and "experts". "Novices" are defined as those students without any educational and technical backgrounds, freshmen and ordinary students. Two classes consist of 74 students. "Experts" are defined as good educational technology majors, graduates with some teaching experience and technical competence who are interested in the learning technology system. There are 23 experts. The experiment takes three months. The study adopts discourse analysis ([18], [19]) to carry through the statistical description. At the end of the experiment, the students are requested to finish three tasks: (1) Write respectively advantages and disadvantages of two-tool-supported teaching situation; (2) "Experts" are required to put forward constructive suggestions; (3) "Experts" are also asked to design the situation in which two tools are used.

6   Data Analysis and Experimental Results

The study gives priority to the data of "novices", with those of "experts" as verifying materials. From the statistical result, the theoretic value of discourse theory of "novices" is 1480, the practical value of discourse is 1198, and valid sample rate is 80.95%, which indicates the number of samples is sufficient and efficient.

6.1 Data Analysis

The COINs model analyzes a knowledge network from three dimensions: connectivity, interaction and sharing. According to the above dimensions and coding system, the researchers perform a corresponding coding and characteristic statistic on the discourse of "experts" and "novices". The results are demonstrated in Tables 2 and 3.

Table 2. Three-dimension analysis of experts' data

Item	ClassCT -Positive	Coverage (87)	ClassCT -Negative	Cverage (95)	ClassKC -Positive	Coverage (65)	ClassKC -Negative	Coverage (90)
C	8	9. 20%	45	47. 37%	7	10. 77%	32	35. 56%
I	39	44. 82%	32	33. 68%	20	30. 77%	27	30.00%
S	40	45. 98%	18	18. 95%	38	58. 46%	31	34. 44%

Table 3. Three-dimension analysis of novices' data

Item	ClassCT -Positive	Coverage (291)	ClassCT -Negative	Cverage (308)	ClassKC -Positive	Coverage (287)	ClassKC -Negative	Coverage (316)
C	36	12. 37%	164	53. 25%	61	21. 25%	158	50. 00%
I	150	51. 55%	81	26. 30%	46	16. 03%	46	14. 56%
S	105	36. 08%	63	20. 45%	180	62. 72%	112	35. 44%

6.2 Experimental Results

From the perspective of the experts, two tools function badly in connectivity, especially the annotation tool. The main reason is that these two tools are developed on the basis of JAVA. In addition, the annotation tool, which needs particular files as its learning objects, finds it more difficult to adapt itself in connectivity to the current classroom network system and the environment. However, in sharing, two tools prove to be more efficient and advantageous, as essential to construct innovative knowledge networks. "Novices" hold nearly similar opinions to those of experts except that they lay more emphasis on the interaction of the annotation tool and sharing of the construction tool. Perhaps in their eyes, content interaction is the key feature of the learning system different from other learning technology system. On the other hand, speediness and visualization of the construction tool provide very important support for the collaborative learning and group brainstorm of "novices". The above data show that in connectivity, the construction tool is better than the annotation tool; but in interactivity, the latter is more valuable; in sharing, the construction tool has more advantages.

7 Conclusion and Prospects

The study proposes a new framework and a technological system of synergistic learning for the knowledge age. Based on an analytical model of CoINs, the study adopts discourse analyses to validate functions and effectiveness of the synergistic learning toolkits from the viewpoints of "novices" and "experts". The synergistic learning technology system is reorganized in terms of sociality of cognitive subject, dynamics of cognitive process and ecology of knowledge construction. Therefore, the instructional system has come to evolve into a social-technical system, thus, a brand new learning theory is necessarily constructed to support the learning reform. The new framework of synergistic learning, to some extent, is capable of dealing with comprehensive instructional challenges, which are concerned about learning objectives, learning diversity, reasonable utilization of cultural tools and cultural burdens of innovation, of the knowledge age. The synergistic learning can be regarded as an attempt, a brand new system to satisfy constructive demands of learning in the knowledge age.

What the paper introduces here is only a small part of the synergistic learning framework focusing on meta-model, information field and knowledge field and technological system. We are carrying out further studies on other fields and their interrelationships and hope to obtain support and collaboration from international colleagues.

References

1. Javirs, P.: Towards a Comprehensive Theory of Learning London: Routledge (2006)
2. Cheng, Y.C.: The Knowledge Base for Re-engineering Schools: Multiple Functions and Internal Effectiveness. International Journal of Educational Management 12(5), 203–224 (1998)
3. Garrison, D.R., Anderson, T., Archer, W.: Critical inquiry in a text-based environment: Computer conferencing in higher education. The Internet and Higher Education 2(2–3), 1–19 (2000)
4. Campbell, P., Cleveland Innes, M.: Emotional Presence in the Community of Inquiry Model: The Students' Viewpoint,
   http://ww.uwex.edu/disted/conference/Resource_library/handouts/05_2024P.pdf,2007-3-9
5. Quinn, C.N.: Making It Matter to the Learner: e-Motional E-Learning, The eLearning Guild's learning solutions: practical applications of technology for learning, (April 3, 2006)
6. Zhiting, Z., Youmei, W., Xiaoqing, G.: Synergistic learning: A new framework of learning technology system for knowledge era. China Educational Technology 4, 5–9 (2006)
7. Haken, H.: Synergetics, An Introduction: on-Equilibrium Phase Transitions and Self-Organization in Physics, and Chemistry, vol. III, p. 191. Springer, Heidelberg (1983)
8. von Krogh, G., Monika, L., Nishiguchi, T.: Knowledge creation: A source of value, pp. 60–88. Macmilian Press LTD (2003)
9. Zhiting, Z.: Synergistic Learning: A New Learning Paradigm in Connected Age. Keynotes on Advanced Seminar of 1st Global ET Summit Conference. Shanghai, China. (July 30, 2006)
10. Koffka, K.: Principle of Gestalt Psychology. Zhejiang Education Publishing House (1999)
11. Shaolun, J.: Psychology of Teaching and Learning. Jiangxi Education Publishing House.1 (1986)
12. Hegel, G.W.F.: Philosophy of Law. The Commercial Press, 126 (1961)

13. McGill, I., Betty, L.: Action Learning. Huaxia Publishing House. 153 (2002)
14. Lave, J., Wenger, E.: Situated Learning: Legitimate Peripheral Participation ECNU Press (2004)
15. Collins, A.: Toward a design science of education. In: Scanlon, E., O'Shea, T. (eds.) New directions in educational technology, Springer, Heidelberg (1992)
16. Wang, Y., Zhu, Z., Luo, H.: Synergistic Learning Technology System and An Analytical Model of CoINS (in press, 2007)
17. Gloor, P.: The Future of Work and Collaborative Innovation Networks
18. http://www.ickn.org/html/ckn_publications.htm,2007-3-9
19. Potter, J., Wetherell, M.: Discourse and Social Psychology, pp. 5–16. China Renmin University Press (2006)
20. Suthers, D.D.: Towards a Systematic Study of Representational Guidance for Collaborative Learning Discourse1. Towards a Systematic Study of Representational Guidance for Collaborative Learning Discourse. Journal of Universal Computer Science 7(3), Electronic publication (2001),
    http://www.jucs.org/jucs_7_3/towards_a_systematic_study

A New Layering Architecture of E-Learning System

Xingwei Hao, Xiangxu Meng, and Xu Cui

School of Computer Science and Technology, Shandong University
250100 Jinan, China
{hxw,mxx}@sdu.edu.cn, cuixu20021981@163.com

Abstract. By nature, an E-Learning system includes two aspects--learning and technologies. In the perspective of learning, learning contents (knowledge) and learning resources are the main parts of an E-Learning system; technologies are only means or tools which will be used to support learning process. With the popularization and deeper application of E-Learning systems, more and more network courses and learning resources have been developed. Accordingly, many problems have being occurred too, such as the difficulty of curriculum developing and updating, the flexibility, expansibility and maintainability of an E-Learning system, etc. On the basis of research about learning contents and their management, i.e., knowledge body of a discipline, we proposed a discipline oriented common knowledge ontology base based layering architecture of E-Learning system. In this developing mode, a common knowledge ontology base (KOB) in a discipline will be built, then through it, the problems of curriculum developing, course contents updating, learning contents reusing among different courses and the learning resources management will be solved, so to ensure the flexibility and practicability of E-Learning systems.

Keywords: E-Learning System Architecture, Knowledge Ontology, Learning Resource Management.

1 Introduction

With the rapid development of knowledge society and the accelerating of knowledge updates, E-Learning has now become one of the most important applications of Internet and has become a very important means of learning. Now, more and more people receive education and update their knowledge through E-Learning.

By nature, E-Learning is an application of information technology in learning, that the main technologies include computer technology, multimedia technology and modern communication technology etc. So, in the perspective of content, E-Learning includes two aspects of learning and technologies; in the perspective of appearance, E-Learning usually takes two kinds of forms--a computer software or a web-based application, i.e. an E-Learning environment or platform, and now the later one is the mainly form in all E-Learning systems.

E-Learning system, especially web-based E-Learning system is by nature a multi-layer structured web application. It is composed of a main directory in a web server which includes some sub-directories, some virtual directories, a large amount of documents and

H. Leung et al. (Eds.): ICWL 2007, LNCS 4823, pp. 218–229, 2008.

databases, all of which constitute the learning resources of an E-Learning system. Due to the characteristics of web application itself, courses developing or course contents updates may lead to great changes of hyperlinks, thus resulting in poor maintainability and expansibility of E-Learning systems. With the development of E-Learning system, as time goes on, the quantity of data in E-Learning system increase rapidly. Meanwhile, the types of learning resources are more various than before. Web pages, ppt documents, images, animations, videos and many other media files have now becoming important learning resources. So, the network curriculum developing and its contents updating , learning resource management, and the maintainability and expansibility of an E-Learning system have now becoming to fundamental problems to be studied and solved in E-Learning applications.

In order to solve the problems occurred in the applications of E-Learning, we proposed a discipline oriented common knowledge ontology base based layering architecture of E-Learning system. In this developing mode, many problems mentioned above will be solved and the flexibility of an E-Learning system can be ensured, so to enhance the practicability of E-Learning systems.

2 Related Research

Since 1996, there is more than 10 years of E-Learning history, a large amount of E-Learning systems have been developed and applied in many fields of education and training. In early days, the research and applications of E-Learning, mainly focused on the Computer-Aided Instruction (CAI), Computer-Based Training (CBT), Web-Based Training (WBT), and other computer aided instructional software. In recent years, with the rapid development and the popularization of multimedia, computer network and Internet, a computer network-based, electronic, digital and multimedia computer aided education, which is referred to as E-Learning, has grown rapidly. It is clear that all the E-Learning systems are the implementation of the traditional class learning in computer network.

E-Learning system or platform is open and so there has no one uniform architecture for all E-Learning systems. In order to develop E-Learning systems, from different aspects, many researchers made their research on the architecture and component of E-Learning systems, which include knowledge flow driven E-Learning architecture, workflow based E-Learning architecture, SCORM-based P2P E-Learning architecture, service-oriented E-Learning architecture and the semantic grid-based E-Learning framework etc [1~12].

In the architecture and component, most E-Learning systems are similar and the implementation technology of E-Learning systems is now almost mature. As an E-Learning system is a system or platform for learning, the realization of learning theory is its fundamental aim. So, in the design of the architecture and component of E-Learning systems, how to express the modern educational thoughts, educational theories, learning theories and educational psychology in an E-Learning system is a very important factor. Additionally, the architecture designing must consider the problems of flexibility and expansibility of an E-Learning system.

3 E-Learning System Layering Architecture Design

A large amount of E-Learning systems or integrated developing environments (such as Web CT, Blackboard Learning System, etc.) have been developed and applied in varies educational or training fields. Although they have different objects, goals and purposes, they are similar in function design. The functions or components usually include network courses and many learning-related parts, such as homework management, communication tools (e.g. online chatting, instant message, bbs and blogs etc.), online testing, learning and assessment function, and some learning affairs management functions.

In order to achieve the web-based learning of computer fundamental courses in our university, we designed and implemented a generalized self-learning platform (GSL). In early days of the development, we designed a three-layer E-Learning system model [13,14], and developed one computer fundamental course, i.e. "The Introduction to Computer", for all non-computer-major students to learn through Internet. Of course, all users connected to Internet can also visit it as a guest learner in a limit rights.

In the following days, we want to develop more courses on the platform, and the former E-Learning system model cannot work well. The mainly problems include: (1) lack of curriculum developing and updating capacity, (2) the problem of knowledge reusing in different courses, and (3) the expression of the relationship between knowledge body and learning objects. So, we proposed a new layering architecture which orients a discipline and is based on a common knowledge ontology base. The new layering architecture is show in Fig.1.

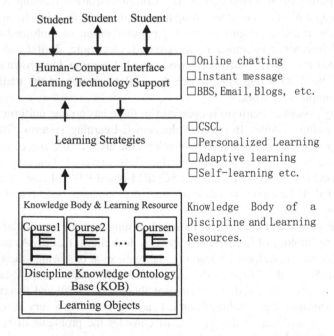

Fig. 1. Discipline knowledge ontology based layering architecture of E-Learning system

In Fig.1, an E-Learning system is divided into three layers: discipline knowledge and learning resource layer, learning strategies layer and human-computer interaction (learning technology support) layer. Discipline knowledge and learning resource layer is the core and most complex layer, it is further divided into three sub-layers including a learning object sub-layer, a discipline knowledge ontology base (KOB) sub-layer and a curriculum sub-layer. The discipline knowledge ontology base stores all knowledge points and their relations in a discipline, which sets up a logic mapping relationship between curriculum contents and learning objects, so to enhance the flexibility of curriculum developing, contents updating and learning resource management, and ensure the expansibility and maintainability of an E-Learning system. In learning strategies layer, some learning strategies based on learning theories are implemented. The learning technology support layer is a user layer, it provides varies communication means, learning tools and personalized views for learners.

4 Discipline Oriented Knowledge Ontology Base Design

4.1 Knowledge Categorization and Cognitive Structure

Cognitive learning theory indicates that learning is the changing process of the cognitive structure in a person's mind. By cognitive structure, simply, it refers to the knowledge structure in a person's mind. In broad senses, cognitive structure is the contents and organizations of all ideas of a person. In narrow senses, it refers to the contents and organizations of a person's knowledge in a specific field. Research in modern educational psychology and cognitive psychology also indicates that the cognitive process, maintenance and transference of different categories of knowledge are different, each having its special characteristics and rules [15,16].

In the study of knowledge categorization, human knowledge is usually divided into two categories: declarative knowledge and procedural knowledge (also called production knowledge). Apparently, this knowledge categorization is rough and not enough for learning practice. In a specific discipline, the declarative knowledge and procedural knowledge should further be divided into sub-categories. For example, in computer fundamental curriculum discipline, we divided the declarative knowledge into five sub-categories, which includes fact, term, concept (simple concept and abstract concept), theorem and device. And the procedural knowledge is divided into three sub-categories including operation skills, algorithm designing and program designing. Each sub-category corresponds to a specific cognitive structure.

4.2 Knowledge Point and Knowledge Ontology

Knowledge point is the elementary unit in knowledge body of a discipline, and it is the most important data in the E-Learning system layering architecture. As the core metadata, the knowledge point is widely used in the course model and learning object metadata model. In order to describe the designing thought of the layering architecture clearly we make the following definitions:

Definition 1. A knowledge point refers to an independent, completely expressed, and independently usable declarative or procedural knowledge entity□such as a fact, a term ,a concept, a theorem, or an algorithm etc.

Definition 2. Knowledge ontology is defined to express the knowledge points and the relations among them, each knowledge point corresponding to one knowledge ontology.

Knowledge ontology expresses the knowledge points themselves and their relations among them. We divide the relations among knowledge points into two kinds: (1) "include" relationship, for example, a complex knowledge point may include some facts and terms, i.e., some simple facts, terms or concepts are usually referred in other relative complex knowledge point. (2) "cognitive sequence" relationship, according to the learning theory of "zone of proximal development" [15], the learning process has a cognitive sequence.

A knowledge ontology includes seven metadata elements: (1) <name> element, it refers to the name of a knowledge ontology, which stores the name or ID of a knowledge point. (2) <alias> element, it refers to the aliases of the knowledge point. (3) <type> element, it refers to the knowledge category of the knowledge point. Different categories of knowledge correspond to different cognitive structures and learning strategies. (4) <include> element, a set of knowledge points that used in the knowledge ontology. (5) <prevs> element, it represents the previous knowledge points set of a knowledge point. (6) <succ> element, it represents the set of its succeeding knowledge points. (7) <refs> element, the set of its related knowledge points, which can be used for associative learning.

In the knowledge ontology model, the sets of previous, succeeding and related knowledge points express the "cognitive sequence" relationship of knowledge points and form a knowledge network [14], and the "include" relationship among knowledge points is expressed by the <include> element.

4.3 Common Knowledge Ontology Base

The knowledge body of a discipline is usually divided into a series of knowledge points, which are expressed via knowledge ontology and are organized in a relational database, that we call the database as discipline common knowledge point ontology base or simply knowledge ontology base (KOB). KOB is a common language for setting up relations among discipline knowledge body, courses and learning resources.

In the definition of knowledge ontology, the "type" field corresponds to knowledge category which corresponding to a specific cognitive structure. A cognitive structure is expressed via a data structure to describe its all cognitive attributes. So, in the KOB, it includes a knowledge ontology data table and more than one cognitive structure data tables. A cognitive structure data table stores data of the description of the knowledge and some knowledge category related attributes of a knowledge ontology.

In the database of KOB, it includes one knowledge ontology data table and some cognitive structure data tables which correspond to knowledge categorization in a discipline. For example, the cognitive structure of an operational skill knowledge includes five fields: problem description, operation steps, reffered knowledge points set and related principles. They relect the aspects that should be grasped in the learning of an operational skill knowledge.

The design goal of the multiple cognitive structure data tables is to reduce the data redundancies. Because the knowledge of facts and terms are relatively simple, it only needs the learners to learn them by heart and there is no specific cognitive structure for them. Additionally,the definition of cognitive structure realized the learning theory of categorization based learning. In addition, knowledge cognitive structure ensures the systematicness and integrality of knowledge in learning, and it is important for associate learning and knowledge memorizing.

5 Learning Resource Management

Learning resources are the carrier of knowledge, and all knowledge is explained via learning resources. In E-Learning systems, they are ultimately represented by various types of data files, including text files, image files, animation files, video files, audio files and any other types of data files.

5.1 Learning Object and Knowledge Point Based Learning Object Metadata Model

Learning resource is often referred to as learning object (LO), i.e., learning object is any digital resource that can be reused to support learning [17]. By nature, learning objects are various types of data files. But, different from ordinary data files, they carry specific knowledge and learning contents; they are designed and organized according to different learning theories, and express the carried knowledge in specific forms and sequences, and hence achieves the explanation of knowledge, i.e. support the knowledge cognition of learners.

In order to set up a logic relationship between learning contents and learning resources, a knowledge point based learning object metadata model is illustrated in Fig.2.

(1) "FileID" refers to the file identifier, including the file path and file name of a learning object.

(2) "MediaType" refers to the file type of the learning resource, such as webpage file (html,xml,etc), pdf file, ppt file, doc file, image file, animation file, video file or audio file, etc.

(3) "kps" refers to a set of knowledge points, which is carried in the learning object; in others words, the set of kps stores the knowledge points that the learning object will explain.

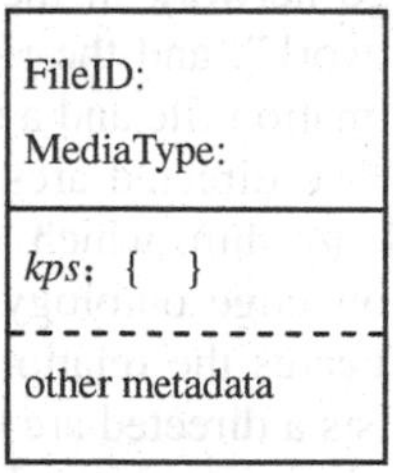

Fig. 2. LO metadata model

In addition, other metadata of IEEE LOM, ADL SCORM or Dublin core can also be included in the above knowledge points based LO metadata model, so as to achieve the learning resource sharing with SCORM E-Learning systems.

The knowledge point based learning object metadata model owns two excellent features: (1) It expresses the semantic meaning of a learning object. The core metadata of the model are knowledge points, which come from the common knowledge ontology base in a discipline. (2) Through knowledge points, a logic relationship between course contents and learning objects can be set up, which ensure the independence of the updates of courses and learning objects. If a new learning objected is registered in the system, the LO will be hyperlinked by any knowledge units that include the same knowledge points with those of the LO including.

5.2   The m:n Mapping Relationship Between Learning Object and Knowledge Point

Built on the definition of knowledge ontology and the learning object metadata model, we can set up a mapping relationship between knowledge point and learning object. An example of the mapping relationship is shown in Fig.3.

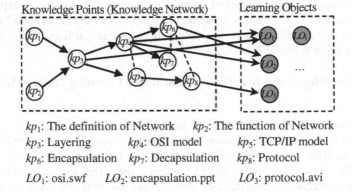

kp_1: The definition of Network kp_2: The function of Network
kp_3: Layering kp_4: OSI model kp_5: TCP/IP model
kp_6: Encapsulation kp_7: Decapsulation kp_8: Protocol

LO_1: osi.swf LO_2: encapsulation.ppt LO_3: protocol.avi

Fig. 3. Mapping relationship between knowledge point and learning object

In Figure 4, the left part is some knowledge points and the corresponding knowledge network in the knowledge unit of network model in the course of "computer network", and the right part lists some learning objects, including a ppt file, a flash animation file and a video file.

The directed arcs between two knowledge points indicate the cognitive sequence relationship, which are expressed via the "succs", "preds" and "refs" attributes of a knowledge ontology. The directed arc from a knowledge point to a learning object indicates the relationship between a knowledge point and a learning object. If there exists a directed arc $<kp_i, LO_j>$, it means that the knowledge point kp_i can be explained via learning object LO_j, in other words, learning object LO_j can be used to explain the knowledge point kp_i.

5.3   Learning Object Base

When a learning object is developed, it can not be used directly in E-Learning systems, it should be registered in the learning object repository. After that, the learning object can be retrieved and used in the E-Learning system. The registration of a learning object includes the metadata description of a learning object and the file identification. The description data of a learning object is stored in a relational database called learning object base (LOB), and all the LO files are organized and stored in different folders according to file types. The learning object base stores the metadata of all registered learning objects, and is indexed on knowledge point for quick retrieving and locating of learning objects in learning process.

6 Courses Developing and Contents Updating

In an E-Learning environment, with the development of discipline, new courses constantly emerge, and the contents of old courses might often need change, so network courses developing and contents updating of old courses have now become a very hard work in E-Learning applications.

According to the discipline knowledge ontology base, we can define a knowledge point based network course metadata model. Upon this model, the developing of a new network course only need to define the course directory structure and to select knowledge points from KOB for every knowledge units (KUs) in the course directory. Because the knowledge points in a KU have been determined, so we can copy all the learning contents of knowledge points included in the KU from the data base of KOB, then the learning contents might be reedited according to the learning objectives of the KU, thus the KU learning contents authoring work becomes easier.

6.1 Knowledge Point Based Course Metadata Model

In traditional, a course is divided into many chapters, sections and subsections, each knowledge unit includes some knowledge points. In an E-Learning system, on the basis of KOB, we can define a knowledge point based network course model. In order to describe the developing and maintenance of a course clearly, we make the formal definition of a course just as bellow:

First, the formal definition of a discipline common knowledge ontology base is defined as:

KOB = {KP_i, | i=1,2,...}

So, a course can be formally defined as the following:

Course = {$Chapter_i$ | i=1,2,...};

Chapter = {$Section_j$, KP_i | j=1,2,..., $KP_i \in$ KOB }

Section = {$SubSection_k$,KP_i | k=1,2,...,$KP_i \in$ KOB}

SubSection = { KP_i | $KP_i \in$ KOB}

The chapter, section and subsection are referred to as knowledge unit (KU) or learning information object (LIO), the KU structure definition is illustrated in Fig 4.

Fig. 4. KU structure

In Fig.4, " KU name" refers to the name of the knowledge unit, which will be displayed in the course directory tree and the KU webpage. "Learning Objective" refers to the learning objectives of the KU. "Learning contents" refers to the contents of the KU (edited in XML). "kps" refers to a set of knowledge points included in the KU.

6.2   KOB Based Content Authoring Method

According to the knowledge point based network course model, each knowledge unit has its learning objectives and learning contents. The developing of a course can be divided into two main steps: course directory structure definition and knowledge unit (KU) contents definition. The course directory structure definition is used to determine the chapters, sections and subsections of a course. The knowledge unit content definition includes determining the learning objectives of a KU, selecting knowledge points from KOB that will be explained in the KU, and authoring the learning contents text. The network course developing algorithm is just as bellow:

Algorithm1: Course Developing Algorithm (CDA)
Step1: Define learning objectives of the course
Step2: According to the course learning objectives, add chapters accordingly, and
 finally get: Course = {Chapter$_i$ I i=1,2,...m};
Step3: Define Chapter$_i$ = {Section$_j$ I j=1,2,...}
 3.1 If the chapter$_i$ not further be divided into sections, go to Step3 to define the
  next chapter;
  3.2 Otherwise, add sections accordingly, and finally get:
   Chapter$_i$ = {Section$_j$ I j=1,2,..., } ;
 3.3 For all Section$_i$ (j=1,2,...,) $\in$ Chapter$_i$, add its all subsections accordingly,
  and finally get:
   Section$_i$ = {SubSection$_k$ I k=1,2,..., }.
Step4: If i<m, go to Step3 to define the next chapter; Otherwise ,go to Step5.
Step5: Edit data of each KU
 5.1 Input and edit the learning objective of the KU;
 5.2 According the learning objective of the KU, select knowledge points for
  the KU from KOB;
 5.3 Call function KU contents authoring algorithm KUCA, reedit the KU
  learning contents.
Step6: End.

In the above course developing and content authoring algorithm, the definition of a course is divided into two main steps: the course directory structure definition and knowledge unit contents definition. The first step is from step1 to step 4, in the end of this step, the course directory is defined. Next, with each knowledge unit, input its learning objectives(Step5.1), select knowledge points from KOB that will be explained in the KU(Step5.2)and edit the learning contents text (Step5.3).

Because the knowledge points that a knowledge unit will explain have been determined, so the work of KU learning contents authoring can be done through copying the metadata of the knowledge points from KOB, which will constitute primitive materials of the learning contents text of the KU, and at last reedit the materials.

Let LC refers to the learning contents of a KU, the cognitive structure based KU content authoring algorithm (KUCA) is as the following:

Algorithm2: Cognitive structure based KU content authoring algorithm (KUCA)

Step1: For each knowledge point $KP_i \in KU$

    1.1 Retrieve KP_i in KOB, copy its metadata from knowledge ontology table and cognitive structure data table of KOB, then combine them to a data variable KP_iData;

    1.2 Add data of KP_i to learning contents of the KU, i.e.

        $LC = LC \cup KP_iData$.

Step2: Edit the Learning contents of KU;

Step3: End.

7   Implementation

According to the new layering architecture, which is discipline oriented and KOB based, we implemented a computer fundamental courses E-Learning platform, the E-Learning platform includes three main components: (1) curriculum developing, the component used for new course developing and course contents update; (2) LCM, which is a component of learning content management module used to maintain the KOB and learning resources; and (3) personalized learning view, it is the learners interface with the system, providing many learning support tools and a personalized view according to different roles and individual profiles.

7.1   Building KOB on Computer Discipline and Curriculum Developing

According to the research of knowledge point and knowledge ontology (see Section 4.2), the function of knowledge point definition in our E-Learning platform is illustrated in

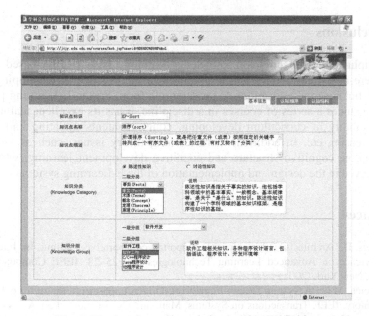

Fig. 5. The interface of knowledge ontology definition

Fig.5. Through the interface, all knowledge points are edited and be stored in KOB, which provides the fundamental data for courses developing, course contents updating, learning contents reusing in different courses and learning resource management etc.

The Course developing and knowledge unit contents authoring algorithm has also been implemented in our E-Learning platform. With the supports of KOB, the development of a new network course only needs to define the course directory structure and its corresponding knowledge points of each knowledge unit, the course contents and their needed learning objects will be retrieved through KOB and LOB (Learning Object Base) automatically. Meanwhile, the updates of the course contents and the change of learning resources could be logically adjusted via the course directory structure, without directly changing the pages of course contents themselves, so the flexibility of the course maintenance is improved greatly.

7.2 Support Multiple Learning Strategies

Built on the KOB, the knowledge categorization and cognitive structure provide flexible learning strategies. The platform supports the following learning strategies: knowledge categorization based learning (includes meaningful learning, associational learning), knowledge network based self-learning (includes personalized and adaptive learning), etc.

After a course developed, it will be released, each knowledge unit corresponds to a webpage to display the learning objective and the learning contents of the KU. At the bottom of the web page, there is a list of knowledge points included in the KU, following with some hyperlinks pointed to the learning objects that can explain the knowledge point. Click a hyperlink of learning object, the corresponding learning object will be displayed in a frame of the webpage.

8   Conclusions

The discipline oriented common knowledge ontology base (KOB) based layering architecture of E-Learning system is proposed in the practice of developing of our computer fundamental curriculum E-Learning platform. For an E-Learning platform, especial includes a series of courses in a discipline, it has its excellent features, such as its flexibility in curriculum developing, course contents updating and learning resource reusing etc. In addition, more learning theory issues, such as knowledge categorization, cognitive structure and cognitive development learning, which have been achieved in the design and implementation of the E-Learning system.

References

1. Suthers, D.: Architectures for computer supported collaborative learning. In: International Conference on Advanced Learning Technologies, pp. 25–28. IEEE Computer Society Press, New York (2001)
2. Dorneich, M.C.: A System Design Framework-Driven Implementation of a Learning Collaboratory. IEEE Transactions on Systems, Man, and Cybernetics—Part A: Systems And Humans 32(2), 200–213 (2002)

3. Kienle, A., Wessner, M.: The CSCL community in its first decade: development, continuity, connectivity. Computer-Supported Collaborative Learning 2006(1), 9–33 (2006)
4. Papanikolaou, K.A.: An Instructional Framework Supporting Personalized Learning on the Web. In: The 3rd IEEE International Conference on Advanced Learning Technologies, pp. 120–124. IEEE Computer Society Press, New York (2003)
5. Shen, R.: An Open Framework for Smart and Personalized Distance Learning. In: Fong, J., et al. (eds.) ICWL 2002. LNCS, vol. 2436, pp. 19–30. Springer, Heidelberg (2002)
6. Mei, Q., Shen, J.: A knowledge flow driven E-Learning architecture design: what is its stratification and how is it personalized. In: International Conference on Computers in Education, pp. 1307–1308. IEEE Computer Society Press, New York (2002)
7. Kong, W., Luo, J., Zhang, T.: A workflow based e-learning architecture in service environment. In: The Fifth International Conference on Computer and Information Technology, pp. 1026–1032. IEEE Computer Society Press, New York (2005)
8. Huang, F.-M., Chao, M.: An architecture of virtual environment for E-Learning (AVEE). In: ICALT 2005, pp. 148–149. IEEE Computer Society Press, New York (2005)
9. Tamura, Y., Yamamuro, T., Okamoto, T.: Distributed and Learner Adaptive E-Learning Environment with Use of Web Services. In: Sixth International Conference on Advanced Learning Technologies, pp. 155–451. IEEE Computer Society Press, New York (2006)
10. Zualkernan, I.A.: HYDRA: a light-weight, SCORM-based P2P E-Learning architecture. In: ICALT 2005, pp. 484–486. IEEE Computer Society Press, New York (2005)
11. Hussain, N., Khan, M.K.: Service-Oriented E-Learning Architecture Using Web Service-Based Intelligent Agents. In: First Internationa Conference on Information and Communication Technologies (ICICT 2005), pp. 137–143. IEEE Computer Society Press, New York (2005)
12. Abbas, Z., Umer, M., et al.: A semantic grid-based E-Learning framework (SELF). In: Fifth IEEE International Symposium on Cluster Computing and Grid Cardiff (CCGrid 2005), pp. 11–18. IEEE Computer Society Press, Washington (2005)
13. Hao, X., Su, X.: A generalized self-learning platform-design and implementation. Journal of Computer Science 31(11), 168–171 (2004)
14. Hao, X., Meng, X.: Research on a Kind of Knowledge Network for Self-learning. In: Pan, Z., Aylett, R.S., Diener, H., Jin, X., Göbel, S., Li, L. (eds.) Edutainment 2006. LNCS, vol. 3942, pp. 116–123. Springer, Heidelberg (2006)
15. Schunk, D.H.: Learning Theories: An Educational Perspective(3rd Edition, Simplified Chinese edition). Pearson Education North Asia Limited and Jangsu Education Publishing House (2003)
16. Lu, B., Zhang, X.: A Tentative Discussion of knowledge categories and instruction. Journal of Nanhua Univesity (edition on Social Science) 1, 73–76 (2001)
17. Wiley, D.A.: Connecting learning objects to instructional design theory (2004), http://reusability.org/read/chapters/wiley.doc

Transformational Techniques for Model-Driven Authoring of Learning Designs

Juan Manuel Dodero[1], Colin Tattersall[2], Daniel Burgos[2], and Rob Koper[2]

[1] Universidad Carlos III de Madrid, Av. Universidad 30,
28911 Leganés, Madrid, Spain
juanmanuel.dodero@uc3m.es
[2] Open Universiteit Nederland, Valkenburgerweg 177
6419 AT Heerlen, The Netherlands
{colin.tattersall, daniel.burgos, rob.koper}@ou.nl

Abstract. Diverse authoring approaches and tools have been designed to assist the creation of units of learning compliant to current learning technology specifications. Although visual and pattern-based editors of Learning Designs (LD) can help to abstract the learning designer from the details of the specifications, they are still far from a high-level, integrated authoring environment. This paper analyzes the major approaches used to transform an abstract LD into a concrete unit of learning (UoL), according to three desired features: the use of patterns and other design techniques to abstract the specific representational details; the difference between the abstract source LD model and the concrete target UoL model; and the possibility of combining multiple models into a single environment. A classification is proposed for the LD techniques commonly found in the analyzed approaches, in order to underline its abstraction from the details of the underlying specifications. We have integrated such LD techniques in a unified Model-Driven Learning Design (MDLD) meta-modeling environment, which has been used to generate UoLs from a number of meta-models. The model-driven development process was studied on the creation of a IMS LD UoL for the Learning Networks' knowledge base.

Keywords: Model-driven development, learning design patterns, IMS Learning Design, unit of learning.

1 Introduction

The increasing adoption of the IMS Learning Design (LD) specification has provided a common ground for the digital representation of learning designs. Learning design deals with exploiting prescriptions from instructional design theory plus examples of best practices and patterns of experience, which are then applied to develop concrete Units of Learning (UoL) [1]. Teachers can avail themselves of LD authoring tools to perform such a complex task, thus creating UoLs that adapt to specific instructional needs. Despite its great expressiveness, IMS LD is far from simple to teachers and learning designers. For instance, to define adaptive UoLs, the level B of the specification must be followed, which requires the definition of technically complex XML-based descriptions of *properties* and *conditions* to describe adaptations [2].

H. Leung et al. (Eds.): ICWL 2007, LNCS 4823, pp. 230–241, 2008.

A recent report from the UNFOLD project shows that most LD tools are still too close to the technical formalisms and underlying specifications of the digital *artifacts* they assist to create [3]. For instance, adding level B elements to a LD may be actually burdensome, since they are too low-level and have to be expressed in XML. The significant shortage of high-level authoring tools prevents teachers from keeping their distance from the specification, so they have to learn and use technical concepts that are far from their pedagogical backgrounds and contexts [4]. This becomes especially difficult if teachers have to learn more than one specification, as it happens in netUniversité [5]; or if they have to create learning content, metadata, and learning designs separately and afterwards integrate them manually, as required by RELOAD [6].

Most computer-assisted authoring environments differentiate between the language used to interact with them (i.e. the *source* language), and the language of the artifact that is eventually generated (i.e. the *target* language). The source LD language can be graphical, as in MOT+LD, or textual, like in the IMS LD XML binding. Graphic tools rely on user-defined visual representations, from which XML descriptions of an IMS LD can be easily generated. However, shapes and drawing elements usually keep too close to the core IMS LD model, as it happens with ASK-LDT [7].

Some graphic tools usually describe a number of models that put together make up the overall source LD. When such generic and shared models are used as learning design elements, the resultant LD can be mapped to a single UoL that is compliant with the IMS LD specification. This approach is taken by MOT+LD [8] to develop models of knowledge, competences, pedagogical structure, materials and delivery, which are eventually transposed to concrete IMS LD UoLs. However, the occurrence of multiple models is not restricted to the LD source, but it also can occur in the target UoL. For instance, an IMS LD UoL can be readily merged with resources described with XHTML [2], QTI [9] and other specifications. In particular, integrating IMS LD and QTI requires clear-cut manipulations of manifest files to bind certain QTI elements (e.g. *score* and *feedback*) with the proper IMS LD Level B properties.

Some works such as the CPM meta-model [10,11] define a UML profile plugged into a commercial meta-CASE environment to provide abstract models, which constitute the basis of a model-based approach to engineer learning designs. Although not strictly comparable to the pedagogically neutral IMS LD, CPM provides a problem-based pedagogical modeling approach that requires knowledge of UML and a vendor tool, which can be still a barrier for teachers and specialists in pedagogy.

To overcome the former issues, learning design patterns have been proposed as a means to incorporate template-based pedagogy in a half-cooked learning design [12]. LD pattern-based tools as Collage [13] are a powerful way to alleviate teachers and designers' inconveniences caused by the undesirable proximity to the IMS LD specification. The seamless integration of patterns into unified LD methods and tools is still required, so they become the foundation of model-based design approaches, which are the focus of this work.

The rest of this paper is structured as follows: first, a characterization of major LD authoring environments is presented, and some challenges observed in the analyzed tools are detailed, specially focused on the use of design abstractions as patterns. Then a classification of relevant pattern and idiom-based LD techniques is provided. An explanation of how such techniques can be integrated in a model-driven development environment is followed, for which a meta-modeling tool and a case study have been developed and tested. Finally, we provide some conclusions and future work.

2 Challenges of LD Authoring

The background challenge found in many authoring approaches is how to raise the level of abstraction at which teachers operate when they create a learning design. Instead of dealing directly with low-level descriptions of LD, software engineering design techniques are commonly used to shortcut the way to the final UoL. This section discusses some issues and provides a characterization of the most widespread authoring tools. The feature selection criterion for the characterization has been the provision of abstraction facilities to isolate users from the specification of the final UoL and resources. Such features are structured in the following categories:

- *Design abstractions*: This category encompasses whether and which learning design abstractions (e.g. patterns) are used to raise the abstraction level, and if different design patterns can be combined and applied to the same UoL. This challenge can be difficult or even meaningless, and it is comparable to the combination of different source models, usually undertaken by defining meta-models and model transformations. Examples of this category are MOT+, CPM and Collage.
- *Source vs. target model*: There is a difference between the source model (i.e. the one to be known by the user to compose an LD) and the target model used by the resultant UoL. For instance, some approaches (e.g. MOD+LD, CPM) are founded on source pedagogical models, which are eventually transposed into the target IMS LD model for the generated UoL, whilst others (e.g. RELOAD, ASK-LDT, Collage) consider IMS LD as both the source and target model.
- *Multiple models*: Some development tools allow the combination of elements from different models or specifications within the same target UoL, while others are model-specific. For instance, the netUniversitè environment [5] allows including IMS LD and QTI elements together in the same UoL through a single authoring environment. Other tools as RELOAD strictly adhere to a number of learning technology specifications, but do not allow combining them in the same UoL. The combination of models can also be carried out on multiple source models, as in MOT+.

A major challenge of existing LD authoring approaches is that the author has to be aware of details related to the categories mentioned above: First, learning design abstractions, such as patterns, must be selected and applied separately, without support to readily combining two or more patterns; second, authors are usually committed to a source model nearly identical to the target model; and third, tools do not usually allow editing learning resources compliant to diverse specifications in the same design.

Our approach is based on the use of meta-models to create source models, which are later transformed and merged without requiring the teacher to be aware the underlying specifications. Transformations are driven by LD patterns and idioms as the fundamental design abstraction. In the following section, transformational techniques used to manipulate and transform source LD models are classified.

3 Transformational Techniques for Learning Design

In software engineering, several design techniques have proven to be helpful in automating software manipulations [14]. These are classified according to the cross-linguality and significance of the transformations required to map, merge and extend software models. Although they are applied on regular software artifacts, they can also be used to map an abstract LD into concrete UoLs. When it comes to LD, such techniques are summarized in the following categories:

- *Shortcutting*: generation of LD instances from parameterized templates that require less coding. Design patterns, idioms and the like are included in this category [15].
- *Mapping*: generation of an LD instance from mixing more than one partly-completed design.
- *Refactoring*: to perform modifications on an LD instance to become more efficient or reusable, without changing its original purpose [16].
- *Extending*: adding a number of LD elements which cannot be represented with a given LD language or it becomes so costly that it is better to use elements from a different language.

3.1 Shortcutting Patterns and Idioms

A design pattern names, abstracts, and identifies the key aspects of a common design structure that make it useful for creating a reusable design [17]. Pattern-based solutions are applied to LD with different levels of abstraction. On one hand, pattern languages define high-level collections of patterns and the rules to combine them, so raising the abstraction level of course design [18]. On a lower abstraction level, when a learning design pattern is specific to an LD language, it becomes an *idiom* [16]. An idiom is a pattern that describes how to implement particular aspects of an LD using the features of a given LD language (notably IMS LD). Although IMS LD can be used to represent higher-level LD patterns, when it comes to generating concrete UoLs, the required transformations have to be aware of IMS LD details such as level B properties and conditions. Idioms provide an abstract expression of such details in IMS LD. Next, a purposeful catalogue of IMS LD idioms is proposed to support the development approach described thereafter.

Although many kinds of IMS LD idioms can be identified, depending on what elements of the IMS LD specification have to do with the idiom, we only selected those that provide a higher-level abstraction for level B elements, like properties and conditions, which are particularly difficult to abstract in authoring tools. Each idiom is described in Table 1 by a UML activity diagram and an associated script containing the binding to the IMS LD information model, which drives the transformation used to generate the UoL. This way, the designer only selects the desired activity idiom from the catalog, and the appropriate transformation is then applied. For brevity we summarize only a handful of IMS LD idioms used to describe common structures of learning activities:

- *Alternative activities* (see Table 1a): Only one of a number of activities is executed depending on a previous condition
- *Forked activities* (see Table 1b): The learning flow is split among a number of concurrent activities, which since then will run in parallel.
- *Rendezvous* (see Table 1c): Two or more concurrent learning activity flows meet on a synchronization point (i.e. the *rendezvous*), and then continue together on a single flow. If there are flows that arrive later, they have to wait for the rest.
- *Guard-synchronized activities* (see Table 1d): The rendezvous synchronization is augmented by the satisfaction of a boolean condition. When it is false, all learning flows must wait; when it becomes true, the behavior is like the rendezvous idiom.

For clarity, the activity idioms described above include only two activities, but the cardinality can be extended by the iterative application of a two-activity idiom, without losing generality. The binding scripts avoid the verbosity of the IMS LD XML binding. From the scripts of Table 1, a simple substitution of parameters —marked with $— is applied to generate the XML-based UoL chunks. These are not still fully-fledged UoLs, since they miss the role and method role-part definition. Nevertheless, they are closer to the sought-after runnable condition of the UoL [19].

3.2 Mapping

The generation of UoL chunks from the idiom scripts is a one-to-one mapping from the model used to express the idiom (i.e. from the idiom script language) to the model in which the UoL chunk is based (i.e. the IMS LD XML binding). Nevertheless, other kinds of transformations may require conformance to more than one model, in which case more complex mappings are required. On the one hand, one-to-many model mappings are useful to keep the user away from knowing more than one model. For instance, the teacher can create an LD containing both activities and assessments without needing to know about IMS LD or QTI and, more importantly, without having to know the way of connecting elements from both specifications —based upon binding level B properties and QTI item variables. On the other hand, many-to-one model mappings (sometimes called model merging) allow the definition of separate aspects on the development of a learning artifact, as well as the division of responsibilities in a group of designers.

One-to-one mappings are used to transform between single meta-models. These mappings can be intra-language or inter-language, depending on the source and target meta-models. In intra-language mappings, a simple sequence of modeling actions describes the transformation from a model to another complying with the same meta-model (for instance, a transformation to enlarge the number of activities of an IMS LD). In inter-language mappings, the source and target meta-models are different (for instance, a transformation from UML to IMS LD). The mapping effort depends on the semantic distance between the concepts of both models (e.g. UML 2.0 activities, lanes, and object nodes versus IMS LD activities, roles, and environments). In such an example, activity diagram lanes are mapped to IMS LD roles, as usually done in the IMS LD specification.

Table 1. IMS LD activity structure idioms. Each idiom is described by a UML activity diagram (left column) and a binding script (right column) from which the IMS LD XML elements are generated.

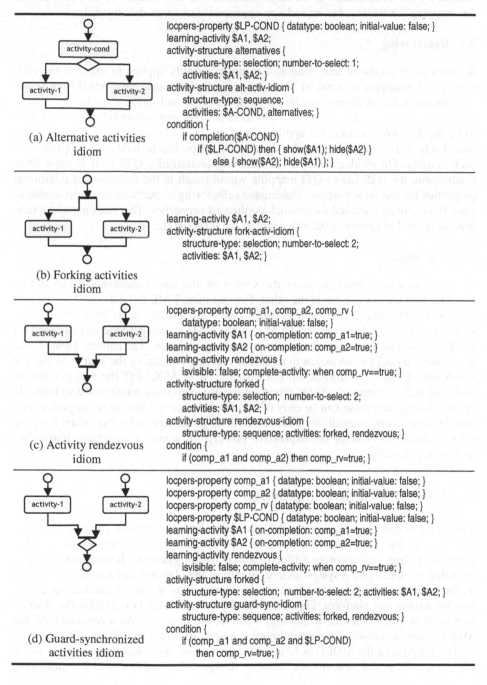

(a) Alternative activities idiom	locpers-property $LP-COND { datatype: boolean; initial-value: false; }
	learning-activity $A1, $A2;
	activity-structure alternatives {
	    structure-type: selection; number-to-select: 1;
	    activities: $A1, $A2; }
	activity-structure alt-activ-idiom {
	    structure-type: sequence;
	    activities: $A-COND, alternatives; }
	condition {
	    if completion($A-COND)
	      if ($LP-COND) then { show($A1); hide($A2) }
	        else { show($A2); hide($A1) }; }

(b) Forking activities idiom	learning-activity $A1, $A2;
	activity-structure fork-activ-idiom {
	    structure-type: selection; number-to-select: 2;
	    activities: $A1, $A2; }

(c) Activity rendezvous idiom	locpers-property comp_a1, comp_a2, comp_rv {
	    datatype: boolean; initial-value: false; }
	learning-activity $A1 { on-completion: comp_a1=true; }
	learning-activity $A2 { on-completion: comp_a2=true; }
	learning-activity rendezvous {
	    isvisible: false; complete-activity: when comp_rv==true; }
	activity-structure forked {
	    structure-type: selection; number-to-select: 2;
	    activities: $A1, $A2; }
	activity-structure rendezvous-idiom {
	    structure-type: sequence; activities: forked, rendezvous; }
	condition {
	    if (comp_a1 and comp_a2) then comp_rv=true; }

(d) Guard-synchronized activities idiom	locpers-property comp_a1 { datatype: boolean; initial-value: false; }
	locpers-property comp_a2 { datatype: boolean; initial-value: false; }
	locpers-property comp_rv { datatype: boolean; initial-value: false; }
	locpers-property $LP-COND { datatype: boolean; initial-value: false; }
	learning-activity $A1 { on-completion: comp_a1=true; }
	learning-activity $A2 { on-completion: comp_a2=true; }
	learning-activity rendezvous {
	    isvisible: false; complete-activity: when comp_rv==true; }
	activity-structure forked {
	    structure-type: selection; number-to-select: 2; activities: $A1, $A2; }
	activity-structure guard-sync-idiom {
	    structure-type: sequence; activities: forked, rendezvous; }
	condition {
	    if (comp_a1 and comp_a2 and $LP-COND)
	      then comp_rv=true; }

In a sense, one-to-many model mappings can be considered as one-to-one mappings between the source model and an instance of the non-explicit meta-model formed by the combination of the target models. For this reason, we do not focus on the mapping cardinality, but on defining appropriate meta-models instead.

3.3 Refactoring

Refactoring is a kind of intra-language mapping usually applied to improve the efficiency or reusability of a model. Although refactoring transformations do not really encompass different abstraction levels for the source and target model, they can be easily automated so that users only have to select the appropriate refactoring method to be applied. For instance, the application of the IMS LD activity rendezvous idiom (see Table 1c) results in adding local personal properties to hold the completion of each activity. On another hand, if each activity contained a QTI item to mark their finalization, the IMS LD-to-QTI mapping would result in the definition of additional properties for the same purpose. Automated refactoring inspections can help to abbreviate the eventual UoL and merge such duplicated properties. This does not add a new functionality, but improves the efficiency of the target UoL.

3.4 Extending

In inter-language mappings, either the source or the target meta-model can define concepts that are not present in the other. For instance, UML 2.0 does not have a form to model roles, like IMS LD does. Such cases are usually dealt by extending the source meta-model. For example, CPM uses the UML extension mechanism based on profiles to augment the set of available modeling elements. On another hand, if the target meta-model has no means to represent certain elements of the source model the target model can lose information. For instance, with ASK-LDT the user can define and configure a library of activity types, which are eventually transformed to IMS LD activities only. But these can be only of two kinds, namely learning or support activities. In these cases, extensibility could be both an advantage and a risk, since it would offer a chance to enhance the expressive power, but it may compromise reusability and interoperability.

4 Model-Driven Learning Design

Transformational LD techniques such as the described above enable the *Model-Driven Learning Design* (MDLD). The intention of MDLD is to develop specific learning technology-supported software artifacts such as learning designs. It enables tools to be provided for specifying a system independently of the platform that supports it, as well as for transforming the system abstract specification into the more concrete specification for a particular platform. Therefore, the objective of MDLD is to raise the abstraction level at which learning technology systems are designed. As a consequence, the MDLD integrates diverse non-representational abstractions to specify an LD.

The purpose of the MDLD is to integrate non-representational techniques in a single environment that relieves the learning designer from lower-level LD authoring tasks. In order to test it in practice, we have built a meta-modeling tool based on Eclipse and the FXL plug-in [20], which provides two complementary views of model-based development:

- The *activity modeler* view (see Figure 1) uses the Business Process Execution Language (BPEL) plug-in to model activities at the PIM level.
- The *transformation modeler* view (see Figure 2) provides a graphic user interface to edit transformation pipelines from the PIM to the PSM level.

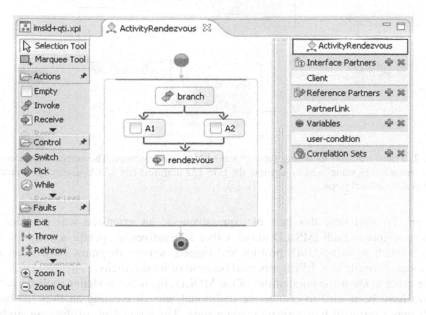

Fig. 1. Activity modeling view of the MDLD environment. The screen represents the BPEL modelling of an activity rendezvous pattern, from which the corresponding IMS LD idiom is later generated.

The model-driven transformation process is defined as a pipeline, which receives a number of source models on the input, and generates other models on the output. This process is accomplished in a number of steps defined through the transformation modeler. On the other hand, graphical editing of the models is carried out with the activity modeler. In its current prototype, the activity modeler allows editing learning activity structures, which are enough to define the IMS LD activity idioms.

The transformation pipeline has to be defined only once —i.e. the teacher is not required to use the transformation modeler. The teacher only has to choose the LD idiom and select the QTI items from the library, and then apply the transformation. On the other hand, the teacher is not forced to define a concrete IMS LD activity structure, but she can simply select it from the library of IMS LD idioms. Nonetheless, the activity modeler provides the learning designer with a higher-level way of dealing with activities.

Activity abstractions are represented with BPEL. The expressive limitations of BPEL are clear (e.g. concerning user roles), since it is not designed for instructional

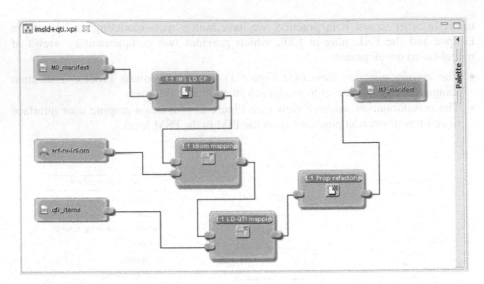

Fig. 2. Transformation modeling view of the MDLD environment. The screen represents the transformation pipeline used to generate the IMS LD manifest file of a UoL through a number of transformational steps.

design. To overcome this lack of expressiveness, an extension was provided by adding scripts to each IMS LD idiom. Other alternatives to specify activity idioms' details, such as using UML profiles and tagged activity diagrams [10], were also explored. Nevertheless, BPEL was used because of its simplicity.

In order to show the possibilities of the MDLD, the meta-modeling tools described above have been used to change the traditional way of creating an IMS LD-based UoL into a series of transformation commands. The target UoL of the case study is based on an adaptive IMS LD taken from the Learning Networks' knowledge base [2], but elements from other specifications have been also incorporated —a set of QTI items grouped in IMS LD activities, which are synchronized by means of level B properties and conditions. Adding such items to a UoL may be a hindrance when the learning designer is not acquainted with the IMS LD and QTI specifications. Therefore, the objective of the case study is to show how non-representational LD techniques included in the MDLD development environment facilitate the creation of an LD exemplar consisting of different models. In particular, the learning design technique used to abstractly represent the activity structure has been the *activity rendezvous* IMS LD idiom.

The transformation pipeline followed in the case study is depicted in Figure 3. From left to right, the input to the pipeline is the M_0 manifest file, which does not contain any IMS LD information at all. First, a content package (CP) transformation is executed to prepare it for holding an IMS Learning Design. The result is the M_1 manifest. Second, M_2 adds to M_1 an empty activity structure according to the activity rendezvous idiom (*act-rv-idiom*). Afterwards, all the activities are filled in with QTI items, which are bound to the UoL by means of two level B properties and one condition (notably to bind the *score* and *feedback* QTI elements), thus resulting in M_3.

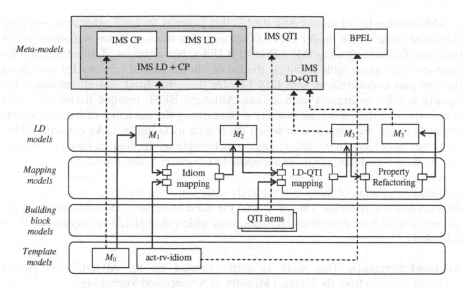

Fig. 3. Scheme of the MDLD transformation pipeline of the case study. Models can represent templates, building blocks, mappings, or exemplars, depending on their granularity level and completion status [19]. Each artifact is an instance of a meta-model from the top of the figure, represented as dashed arrows.

Since the LD-QTI mapping added some redundancy on properties when it is combined with the rendezvous idiom, a final refactoring stage is executed to overcome this issue.

The complete MDLD process delivers the M_3' UoL, which becomes functionally identical to M_3, but less verbose in using level B properties. Artifact M_3 contains elements from both IMS LD and QTI specifications. To generate this, it was only required to select the LD idiom and QTI items from respective libraries containing templates and building blocks. According to the terminology of Hernández-Leo *et al.* [19], M_3 and M_3' are exemplars (i.e. ready-to-run UoLs); M_1 and M_2 are LD templates (i.e. partly completed exemplars), M_0 is a non-LD template; QTI items are building blocks (i.e. partly completed UoL chunks).

5   Conclusion and Future Works

This paper presents a characterization of LD techniques aimed at providing high-level LD authoring environments. Relevant design pattern-based approaches are classified, enlarged with IMS LD idioms, and combined in a model-driven learning design environment which enables the overall objective of distancing the author from the IMS LD specification. The MDLD environment is based on the use of meta-models and idiom-based transformations to manipulate multiple source models and produce the eventual UoL. With the help of the MDLD environment, a learning designer can generate an IMS LD UoL that combines several learning technology specifications without requiring a detailed knowledge of them.

Although the list of idioms described in this paper is far from exhaustive —it only contained those which model IMS LD activity structures—, it was sufficient to test how they facilitate creating IMS LD level B UoLs. Nevertheless, if different LD roles were involved along with activities, the list of idioms should be extended to express the role-part collaborations with IMS LD. On the other hand, not all languages are equally suitable to express such idioms. Although BPEL resulted useful due to its simplicity, its expressive limitations (e.g. concerning the modeling of user roles) corresponds to the mapping case in which the source meta-model lacks concepts which the target model has. In the future, other transformational techniques based on extending the source modeling language are needed to overcome such limitations.

As a consequence, not all abstract modeling languages are equally suitable for LD authoring, and none of them is completely satisfactory to model complex aspects of the IMS LD specification. This motivated the need to define a Domain-Specific Language (DSL) for the educational domain, with which the MDLD environment can be extended.

Acknowledgements. This work is partly funded by the MODUWEB project (TIN2006-09768) from the Spanish Ministry of Science and Technology.

References

1. Koper, R.: An introduction to learning design. In: Koper, R., Tattersall, C. (eds.) Learning Design: A Handbook on Modelling and Delivering Networked Education and Training, pp. 3–20. Springer, Berlin (2005)
2. Koper, R., Burgos, D.: Developing advanced units of learning using IMS Learning Design level B. Advanced Technology for Learning 2(4), 252–259 (2004)
3. Burgos, D., Griffiths, D.: The UNFOLD Project. Understanding and Using Learning Design. Open University of The Netherlands, Heerlen (2005)
4. Griffiths, D., Blat, J.: The role of teachers in editing and authoring units of learning using IMS Learning Design. Advanced Technology for Learning 2(4), 243–251 (2005)
5. Giacomini, E., Trigano, P., Sorin, A.: A QTI editor integrated into the netUniversitè web portal using IMS LD. Journal of Interactive Media in Education 9 (2005)
6. Milligan, C.D., Beauvoir, P., Sharples, P.: The Reload learning design tools. Journal of Interactive Media in Education 7 (2005)
7. Sampson, D.G., Karampiperis, P., Zervas, P.: ASK-LDT: A Web-based learning scenarios authoring environment based on IMS Learning Design. Advanced Technology for Learning 2(4) (2005)
8. De la Teja, I., Lundgren-Cayrol, K., Paquette, G.: Transposing MISA learning scenarios into IMS units of learning. Journal of Interactive Media in Education 13 (2005)
9. Vogten, H., Martens, H., Nadolski, R., Tattersall, C., Van Rosmalen, P., Koper, R.: Integrating IMS Learning Design and IMS Question and Test Interoperability using Copper-Core Service Integration. In: Proc. of the Learning Networks for Lifelong Competence Development Workshop, Sofia, Bulgaria, p. 43 (2006)
10. Nodenot, T., Laforcade, P., Sallaberry, C., Marquesuzaa, C.: A UML profile incorporating separate viewpoints when modeling co-operative learning situations. In: Proc. of the First International Conference on Information Technology: Research and Education, p. 605. IEEE Press, Newark, USA (2003)

11. Nodenot, T., Marquesuzaa, C., Laforcade, P., Sallaberry, C.: Model-based engineering of learning situations for adaptive web based educational systems. In: Proc. of the Thirteenth International World Wide Web Conference, p. 94. ACM Publications, New York (2004)

12. McAndrew, P., Goodyear, P., Dalziel, J.: Patterns, designs and activities: unifying descriptions of learning structures. International Journal of Learning Technology 2(2), 216–242 (2006)

13. Hernández-Leo, D., Villasclaras-Fernández, E.D., Jorrín-Abellán, I.M., Asensio-Pérez, J.I., Ruiz-Requies, I., Rubia-Avi, B.: COLLAGE: A collaborative learning design editor based on patterns. Educational Technology and Society 9(1), 58–71 (2006)

14. Caplat, G., Sourrouille, J.L.: Model mapping using formalism extensions. IEEE Software 22(2), 44–51 (2005)

15. Buschmann, F., Meunier, D., Rohnert, H., Sommerlad, P., Stal, M.: Pattern-Oriented Software Architecture. A System of Patterns, vol. 1. Wiley, Chichester (1996)

16. Fowler, M., Beck, K., Brant, J., Opdyke, W., Roberts, D.: Refactoring: Improving the Design of Existing Code. Addison-Wesley, Reading (1999)

17. Gamma, E., Helm, R., Johnson, R., Vlissides, J.: Design Patterns: Elements of Reusable Object-Oriented Software. Addison-Wesley, Reading (1994)

18. Bergin, J.: A pattern language for initial course design. ACM SIGCSE Bulletin 33(1), 282–286 (2001)

19. Hernández-Leo, D., Harrer, A., Dodero, J.M., Asensio-Pérez, J.I., Burgos, D.: A Framework for the Conceptualization of Approaches to Creating by Reusing Learning Design Solutions. Journal of Universal Computer Science 13(7), 750–760 (2007)

20. Reichel, C., Oberhauser, C.R.: XML-based Programming Language Modeling: An Approach to Software Engineering. In: Proc. of SEA, November 2004, MIT Cambridge, Cambridge (2004)

Automatic Question Generation for Learning Evaluation in Medicine

Weiming Wang[1,2], Tianyong Hao[2], and Wenyin Liu[2]

[1] School of Computer, Wuhan University, Wuhan, PR China
{whu.wweiming}@gmail.com
[2] Department of Computer Science, City University of Hong Kong,
Hong Kong SAR, PR China
{tianyong, csliuwy}@cityu.edu.hk

Abstract. An approach of automatic question generation from given learning material of medical text is presented in this paper. The main idea is to generate the questions automatically based on question templates which are created by training on many medical articles. In order to provide interesting questions, our research focuses on medical related concepts. This method can be used for evaluation of learner's comprehension after he/she finished a reading material. Different from traditional learning system the articles and questions are all prepared beforehand; participants can learn whatever new input medical articles with the help of automatic question generation.

Keywords: Question Generation, Nature Language Generation, Question-based, E-Learning, Learning Evaluation.

1 Introduction

With the continuing development of technical knowledge and expertise, people are required to update their knowledge timely. Continuing education is a good approach to keep up with technical development. Easy usage of web-based courses has potential value to learn and enhance personal knowledge. Though more and more websites provide easy access to useful learning material of specific domain, most of them fail to test the performance of the participants and thus result in poor usage. So, new technologies need to be developed to take full advantage of this learning environment.

Evaluation is an essential aspect of course learning. It is definitely helpful for any participant to test the reliability of his comprehension towards given material. Answering questions related to the course is an effective way of evaluation. One of the most important uses of questions is reflection, improving our understanding of things we have found out. To successfully respond to a question, the participant is often to integrate several skills and processes such as prior knowledge and knowledge from course material. As a result, seeking answers for specific questions leads to more in-depth understanding. Studies investigation found that more questions in the same topic can improve the level of understanding while answering different questions on the same topic area [1]. This occurs even no standard answers are given to participant.

H. Leung et al. (Eds.): ICWL 2007, LNCS 4823, pp. 242–251, 2008.

This paper describes a medical E-Learning system which generates the questions from free text documents as part of learning. We propose an approach to automatic question generation from medical documents based on question templates. The basic idea is to build question set automatically for given learning material. We have created lots of question templates on many medical articles with the help of some NLP tools. Questions are all generated based on these templates. Traditionally, learning articles in the evaluation system are prepared beforehand. Participants won't benefit from a learning system if the database does not contain desired content. In our system, participants can input whatever medical texts they want to study. And they will also benefit from automatic test since it provides immediate feedback, online grading, and online submission.

We have built a prototype and created 23 question templates. 100 medical articles on headache were tested and results show that our system achieves 88% accuracy in finding the relevant questions. And 83% of these generated questions were correctly answered.

The paper is organized as follows: Section 2 introduces some related work about question generation and learning evaluation. In Section 3 question templates which define rules of question matching and answering are presented. The question generation including processes such as article analysis and template matching are discussed in Section 4. We present the experimental results in Section 5 and the last section summarizes our current research and speculates on what the future may bring.

2   Related Work

With large number of courseware being delivered online, more and more testing and evaluation systems are currently available [2][3]. These systems normally come with database support and hence formulating different kinds of objective questions, automatic grading and records keeping for advices are all possible. Although they provide excellent support managing of related records to evaluate their understanding, but most of the tests are provided beforehand and none of them support automatic question generation.

Question generation has received great attention in recent year. It's a subclass of Natural Language Generation (NLG) which plays an important role in learning environments, data mining, information extraction and a myriad of other applications[4]. Some of them declare that they present domain-independent question generation system. However, it makes no difference with traditional Database[5]. Eriks Sneiders introduces a template-based approach to generate questions on four kinds of entities [6]. The entities in their system are person name, location, organization, or time which may get from Name Entity Recognizer (NER) tools, such as Stanford NER [7]. As a result, it fails to produce interesting questions to help improve comprehension.

This paper proposes a new evaluation system based on automatic question generation. Questions are generated from plain texts in medical area for learning.

3   Question Template Generation

3.1   Question Template

Question templates are essential to this automatic question generation approach from which questions are generated. A template represents a class of questions with same structure. There are four components in a common template: question, entries, keywords and answer. Question and the answer are the output from medical documents for learning. Entries and keywords are used for template matching. The significant innovation is entity slots - free space for data instances of medical terms, which make it possible to tailor traditional questions and include data instances from the taxonomy database [6]. Once a template is created for a test, multiple equivalent questions can be generated according to this template as necessary.

In this paper, we focus on only common medical entities, such as <Disease>, <Medicine>, <Cause>, <Therapy>, <Symptom> and <Device>. Our purpose is to find the best template and apply it to given sentences. The rules for matching and answering associated to a template are given in advance. When a question is generated, the exact answers are also generated according to the rules defined in given question template. A sample template is given as follows:

Question: "what is the symptom for <Disease>?"
Required Entries: symptom, disease;
Keywords: feel, experience, accompany
Related Answer: <symptom>.

When a sentence matches this template, we generate the exact question by replace the <Disease> with the special disease. At the same time, the relevant symptoms in this sentence are generated as the answers to this question.

3.2   Template Generation

In our system, question template plays an important role for automatic question generation. Questions are generated for medical documents with the help of these templates.

We have created nearly one hundred templates in every aspect of medical domain. Question templates are mainly created by experts based on the parsed articles, but not absolutely. With some basic medical knowledge, participants can provide satisfactory templates themselves. We give an example as follows:

(1) The <Medicine>angiotensin converting enzyme (ACE) inhibitors </ Medicine > and the <Medicine> angiotensin receptor blocker (ARB) </ Medicine > drugs both affect the <Substance>renin-angiotensin hormonal </Substance> system, which, as mentioned previously, helps regulate the blood pressure.

(2) As an added benefit, <Medicine> ACE inhibitors </Medicine> may reduce an <finding> enlarged heart </finding> (left ventricular hypertrophy) in patients with hypertension.

(3) <Medicine>ARB</Medicine> drugs are also suitable as first line agents to treat <Disease> hypertension </Disease>.

(4) In patients who have <Disease>hypertension</Disease> in addition to certain second diseases, a combination of an <Medicine>ACE inhibitor </Medicine> and an <Medicine>ARB</Medicine> drug may be effective in controlling the hypertension and also benefiting the second disease.

(5)<Medicine>angiotensin converting enzyme (ACE) inhibitors </Medicine> or <Medicine> angiotensin receptor blocking (ARB)</Medicine> drugs are the drugs of choice in patients with <Disease>heart failure</Disease >, <Disease> chronic kidney failure</Disease> (in diabetics or non-diabetics), or <Disease> heart attack (myocardial infarction) </Disease> that weakens the heart muscle (systolic dysfunction).

(6) <Medicine>Acetaminophen</Medicine> is used for the relief of <Disease > fever </Disease> as well as aches and <Symptom>pains</Symptom> associated with many conditions.

(7) There are three types of cough medications available OTC for the temporary relief of <Symptom> cough </Symptom> due to a <Disease>cold </Disease>. They are oral cough < Substance > suppressants</Substance>, <Substance> oral expectorants </Substance>, and <Medicine>topical (externally applied) medicines</Medicine>.

These sentences are talking about medicine related to special disease, so we define the question template as follow. The **question**: What medications are used in <Disease>? <Medicine> and <Disease> are **required entities** in the template. <Substance >and <Symptom> are optional ones. In our analysis we also found that some keywords are tightly related to the template. The semantic interpretation is driven by syntactic phenomena that indicated semantic predicates including nouns, verbs and adjectives. In this template, we define these keywords for interpretation:

Nouns: drug, medicine, effect.

Verbs: help, use,release, improve.

Adjectives: suitable, effective.

The main role of keywords is to indicate relationships and relevant attributes of key concepts represented by entity slots. In the above template, we use the content of <Medicine> as the answer to these questions generated from this template.

3.3   Guideline of Question Generation

There are different kinds of questions. However, some criterions are necessary defined to prevent from arbitrarily generation. The most important points are answerable, interesting and medical-related. The questions we will less generate are shown as follows:

1. **Interesting but not easy to answer**
   There is a common question for every article: "What's the article are mainly about?" It does absolutely an interesting question for every article. However

it's hard to answer automatically though readers can confer the main idea from the abstract based on the findings of therapy, disease, Medicine and so on.

2. **Easy to answer but not interesting enough**

   We may generate this question: what's the relation between <Disease> and <Therapy> ? It does really reveal something. However, it is too common to find the exact knowledge from this question. So we pay less attention on this in this paper.

3. **Less content-related**

   It's easy to get the person name, location, organization, time from articles with the help of the common NER tools. We can also generate questions through "who" in place of person name, "where" in place of location, and "when" to time. However, these questions are less related to medical so that they should no be selected. Question is approach for learning and they should reveal the level of understanding and help participants to build more reliable understanding of the articles effectively.

3.4 Scoring Templates

In general, a good question template should have ability of distinguishing relevant data instances and ignore irrelevant data instances. In the above, we just show some intuitive impression about interesting, answerable and content-related. We have introduced a method to calculate the weight of the templates for template selection. The higher the weight, the more possibility the templates are selected for questions. There are two factors affect the weight:

1. Number of concepts and what kinds of concept exist in the sentence. The more concepts, the higher weigh.
2. Evaluation to questions generated from this template. These weights would change according to students' evaluation toward questions. There are many reasons for this: generated questions are not interesting or useful, or the answers of this template are often disappointed.

$$w_m = (1 - \frac{b}{n})(1 + \lg k) \prod_{i=1}^{k}(1 + \lg n_i)w_0$$

w_m: Weight of the template.

   w_0: Initial weight, usually set 1.0.

b: Number of negative evaluations towards this template;

n: Number of total questions generated from this template;

k: Number of total concept kinds;

   n_i: Number of total words of the i-th concept.

4   Automatic Question Generation

The learning system is a new testing system that allows for dynamic generation of questions, from which participants can make a good comprehension by seeking the true answer and thus improve the effect of learning. General architecture of automatic question generation is shown in in Figure 1. Medical articles were parsed by MMTx [8] to identify the medical terms and classify them to different classes. We extract medical concepts according to UMLS (Unified Medical Language System [9] [10]).

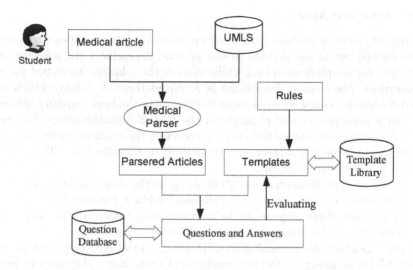

Fig. 1. Architecture of Automatic Question Generation

The research is based on UMLS. It is constructed to "understand" the meaning of the language of biomedicine and health. There are three UMLS Knowledge Sources: the Metathesaurus, the Semantic Network, and the SPECIALIST Lexicon, in which concepts, categories and Lexicon for indices are described separately. The current release contains over 1 million biomedical concepts and 5 million concept names, 135 semantic types and 54 relationships.

MetaMap, a component of the Semantic Knowledge Representation (SKR) project, was designed to map arbitrary text to concepts in the UMLS Metathesusus. MetaMap Transfer(MMTx) is a JAVA implementation of the MetaMap, which maps the noun phrases in the text to the best matching UMLS concept or set of concepts that best cover each phrase [8][11]. For each medical phrase, MetaMap generates synonyms, acronyms, abbreviations, spelling variants using the UMLS SPECIALIST lexicon. In our clinical QA system, we use these terms are for query expansion.

Based on these specific medical concepts from UMLS extracted by MMTx, we select the most similar templates related to this sentence stored in Template library created beforehand. We then generate questions and answers according to the selected template and the semantic interpretation of the medical sentences. When a participant learns an article, the related questions are automatically generated for learning.

We also calculate interesting weight for each question. The higher the template weight, the more chances to be selected for question generation. The participants can determine the questions whether it is interesting or not and thus affect the weight of the question templates. Reversely, this action will affect the question generation.

4.1   Sentence Analysis

he role of sentence analysis is to produce semantic interpretations which can be used by the rest of the system. In our system, it produces the relevant medical concepts for template matching whilst convey the relations identified for answer generation. The domain knowledge is acquired through MMtx, which use the UMLS lexicon along with some rules to determine the best mapping between the text of a noun phrase and concepts in the UMLS Metathesaurus. The relevant UMLS concepts are obtain from each sentence in the medical documents, such as Influenza identified as <Disease>, Hemodialysis identified as <Therapy>. The examples are given as follows:

(8) <Therapy>Hemodialysis</Therapy> is the most common method used to treat advanced and permanent <Disease>Kidney Failure</Disease>.

(9) Because there appears to be a connection between <Medicine>aspirin </Medicine> and <Disease> Reye's syndrome <Disease>.

(10) <Doctor>Anesthesiologists</Doctor> in the ICU help patients recover from ARDS by using a <Device>mechanical ventilator </Device> to help oxygenate and ventilate the patient. Sometimes this requires sedating patients into a drug-induced <Symptom> coma </Symptom> so that they aren't too anxious and "fight" the ventilator.

(11) <Medicine>aspirin</Medicine> is no longer used to control flu-like symptoms or the symptoms of <Disease> chickenpox <Disease> in minors.

(12)<Disease>Influenza</Disease>, commonly known as the <Disease> flu </Disease>, is an infectious disease of birds and mammals caused by an <Virus> RNA virus</Virus> of the <Virus>family Orthomyxoviridae </Virus> (the influenza viruses).

After this process, medical concepts are identified from medical sentences. We discard sentences with less than two medical entity kinds for they do little help for question generation. The left sentences are further processed for semantic interpretation to generate the phrase-level answer.

4.2   Templates Matching

As we know, the questions are generated based some created question template in our system. Each template has defined its required entities and relevant keywords for matching. After the sentence analysis stage, we have obtained all medical concepts in the sentences. A sentence will match the template if the sentence contains all required entities and at least exists one of the keywords. By matching the entities and keywords, the system makes subtler conclusion about the closeness between the question templates and the sentences. The algorithm to find candidate template for a sentence is as follows:

```
For each template in template base
{
    If (exist all required entities) and (!exist forbidden entities)
    {
        If (sentence exist one of the required keywords)
            Add this template to candidate templates
    }
}
```

4.3 Answer Generation

In this stage, we generate the phrase-level answers for the generated questions. Semantic interpretation of the original sentence serves as the bridge. The UMLS Semantic Networks has defined a set of useful and important relationships, or semantic relations that exist between medical concepts. Such as, Therapeutic or Preventive Procedure **treats** Disease or Syndrome. We have defines some mapping rules between the keywords and the UMLS Semantic relations and generate the semantic interpretation based on these semantic relations. For example, in sentences (8), the semantic interpretation is given as follow: Hemodialysis **treats** Kidney Failure.

The semantic types of the answer are clearly defined in the question templates. To generate the exact answer, we match the semantic type and the semantic interpretation.

4.4 Question Selection

Questions are generated for learner to test the reliable of their understanding and make online assessment possible. For evaluate test we have made some rules for that:

1. Syntax difference
   Different types of questions are encouraged. A test shouldn't be full of the same questions: what's the symptom of ¡Disease¿? Even the diseases may be different. We will choose different templates for different questions.
2. Semantic difference
   Question should not ask the same point. There may be several relevant candidate templates, but we won't generate different questions for a single sentence. The template with max weight will be selected as the final choice which will make much completer use of all knowledge from the sentence.
3. Number of questions
   The questions in a test shouldn't too many or too few. We generate 5-10 questions for a articles, usually about 1 sentence for each 100 words.

4.5   Grading and Evaluation

Immediate feedback is important for the participants to know whether their understandings are reliable. The levels of comprehension are reflected by the answering given by participants. After the participants finished the test, we present the scores according to their answering. The scores are calculated the semantic similarity between the answering and generated answers.

5   Experiments and Results

We have built an automatic question generation system and test 100 medical articles using 23 created templates on every aspect of headache. The experiment was conducted on six people with different levels of medical knowledge and the terminology. Each participant answers more than 10 articles to test the accuracy of the question generation system and the ability to help enhance the comprehension.

The experiment results are listed in Table 1, in which the columns are: articles, left medical sentences, accurate questions, and correctly answered.

Table 1. Experiment result

Articles	Question Templates	Accurate Questions	Correctly Answered
100	23	88%	83%

From the result, we can find that most of the medical sentences are correctly questioned and answered. The mistakes are mainly from the created templates. The defined entries and keywords are insufficient to represent the relationships in these templates. There are some sentences satisfying the matching rules, which are derived from associated entries and keywords, cannot apply this template. And we find that low-ability participants profit more from the generated questions than the average-ability participants, which may because the questions generated are factual one.

6   Conclusions and Future Work

The main contribution of this research is online assessment through automatic question generation, answering and grading.

It would be very easy to construct a medical learning system with the help of this research. No additional personal work is needed to build the question database or grading. Participants will benefit from this automatic question generation system for the online testing and immediate feedback.

The disadvantage of our method is that the generated questions are factual and may be less meaningful than the manual questions. Furthermore, it is time consuming to parse the articles and obtain the semantic interpretation for each sentence, especially for long articles. The current method of question generation is mainly based on a single sentence. This would result in missing some important information and might bring weird questions. More works will be done in the future, including:

- more helpful questions automatic generation and giving convictive answers.
- giving more relevant mapping and answering rules with the help of UMLS.

Acknowledgements

The work described in this paper was fully supported by a grant from City University of Hong Kong (Project No. 7002137), the National Grand Fundamental Research 973 Program of China under Grant No.2003CB317002.

References

1. Shavelson, R.J., Berliner, D., Ravitch, M., Loeding, D.: Effects of Position and Type of Question on Learning from Prose Material: Interaction of Treatments with Individual Differences. Journal of Educational Psychology 65(1), 40–48 (1974)
2. Tinoco, L.C., Fox, E.A., Barnette, N.D.: Online evaluation in WWW-based courseware. In: Proceedings of the twenty-eighth SIGCSE technical symposium on Computer science education, pp. 194–198. ACM Press, New York (1997)
3. Bade, D., Nüssel, G., Wilts, G.: Online Feedback by Tests and Reporting for eLearning and Certification Programs with TCmanager. In: Proceedings of the 13 thInternational World Wide Web Conference on Alternate track papers, pp. 432–433 (2004)
4. Lauer, T.W.: Questions and information: Contrasting metaphors. Information Systems Frontiers 3(1), 41–48 (2001)
5. Merzbacher, M.: Automatic Generation of Trivia Questions. In: Hacid, M.-S., Raś, Z.W., Zighed, A.D.A., Kodratoff, Y. (eds.) ISMIS 2002. LNCS (LNAI), vol. 2366, pp. 123–130. Springer, Heidelberg (2002)
6. Sneiders, E.: Automated Question Answering: Template-Based Approach. PhD thesis, Royal Institute of Technology and Stockholm University (2002)
7. Finkel, J.R., Grenager, T., Manning, C.: Incorporating non-local information into information extraction systems by gibbs sampling. In: Proceedings of the 43rd Annual Meeting of the Association for Computational Linguistics (ACL 2005), Ann Arbor, Michigan, Association for Computational Linguistics, June 2005, pp. 363–370 (2005)
8. Meystre, S., Haug, P.J.: Evaluation of Medical Problem Extraction from Electronic Clinical Documents Using MetaMap Transfer (MMTx). Stud Health Technol Inform 116, 823–828 (2005)
9. Lindberg, D.A., Humphreys, B.L., McCray, A.T.: The Unified Medical Language System. Methods Inf. Med. 32(4), 281–291 (1993)
10. Campbell, K.E., Oliver, D.E., Shortliffe, E.H.: The Unified Medical Language System: Toward a Collaborative Approach for Solving Terminologic Problems. Journal of the American Medical Informatics Association 5(1), 12–16 (1998)
11. Aronson, A.R.: Effective mapping of biomedical text to the umls metathesaurus: the metamap program. In: Proceedings of the AIMA, pp. 17–21 (2001)

A Cloze Test Authoring System and Its Automation

Ayako Hoshino and Hiroshi Nakagawa

University of Tokyo
{hoshino, nakagawa}@dl.itc.u-tokyo.ac.jp

Abstract. This paper presents a pilot system and discusses its possible extensions. In the first sections, we present a web-based test authoring system for English grammar and vocabulary. It assists language teachers to make questions on arbitrary input texts, such as online news. The system employs the techniques of NLP (Natural Language Processing) and is compared with other studies in the same field. In the latter sections we discuss some extensions of the system. First, we show a method of automatically acquiring the grammar targets. Secondly, we discuss an extension to a computer-adaptive question generator which interacts with students. We describe the design of the extended system and focus on the difficulty predictor, one of the major components needed. Then we present some primary results of the difficulty prediction task. Finally, we compare existing systems and discuss their use and evaluations.

Keywords: Test Authoring System, Language Testing, Natural Language Processing, Computer-Adaptive Testing.

1 Introduction

Sakumon (Beta version) is a test-making assistance system which had been made available on the web in January 2007. In comparison with other automatic question generators, which have been studied in the field of NLP (Natural Language Processing), the main characteristic of Sakumon is that it works as an assistant to the user: it helps the user to choose an article, highlights grammar targets, suggests possible choices for the wrong alternatives and formats the questions in a printer-friendly way.

In developing an assistant system, we explore the use of NLP for the purpose of cloze test making. Recent years have seen a large advance in technologies to analyze natural language, such as a sentence parser. A sentence parser analyzes a sentence in a nested phrase structure. Also there are more available NLP resources such as machine-readable dictionaries and thesauri. Aside from that, there are more available online texts and corpora, which is a large collection of texts, on the World Wide Web. There has always been a growing interest in educational applications in NLP [1] [2], while NLP techniques and resources keep advancing. One of our motivations is to see if the state-of-the-art NLP is practical for an educational purpose.

The system is designed to semi-automatically make questions in a given input text. We use online news articles as a source text. The reasons for using online news are; first, news texts are properly written compared with other sources on the web. Secondly, their topics are suitable for foreign language education. Also, they are up-to-date so a quick

H. Leung et al. (Eds.): ICWL 2007, LNCS 4823, pp. 252–263, 2008.

question making benefits. The result of user evaluation was quite favorable [3], with its overall usefulness and usability approved by ten out of ten English teachers.

Despite the usefulness and its usability, the system remains an authoring assistance; it does not make the most of the advantages of a web-based learning system, which is, for example, being adaptive to the students. A human teacher cannot control administration of questions for each student even with an authoring assistance system. Therefore, in this paper, we pursue automation the process of question making to fully enjoy the possibility of web-based learning and computerized testing. A system which tailors a test based on each student's ability would be appreciated for working on their own. The quality of the questions is encouraging enough to assume that we only have to extend the current system.

The current system supports only multiple-choice fill-in-the-blank type questions, which in the title we referred to as **cloze** for short, hence we deal with only questions in this format in the rest of the paper.

The paper is organized as follows. Section two reviews works mainly in the field of natural language processing. Then we describe the current system in section three. Section four discusses how to extend the system to an adaptive question generation system. Section five describes the difficulty prediction task as the first step toward an adaptive question generation system. Finally, we conclude the paper comparing the three types of systems: an automatic question generator, an assistance system, and an adaptive question generator.

2   Related Works

There are recently some attempts to automatically generate multiple-choice cloze questions. In principle they take input texts and generate questions by removing some words from a sentence. Although the method for providing the wrong alternatives or *distractors* varies from research to research, the main idea is to select similar words to the correct answer, as in one research stated; "Syntax, rather than football or sport, is more appropriate for a distractor of the correct answer semantics"[4].

In selecting similar words, machine-readable dictionaries are used in most of the studies. Mitkov et al. Liu and Brown [5] used WordNet[1], and Sumita [6] and Kunichika [7] used their in-house thesauri. Typically, they retrieve similar or related words (synonyms, antonyms, hypernyms, hyponyms, etc.) by consulting a machine-readable thesaurus and in their respective metrics select the most appropriate ones for the distractors. In Sumita's study, they first retrieved similar words by consulting a thesaurus and then filtered out the distractors that can result in a multiple right answers.

Liu et al., Sumita et al. and Brown et al. generate cloze or fill-in-the-blank questions on text, while Mitkov and Kunichika generated question sentences with conversion patterns that change declarative sentences into interrogatives. The type of question targeted in most of the studies is vocabulary type. Kunichika et al. report that their system is also capable to produce reading comprehension questions.

This is among the first study that uses NLP techniques to generate grammar type questions. Chen generated grammar questions using regular expressions and

---

[1] An online lexical reference system by Princeton University. (http://wordnet.princeton.edu/)

part-of-speech tagged texts [8], while in this study we use parse results. While other studies present automatic systems, we also provide an interactive system which works as an assistance for a teacher. Except for those features, we adopted common methods in above studies: the format of the resulting questions is multiple-choice, fill-in-the-blank embedded in a given text. The resource we used for vocabulary distractors is WordNet.

3 The Current System

In this section, we present the current version of Sakumon system. We first explain its function from the users' viewpoint, along with the three sequenced screens: 1. Article Selection, 2. Question Making and 3. Confirm and Print. Then, a mechanism of the grammar targets, which is the main feature, is explained. The first extension, which is automatic acquisition of grammar targets, is presented here. Finally, the pedagogical value of the system is discussed. For more information on this system, see [3].

Screen 1: Article Selection

On the first screen the system helps the user to choose an article on which she is going to make questions. It shows the list of articles it has in its article pool. An article is shown as a list item with its news source, date, title and number of words. The user can see more information on the article, such as its lead (the first 10 words of the article), vocabulary level (Kincaid score) and grammar targets included and their times of appearance by putting the cursor on a list item.

The user can narrow down this list of articles with conditions on grammar targets and/or vocabulary levels. The system has a menu bar on which the user can specify conditions by clicking on the checkboxes or selecting from combo boxes. When the conditions are specified, the system returns a list of (the only and all) articles that meet the conditions. The user can choose an article with the grammar targets she wants to test and in a desired difficulty level. For example, the user can choose an article which contains sentences in perfect present tense and within a difficulty level of 5~6 in Kincaid.

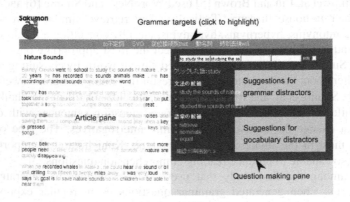

Fig. 1. Question Making Screen

Screen 2. Question Making

When the article is selected, the screen moves on to question making page (Figure 1). The system assists the user's making blanks on the passages and deciding the wrong alternatives. Article text is shown on the left side and the question making area is on the right side. In the article text, the words that have distractor suggestions are clickable and shown in black. The words that have no suggestions (proper nouns, articles, etc.) are unclickable and shown in gray. When the user clicks on a word or a highlighted phrase in the article, the system replaces the word/phrase with a blank and shows it on question making pane as the right answer, along with three input forms. At the same time, the suggested alternatives are shown on question making pane, which fill the forms when clicked.

Menu on question making pane shows the grammar targets contained in the article. When a target is clicked, the corresponding phrases in the article are highlighted (black turns red and gray turns orange). When a particular phrase is selected by the user's click on the article text, the suggestions for grammar distractors as well as the ones for vocabulary distractors[2] appears on question making pane. By selecting one from grammar distractor suggestions and one from vocabulary distractor suggestions, the third field is automatically filled with the combination of the grammar distractor and the vocabulary distracor, resulting in a symmetric set of alternatives. For example, when the original sentence is "We are planning [to go to the theater]", the suggestions for grammar distractors are "to going to the theater", "go to the theater" and "went to the theater". The system also provides the suggestions for vocabulary distractors, which are, say, "give", "keep" and so on. When the user selects the first suggestions from the both kinds of suggestions ("to going to the theater" and "to give"), the third distractors are automatically filled in with their combination: "to giving to the theater". The resulting question is:

We are planning [   ] to the theater.

going, 2. to go, 3. giving 4. to give

Screen 3: Confirm and Print

When the questions are completed and the user clicked the submit button, the system shows the resulting questions in a test format. On moving to this page from question making page, blanks containing phrases shrink where appropriate. In the example "We are planning [to go] to the theater", the phrase "to go to the theater" is retrieved from the blank. The blank shrinks so it contains only "to go", since the rest of the phrase "to the theater" is the same in all alternatives. The user is allowed to modify the distractors on this screen. When "print" button clicked, the screen provides forms for the date, the name of a test taker and the answer boxes.

The Core Feature: Grammar Targets

One of the core features of this system is what we call the grammar targets. The system has a set of grammar targets which mark up the corresponding phrases in the text and

---

[2] The method we used to decide suggestions for vocabulary distractors is based on the theory introduced in [10] and adapted in a previous study [11].

convert the phrase into possibly incorrect ones to produce distractor suggestions. It is this component which makes it possible to count the times of appearance in advance and to provide grammar questions upon the user's clicking. When an article is added to the article pool, it goes through various preprocessings among which is marking up with grammar targets.

There are 10 grammar targets in the current system (See [3]), which are chosen among the most frequent grammar targets in BNC [9].

Each grammar target is composed of one matching pattern and three generation patterns. A matching pattern is a pattern written for a parse tree and it finds phrases that contain the target, whether it is the whole sentence or a part of the parse tree. As in Figure 2, the matching pattern for SVO structure finds the pattern in a subordinate clause, "the culprit did that". A generation pattern is a pattern that converts a parse tree by altering the parse tree, as in Figure 3, "... how the culprit did that" is changed into "... how did the culprit that". Note that "the culprit" is a noun phrase which consists of two words. This is an advantage of using the parse tree, in comparison with regular expressions to a sequence of part-of-speech-tagged result; the pattern can be captured, and moved around however a phrase is longer or complicated.

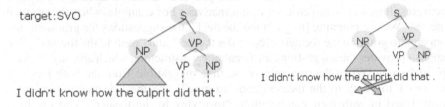

Fig. 2. Matching Pattern   **Fig. 3.** Generation Pattern

A generation pattern can again be decomposed into a sequence of operations. For example, in Figure 4, the process of obtaining the converted phrase is 1) to remove the VP (verb phrase) which contains the word "did" 2) to insert the VP in the leftmost in S. We call this sequence of operations path and show the method of automatically acquiring grammar targets from human made question data.

Path Analysis

We devised a method to obtain grammar targets automatically from human-made questions. We use dynamic programming to retrieve a path from the correct answer to a wrong answer. DP or dynamic programming is a technique to find the shortest (i.e. with minimum cost) path from one string to another among the possible paths. When a question is given, our path analyzer takes a pair of the correct answer and one of the three wrong alternatives and extracts a path from one (i.e. correct answer) to the other (i.e. distractor). Then this path is used as a generating pattern of a grammar target. Table 1 shows the list of operations along with their cost as we employed in this task.

Table 1. Operations used in Path Analysis

Operation	Cost	Example
DELETION	5	"to go" -> "go"
INSERTION	5	"go" -> "to go"
CHANGE_WORD	4	"go" -> "along"
CHANGE_WORD_SAMESTEM	3	"decide" -> "decision"
CHANGE_LEXICAL_ITEM	2	"had" -> "went"
CHANGE_INFLECTION	1	"have" -> "had"

Usually, only three operations are used to find a path from one string to another: DELETION, INSERTION and CHANGE. This method is called edit distance. Our technique is modified version of edit distance. Instead of character-based operations, we use word-based ones. We elaborated the CHANGE operation; if the two words in comparison don't have in common neither of the part-of-speech, the lexical item or the stem of a word, then CHANGE_WORD is performed, if they have the same stem (as "decide" and "decision") then CHANGE_WORD_SAMESTEM is performed, if they have a lexical item in common but have different inflection then CHANGE_LEXICAL_ITEM is performed, if they have the same lexical item but are in different inflection forms then CHANGE_INFLECTION is performed. We set the cost of each operation so that CHANGE_INFLECTION, CHANGE_LEXICAL_ITEM, CHANGE_WORD_SAMESTEM and CHANGE_WORD are favored in this order.

The result of 800 questions from TOEIC preparation books shows that in 90 percent of the cases the path from the correct answer to a distractor takes two operations at most. About 70 percent of the paths consist of single path of CHANGE_LEXICAL_ITEM, CHANGE_WORD_SAMESTEM or CHANGE_ WORD, which means 70 percent of the distractors are vocabulary ones, and consequently, the rest of the distractors are grammar ones. We are planning to include retrieved paths as generation rules in a future version.

Pedagogical Values of the System

The major pedagogical value is the speed or efficiency. The system quickens the process of question making up to the point that it is possible to use online texts in, for example, mini-tests in the classroom. This is not easy if the teacher makes tests with pens and papers. The system presents distractor suggestions and does inflection, so a teacher risks less spelling mistakes and can concentrate on the quality of questions.

Aside from efficiency, there are some pedagogical values of this system. First, it helps the teachers to diagnose grammatical knowledge of students. In this system, the resulting questions are labeled with grammar targets and vocabulary items. When the teacher summarizes the result of a test, he/she can do that according to grammar targets and vocabulary items, rather than according to each question as in tests that has been made in a conventional way.

The next section discusses how to make the most of this advantage and extend this system to a computer adaptive one.

4 Computer Adaptive System

Now we discuss the possibility of extending this system to a computer adaptive question generator. In CAT (Computer Adaptive Testing), the system has an 'item pool' which contains ready-made questions. In interacting with testees, the system selects the next question to be administered for each testee based on his/her previous responses. It is said that 100~200 items should be kept in the item pool and old items should be replaced routinely to avoid overexposure.

Instead of having an item pool, our extended question generator system will have an 'article pool', from which questions are generated on demand. There is no need of maintaining questions; you will only have to add articles which are preprocessed automatically and stored to the article pool. The difference from the current authoring system is that the selection of blank positions and alternatives, which are done manually, should be automated. Figure 4 shows the system diagram (in blueprint) of a computer adaptive question generator.

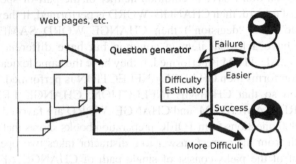

Fig. 4. The System Diagram of Computer Adaptive Question Generator

The system takes web pages, etc. as input and automatically generates questions which are stored within the question generator. This process is done by selecting all possible blank positions and randomly selected distractors from distractor suggestions. Then one of the questions is administered to the user (this time, a student). If the user's response is successful, the system administers a more difficult one as a next question. If the user's response is a failure, the system administers an easier question. The core component in this computer adaptive system will be the difficulty estimator, which can estimate difficulty of a question in an automatic way.

This adaptation is based on IRT (Item Response Theory). In IRT, each item i.e. question has an item response function, which expresses the probability of a testee's giving a correct response given his/her ability [12] [13]. Item response function has at most three parameters: difficulty, discrimination and guessing values. The 1-parameter model (the Rasch model) takes into consideration difficulty parameter only. The 2-parameter model allows the items to have different discrimination values, and the 3-parameter model includes a parameter for odds of getting a correct response by a random guess.

Now we already know the third parameter: 25 percent when the number of alternatives is four. At this moment, we do not know how to decide a discrimination value of a question, but this parameter is optional. We decided that we should first adopt one-parameter model. So it is the difficulty value which is needed and which is sufficient for the current system to be extended to an IRT-based adaptive system. In fact, the one-parameter model is always favored because of its stability. Other components needed, aside from a difficulty predictor, are the interface for student users and the student profile that maintains record of the students' responses and the system's assumption of their ability, which can be stored in a database.

5 Difficulty Prediction Task

To our knowledge, there was no preceding work on predicting difficulty of the type of questions dealt in this paper. As a first attempt, we try to solve this task in the framework of machine learning.

A machine learning task, specifically supervised machine learning, is a task to predict the labels of unlabelled instances (called 'test data') given a set of labelled instances (called 'training data'). An instance is usually expressed as an array of 'features', which express certain characteristics of an instance with real value, discrete value or binary value. Various techniques have been developed for this task among which we employ Instance-Based (IB1), naive Bayes, J48 decision tree and RBF network. We used weka experiment toolkit. (http://www.cs.waikato.ac.nz/ml/weka/)

Experimental Settings

As a first step, we set up a binary-classification version of this task. The machine has to label a question with either of "easy" or "difficult". As a training data, we use questions from TOEIC preparation books. The type of questions is of part 5 and 6 in the renewed version of TOEIC and the total number of questions was 208. For each question, percentage of students with the correct answer is given in the book. These percentages are based on the result of the exams in a TOEIC preparation school.

It should be noted that these percentages are actually observed values and expected to contain various kinds of errors (measurement error, etc). They may also be affected by the order of the questions in the test, students' tendency, etc. so we are not sure how accurately these values reflect difficulty of questions. Taking this issue in consideration, we sampled 80 questions with the highest percentage (correct responses > 63.9 percent) and 80 questions with the lowest percentage (correct responses < 50 percent) which are labelled "easy" and "difficult" respectively.

Features in machine learning should be characteristics of an instance that can be extracted automatically since the process of learning has to be done automatically. Under this limitation we used the features shown in Table2.

The first group of features 'Path features' are the features which are extracted using path analysis introduced in Section three 'Vocabulary features' are extracted using a word frequency list. This is based on an idea that a question's difficulty is dependent on difficulty of the words in it, and difficulty of a word is reflected in the word frequency (easy words are used more often, difficult words are less often). We use the Adam Kilgarriff's word frequency list, which is used in some of the studies reviewed in Section two.

Table 2. Features in Difficulty Prediction Task

Group	Name	Explanation
Path features	lengthmax lengthmin includechangeinfl includechangelex includechangesamestem includechangew	- the number of operations in the longest path - the number of operations in the shortest path - a Boolean value expresses if any of the paths includes CHANGE_INFLECTION -a Boolean value expresses if any of the paths includes CHANGE_LEXICAL_ITEM - a Boolean value expresses if any of the paths includes CHANGE_WORD_SAMESTEM - a Boolean value expresses if any of the paths includes CHANGE_WORD
Vocabulary features	freqminsent freqmaxsent freqmin freqman	- the lowest frequency of a word in the sentence - the highest frequency of a word in the sentence - the lowest frequency of a word in the correct answer - the highest frequency of a word in the correct answer
Other features	sentence_length blank_length pos_arr num_samepos	- length of the sentence (in words) - blank length (in words) - pos sequence of the correct answer - number of the distractors that has the same part-of-speech sequence as the correct answer

Using the above features, we evaluated the performance of different learning algorithms: IB1, the most primitive classifier, which labels as the closest train instance in Euclidian distance, naïve Bayes, which compute the probability of an instance's having a certain label using the Bayes theorem, J48 decision tree builds a model expressed in a collection of rules in the form of branches on a tree and RBF network builds a model with a network whose nodes have multiple radial basis functions.

Results and Discussion

We performed the 10-fold cross-validation procedure commonly used to evaluate a classifiers performance. We split the data into 10 sets. The classifier is first trained on the first nine sets (72 instances) and tested on the last one set (8 instances). Then it is

Table 3. Result of Difficulty Prediction

	Label	Precision	Recall	F-score	Correct instances
IB1	Difficult Easy	0.512 0.514	0.550 0.475	0.530 0.494	51.25 %
naive Bayes	Difficult Easy	0.539 0.549	0.600 0.488	0.568 0.517	54.375 %
J48	Difficult Easy	0.582 0.629	0.713 0.488	0.640 0.549	**60 %**
RBF network	Difficult Easy	0.616 0.598	0.563 0.650	0.588 0.623	**60.625 %**

trained on the first eight sets and the last set, and tested on the ninth set. This process is repeated until each set is used nine times for training and once in testing. A summary of the result is shown in Table 3.

Table 3 shows the details on precision, recall and F-score which are commonly used in machine learning task. The last column shows the percentage of correctly labelled instances, which summarizes the performance of the learning algorithms.

Despite the sampling that makes it easier for the machine to achieve high scores than using the whole textbook of questions, the observed performances of the algorithms were far from accurate. The result of IB1 was almost chance level. The naive Bayes was only slightly above. However, J48 and RBF network achieved 60 percent, with the highest score in retrieving the 'difficult' questions (recall 0.713).

We analysed which features contributed to the accuracy of the learners. Weka's Chi squared feature evaluation listed the features in the following order: pos_arr, **lengthmax**, freqmaxsent, **lengthmin**, blank_length, sentencelength, num_samepos, **includechangelex**, **includechangesamestem**, **includechangew**, freqmax, freqminsent, **includechangeinfl**, freqmin (path related features in **bold**, vocabulary related features underlined). Except for freqmaxsent, vocabulary related features tend to contribute less than path related features. Figure 5 shows distributions of the two labels in three features, num_samepos, freqmaxsent and includechangelex. When the distribution the label is skewed, rather than equally distributed over the feature values, the feature is more informative. We can also see the tendencies of each feature by taking look at distributions of feature values.

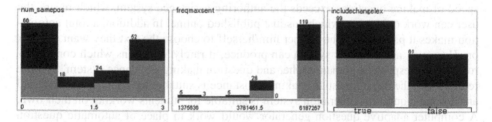

Fig. 5. Distribution of Feature Values

Black shows the 'easy' instances and gray shows 'difficult' instances. From the chart of num_samepos (leftmost), we can see that a question becomes more difficult as the number of distractors which has the same pos sequence increases. From the chart of freqmaxsent (center), we can see that the distribution of the labels is not very skewed. From the chart of includechangelex (rightmost), we can see that a question tends to be difficult when one of the paths includes CHANGE_LEXICAL_ITEM.

To summarize the results of the experiment; 1) the overall performance is not very high 2) the decision tree approach and RBF network works better than other algorithms used 3) path features contribute the accuracy 4) vocabulary features have little contribution. In order to improve the performance, we are going to further elaborate the features on path as well as to consider better measures for vocabulary difficulty. As for the vocabulary features, it is possible that difficulty of a word is not reflected in the word frequency accurately enough. Currently we are seeking a better measurement for word difficulty.

6 Conclusions

In this paper, we have presented an online test-making assistance system, Sakumon and discussed its extensions. We focused on its grammar targets as one of the core features. We introduced the path analysis which is devised to extract generation patterns for distracters. Furthermore, we have presented the design of computer adaptive question generator as an extended system of the current authoring assistance system. The core component needed for this extension is an automatic difficulty estimator. Using the framework of machine learning, we set up an experimental setting for the difficulty prediction task and showed some primary results. The task remains tough for the employed methods, but the feature evaluation brought some insights for possible improvements.

Finally we compare different types of question making systems. So far we have seen, including the one in blueprint, three types of systems: automatic question generation systems as we have reviewed in Section two, a question making assistance system and finally, a computer adaptive question generator presented in Section four. The major virtue of an automatic question generation is low or non cost questions for the learners. There is no need for human teachers so the learner can practice as many times as s/he wants without worrying him/herself by running out of questions. Also, the speed of making questions exceeds the authoring assistance system, which means the user can work on the text which has just published online. In addition, a total automation makes it possible for the learner him/herself to choose the text they want to work on. However, an automatic system can produce, if rarely, questions which contain errors. In this respect, "a human teacher and question making assistance system" is more reliable. So, the use of question making assistance is suitable for a high-stake test, and an automatic question generation system is suitable for students working on their own. A computer adaptive question generator would work in place of automatic question generators, but would provide a better means of assessment. It not only offers a limitless number of questions on latest texts, but also it actively tries to assess the level of students.

The quality of a question generator has been evaluated by the questions' being valid, which means the questions are errorless and the percentage of getting the correct answer does not contradict the students' level. The errorlessness is typically measured by the questions' not having multiple correct answers, and the validity of questions is typically measured by their "discrimination value". The previous studies have shown that their methods do well in the mentioned measures. When those measures satisfied, another measure should be cared about, which is, "the difficulty level". For example, the example question used in Section three ("go to the theater" example) is errorless, valid and suitable for beginners, but not suitable for intermediate or advanced learners. As in this example, the quality of questions is dependent on the difficulty level of the student. Therefore an automatic question generator should be also evaluated with respect to its ability of generating questions in an appropriate difficulty level.

References

1. Gamper, J., Knapp, J.: A Web-based Language Learning System. In: Fong, J., et al. (eds.) ICWL 2002. LNCS, vol. 2436, pp. 106–118. Springer, Heidelberg (2002)
2. Gamper, J., Knapp, J.: A Review of Intelligent CALL Systems. Computer Assisted Language Learning 15(4), 329–342 (2002)
3. Hoshino, A., Nakagawa, H.: Assisting cloze test making with a web application. In: Proc. SITE 2007, San Antonio, U.S, pp. 2807–2814 (2007)
4. Mitkov, R., Ha, L.: Computer-aided generation of multiple-choice tests. In: Proc. HLT-NAACL 2003 Workshop on Building Educational Applications Using Natural Language Processing, Edmonton, Canada, pp. 17–22 (2003)
5. Brown, J., Frishkoff, G., Eskenazi, M.: Automatic question generation for vocabulary assessment. In: Proc. HLT/EMNLP 2005, Vancouver, B.C. (2005)
6. Sumita, E., Sugaya, F., Yamamoto, S.: Measuring Non-native Speakers' Proficiency of English by Using a Test with Automatically-Generated Fill-in-the-Blank Questions. In: Proc. the Second Workshop on Building Educational Applications Using NLP, Ann Arbor, Michigan, pp. 61–68 (2005)
7. Kunichika, H., Urushima, M., Hirashima, T., Takeuchi, A.: A Computational Method of Complexity of Questions on Contents of English Sentences and its Evaluation. In: Proc. of ICCE 2002, Auckland, NZ, pp. 97–101 (2002)
8. Chen, C.Y., Liou, H.C., Chang, J.S.: FAST - An Automatic Generation System for Grammar Tests. In: Proc. ACL 2006, Sydney, Australia (2006)
9. Tateno, J., Sano, H., Aizawa, H., Nakamura, T., Morita, Y.: Producing English Educational Materials form the BNC and releasing them on the Web. IEICE Technical report, Tokyo, JAPAN, TL2005-18~26, pp. 7–12 (2005)
10. Conium, D.: Preliminary inquiry into using corpus word frequency data in the automatic generation of English language cloze tests. CALICO Journal 16(2-4), 15–33 (1997)
11. Brown, J.D.: Testing in language programs. Prentice Hall Regents, Upper Saddle River (1996)
12. Shizuka, T., Takeuchi, O., Yoshizawa, K.: Basic Concepts in Foreign Language Educa-tion Research and Testing. Kausai Daigaku publishing, JAPAN (2002)
13. Barker, F.: The Basics of Item Response Theory (2001), http://edres.org/irt/

A Web-Based E-Testing System Supporting Test Quality Improvement

Gennaro Costagliola, Filomena Ferrucci, and Vittorio Fuccella

Dipartimento di Matematica e Informatica – Università degli Studi di Salerno,
Fisciano(SA), Italy
{gcostagliola,fferrucci,vfuccella}@unisa.it

Abstract. In e-testing it is important to administer tests composed of good quality question items. By the term "quality" we intend the potential of an item in effectively discriminating between strong and weak students and in obtaining tutor's desired difficulty level. Since preparing items is a difficult and time-consuming task, good items can be re-used for future tests. Among items with lower performances, instead, some should be discarded, while some can be modified and then re-used. This paper presents a Web-based e-testing system which detects defective question items and, when possible, provides the tutors with advice to improve their quality. The system detects defective items by firing rules. Rules are evaluated by a fuzzy logic inference engine. The proposed system has been used in a course at the University of Salerno.

Keywords: e-Testing, Computer Aided Assessment, CAA, item, item quality, questions, eWorkbook, Item Response Theory, IRT, Test Analysis, online testing, difficulty, discrimination, multiple choice, distractor.

1 Introduction

E-testing systems are more and more widely adopted in academic environments combined with other assessment means. Through these systems, tests composed of several question types can be presented to the students in order to assess their knowledge. *Multiple Choice* question type is extremely popular, since, among other advantages, a large number of its outcomes can be easily corrected automatically. The experience gained by educators and the results obtained from several experiments [1] provide some guidelines for writing good *multiple choice* questions (*items*, in the sequel), such as: "use the right language", "avoid a big number of unlikely *distractors* for an item", etc.

It is possible to evaluate the effectiveness of the items, through the use of several statistical models, such as *Item Analysis* (*IA*) and *Item Response theory* (*IRT*) [2]. They are both based on the interpretation of statistical indicators calculated on test outcomes. The most important of them are the *difficulty* indicator, which measures the difficulty of the items, and the *discrimination* indicator, which represents the information of how well an item discriminates between strong and weak students. More statistical indicators are related to the *distractors* (wrong options) of an item.

H. Leung et al. (Eds.): ICWL 2007, LNCS 4823, pp. 264–275, 2008.
© Springer-Verlag Berlin Heidelberg 2008

An item with a high value for *discrimination* is a good item, that is, an item that is answered correctly by strong students and incorrectly by weak ones, on average. Furthermore, in this study we regard as more efficient those items whose calculated *difficulty* tends to be closer to the difficulty guessed by the tutor. In a test, in order to better assess a heterogeneous class with different levels of knowledge, it is important to balance the difficulty of the items: tests should be composed of given percentages of difficult (25%), medium (50%) and easy (25%) items. If the tutor succeeds in giving the desired difficulty level to an item, he/she can more easily construct balanced tests which assess students on the desired knowledge.

Despite the availability of guidelines for writing good items and statistical models to analyze their quality, only a few tutors are aware of the guidelines and even fewer are used with statistics. The result is that the quality of the tests used for exams or admissions is sometimes poor and in some cases could be improved. Although it is almost impossible to compel the tutors to read manuals for writing good test assessment, it is possible to give them feedback on their items' quality, allowing them to discard defective items or to modify them in order to improve their quality for next use and, at the same time, to learn how to write good items from experience.

This paper presents a Web-based e-testing system which helps the tutors to obtain good quality assessment items. By item quality we intend the potential of an item in effectively discriminating between strong and weak students and in obtaining a tutor's desired difficulty level. After a test session, the system marks the items: good items are marked with a green light. For poor quality items there are two different levels of alarm: *severe* (red light), for items which should be discarded, and *warning* (yellow light) for items whose quality could be improved. For the latter ones, the system provides the tutor with suggestions for improving item quality. Aware of defective items, and helped by the suggestions of the system, the tutor can discard or modify poor items. Improvable items can be re-used for future tests.

Quality level and eventual suggestions are decided through a rule-based classification [3]. Fuzzy logic has been used in order to obtain a *degree of fulfillment* of each rule. Rules have been preferred over other frequently used classification methods, such as hierarchical methods [4], K-means methods [5] and correlation methods due to the following reasons:

- *Knowledge availability*. Most of the knowledge is already available, as witnessed by the presence of numerous theories and manuals on psychometrics.
- *Lack of data*. Other types of classification based on data would require the availability of large data sets. Once they have gathered, in such a way to have statistically significant classes to perform data analysis, such methods might be exploited.

The system has been carried out by adding the formerly described features to an existing Web-based e-testing system: *eWorkbook* [6], developed at *University of Salerno*, which has been equipped with an *Item Quality Module*. A first experiment has been carried out in a course at the University of Salerno.

The paper is organized as follows: section 2 gives some concepts about the knowledge on which the system is based. In section 3, the system is defined, following the steps of a classical methodology for fuzzy systems definition. In section 4, we briefly discuss the implementation of the quality module and its integration in the existing e-testing system. Finally, section 5 presents an experiment and a discussion of its results. The paper concludes with a brief survey on work related to ours, several final remarks and a discussion on future work.

2 The Knowledge-Base

Our system makes use of *multiple choice* items for the assessment of students' knowledge. Those items are composed of a *stem* and a list of *options*. The stem is the text that states the question. The only correct answer is called the *key*, whilst the incorrect answers are called *distractors* [1].

Test results can be statistically analyzed to check item quality. As mentioned in the previous section, two main statistical models are available: *IA* and *IRT*. Several studies, such as the one in [7], make a comparison between the two models, often concluding that they can both be effective in evaluating the quality of the items. For our study, *IA* has been preferred over *IRT* for the following main reasons: it needs a smaller sample size for obtaining statistically significant indicators and it is easier to use *IA* indicators to compose rule conditions. The following statistical indicators are calculated by our system for each item answered by a significant number of students:

- *difficulty*: a real number between 0 and 1 which expresses a measure of the difficulty of the item, intended as the proportion of learners who get the item correct.
- *discrimination*: a real number between -1 and 1 which expresses a measure of how well the item discriminates between good and bad learners. *Discrimination* is calculated as the *point biserial* correlation coefficient between the score obtained on the item and the total score obtained on the test.
- *frequency(i)*: a real number between 0 and 1 which expresses the frequency of the i-th option of the item. Its value is calculated as the percentage of learners who choose the i-th option.
- *discrimination(i)*: a real number between -1 and 1 which expresses the discrimination of the i-th option. Its value is the point biserial correlation coefficient between the result obtained by the learner on the whole test and a dichotomous variable that says whether the i-th option was chosen (yes=1, no=0) by the learner or not.
- *abstained_freq*: a real number between 0 and 1 which expresses the frequency of the abstention (no answers given) on the item. Its value is calculated as the percentage of learners who didn't give any answer to the item, where allowed.
- *abstained_discr*: a real number between -1 and 1 which expresses the discrimination of the abstention on the item. Its value is the point biserial correlation coefficient between the result obtained by the learner on the whole test and a dichotomous variable that says whether the learner refrained or not (yes=1, no=0) on the item.

Discrimination and *difficulty* are the most important indicators. They can be used for both determining item quality and choosing advice for tutors. As experts suggest [8], a good value for *discrimination* is about 0.5. A positive value lower than 0.2 indicates an item which does not discriminate well. This can be due to several reasons, including: the question does not assess learners on the desired knowledge; the stem or the options are badly/ambiguously expressed; etc. It is usually difficult to understand what is wrong with these items and more difficult to provide a suggestion to improve them, so, if the tutor cannot understand the problem her(him)self, the suggestion is to discard the item. A negative value for *discrimination*, especially if joined with a positive value for the discrimination of a *distractor*, is a sign of a possible mistake in choosing the key (a data entry error occurred). In this case it is easy to recover the item by changing the key.

If *difficulty* is too high (>0.85) or too low (<0.15), there is the risk of not correctly evaluating on the desired knowledge. This is particularly true when such values for *difficulty* are sought together with medium-low values for *discrimination*. Furthermore, our system allows the tutor to define the foreseen difficulty for an item. Thus, the closer a tutor's estimation of item *difficulty* is to the actual calculated difficulty for that item, the more reliable that item is considered to be. When *difficulty* is too high or underestimated, this can be due to the presence of a *distractor* (noticed for its high frequency) which is too plausible (it tends to mislead a lot of students, even strong ones). Removing or substituting that *distractor* can help in obtaining a better item. Sometimes, the item has its intrinsic difficulty and it can be difficult to adjust it, so the suggestion can be to modify the tutor's estimation.

As for *distractors*, they can contribute to a good item when they are selected by a significant number of students. When the frequency of the *distractor* is too high, there could be an ambiguity in the formulation of the stem or of the *distractor*. A good indicator of *distractors'* quality is their discrimination, which should be negative, denoting that the *distractor* was selected by weak students. In conclusion, a good *distractor* is the one which is selected by a small but significant number of weak students.

High abstention is always a symptom of high difficulty for the item. When it is accompanied by a high (not negative or next to 0) value for its discrimination and a low value for item *discrimination*, it can tell that the question has a bad quality and it is difficult to improve it.

3 The Fuzzy System

The system for the evaluation of item quality is *rule-based*: the rules use, as *linguistic variables*, statistical indicators calculated after a test *session*. By this term we mean the time necessary to administer several items to a statistically significant number of students. The value of this number is set in the configuration of the system.

The system works by performing a *classification* of the items. Several classes of items have been identified, and each class is associated to a *production rule*. The *degree of fulfillment* of a rule tells the membership of the item to the corresponding class. The classification is performed by selecting the class for which the *degree of fulfillment* is the highest.

3.1 Variables and Fuzzyfication

The set of variables used are reported, together with an explanation of their meaning and the set of possible values they can assume (*terms*), in table 1. These variables are directly chosen from the statistical indicators presented in section 2 or derived from them.

Table 1. Variables and terms

Variable	Explanation	Terms
discrimination	Item's discrimination (see sec. 2)	Negative, low, high
difficulty	Item's difficulty (see sec. 2)	Very_low, medium, very_high
difficulty_gap	The difference between the tutor's estimation of item's difficulty and the difficulty calculated by the system	Underestimated, correct, overestimated
max_distr_discr	The maximum discrimination for the *distractors* of an item	Negative, positive
max_distr_freq	The maximum (relative) frequency for the *distractors* of an item.	Low, high
min_distr_freq	The minimum (relative) frequency for the *distractors* of an item	Low, high
distr_freq	The (relative) frequency of the *distractor* with maximum discrimination for an item	Low, high
abst_frequency	The frequency of the abstentions for an item	Low, high
abst_discrimination	The discrimination of the abstentions for an item	Negative, positive

The variables *discrimination* and *difficulty* are the same indicators for item *discrimination* and *difficulty* defined in section 2. The same discourse is valid for the variables related to the abstention, *abst_frequency* and *abst_discrimination*. *difficulty_gap* is a variable representing the error in tutor's estimation of item *difficulty*. Through the system interface, the tutor can assign one on three difficulty level to an item (easy = 0.3; medium = 0.5; difficult = 0.7). *difficulty_gap* is calculated as the difference between the tutor estimation and the actual difficulty calculated by the system.

Three variables representing the frequency of the *distractors* for an item have been considered: *max_distr_freq*, *min_distr_freq*, *distr_freq*. Their value is not an absolute frequency, but relative to the frequency of the other *distractors*: it is obtained by dividing the absolute frequency by the mean frequency of the *distractors* of the item. In the case of items with five options, as our system has been tested, their value is a real number varying from 0 to 4.

3.2 Membership Functions

As for the membership functions of fuzzy sets associated to each term, *triangular* and *trapezoidal shapes* have been used. Most of the values for the bases and the peaks have been established using the expertise. Only for some variables, the membership functions have been defined on an experimental basis.

While we already had clear ideas on how to define some membership functions, we did not have enough information from the knowledge-base on how to model membership functions for the variables related to abstention (*abst_frequency* and *abst_discrimination*). A calibration phase was required in order to refine the values for the bases and peaks of their membership functions. As a calibration set, test results from the *Science Faculty Admission Test* of the last year (2006) were used. The calibration set was composed of 64 items with 5 options each. For each item, about one thousand records (students answers) were available, even if only a random sample of seventy of them was considered. Test items and their results were inspected by a human expert who identified items which should have been discarded due to low *discrimination* and anomalous values for the variables related to abstention. We have found 5 items satisfying the conditions above: the mean values for *abst_discrimination* and *abst_ frequency* were, respectively, 0.12 and 0.39.

Due to the limited size of the calibration set, the simple method of choosing the peaks of the functions at the mean value, as shown in [4], has been used. When more data will be available, a more sophisticated method will be used for the definition of membership functions, such as the one proposed in [9]. Charts for the membership functions are shown in figure 1.

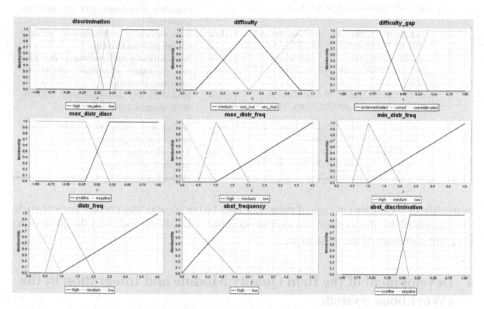

Fig. 1. Membership Functions of the Fuzzy Sets

3.3 Rules

From the verbal description of the knowledge presented in section 2, the rules summarized in table 2 have been inferred. The first three columns in the table contain, respectively, the class of the item, the rule used for classification and the item state. For items whose state is yellow, the fourth column contains the problem affecting the item and the suggestion to improve its quality.

Conditions in the rules are connected using AND and OR logic operators. The commonly-used *min-max* inference method has been used to establish the *degree of fulfillment* of the rules. All the rules were given the same *weight*, except for the first one. By modifying the weight of the first rule, we can tune the sensitivity of the system: the lower this value, the higher the probability that anomalies will be detected in the items. Some rules suggest to perform an operation on a *distractor*. The *distractor*

Table 2. Rules for Item Classification

Class	Rule	State	Problem and Suggestion
1	discrimination IS high AND abst_discrimination IS negative WITH 0.9	Green	/
2	discrimination IS low AND abst_frequency IS high AND abst_discrimination IS positive	Red	/
3	difficulty IS very_low AND discrimination IS low	Red	/
4	difficulty IS very_high AND discrimination IS low AND max_distr_freq IS high	Yellow	Item too difficult due to a too plausible *distractor*, delete or substitute *distractor x*.
5	difficulty_gap IS overestimated AND discrimination IS low	Yellow	Item difficulty overestimated, avoid too plausible *distractors* and too obvious answers.
6	difficulty_gap IS overestimated AND discrimination IS NOT low	Yellow	Item difficulty overestimated, modify the estimated difficulty.
7	difficulty_gap IS underestimated AND max_distr_freq IS high	Yellow	Item difficulty underestimated due to a too plausible *distractor*, delete or substitute *distractor x*.
8	difficulty_gap IS underestimated AND max_distr_freq IS NOT high	Yellow	Item difficulty underestimated, modify the estimated difficulty.
9	max_distr_discr IS positive AND discrimination IS negative	Yellow	Wrong key (data entry error), select option *x* as the correct answer.
10	discrimination IS high AND max_distr_discr IS positive AND distr_freq IS NOT low	Yellow	Too plausible *distractor*, delete or substitute *distractor x*.

to modify or eliminate (in case of rules 4, 7 and 10) or to select as correct answer (rule 9) is signaled by the system. An output variable x has been added to the system to keep the identifier of the *distractor*.

4   Development of the Item Quality Module and Integration in the eWorkbook System

A software module for the evaluation of item quality has been implemented as a Java *Object Oriented* framework. In this way, it would have been easily integrated in any e-testing java-based system. For each item, the module performs the classification, by implementing the following functionalities:

- Implementation of an *Application Programming Interface* (*API*) for the construction of a data matrix containing all the students' responses to the item.
- Calculation of the statistical indicators, as described in section 2.
- Substitution of the variables, evaluation of the rules and choice of the class which the item belongs to.

Implementation of a suitable *API* for obtaining the *state* of an item (*green*, *yellow*, *red*) and, in case of yellow, of the *suggestions* for improving the item. It is worth noting that suggestions can be internationalized, that is, they can easily be translated into any language by editing a text file.

A free java library implementing a complete Fuzzy inference system, named *jFuzzyLogic* [10] has been used. The system variables, fuzzyfication, inference methods and the rules have been defined using *Fuzzy Control Language* (*FCL*) [11], supported by the *jFuzzyLogic* library. The advantage of this approach, compared to a hard-coded solution, is that membership functions and rules can be changed only by editing a configuration file, thus avoiding to build the system again. Data can be imported from various sources and exported to several formats, such as spreadsheets or relational databases. The data matrix and the results can be saved in persistent tables, in order to avoid to perform calculations every time they must be visualized.

4.1 eWorkbook

eWorkbook is a Web-based e-testing system that can be used for evaluating learner's knowledge by creating (the tutor) and taking (the learner) on-line tests based on *multiple choice* question types. The questions are kept in a *hierarchical* repository. The tests are composed of one or more sections. There are two kinds of sections: *static* and *dynamic*. The difference between them is in the way they allow question selection: for a static section, the questions are chosen by the tutor. For a dynamic section, some selection parameters must be specified, such as the difficulty, leaving the system to choose the questions randomly whenever a learner takes a test. In this way, it is possible with *eWorkbook* to make a test with banks of items of different difficulties, thus balancing test difficulty, in order to better assess a heterogeneous set of students. *eWorkbook* adopts the classical *three-tier* architecture of the most common *J2EE* Web-applications. The *Jakarta Struts framework* has been used to support the *Model 2* design paradigm, a variation of the classic *Model View Controller* (*MVC*) approach. In our design choice, Struts works with *JSP*, for the View, while it interacts with *Hibernate* [12], a powerful framework for *object/relational persistence* and query service for Java, for the Model. The application is fully accessible with a Web Browser. No browser plug-in installations are needed, since its pages are composed of standard HTML and *ECMAScript* [13] code.

4.2 Integration

The integration of the new functionalities in *eWorkbook* has required the development of a new module, named *Item Quality Module*, responsible for instantiating the framework and providing import, export and visualization functionalities. Import of data was performed by reading data from *eWorkbook*'s database and by calling the *API* to fill the data matrix of the framework. The interface for browsing the item repository in *eWorkbook* has been updated in order to show item's performances (*difficulty* and *discrimination*) and state (*green, yellow* or *red*). In this way, defective items are immediately visible to the tutor, who can undertake the opportune actions (delete or modify). A screenshot of the item report is shown in figure 2a.

Furthermore, the system has been given a *versioning functionality*: once an item is modified, a newer version of it is generated. Through this functionality, the tutor can analyze the entire lifecycle of an item. In this way, the tutor can have feedback on the trend of statistical indicators over time, making sure that the changes he/she made to the items positively affected their quality. Figure 2b shows the chart of an item improved across two sessions of tests. The improvement is visible both from the increase in the item *discrimination* (the green line), and in the convergence of the calculated difficulty with the tutor's estimation of the difficulty (the continuous and dashed red lines, respectively).

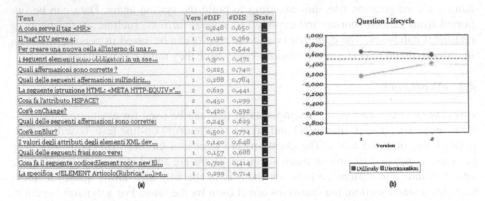

Text	Vers	#DIF	#DIS	State
A cosa serve il tag <HR>	1	0,248	0,650	
Il "tag" DIV serve a:	1	0,192	0,369	
Per creare una nuova cella all'interno di una r...	1	0,212	0,544	
I seguenti elementi sono obbligatori in un ese...	1	0,300	0,471	
Quali affermazioni sono corrette ?	1	0,225	0,740	
Quali delle seguenti affermazioni sull'indiriz...	1	0,288	0,784	
La seguente istruzione HTML: <META HTTP-EQUIV="...	2	0,619	0,441	
Cosa fa l'attributo HSPACE?	2	0,450	0,299	
Cos'è onChange?	1	0,420	0,592	
Quali delle seguenti affermazioni sono corrette:	1	0,245	0,629	
Cos'è onBlur?	1	0,500	0,774	
I valori degli attributi degli elementi XML dev...	1	0,140	0,648	
Quali delle seguenti frasi sono vere:	1	0,157	0,688	
Cosa fa il seguente codice:Element root= new El...	1	0,720	0,414	
La specifica <!ELEMENT Articolo(Rubrica*,...)>s...	1	0,299	0,714	

(a)   (b)

Fig. 2. Screenshots From the eWorkbook System Interface

5   Use Case in a University Course

A first experiment has consisted of using the system across two test sessions in a university course, and measuring the overall improvement of the items in terms of discrimination capacity and matching to a tutor's desired difficulty. A database of 50 items was arranged for the experiment. In the first session, an on-line test, containing a set of 25 randomly chosen items, was administered to 60 students. After, items were inspected through the system interface in order to check those to substitute or modify. Once the substitutions and modifications were performed, the modified test was administered to 60 other students.

Figure 3a shows a table, exported in a spreadsheet, containing a report of the items presented in the first test session and their performances. The item to eliminate are highlighted in red, while those to modify are highlighted in yellow. According to the system analysis, 5 out of 25 items must be discarded, while 4 of them must be modified.

Actually, among the items to modify, for two of them (those with id 1-F-4 and 1-E-1) the *difficulty* was underestimated due to a *distractor* that was too plausible (class 7), which was substituted with a new *distractor*. In another case (1-B-16), the difficulty was different from that estimated by the tutor, due to the intrinsic difficulty of the item (class 8). The action undertaken was to adjust tutor's estimation of the difficulty. Lastly, the item with id 1-F-1, with a negative *discrimination*, presented a suspect error in the choice of the key (class 9). By inspecting the item, the tutor verified that the chosen key was not correct, even though the *distractor* labeled correct by the system was not the right answer: simply, the item did not have any correct answer. The text of the key was modified to provide the right answer to the stem.

A new test was prepared, containing the same items of the previous, except for the 5 discarded ones, substituted by 5 unused items, and for the 4 modified ones, which were substituted by a newer version of themselves. A new set of sixty students participated in this test. In the analysis of test outcomes, our attention was more focused on the eventual improvement obtained than on the discovery of new defective items. Figure 3b shows the report of the second test session. The values of *discrimination* and *difficulty*, changed in respect to the same rows of the session 1 table, are highlighted in yellow.

To measure the overall improvement of the new test, in respect to the previous one, the following parameters were calculated for each of the two tests:

- the mean of the *discrimination* indicator for the items;
- the mean of the differences |*tutor_difficulty* – *difficulty*| for the items of the tests;

As for parameter 1, we have observed an improvement from a value of 0,375, obtained in the first session, to a value of 0,459, obtained in the second session. The percentage of increment is 22,4%. As for parameter 2, we had a decrement in the mean difference between the difficulty estimated by the tutor and the one calculated by the system of 17,8%, passing from a value of 0,19 to 0,156 across the two sessions.

(a)

Question Id	Options	Correct	Discrimination	Tutor Diff	Difficulty
1-F-1	5	1	-0,04	0,7	0,76
1-B-10	5	3	0,51	0,5	0,24
1-B-6	5	4	0,6	0,5	0,58
1-A-19	5	4	0,22	0,5	0,29
1-D-2	5	2	0,7	0,5	0,82
1-B-4	5	5	0,42	0,5	0,34
1-A-13	5	1	0,33	0,3	0,08
1-F-4	5	3	0,32	0,5	0,79
1-B-18	5	4	0,55	0,3	0,53
1-A-15	5	5	0,37	0,5	0,66
1-B-2	5	5	0,59	0,5	0,45
1-E-4	5	4	0,4	0,5	0,79
1-C-1	5	1	0,07	0,5	0,39
1-B-12	5	4	0,48	0,3	0,74
1-A-24	5	2	0,36	0,3	0,37
1-D-3	5	5	0,15	0,5	0,53
1-C-4	5	1	0,16	0,5	0,74
1-B-16	5	3	0,41	0,5	0,76
1-A-9	5	3	0,57	0,3	0,53
1-B-20	5	5	0,38	0,3	0,47
1-A-2	5	2	0,21	0,3	0,34
1-B-8	5	5	0,49	0,5	0,29
1-C-5	5	1	0,17	0,7	0,87
1-B-15	5	4	0,52	0,5	0,42
1-E-1	5	4	0,44	0,5	0,87
Average Discrimination			0,3752		
Average Difficulty Gap			0,19		

(b)

Question Id	Options	Correct	Discrimination	Tutor Diff	Difficulty
1-F-1	5	1	0,48	0,7	0,67
1-B-10	5	3	0,51	0,5	0,24
1-B-6	5	4	0,6	0,5	0,58
1-D-4	5	3	0,08	0,5	0,76
1-D-2	5	2	0,7	0,5	0,82
1-B-4	5	5	0,42	0,5	0,34
1-A-13	5	1	0,33	0,3	0,08
1-F-4	5	3	0,47	0,5	0,43
1-B-18	5	4	0,55	0,3	0,53
1-A-15	5	5	0,37	0,5	0,66
1-B-2	5	5	0,59	0,5	0,45
1-E-4	5	4	0,4	0,5	0,79
1-A-17	5	5	0,44	0,3	0,45
1-B-12	5	4	0,48	0,3	0,74
1-A-24	5	2	0,36	0,3	0,37
1-D-3	5	5	0,15	0,5	0,53
1-A-23	5	3	0,38	0,3	0,32
1-B-16	5	3	0,41	0,7	0,76
1-A-9	5	3	0,57	0,3	0,53
1-B-20	5	5	0,38	0,3	0,47
1-F-3	5	5	0,76	0,5	0,72
1-B-8	5	5	0,49	0,5	0,29
1-B-5	5	5	0,66	0,3	0,5
1-B-15	5	4	0,52	0,5	0,42
1-E-1	5	4	0,37	0,5	0,58
Average Discrimination			0,4588		
Average Difficulty Gap			0,1556		

Fig. 3. Report of the Test Sessions

6 Related Work

Several different assessment tools and applications to support blended learning have been analyzed, starting from the most common Web-based E-Learning platforms, such as *Moodle* [14], *Blackboard* [15], and *Questionmark* [16]. These systems generate and show item statistics parameters but they do not interpret them, so they do not advise or help the tutor in improving items erasing anomalies revealed by statistics. A model for presenting test statistics, analysis, and to collect students' learning behaviors for generating analysis result and feedback to tutors is described in [17]. *IRT* has been applied in some systems [18] and experiments [19, 20] to select the most appropriate items for examinees based on individual ability. In [19], the fuzzy theory is combined with the original *IRT* to model uncertainly learning response. The result of this combination is called *Fuzzy Item Response Theory*.

A work closely related to ours is presented in [21]. It proposes an e-testing system, where rules can detect defective items, which are signaled using traffic lights. It proposes an analysis model based on *IA*. Statistics are calculated by the system both on the items and on the whole test. Unfortunately, the four rules on which the system is based seem to be insufficient to cover all of the possible defects which can affect an item. Moreover, these rules are not inferred from a solid knowledge-base and use crisp values (i.e., one of them, states that an option must be discarded if its frequency is 0, independently from the size of the sample). Furthermore, it does not contain any experiment which demonstrates the effectiveness of the system in improving assessment. Nevertheless, this work has given us many ideas, and our work can be considered a continuation of it.

7 Conclusion

In this paper we have presented an e-testing system, capable of improving item quality, through the re-use of the items across subsequent on-line test sessions. Our system's rules use statistical indicators from the *IA* model to detect anomalies on the items, and to give advise for their improvement. Obviously, the system can only detect defects which are visible by analyzing results of item and *distractor* analysis.

The strength of our system is in the possibility for all the tutors, and not only experts of assessment or statistics, to improve test quality, by discarding or, where possible, by modifying defective items. An initial experiment carried out at the University of Salerno has produced encouraging results, showing that the system can effectively help the tutors to obtain items which better discriminate between strong and weak students and better match the difficulty estimated by the tutor. More accurate experiments, involving a larger set of items and students, are necessary to effectively measure the system capabilities.

Our system performs a classification of items, carried out by evaluating fuzzy rules. At present, we are collecting data on test outcomes. Once a large database of items and learner's answers is available, there will be the possibility of exploiting other methods of classification, based on data, such as hierarchical methods, K-means methods, and correlation methods.

References

1. Woodford, K., Bancroft, P.: Multiple Choice Items Not Considered Harmful. In: 7th Australian conference on Computing education, Newcastle, Australia, pp. 109–116 (2005)
2. Hambleton, R.K., Swaminathan, H.: Item Response Theory– Principles und Applications, Kluwer Academic Publishers Group, Netherlands (1985)

3. Zadeh, L.A.: Fuzzy Sets and Their Applications to Pattern Classification and Clustering. World Scientific Publishing Co. Inc, River Edge, NJ, USA (1977)
4. Bardossy, A., Duckstein, L.: Fuzzy Rule-Based Modeling with Applications to Geophysical, Biological, and Engineering Systems. CRC Press, Boca Raton, USA (1995)
5. Lloyd, S.: Least Squares Quantization in PCM. IEEE Transactions on Information Theory 28 (2), 129–137 (1982)
6. Costagliola, G., Ferrucci, F., Fuccella, V., Gioviale, F.: A Web-based Tool for Assessment and Self-Assessment, In: 2nd International Conference on Information Technology: Research and Education, pp. 131–135 (2004)
7. Stage, C.: A Comparison Between Item Analysis Based on Item Response Theory and Classical Test Theory. A Study of the SweSAT Subtest READ (1999), http://www.umu.se/edmeas/publikationer/pdf/enr3098sec.pdf
8. Massey: The Relationship Between the Popularity of Questions and Their Difficulty Level in Examinations Which Allow a Choice of Question. Occasional Publication of The Test Dev. and Res. Unit, Cambridge
9. Civanlar, M.R., Trussel, H.J.: Constructing membership functions using statistical data. Fuzzy Sets and Systems 18, 1–14 (1986)
10. jFuzzyLogic: Open Source Fuzzy Logic (Java), http://jfuzzylogic.sourceforge.net/html/index.html
11. FCL: Fuzzy Control Prog. Committee Draft CD 1.0 (Rel. 19 Jan 97), http://www.fuzzytech.com/binaries/ieccd1.pdf
12. Hibernate, http://www.hibernate.org
13. ECMAScript, Standard ECMA-262, ECMAScript Language Specification, http://www.ecma-international.org/publications/files/ECMA-ST/Ecma.262.pdf
14. Moodle, http://moodle.org
15. Blackboard, http://www.blackboard.com
16. Questionmark, http://www.questionmark.com
17. Hsieh, C.T., Shih, T.K., Chang, W.C., Ko, W.C.: Feedback and Analysis from Assessment Metadata in E-Learning. In: 17th International Conference on Advanced Information Networking and Applications, Xi'an, China, pp. 155–158 (2003)
18. Ho, R.G., Yen, Y.C.: Design and Evaluation of an XML-Based Platform-Independent Computerized Adaptive TestingSystem. IEEE Transactions on Education 48(2), 230–237 (2005)
19. Chen, C.M., Duh, L.J., Liu, C.Y.: A Personalized Courseware Recommendation System Based on Fuzzy Item Response Theory. In: IEEE Int. Conf. on e-Technology, e-Commerce and e-Service, Taipei, Taiwan, pp. 305–308 (2004)
20. Sun, K.T.: An Effective Item Selection Method for Educational Measurement. In: International Workshop on Advanced Learning Technologies, pp. 105–106 (1967)
21. Hung, J.C., Lin, L.J., Chang, W.C., Shih, T.K., Hsu, H.H., Chang, H.B., Chang, H.P., Huang, K.H.: A Cognition Assessment Authoring System for E-Learning. In: 24th Int. Conf. on Distributed Computing Systems Workshops, pp. 262–267 (2004)

A Novel Architecture for E-Learning Knowledge Assessment Systems

Krzysztof Gierłowski and Krzysztof Nowicki

Gdansk University of Technology
{krzysztof.gierlowski, krzysztof.nowicki}@eti.pg.gda.pl

Abstract. In this paper we propose a novel E-Learning system, dedicated strictly to knowledge assessment tasks. In its functioning it utilizes web-based technologies, but its design differs radically from currently popular E-Learning solutions which rely mostly on thin-client architecture. Our research proved that such architecture, while well suited for didactic content distribution systems is ill-suited for knowledge assessment products.

In our design we employed loosely-tied distributed system architecture, strict modularity, test and simulation-based knowledge and skill assessment and an our original communications package called Communication Abstraction Layer (ComAL), specifically designed to support communication functions of E-Learning systems in diverse network conditions (including offline environment). The system was tested in production environment on Faculty of Electronics, Telecommunications and Informatics, Technical University of Gdansk with great success, reducing staff workload and increasing efficiency of didactic process. Tests also showed system's versatility as the system was deployed in environments of classroom, remote and blended learning.

Keywords: knowledge and skill assessment, distributed system, modular, didactic simulation.

1 Introduction

The task of knowledge assessment is one of the fundamental elements of didactic process. It was also one of the first didactic tasks to be conducted by various electronic learning devices employed to support didactic process.

Currently there are many E-Learning solutions supporting knowledge assessment both as their main functionality or as an additional module [1,2].

Almost any advanced E-Learning tool offers this functionality. In light of those facts we could conclude that this area of E-Learning is a well explored one and suitably supported in practical E-Learning products.

Our experience with E-Learning systems both as their users and designers, leads us to conclusion that the above statement is far from correct. Vast majority of currently available electronic knowledge assessment tools are extremely similar and offer strictly limited functionality. Such products offer almost exclusively knowledge assessment based on various choice tests and their automatic grading mechanisms most often are not very comprehensive and fit to support different grading scenarios.

In complex E-Learning systems knowledge assessment functionality is treated as mandatory element, but also receives no special consideration, which often results in

H. Leung et al. (Eds.): ICWL 2007, LNCS 4823, pp. 276–287, 2008.

a simple implementation of choice test. Specialized knowledge testing solutions (employed for example by Microsoft during their computer proficiency exams) include more advanced mechanisms, like adaptive question selection, but they are few and still do not go beyond the basic scenario of choice test [3,4].

Apart from these weaknesses, one of the most serious problems with currently available products and especially the most popular ones based on web-based thin-client architecture, is their strict dependence on network connectivity. Majority of such products require constantly active network connection during E-Learning session and few are fit to function under other circumstances, such as periodic or no network connectivity, and still remain a part of managed E-Learning system. The quality of network service is also a factor in case of many of such products [5].

Having analyzed above limitations of currently available knowledge assessment products, we designed and created our own dedicated knowledge assessment system. It was designed to provide highly modifiable platform for various knowledge testing tools, able to provide its functions in any network connectivity conditions (including no connectivity scenario). The system can scale from very simple setup (adequate for servicing a single exercise) to a large, distributed solution fit to support an enterprise. Strictly modular architecture allows users to employ only a selected set of its mechanisms and extremely easily integrate it with third-party solutions. The selection of employed modules depends completely on user needs – there is no mandatory control module or management platform which must be present.

We created a number of client modules with full support for low/no-connectivity scenarios, for example:

- the classic, but highly configurable and versatile, multiple choice knowledge testing solution,
- an unique simulation-based knowledge and skill assessment module, dedicated to exercises concerning Asynchronous Transfer Mode (ATM) and Frame Relay,
- a module allowing a real-time grading of students performance during exercises.

Our system also addresses security aspects of remote, computer based knowledge testing, in both test distribution and results gathering preserving user anonymity to unauthorized parties.

As an key element of the system, we have created an innovative Communication Abstraction Layer (ComAL) - a set of mechanisms designed to provide E-Learning system designers with API containing a comprehensive set of communication functions which can make an E-Learning system independent of underlying network connectivity conditions. ComAL completely isolates E-Learning solution programmer from the details of network communication and can be employed to easily create networked E-Learning solutions, **allowing creation of an integrated, managed E-Learning system even in environment without network connectivity**.

2   Overall System Design

During design and creation of our system we aimed to provide a solution fit to accommodate needs to assess students knowledge in the widest possible set of scenarios. To fulfill this task we considered its following aspects:

- compatibility with the widest possible set of hardware and operating systems,
- ability to function in variety of network connectivity environments (including lack of such connectivity) while still retaining capability to function as globally managed solution,
- security and reliability of the system, including safety of the system itself, test content, students' solutions and personal data,
- information storage and manipulation capabilities, to allow creation of central database of results and grades, complete with easy access methods,
- knowledge assessment functionality including: multiple choice tests with highly customizable automatic grading and real time grading by a teacher,
- comprehensive management interfaces for administrators and teachers,
- ease of deployment, customization, modification and integration with third-party solutions.

To fulfill these requirements, we have chosen a client-server architecture for our system, which is a pretty standard solution today, but in contrast to the most common practice we decided to abandon thin-client technology in favor of full-client approach.

From our experience, web-based thin-client architecture despite its undisputed compatibility and ease of deployment, is not especially well suited for knowledge assessment systems, as it requires a constant network connectivity for operation and lacks a sufficient degree of control over user environment, which impairs system reliability and allows unauthorized actions on part of the users. Operating system and web browser security mechanisms are also an important issue here, as their incorrect configuration can lead to abnormal or partial client software behavior [6].

Full-client approach allows client to conduct much wider range of operations compared to thin-client. This allows inclusion of more advanced internal mechanisms providing improved functionality, much better reliability and security of client operation. With proper design full-client utilizing web-based technologies can also operate independently of server which gives our system versatility, necessary to handle limited network connectivity scenario. It also helps to create strictly modular system architecture and provide high level of scalability (as many tasks can be conducted client-side and data transfers minimized).

The most serious limitations of full-client approach, deployment and system compatibility, are also possible to overcome by employing easily deployable, platform independent clients (for example Java-based). Such solution allows for all advantages of full-client and web-based technologies, while still retaining high level of hardware and system compatibility and easy (even web-based) deployment.

The second of our fundamental design decisions was maintaining a strict modularity of our product. All basic elements are constructed as modules capable of operating independently, and are employing only standardized, self-describing data format for inter-module data transfer - Extensible Markup Language (XML). The format is compatible with QTI (Question & Test Interoperability) version 2 specification [7], but defines additional extensions.

Modular system structure complicates design and implementation, as it requires the use of additional inter-module communication mechanisms, but these difficulties are easily compensated by our ComAL API, described in later chapter.

On the other hand modular structure brings enormous advantages, as it is possible to substitute customized solutions in place of some standard modules or include additional elements into standard system data paths to provide additional data analysis/translation functionality. Advantages of these possibilities are clear, as they allow easy modification and customization of the system, including creation of dedicated interfaces for third-party systems and applications. Moreover, there are already many such solutions accepting XML input and providing XML output (for example MS Office, OpenOffice etc.).

There is also a possibility which had proven even more useful then these mentioned above during test deployments of our system – it is possible to deploy only selected elements and/or integrate it directly with third-party solutions supporting XML language.

An ability to deploy only a chosen set of modules allows for deployment precisely tailored to individual needs. If system user is interested only in simple multiple choice solution for a small number of students there is no need for a system server – it is enough to deploy only a testing/grading module and read resulting offline data files directly with MS or Open Office. In an opposite situation, where the user is interested only in system's data storage and access functions, he can easily deploy the system's server part, substituting its clients with his own, as long as they support XML output or can provide appropriate translating interface.

Fig. 1. Partial system deployment and integration with 3rd party solutions

This partial-deployment ability also makes transition to new system much easier, as it can be conducted in phases, by gradually exchanging existing infrastructure with modules of the system.

3   Communication Abstraction Layer

One of key elements of modular system are inter-module communication mechanisms. The task of providing local communication (between modules on the same machine) is relatively simple, because we can precisely predict environment characteristics.

Remote connectivity (communication between modules on different machines) is another matter as it is dependent on various characteristics of available network infrastructure and providing reliable communication, satisfying quality of service requirements of an E-Learning system in wide range of network scenarios and conditions is a difficult and work intensive task [5]. Its complication and cost most often lead to abandoning such attempts and creation of products which require constant and stable network connectivity lacking mechanisms for handling other scenarios (for example: the popular thin-client architecture) or employ no advanced communication functions at all.

While such approach may be sufficient for didactic content distribution systems, knowledge assessment requires a higher degree of communication between client (which interacts with user) and server part of the system (usually responsible for control, management, task assignment and results gathering).

To help developers in building a robust, networked E-Learning systems we have created a set of mechanisms called Communication Abstraction Layer (ComAL) specifically designed to provide network communication functions required by E-Learning environment. This set of mechanisms can employ a variety of communication methods, automatically choosing the one most appropriate for current working conditions, and is responsible for all communication tasks – both local and remote. It isolates E-Learning system developer from particulars of implementing a network communication mechanisms by providing him with high level API.

From our experience in developing networked E-Learning systems, we divided most often encountered network conditions into four scenarios:

- Local Area Network – efficient and reliable, permanent network connectivity.
- Internet – an environment where we have a permanent network connectivity at our disposal, but there are no Quality of Service (QoS) or reliability guarantees.
- Periodic connectivity – most commonly encountered in case of dialup connections.
- Offline – there is no network connectivity, but there is still a possibility of communication by offline methods (floppy, CD/DVD, USB-storage...).

ComAL provides dedicated means for maintaining a stable communication in all of these environments, and is able to detect the correct scenario automatically and keeps monitoring the situation to detect if the scenario changes.

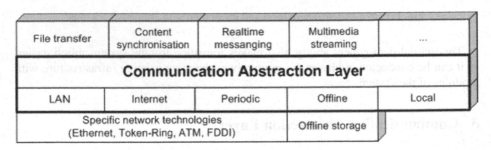

Fig. 2. Overall ComAL architecture

The provided set of communication functions available to E-Learning system creator can accommodate a wide variety of application types, ranging from sending a simple messages, through high volume file transfers and content synchronization, to reliable, real-time interactive message exchanges and multimedia transmissions. Of course, not all of these functions can be made available in all of the above scenarios. To deal with such limitations, ComAL provides feedback mechanisms informing higher application layers about functionality available under current network conditions, state of currently conducted communication activities, overall status of network connectivity and its changes.

For transport of data ComAL currently employs: direct TCP and UDP connectivity, SOAP over HTTPS, encrypted SOAP over SMTP and advanced, secure file export/import functions. Some of these methods (SMTP and file-based) allow communication between system modules behind NAT. Moreover, we are currently developing a media proxy module functionality, allowing destinations behind NAT to communicate with TCP/UDP and indirect (but still secure) SOAP over HTTPS.

All communications can be protected with use of strong security mechanisms, providing their confidentiality, integrity and mutual authentication of communicating parties. The ComAL utilizes both symmetric and public-key cryptography and supports automatic key/certificate generation for clients.

We believe that creation of such abstraction layer, able to free E-Learning system developers from difficult, specialized, costly and work consuming design and implementation of network communication functions can encourage creation of advanced solutions, taking full advantage of potential provided by a networked environment. It has been utilized in a number of our E-Learning products [6,8,9], greatly reducing design complexity and implementation work required. It was also successfully employed to extend functionality of strictly local E-Learning solution, to allow network based management.

ComAL is a basis of all inter-module communication in our knowledge assessment system, enabling our system to function as manageable entity in most diverse communication scenarios.

4 System Architecture

As our knowledge assessment system follows a client-server design, its modules can be divided into two basic groups: client and server modules. Communication between system elements is conducted with use of ComAL to support various network environments.

Client modules interact directly with student or teacher during didactic process and are responsible for providing majority of system's functionality in accordance with configuration information obtained from servers and under their control. Results of knowledge assessment conducted by client modules are returned to servers for processing and storage.

There can be many client modules providing different types of knowledge assessment or supporting functions. Currently we have implemented the following client modules:

- Test-based knowledge assessment module.
- Unique simulation-based E-Learning model, allowing knowledge and skill assessment.
- Teacher's interface for grading student's progress during training session.

All of these modules are able to function as independent applications and support full ComAL capabilities, including strictly offline scenario – in such case configuration and test packages are provided to them as cryptographically protected files (automatically generated by server), and results are returned to server in the same way. Also they are able to monitor presence of network connectivity and initiate automatic upload of results gathered in offline mode.

Server part of the system is a distributed database containing both didactic content and system's complete configuration information. A single server consists of a database (most often an SQL server) and a system maintenance module responsible for creating and maintaining distributed information base. It also provides a web-based administrative interface allowing administrator to create and control the system.

An administrator is responsible for creating a distributed system architecture by defining communication links between system server, and deciding which of ComAL transport mechanisms are permitted for each link. If a server cannot maintain current transport mechanism it will switch do less demanding one if such is permitted, otherwise it will mark link as down. A simple link-state path selection protocol is then used to ensure communication between all nodes, utilizing as link metrics information from ComAL network monitoring mechanisms.

Over such communication structure works a data indexing mechanism, allowing full access to distributed information base from any system node. This distributed database includes complete information about system-wide configuration (system structure, global users and access rights, link states, distributed database state) which is replicated to all servers and didactic content (test content, grading rules, student lists, test results and grades etc.) which is kept locally on specific server and is not replicated, but can be accessed from any server if there is connectivity present.

Such architecture allows largely independent operation of particular server (supporting for example a single course or organization department), while still allowing administration of the system as a whole and easy access to information stored on different servers. It will give various teachers or departments the freedom of independent operation and still provide means of global data access. As a result servers can be connected and disconnected from the distributed system at will.

If a given server will communicate with client modules, it must be supplemented by a client communication module. It is responsible for client-server communications, supplying client modules with configuration and didactic content, gathering and processing incoming results and providing teacher's interface to the system.

Teacher's interface allows its user to create test packages and assign it to specific combination of students, network workstations or time frames – it is possible to provide student witch a choice of available tests. Such test package contains all information to conduct a test, namely: test content adequate for specific client module, grading rules and additional information concerning test execution (time limit, randomization of content, means of results upload etc.).

Teacher's interface allows a full read access to gathered results and ability to modify or add data concerning teacher's own tests, as well as generation of various reports and statistics. There is also an option of importing external data in XML format into the system and exporting system data in the same format.

5 Client Modules

Client modules are critical for the system as they are its point of contact with the student, responsible for many essential tasks, such as presentation of test content, enforcing configured test conditions (time, test randomization, etc.), performing it and sending all necessary information back to the system for processing and storage, etc. The grading of tests can be conducted client-side, by client modules, or server-side, by client communication module. Server side grading is more secure but less scalable and versatile solution.

5.1 Test-Based Knowledge Assessment Module

This first and most often employed client module of our system allows knowledge assessment by means of diverse choice tests. While the method itself is very popular in case of E-Learning products, we designed this module to provide functionality unique among similar products.

Module's user interface allows presentation of wide range of multimedia content including formatted text, bitmap and vector graphics, sound and movies which provides teacher with great versatility when preparing test content. Test questions can be randomly selected from a larger set, and order of both questions and answers can be randomized.

Included automatic grading mechanisms support both single and multiple choice questions in single test, and use simple scripting language which allows to utilize any of popular methods of assigning points for test answers. The total test result can be normalized to a provided value and/or mapped to a grade. The module returns to server or external application a complete information about student's solution (which can be later used by, for example, server side grading mechanisms), such as: personal data, test id, timeframe of test, client-side grading results of all questions and total grade, all answers, operating system computer name and user name, IP address etc.

Module configuration allows teacher to enforce various additional test characteristics, such as necessity of solving questions in order, lack of ability correct already answered questions, time limit for a whole test or every single question etc.

Apart from already described functionality, one of our primary priorities was to take full advantage of ComAL communication capabilities allowing the software to function as part of managed system even without network connectivity. Such scenario is most often ignored by designers of modern E-Learning solutions as it prohibits the use of web-based thin-client architecture. At the same time it is a very popular scenario in case of network-related courses, as obtaining network connectivity is often the final goal of laboratory exercises on the subject.

The module is fully capable of independent offline operation according to encrypted and protected configuration files and course packages. In such case results are stored in similar files and can be decrypted by the module at teachers request to manually transfer them to the server or other application such as MS Excel. The module can also detect available network connectivity and update its status by obtaining new configuration settings/course packages from the server and uploading cached test results automatically.

As a result we have at our disposal one of the most advanced (apart from adaptive choice tests) knowledge testing products utilizing choice test method, which can function as a standalone application or as a part of managed system regardless of network connectivity available, due to integrated ComAL functionality.

5.2 Didactic Model of Connecting LAN Systems by WAN Networks

"Didactic model of connecting LAN systems by WAN networks" has been developed as a part of our research concerning simulation-based didactic and E-Learning tools. It is a didactic simulator [10], designed and implemented according to results of our original research of such educational tools [6,8].

Our simulator covers various technologies that allow computer data traffic through Asynchronous Transfer Mode (ATM) and Frame Relay wide area networks, for example: Classical IP over ATM (CLIP), LAN Emulation (LANE) or Multiprotocol over Frame Relay (MPoFR).

Due to its original design [8] it can be employed in a variety of didactic roles:

- knowledge distribution – a comprehensive, context sensitive help system is included, containing theoretical information concerning various elements of simulated environment. Coupled with simulator's ability to illustrate the knowledge with interactive, modifiable examples it creates a highly efficient knowledge distribution solution.
- skill development – didactic simulation product is one of the best tools for building practical skills on the base of theoretical knowledge, bridging theory and practice.
- self study and experimentation – didactic simulation product (with its ability to save and restore simulated system state) can be used by students for self study, as they are able to experiment in real-like environment without fear of damaging or critically misconfiguring the equipment.
- design, troubleshooting and optimization exercises – ability to interact with much more complicated systems than possible under laboratory conditions allows for these highest level exercises, able to build not only basic skills but also give user experience in efficiently dealing with these complex tasks.

Among these roles a knowledge and skill assessment can also be found – our simulation product includes mechanisms for automatically measuring various aspects of simulated system performance (available bandwidth, data loss, transmission delay etc.), which allows automatic grading mechanisms to assess competence of simulated system's designer and administrator.

The module is able to receive task files by ComAL from the server. A tasks file consists of a starting simulation setup, a set of goals which user must reach (for example: create connectivity between selected devices, optimize system efficiency by a certain threshold etc.) and grading rules. User's solutions along with their grades are uploaded to the server.

The module was originally created as a standalone application supporting SCORM-compliant data files [11], but by employing a dedicated interface interacting with product's information store and ComAL communication functionality it has been upgraded to a networked product, able to fully integrate with our knowledge assessment system. Modifications of product code were not necessary to archive that result, and that fact can be considered as another evidence of ComAL vast usefulness and versatility. A number of minor user interface modifications were also made to improve functionality of the product.

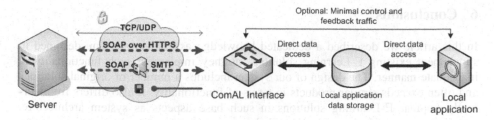

Fig. 3. Integration of local E-Learning solution with networked system with ComAL-database interface

A didactic simulator can be a powerful E-Learning tool as its capabilities cover wide range of scenarios. Its inclusion of as a module in our system offers us a unique ability to test not only theoretical knowledge, but also student's ability to employ it in a given situation (user's skill), and even his efficiency in dealing with various real-life situations (experience). These test can be conducted in both simple and very complex systems, which would otherwise never be available for didactic tasks.

5.3 Real-Time Grading Module

Real-time grading module has been designed to support classical theoretical and laboratory exercises. It is an interface for a teacher, allowing him to grade students during such activities, by marking their progress through assigned tasks.

The main element of the module's user interface is a table containing all students participating in the current class in the rows and task numbers in columns. A teacher can assign percent grades (including above 100% for exceptional performance) for specific tasks, and the system will calculate resulting total grade automatically and in real-time.

The list of students can be obtained from the system server or any other application with use of any ComAL-supported mechanisms including offline files. For example, if students are required to take an entry test before the class, their list, complete with additional information such as their place number and entry test grade will be displayed. Of course other means of creating such list can also be used (such as dedicated system module for checking in or a teacher prepared list) and provided to module by the server automatically or by simple file import.

Apart from user list, module can also take into account different point weights for different tasks, and such information is obtained by the module in the same way as the list of students.

This module can be an enormous help for a teacher, as he has complete information about his students at his disposal including name, place, and if entry test was taken, its result. That way he knows the entry level of theoretical knowledge of his students and can assign his attention accordingly. Also student's progress during current class is easy to track and graded automatically. Results can be uploaded to system server via any of ComAL transport methods.

6 Conclusions

In this article we described a dedicated knowledge assessment system, designed to supplement existing E-Learning solutions, as they implement such functionality in inadequate manner. The design of our system includes a number of original solutions and often exceeds similar products in terms of functionality. It also differs from currently popular E-Learning solutions in such base aspects as system architecture, because our research shows that knowledge assessment functionality requires significantly different approach then content distribution tasks which constitute most of popular E-Learning systems' functionality. Our system relies heavily on web-based technologies (Java, XML, HTML, standardized media files, streaming media, SOAP, SMTP, MIME, etc.), but their usage differs from currently popular trends.

The uniqueness of our E-Learning solution lies in its architecture of independent modules, full-client approach, distributed server-side structure and inclusion of ComAL functionality.

As a result we have a system which can be deployed fully or partially and easily integrated with third party solutions. Possible deployment scenarios range from a single workstation with knowledge testing module exporting results to MS Excel, to a collection of interconnected servers (each controlling a large number of knowledge-testing client modules) allowing global information searches. The system has proven to be extremely scalable. Complication of system configuration also scales, which means that simple setups are as easy to prepare and maintain as installing and running a standalone application, while only more advanced require system configuration and administration.

Distributed server part configuration is also easy due to automatic information routing mechanisms. System servers function independently and can be connected and disconnected from the system almost at will with no impairment of their basic functionality, apart from global search ability. That independence allows various departments of an organization to autonomously organize their own elements of the system and retain access to full system information base.

Client modules are implemented in full-client version, as our research proves it to be superior to thin-client approach in case of knowledge assessment systems, in contrast with systems mainly devoted to didactic content distribution.

Our, currently implemented, client modules allow both classical knowledge assessment by use of choice tests and unique functionality of skill assessment by employment of didactic simulation-based tool. There is also a module allowing teacher to easily grade students during classroom exercises and interface to import/export XML data between the system and external sources.

All system modules employ our original ComAL communication package designed especially for E-Learning systems. Allows E-Learning product designers to use communication functions independent of available network connectivity, and allows dynamic environment detection and automatic selection of data transmission mechanisms including strictly offline methods (automatically controlled file import/export). Such functionality allows creation of centrally managed systems even in environment where there is no network connectivity available.

All of these traits make our system one of the most versatile, expandable and easy to deploy knowledge assessment solutions available.

To test its efficiency in production environment we deployed the system in selected classes (mainly computer science, and computer networks) of Faculty of Electronics, Telecommunications and Informatics, Technical University of Gdansk during last two years. A total of over 2000 students participated in the tests generating about 20000 separate test results.

The system allowed to drastically reduce workload of the teachers by automatically creating attendance list, conducting and grading tests and generating lists of results. It also allowed to minimize number of errors occurring in this process by about 70%. It was also well received by students, as it allowed to minimize the time required to obtain their grades.

A combination of test-based knowledge assessment and real-time grading modules, has been particularly effective during laboratory exercises, as it allowed to instantly grade exercises composed of theoretical test and practical laboratory work. Its ability to function in offline environment and upload results when connectivity becomes available made it suited even for computer networks laboratories.

References

1. Sakai: Collaboration and Learning Environment for Education,
   http://sakaiproject.org/
2. Moodle Course Management System, http://moodle.org/
3. Learning Management Systems 2004, Bersin & Associates (2004)
4. Jesukiewicz, P., Slosser, S., Hu, X.: A.D.L Initiative Status and ADL Co-Lab Network (2006)
5. Gierłowski, K., Gierszewski, K.: Analysis of network infrastructure and QoS requirements for modern remote learning systems. In: Proceedings of the 15th International Conference on Systems Science (2004)
6. Nowicki, K., Gierłowski, K.: Implementation of Didactic Simulation Models in Open Source and SCORM Compliant LMS Systems. In: Proceedings of XXVIth International Autumn Colloquium, Advanced Simulation of Systems, pp. 161–166 (2004)
7. QTI Public Draft Specification Version 2,
   http://www.imsproject.org/ question/
8. Gierłowski, K., Nowicki, K.: Simulation of Network Systems in Education. In: Proceedings of the XXIVth Autumn International Colloquium Advanced Simulation of Systems, pp. 213–218 (2002)
9. Gierłowski, K., Nowicki, K., Uhl, T.: Didaktische simulationsmodelle für E-Learning in der IK-ausbildung. In: 7th Workshop Multimedia für Bildung und Wirtschaft (2003)
10. Kindley, R.: The Power of Simulation-based E-Learning. The E-Learning Developers' Journal (2002)
11. SCORM, 3rd Edition Documentation, Advanced Distributed Learning (2004),
    http://www.adlnet.gov/

An Assessment Tool for Judging the Overall Appearance of Chinese Handwriting Based on Opinions from Occupational Therapists

Ka Ki Li[1], Howard Leung[1], Sutie Lam[2], and Cecilia Li-Tsang[2]

[1] Department of Computer Science, City University of Hong Kong,
Tat Chee Avenue, Kowloon, Hong Kong SAR
{kakili, howard}@cityu.edu.hk
[2] Department of Rehabilitation Science, The Hong Kong Polytechnic University,
Hung Hom, Kowloon, Hong Kong SAR
{rssutie, rscecili}@inet.polyu.edu.hk

Abstract. Children's handwriting performance is a part of concern by parents, teachers and researchers, because learning to write is a major and critical task for children. An assessment tool capable of evaluating students' handwriting automatically can help teachers to provide feedback to students and to find out more objectively the specific problems identified. In this paper, we propose an assessment tool for judging the overall appearance of the student's Chinese handwriting by finding different geometric transformed parameters of a Chinese character with respect to a template character. By cross-validation with a team of occupational therapists who are more experienced in assessment of handwriting performance, it is hoped that a more reliable handwriting evaluation is received. The proposed tool has been integrated into a web-based system for assisting children to write correctly and precisely.

Keywords: Chinese handwriting education, Handwriting analysis, Pattern recognition, Handwriting difficulty.

1 Introduction

The Education and Manpower Bureau of the Hong Kong Special Administrative Region Government reported that there were 948 children with specific learning difficulties identified in 2001/2002 [1]. The Heep Hong society, a local organization to provide professional training and education to children of different abilities, found that 5-10% of the Hong Kong school-aged children have reading and writing difficulties. This group of children also experience difficulties in academic achievement, social participation and integration, psychological well-being [2][3][4][5] which affect their adulthood [6]. It is thus important for children to grasp proper handwriting skills.

In learning the Chinese and English language, writing is one of the main learning objectives [8]. In order to let all students write both Chinese characters and English letters with neatness and accuracy (Primary 1 to Primary 3) in a reasonable speed

H. Leung et al. (Eds.): ICWL 2007, LNCS 4823, pp. 288–299, 2008.
© Springer-Verlag Berlin Heidelberg 2008

(Primary 4 to Primary 6) [7], special provision, techniques and facilities are required to help them fully develop their potential, achieve independence as much as possible, and be well-adjusted in the community [9]. Thus, many researchers [10][11][12] have proposed different kinds of tools in assisting teachers and children in teaching handwriting skills. Most of these tools were developed overseas and mainly focus on English handwriting. In fact, there is a strong demand to develop a tool that enhances the Chinese handwriting education since writing Chinese characters is a more complex process. Each Chinese character may contain several strokes and children have to remember the stroke sequence, position of components, the shape of the strokes, the direction of the strokes and other criteria, including size, alignment and shape of the characters. It is difficult, as a result, for teachers to point out all the handwriting errors precisely given static handwritings in an exercise book.

Some studies [13][14][15][16][17] had been done by researchers in facilitating Chinese handwriting education. They targeted for Chinese characters by extracting some global features to determine how similar they are matched to a given model. A web-based education system [18][19] with automatic feedback and analysis tool [20][21][22] was proposed for assisting children in learning Chinese handwriting. The system points out whether a written character contains incorrect stroke sequence and gives correct order by a minimal feedback algorithm if needed. Besides, this system is capable of distinguishing and locating stroke production errors such as extra stroke, missing stroke, broken stroke and concatenated stroke.

In this paper, an assessment tool for measuring the overall appearance of a character is proposed. The tool points out if student's handwriting is acceptable in its size and orientation by comparing with a template. According to the analysis by occupational therapists who have experiences in assessment of children's handwriting [23], the scale, rotation and shear problems usually exist, especially the scaling cases. The analysis is focused on those useful elements for exploring various factors affecting a child's handwriting, namely, visual perception (VP), visual motor integration (VMI) and grip modulation (GRIP), ocular motor control, which are key factors affecting handwriting performance in addition to factors like memory, attention span etc. The proposed tool was integrated into a web-based system (http://vache.cs.cityu.edu.hk/ccls) [18][19] so that the system can check on a handwritten character based on its appearance and correctness in the stroke level.

The organization of the paper is as follows: In Section 2, we illustrate the framework of our proposed system. Results are shown in Section 3, while the conclusion and future work are discussed in Section 4.

2 Framework of Proposed Tool

In our tool, a standard template character written by a primary school teacher is loaded as reference. The student practices his/her handwriting inside a 150×150 pixels square grid by observing the animation of the template. Once the character is written, our tool evaluates if its size and orientation is acceptable. The handwriting is classified as acceptable if its scale factor (K), rotation factor (θ) and shear factor along x-axis (m_x) and y-axis (m_y) are all within the corresponding threshold values. Otherwise, characters are either reported as too large, too small or too tilted.

2.1 System Flow

The system flow is shown in Fig. 1. The input character is stored in online format in which the 2D coordinates of the strokes are saved. The handwritten character and the teacher's template are first pre-processed for normalization purpose. Afterwards, a rough scale factor (K_0) and a rotation factor (θ_0) are estimated for getting a more accurate stroke correspondence. With the stroke correspondence information, the transform parameters can be found. Each transform parameter is compared against a threshold that is obtained from the evaluation of three occupational therapists in Department of Rehabilitation Science, The Hong Kong Polytechnic University. A warning message is given whenever poor handwriting appearance is detected. If the quality of appearance is good enough, the characters will then be sent to another module for checking the correctness of the handwriting [20][21][22].

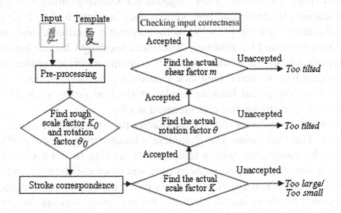

Fig. 1. The system flow of our handwriting evaluation tool

2.2 Pre-processing

As handwriting variation and unstable handwriting speed may cause the written characters to contain irregular sample points, two major pre-processing techniques, namely smoothing and equi-distance re-sampling, are applied before performing any analysis. Smoothing is used to reduce pen jittering. Besides, equi-distance re-sampling is applied to avoid uneven distribution of points due to the unstable handwriting speed. Every stroke contains p feature points after re-sampling.

2.3 Rough Estimation of Scale Factor K_0 and Rotation Factor θ_0

Scale factor K_0 and rotation factor θ_0 between the template and the input character are roughly estimated before finding the stroke correspondence. The rough estimation allows our tool to determine the stroke corresponding more precisely in the next step. The rough scale factor K_0 is found to be the ratio of the template's height (width) to the input character's height (width). The rough rotation factor θ_0 is the angle with which after rotating, its orientation is similar to that of the template. The rough rotation factor θ_0 can be found by comparing the histograms between the input handwriting and the template. The Cartesian coordinates of the input handwriting and the template are converted to the polar coordinates. Histograms of the polar coordinates distributions are plotted in the range from $-\pi$ to π radians at 360 equal intervals. Fig. 2a and Fig. 2b illustrate the histograms of a given template and input character respectively. The histogram of the input character is shifted by 1 interval in each trial and is compared with the template histogram. The rough rotation factor θ_0 is the rotation angle in which the histogram distribution of the template and the shifted histogram distribution of the input are the most similar as shown in Fig. 2c.

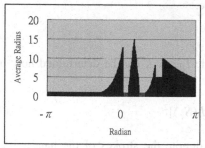

(a) Data distribution of template

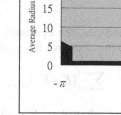

(b) Original data distribution of input

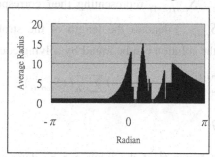

(c) Template and input are similar after input is shifted towards left by 28 intervals

Fig. 2. Histograms for finding the rough rotation angle θ_0

2.4 Stroke Correspondence

After finding the rough transform parameters, the input character is scaled by K_0 and rotated at θ_0 radians so that the accuracy of the stroke matching between the template and the input character can be enhanced. Stroke correspondence is determined from global matching by minimizing the total cost between strokes. Hungarian method is used to find the minimum cost between stroke pairs. The overall cost linearly combines the distance cost defined in equation (1) and the direction cost defined in equation (2).

Distance cost between a stroke pair:

$$C_{Dist} = \frac{1}{p} \sum_{i=1}^{p} \sqrt{(x_i^S - x_i^T)^2 + (y_i^S - y_i^T)^2} \qquad (1)$$

Distance cost between a stroke pair:

$$C_{Dir} = \frac{1}{p-1} \sum_{i=1}^{p-1} \sin \left| \arctan\left(\frac{y_{i+1}^S - y_i^S}{x_{i+1}^S - x_i^S} \right) - \arctan\left(\frac{y_{i+1}^T - y_i^T}{x_{i+1}^T - x_i^T} \right) \right| \qquad (2)$$

where S is the input stroke and T is the template stroke; (x_i^S, y_i^S) and (x_i^T, y_i^T) denote the coordinates of the ith point in an input stroke and template stroke respectively; p is the number of the total sample points in a stroke.

2.5 Scale Factor K

With stroke correspondence, the optimum scale factor K can be determined now by minimizing the following objective function:

$$\sum_{i=0}^{n-1} [K \times L(S_{corr(i)}) - L(S_i')]^2 \qquad (3)$$

where n is the number of strokes; $S'_0, \ldots S'_{n-1}$ denote the strokes of the handwritten character with $S_{corr(0)}, \ldots, S_{corr(n-1)}$ representing their corresponding strokes of the template character; $L(S_{corr(i)})$ denotes the length of the stroke $S_{corr(i)}$. This is a quadratic equation, and the solution can be found by solving equation (4).

$$K = \sum_{i=0}^{n-1} L(S_{corr(i)}) \times L(S_i') / \sum_{i=0}^{n-1} L(S_{corr(i)})^2 \qquad (4)$$

2.6 Rotation Factor θ

A more precise rotation factor θ of the input can be determined using the stroke correspondence information. The rotation factor θ that minimizes the objective function below:

$$\sum_{i=0}^{n-1} L(S_{corr(i)}) \left\| \Theta_{corr(i)} - \theta - \Theta_i' \right\|^2 \qquad (5)$$

where n is the number of strokes; $S'_0, \ldots S'_{n-1}$ denote the strokes of the input character with $S_{corr(0)}, \ldots, S_{corr(n-1)}$ representing their corresponding strokes of the template character; $\Theta_{corr(i)}$ denotes the orientation and $L(S_{corr(i)})$ denotes the length of the stroke $S_{corr(i)}$. The optimum rotation factor θ for the input character can be found according to equation (6).

$$\theta = \sum_{i=0}^{n-1} L(S_{corr(i)}) \left\| \Theta_{corr(i)} - \Theta_i' \right\| / \sum_{i=0}^{n-1} L(S_{corr(i)}) \tag{6}$$

2.7 Shear Factors m_x and m_y

Given the coordinates of an input handwriting and a transform matrix, it is possible to determine the new coordinates after translation, scaling, rotation and shearing. The mathematical representation is defined as equation (7):

$$\begin{pmatrix} x_i^{S'} \\ x_i^{S'} \end{pmatrix} = \begin{pmatrix} 1 & m_x \\ m_y & 1 \end{pmatrix} \begin{pmatrix} \cos\theta & -\sin\theta \\ \sin\theta & \cos\theta \end{pmatrix} \begin{pmatrix} K & 0 \\ 0 & K \end{pmatrix} \begin{pmatrix} x_i^S \\ y_i^S \end{pmatrix} + \begin{pmatrix} T_x \\ T_y \end{pmatrix} \tag{7}$$

where $x_i^{S'}$ and $y_i^{S'}$ are the new x- and y-coordinates of point i after transformation; x_i^S and y_i^S are original position of point i; θ is the rotation angle in radian; K is the scale factor; m_x and m_y are shear factors along x-axis and y-axis respectively; with translations T_x and T_y. On the other hand, the transform parameters (K, θ, m_x, m_y, T_x, T_y) can be determined if the corresponding strokes are correctly matched and sufficient information is provided. In section 2.5 and 2.6, the scale factor K and the rotation factor θ are determined, they can be substituted to the transform matrix T to find the shear factor m_x and m_y. To get the shear factor along x-axis m_x, the equations $\begin{pmatrix} x_i^T \\ y_i^T \end{pmatrix} = \begin{pmatrix} 1 & m_x \\ 0 & 1 \end{pmatrix} T_{SR} \begin{pmatrix} x_i^S \\ y_i^S \end{pmatrix}$ should be solved, where T_{SR} is the transform matrix consisted of scaling and rotation; x_i^S and y_i^S denotes the x- and y-coordinates of point i in the input character; x_i^T and y_i^T are the x- and y-coordinates of point i in the template; It should be noted that there is no unique solution for m_x, as there are many corresponding points between the template and the input. m_x should be solved in the least square sense, meaning that the optimum shear factor m_x should yield the minimum value for the expression $\sum_i \sqrt{\left(x_i^S - x_i^T \right)^2 + \left(y_i^S - y_i^T \right)^2}$. Similarly, to get the shear factor along y-axis m_y, the same method is applied with another matrix: $\begin{pmatrix} x_i^T \\ y_i^T \end{pmatrix} = \begin{pmatrix} 1 & 0 \\ m_y & 1 \end{pmatrix} T_{SR} \begin{pmatrix} x_i^S \\ y_i^S \end{pmatrix}$ and

it is solved again in the least square sense.

2.8 Evaluation

Transform parameters, scale factor (K), rotation factor (θ) and shear factor along x-axis (m_x) and that of y-axis (m_y) are found according to the sequence as shown in Fig. 1. For instance, if the scale factor is over its threshold, our tool tells the student that his/her character is either too large (Fig. 3a) or too small (Fig. 3b). For

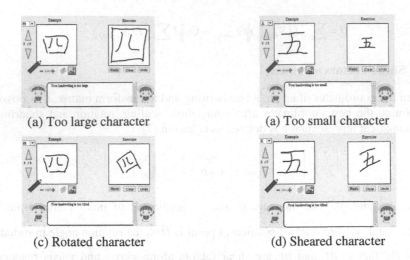

(a) Too large character   (a) Too small character

(c) Rotated character   (d) Sheared character

Fig. 3. Checking appearance of characters by the tool

a character that is rotated (Fig. 3c) or sheared (Fig. 3d), the tool indicates that the character is too tilted.

3 Experiment

In this section, the experiments for finding the threshold values and the evaluations on the tool are discussed.

3.1 Data Collection

Some users were asked to write 20 characters by a Flash application with a tablet. Fig. 4a shows the characters that were chosen to be written by users and Fig. 4b shows the tool for collecting the user's handwritings. The size of each square grid in the tool is 100×100 pixels. New handwriting samples were generated by varying different transform parameters. The transform parameters, including scale factors, rotation factors and shear factors, were recorded for analysis purpose at later stage.

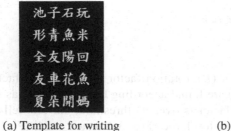

(a) Template for writing   (b) Tool for collecting handwriting

Fig. 4. Data collection

3.2 Data Evaluation

Samples were sent to three occupational therapists in Department of Rehabilitation Science, the Hong Kong Polytechnic University, for evaluation. They are experienced in evaluation of Chinese handwriting performance. Feedback given by the therapists included whether the characters were acceptable in their scale factor, rotation angle or shear unit. By utilizing the subjective evaluation from experts, more reliable and accurate thresholds could be defined.

3.3 Finding Threshold Value

Scale threshold. Fig. 5a shows a set of scaled characters used in the experiment. In Fig. 5b, a set of data was generated based on the characters shown in Fig. 5a with different scale factors. Therapists looked at each set of data and circled those characters that were not acceptable in size. The distribution of scale factors between acceptable characters and unacceptable characters in 1200 samples is shown in Fig. 6. The threshold of small size character is 0.64 and that of enlarged character is 1.425.

(a) Characters in solid line circle were small; Characters in dash line circle were too large

(b) Same set of data but they were in different size; "雨" and "陽" were smaller in this set

Fig. 5. Data used in finding scale factor

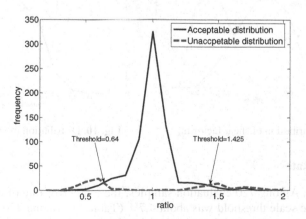

Fig. 6. Distribution of scale factors

Rotation threshold. A total of 1200 samples with rotation angles between 0.6 radians and -0.6 radians were generated to perform the experiment. Samples of rotated characters are shown in Fig. 7. Two occupational therapists were assigned to determine whether each character was acceptable. The distribution of rotation angles is shown in Fig. 8. Two threshold values, -0.19 radian and 0.165 radian, are found. To be more tolerant, ±0.19 radians is taken as threshold such that our tool is less sensitive to noise.

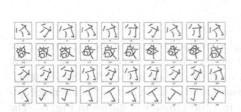

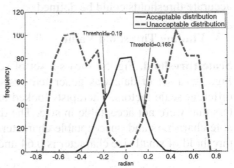

Fig. 7. Data set used in finding rotation factor

Fig. 8. Distribution of rotation factors

Shear threshold. Two threshold values, namely the shear threshold along x-axis m_x and the shear threshold along y-axis m_y, were determined in this experiment. 600 samples with or without shear problem were used to find the threshold. From Fig. 9, the thresholds of the shear factor m_x are -0.253 shear units and 0.155 shear units. From Fig. 10, the threshold values of another shear factor m_y are -0.175 shear units and 0.21 shear units respectively.

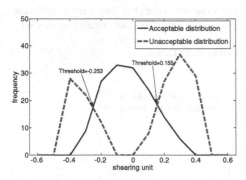

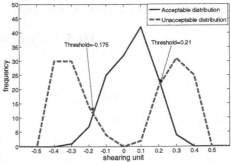

Fig. 9. Distribution of shear factor m_x

Fig. 10. Distribution of shear factor m_y

3.4 Error Rate

Scaling case. Among 720 evaluation samples, the total error rate of evaluating handwriting by the scale threshold was about 4.7% (Table 1). Among 720 evaluation samples, the total error rate of evaluating handwriting by the scale threshold was about 4.7% (Table 1). Fig. 11 shows a set of characters used in the experiment, the size of the highlighted characters looked similar. However, only the character circled by solid line was classified as too large by human judgment. In fact their scale factors *K* were all within the threshold. As the human evaluation is not always consistent, some bias might exist in the detection.

Table 1. Error rate in judging the size of character

	Accepted	Unaccepted	Total
Therapists' Evaluation	657	63	720
Correct Evaluation	640	46	686
Incorrect Evaluation	17	17	34
Error Rate (%)	2.5	26	4.7

Rotation case. Totally 1200 samples with rotation characteristics were tested. Threshold value defined in section 3.3 was applied to examine whether the samples were acceptable. Results were compared with the subjective evaluation result done by 2 occupational therapists. The testing result is shown in Table 2. The correct evaluation rates were about 90%.

Table 2. Error rate in judging the rotation of character

	Accepted		Unaccepted		Total	
	OT1	OT2	OT1	OT2	OT1	OT2
Therapists' Evaluation	176	145	424	455	600	600
Correct Evaluation	154	138	391	406	545	544
Incorrect Evaluation	22	7	33	49	55	56
Error Rate (%)	12.5	4.8	7.8	10.7	9.1	9.3
Correct Rate (%)	87.5	95.2	92.2	89.3	90.9	90.7

Shearing case. It is more difficult for judging whether a character is being sheared, as some Chinese characters are already slightly tilted when they were created. Human judgment on these characters might consider them as correct, but in our tool, just by using the thresholds, they were counted as incorrect (Fig. 12). Conversely, some characters were not sheared during creation but they were recognized as sheared by human judgment. This leaded to a larger inconsistency between the decision made by the threshold and that of the human judgment (Table 3).

Fig. 11. Characters with similar size but only the character circled in solid line was considered as too large by human judgment

Fig. 12. Character accepted by human but broke the threshold slightly in our system

Table 3. Error rate in judging the shearing of characters

	Accepted	Unaccepted	Total
Therapists' Evaluation	439	361	800
Correct Evaluation	355	227	582
Incorrect Evaluation	84	134	218
Error Rate (%)	19.1%	37.1%	27.3%

4 Conclusion and Future Work

In this paper, we proposed a tool to determine if a Chinese character was acceptable in its scale factor, rotation angle and shear unit. The samples were evaluated by occupational therapists who gave us reliable ground truth to predict the optimistic conditions in classifying good and poor handwriting. Three threshold values, namely, the rotation threshold, scale threshold and shear threshold were defined according to the expert's feedback. The tool had been integrated into an online web-based system (http://vache.cs.cityu.edu.hk/ccls/) for assisting children in handwriting education.

The practical value of our tool can be examined in the coming future as the online system is scheduled to be used in a handwriting training program. Other important criteria for analyzing children handwriting performance, such as the structure of a written Chinese character, spatial relationships, and orientation of components, were not studied in this paper. They will be explored in future study. In addition, a more comprehensive tool, including detecting and locating handwriting errors and checking the legibility of handwriting, will be developed to assist both children and teachers in learning Chinese handwriting.

Acknowledgments

The work described in this paper is fully support by a grant from City University of Hong Kong (Project No. 7001711).

References

1. Lam, C.C.C.: Developmental dyslexia. Public Health and Epidemiology Bulletin 12(1) (2003)
2. Opper, S.: Hong Kong's Young Children: Their early development and learning. The Hong Kong University Book Press, Hong Kong (1996)
3. Mancini, M.C., Coster, W.J.: Functional Predictors of School Participation by Children with disabilities. Occupational Therapy International 11(1), 12–25 (2004)
4. Rosenblum, S., Parush, S., Weiss, P.L.: Computerized Temporal Handwriting Characteristics of Proficient and Non-Proficient Handwriters. The American Journal of Occupational Therapy 57(2), 129–138 (2003)
5. Preminger, F., Weiss, P.L., Weintraub, N.: Predicting Occupational Performance: Handwriting Versus Keyboarding. The American Journal of Occupational Therapy 58(2), 193–201 (2004)
6. Sutton Hamilton, S.: Evaluation of clumsiness in children. American Family Physician 66(8), 1435–1440 (2002)

7. Curriculum Development Council, HKSAR, CDC Chinese Language Education Key Learning Area Curriculum Guide (P1 - S3). HKSAR: Education and Manpower Bureau (2002)
8. Curriculum Development Institute, HKSAR, CDC Chinese Language Curriculum Guide (Primary 1-6). HKSAR: Education and Manpower Bureau (2004)
9. Education and Manpower Bureau, HKSAR. ebook: 《小一學生之學習情況量表》使用手冊。. The Hong Kong SAR Government, The Education and Manpower Bureau (2004) (Retrieved April 28, 2005), http://eii.emb.hkedcity.net/pdf/data01.01.pdf
10. Kulesh, V., Shaffer, K., Sethi, I., Schartz, M.: Handwriting Quality Evaluation. In: Proc. Intl. Conf. Advances in Pattern Recognition, pp. 157–165 (2001)
11. Djeziri, S., Guerfali, W., Plamondon, R., Robert, J.M.: Learning handwriting with pen-based systems: computational issues. Pattern Recognition 35(5), 1049–1057 (2002)
12. Robert, J.M., Djeziri S., Audet, M., Plamondon, R.: Scriptôt: pen-based software to support handwriting learning in primary schools, Technical Report, Ecole Polytechnique Montreal (1999)
13. Kim, D.H., Kim, E.-J., Bang, S.Y.: A Variation Measure for Handwritten Character Image Data Using Entropy Difference. Pattern Recognition 30(1), 19–29 (1997)
14. Ozaki, M., Adachi, Y., Ishii, N., Koyazu, T.: CAI System to Improve Hand Writing Skills by means of Fuzzy Theory. In: Proc. IEEE Intl. Conf. on Fuzzy Systems and the Second Intl. Fuzzy Engineering Symposium, pp. 491–496 (1995)
15. Chou, S.L., Yu, S.S.: Sorting Qualities of Handwritten Chinese Characters for Setting up a Research Database. In: Proc. Intl. Conf. on Document Analysis and Recognition, pp. 474–477 (1993)
16. Kato, T.: Evaluation System for hand-written characters. In: Kato, T. (ed.) Proc. Machine Vision Applications in Character Recognition and Industrial Inspection, pp. 73–82 (1992)
17. Leung, H., Komura, T.: Web-Based Handwriting Education with Animated Virtual Teacher. In: Liu, W., Shi, Y., Li, Q. (eds.) ICWL 2004. LNCS, vol. 3143, pp. 293–300. Springer, Heidelberg (2004)
18. Tang, K.-T., Li, K.K., Leung, H.: A Web-based Chinese Handwriting Education System with Automatic Feedback and Analysis. In: Liu, W., Li, Q., Lau, R.W.H. (eds.) ICWL 2006. LNCS, vol. 4181, pp. 176–188. Springer, Heidelberg (2006)
19. Tang, K.-T., Leung, H.: VACHE: A Ubiquitous Chinese Handwriting Education System. In: 1st International Conference on Ubiquitous Information Management and Communication
20. Tang, K.-T., Leung, H.: Reconstructing the Correct Writing Sequence from a Set of Chinese Character Strokes. In: Matsumoto, Y., et al. (eds.) ICCPOL 2006. LNCS (LNAI), vol. 4285, pp. 333–344. Springer, Heidelberg (2006)
21. Tang, K.-T., Leung, H.: Teaching Chinese Handwriting by Automatic Feedback and Analysis for Incorrect Stroke Sequence and Stroke Production Errors. In: 14th International Conference on Computers in Education (ICCE 2006), pp. 101–114 (2006)
22. Tsang, K., Leung, H.: Teaching Stroke Order for Chinese Characters by Using Minimal Feedback. In: Lau, R.W.H., et al. (eds.) ICWL 2005. LNCS, vol. 3583, pp. 135–145. Springer, Heidelberg (2005)
23. Tseng, M.-h.: Factorial Validity of the Tseng Handwriting Problem Checklist. J. Occup. Ther. Assoc. ROC 11, 13–27 (1993)
24. Burkard, R.E., Cela, E.: Linear Assignment Problems and Extensions. In: Pardalos, P.M., Du, D.-Z. (eds.) Handbook of Combinatorial Optimization, pp. 75–149. Kluwer Academic Publishers, Dordrecht (1999)

WILLIE – A Web Interface for a Language Learning and Instruction Environment

Werner Winiwarter

University of Vienna, Department of Scientific Computing,
Universitätsstraße 5, A-1010 Vienna, Austria
werner.winiwarter@univie.ac.at

Abstract. In this paper we present WILLIE, a Web-based language learning tool for Japanese, which provides the language students with a comfortable interface to lexical, syntactic, and translation knowledge. The linguistic data is derived automatically from a large parallel corpus by using a Japanese-English machine translation system, which we developed in our previous research. The system randomly chooses translation examples to present them to the students using JavaScript to dynamically open pop-up windows with additional, clearly arranged color-coded information. WILLIE has been implemented in Amzi! Prolog, using the Amzi! Logic Server CGI Interface to develop the Web application.

1 Introduction

In our research work, we use the bilingual data from the JENAAD corpus [14], which contains 150,000 Japanese-English sentence pairs from news articles. During previous research we had implemented *WETCAT* [15], a Web-based machine translation system. It follows a rule-based transfer approach (see [12,13,1]) to achieve high translation quality, however, all the transfer rules are learnt fully automatically from the translation examples in JENAAD by using structural matching between the parse trees for source and target language.

With *WILLIE*, a Web Interface for a Language Learning and Instruction Environment, we wanted to fully exploit the linguistic knowledge derived from JENAAD by using the generic and intuitive rule formalism developed for WET-CAT to convey detailed information about the individual steps involved in the translation of a Japanese sentence. The system randomly selects Japanese sentences so that the students can inspect them both at the surface level as well as regarding syntactic and transfer knowledge. All the linguistic information is only displayed to the students on demand via dynamic pop-up windows implemented in JavaScript. This user interface design choice was motivated by the objective not to overload the students with too much redundant data. On the contrary, we want to make the learning experience more interactive and interesting, e.g. in that the students only click on an item if they do not know the answer or if they want to verify their solutions.

It is our intention to extend WILLIE with additional functionality towards a fully-fledged intelligent language tutoring system by building on the results

H. Leung et al. (Eds.): ICWL 2007, LNCS 4823, pp. 300–311, 2008.

and experiences of other successful intelligent tutoring systems for Japanese, in particular Robo-Sensei [10] (based on BANZAI [8,9]). Especially the use of our linguistic analysis techniques to manage sophisticated exercises by processing student input and generating meaningful feedback seems a very promising direction as indicated by several studies [4,5,6,7,11,17,18,19].

The main research issue involved in our work is thus how to bridge the gap between machine translation and computer-assisted language learning to make full use of the wealth of linguistic data contained in parallel corpora, to create a lucid explanation of the translation process, and to find the best representation format to convey this information to the language student.

The rest of the paper is organized as follows. After a brief overview of the system architecture in Sect. 2, we describe the lexical analysis and parsing of Japanese sentences in Sect. 3. Next, we provide a short introduction into our rule formalism to represent the transfer knowledge, and explain the generation of the color-coded visualization of the incremental transfer steps in Sect. 4. Finally, we show in Sect. 5 how we compute the surface form of the sentence translation as well as context-specific word translations.

2 System Architecture

WILLIE was implemented in Amzi! Prolog, which offers an expressive declarative programming language within the Eclipse Platform, powerful unification operations for the efficient application of the transfer rules, and full Unicode support for Japanese characters. In addition, Amzi! Prolog comes with several APIs, in particular the Amzi! Logic Server CGI Interface, which we used to develop our Web interface.

WILLIE's system architecture is outlined in Fig. 1. The modules adapted from the WETCAT machine translation system are shaded, all the other modules have been newly implemented for WILLIE. The student's Web browser sends CGI calls to the Web server, which calls the CGI application to return dynamically generated JavaScript documents. The CGI application consists of a C program responsible for starting the Amzi! Logic Server and loading the Prolog CGI script. All user input and CGI variables are asserted as facts to the Prolog logicbase before calling the Prolog part of the CGI Amzi! interface. This Prolog wrapper performs the necessary CGI bookkeeping functions and calls predicates defined in the Prolog script implementing the language learning tool.

Whenever the student asks for a new translation example, the system *randomly selects* a Japanese sentence from the 150,000 sentences in the JENAAD corpus. The sentence is first analyzed by the *tagging* module, which produces the correct segmentation into a list of word tokens annotated with part-of-speech tags. Next, the token list is converted into a parse tree by the *parsing* module. The *transfer* module traverses the parse tree top-down and applies the transfer rules in the rule base to transform the Japanese parse tree into a corresponding

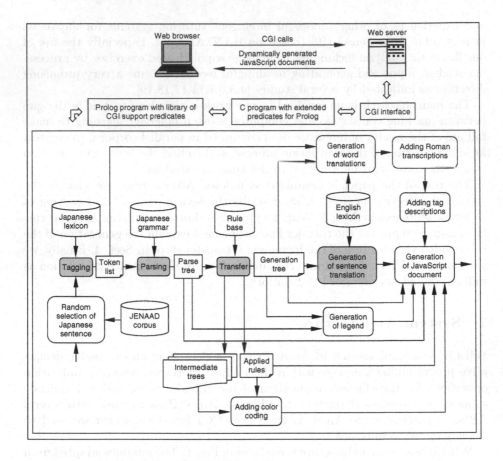

Fig. 1. System architecture

English generation tree. All intermediate trees and applied rules are stored for the display of the incremental transfer steps to the student. The final task of the translation process is the *generation* of the surface form of the sentence translation by flattening the structured information in the generation tree. Although we could directly use the English translations from the JENAAD corpus, we chose not to do so in view of a planned extension of WILLIE towards the translation of free input entered as part of interactive student exercises.

We enhance the lexical data in the token list with context-specific *word translations* derived from the generation tree and add *Roman transcriptions* of Japanese words as well as plain text *tag descriptions*. To improve the comprehensibility of the tree diagrams, we dynamically generate a *legend* with descriptions of all constituent categories and feature values in both parse tree and generation tree. Finally, we apply *color coding* to the intermediate trees to convey the semantics of the applied transfer rules. All the information is gathered and combined to generate the *JavaScript document* to be sent back to the student.

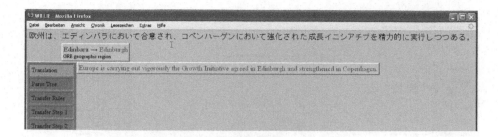

Fig. 2. Example of lexical data

3 Lexical Data and Parse Trees

The student reaches WILLIE through a portal page, which provides instructions about how to use the system. As described before, the system randomly selects a translation example and returns a dynamically generated JavaScript page, which contains the Japanese sentence at the top and a menu bar at the left. At first, only the source sentence is visible, all lexical data is displayed in dynamic pop-up windows when moving the curser over the individual words (see Fig. 2). The English translation of the sentence can be toggled on or off by clicking on "Translation" in the menu bar.

The lexical data for each word includes the Roman transcription, the context-specific translation, and the part-of-speech tag. To compute this information, the tagging module first has to perform the correct segmentation of the Japanese sentence. For this purpose it accesses the Japanese lexicon, which was compiled automatically by applying the morphological analysis system ChaSen [3] to the JENAAD corpus. We map the numerical part-of-speech tag codes used by ChaSen to three letter acronyms and add textual descriptions. For conjugated words, we also indicate the Roman transcription of the base form and tags for conjugation type and conjugation form in parentheses (see Fig. 3). Finally, we add context-specific word translations (see Sect. 5).

By moving the cursor over "Parse Tree" in the menu bar, the student can open a pop-up window containing a nicely formatted display of the Japanese parse tree (see Fig. 3). The pop-up window remains open until the student either chooses another option from the menu bar or explicitly clicks on "Parse Tree" to close the pop-up window again. The same functionality applies to all the other entries in the menu bar except "Translation" and "Legend", which are toggled.

The parse tree is computed by the parsing module with the assistance of the Definite Clause Grammar preprocessor of Amzi! Prolog by applying the Japanese grammar to the token list. We model a sentence as a list of *constituents*, which are defined as compound terms of arity 1 with the *constituent category* as principal functor. With regard to the *argument* of a constituent we distinguish two cases:

- a *simple constituent* either represents a word with its part-of-speech tag as atom/atom or a feature value as atom,
- a *complex constituent* models a phrase as a list of subconstituents.

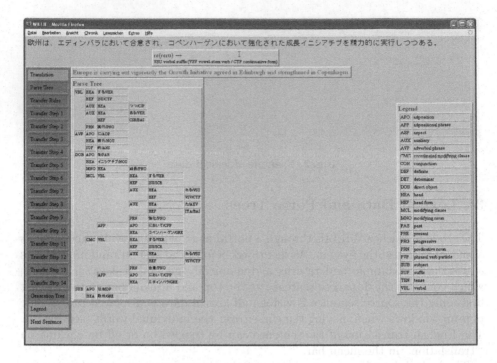

Fig. 3. Example of parse tree

All the acronyms used in the parse tree and the generation tree (see Sect. 5) are collected and annotated with plain text descriptions to generate an alphabetically sorted legend, which can be toggled on or off as mentioned before. For conjugated words the lexical data is divided into the two constituents HEA (head) and HEF (head form). The former has the argument base_form/part-of-speech, the latter conjugation_type/conjugation_form.

4   Transfer Rules and Steps

In our approach we have developed a very generic formalism to represent translation knowledge. We divide a translation into a sequence of translation steps, where each step is the application of one transfer rule. There only exist three different types of transfer rules: a *word transfer rule* translates the argument of a simple constituent, a *constituent transfer rule* translates both the category and the argument of a complex constituent, and a *phrase transfer rule* allows to define elaborate conditions and substitutions on the argument of a complex constituent.

All the transfer rules are actually stored as Prolog facts in the rule base. The rule base is created automatically by using structural matching between parse trees of translation examples from the JENAAD corpus. For that purpose we also have to tag and parse the English sentences from the corpus. The English lexicon used by the English tagging module has been built automatically by applying the MontyTagger [2] to the JENAAD corpus. The grammar rules used by the English parsing module are again written in Definite Clause Grammar syntax.

The acquisition module traverses the Japanese and English parse tree for a translation example and derives new transfer rules. The search for new rules starts at the sentence level by recursively mapping the individual subconstituents of the Japanese sentence. We also perform a consolidation run on the complete set of rules, which generalizes rules to avoid overtraining and to increase the coverage for new unseen data. For more details on the acquisition process and a more formal treatment of the rule formalism we refer to [16].

In the following, we list three illustrative examples of transfer rules (using Roman transcriptions for the ease of the reader):

1. WTR(shijō/NOU, market/NN).
2. CTR(MNO, MAJ, keizai/NOU, [HEA(keizai/NOU)], [HEA(economic/JJ)]).
3. PTR(CL, suru/VER, [APP([APO(ni totte/CPP), HEA(hatten/PNO) | X1])], [APP([APO(for/IN), HEA(progress/NN) | X1])]).

Rule 1 is the default translation of the noun shijō as the noun market. Rule 2 changes the modifying noun (MNO) keizai into the modifying adjective phrase (MAJ) economic. The third argument of the rule is the *head condition*, it is used as an index for the fast retrieval of rule candidates during transfer.

Rule 3 states that for any clause (CL) with head verb suru, the adpositional phrase (APP) "X1 hatten ni totte" has to be replaced by the adpositional phrase "for X1 progress".

The first argument is the *category condition*. CL is an example of a generalized constituent category, the other one being NP (noun phrase). The rule can be applied if the constituent category of the input is subsumed by the generalized category. The second argument is again the head condition, for a clause it is tested on the head of the verbal. Both constituent and phrase transfer rules may contain *shared variables for unification* as shown in Rule 3. This makes it possible to translate only certain parts of the input and to leave the rest intact.

One important requirement for the efficient and robust implementation of the transfer module is that the *argument condition* in the third argument of a phrase transfer rule has to be understood as a subset condition. For example, in Rule 3 it is necessary that the clause contains an adpositional phrase at an arbitrary position with the adposition (APO) "ni totte" and the head noun hatten, both again at arbitrary positions. All other elements of the clause and the adpositional phrase are appended unchanged to the translated required elements.

The language student can inspect the transfer rules used to translate a Japanese sentence by moving the mouse over the "Transfer Rules" entry of the menu bar. The rules are displayed as a numbered tabular list sorted by the sequence of their application (see Fig. 4).

The transfer module traverses the Japanese parse tree top-down and searches the rule base for transfer rules that can be applied. At the top level we first

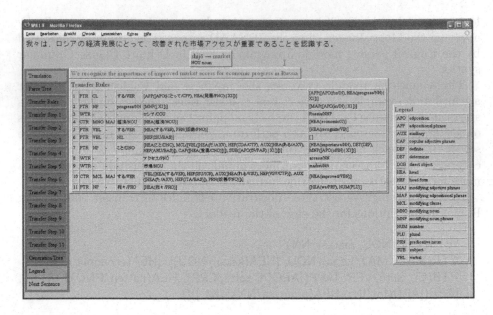

Fig. 4. Example of transfer rules

try to find suitable phrase transfer rules. To apply a phrase transfer rule, we collect all rule candidates that satisfy the condition part and then rate each rule and choose the one with the highest score. The most difficult subtask is the verification of the argument condition because it involves testing for set inclusion at the argument level as well as recursively testing for set equality of arguments of subconstituents.

If no more rules can be applied at the sentence level, each constituent in the sentence is examined separately. We first search for constituent transfer rules before we perform a transfer of the argument. The latter involves the application of word transfer rules for simple constituents, whereas the top-level procedure is repeated recursively for complex constituents. We also perform some common standard transformations. The two most important ones are:

- the removal of redundant Japanese particles that only indicate the relationship of a phrase to the embedding phrase, which is already expressed through the category of the complex constituent,
- the addition of the coordinating conjunction "and", which is often not explicitly expressed in Japanese.

To give the students a better understanding of the translation process, we provide them with the possibility to inspect the conditions and transformations of each rule application in detail.

For each transfer step we show the applied rule and, side-by-side, the intermediate trees before and after the application of the rule (*source tree* and *target tree*). There exists a menu entry for each individual transfer step in the menu

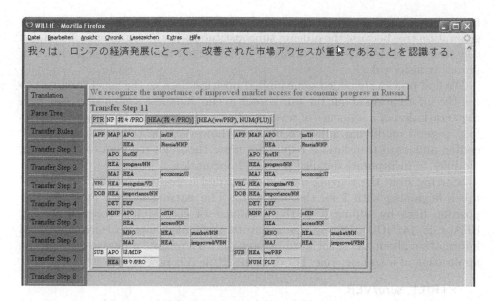

Fig. 5. Example of transfer step

bar so that the students can slide the mouse over the entries to get an animated view of how the Japanese parse tree gradually changes into the completely translated English parse tree, i.e. the generation tree to compute the final sentence translation.

As can be seen in Fig. 5, we use color coding of source and target trees to convey the semantics of a rule application to the student. We use the following colors for this purpose:

- *blue*: category condition,
- *green*: head condition,
- *violet*: argument condition,
- *orange*: translation of required elements,
- *yellow*: standard transformation.

In the example in Fig. 5, one can easily see that the constituent category SUB is subsumed by NP, the head condition wareware/PRO is satisfied, the argument condition is identical to the head condition, and the translation of the Japanese pronoun wareware is therefore the personal pronoun we/PRP with an additional feature value NUM(PLU) to indicate number plural. Finally, the modifying particle WA/MDP, marking the subject of this sentence, is eliminated.

The main problem with computing the correct color coding is to find the exact location in the intermediate trees where to apply the coloring. The same is true for the generation of the context-specific word translations (see Sect. 5).

Since the original intended use of the system was for machine translation, flexibility and robustness were the two main requirements. Unfortunately, this implied that there remained no trace of the original word order in the resulting generation tree because the order of subconstituents in the arguments of complex constituents could have been arbitrarily rearranged through the application of phrase transfer rules.

We had previously added some limited position data to the generation tree to use the information about the word order in the Japanese sentence to deal with the translation of a sequence of several subconstituents with identical categories (e.g. several modifying adjective phrases), however, the computation of color coding and word translations required a more thorough redesign of all existing modules to incorporate detailed position information.

Starting from the tagging module, we added a position index to each word token beginning with 1 for the first word. The parsing module preserves this position data by adding it to the argument of each simple constituent, e.g. HEA(shijō/14/NOU). During rule acquisition, we also have to learn additional information about the exact word mapping if we translate a phrase through the application of a transfer rule. For example, Rule 3 is now stored as:

```
PTR(CL, suru/VER,
[APP([APO(ni totte/X1/CPP), HEA(hatten/X2/PNO) | X3 ])],
[APP([APO(for/X1/IN), HEA(progress/X2/NN) | X3 ])]).
```

This means that we use again shared variables for unification to preserve the position data during the application of rules by the transfer module. If there is no corresponding word in the other language, then free variables are used, i.e. they do not affect the satisfiability of the rule. Finally, it is also possible to map one Japanese word to several words in English by using the same variable, e.g.:

```
PTR(VBL, suru/VER,
[HEA(suru/X1/VER), PRN(jikkō/X2/PNO)],
[HEA(carry/X2/VB), PVP(out/X2/IN)]).
```

In Japanese grammar, there exist predicative nouns (also called "sahen nouns") that can be used together with the verb suru ("to do") to derive a new verb, like "to integrate" from "integration". In this example, the predicative noun (PRN) jikkō is translated as "carry out", i.e. a phrasal verb with the phrasal verb particle (PVP) out. Therefore, in this situation, a free variable is assigned to the position data of suru, and the position of jikkō is propagated to both carry and out so that later the complete context-specific translation "is carrying out" is assigned to jikkō.

During transfer we store all the intermediate trees with the position information intact. In addition, we number the applied rules and store them together with additional position data depending on the rule type:

- *word transfer rules*: the position of the simple constituent,
- *constituent transfer rules*: the positions of the head elements of the old and new complex constituent,
- *phrase transfer rules*: the positions of the head elements of the complex constituent before and after applying the rule to its argument.

In addition to the applied transfer rules, we also have to store the information about which standard transformations were performed during transfer to guarantee the correct color coding as shown before. To be able to assign each standard transformation to the correct transfer step, we indicate the rule number and the token that has been removed or inserted. In addition, we keep track of the position of the eliminated element, or, for inserted elements, the position of the head of the embedding phrase.

All this information is used by the color coding module to assign the correct color to the individual cells of the tabular display. For that purpose we perform a top-down traversal of the source and target tree and look for the constituent to which the rule is applied. Depending on the rule type, we have to distinguish the following cases:

- *word transfer rules*: the argument of the simple constituent is painted violet in the source tree and orange in the target tree,
- *constituent transfer rules*: the category is painted blue in the source tree and orange in the target tree,
- *phrase transfer rules*: the category is painted blue in the source tree, except for rules at sentence level,
- *standard transformations*: the category and the argument is painted yellow in the source tree for eliminations, in the target tree for insertions.

If the anchor constituent has been found for a constituent or phrase transfer rule, then the argument condition and its translation is analyzed recursively. The categories and arguments of all matching subconstituents are colored violet in the source tree and orange in the target tree, except for the argument of the head condition, which is colored green in the source tree.

5   Translations

The final task on the way to a completely translated Japanese sentence is the generation of the surface form of the English sentence as character string.

The input to the generation module is the *generation tree*, i.e. the final parse tree after applying all transfer rules. The generation tree can be inspected side-by-side with the original Japanese parse tree by moving the mouse over the corresponding menu entry.

The generation module traverses the generation tree top-down and transforms the argument of each complex constituent into a list of surface strings. The list is computed recursively from the subconstituents and flattened afterwards. The correct surface form for words with irregular inflections is computed by accessing the English lexicon.

In addition to the sentence translation, as mentioned before, we add context-sensitive word translations to the lexical entries in the token list. In a first processing step, we flatten the information in the generation tree by traversing it top-down and asserting a dynamic fact for each simple constituent indicating the position, the constituent category, and the argument. In addition we assert dynamic facts for complex constituents that influence the generation of word translations, e.g. genitive noun phrases.

Next, we process the token list from left to right. The default treatment for a lexical entry is to use the English token if a single dynamic fact exists for that list position. Otherwise, the word translation is left empty.

If there exist several dynamic facts for a position, they are used to generate the correct surface form of conjugated words as well as concatenate the individual elements of phrases.

Most problems with the assignment of word translations to the correct positions in the token list have already been resolved through the extension of the acquisition module (see Sect. 4). Therefore, there remain only few special cases to be dealt with, e.g. for predicative nouns, the features regarding conjugation have to be collected from the next position for the verb suru to produce the correct surface form. Finally, we also have to ensure the correct placement of:

- words inserted through standard transformations,
- commas and other punctuation marks,
- words inserted due to complex constituents, e.g. "to" in a modifying to-infinitive clause.

6   Conclusion

In this paper we have presented a Web-based language learning tool for Japanese, which has been developed based on an existing machine translation system. WILLIE randomly selects translation examples and displays detailed information about lexical, syntactic, and translation knowledge by using dynamic JavaScript pop-up windows and color coding. We have finished the implementation of the system including a first local prototype configuration of the Web server to demonstrate the feasibility of the approach.

Future work will focus on making WILLIE available to students of Japanese studies at our university to receive valuable feedback from practical use, in particular regarding usability. In addition, we are planning to make a demo version of WILLIE publicly available in the near future.

Although WILLIE is already a very useful tool for language students, we also see it only as a first step towards the larger aim of developing an intelligent language tutoring system. We want to extend WILLIE so that it is possible for the student to enter free input to be analyzed. This should then be embedded into interactive exercises with meaningful feedback.

Acknowledgements

We are deeply grateful to Amzi! inc. for supporting our research with a complimentary Professional Edition of Amzi! Prolog + Logic Server.

References

1. Hutchins, J.: Machine translation and computer-based translation tools: What's available and how it's used. In: Bravo, J.M. (ed.) A New Spectrum of Translation Studies, University of Valladolid, pp. 13–48 (2004)
2. Liu, H.: MontyLingua: An End-to-End Natural Language Processor with Common Sense, MIT Media Lab (2004)
3. Matsumoto, M., et al.: Japanese Morphological Analysis System ChaSen Version 2.0 Manual. NAIST Technical Report, NAIST-IS-TR99009 (1999)
4. Nagata, N.: Intelligent computer feedback for second language instruction. Modern Language Journal 77(3), 330–338 (1993)
5. Nagata, N.: An effective application of natural language processing in second language instruction. CALICO Journal 13(1), 47–67 (1995)
6. Nagata, N.: Computer vs. workbook instruction in second language acquisition. CALICO Journal 14(1), 53–75 (1996)
7. Nagata, N.: An experimental comparison of deductive and inductive feedback generated by a simple parser. System 25(4), 515–534 (1997)
8. Nagata, N.: BANZAI: An application of natural language processing to Web based language learning. CALICO Journal 18(4), 583–599 (2002)
9. Nagata, N.: BANZAI: Computer assisted sentence production practice with intelligent feedback. In: Proc. of the 3rd Intl. Conf. on Computer-Assisted Systems for Teaching and Learning Japanese, San Diego, USA (2002)
10. Nagata, N.: Robo-Sensei: Personal Japanese Tutor, Cheng & Tsui (2003)
11. Nagata, N., Swisher, M.V.: A study of consciousness-raising by computer: The effect of metalinguistic feedback on second language learning. Foreign Language Annals 28(3), 337–347 (1995)
12. Newton, J. (ed.): Computers in Translation: A Practical Appraisal. Routledge (1992)
13. Somers, H. (ed.): Computers and Translation: A Translator's Guide. John Benjamins (2003)
14. Utiyama, M., Isahara, H.: Reliable measures for aligning Japanese-English news articles and sentences. In: Proc. of the 41st Annual Meeting of the ACL, Barcelona, Spain, pp. 72–79 (2003)
15. Winiwarter, W.: WETCAT – Web-enabled translation using corpus-based acquisition of transfer rules. In: Proc. of the 3rd IEEE Intl. Conf. on Innovations in Information Technology, Dubai, United Arab Emirates (2006)
16. Winiwarter, W.: Automatic acquisition of translation knowledge using structural matching between parse trees. In: Proc. of the First Intl. Conf. on the Digital Society, Guadeloupe, French Carribean (2007)
17. Yang, J., Akahori, K.: Development of computer assisted language learning systems for Japanese writing using natural language processing techniques: A study on passive voice. In: Proc. of the AIED-Workshop on Intelligent Educational Systems on the World Wide Web, Kobe, Japan (1997)
18. Yang, J., Akahori, K.: An evaluation of Japanese CALL systems on the WWW. Comparing a freely input approach with multiple selection. Computer Assisted Language Learning 12(1), 59–79 (1998)
19. Yang, J., Akahori, K.: Error analysis in Japanese writing and its implementation in a computer assisted language learning system on the World Wide Web. CALICO Journal 15(1-3), 47–66 (1998)

E-Learning and Deaf Children: A Logic-Based Web Tool

Rosella Gennari and Ornella Mich

KRDB, CS Faculty, Free University of Bozen-Bolzano
Piazza Domenicani 3, 39100 Bolzano, Italy
gennari@inf.unibz.it, mich@itc.it

Abstract. LODE is a LOgic-based web tool for Italian DEaf children. LODE stimulate them to globally reason on an e-story written in a verbal language, such as Italian. In this paper, we focus on temporal reasoning; children are invited to reason on a temporally rich e-story through apt exercises and with the support of an automated reasoner. To the best of our knowledge, LODE is the first E-Learning tool for Italian deaf children that aims at stimulating global reasoning on whole e-stories.

Keywords: E-Learning platforms and tools; pedagogical issues.

1 Introduction

Learning to read and write effectively is a difficult task for deaf people: "Deaf children have unique communication needs: unable to hear the continuous, repeated flow of language interchange around them, they are not automatically exposed to the enormous amounts of language stimulation experienced by hearing children" [23]. According to some findings, their reading ability does not often go beyond that of an eight-year old child [19].

In particular, as highlighted in [3], deaf people tend to reason on single episodes and show difficulties in formulating global relations, such as temporal relations, between episodes of a narrative in a verbal language[1]. This attitude can also depend on the kind of "literacy interventions addressed to deaf children" which tend to "focus on single sentences and the grammatical aspects of text production" [3]. An innovative literacy e-tool for them should thus elicit global deductive reasoning on narratives: we aim at developing an E-Learning tool of this type, namely, LODE, a LOgic-based e-tool for DEaf children.

In this paper we restrict our attention to global reasoning with qualitative temporal relations. To assist the child in inferring the "correct" temporal relation, LODE employs an automated reasoner, namely, a constraint programming system. The essential background on automated temporal reasoning is provided in Sect. 2. The core part of this paper is Sect. 3, which presents the educational

---

[1] Here, the term *verbal language* refers to any oral-auditive language with words as lexical units; by contrast, *sign languages* are gestural-visual languages with signs as lexical units and no written form, and are mainly developed in deaf communities.

H. Leung et al. (Eds.): ICWL 2007, LNCS 4823, pp. 312–319, 2008.

tasks of LODE. Sect. 4 compares LODE to other E-Learning tools for deaf children, and Sect. 5 concludes with a preliminary assessment of our LODE prototype and an evaluation plan for LODE.

2   LODE and Automated Temporal Reasoning

Temporal Reasoning is a branch of Artificial Intelligence (AI) and involves the formal representation of time and a computational reasoning system for this. An instance of a temporal reasoning problem is provided in the following excerpt from a LODE tale, a simplified version of *The Ugly Duckling* by H.C. Andersen.

> Mammy duck is brooding: she has five eggs, four are small, and one is big. All of a sudden, while she is still brooding, the small eggshells crack and four little yellow ducklings peep out. Mammy duck watches the big egg but sees no signs of cracking... So she decides to keep on brooding. After some days, while she is brooding, also the big eggshell cracks and an ugly grey duckling peeps out...
>
> **Task:** *do the small eggshells crack* before *the big eggshell cracks?*

Here we adopt intervals as the primitive entities for *formally representing time*; each interval is uniquely associated with a time event. Between any two pairs of events, there is an *atomic Allen* relation, namely, a relation rel of the form

$$\text{before, meets, overlaps, starts, during, finishes, equals}$$

or its inverse rel^{-1}; see Fig. 1 for an intuitive graphical representation of the atomic Allen relations between two events, $e1$ and $e2$. The Allen relations are

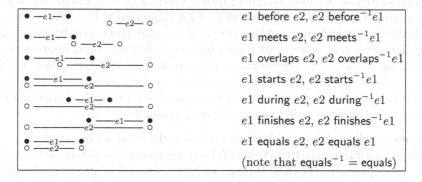

	$e1$ before $e2$, $e2$ before$^{-1}e1$
	$e1$ meets $e2$, $e2$ meets$^{-1}e1$
	$e1$ overlaps $e2$, $e2$ overlaps$^{-1}e1$
	$e1$ starts $e2$, $e2$ starts$^{-1}e1$
	$e1$ during $e2$, $e2$ during$^{-1}e1$
	$e1$ finishes $e2$, $e2$ finishes$^{-1}e1$
	$e1$ equals $e2$, $e2$ equals $e1$
	(note that equals^{-1} = equals)

Fig. 1. The atomic Allen relations

employed whenever temporal information boils down to qualitative relations between events, such as "The small eggshells crack *while* Mammy duck broods"; in terms of the Allen relations, the sentence states that the relation "during" holds between the event "the small eggshells cracks" and the event "Mammy duck broods". As *automated reasoning system*, LODE employs ECL^{i}PS^e, a constraint programming system [2]. Once a temporal reasoning problem is formalised in the language of ECL^{i}PS^e, it can be *solved* by this. For instance, ECL^{i}PS^e can be invoked to solve the following tasks: to decide on "the big eggshell cracks after the small eggshells crack"; to infer all the Allen relations between the events "the big eggshell cracks" and "the small eggshells crack", implicit in the problem and consistent with it. For a survey on temporal reasoning and constraint programming, we refer the reader to [10].

3   LODE and Its Educational Tasks

Temporal global reasoning on texts written in a verbal language can be problematic for deaf children, as outlined in Sect. 1. LODE aims at tackling this issue with the help of famous stories for children. More precisely, LODE presents a list of e-stories the child can choose among. They are simplified versions of traditional children tales, such as *The Ugly Duckling*, so that the language is more suitable to an eight-year old deaf child; they are also enriched with explicit temporal relations so as to focus the attention of the child on temporal reasoning. The child has to choose a story from the list in order to begin his/her exercise session. We explain the educational exercises of LODE in Subs. 3.1 and outline the visual interface of LODE in Subs. 3.2.

3.1   Educational Exercises

Once the child chooses an e-story, he/she can start reading it. Words which are unusual for deaf children are explained in an e-dictionary of LODE; there, each word is illustrated by means of an image and a short textual explanation; example sentences are also available; future versions of LODE will also feature a translation of these words into Italian Sign Language (LIS). The dictionary simplifies the comprehension of the story and the association grapheme-meaning in beginning readers, a step which may be necessary with young deaf users.

Then the chosen story is presented, split across different pages. There are two or three sentences with an explanatory image on each page. Every few pages, the child starts a new exercise session for *reasoning* on the tale. LODE features two reasoning exercise types: comprehension; production.

Comprehension. In *comprehension exercises*, the child is presented with temporal relations connecting events of the story; the relations may be implicit in it. More precisely, the child is proposed four temporal relations; each relation corresponds to an atomic Allen relation. The child is asked to judge which relations are inconsistent with the text he/she has already read, playing the role of the 'teacher' who eliminates the incoherent ones. The four cases are constructed with the assistance of the ECL^{i}PS^e automated reasoner to determine which temporal relations are (in)consistent with the narrative.

Production. In the *production exercises*, the children are shown scattered sentence units extracted from the given story; then he/she is asked to compose a grammatically correct sentence with them, forming a temporal relation consistent with the story and which may be implicit in the story. For instance, suppose that the available sentence units are: BEFORE, WHILE, AFTER, MAMMY DUCK BROODS, THE DUCKS, SWIM. Two are the possible correct sentences the child can compose, consistent with the tale. The first one is: MAMMY DUCK BROODS BEFORE THE DUCKS SWIM. The second sentence is: THE DUCKS SWIM AFTER MAMMY DUCK BROODS. If the child composes a wrong sentence, because it is ungrammatical or inconsistent with the story, LODE will provide suggestions to correct the sentence with the help of the automated reasoner ECL^{i}PS^e and a natural language processor for Italian.

The difficulty of the reasoning exercises increases with the portion of the story the child has to reason on. The first and simpler exercises relate two temporal events which occur in the portion of the tale, temporally rich, that the child has just read. If the score reached so far by the child is reasonably good, then LODE proposes the more challenging tasks, namely, those that require a deep global understanding of the story and the creation of global temporal relations: these exercises relate two temporal events, one of the current session and the other of a previous session—the farther is this session the more difficult is the exercise.

Moreover, note that the comprehension exercises focus on stimulating global inferences between events of the story; the production exercises demand this and something else, that is, to compose parts of the story. Therefore, the production exercises also aim at teaching children Italian grammar.

3.2   Visualisation

Deaf children are *essentially visual learners* [21], with (visual) learning strategies of their own; thus LODE employs cartoons and images for assisting children in the story narration and exercises. In a LODE story, each significant temporal event is illustrated with an image; this should help children in focusing on the temporal event and comprehending it; note that the visual aid is important because deaf children do not usually know tales[2]. As LODE is a tool for improving the reading capabilities of deaf children, the text is visually predominant so as to capture the child's attention.

An animated cartoon agent will also assist children through the different educational tasks; it will stimulate children with positive feedback to maintain their attention alive. As highlighted by Stokoe, quoted in [21], a sign language such as LIS and the verbal language of the same nation tend to be very different languages. As LODE aims at being an E-Learning tool for reasoning 'on' e-stories in a verbal language, its users are solicited to reason 'in' verbal Italian; thus instructions in the reasoning exercises are not provided in LIS. LIS videos will instead be employed in the dictionary as a support tool for LIS signers.

---

[2] Private communication with ENS, Italian National Institute for the Assistance and Protection of the Deaf.

The visual representation of the Allen relations in the comprehension exercises is still an open issue. In the remainder we present two visualisations, one is *textual*, the other is *spatial*; in both, each event is represented by means of an image. For an example, see Fig. 2. In the *textual visualisation*, the two images representing the events are connected by an arc labelled by one of the atomic Allen relations. This visualisation is easy to implement and compact in size; however, children must precisely understand the semantics of the Italian writing of the Allen relations. In the *spatial visualisation*, an atomic Allen relation between the two events is rendered by the spatial position of the relative images of the events along the timeline. Once the children get familiar with this visualisation, the semantics of the relations is likely to be more intuitive to them. Note that the two visualisations differently represent hence differently stimulate the reasoning of children on temporal relations: the spatial visualisation exploits spatial information and reasoning; the textual visualisation represents relations and stimulates reasoning on them with text only.

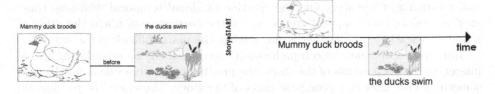

Fig. 2. A visual representation of the Allen temporal relation before with the textual method (on the left) and the spatial method (on the right)

4   Related Work

Currently, computer science research for deaf or hearing impaired people seems to mostly focus on applications for sign languages, such as LIS, e.g., [5, 15]. Considerable less attention seems to be devoted to the development of E-Learning tools for improving the literacy of deaf children in verbal languages. In the remainder, we overview some E-Learning tools for deaf children which are related to LODE.

In Italian. In Italy, three learning tools were developed in between 1997–1998 to tackle specific aspects of verbal Italian lexicon or grammar: *Articoli* [4] aims at teaching Italian articles (e.g., gender agreement); *Carotino* [6] is an interactive tool for teaching simple Italian phrases; *Pro-Peanuts* [20] deals with the correct use of pronouns. These tools are not developed only for deaf children.

We also found references to a tool developed in 1994, *Corso di Lettura* [8]; according to its specifications, the tool aims at improving the reading capabilities of hearing-impaired children. In order to facilitate the integration of a deaf girl into an Italian primary school, teachers and students of the school created *Fabulis* [9], a collection of famous stories for children narrated using text and images, based on gestures and LIS signs. Another application born at school is *Nuvolina* [18], the result of a project realised in a fourth class of an Italian primary school: it is a multimedia tale with contents in Italian, English and French, written and spoken; the version in verbal Italian is also presented in LIS videos. Another bilingual tool is *Gli Animali della Savana* [1], a multimedia software based on text, images and videos, featuring an actor who translates the written text in LIS; assisted by a cartoon (a lion), the user navigates through a series of pages presenting the life of 10 wild animals. A more recent and ambitious project is *Tell me a Dictionary* [14, 22], the purpose of which is to offer both deaf and hearing children an interactive instrument to discover and compare the lexicon of LIS and Italian.

In English. The primary goal of ICICLE [13, 16] is to employ natural language processing and generation to tutor deaf students on their written English. ICICLE's interaction with the user takes the form of a cycle of user input and system response. The cycle begins when a user submits a piece of writing. The system then performs a syntactic analysis on the writing, determines its errors, and returns tutorial feedback to make the student aware of the nature of his/her errors.

CornerStones [17] is an approach to literacy development for primary-school children who are deaf or hard of hearing. Academic experts in literacy and deafness, and teachers of deaf students participated in its development. Cornerstones developers were most concerned with three key areas of literacy: first, identification of words in print, second, in-depth knowledge of words, and third, story comprehension. An essential element of Cornerstones is a story taken from the PBS's literacy series *Between the Lions*, complemented by versions of the story in American Sign Language and other visual-spatial systems for communicating with deaf children. Cornerstones developers evaluated their system with children and teachers and results of their evaluation demonstrated an increase in students' knowledge of selected words from pre-test to post-test.

FtL was not intended exclusively for deaf or hard of hearing children, but they have also been considered as potential users [7]. FtL is a comprehensive computer-based reading program designed to teach beginning and early readers to read accurately and fluently. It consists of three integrated components: (1) a Managed Learning Environment (MLE) that tracks and displays student progress and manages an individual study plan for each student; (2) Foundational Skills Reading Exercises, which teach and practice basic reading skills, such as alphabet knowledge and word decoding; (3) Interactive Books, which integrate human language and animation technologies to enable conversational interaction with a Virtual Tutor that teaches fluent reading and comprehension of text. Summative evaluation of FtL produced learning gains for letter and word recognition for kindergarten students.

Comparison. According to our overview of Italian and non-Italian projects for deaf children, LODE is the first web E-Learning tool that tackles literacy issues of deaf children which go beyond the syntax and grammar of a verbal language; that is, it addresses *global deductive reasoning* on whole e-stories, with the support of an automated reasoner.

5   Conclusions

This paper presented an innovative E-Learning tool for deaf children, namely, LODE: the tool aims at stimulating global reasoning on written e-stories. As outlined in Sect. 1, this is a problematic issue for many deaf children. In Sect. 3, we explained the educational exercises of LODE and the role of the automated reasoner in their construction and resolution; for a survey of the architecture of LODE, we refer to [11, 12]. In Sect. 4, we overviewed and compared E-Learning tools addressing literacy problems of deaf children. According to our overview and to the best of our knowledge, LODE is the first web-based E-Learning tool which aims at stimulating global deductive reasoning on whole e-stories in a verbal language. Currently, we are concentrating on global temporal reasoning; in the future, we are going to extend LODE to other kinds of global reasoning on narratives, addressing problems which may be critical for deaf children and that can be tackled with the assistance of an automated reasoner. LODE, now in prototype form, is being evaluated into three main phases. The first evaluation phase is almost over; a cognitive psychologist, a logopaedist, LIS interpreters and teachers for deaf children tested a preliminary version of LODE and provided us with positive informative feedback on its learning goals and strategies. The second and third evaluation phases will directly involve deaf children; the second phase will be done with the assistance of a teacher for deaf children; the third phase will involve children at home. The second evaluation phase tests the usability of LODE, in particular, it tests which is the most effective way of visually representing the Allen relations and the LODE exercises in general. The third evaluation phase aims at delivering the final design solution, focusing on the user's satisfaction.

Acknowledgments. Among the others, we wish to thank B. Arfé, T. Di Mascio, the ENS and Talking Hands from Trento (in particular, N. Hy Thien and F. De Carli), M. Valente, and the anonymous referees for their valuable comments.

References

[1] Gli Animali della Savana (Retrieved May 21, 2007), http://www.areato.org/noquadri/ausiliDinamici/AusDnm_00_Titolo.Asp?IDAUSILIO=106&FORMATO=G

[2] Apt, K.R., Wallace, M.G.: Constraint Logic Programming using ECLiPSe. Cambridge University Press, Cambridge (2006)

[3] Arfé, B., Boscolo, P.: Causal Coherence in Deaf and Hearing Students' Written Narratives. Discourse Processes 42(3), 271–300 (2006)

[4] Articoli: (Retrieved May 21, 2007),
http://www.anastasis.it/AMBIENTI/NodoCMS/CaricaPagina.asp?ID=36
[5] Bartolini, S., Bennati, P., Giorgi, R.: Sistema per la Traduzione in Lingua Italiana
dei Segni: Blue Sign Translator / Wireless Sign System. In: Proc. of the 50th AIES
National Conference (2004)
[6] Carotino: (Retrieved May 21, 2007),
http://www.anastasis.it/AMBIENTI/NodoCMS/CaricaPagina.asp?ID=40
[7] Cole, R., Massaro, D., Rundle, B., Shobaki, K., Wouters, J., Cohen, M., Beskow,
J., Stone, P., Connors, P., Tarachow, A., Solcher, D.: New Tools for Interactive
Speech and Language Training: Using Animated Conversational Agents in the
Classrooms of Profoundly Deaf Children
[8] di Lettura, C.: (Retrieved May 21, 2007),
http://www.anastasis.it/AMBIENTI/NodoCMS/CaricaPagina.asp?ID=35
[9] Fabulis: (Retrieved May 21, 2007), from http://www.bonavitacola.net/fabulis/
[10] Gennari, R.: Temporal Reasoning and Constraint Programming: A Survey. CWI
Quarterly 11(2–3) (1998)
[11] Gennari, R., Mich, O.: LODE: A Logic-based E-Learning Tool for Deaf Children.
Technical report, KRDB, Free University of Bozen-Bolzano (2007)
[12] Gennari, R., Mich, O.: LODE: Global Reasoning on e-Stories for Deaf Children.
In: Apolloni, B., Howlett, R.J., Jain, L. (eds.) KES 2007, Part III. LNCS (LNAI),
vol. 4694, pp. 678–685. Springer, Heidelberg (2007)
[13] ICICLE. (Retrieved May 21, 2007), http://www.eecis.udel.edu/research/
icicle/
[14] Insolera, E., Militano, G., Radutzky, E., Rossini, A.: Pilot Learning Strategies in
Step with New Technologies: LIS and Italian in a Bilingual Multimedia Context
'Tell me a Dictionary'. In: Vettori, C. (ed.) Proc. of the 2nd Workshop on the
Representation and Processing of Sign Languages, LREC (2006)
[15] Mertzani, M., Denmark, C., Day, L.: Forming Sign Language Learning Environments in Cyberspace. In: Vettori, C. (ed.) Proc. of the 2nd Workshop on the
Representation and Processing of Sign Languages, LREC (2006)
[16] Michaud, L.N., McCoy, K.F., Pennington, C.: An Intelligent Tutoring System for
Deaf Learners of Written English. In: Proc. of ASSETS (2000)
[17] NCAM-CornerStones: (Retrieved May 21, 2007),
http://ncam.wgbh.org/cornerstones/overview.html
[18] Nuvolina (1998) (retrieved May 21, 2007),
http://www.areato.org/noquadri/ausiliDinamici/AusDnm_01_Dettaglio.
Asp?IDAUSILIO=229\&IDSEZIONE=5\&FORMATO=G\&VETRINA=N
[19] Paul, P.V.: Literacy and Deafness: The Development of Reading, Writing, and
Literate Thought. Allyn & Bacon (1998)
[20] Pro-peanuts (1998) (retrieved May 21, 2007),
http://www.ciscl.unisi.it/persone/chesi/laurea/str.htm
[21] Sacks, O.: Seeing Voices: A Journey into the World of the Deaf. Vintage Books
(Italian version: "Vedere Voci", Adelphi, 1999 (1989)
[22] Tell me a Dictionary (2005), (retrieved May 21, 2007),
http://www.lismedia.it/demo01/home.html
[23] UNESCO. Education of Deaf Children and Young People. Guides for Special
Needs Education. Paris (1987)

A Virtual Chinese Hairy Brush Model for E-Learning

Bendu Bai[1,2], Kam-Wah Wong[2], and Yanning Zhang[1]

[1] Northwestern Polytech University,
School of Computer Science, Xi'an 710072, China
[2] City University of Hong Kong,
School of Creative Media, Kowloon, Hong Kong China
{baibendu, smkam}@cityu.edu.hk,
ynzhang@nwpu.edu.cn

Abstract. The increasing demands of education, reduction of study cost and study without location limitation have encouraged developers providing different types of learning and educational systems. This paper presents a virtual Chinese hairy brush painting environment which can be used as a digital tool for learning or creating Chinese calligraphy or Chinese painting. The framework comprises two components: brush geometry model and brush dynamic model. Instead of simulating the brush using bristles, we use points to simulate the whole brush bundle, which can drastically decrease the complexity inherent in the conventional bristle-level approach; our brush dynamic model describes the behavior of the real brush's deformation in terms of the interaction of the external and internal forces with the virtual writing paper. A spring network is derived to calculate the physical deflection of brush according to the force exerted on it. A prototype system has been implemented based on this framework, with which high-quality digital painting and calligraphy artwork can be produced.

1   Introduction

Web-based teaching and learning has been explored and studied by many researchers. This paper presents a virtual Chinese hairy brush painting environment which can be used as a digital tool for learning or creating Chinese calligraphy or Chinese painting. The Chinese have been painting with hair brushes and ink on paper over two thousands years. Chinese calligraphy was thought to be the highest and purest form of Chinese painting. Traditional Chinese hair brushes are made from animal hairs and the ink are made from pine soot and animal glue. With the development of modern computers, to design and develop a digital painting environment that simulates Chinese brush has attracted a lot of researchers. Moreover, the increasing demands of education, reduction of study cost and study without location limitation have encouraged developers providing different types of learning and educational systems.

However, most of the related researches focus on the visual quality of the output rather than the running efficiency of the system. For a web-based learning

H. Leung et al. (Eds.): ICWL 2007, LNCS 4823, pp. 320–330, 2008.

system, the efficiency is relatively important. In this paper we presents a model that is simple and efficient enough for web-based learning purpose.

1.1 Related Work

Recently, several physically-based 3D brush models have been proposed and we will review only those are directly related to our work. The first purely physically based 3D brush model was proposed by Saito [6]. Saito used energy optimization to determine the brush deformation. His model accounted for brush stiffness, friction and kinetic energy. However, the model can not simulate brush spreading. Wong et al. [7] modeled a calligraphy brush as an inverted cone, with some ellipses to synthesize Chinese calligraphic writings. Since their model pay no attention to the brush tip while drawing stroke, it fails to produce the biased-tip strokes. Baxter et al. [1] modeled the western brush as spring-mass systems, but the model was still lacking of the effect of brush spreading or splitting. Xu et al. [8][9] presented a more complex geometry which can split into smaller tufts, but the bulk of the brush must penetrate the paper in the drawing process which leads to unrealistic brush footprints. Chu and Tai [2][3][4] delivered a very convincing model for Chinese calligraphy that included factors such as plasticity, tip spreading, and pore resistance. Like Saito, Chu and Tai also used energy optimization for the brush dynamics, but their approach had to solve a static constrained minimization problem by using local sequential quadratic programming(SQP). Although the method of SQP can avoid solving stiff differential equations, it is still complex in computation due to the iterations of SQP.

2 The Brush Model

Our aim is to provide a simple but efficient brush model for interactively creating oriental artworks with computer. Since a typical real brush may consist of thousands or even tens of thousands of individual bristles, physically simulating each and every bristle is not practical based on present hardware capability. Inspired by the fact that artists use real brush with elastic bristles to draw strokes, and based on the physical characteristics of the motion of brush, we convert simulating the complex physical deformation of bristles to simulating the footprint variation of brush, since the final effect is determined by the latter. For this purpose, we simplify the geometric representation of brush to be a collection of points instead of hair threads and use it as the basic unit to construct a 3D brush bundle.

2.1 Brush Basic Unit

In a real brush, the hairs distribute non-uniformly alone the radius. The density of hairs in the center area is much thicker than that near the boundary. Crowded hairs are obviously found in the center, and loser around the brush boundary.

According to this role, we design the brush basic unit (BU) as shown in Fig.1. Then, a 3D virtual brush in static state can be built using a series of BU (see

Fig. 1. The brush basic unit

Fig.1) with the different sizes, starting from brush tip to the brush root (see Fig.2). Obviously, the smallest BU may only have one dot. However, for hair brush, a small brush tip including only one dot does not have a practical meaning. Our experiments show that the tip of the brush including four dots is a minimum.

Fig. 2. The single brush bundle

2.2   Brush Dynamics

Brush dynamic model describes the deformation of the brush bundle at every instance of brush movement. In real-life Chinese calligraphy, a typical stroke usually includes three stages: Qibi (press), Yunbi (move) and Tibi (lift). During different stage the brush dynamic model should have different footprint when the brush is pressed onto or lifted from the paper.

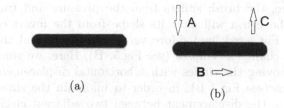

(a)

(b)

Fig. 3. (a) A stroke generated by our model. (b) The moving direction of the brush during a single stroke.

Qibi. Fig3.(a) shows a horizontal stroke. As the artist writes the stroke, firstly he presses the brush vertically against the paper until the brush tip reaches the writing paper (see arrow A of Fig3.(b)). Starting from the moment when the brush touched the paper, with the brush continually moving downward(i.e., brush only moves along z-axis), to the moment when the brush is beginning to move on the paper surface (i.e. brush moves along x-axis or y-axis), is the stage of Qibi.

During this stage, the brush is dipped with ink. The attractive force between ink and hair molecules holds the hair together. Moreover, in real-life calligraphy writing, usually only the tip of the brush is to paint in the Qibi stage. Although the force that the brush suffers in the stage is rather complex, such as the external pressure and the internal friction between wet bristles, the footprint in a real-life writing process looks like a circular disk according to our observations. Therefore, our brush model in Qibi stage is designed as a series of concentric circular disks, which are laid to lap over each other onto the cross-sectional plane (as shown in Fig.4. A). This simple representation is computationally efficient and quite similar to the observed reality.

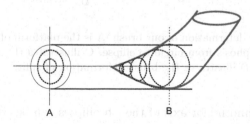

Fig. 4. The dynamic deformation of our brush during the different stage of a single stroke

Yunbi. The stage of Yunbi starts from which the artist drugs the brush along the path of the stroke (see arrow B of Fig3.(b)). At the very beginning of the stage, the artist will continually press the brush against the paper surface, as far as the stroke width reaches certain value which the painter wants the stroke to be.

During this stage, the brush suffers from the pressure and friction with the paper, so that the brush will alter its shape from the invert cone to a bent invert cone (see Fig.4 red line). Moreover, the pressure and the friction also make the circles change as ellipses (see Fig.5. B). Here, we simulate the bent brush through moving the circles with a horizontal displacement along x-axis of the paper plane(see Fig.4 B). In order to maintain the smoothness of the stroke boundaries, the displacement between two adjacent circle should meet the constrain as follows

$$r_i - r_{i-1} \leq d_i \leq 2(r_i - r_{i-1}) \tag{1}$$

where d_i represent the displacement between the ith circle and the $(i-1)$th circle, r_i represents the radii of the ith circle, and r_{i-1} is the radii of the adjacent of the ith circle nearer to the brush tip.

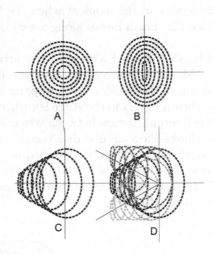

Fig. 5. The dynamic deformation of our brush. A is the platform of our model. B illustrates brush anamorphosis from circle to ellipse. C illustrates the deformation during the stage of Yunbi . D illustrates the brush deformation of split.

The major axis and minor axis of the ith ellipses can be computed by follow equations

$$majoraxis(u_i) = r_i k_u, \quad minoraxis(v_i) = r_i k_v \tag{2}$$

where k_u are the deformation constant of major axis, and k_v is the deformation constant of minor axis. Typically, k_u and k_v are from 1.0 to 1.5 and from 1.0 to 0.5, respectively.

Tibi. The stage of Tibi describes the process that the brush was lifted from the writing paper, which can be found at the end of the stroke (see arrow C of Fig.3.(b)). During this stage, a moist brush is deformed. In order to return the bent brush to its original shape, the flexible force has to overcome the resistance of molecular friction. Due to the effect of this internal frication, the bent brush does not entirety revert to its original shape. We formulate the energy function based on the principle of conservation of energy when the brush was pressed or lifted as follows:

$$E_{press} = E_{bend} + E_{fric} \tag{3}$$

$$E_{lift} = E_{bend} - E_{fric} \tag{4}$$

$$E_{press} = E_{lift} \tag{5}$$

where E_{bend} is the brush bent energy, and E_{fric} is the internal energy of molecular friction when the brush was pressed or lifted. Then, we deal with the problems by using a spring network to approximate the behavior of the deformations. We use bend springs at each joint point between cone major axis and circles to model the bending deformation of the brush. The relationship between the amount of bent displacement and the spring force can be closely approximated by using Hooke's law [5]:

$$F_s = -F_x = -kx \tag{6}$$

where F_s is the equal and opposite restoring force of the spring on the stretch node, k is the spring constant, and x is the displacement of a node position under the influence of a force F_x. Taking the definition of the Hooke's law (Equation 6) into Equation 3 and 4, we thus have our energy functions as:

$$E_{press} = E_{bend} + E_{fric} = -k_b d_i - k_f d_i \tag{7}$$

$$E_{lift} = E_{bend} - E_{fric} = -k_b d_j + k_f d_j \tag{8}$$

where k_b and k_f are the bent spring constant and the internal friction constant, d_i (d_j) is the displacement of spring node between the ith (jth) circle and the $(i-1)$th ($(j-1)$th) circle. The value of d_i, d_j should satisfy the constraint of formula (1).

2.3 Splitting Brush

The effect of splitting brush results from the brush deformation, the decrease of the volume of the ink, and rapid moving of the brush.

With a single brush bundle, it is impossible to achieve the effect of brush splitting. To deal with the problem, Xu [8] proposed a two-level hierarchical brush geometry model. The main advantage of Xu's model lies in modeling the complex geometry of a realistic split brush as several similar cluster using the comparability of the hair macros. We cope with the problem by using a similar approach, with some necessary modifications due to a different primitive model adopted in our framework.

According to our brush basic unit (BU), we use a simple algorithm to achieve the splitting effect. Since the amount of ink plays an important role in the process of brush splitting, we firstly set an initial ink value for entire brush bundle(the ink model will be discussed in next section). For every instant t, we check the decrease of the amount of ink and the deformation of the brush tip. When the ellipse of the brush tip reaches its limit($k_u = 1.5$) and the amount of ink reduce to a threshold, a new primitive brush generates. Then, we use the affine transformations composing the parent brush bundle and the new sub-brush bundle together. Each sub-brush bundle can be classified as a collection of vertices as shown in Fig.1. We use the same brush model for the split brush bundle because it can reduce the number of models that need to be generated. This is helpful to build a complex model by a single model, as which allows Graphical Processing Unit(GPU) to work on a smallest set of vertices at a time.

Fig.5. D shows a model with one parent brush bundle and two sub-brush bundles. By this method, with less than 6 sub-brush bundles, we have not only modeled the complex geometry of a split brush, but also diminish the computational time.

Ink Depositing Model. The ink model describes the process of ink depositing in which brush geometry model is instanced and transformed into a real screen presentation. During the painting process, the brush sweeps paper plane along a stroke path which transfers the brush footprint to the paper plane on each pass. To simulate the decrease of the amount of the ink, we define a parameter c_i (1.0-0.0) for the ink consumption at unit interval of the brush bundle's the ith ellipse. When the single brush bundle split into several bundles, each ellipse of the new sub-brush bundles will have the same value as the ellipse on the same contour line of the main brush bundle. Therefore, the amount of ink of the ith ellipse at instance t is

$$e_{i,t} = 1 - \sum_{j=1,\dots,t} c_{i,j}. \tag{9}$$

Here, in terms of efficient computation, we suppose that

$$c_{i,t} = c_{i,t+1}. \tag{10}$$

Suppose we are drawing a stroke, we want to have a brush that gradually adds color so that each points of a footprint contributes a little more ink with whatever is currently in the image. To do so, we simulate the process using alpha blending with OpenGL. The blending functions that use the source and the destination blending factor are GL_SRC_ALPHA and GL_ON_MINUS_SRC_ALPHA. To avoid the alias brush shape, we vary the alphas across the brush to make the brush add more ink in the middle and less on the edges. The process of the ink deposition is optimized by GPU's hardware implementation. As a result, the CPU can offload the rendering processing to do physics simulation, and therefore increase system performance.

3   Implementation Results

We have implemented a prototype system based on our brush model. Our system was written in c++ using Microsoft Visual C++6.0. All graphical rendering operations are accelerated by using OpenGL on the GPU. In the current implementation, on a 2GHZ Pentium 4 with NVIDIA GeForce FX 5200 display card, our system runs in real-time at 60 frames per second.

Figures 6 and 8 show some sample calligraphy and strokes obtained using our prototype system. A calligraphy horizontal stoke shown in Fig 6 (a) was written with a dipped sufficiently ink brush. Fig 6 (b) and (c) illustrate the effect of ink diffusion due to the decrease of the amount of ink and the the amount of the time that the brush spent in contact with the paper.

Although the examples shown in the figures 6(a),(b),(c) are very simple strokes, it proves that the proposed model is able to simulate the different shading effects along and across the width of a calligraphic stroke, which was not reported by the other systems so far.

Fig 6 (d) and (e) illustrate the effect of brush split generated by a dry and multi-tuft brush. Fig 7 to fig 10 show some comparisons between the digitized real calligraphy sample and the imitation artwork created by our prototype system. It proves that very realistic-looking calligraphy artwork can be generated by our brush model.

4   Conclusion and Application

We have presented a novel model for virtual brushes that can produce the effects needed by the digital Chinese calligraphy. The model is very simple but efficient, which is essential for a web-based learning system. With the proposed model, realistic Chinese calligraphy artwork can be generated effectively with direct manipulation. Major advantages of our model over previous works are

- We use a collection of points instead of hair threads as the basic unit to construct a 3D brush bundle, so that we convert simulating the complex physical deformation of bristles (as the way in most previous models did) to simulate the footprint variation of brush, which can efficiently decrease the complexity of physical simulation.
- We formulate the brush dynamics as a set of energy function according to the force exerted on it. A spring network is derived to calculate those energy function. This method significantly improves the brush's appearance, producing the plastic effect of brush that user expect.

Up to now, our research mainly focused on modeling a medium stiff hair brush. It is expected that our model can also mimic other kinds of brushes by modifying the bent spring parameter. Moreover, only a vertical brush dynamic model was simulated presently. In order to simulate a hairy brush in Chinese painting, a slant angle brush dynamic model should also be studied.

In Chinese traditional calligraphy, in order to achieve good calligraphic artwork, artist takes a great deal of experimenting and practice. How to control the pressure of the brush and to maintain elasticity during the pressing-downs and raising-ups in moving the brush is indeed a major technique in Chinese art. Speed of the brush is just as important as pressure. Speed affect the flow of the

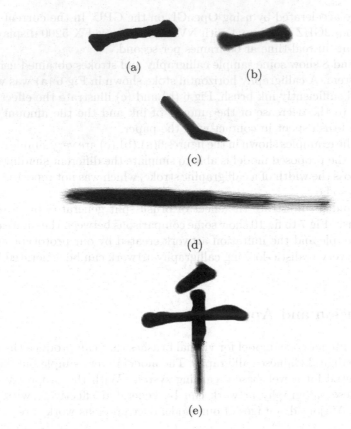

(a)

(b)

(c)

(d)

(e)

Fig. 6. Sample calligraphy stoke from our prototype system to illustrate the impact of the variety of the ink. (a) A horizontal stroke with full-inking. (b) A horizontal stroke with medium-inking. (c) Blade-like calligraphic stroke with medium-inking. (d) Made with a drying splitting brush. (e) Character 'thousand' made with a drying splitting brush.

ink and the texture of a line; it creates the feeling of motion within a line (see Fig 6 (d) and (e)). This takes arduous labor and long practice before full control is gained, especially the changing of pressure while doing one stroke, such as press-lift-press, or vice versa.

In learning to write, school children were usually taught to practice it by facsimile the artwork of famous artistes. Fig 8 (a) is the facsimile template of the stroke 'Ti', which illustrates the flow of the stroke 'Ti'. Beginner put a paper on the template, then facsimile the stoke again and again. Nowadays, computer are widely used in our daily life. Base on our system we can develop a Chinese calligraphy learning and practice system, which not only is convenient for learning writing, but also economizes on paper, which has practical significance.

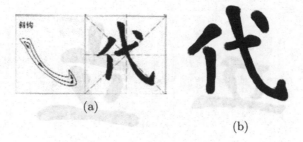

(a)

(b)

Fig. 7. (a) Digitized image of a real art work. (b) The image generated by our prototype system.

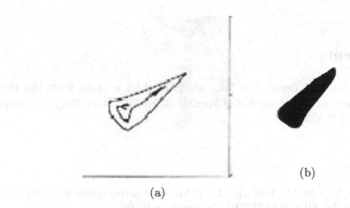

(b)

(a)

Fig. 8. (a) Digitized image of a real art work. (b) The image generated by our prototype system.

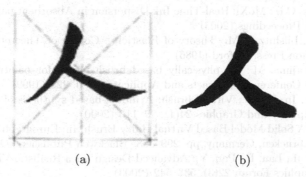

(a)

(b)

Fig. 9. (a) Digitized image of a real art work. (b) The image generated by our prototype system.

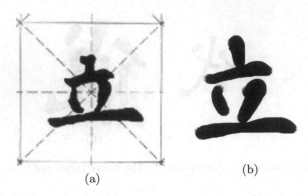

(a)   (b)

Fig. 10. (a) Digitized image of a real art work. (b) The image generated by our prototype system.

Acknowledgments

The work described in this paper was fully supported by a grant from the Research Grants Council of the Hong Kong Special Administrative Region, China [Project No. CityU 121205]

References

1. Baxter, B., Scheib, V., Lin, M., Manocha, D.: DAB: Interactive haptic painting with 3D virtual brushes. In: SIGGRAPH 2001 Proceedings (2001)
2. Chu, N.S., Tai, C.L.: An efficient brush model for physically-based 3D painting. In: Proc. of Pacific Graphics (2002)
3. Chu, N.S., Tai, C.L.: Real-Time Painting with an Expressive Virtual Chinese Brush. IEEE Computer Graphics and Applications 24(5), 76–85 (2004)
4. Chu, N.S., Tai, C.L.: MoXi: Real-Time Ink Dispersion in Absorbent paper. In: SIGGRAPH 2005 Proceedings (2005)
5. Landau, L.D., Lifshitz, E.M.: Theory of Elasticity, Course of Theoretical Physics, vol. 7. Pergamon Press, Oxford (1986)
6. Saito, S., Nakajima, M.: 3D physically based brush model for painting. In: SIGGRAPH 1999 Conference Abstracts and Applications, p. 226 (1999)
7. Wong, H.T.F., Ip, H.H.S.: Virtual brush: A model-based synthesis of Chinese calligraphy. Computers and Graphics 24(1), 99–113 (2000)
8. Xu, S., et al.: A Solid Model Based Virtual Hairy Brush. In: Eurographics 2002 Proceedings, Saarbrucken, Germany, pp. 299–308. Blackwell Publishers, Oxford (2002)
9. Xu, S., Tang, M., Lau, F., Pan, Y.: Advanced Design for a Realistic Virtual Brush. Computer Graphics Forum 22(3), 533–542 (2003)

Exploratory Learning for Computer Networking

Colin Allison, Alan Miller, Kristoffer Getchell, and Thomas Sturgeon

School of Computer Science, University of St Andrews, Jack Cole Building,
North Haugh, St Andrews, FIFE, KY16 9SX, Scotland
{colin, alan, kg, tommy}@cs.st-andrews.ac.uk

Abstract. Computer networking is a dynamic and naturally engaging subject which is important to many aspects of life. There are, however significant challenges to be overcome before a student can engage with the dynamism of the subject. These can be categorised as barriers of time, space and access. From the perspective of time, many of the interactions occur at timescales that are outside of the range of human perception; from the perspective of space, a student's location will often define their view of the network; from the perspective of access, programming skills are often required. We have sought to address these challenges through the creation of network learning objects designed to be used in lectures, laboratories or by remote learners. In this paper we assert the effectiveness of an exploratory approach to the teaching of networking and identify technologies which aid the development of exploratory learning environments.

Keywords: TCP, WiFi, Exploratory Learning, Computer Networks.

1 Introduction

It is hard to overstate the importance of computer networking in the modern world as more and more features of daily life rely upon network connections, from mobile phones to web browsers to "mission critical" monitoring systems. Consequently, it is a major requirement for Computer Science and Information Technology curricula to foster effective learning in this area. In keeping with a broadly socio-constructivist theory of learning we believe that effective learning is most likely to take place when a student learns through *doing*, sometimes referred to as *experiential learning*. Experience comes from interaction rather than passive presence, and students are more likely to be engaged with, and seek to understand a topic, if they can interact with some artifacts or manifestations of it. The interaction may be with simple animations, simulations, or real world contexts. Exploratory learning environments allow students to follow their own learning trajectories through interaction with suitably sculpted learning objects. Learning through experimentation is a specific type of exploration, and an approach we seek to inculcate in all scientific discovery. Accordingly, a laboratory, real or virtual, is a very useful facility. As a further consideration, lasting understanding is rarely achieved through a single illumination – it more typically involves crossing the line between puzzlement and comprehension on several

H. Leung et al. (Eds.): ICWL 2007, LNCS 4823, pp. 331–342, 2008.
© Springer-Verlag Berlin Heidelberg 2008

occasions, and from different perspectives. Hence one of the benefits of exploratory learning environments is that they can be revisited as often as the learner wishes.

Computer networking is well supported by established texts, for example [1-4], but these texts and traditional lectures are not enough to create an effective learning environment, especially where time is limited and networking is only one of many topics in a crowded curriculum. The approach we have taken is to create exploratory learning environments that are interactive, realistic, highly available, and can either complement traditional teaching in a blended learning approach, or be used to directly support distance learning.

The following two sections describe case studies of exploratory learning environment design and implementation. These are, in chronological order: TCPView [5] and the WiFi Virtual Laboratory (WiFiVL) [6]. Following on from these case studies a brief review of related work is given. Some current work in progress on a new learning environment is then described before concluding and discussing future work.

2 TCPView

TCP currently carries over 85% of all Internet traffic and is a complicated protocol, providing a reliable, full duplex, end-to-end, byte stream abstraction on top of the best effort Internet Protocol (IP) for application-level protocols and programs. TCPView seeks to support exploratory learning and complement the traditional "texts and lectures" approach by: i) emphasising the use of interactive diagrams and animations; ii) exploiting the use of interactive 2D visualisations; iii) supporting varying levels of conceptual complexity so it can be used from first year undergraduate through to postgraduate level; iv) introducing novel 3D visualisations of TCP efficiency; v) providing a comprehensive set of references to key publications, standards documents and protocol stack implementations.

The original implementation used Java applets for all graphical content. After some experimentation and review it was decided to use Flash for certain types of interactive animations as it better supports a movie frame approach with standard {stop, start, pause, single-step} buttons. For interactive animations it was decided to use alternate visual metaphors to represent the same protocol feature. Figs. 1 and 2 are snapshots from two animations which represent the same "TCP Open" protocol feature. The well known TCP state-transition diagram, found in the original RFC standards document [7] and reproduced in most texts, is also presented as an interactive animation with options to highlight different transitions to help understand the respective client and server states, the macro state and the micro state. Similarly the oft drawn *sawtooth* graph is interactive so the user can experiment with varying the probabilities of packet loss to see how that affects the congestion window maintained by the transmitter (see Fig. 3). The 3D efficiency grapher is based on work by Ruddle, Allison and Lindsay [8, 9] and represents a depth of view into TCP that is not typically presented in text books (see Fig. 4).

Fig. 1. A Packet Exchange animation

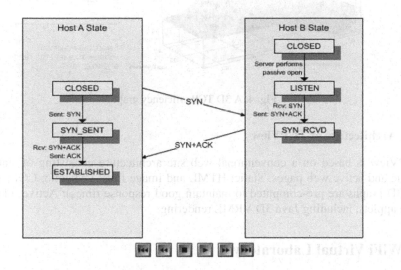

Fig. 2. A Time-Event animation

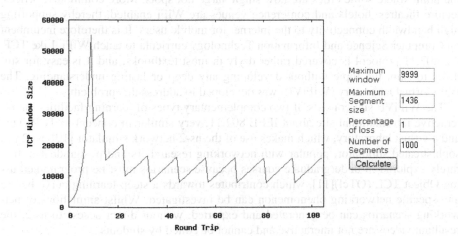

Fig. 3. An interactive TCP Congestion graph

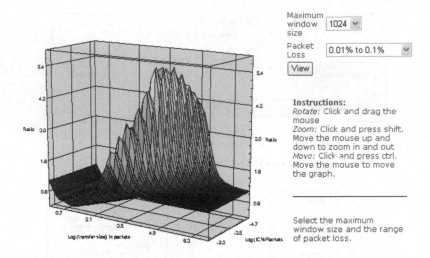

Fig. 4. A 3D TCP efficiency graph

2.1 Architecture of TCPView

TCPView is based on a conventional web site architecture consisting of static, dynamic and active web pages. Static: HTML and image files; Dynamic: CGI (some of the 3D graphs are pre-computed to maintain good response times); Active: Flash and Java applets, including Java 3D VRML rendering.

3 WiFi Virtual Laboratory

IEEE 802.11 wireless networking protocols have become increasingly pervasive, to the point where some cities are now single large hot spots. More commonly, offices, lecture theatres, hotels and conference venues are WiFi enabled, thereby supporting high bandwidth connectivity to the Internet for mobile users. It is therefore incumbent on Computer Science and Information Technology curricula to teach WiFi. Like TCP, the 802.11 protocol is covered rather dryly in most textbooks, and it is easy for students to skim the topic without developing any deep or lasting understanding. The WiFi virtual laboratory (WiFiVL) was developed to address this problem.

The WiFiVL site consists of two complementary types of learning facilities, an interactive informational site about IEEE 802.11, very similar in concept to TCPView, and a virtual laboratory, which makes use of the ns-2 network simulator [10]. ns-2 is a sophisticated simulator, popular with networking researchers and postgraduates. It is rarely explored in undergraduate courses because scenarios must be programmed using Object TCL (OTcl)[11], which contributes towards a steep learning curve before any specific networking phenomenon can be investigated. Whilst animations of networking scenarios can be generated and exported, without direct access to ns-2, the resultant videos are not interactive and cannot be edited by students.

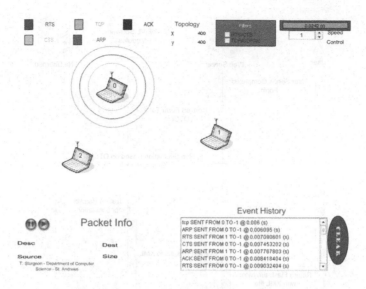

Fig. 5. Output from a WiFiVL simulation

WiFiVL enables transparent use of ns-2 for 802.11 simulations through any web browser. The input is taken from users through an HTML form or alternative front end, and the output is a Flash animation that can be paused, rewound, and speed controlled (see Fig. 5). Users can add nodes, create traffic links between nodes, specify higher level protocols such as FTP/TCP or UDP, specify either the start and stop times for links or the amount of data to be transferred, and other parameters such as signal reach. Once a student is familiar with setting up simple simulations they can be asked to carry out virtual scientific experiments, such as creating the hidden or exposed terminal scenarios. By referring to dynamically generated graphs, users are able to see changes in network behaviour by monitoring the different types of packets being sent onto the network.

3.1 Architecture of WiFiVL

The parameters for a simulation are gathered from a submitted HTML form and used to build an OTcl input. The OTcl is passed to the ns-2 server which generates a simulation event list and a network animation (.nam) file. The .nam file is translated to XML which is returned to the user's browser (see Fig. 6).

One of the main technical challenges was the use of Flash to display a discrete event simulation, where events are scheduled against the simulation time base. The particular combination of Flash and ActionScript was chosen because it is available cross-platform, it is commonly bundled or installed with popular browsers and it is capable of displaying high quality animations. However ActionScript, unlike Java, does not provide threads with "sleep" or timing capabilities, which are necessary for switching between events in simulations.

This challenge has led to an innovation, the development of a scheduled execution stack written in ActionScript. The scheduler is implemented as an ActionScript class

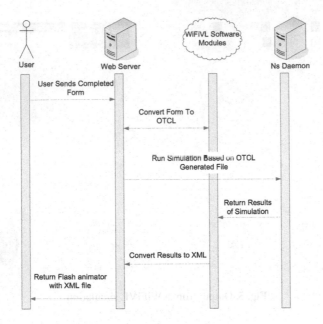

Fig. 6. Architecture of the WiFiVL

that controls the execution of simulation events in Flash (see Fig. 7). The scheduler processes a list of events that are to be executed in the future. This has been implemented as an XML file. The events list is checked with every new frame to see if any events need to be animated and thus removed from the list. The animation of a sequence involves mapping real time to simulation time. While the Flash animation is being displayed to the user a new frame is called periodically. This interval and event are used as a slice of execution time in the system. The speed of animation is 50 frames per second, with each frame considered to be 1/35000 (s) of simulation time. This divisor can be changed by the user to control the speed of playback.

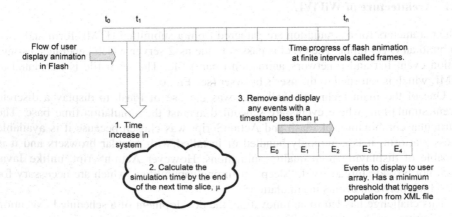

Fig. 7. Event switching in Flash

4 Evaluation

TCPView and WiFiVL are used as an integral part of the core Computer Science curriculum at the University of St Andrews. They have both been evaluated and positively received by students [12]. We have conducted a systematic evaluation of both systems whilst they have been used as part of the 3rd year Data Communications and Networks module which was taken by 34 students. This evaluation looked at system usability, perceived and observed educational value and system performance.

In both cases, supervised lab sessions were undertaken as part of the course. At the start of these lab sessions, a brief introduction to the topic of the session and to the tools of the session (either TCPView or WiFiVL) was given. Students were asked to work through lab sheets which involved answering questions relevant to the subject area by setting up simulations or interacting with demonstrations. They were required to write up and submit this work which was formatively and summatively assessed.

During the lab sessions, passive observers took notes on students' interactions with the systems, their effectiveness in completing the lab sheets and system performance. Interviews were also conducted with lecturers, students and tutors. At the end of each session students were asked to complete two questionnaires addressing system usability and educational value.

The System Usability Scale (SUS) [13] was used to evaluate the intuitiveness of the user interface. SUS uses a Likert scale where users are asked to rate a statement from strongly agree (1) to strongly disagree (5). The results are converted into a value between 0 and 100 representing the usability of a system, where a higher result represents better usability. One advantage of SUS is its widespread use which facilitates understanding of the results and comparison between different systems. The second questionnaire addressed educational content. It was modeled on SUS, using 10 questions to solicit user responses. The questions used were domain specific, for example, for the WiFiVL lab one question was: "Constructing and playing a simulation of the hidden terminal problem helped me understand it". In the TCPView session, questions were similarly tailored to the topic, for example: "The visualisation of TCP efficiency helped me understand the protocol."

4.1 TCPView Evaluation

The graph in Fig. 8 highlights the results returned in the TCPView evaluation. As can be seen in the graph, the results are skewed to the right indicating a broadly positive SUS response from users.

On a scale from 1 to 5, with 1 being strongly disagree and 5 being strongly agree, the average response for the cohort was 4.1 for the question "I would imagine most people would be able to use this system very quickly" and 2.2 for question 8, "I found the system very cumbersome to use", indicating that the respondents agreed with the first statement and disagreed with the second. Individual SUS scores were calculated for each respondent. The upper quartile of the resultant scores was 78.8, the lower quartile 63.8, with a median of 70.0. These results are consistent with our observations and comments solicited in interview, and strongly suggest that users found the system easy to learn and intuitive to use.

In terms of perceived educational value, similar results were obtained with the cohort returning a median score of 77.5, an upper quartile 87.5 and a lower quartile of 60.0. In particular the users found that the animations provided believable information, responding to the question with an average score of 4.5. Users also strongly confirmed that they could easily follow TCP connection open and closure state transitions using the system, returning an average score of 4.3.

Whilst TCPView is designed to support individuals learning at their own pace, a strong sense of team working was witnessed in all evaluation sessions, with neighboring students routinely grouping together whilst referring to TCPView in order to collaboratively develop their understanding before completing their own answers to the lab sheets.

In addition to the TCPView site, students were frequently witnessed accessing additional information sources using the links section of TCPView as well as popular search engines such as Google. The sections of the Wikipedia online encyclopedia relating to the TCP protocol [14] were also popular amongst many of the evaluation participants. When accessing external sites, most students made use of multiple browser windows, or tabs, to allow them to quickly switch between the TCPView site pages and those provided by external information resources. On occasion students working in groups coordinated their efforts, using multiple neighboring computers to simultaneously display TCPView and external pages; thereby allowing them to easily confirm their understanding using multiple data sources in parallel.

TCPView was designed to minimise the need for real time calculations and consequently server performance is similar to that of static web pages. The server was easily able to handle the load placed on it by 30-40 simultaneous users.

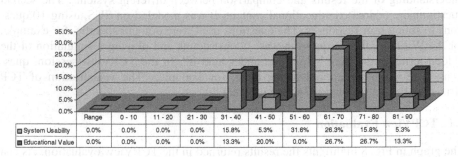

	Range	0 - 10	11 - 20	21 - 30	31 - 40	41 - 50	51 - 60	61 - 70	71 - 80	81 - 90
System Usability	0.0%	0.0%	0.0%	0.0%	15.8%	5.3%	31.6%	26.3%	15.8%	5.3%
Educational Value	0.0%	0.0%	0.0%	0.0%	13.3%	20.0%	0.0%	26.7%	26.7%	13.3%

Statistical Measure	System Usability Score	Educational Value Score
Max, Min, Mean	100.0, 42.5, 70.4	97.5, 50.0, 70.0
UQ, LQ, Median	78.8, 63.8, 70.0	87.5, 60.0, 77.5
Inter Quartile Range	15.0	27.5

Fig. 8. TCPView System Usability Scale and Educational Value Scores Breakdown

4.2 WiFiVL Evaluation

The results obtained from the SUS evaluation of WiFiVL are shown in the graph in Fig. 9. The results indicate that users found the system relatively easy to learn and intuitive to use. The lower quartile SUS score was 52.5, the median 61.3 and the upper quartile 71.9. These scores are good; however they are systematically lower than those for the TCPView site. This, in part, reflects the fact that the WiFiVL allows for more complex interactions than TCPView. Hence there is a steeper learning curve which we feel is rewarded by the existence of a richer set of interactions. This conclusion is supported when responses to the educational content are considered. For example, in response to the question "I feel I have learned something by using this system", an average score of 3.9 was returned. Users also strongly agreed that "constructing and playing a simulation of the hidden terminal problem helped me understand it", returning an average score of 3.9. Considering the scores for all questions for this questionnaire, the upper quartile was 76.9, the median 67.5 and the lower quartile 50.0. This indicates that the learners found the system to be educationally beneficial.

In addition to the lab session, student performance in answering questions on WiFi in examinations has been evaluated and is presented in some detail in [12]. The results showed that a higher percentage of students who had used WiFiVL opted to answer a question on WiFi than those who had not accessed WiFiVL.

Whilst the number of students scoring at the very high level did not change, there were fewer students who performed poorly. The decrease in poor performance indicates that WiFiVL has helped students grasp the basics of the 802.11 protocol. These are strongly positive results. Direct observation and informal interviews were conducted which confirmed that students found the WiFiVL beneficial.

A systems performance evaluation of WiFiVL was undertaken. The findings indicate that a single server such as a 1GHz Pentium 3, producing a varied load of simulations at an average rate of one every 20 ms, can serve a class of approximately 80 students while maintaining a response time of one second. In the case of a simple scenario such as two nodes and one data transfer the response time indicates that a much larger class could be supported without degradation.

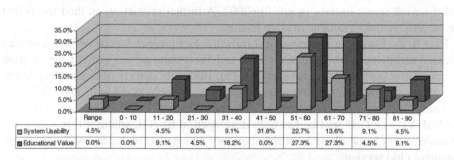

Statistical Measure	System Usability Score	Educational Value Score
Max, Min, Mean	100.0, 10.0, 61.4	97.5, 25.0, 64.3
UQ, LQ, Median	71.9, 52.5, 61.3	76.9, 50.0, 67.5
Inter Quartile Range	19.4	26.9

Fig. 9. WiFiVL System Usability Scale and Educational Value Scores Breakdown

WiFiVL is still evolving and many of the operating issues currently experienced are concerned with the nature of the simulation visualisation. For example, as elapsed network time in microseconds is slowed down by orders of magnitude for the animation there are periods where nothing appears to be happening. In future versions these "idle" phases will be flagged and may be skipped by the user.

A facility for collaborative parameter setup, and the storage, retrieval and sharing of specific simulations is being developed. Highly structured virtual scientific experiment support using IMS-Learning Design [15] is also being investigated.

5 Related Work

In this paper our focus is the development of exploratory learning environments. Although there are many innovative and interesting approaches to teaching computer networking, relatively few are well documented, non-commercial, and provide facilities via the ubiquitous web browser to support exploration. A notable exception is found in the approach adopted by Mark Holliday of Western Carolina University [16], which aims to make the principles of computer networks accessible to both computer science majors and other non-computer science students. Java applets are used to present an animated interface to the learner. The applets serve two roles; firstly they provide a visual representation of different scenarios and secondly they act as a vehicle for experimentation, allowing the learner to explore at their own pace. Sliding window protocols and 802.3 (Ethernet) are among the topics supported.

The potential of using ns-2 for educational purposes has been recognised elsewhere, notably at the Information Sciences Institute, University of Southern California where ns-2 is maintained. A web page is dedicated to "Ns and Nam with Peterson and Davies' Computer Networks" [17]. Unfortunately, there are not many animations, and the work seems to have stopped in 2002. A further restriction on their use is that the outputs are only available in .nam format.

ELeGI, the European Learning Grid Infrastructure project, has developed a service oriented architecture which exploits Grid and Web standards to support the creation of innovative learning environments [18, 19]. Research aspects of exploratory learning in general include "E-Learning architectures", such as ELeGI, and "Units of Learning" support schema such as IMS-Learning Design (IMS-LD) [15]. A version of the WiFiVL as a Grid service has been developed in ELeGI, where it forms part of a larger Wireless Networking Virtual Laboratory which also includes a sensor network simulator Grid service.

IMS-LD provides a framework that can be used to formally describe an educational scenario. A learning design is a method which allows learners to accomplish particular objectives by undertaking activities that interact with a learning environment, gaining knowledge as they progress. By supporting multiple delivery methods IMS-LD allows learning objects to be transferred and reused in any number of different learning scenarios.

6 Work in Progress: Active Learning with Planetary Objects

Network programming exercises in educational contexts often face several limitations. If a popular teaching language such as Java is used then lower level entities, such as IPv4 and ICMP datagrams, cannot be constructed from scratch. Institutional firewalls often preclude generation and observation of traffic on wide area Internet paths and experiments carried out on local, or campus area networks do not typically display characteristics reflecting congestion, loss, delay and variance in times that are found on the global Internet.

Active Learning with Planetary Objects (ALWPO) [20] seeks to overcome these limitations by exploiting the PlanetLab overlay network [21]. PlanetLab was introduced to support network research across the global Internet. Nodes are exempted from institutional firewalls as all security is enforced within the customised Linux OS that is used. There are over eight hundred Planet Lab nodes spread across the world, and any participating institution can request a "slice" consisting of any subset of these nodes. This means, for example, that an experiment could be set up from a Scottish node which involves transferring data streams from Brazil to China. PlanetLab is used primarily for research and ALWPO is relatively unusual in using it for education. Most PlanetLab users are researchers who have a set of programming skills and low-level systems expertise that is not present in undergraduates. Accordingly, the main challenge for ALWPO is to make low-level datagram creation and the sending and observation of packets accessible to students who have limited time and minimal low level programming skills. We are addressing this challenge through the creation of an easy to use web-based GUI.

7 Conclusions

We have identified challenges in supporting effective learning about computer networking and described how we are meeting them through the use of web technologies for exploratory learning. Two case studies have been described which reflect different but complementary approaches. TCPView features interactive animations and graphing facilities whilst WiFiVL goes further by providing a virtual laboratory based on the ns-2 network simulator. A third approach, ALWPO, is a work in progress which will make it possible for students to easily create, send and observe datagrams on the real wide area Internet.

We see the next major stage in the evolution of the exploratory approach involving the refinement of learning environment components and services, and the provision for creating, storing and sharing virtual scientific experiments. For example, all the environments contain elements that can be used for different aspects of TCP education, but this currently involves jumping between web sites with different contexts, presentational themes and technical foci. It would be highly useful if a lecturer could easily select just the aspects of TCPView, WiFiVL and ALWPO that they want for a particular class and organise them into a bespoke learning environment.

Acknowledgements

The TCPView, WiFiVL and ALWPO projects have been partially supported by both the UK's Higher Education Academy for Information and Computer Sciences Development Fund, and the University of St Andrews Fund for Initiatives in Learning, Teaching and Assessment. These projects would have not have progressed as far as they have without this valued assistance.

References

1. Comer, D.: Computer Networks and Internets. Prentice-Hall International Editions (1999)
2. Kurose, J.F., Ross, K.W.: Computer Networking. Addison-Wesley, Reading (2001)
3. Peterson, L., Davie, B.: Computer Networks. Morgan Kaufmann, San Francisco (2003)
4. Tanenbaum, A.S.: Computer Networks. Prentice-Hall, Englewood Cliffs (2002)
5. TCPView, http://tcp.cs.st-andrews.ac.uk/
6. WiFi Virtual Laboratory, http://wifi.cs.st-andrews.ac.uk/
7. RFC 739: Transmission Control Protocol, http://www.ietf.org/rfc/rfc0793.txt?number=793
8. Lindsay, P., Ruddle, A., Allison, C.: Visualisation of TCP Behaviour. In: 3rd Annual Postgraduate Symposium on the Convergence of Telecommunications, Networking and Broadcasting, JMU, Liverpool, UK (2002)
9. Ruddle, A., Allison, C., Nicoll, R.: Analysing the Latency of WWW Applications. In: Software Practice and Experience, pp. 1301–1322. Wiley, Chichester (2003)
10. The Network Simulator - ns-2, http://www.isi.edu/nsnam/ns/
11. Object Tcl Extensions, http://bmrc.berkeley.edu/research/cmt/cmtdoc/otcl/
12. Sturgeon, T., Miller, A., Allison, C.: A WiFi Virtual Laboratory. In: 7th Annual Conference for the Higher Education Academy Subject Network for Information and Computer Science, Higher Education Academy, Dublin, Ireland (2006)
13. System Usability Scale, http://en.wikipedia.org/wiki/System_Usability_Scale
14. TCP, http://en.wikipedia.org/wiki/Transmission_Control_Protocol
15. Learning Design Best Practice and Implementation Guide. IMS Global Learning Consortium (2003)
16. Holliday, M.: Animation of Computer Networking Concepts. ACM Journal of Educational Resources in Computing 3(2), 1–26 (2003)
17. Ns and Nam with Peterson and Davie's Computer Networks, http://www.isi.edu/nsnam/ns/edu/peterson_and_davie.html
18. Allison, C.: Learning from E-Learning: Initial Experiences from the European Learning Grid. In: Developing a Framework for E-Learning, University of Greenwich, UK (2006)
19. Allison, C., et al.: Services, Semantics and Standards: Elements of a Learning Grid Infrastructure. Applied Artificial Intelligence 19(9–10), 861–879 (2005)
20. Oliver, I., et al.: Using Disruptive Technology for Explorative Learning. In: 12th ACM CSE Annual Conference on Innovation and Technology in Computer Science Education, ACM Press, Dundee, UK (2007)
21. PlanetLab – An open platform for developing, deploying, and accessing planetary-scale services, http://www.planet-lab.org/

Application of an Online Judge & Contester System in Academic Tuition

Adrian Kosowski[1], Michał Małafiejski[1], and Tomasz Noiński[2]

[1] Department of Algorithms and System Modeling, Gdańsk University of Technology
Narutowicza 11/12, 80-952 Gdańsk, Poland
[2] Computer Architecture Department, Gdańsk University of Technology
Narutowicza 11/12, 80-952 Gdańsk, Poland
{kosowski,mima,noix}@sphere.pl

Abstract. The paper contains a description of the SPOJ online judge and contester system, used for E-Learning of programming, which has been successfully applied in the tuition of students at the Gdańsk University of Technology. We study the implementation of the system with security demands and present our experiences connected with the use of such systems in academic courses at an undergraduate and graduate level in the last four years.

1 Introduction

Gaining experience in the design and analysis of algorithms and data structures is one of the most important steps of the initial part of the learning process for students of computer science. The management of related courses can be easily automated using E-Learning platforms, such as Blackboard [1] or Moodle [2]. However, due to the very nature of programming assignments, for such courses one further step of automation is possible: the E-Learning platform may not only serve as an online document repository and communication medium, but may also perform tasks related to the automated assessment of user-submitted programs.

Historically, such an approach was first adopted for early programming contests, mainly in order to decrease the strain on the staff responsible for grading, and to ensure an entirely impartial and immediate judgment of submissions from all participants. This lead to an increase of popularity of similar systems designed for training purposes, usually in the form of websites known as *online judges*, providing their services to potential contestants and other enthusiasts intent on improving their programming skills. But the application of online judges in formal E-Learning, especially in compulsory university tuition for computer science students, turns out to be a somewhat more complex process, which has only recently started gaining popularity [3, 4].

Herein we present some results of the first four years of operation of the SPOJ online judge system [5], which was developed in the years 2003–2007 [6, 7]. At present it is, to the best of our knowledge, the only online judge system designed

H. Leung et al. (Eds.): ICWL 2007, LNCS 4823, pp. 343–354, 2008.

specifically to serve as a convenient web-based host platform for multiple, possibly simultaneous, E-Learning courses in programming (with a special focus on algorithm-related aspects).

The SPOJ system can be seen as an implementation of two concepts: an online judge and an E-Learning platform. The objective of an *online judge* is automatic evaluation of user-submitted programs. Such programs, being solutions to specifically stated problems, are typically compiled and run on a given set of input data. The output of programs is then evaluated — either simply by comparison (with output known to be correct) or with a dedicated *judge* program. Such a *judge* is necessary especially in case of problems with multiple correct answers. An example would be a problem of finding the shortest path in a graph: there might be multiple shortest paths in a given graph. In such situation, it is most convenient to write a judge program which only knows the length of shortest paths for every test-case and knows how to tell if output of the program is a correct path in the graph. In extreme cases, it is not even necessary to know the correct solution to be able to write a program which assess correctness.

SPOJ allows not only for binary-evaluated problems with only two choices — a correct or incorrect solution. Solutions to problems might be associated with a *score*, e.g. being the number of positively solved test-cases. It might also be used for optimization problems, where many solutions might be acceptable, but the score depends on the quality of the result.

2   Conducting University Courses with SPOJ

The SPOJ system has in the last four years been applied in the teaching of many algorithmic and programming courses at the university, even in mathematical and theoretical courses, like logic and set theory or cryptography. The large number of more than 30 programming languages makes it possible to compare advantages and disadvantages of languages and different paradigms of programming: structural, object-oriented and functional. In this section we describe our experiences of using the online judge and contester system. We focus on those courses in which the staff was able to communicate personally with the students participating in the course at weekly or biweekly intervals (rather than pure E-Learning courses). Most were accompanied by regular lectures, and some also by classroom exercises.

2.1   Human and Automatic Grading

A comparison of human and automatic grading can be found in [3,4], where the relative merits of both grading systems are discussed in detail based on a single programming course at the National University of Singapore.

The automatic grading model of the SPOJ system tries to overcome the disadvantages of human grading. The system is assumed to collect all the electronic submissions and checks its correctness and efficiency in real-time. This makes it much easier to evaluate the correctness, time efficiency and resource usage of programs for both random and worst-case instances of test data. Some complementary elements of the assignment, such as user interface designs, additional documentation, or source code quality, may still be optionally assessed by a human grader (the human factor is crucial when designing large business applications, but far less important when teaching programming languages, design and analysis of algorithms or advanced topics like numerical and probabilistic methods at an undergraduate level). The rapid feedback allows students to eliminate many source code errors at once. The experience gained while designing dozens of *correct* programs allows them to avoid logical and design errors in the future. Other advantages include grading consistency, no special treatment, rejudgeability (in case of staff errors), and easier adaptability of programming assignments to participants.

The SPOJ system realizes the E-Learning paradigm: the individual work of students can be performed at home or at university, or generally at any place with Internet access. This is in keeping with trends in information technology societies with access to knowledge and education via web technologies.

2.2   Academic Courses and Programming Challenges

For the four last years, SPOJ has been used in more than ten courses, as well as for programming interest groups of different universities. In this section we present a detailed analysis of the courses in Gdańsk and the specific demands of each of them.

Online Contester for Undergraduate Courses. The introductory level of the programming skills is approached on the two basic courses at the first year: Fundamentals of Programming, and Design and Analysis of Algorithms, where the students learn the C/C++ programming languages and study data structures (heaps, binary search trees and graphs) and dozens of algorithms (sorting, set operations, hashing, graph algorithms, pattern recognition, geometry algorithms, etc...). The students have to choose the appropriate data structure and design an efficient algorithm with a bounded computational complexity to solve each of about 50 easy and hard problems with a strict specification and i/o examples.

Besides these two courses, we experimented with using the online judge on mathematical courses, like Logic and Set Theory, where many of pure theoretical concepts could be adopted to its algorithmic versions, for example recognizing the cardinal numbers, satisfiability problems, equivalence axioms or calculator of (infinite) ordinal numbers. The proposed new methods of teaching pure theoretical topics meet with a great approval from students (most of them from computer science faculty).

Online Contester for Graduate Courses. At first glance, advanced algorithmic and theoretical topics do not seem compatible with automated grading, but we have successfully managed to teach them using the online judge and contester system on the graduate courses: Differential Numerical Methods, Computer Modeling of Systems (probabilistic aspects of random sequences, advanced numerical modelling problems in engineering), Internet Modeling (analysis of search engine strategies, routing algorithms, small-world graph phenomenon), Combinatorial Algorithms, Discrete Optimization Algorithms and Graph Theory (advanced algorithms including numerous matching and flow-based problems), Fundamentals of Cryptography, Dynamics of Object-Oriented Programs (advanced dynamic aspects of the STL library for the C++ programming language), Scripting Languages (Perl, Python), Design of Expert Systems (CLIPS). The problems were usually long-term assignments, requiring solid basics in theory and time to design and analyze the correct approach to solving them. In a few isolated cases, the system was used only as a repository with the automated plagiarism detection facility of source codes, which were graded manually by the staff members.

Online Contester for Programming Contests. Currently, SPOJ is a platform bundling many local, regional and international programming contests, organized in different manners: from the very shortest which last a few hours, through contests of one or several days, to month or year-long programming leagues. The contest organizers come from different countries and frequently organize the entire contest in their native language.

It is worth pointing out that in terms of the amount of work required, organizing such a programming contest is comparable with organizing a course for students. Some tasks are drawn from the archive set of more than 1500 available problems, the remainder are original tasks put forward by contest setters. The ranking system is flexible, allowing the contest setter to generate participant rank list tables in arbitrary format, using a plugin software module which can be designed and installed by the contest setter (without requiring the supervision of system administrators), or chosen from a predefined set.

2.3   Implications of the SPOJ System for Computer Science Courses

Having integrated the online judge and contester system with the academic tuition system at the Gdańsk University of Technology and taking into account four years' experience with the system, we attempt to formulate some conclusions which describe the major advantages and disadvantages of using such a system in teaching at an academic level.

General Concerns. First of all, from the point of view of staff members the system has the positive effect of reducing the amount of effort required to evaluate programs delivered by students. Instead of this, the tutors can devote their time to describing ideas of how to solve the problem to those students who require assistance. Moreover, it is quite easy to adaptively modify the hardness of a single problem so as to match the level of students at different levels of proficiency, e.g. by using the mechanism of multiple test cases of varying difficulty.

From the students' point of view, there have been many important advantages: instantaneous feedback on the quality of the submitted solution, simple and unvarying principles of grading the solutions, an unlimited number of attempts allowed to solve the problem (for most courses), different points for solutions of different quality, consistency (accepted solutions in the system are treated as accepted by all staff members, unless other rule violation is detected). The system also helps develop the ability to create (and possibly share) good generators of test data and sequences used for debugging purposes. At an initial level, it teaches students to correctly interpret the limited feedback provided by the operating system and software layer of the online judge to detect the location of errors in programs.

Distribution of Grades. The distribution of grades in a SPOJ-based contest can be easily influenced by its organizer by manipulating the number of assignments and the grading systems with restricted deadlines. One interesting effect may be achieved by giving students a large number of assignments to choose from (with the maximum score exceeding the number of points required to achieve the maximum grade even several times). This is especially advantageous for students in their initial year: it encourages them to choose problems which they are capable of solving, at in this way to improve their skills at their own level. Achieving a pass grade is dependent mainly on the amount of work done. An example for the course in the Design and Analysis of Algorithms is presented in Fig. refplot1. It can be observed that a relatively small number of students are directly below the pass threshold; this is the result of self-motivation of the student (and not the flexibility and sympathetic approach of the staff, since grading is entirely automatic). The awareness of the current score helps students better allocate time spent on solving next assignments, or perhaps skipping them if there are more pressing concerns. But as is evident from the figure, a large proportion of the students go far beyond the score required for the maximum grade, trying to do as many of the assignments as possible for their own benefit and enjoyment.

The conversion of points to grades is up to the individual preferences of the course supervisor. In general, it is easiest to fix a scale in advance and make it known to the students. This can sometimes result in a deviation of the distribution of grades from the Gaussian distribution, with a noticeable inversion of counts of the two topmost grades. Such an effect is explained by some of the students in the top 10th to 25th percentile taking more interest in the course than they would normally do, and is as a rule acceptable from the point of view of university authorities.

Statistical Properties. One of the most interesting properties which become evident when applying an online judge is that as a rule students skilled at programming achieve good results more effortlessly than unskilled programmers achieve a minimum pass grade (though, as seen from Fig. 1, those who try consistently usually manage it). This is especially true for algorithm courses in which it is important to write entirely correct programs. Less skilled programmers

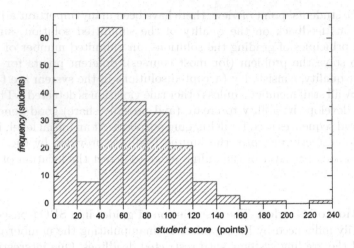

Fig. 1. Distribution of participant score for a sample E-Learning course for undergraduate students (pass threshold is 40 points, top grade threshold is 100 points)

tend to write longer and worse designed sections of code for the same actions, thus spending more time programming and especially debugging code. Figure 2 shows the change of the amount of source code created (measured by a parameter known as McCabe's cyclomatic complexity [8]) per single point earned in the previously considered Design and Analysis of Algorithms course, for students who achieved a different final rank in the course. The range in between the two dashed vertical lines represents ordinary students who pass the course, but do not solve problems after receiving top grades; throughout most of this range the effort per point gained decreases when moving towards top-ranked students. To the left of left vertical line the effort increases, since the top students decide to solve some of the toughest problems for their own benefit. In the right part of the graph, the effort per point also decreases slightly, in the range where students choose only the very simplest problems required for a pass. The other plot in Fig. 2 is a measure of source documentation; there is a slight, but clear correlation between the rank of the student and the amount of documentation in the code. The observation that the quality of source code improves maintainability and helps decrease debugging time is made by most of the students, even when the staff does not impose any code quality requirements on the assignments submitted to the online judge.

Student Work Model. It is undeniable that the application of SPOJ influences the model of work of students throughout the term. To begin with, the system has been found to have a marked disciplining effect, compelling students participating in the course to treat all upcoming deadlines seriously, since they are enforced by the judge (it is also impossible e.g. to submit a semi-completed

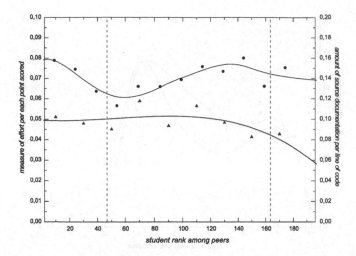

Fig. 2. Averaged measures of solution source code characteristics as a function of student rank (from top rank 1 to bottom 190): participant's coding effort per unit of gain (circles, left); an exemplary measure of participant's code quality (triangles, right)

project directly before the deadline, hoping for partial points). There are in general two approaches to deadlines for SPOJ assignments: one consists in automatically cutting off the possibility of submission after a given date and time, the other — in automatically adding penalty points for late submissions, depending on their lateness. Some course supervisors also choose to reward early submissions with a bonus score. Figures 3 and 4 show student activity in the days preceding and following the deadline for a sample programming problem of implementing an interpreter of a simple functional programming language. The problem was disclosed to the students 15 days before the deadline, and submission of solutions was allowed from 10 days before the deadline to 20 days after the deadline; solutions could be submitted by each student an unlimited number of times. The score of a submission was assessed as 0 points for an incorrect submission or 5 to 10 points for a partially correct submission, also depending on its efficiency. The total score of a user was increased by a bonus of 0.25 points per day for early submission and a penalty of 0.5 per day for late submission. Figure 3 shows that there are two main periods of peak activity: directly after submitting becomes possible (since then most of the top students attempt to solve the problem) and directly before the deadline. Figure 4 shows values of two characteristics for each day, averaged over all students submitting on the given day: the count of submissions made per single point earned and the maximum score achieved. Maxima of the count curve correspond to solving days with low success rates — usually directly after a large group of students starts submitting, but before they develop a satisfactory solution. The descent after the left peak of this curve corresponds to the maximum of the quality curve,

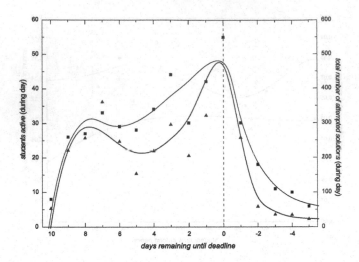

Fig. 3. Contest activity for a selected problem as a function of the number of days remaining till the deadline: number of active students (squares, left) and total number of submitted solutions per day (triangles, right)

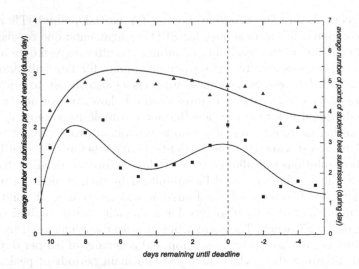

Fig. 4. Change of average characteristics of solutions submitted to a problem as a function of the number of days remaining till the deadline: number of solutions submitted per student per day with respect to the total number of points earned in consequence (squares, left); average number of points of all active students' best solutions on a given day (triangles, right). Bonus points and penalties dependent on submission date are not included.

and marks the dates on which most of the skilled "pioneers" manage to solve the problem. After this date the problem is solved by the predominant group of students, with slightly inferior programming skills, and the quality curve shows a gradual decline.

The presented example may be considered representative of most programming assignments at SPOJ, but the exact distribution of activity is affected by events such as bank holidays or mid-term examinations and may be different in some cases. The number of waves of activity may increase from 2 to 3 or more if the assignment is available for more than two weeks; nevertheless the wave directly before the deadline is always the largest. There are also rare exceptions to the changes of solution quality characteristics in time. For example, if the main difficulty of the problem consists in its idea (finding the right approach), then the characteristics can reflect an apparent decrease of difficulty of the problem in time, as word spreads among the students on how to solve the problem.

3   System Architecture, Security and Performance Evaluation

In order to increase maintainability and security, the SPOJ system is divided into several modules. Most components communicate with each other via SQL database. It is a simple solution and makes it unnecessary to implement dedicated network protocols, as components mostly do not communicate with each other directly.

The user-visible component is the web interface. It is the only interface a regular user really needs access to (optionally, users can receive confirmation mails for each submission via the *mail* component). Another crucial component is a *checker*. It is responsible for compiling, running and judging submitted programs in a secure manner. Typically there are more than one, grouped by processor speed into *checker groups*.

SPOJ currently spans across three dedicated server nodes with four processors each: a publicly-available master node and two slaves in an internal subnetwork. While slave nodes host only *checker* components, master node runs the rest — including SQL server and the WWW component. Each node has four physical processors and each checker host four *checker* components, so there are currently eight indistinguishable *checkers* in this deployment.

In an online judge system, security is absolutely crucial. SPOJ is open not only for university students attending programming courses, but also for anonymous participants from the Internet. Potentially users may have malicious intentions and they might benefit from bypassing security restrictions if they were able to. A successful attacker might influence students' grades, deciding about failing or passing a course, or choose the winners of a short-term contest with money prizes.

SPOJ users have diverse permissions. While certain people, like course teachers or contest committee, should be able to see sources and results of programs written by a group of participants, a regular user should at most be given only the possibility to retrieve his already submitted programs and see limited feedback information about the results. SPOJ puts its users into five main categories: system administrators, problem-setters, contest-setters, regular users and non-registered users with different privileges.

Modularization is an important part of securing a system. SPOJ is a sufficiently large project to be separated into several components, not necessarily trusting each other. Therefore, potential damage caused by compromising a single component is hopefully minimized. Components are run on separate physical systems or at least with different privileges. It is also essential that *checker* computers do not have access to the Internet, so even after being compromised their value for an attacked is very limited. An additional layer of security is provided by an isolated backup server, performing daily database snapshots and also storing all submitted programs before they are being compiled and run.

Running programs from untrusted users in a secure manner is the hardest and probably most vulnerable part of the system [3]. User interface to the system is www-based, so only standard http ports are exposed to a potentially malicious user. An attacker is forced to perform remote attacks against a web application, which exposes only a small part of the system. However, running compiled programs is an entirely different matter. Programs are run locally on dedicated machines and a potential attacker has considerably more attack vectors: he can conduct local attacks against the checker software as well as against the program's interpreter or the operating system.

There are two approaches to restricting user-submitted programs in an online judge environment:

- programming language level,
- operating system level.

The former approach, restricting a program on the programming language level might seem tempting at first. For a compiled language like C++ or Pascal it might mean scanning the source code for unwanted constructs (like certain function calls) or modifying the compiler or libraries so it does not allow operations from of a prepared black-list. However, it would be quite error-prone, as it is easy to forget about one "dangerous" function, not black-list it and therefore make SPOJ vulnerable. Also, in a low-level language like C it is possible to prepare a specially-crafted piece of machine code, insert it into a table and execute it by a low-level cast.

Although this approach does not seem reasonable for the reasons given, programs in some languages (especially interpreted ones) could be securely restricted in this way. One example might be Java, with a powerful security infrastructure at the JVM (java virtual machine) level. Anyway, in a multi-language online judge system like SPOJ restrictions at this level can only be used as an additional layer of security and it seems obvious that restrictions at operating system level are most important.

All checker computers are running Debian GNU/Linux. A stable Linux 2.6 kernel has been additionally hardened with grsecurity patches [9]. Untrusted programs have to be executed very carefully. The most obvious restriction is running such a process as a separate user, so that the operating system ensures this process cannot send signals to other processes in the system. SPOJ also utilizes `chroot()` - a very powerful Linux system call. It allows creating filesystem sandboxes, different for every programming language allowed by SPOJ. Grsecurity patches extend chroot-jail's semantics, imposing additional restrictions on a chrooted process.

Another heavily used Linux features are *rlimits*, i.e. per-process resource limits - especially for memory and time used. Although `RLIMIT_CPU` limits cpu time spent by a process, it does not take into account time spent on waiting for blocking system calls like `sleep()`. A malicious user might send a program which, for example, almost does not use any cpu time at all, but sleeps for two days, hogging the checker machine. Such a situation is prevented by another wall-time limit, imposed by a dedicated process watching the untrusted processes. It is also worth noting that any user submitted program is considered untrusted. Not only solutions to the problems, but also problem-setter-submitted judges, contest-setter submitted ranking generator programs and even compilation. Treating compilation process as unsafe might seem excessive, but in reality there are many languages letting the programmer do some cpu-intensive work at compile-time. For example, without a time-limit for compilation, an attacker might monopolize a *checker* with a C++ program that uses tricky templates or with a C program beginning with "`#include </dev/urandom>`".

Some restrictions would be easier to apply if it was possible to request that all user-submitted programs use exactly one system process and one thread. Unfortunately, some compilers or interpreters enforce use of threads even for the simplest program. For example, a Java "`Hello world!`" program spawns about 6 system threads (with Linux and the newest stable version of Sun's JVM at the moment of writing). Multiple system processes also make it harder to kill untrusted processes reliably. In addition, it is worth noting that mainline Linux uses an unreliable, sample-based algorithm for measuring processes' CPU time (for performance reasons). For a system like SPOJ, Linux kernel had to be patched to use more reliable mechanisms: using processor tick counters instead of wall time and measurement on every context switch instead of sampling.

4 Conclusions and Future Work

In the last four years the SPOJ system has proved to be a robust and secure E-Learning platform for programming assignments. As shown by the example of the Gdańsk University of Technology, and also other universities, it can be of much help in academic tuition — both alleviating much work from the teaching staff and providing a fair and educational programming course for the students. It does of course display some of the shortcomings of a typical E-Learning platform, resulting from the lack of personal communication between students and staff. However these effects can usually be countered by the internal mechanisms of the SPOJ system (ensuring that students always solve problems at their own level of advancement) or by constructing additional communication channels between students and staff.

In the future we plan to extend the functionality of the SPOJ system both in the layer of the online judge and web-based E-Learning platform. An extension of the judging system will allow for the automated grading of programs working in a dynamic environment, such that input provided to the program depends on its previous output, for use in game theory problems and physical modeling and simulation. In a more general case, this feature could be used in problems where one program competes or cooperates with other programs submitted by different participants.

Finally, for the E-Learning platform, a lot of user feedback suggests the introduction of more flexible communication mechanisms, known informally as "web 2.0". One of the proposed changes would introduce a wiki-like page structure to the contest, allowing staff members enhanced collaborative management of site content. This would also stimulate official discussions between students, and also allow for parallel versions of the same assignment problems, such as translations into different languages, or simplified texts with hints on the solution method.

Acknowledgment

The authors would like to express their gratitude to the TASK Academic Computer Center [10] for hosting the SPOJ system on its hardware.

References

1. Blackboard: http://www.blackboard.com/
2. Moodle Project: http://moodle.org/
3. Cheang, B., Kurnia, A., Lim, A.: Online judge. Computers and Education 36, 299–315 (2001)
4. Cheang, B., Kurnia, A., Lim, A., Oon, W.-C.: On automated grading of programming assignments in an academic institution. Computers and Education 41, 121–131 (2003)
5. Sphere Online Judge: Gdansk University of Technology, http://www.spoj.pl/
6. Kosowski, A., Małafiejski, M., Noiński, T.: Security in the Sphere Online Judge system. In: XIII Conference on Networks and Computer Systems, Łódź, Poland, pp. 663–670 (2005) (In Polish)
7. Janczewski, R., Kosowski, A., Małafiejski, M., Noiński, T.: Application of SPOJ cooperative contest management in the university tuition system (in polish). Annals of the Gdansk University of Technology 10, 365–370 (2006)
8. McCabe, T.: A complexity measure. IEEE Transactions on Software Engineering SE-2(4) (1976)
9. The Grsecurity Project: http://www.grsecurity.net/
10. TASK Academic Computer Centre: http://www.task.gda.pl/

Assessing the Learners' Motivation in the E-Learning Environments for Programming Education

Yasuhiro Takemura[1], Hideo Nagumo[2], Kuo-Li Huang[3],
and Hidekuni Tsukamoto[4]

[1] Department of Character Creative Arts, Osaka University of Arts, Osaka, Japan
yasuhi-t@osaka-geidai.ac.jp
[2] Department of Social Welfare and Psychology, Niigata Seiryo University,
Niigata, Japan
nagumo@n-seiryo.ac.jp
[3] Department of Visual Communication Design, Southern Taiwan University of
Technology, Tainan, Taiwan
z3z@mail.stut.edu.tw
[4] Department of General Education, Osaka University of Arts, Osaka, Japan
hide1123@osaka-geidai.ac.jp

Abstract. In this paper, a pedagogical system to visualize the students' motivation states for learning programming is proposed. This system can be used in E-Learning environments so that the instructors can assess the students' motivation states in real-time. This system is based on the *Systematical Information Education Method* (SIEM) assessment standard proposed by Dohi [1], which is used to assess the students' motivation to learn programming. In order to visualize the students' motivation states, the correlations between the factors in the SIEM assessment standard are mapped on the width of the arcs of the graph whose nodes are the factors in the standard. As the preliminary experiments, the introductory programming courses were offered to the students in the art design and digital design faculties at two universities. It has been found that in order to maintain or raise students' motivation it is more important to allow students to enjoy viewing the final results (artwork) of the programming than to make them strive to create more beautiful artwork.

1   Introduction

In E-Learning systems that utilize the computer networks, it is difficult to grasp the students' motivation to learn because there is little face-to-face communication between the instructors and the students. Even in the face-to-face sessions, it is very important to understand the students' motivation states because it will enable the instructors to make very effective teaching strategies. In recent E-Learning systems, there have been a lot of improvements in the function of getting feedback from the students, and that of offering the course materials that are suitable to each student based on his/her personal profile [2]. However,

H. Leung et al. (Eds.): ICWL 2007, LNCS 4823, pp. 355–366, 2008.

there have been few systems that allow the instructors to assess the students' motivation states. In this paper, a pedagogical system to visualize the students' motivation states for learning programming is proposed.

In this system, the students' motivation states are evaluated through some evaluation items that are based on the *Systematical Information Education Method* (SIEM) assessment standard proposed by Dohi [1]. The SIEM assessment standard is a metric that can be used to objectively measure students' motivation levels to learn programming. There are nineteen evaluation items in this standard and they are grouped into four factors. This assessment standard will be explained in section 4. In order to visualize the students' motivation states, the correlations between the factors in the SIEM assessment standard are averaged, and the average values are mapped on the width of the arcs of the graph whose nodes are the factors in the standard. With this graph, which we call the *correlation structure graph*, it is easy to grasp which factor would affect the students' motivation most, and the instructors would be able to use this information to adjust their strategies to give instructions.

As the preliminary experiments, the introductory programming courses were offered to the students at two universities: university A in Japan, and university B in Taiwan. The motivation levels of the students were evaluated using the SIEM assessment standard. Since our interest was related to the appreciation of beauty, an artistic programming environment called Processing [3] was used in these experiments, and the students at the universities were in the art design faculty and digital design faculty. Those students learn programming because some artistic works are directly created through programming. Also, they will be able to improve their environments for creation if they really understand the mechanisms of the computer application they use for creating their work by learning computer programming [4]. Processing has the following attractive features for using in the introductory programming courses: (1) Fine artwork can be created from relatively simple codes, (2) It is open source and is widely available, and (3) The syntax in Processing is similar to the one in Java, which is a widely used programming language.

The teaching materials used in these experiments were designed in accordance with the ARCS motivation model [5] as much as possible so that the students would be adequately motivated. The ARCS motivation model is a widely used educational theory that describes the factors involved with the motivation to learn, and was introduced by J. M. Keller [5]. This model will be explained in section 3.

The motivation for learning has been studied by many researchers. R. Pekrun, T. Goetz, and W. Titz evaluated the attitude of students toward learning, and confirmed that the academic emotion of students correlates to achievement, motivation to learn, and self-regulated learning [6]. For programming education, M. Feldgen and O. Clúa studied students' favorite exercises among calculus, engineering, business, and games by analyzing their homework. They verified that the students' preferred context was games [7]. In order to minimize the drop-out rate of the students in the distance education courses, W. Jun, L. Gruenwald, J. Park, and S. Hong introduced a new model to provide motivation to students [8]. Their model is based on the principles of *constructivism*. Their model provides students' motivation according to the four types of interactions: students-teachers, students-students, students-contents, and students-experts. Also for keeping attrition rate low, Z. W. Abas and his team developed a motivation model based on Horton's recommendations for a motivating environment to help sustain the students' interest [9].

2   The Programming Courses

In university A, six among the 14 classes of the "Introduction to Information Technology" course were used to teach programming. The class met once a week, and the duration of each class was 90 minutes. Therefore, nine hours in total was used for teaching programming. There were 84 second-year students in the class and all of them were from the art design faculty (character design). In university B, programming was taught in the "Computational Figures and Animation Processing" course. This was an intensive lecture and it took four days: three hours on the first day, three hours on the second day, six hours on the third day, and six hours on the fourth day. Therefore, 18 hours in total was used for the course. The duration of one class was 50 minutes. There were 53 students in the class, and they were all from the digital design faculty (Information Communication, Visual Communication Design, Multimedia and Entertainment Science, and Graduate School of Digital Content and Animation). There were all year levels of students, from first-year to graduate school, mixed in the class.

The common syllabus for the two courses is shown in Table 1. As shown in the table, the course contained 14 topics (not in the same duration). The course started with an introduction to computers and an introduction to Processing,

Table 1. Syllabus of the programming courses

Topic	Title	Contents
1	Computers and Processing	hardware and software, characteristics of Processing
2	How to use Processing	statements and comments, coordinates, basic figures, color
3	Variables	variables, arrays
4	Repetition	for sentence, nested for
5	Conditional branch	if sentence
6	Creation of 2D figures	creation and appreciation of 2D figures
7	3D Figures	commands for drawing 3D figures
8	Displaying images	images, background images
9	Algorithms of animation	the algorithm for creating moving images
10	Mouse input	mouse click, coordinates of a mouse point
11	Bezier curves	creation of artwork with Bezier curves
12	Fractal figures	fractal figures, creation of artwork with fractal figures
13	Creation of animation	creation of animation
14	Conclusions	concluding remarks

and then moved on to how to use the Processing programming environment. It was followed by the basics of programming, such as variables, repetition, and conditional branches. In topic 6 (Creation of 2D figures), the first free design assignment was given to the students, and they designed artwork without animation effects. After that, 3D figures were briefly introduced, and the ways to display images were taught. The ways to make animation and the ways to make the students' artwork interactive with mouse input were taught next. In topic 11 and 12, the functions to generate Bezier curves and Fractal trees were taught so that the students could make attractive animation. In topic 13 (Creation of animation), the second free design assignment was given to the students, and they designed artwork with animation. The course was summarized in the last class.

3   The ARCS Motivation Model

For designing our introductory programming courses with Processing, the ARCS motivation model [5] played a very important role. In particular, our teaching materials used in this study were designed in accordance with the ARCS motivation model as much as possible. This model assumes that there are four factors in motivation: *attention, relevance, confidence,* and *satisfaction.* This model also gives the sub-level categories of the characteristics of motivation for each factor.

The first factor of the ARCS motivation model is *attention.* To be motivated for learning, the attention of the students must be aroused and maintained. This characteristic of motivation has three sub-level categories: A.1. *perceptual arousal,* A.2. *inquiry arousal,* and A.3. *variability. Perceptual arousal* is meant to arouse attention by using the visual function of the computer. The aesthetic satisfaction of the resulting artwork can be used as this stimulus. *Inquiry arousal* is meant to arouse curiosity in the students. In order to raise the students' curiosity levels, they were asked to guess the codes of some given works of art instead of guessing the artwork from the given codes. *Variability* is important for maintaining students' interest. In order to arouse *variability*, works of art can be changed from still images to moving images, and to the artwork that receives mouse input.

The second factor of the ARCS motivation model is *relevance.* The students might ask why they should learn programming, and wonder if there is any relation between programming and their sense of value, experiences, career, and so on. If these questions are answered adequately, the motivation levels of the students will be raised. This motivation characteristic has three sub-level categories: R.1. *goal orientation,* R.2. *motive matching,* and R.3. *familiarity. Goal orientation* was naturally met because the students were in the art and digital design faculty. For *motive matching,* the students must be provided with appropriate choice, responsibilities, and influences. The students were asked to create their own artwork in their free assignments. For *familiarity,* the students were asked to create symmetrical 2D patterns with which students are familiar using repetition and conditional branch.

The third factor of the ARCS motivation model is *confidence*. This characteristic of motivation has three sub-level categories: C.1. *learning requirements*, C.2. *success opportunities*, and C.3. *personal control*. For enhancing *learning requirements*, some examples that are similar to the exercise problems were shown to the students. In order to give students *success opportunities*, some example problems in which changing some parameters would create very attractive artwork were given to the students. For *personal control*, the students could use their own creativity to create their original work, in which case the students were able to attribute their success to their own talent.

The fourth factor of the ARCS motivation model is *satisfaction*. This characteristic of motivation has three sub-level categories: S.1. *natural consequences*, S.2. *positive consequences*, and S.3. *equity*. Natural consequences could be satisfied simply because the students could use their newly acquired knowledge in their own work. For *positive consequences*, the students' works of art were appreciated thereby providing reinforcement to the students' success. For *equity*, the students were encouraged to continue learning Processing so that they could embed their positive feelings about their accomplishments in their studies.

4   Evaluation Method of Motivation

4.1   The Assessment Standard

For measuring students' motivation levels, the SIEM assessment standard [1] was used. This standard uses the ARCS motivation model [5] as the background theory, and many evaluation items in this standard are related to the sub-levels in the ARCS motivation model. There are nineteen evaluation items in the SIEM assessment standard, and are grouped into four factors: Factor 1 *Class Construction Factor*, Factor 2 *Spontaneity Factor*, Factor 3 *Interaction Factor*, and Factor 4 *Attendance Factor*. We added one more group that contains two evaluation items related to the artwork generated by Processing because our particular interest was whether the appreciation of beauty would arouse the motivation of the students to learn. The added items were tested independently from other groups.

In the article [1], the time series evaluation using the SIEM assessment standard was conducted three times in a semester: early in the semester, halfway through, and late in the semester. The evaluation was conducted in the same way in our experiment. Each evaluation item is presented using a five-point *Likert* scale.

The evaluation items of the SIEM assessment standard as well as the added evaluation items are shown in Table 2. In this table, the added items are item (20) and item (21). Item (20) is similar to item (5), but its question is more specific and related to the results of Processing programming instead of general programming. Item (21) is similar to (9), but its question is more specific to Processing.

Table 2. SIEM assessment standard with added evaluation items

Factor 1: Class construction factor	
(1) Success opportunity	Do you think you have gained a sense of accomplishment by learning and comprehending classroom instruction?
(2) Familiarity	Do you think that the course contains friendly content?
(3) Pleasure	Do you think this programming class is enjoyable?
(4) Comprehension	Do you think that the programming course is easy to comprehend?
(5) Perceptual arousal	Do you think it's fun to see how the program you design and input works?
(6) Significance	Do you think the purpose and the significance of the course is clear?
(7) Curiosity arousal	Do you think your curiosity is aroused in class?

Factor 2: Spontaneity factor	
(8) Usefulness future	Do you think that the knowledge learned in this class will be useful in the future?
(9) Improvement effort	Do you think you want to study more about computer programming?
(10) Self control	Do you think you want to study in your own unique way by utilizing the knowledge gained in your classes?
(11) Self goal	Do you think that the learning goal which you should attain is clear?

Factor 3: Interaction factor	
(12) Communication	Do you think you communicate well with your teacher and fellow students?
(13) Positive consequence	Do you think that teachers and fellow students are friendly to you?
(14) Equity	Do you think the assignment corresponds with the course contents?

Factor 4: Attendance factor	
(15) Attendance enthusiasm	Do you think your class motivates you enough not to be absent?
(16) Activation scale	Do you think you are active in class?

MV evaluation items	
(17) Importance	Do you think studying computer programming is crucial?
(18) State recognition	Do you think you have acquired enough computer knowledge and skills?
(19) Expectation	Do you think you would like to gain more computer knowledge and skills?

Evaluation items for Processing	
(20) Perceptual arousal	Do you think it's fun to see the results of Processing programming?
(21) Improvement effort	Do you think you want to strive to create more beautiful artwork with Processing?

Though all of the items are used for evaluating students' motivation levels, there are two particular items, (17) and (19), which are used to calculate the motivation index (abbreviated as "MV" in this paper). MV is calculated as Equation (1).

$$MV = (17) \text{ Importance} \times (19) \text{ Expectation} \tag{1}$$

In a prior study, it has been found that there was a correlation between the added items about Processing, (20) and (21), and the items that were used to calculate MV, (17) and (19) [10]. In other words, there was a correlation between the aesthetic satisfaction and the motivation levels to learn programming.

4.2   Analysis Method

The data of the SIEM assessment standard were analyzed, and the *correlation structure graphs* are drawn in the following manner. In **P1** the general tendency of the learners is analyzed. In **P2** the correlation coefficients between evaluation items are calculated. In **P3** the correlation coefficients calculated in **P2** are transferred into the values that represent the correlation between each pair of the four factors in SIEM assessment standard, the factor of MV evaluation items, and the factor of the evaluation items about Processing. In **P4** the *correlation structure graph* is drawn using the values that represent the correlations calculated in **P3**. In **P5** this structure is visually analyzed.

P1 The basic statistics (mean, maximum, minimum, and variance) of the SIEM assessment standard are calculated.

P2 The correlation coefficients between each pair of the evaluation items are calculated.

P3 The correlation coefficients calculated in **P2** are processed statistically.

　P3.1 The significance of the correlation coefficients is tested using the table of "distribution percentage point of correlation coefficients," and the significant correlation coefficients are extracted.

　P3.2 The mean, S_{xy}, of the significant correlation coefficients, between the items in Factor X and those in Factor Y is calculated.

　P3.3 The ratio, F_{xy}, of the significant correlation coefficients, between the items in Factor X and those in Factor Y is calculated.

　P3.4 The correlation, R_{xy}, between Factor X and Factor Y is calculated with the following equation:

$$R_{xy} = S_{xy} \times F_{xy}.$$

　P3.5 The correlation R_{xy} is transferred to the integer value, M_{xy}, used in the *correlation structure graph* system with the following equation:

$$M_{xy} = \text{INT}(R_{xy} \times 10).$$

P4 M_{xy} is input into the *correlation structure graph* system, and the correlations among Factor 1 through Factor 4, the factor of Processing, and the factor of MV are drawn as the graph in which the width of each arc corresponds to M_{xy}.

P5 The widths of the arcs of the graph are visually analyzed.

5   Experimental Results

The students' motivation to learn programming was evaluated using the questionnaires mentioned in section 4.

5.1   The General Tendency

The values of MV measured at different times at the two universities are shown in Table 3. Although MV taken early in the course at university A (17.1) was slightly higher than that of university B (17.0), MV became much higher at university B when it was taken late in the course. At university A, the time series evaluation of MV shows a decreasing tendency, while at university B, it shows an increasing tendency. A similar decreasing tendency of MV was reported in [1]. Since the teaching materials of programming become more difficult as time progresses, it is understandable to have decreasing tendency of MV. It is rather surprising to see the increasing tendency of MV at university B.

Table 3. MV of the students in the two universities

	Items	University A			University B		
		Early	Middle	Latter	Early	Middle	Latter
Total	Mean	17.1	13.9	12.7	17.0	17.7	18.9
	Maximum	25	25	25	25	25	25
	Minimum	6	1	1	8	8	9
	Variance	25.0	37.0	31.7	18.4	23.2	23.5
	Total	484	391	357	611	638	679
High group $10 \leq$ MV	Ratio	37.9%	10.3%	10.3%	38.9%	47.2%	50.0%
	MV mean	21.8	25.0	23.3	21.4	22.1	23.1
Medium group $10 \leq$ MV < 20	Ratio	51.7%	62.1%	48.3%	52.8%	50.0%	47.2%
	MV mean	14.7	15.1	14.2	14.4	14.2	15.0
Low group MV < 10	Ratio	10.3%	27.6%	41.4%	8.3%	2.8%	2.8%
	MV mean	8.0	5.6	7.3	8.0	8.0	9.0

In order to analyze the change in motivation of the students further, the average value of each factor in the SIEM assessment standard and the average value of Processing factor were calculated. Fig. 1 shows the transition of those values as well as MV. This figure suggests that there was a significant decreasing tendency in Factor 1 and Factor 2 for university A, and increasing tendency in Factor 1, Factor 2, and Factor 3 for university B.

To confirm this conjecture, t-test between the same evaluation items at different times were conducted, and the resulting p-values are shown in Table 4. In this table, the p-values less than or equal to 0.05 are highlighted with boldface letters. It can be noticed that there are many p-values that are less than or equal to 0.05 in Factor 1 and Factor 2 when t-test was conducted between Early and Middle for University A (third row from the top). Therefore, there is a statistical significance between the same evaluation items taken early in the course and of those taken halfway through the course for many items in Factor 1 and Factor 2, of a significant level of 5%. This fact proved that Factor 1 and Factor 2 for university A had actually dropped. Also, some p-values less than 0.05 can be found in the rows of university B for items (2), (6), (7), (11), and (12). In this case, the average values of those evaluation items actually increased.

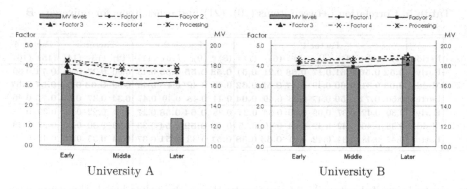

Fig. 1. Transition of the average value of each factor and MV

Table 4. t-test between the same evaluation items at different times

Univ.	Between	Factor 1							Factor 2			
		(1)	(2)	(3)	(4)	(5)	(6)	(7)	(8)	(9)	(10)	(11)
A	Early and Middle	**0.02**	0.06	**0.01**	**0.00**	0.18	**0.05**	**0.01**	**0.00**	**0.00**	**0.01**	0.66
	Middle and Latter	0.49	0.60	0.61	0.77	0.41	0.57	1.00	0.86	0.17	0.87	0.92
B	Early and Middle	0.49	0.66	0.83	0.15	0.82	0.80	0.62	0.70	0.30	0.21	**0.05**
	Middle and Latter	0.32	**0.01**	0.09	0.15	0.05	**0.04**	**0.03**	0.21	0.34	0.13	0.64

Univ.	Between	Factor 3			Factor 4		Processing	
		(12)	(13)	(14)	(15)	(16)	(20)	(21)
A	Early and Middle	0.64	0.56	0.25	**0.01**	0.26	0.06	**0.00**
	Middle and Latter	0.86	0.60	0.85	1.00	0.74	0.27	0.71
B	Early and Middle	0.47	1.00	0.74	0.28	0.29	0.06	0.64
	Middle and Latter	**0.00**	0.10	0.42	1.00	0.21	0.77	0.77

In order to investigate what made this rise in motivation of the students at university B, the correlation coefficients between the two evaluation items about Processing, (20) and (21), and other evaluation items were calculated. Those coefficients for university B are shown in Table 5. In this table the correlation coefficients greater than 0.5 are highlighted with boldface letters.

It can be found in this table that most of the items in Factor 1, Factor 2, and Factor 3 correlate to item (20) but not to item (21), though the items in Factor 2 correlate to both item (20) and item (21). This fact implies that in order to maintain or raise students' motivation it is more important to allow students to enjoy viewing the final results (artwork) of the programming than to make them strive to create more beautiful artwork, since the question for item (20) is "Do you think it's fun to see the results of Processing programming?" and the one for item (21) is "Do you think you want to strive to create more beautiful artwork with Processing?".

At university A, the grade of the course was determined by only one final assignment. Therefore it could be that the students at university A had to strive

Table 5. Correlation between items (20), (21) and other items for university B

Item	Period	Factor 1							Factor 2				Factor 3			Factor 4	
		(1)	(2)	(3)	(4)	(5)	(6)	(7)	(8)	(9)	(10)	(11)	(12)	(13)	(14)	(15)	(16)
(20)	Early	0.52	0.56	0.61	0.17	0.68	0.21	0.51	0.53	0.55	0.53	0.43	0.00	0.27	0.45	0.71	0.30
	Middle	0.63	0.31	0.60	0.49	0.87	0.55	0.62	0.49	0.49	0.41	0.40	0.39	0.63	0.59	0.57	0.57
	Latter	0.50	0.71	0.59	0.47	0.48	0.49	0.64	0.44	0.48	0.40	0.47	0.34	0.37	0.55	0.75	0.46
(21)	Early	0.30	0.42	0.37	0.09	0.30	0.33	0.23	0.38	0.64	0.58	0.27	-.06	0.22	0.44	0.39	0.33
	Middle	0.38	0.40	0.42	0.42	0.44	0.40	0.35	0.43	0.52	0.54	0.33	0.23	0.30	0.29	0.27	0.33
	Latter	0.42	0.48	0.34	0.42	0.21	0.63	0.58	0.51	0.33	0.51	0.37	0.34	0.35	0.45	0.48	0.42

to create beautiful artwork. At university B, on the other hand, the grade was determined by two exams, two assignments, two quizzes, and class attendance. Therefore, it could be that the students at university B enjoyed creating artwork with Processing more than the students at university A, and hence their motivation was maintained.

5.2   Analysis of the *Correlation Structure Graph*

The *correlation structure graphs* for the programming courses in university A and university B are shown in Fig. 2. In the *correlation structure graph* of university B, the width of the arc between Aesthetics (questions about Processing) and Factor 2 (*Spontaneity*) does not change much. However, the corresponding

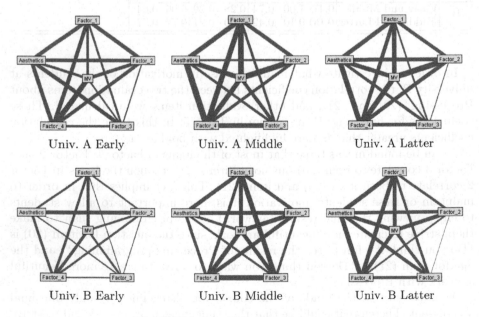

Univ. A Early   Univ. A Middle   Univ. A Latter

Univ. B Early   Univ. B Middle   Univ. B Latter

Fig. 2. The *correlation structure graphs*

arc of university A decreases from Early to Middle (although it increases from Middle to Latter). This fact suggests that the appreciation of beauty could not arouse *spontaneity* of the students at university A. The main difference between university A and university B is the duration of the courses. At university A, it was six weeks and class met once per week, while at university B, it was four days (intensive lecture). The students at university A had worked on the programming for almost four weeks when the second questionnaire was administered. Therefore, it is assumed that many students were tired of programming because of the long duration, and were working on the codes just because they wanted to finish the assignments, but not because they wanted to create more beautiful artwork. On the other hand, the students at university B could maintain the relation between appreciation of beauty and *spontaneity* until the second questionnaire was administered because they had worked on programming only for three days.

A similar thing could be said about the relation between Aesthetic and Factor 3. In this way, it is possible to assess the motivation of the students to learn programming by visually analyzing the *correlation structure graphs*.

6   Conclusions

An introductory programming course was offered to the students in the art design faculty and digital design faculty at two universities (A and B), and the factors that raise the motivation of the students to learn programming were analyzed. The programming environment used was Processing which can produce fine artwork with relatively simple codes. The teaching materials were designed in accordance with the ARCS motivation model as much as possible so that the students were adequately motivated to learn. In order to evaluate the students' motivation levels, the SIEM assessment standard was used.

In the time series analysis of motivation, it was found that the students' motivation increased at university B, while it dropped at university A. Looking at each factor of the SIEM assessment standard, there was decreasing tendency in class construction factor and spontaneity factor for university A, and increasing tendency in class construction factor, spontaneity factor, and interaction factor for university B. The correlation between the evaluation items about Processing and other items for university B reveals that in order to maintain or raise students' motivation it is more important to allow students to enjoy seeing the final results (artwork) of the programming than to make them strive to create more beautiful artwork. It was also found that it was possible to assess the students' motivation states to learn programming by visually analyzing the *correlation structure graphs*.

In future work, we plan to include the process to display the *correlation structure graphs* in our E-Learning systems, and investigate if it would improve our programming education.

Acknowledgments

This work was partly supported by Grants-in-Aid for Scientific Research of Scientific Research (C) No.19500832 from Japan Society for the Promotion of Science.

References

1. Dohi, S., Miyakawa, O., Konno, N.: Analysis of the Introduction to the Computer Programming Education by the SIEM Assessment Standard. In: Proceedings of the 6th International Conference of Information Technology Based Higher Education and Training. Session F4A, pp. 8–13 (2005)
2. Leung, E.W.C., Li, Q.: A Model for Personalized Course Material Generation Based on Student Learning Abilities and Interests. In: Liu, W., Li, Q., Lau, R.W.H. (eds.) ICWL 2006. LNCS, vol. 4181, pp. 25–37. Springer, Heidelberg (2006)
3. Fry, B., et al.: Processing 1.0 (BETA) (2007), http://processing.org
4. Takemura, Y., Matsumoto, K., Inoue, K., Torii, K.: A statistical analysis on the order of understanding for the Java programming language. In: Proceedings of the 7th World Multiconference on Systemics, Cybernetics and Informatics (SCI2003), vol. 16, pp. 294–299 (2003)
5. Keller, J.M., Suzuki, K.: Use of the ARCS motivation model in courseware design, ch.16. In: Jonnasen, D.H. (ed.) Instructional designs for microcomputer courseware, pp. 401–434. Lawrence Erlbaum Associates, USA (1987)
6. Pekrun, R., Goetz, T., Titz, W.: Academic Emotions in Students' Self-Regulated Learning and Achievement: A Program of Qualitative and Quantitative Research. Educational Psychologist 37(2), 91–105 (2002)
7. Feldgen, M., Clúa, O.: Games as a Motivation for Freshman Students to Learn Programming. In: Proceedings of the 34th ASEE/IEEE Frontiers in Education Conference. Session S1H, pp. 11–16 (2004)
8. Jun, W., Gruenwald, L., Park, J., Hong, S.: A Web-Based Motivation-Supporting Model for Effective Teaching-Learning. In: Fong, J., Cheung, C.T., Leong, H.V., Li, Q. (eds.) ICWL 2002. LNCS, vol. 2436, pp. 44–55. Springer, Heidelberg (2002)
9. Abas, Z.W.: Incorporating Motivational Elements in a Web-Based Learning Environment for Distance Students: A Malaysian Experience. In: Zhou, W., et al. (eds.) ICWL 2003. LNCS, vol. 2783, pp. 396–410. Springer, Heidelberg (2003)
10. Takemura, Y., Nagumo, H.: Analysis of the Relationship between Motivation for Learning Computer Programming and Computational Figures. In: Poster Paper Notes of the 14th International Conference on Computers in Education (ICCE2006), pp. 49–52 (2006)

Using Constraint-Based Modelling to Describe the Solution Space of Ill-defined Problems in Logic Programming

Nguyen-Thinh Le and Wolfgang Menzel

University of Hamburg, Department of Informatics
Vogt-Kölln-Str. 30
D-22527 Hamburg, Germany
{le, menzel}@informatik.uni-hamburg.de

Abstract. Intelligent Tutoring Systems have made great strides in recent years. Many of these gains have been achieved for well-defined problems. However, solving ill-defined problems is important because it can enhance the cognitive, metacognitive and argumentation skills of a student. In this paper, we demonstrate how to apply the constraint-based modelling approach to describe the solution space of ill-defined problems in logic programming. This technology has been integrated into a web-based ITS (INCOM) and has been evaluated with student solutions from past examinations.

Keywords: Ill-defined problems, error diagnosis, logic programming, constraint-based modelling, ITS.

1 Introduction

Intelligent Tutoring Systems (ITS) have made great strides in recent years. Many of these gains have been achieved for well-defined problems such as geometry, Newtonian Mechanics, and system maintenance [1]. However, by solving ill-defined problems students can gain more benefits:

1. Enhancement of cognitive skills: well-developed domain knowledge is a primary factor in solving ill-defined problems [2]. In solving ill-defined problems, students apply their domain knowledge in a meaningful way instead of storing a chunk of concepts in a memory [3].
2. Enhancement of metacognitive skills: ill-defined problems require solvers to control and regulate the selection and execution of a solution process [4], [5]. In the ill-defined problem solving process, students employ their meta-cognitive skills, such as changing strategies, modifying plans and reevaluating goals in order to reach an optimal solution [3].
3. Enhancement of argumentation skills: since ill-defined problems require students to consider alternative solutions, successful students can provide evidence for their solution [6]. Therefore, students gain practice justifying their solution in a logical way to persuade others.

H. Leung et al. (Eds.): ICWL 2007, LNCS 4823, pp. 367–379, 2008.
© Springer-Verlag Berlin Heidelberg 2008

For this purpose, we focus our research on a web-based programming ITS which supports students learning logic programming by solving ill-defined problems. Prolog is one of the most widely used logic programming languages. Prolog is considered to be difficult to learn because of the non-determinism of program execution, the under-specification of programming constructs and the concept of recursive programming which is the most important programming technique [7]. In general, the domain of programming is infinite. For a given programming task, there is no single solution, but many strategies to design a solution. For a strategy, there are many ways to implement them.

How can an ITS diagnose errors in the student solution for an ill-defined problem? Over the last two decades, numerous error diagnosis approaches in the domain of programming languages have been devised, such as program transformation [8], program verification [9], plan and bug library [10], model tracing [11] and constraint-based modeling (CBM) [12]. Among these, model tracing is used by cognitive tutors which are among the most successful ITS today [13]. However, those approaches have been applied to problems with a lower degree of ill-definedness. An ill-defined problem has not only a simple correct solution, rather many or even uncountably many. In this paper, we introduce the CBM approach to cope with the solution space for ill-defined problems in logic programming. In the next section, we review the characteristics of ill-definedness in the literature and argue why logic programming problems provided by INCOM are ill-defined. The solution space for a programming problem in Prolog is described in the third section. In the fourth section, we introduce CBM and how we apply it to model the solution space for a Prolog problem. In the fifth section we show our evaluation result. Our conclusions and future works are summarized in the last section.

2 Ill-defined Problems[1]

There is no formal definition in the literature of what constitutes a "well-defined problem". Instead, we must be content with requirements which have been proposed as criteria a problem must satisfy in order to be regarded as well-defined: 1) a start state is available; 2) there exist a limited number of transformation steps which are relatively easily formalized; 3) evaluation functions are specified and 4) the goal state is unambiguous [14]. If one or several of these conditions is violated, the problem is considered ill-defined [15]. Most researchers agree that a design problem is a representative of ill-defined problems [16], because the start state is underspecified, there is no predefined set of rules for completing the task, and it is difficult to evaluate when a "best" result has been attained. However, "the boundary between well-defined and ill-defined problems is vague, fluid and not susceptible to formalization" [17]. Thus, this vagueness and relativity should simply reflect the continuum of degrees of definiteness between the well-defined and ill-defined ends of the problem spectrum. Those problems, which lie somewhere in the middle between well-defined and ill-defined ends, may have well-specified start and goal states, but underspecified transformation rules or evaluation

---

[1] In this paper we have chosen the term ill-defined problem. The terms ill-structured and ill-defined are used interchangeably in the literature. To avoid confusion, we use the latter one.

functions because 1) there are multiple representations of knowledge with complex interactions; 2) the ways in which the rules apply vary across cases nominally of the same type [18] and 3) there are only aesthetic value judgments, but no quantitative measurements available.

Most programming problems, which are used to tutor Prolog, are simple and might have well-defined start as well as goal states. The problem text can be well specified and a solution can be verified whether it solves the given problem correctly. However, the activity of solving a Prolog programming problem is a design problem. The solution space is mainly spanned by using different Prolog primitives or applying mathematical rules. Furthermore, one can modularize a program in order to make the code clearer, easy maintainable and reusable, but all these criteria are highly subjective. That is why Prolog programming problems are ill-defined.

3   Solution Space for a Logic Programming Problem

We consider only Prolog programs without cuts, disjunctions or if-then-else operators. No assert, retract, abolish or similar database-altering predicate can be used. The set of built-in predicates which can be employed by the programs are: =, =.=, =\=, ==, \==, >, >=, <, =<, =.., +, -, *, /, ^ and 'is'. Auxiliary predicates are provided explicitly or can be defined by users.

To solve a logic programming problem, there are many solutions. The solution space results from a variety of Prolog primitives and programming techniques which describe standard solution strategies. The solution space is also determined by a set of general principles of Prolog. Furthermore, it is restricted by an appropriate predicate declaration which is developed interactively with the student prior to the implementation itself. The declaration information is used to gather the intention of the student, and to understand subsequent implementation of the student solution. In the following, we describe the solution space for a given problem in more detail.

Solution space spanned by Prolog primitives: a predicate is composed of a clause head and a clause body. A clause body contains several subgoals. Table 1 shows the possible variations of a clause head and of its subgoals. This collection is not a complete one, but also reflects specific restrictions imposed by the system. The following types of clause head and subgoals can be distinguished:

Clause head: a clause head is the first part of a clause of a predicate. The definition for a clause head must adhere to the predicate declaration: clause type (a base case, a recursive case or a non-recursive clause), argument types (atom, number, list or arbitrary) and argument modes (+, -, ?). A clause head may vary depending on the clause body, i.e. a (de)composition or a unification either takes place in the clause head implicitly or in the clause body explicitly.

Recursive: a recursive subgoal has the same functor and the same arity as its clause head. Arguments of a recursive subgoal inherit declaration information from the clause head such as: types, modes and argument meaning.

(De)-composition: a (de)composition subgoal composes an argument using other variables or decomposes an argument into several variables or constants. A (de)composition can be established implicitly at an argument position or can be represented explicitly as a separate subgoal.

Arithmetic test: an arithmetic test subgoal is used to compare two bound arguments which are of type number. There are two classes of arithmetic test subgoals. The first one applies the operators: <, >, =< and >= to test whether a number is greater/smaller than another one. The second class applies the operators: =:= and =\= to test whether two numbers are equal or not. The operands of the operators can be transposed because they are commutative.

Calculation: a calculation subgoal is used to compute an arithmetic expression using the operator 'is'. It requires that the variables on the right hand side of the subgoal are bound; otherwise the evaluation cannot be executed. We consider the following arithmetic operators: +, -, *, /, ^ and three forms for an arithmetic expression are distinguished: 1) Normal form: $A°X\pm B°X$; 2) Applying the distributive law and 3) Applying the commutative law where the operator $\pm$ is either + or -, and the operator $°$ is either * or /. Currently, we do not perform any transformation for exponential expressions: $(X+Y)^A$. We just consider the neutral elements: $X^1=X$ and $X^0=1$. The basis is regarded as an arithmetic expression with possible variants.

Unification: a unification subgoal unifies two variables or assigns a value to a variable using the operator =. The unification subgoal is referred to as an explicit unification. An unification can also occur if two different argument positions have the same variable name and this case is called implicit unification or co-reference.

Term test: a term test subgoal checks whether two terms are equivalent using the operators: == and \==. We also include the operator \= into the subgoal class because it tests whether two terms are not unifiable. All three operators are commutative.

Relation: a subgoal is a relation if a database is provided in which an appropriate relation is defined as a collection of facts. A relation can not be transformed.

Helper predicates: we restrict the space of helper predicates to the ones which build accumulation over lists or which are defined without using recursion. In general, the space of helper predicates is open-ended.

Table 1. Normal form and variation of clause heads/subgoals

Head/Subgoal	Normal form	Variants
Clause head	p(X,Y):-X=Y. q(X,Y):-X=[H|T].	p(X,X). q([H|T],Y).
Recursive	p([H|T],Y):-p(T,Y)	p([H|T],Y):-p(T,Y)
(De)composition	Explicit: p(X,Y):-X=[H|T], p(T,Y).	Implicit: p([H|T], Y) :- p(T,Y).
Arithmetic test	X<Y A=:=B A=\=B	Y>X; X-Y<0; Y-X>0; 0>X-Y; 0<Y-X; B=:=A B=\=A
Calculation	$A°X\pm B°X$	distributive: $(A\pm B)°X$ commutative: $X°A\pm B°X$, $A°X\pm X°B$, $X°(A\pm B)$
Unification	Explicit: p([H1|T1],[H2|T2]):- H1=H2, p(T1,T2).	Implicit: p([H|T1],[H|T2]):-p(T1,T2).
Term test	A==B; A\==B; A\=B	B==A; B\==A; B\=A
Relation	query(A,B,C)	query(A,B,C)
Helper predicate	help(A,B,C)	help(A,B,C)

Solution space spanned by patterns: to solve a problem in logic programming many programming techniques can be applied and combined. The programming techniques underlying a predicate definition determine the strategy of a problem solution. For example, to solve the problem of processing all elements of a list, one can choose between recursion by processing many elements or only one element. If only one element is processed, there are several possible alternatives: naive recursion, inverse recursion, recursion using an accumulation predicate or applying the railway-shunt [19]. Hence, for a given problem of Prolog programming, there are typical solution strategies which we refer to as patterns. The number of patterns spans the solution space for a given problem in logic programming.

Solution space spanned by a set of general principles of Prolog: the general principles of Prolog assure that a Prolog predicate definition is executable. The following is a subset of general principles of Prolog, which is not an exclusive list: variables on the RHS of a calculation subgoal must be bound; variables of arithmetic test and of term test subgoals must be bound; for a recursive implementation, at least a base (recursive) case is required.

Solution space spanned by the choice of names for variables and predicates: as we do not want to restrict students to a small space of solutions, they are allowed to choose any names for variables and predicates as they do without an ITS system. Therefore, the solution space for a programming problem in Prolog also becomes open with respect to the choice of names for variables and predicates.

Helper predicates: can be defined according to individual needs. There are two reasons to define a helper predicate: 1) to execute a necessary subtask and enable the re-usability and 2) to keep the code in the main predicate definition simple. Thus, the space of helper predicates which might be defined by each individual is open-ended.

4 Applying CBM Approach

4.1 Constraint-Based Modeling

The CBM approach has been proposed in [12] to model general principles of a domain as a set of constraints. A constraint is represented as an ordered pair consisting of a relevance part and a satisfaction part: Constraint C = <relevance part, satisfaction part> where the relevance part represents circumstances under which the constraint applies, and the satisfaction part represents a condition that has to be met for the constraint to be satisfied. Constraints are not only used to circumscribe facts, principles or conditions of a domain, they can also be used to specify the requirements of a task or to handle solution variations. Using the relevance part constraints can be tailored according to the semantics which represent the requirements of the given task [19]. If a constraint is violated, it indicates that the student solution does not hold principles of a domain or it does not meet the requirements of the given task. To evaluate constraints, we define a formal representation for constraints: ***constraint(Id, Type, Relevance,***

Satisfaction, Severity, Position, Hint[2]. Information about relationships between structural elements of a given Prolog program and a given predicate declaration are stored in three types of assertions: headarg, bodyarg and argmode where headarg and bodyarg contain information about each argument in the clause head and in the clause body, respectively. If an assertion of type argmode exists, it denotes that the argument is bound, after its corresponding subgoal has been executed [19]. As a result, the relevance and satisfaction parts of a constraint can be specified as conjunctions of assertions. The constraint evaluation is carried out as follows: first, the relevance part of the constraint is matched against a set of assertions. If there is a match, i.e. the constraint is relevant to the program, and then the satisfaction part is matched against the same set of assertions. If the satisfaction part is also fulfilled, then the Prolog program is considered to be correct with respect to that constraint. Otherwise, it indicates a shortcoming in the program and the corresponding information will be returned for instructional purposes: error location, constraint severity and hint encoded in the constraint [20].

4.2 Applying CBM to Model a Solution Space

There are two classes of constraints: semantic constraints and Prolog general constraints. The first one includes constraints which examine whether a solution object satisfies the requirements of a given problem. Constraints of the latter class examine whether the solution object fulfills general principles of Prolog. Prolog general constraints can be constructed as demonstrated in [19]. Semantic constraints are constructed based on a semantic table which contains information required to solve a given problem. Clause heads and subgoals in the semantic table are represented in normal forms (Table 2). The normal form representation reveals the underlying programming techniques and thus, the diagnosis becomes more accurate.

Table 2. An example of a semantic table

Head	Subgoal	Description
salary(OldL,NewL)	OldL=[] NewL=[]	Old list is empty New list is empty
salary(OldL,NewL)	OldL=[N,S|T] NewL=[N,Snew|Tnew] S=<5000 Snew is S+S*0.03 salary(T,Tnew)	N, S: name, salary build a new salary list Salary less than 5000 Salary is increased Decompose old salary list recursively

From this table, *headarg, bodyarg* and *argmode* assertions can be extracted. They are referred to as semantic assertions, while similar ones derived from the student

---

[2] Id is an unique identification; Type is one of pattern, general, head, recursive, arithmetictest, termtest, (de)composition, unify or calculation; Relevance is a relevance part; Satisfaction is a satisfaction part; Severity indicates the severity of the constraint, it ranges between zero if the constraint is important and one if it is informative; Position indicates the error location; Hint is an instructional message.

solution are referred to as student assertions. Assertions are used to construct semantic constraints. The diagnosis is carried out as an interaction of hypothesis generation and hypothesis evaluation. Hypotheses are interpretation variants for the student solution, which are generated by mapping the elements of the student solution to the ones of the generalized sample solution. At the same time, the systematic variations of the sample solution, which are created by applying transformation rules, are also considered. Every interpretation hypothesis is evaluated based on the relevant constraints. In addition, the score of the constraints, which are violated by the selected hypothesis, is computed based on a multiplicative model. That score is used to take a decision for the most plausible interpretation. Diagnostic information about the shortcomings of the student solution can be gained from constraint violations as well as from the hypothesized mapping between the student solution and the generalized sample solution.

From the vertical view, the interaction of hypothesis generation and hypothesis evaluation takes place on different levels subsequently: 1) Selection from the alternative sample solutions in the semantic table; 2) Mapping of the clauses; 3) Mapping of the subgoals within a clause; 4) Mapping of arguments and operators; 5) Mapping of summands in an arithmetic expression; 6) Mapping of factors and algebraic signs in a summand. The two steps hypothesis generation-evaluation also allows us to cover the solution space spanned by the choice of names for variables and predicates. The hypothesis generation step maps corresponding elements between student assertions and semantic assertions without considering variable names or predicate names, and the evaluation step examines created mappings.

4.3 Applying CBM and Transformation to Model a Solution Space

A programming technique or a construct can be varied in different ways. Especially, arithmetic expressions can be transformed using the commutative or distributive law. In order to represent a space of alternatives for a programming technique or a construct, we have to define transformation rules. Currently, we do not consider recursively embedded arithmetic expressions. Our system just copes with arithmetic expressions without nesting, for example: A*(B+C). For such arithmetic expressions, the following transformation rules are required:

Rule 1: transforms the normal form to the simplified form applying the distributive law: $A°X ± B°X \longrightarrow (A±B)°X$, where the operator ° is either * or /. If A and B are numbers, then $(A±B)°X$ can be transformed to $M°X$ where $M=A±B$;

Rule 2: transforms a product term applying the commutative law: A*B -> B*A.

Transformation rules are also required to cover solutions, for which helper predicates are required. If the student wants to keep the code in the main predicate definition clear and simple, then he can define a helper predicate. Applying the unfolding/folding techniques proposed in [21], it is possible to transform a student solution with a helper predicate to an equivalent one without, if not both the main predicate and the auxiliary predicate apply the recursion technique. The solution without helper predicates is supposed to correspond to one of the generalized sample solutions in the semantic table. If both the main predicate and the helper predicate require recursion as part of the solution strategy, the definition of the helper predicate must be included in the semantic table.

4.4 Applying CBM and Pattern Candidates to Model a Solution Space

The variation of a subgoal (clause head) requires considering arguments within that subgoal (clause head). A pattern variant differs from others not only at argument positions in one subgoal, but also in many subgoals. Therefore, the generalized constraint template above cannot be applied directly to define constraints which span the space of patterns. Syntactically, a constraint, which should cover the space of patterns, requires to consider many subgoals (clause heads) in its relevance part. The following problem exercise illustrates this issue:

Compound interest: An amount of money S will be charged with an annual interest rate (i.e. R=0.05) and rises exponentially. Define a predicate to compute the amount of money after X years of investment.

For the problem above we can apply four different patterns: *analytic, tail recursive, increasing recursive and decreasing recursive.* Possible solutions according to the last two patterns are shown in Table 3. We can notice that those solutions differ from each other remarkably. Even though the *increasing recursive* and the *decreasing recursive* solutions seem to have many structures in common, from the view of underlying programming techniques, they are quite different. The predicate in the *increasing recursive* solution calls itself until the variable New_Period is bound, and then the second subgoal, an arithmetic calculation, tests the bound value of New_Period in relation to the bound value X (number of investment years). If the test succeeds, the new sum is calculated, otherwise, the recursive subgoal is called again. In another solution New_Period is calculated by decrementing X, as long as X is greater than 1, the new investment sum is computed until New_Period is zero.

Table 3. Possible solutions for the problem *Compound interest*

Pattern	Solution

Increasing recursive	`in_inv(S,_,0,S).`
	`in_inv(S,R,X,End_S):- in_inv(S,R,New_Period,New_S),`
	`X is New_Period+1, End_S is New_S+R*New_S.`

Decreasing recursive	`de_inv(S,_,0,S).`
	`de_inv(S,R,X,End_S):-X>0, New_Period is X-1,`
	`de_inv(S,R,New_Period,New_S), End_S is New_S+R*New_S.`

Hypothesis: It is possible to define a constraint which models a common space of solutions for both patterns *increasing recursive* and *decreasing recursive.*

Attempt 1: Define <u>Constraint P1</u> without using transformation. We select assertions from the semantic table to describe the *decreasing recursive* pattern as the relevance part of a constraint, and the satisfaction part requires that the student solution satisfies either the *increasing recursive* or the *decreasing recursive* pattern.

P1<Relevance>: in the semantic table, a recursive subgoal R, an increment calculation subgoal A: X is V+1, a calculation subgoal A, and a base case Cbase exist and should fulfill the following conditions: R precedes A; V also exists in R at the position p(V); p(V) is equal to the argument position of X in the clause head; The argument at position p(V) in Cbase is bound to a constant.

P1<Satisfaction>: in the student solution, either condition set A or condition set B should be satisfied:

Condition set A: there should exist a recursive subgoal SR, an increment calculation SA: SX is SV+1, and a base case SCbase, which meet following requirements: SR precedes SA; SV exists in SR at the position p(SV); p(SV) is equal to the argument position of X in the clause head; The argument at position p(SV) in SCbase is bound to a constant.

Condition set B: there should exist a recursive subgoal SR, a decrement calculation subgoal SC: SV is SX-1, and a base case SCbase, which meet the following requirements: SR precedes SC; SV exists in SR at the position p(SV); p(SV) is equal to the argument position of SX in the clause head; The argument at position p(SV) in SCbase is bound to a constant; An arithmetic test subgoal SX>0.

Suppose, Solution SP3 (Appendix) for the problem *Compound interest* should be evaluated. The relevance part of Constraint P1 is always evaluated to true because it is a conjunction of semantic assertions. However, SP3 will not satisfy Constraint P1 because the calculation subgoal neither satisfies the condition set A nor set B. As a result, Constraint P1 is not useful due to following problems: 1) the student solution is implemented according to either the *increasing recursive* or the *decreasing recursive* pattern. But in case of an erroneous solution, this distinction is not reflected in the diagnostic results because the constraint simply evaluates to false without indicating the strategy used by the student probably. 2) The relevance part of Constraint P1 is so complex that errors in the student solution can not be reliably localized.

Attempt 2: Define a constraint applying the DRP-IRP rule to transform the decreasing recursive (DRP) to the increasing recursive pattern (IRP).

DRP-IRP Rule: copy the base case of DRP: de_inv(S,_,0,S); copy the clause head of the recursive case of DRP: de_inv(S,R,X,End_S); remove the arithmetic test subgoal of DRP; convert the decrement subgoal of DRP to increment subgoal: N_Period is X-1 → X is N_Period+1; concatenate the recursive subgoal of DRP to the front of the increment subgoal; concatenate the increment subgoal with other subgoals of the recursive case of DRP; the new form is the IRP.

We now evaluate Constraint P1 on a predicate which uses arithmetic recursion as follows: 1) Assuming, a solution is coded according to *decreasing recursive* pattern (called SEM_DRP). We apply DRP-IRP Rule to SEM_DRP resulting in a predicate SEM_IRP which uses *increasing recursive* pattern; 2) evaluate Constraint P1 based on either SEM_DRP or SEM_IRP; 3) SEM_DRP or SEM_IRP, which causes fewer constraint violations, is taken as the one which apparently has been implemented in the student solution. However, the transformation rule is very complex and it is difficult to verify its correctness.

To avoid the constraint complexity as in Attempt 1 and the necessity to apply a transformation as in Attempt 2, the semantic table is extended to contain two candidates for the two patterns. The student solution is evaluated based on semantic assertions. The pattern candidate, which causes the least constraint violation, is taken as the most plausible explanation for the student solution.

5 Evaluation

The efficacy of an ITS depends on the accuracy of diagnosis. We conducted an off-line test by selecting appropriate exercises from past written examinations and integrated them into INCOM. Then, we collected student solutions for those exercises. The examination candidates should have attended a course in logic programming which was offered as a part of the first semester curriculum in Informatics. The purpose of the evaluation is to find out whether the solution space modeled by CBM covers possible student solutions, and thus the ITS was able to give appropriate diagnostic information.

Sofar, we conducted the evaluation with three exercises tasks (Appendix A). Each of the exercise tasks requires different skills to solve. For the first one, students should be able to handle recursion, arithmetic calculation, arithmetic test, and (de)composition of a list structure. The second one requires students to cope with arithmetic calculation and database relationships. The last one requires the skill of implementing a recursive subgoal, using unification and (de)composition.

While collecting student solutions from past examinations we filtered out solutions which are not sufficiently elaborated for applying a diagnosis, i.e. fragmentary clauses. Furthermore, we added appropriate predicate declarations, because students were not asked to provide that information about meaning, types and modes of each argument position. An expert marks the position of errors in the student solution, and looks for a list of possible constraints which might be violated. Finally, we run the diagnosis on the student solution resulting in a list of constraint violation hypotheses. If both lists are in agreement, the automatic diagnosis is in accordance with the one of the expert. Each student solution is a test case.

Table 4. Evaluation of student solutions

Exercise	Participants	Solutions	Solutions not diagnosed
1	20	11	0
2	20	5	2
3	39	10	0

We summarize the number of participants who had to solve the exercises and the number of collected solutions which are diagnosable in Table 4. The system INCOM could diagnose almost all collected solutions correctly except two of them: SP1, SP2 (Appendix A). In one case the solution contained a disjunction operator ';' which is currently not supported. In the other case the semantic table was incomplete, since it did not contain a pattern candidate implementing an accumulator.

6 Conclusion and Future Works

We have discussed how the CBM technique can be applied to describe the solution space of ill-defined problems in logic programming. There are three cases when we should apply constraints: 1) Constraints without transformation are particularly well suited to describe an object for which there is a small number of variants as long as the conditions are not too complex. If the complexity of a constraint becomes too high, the author risks that the relevance part of the constraint will not be fulfilled by an erroneous solution or that the error committed by the student cannot be diagnosed precisely enough. Therefore, we should use constraints without transformation primarily to examine objects at the argument level of a Prolog predicate definition. 2) Constraints with transformation can be applied to objects, which may have many variants, i.e. an arithmetic expression that can be modified using the distributive or commutative law. We suggest describing only transformation rules which are verifiable. 3) Pattern candidates are required if it is not possible to define a transformation between them or a transformation rule can not be verified. Normally, pattern candidates have a large degree of dissimilarity. They are distinguished from each other not only at the argument level but also at the subgoal and clause level and thus, a transformation becomes very complex. As a consequence, it is almost not possible to verify the correctness and the generality of the transformation. Therefore, a normalized pattern candidate should be provided.

This technology has been integrated into a web-based ITS and the system has been evaluated with student solutions from past examinations. The evaluation results pointed out that the CBM was able to cover 24 of 26 student solutions for the exercises in Appendix A. The disadvantage of this approach is that we have to define enough pattern candidates to represent the different programming strategies for which no transformation rules between patterns can be defined and verified. This is not always an easy task for a very ill-defined problem. We will extend INCOM with new exercises and test cases to demonstrate the effectiveness of the CBM approach.

References

1. Lynch, C.F., Ashley, K.D., Aleven, V. Pinkwart, N.: Defining Ill-Defined Domains; A literature survey. In: Proceedings of the Workshop on ITS for Ill-Defined Domains, the 8th Conference on ITS, pp. 1–10 (2006)
2. Roberts, D.A.: What counts as an explanation for a science teaching event? Teaching Edu.3, 69–87 (1991)
3. White, B.Y., Frederksen, J.R.: Inquiry, modeling, and metacognition: Making science accessible to all students. Cognition and Instruction 16(1), 3–18 (1998)
4. Gick, M.L.: Problem-solving strategies. Educational Psychologist 21, 99–120 (1986)
5. Jacobs, J.E., Paris, S.G.: Children's metacognition about reading: Issues in definition, measurement, and instruction. Educational Psychologist 22, 255–278 (1987)
6. Voss, J.F., Post, T.A.: On the solving of ill-structured problems. In: Chi., Glaser., Farr (eds.) The nature of expertise, Lawrence Erlbaum, Mahwah (1988)
7. Taylor, J., Boulay, B.D.: Studying novice programmers: Why they might find learning Prolog hard. In: Rutkowska., Crook (eds.) Computers, Cognition & Development: Issues for Psychology & Education, Wiley, New York (1987)
8. Vanneste, P.: A Reverse Engineering Approach to Novice Program Analysis, PhD thesis. KU Kortrijk (1994)
9. Murray, W.: Automatic Program Debugging for Intelligent Tutoring Systems. Morgan Kaufmann, Los Altos (1988)
10. Weber, G.: Episodic learner modeling. Cognitive Science 20, 195–236 (1996)

11. Anderson, J.R., Reiser, B.J.: The Lisp Tutor, BYTE, 159—175 (April 1985)
12. Ohlsson, S.: Constraint-based student modeling, in Greer, McCalla, Student Modelling: The Key to Individualized Knowledge-based Instruction, Berlin, pp. 167–189 (1994)
13. Koedinger, K.R., Anderson, J.R., Hadley, W.H., Mark, M.: Intelligent tutoring goes to school in the big city. International Journal of AI in Education 8(1), 30–43 (1997)
14. Jonassen, D.H., Tessmer, M., Hannum, W.H.: Task analysis methods for instructional design. Erlbaum, Mahwah (1999)
15. Ormerod, T.C.: Planning and ill-defined problems. In: Morris, R., Ward, G. (eds.) The Cognitive Psychology of Planning, Psychology Press, London (2006)
16. Goel, V.: Comparison of well-structured & ill-structured task environments and problem spaces. In: Proceedings of the 14th annual conference of the cognitive science society, Erlbaum, Hillsdale, NJ (1992)
17. Simon, H.: The structure of ill-structured problems. AI 4, 181–201 (1973)
18. Spiro, R.J., et al.: Cognitive Flexibility, Constructivism and Hypertext. Random Access Instruction for Advanced Knowledge Acquisition in Ill-Structured Domains. Educational Technology 31(5), 24–33 (1991)
19. Le, N.-T.: Using prolog design patterns to support constraint-based error diagnosis in logic programming. In: Ashley, K., et al. (eds.) Proc. of the Workshop on ITS for Ill-Defined Domains, the 8th Conf. on ITS, pp. 38–46 (2006)
20. Le, N.-T.: INCOM: A constraint-based tutoring system for logic programming. Report, FBI-HH-B-280/07, University of Hamburg, Department of Informatics
21. Tamaki, H., Sato, T.: Unfold/fold transformations of logic programs. In: Proceedings of 2nd International Conference on Logic Programming, Sweden, pp. 127–138 (1984)

Appendix A: Exercises for Evaluation and Selected Student Solutions

Exercise 1: A salary database is implemented as a list whose odd elements represent names and even elements represent salary in €. Define a predicate to create a new salary list according to following rules: 1) Salary less equal 5000€ will be raised 3%; 2) 2% for salary over 5000 €. Notice: the notation of 3% and 2% corresponds to 0.03 and 0.02 in Prolog, respectively.

Exercise 2: The income of a company is implemented as a collection of facts in Prolog: *invoice(InvoiceNr, ClientNr, Amount, Date)* where Amount is a sum of money in old German Mark. Please, define a predicate invoice_e/4, to convert invoices from German Mark into Euro.

Exercise 3: A list represents numbers of audience for a series of TV programs. Each list element contains a sublist with information about the TV station, the program title and the number of audience (in Tsd). The list is ordered in descending order according to the number of audience and is implemented as an argument of the predicate audience/1 in the database of the Prolog system: *audience([[TV1,Pro1,5300], [TV2, Pro2, 4200],...,[TVn,ProN,3000]])*. Please, define a predicate which builds a new list of programs for a given name of TV station. Notice that the original order should be kept and the operator not/1 is provided to negate unification.

SP1 for Exercise 2:

```
plus([], L2, L2).
plus(Gehalt,L2,R):-
   Gehalt=[Kopf|Rest], Rest=[Kopf1|Rest1], Kopf1<=5000, NKopf1 is
Kopf1*1.03, plus(Rest1,[L2|Kopf,NKopf1],R]);
   Gehalt=[Kopf|Rest], Rest=[Kopf1|Rest1], Kopf1>5000, NKopf1 is
Kopf1*1.02, plus(Rest1,[L2|Kopf,NKopf],R).
```

SP2 for Exercise 2:

```
gehalttarif(Gehaltvorher,Gehaltnachher):-
   gtacc(Gehaltvorher,[],Gehaltnachher).
gtacc([GLvorName,GLvorDM|GLvorTail],Acc,GLnach):-
gtacc(GLvorTail,[GLvorName,GLneuDM|Acc],GLnach),
        (GLneuDM is GlvorDM*103/100,Gehalt<=5000);
        (GLneuDM is GLvorDM*105/100, Gehalt>5000).
Gtacc([], Acc, Acc).
```

SP 3 for the problem Compound interest:

```
invest(S,_,0,S).
invest(S,R,X,End_S):-
   X is New_P-1, invest(S,R,New_P,New_S), End_S is New_S+R*New_S.
```

A Web Application for Mathematics Education[*]

Ana Paula Tomás[1,2], José Paulo Leal[1,2], and Marcos Aurélio Domingues[2]

[1] Departamento de Ciência de Computadores, Faculdade de Ciências,
Universidade do Porto, Portugal
{apt,zp}@dcc.fc.up.pt
[2] Laboratório de Inteligência Artificial e Ciência de Computadores,
Universidade do Porto, Portugal
marcos@liacc.up.pt

Abstract. AGILMAT is a web application designed to help students learn Mathematics, with focus on high-school algebra and calculus drills. A modular and extensible architecture and a wizard-based configuration interface decoupled from the system core are major design features of AGILMAT. The drill expressions are specified by grammars and constraints imposed by default profiles and user options, so that AGILMAT may support distinct learning levels and stages. The core system uses symbolic manipulation and automated reasoning to provide correct answers for the drills. The paper shows how AGILMAT may be used to create and customize drills automatically.

1 Introduction

Improving proficiency in mathematics stands at the top of educational priorities in Portugal, as well as in many countries. Although it is a fact that some students lack mathematical skills, the main reason for the lack of success in mathematics is that too often students memorize how to work out a specific drill but do not grasp the concepts underlying the solution steps. Some students even prefer quick practical rules with no mathematical basis, such as *"to see if $|x| > b$ should be rewritten as $x < -b \vee x > b$ or as $x < -b \wedge x > b$, rotate $>$ by $90°$ clockwise"*.

Over the last three decades applications of computers in mathematics education as a supplement to regular class or as a primary means of instruction became more and more widespread [1,2,11]. The fast growth of Internet has also fostered a significant breakthrough in computer assisted learning. Sophisticated web-based learning environments are being developed also for mathematics education, some offering authoring tools for creating courseware, assignments and exams, some being used for training, assessment and contests [5,8,15,18]. Nevertheless, designing courseware material for E-Learning is still quite time-consuming, even when instructors may count on E-Learning authoring tools [5,15]. Advances in computer technology shall therefore be exploited to develop really re-usable and customizable contents, for personalized E-Learning.

[*] Partially supported by AGILMAT (POSI/CHS/48565/2002), funded by Fundação para a Ciência e Tecnologia, under POSI, co-funded by EU/FEDER.

H. Leung et al. (Eds.): ICWL 2007, LNCS 4823, pp. 380–391, 2008.
© Springer-Verlag Berlin Heidelberg 2008

AGILMAT project (www.ncc.up.pt/AGILMAT/) aims to develop tools to automatically create and solve mathematics drills, for computer aided training or assessment. Drill and practice, together with exposition, are still the main modes of instruction in Mathematics. Nevertheless, very often drills created by online exercise systems lack pedagogical interest, as they tend to be too hard-wired and just correspond to randomly generated instances of the same problem template [18].

In contrast to the most usual practice, the analysis of algebraic procedures that students should learn and apply in a given curriculum plays a central role in AGILMAT. In particular, for the abstraction of problem templates and their formal description, we try to understand how these algorithms condition the drills that may be created and solved automatically [16]. The expressions that arise in the exercises are specified by constrained grammars and refined by default profiles and user options.

AGILMAT supports different initial settings by parametrizing the interface, generator and solver. The user is given the possibility to further refine some of these parameters so as to customize the exercises. The released prototype[1] allows users to create hundreds of examples and their one-line solutions, about univariate functions. Drills currently supported are directed to high school students and mathematics teachers (grade levels 10 to 12). We may explore the advantages of this tool as a means for learning fundamental notions. For example, by making students understand and justify why the one-line solutions produced by the system are correct. The possibility of using AGILMAT for this purpose was validated in informal demos of the system to high-school students and teachers.

AGILMAT implementation integrates different technologies and programming languages. Pursuing the line of [16,17], the core system is implemented in a Prolog-based constraint logic programming language [10,13,14] to support constraints on the exercises.

The framework that supports AGILMAT's interface is described in [3,6]. It is loosely inspired in the model-view-controller (MVC) pattern and implemented on a Java servlet container (J2EE Web Application, using the Apache Tomcat Servlet Container, version 5.5). A main feature is the fact that it can be extended without requiring code programming. The hot spots of such framework are XML configuration files to define the interface data, how this data is mapped into the system's commands, and how commands output and the interaction state is mapped into web formatting languages. With this approach the web interface is kept separated from the system it controls, it is easy to define and modify, and is able to capture enough domain knowledge to be a real advantage for the novice or sporadic user.

The rest of the paper is structured as follows. In Section 2, we show how AGILMAT may be used to create and customize drills automatically. Section 3 presents its architecture in brief and some implementation details. In Section 4, we address ongoing work that aims at extending the prototype and discuss some

---

[1] The released version of AGILMAT is available at www.ncc.up.pt:8080/Agilmat.

of the theoretical problems inherent to mathematical knowledge management that we have to circumvent.

2   Generating Exercises

AGILMAT's front-end is a web application that collects a set of options that will control the generation of exercises. Figure 1 presents AGILMAT initial interface where the user can generate a set of exercises defining only a minimal set of options.

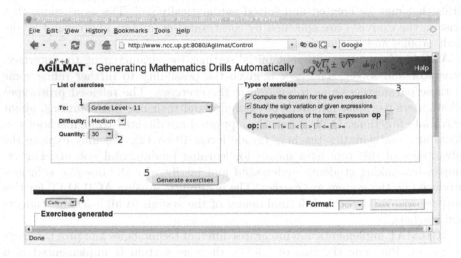

Fig. 1. Screen of the main interface of AGILMAT

The location of these options in the users interface is highlighted in Figure 1. Each one is numbered and its purpose is described below.

Option 1 - Defines a profile of exercises that will be generated, set to "Grade Level - 11" in the example. This makes the system initialize the range of each parameter of AGILMAT's back-end with suitable default values (defined by such profile). These values may correspond not only to grade levels but also to specific topics of the curricula. The advantage of this option is to allow novice users to generate exercises for their particular needs without having to set a large number of parameters.

Option 2 - Defines the maximum number of expressions that will be generated for the exercises, set to "30", in the figure.

Option 3 - Defines the types of exercises that will be generated. The user can use this option to choose the types of exercises that he/she does want, such as "Compute the domain for the given expressions", "Study the sign variation of given expressions" and "Solve (in)equations". Exercise sheets may contain several different types of exercises. We set the option to "Compute the domain for the given expressions" and "Study the sign variation of given expressions".

Option 4 - Turns on and off the cache system. On "Cache on" the system gets exercises from the ones cached, if there are some. Otherwise, AGILMAT will generate fresh exercises.

Option 5 - Finally, if we press "Generate exercises", some exercises will be displayed in the bottom of the screen, as we show in Figure 2.

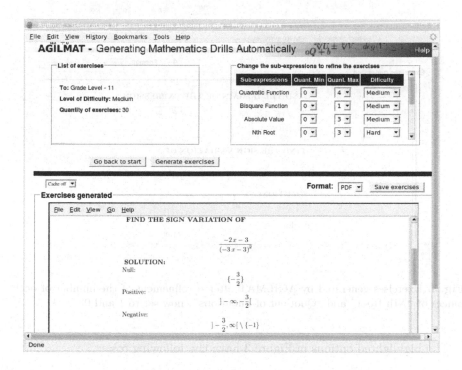

Fig. 2. Examples of exercises created by AGILMAT

2.1 Refining the Exercises

The user can refine exercise generation by setting different values for particular parameters of AGILMAT's back-end. After the first step, the interface header changes to present a comprehensive set of parameters that control variables in AGILMAT's back-end. The parameters, their range and default values depend on the basic profile defined previously. Figure 2 shows the parameters that would be made available under the conditions imposed by the selections made in the previous panel. If the user changes, for instance, his requirements on the number of occurrences of "Nth Root" (to be exactly 1) and "Quotient of Functions" (to be 0) and asks AGILMAT to generate exercises, then all the expressions will contain exactly one radical and no quotient, as we see in Figure 3.

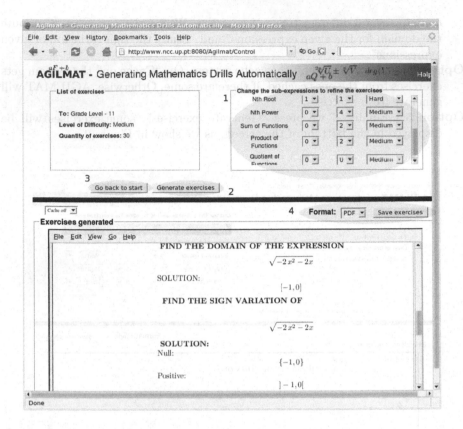

Fig. 3. Exercises generated by AGILMAT after a refinement of the number of occurrences of "Nth Root" and "Quotient of Functions", now set to 1 and 0

The highlighted options in Figure 3 have the following roles:

Option 1 - Allows the user to change the number of occurrences of a particular constructor (or sub-expression) that can arise in the exercises, as well as its difficulty level. Three difficulty levels are supported currently – easy, medium and hard – mapped internally to integer values or ranges, that are defined in the selected profile.

Option 2 - To generate exercises again, the user presses the button "Generate exercises".

Option 3 - The user can return to the initial interface by pressing the button "Go back to start".

Option 4 - Generated exercises can be saved in different formats by pressing "Save exercises". Formats currently supported are HyperText Markup Language (HTML), Portable Document Format (PDF) and PostScript (PS) and XML - Question & Test Interoperability (XML - QTI), although for the released version, the available format is restricted to PDF.

The user may go on redefining or refining the parameters. Within AGILMAT core system, the difficulty level is modeled as a sum of ranks given to the basic functions involved in the expressions and to their composition. The user may partially tune this level by changing the selections in the "Difficulty" menus (see Figure 3, option 1).

In Figure 4, we see another excerpt of an exercise sheet. This random example

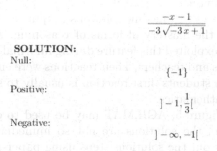

FIND THE SIGN VARIATION OF

$$\frac{-x-1}{-3\sqrt{-3x+1}}$$

SOLUTION:
Null:
$$\{-1\}$$

Positive:
$$]-1,\frac{1}{3}[$$

Negative:
$$]-\infty,-1[$$

Fig. 4. Requiring one radical and one quotient

was created by setting the number of occurrences of "Quotient of Functions" to 1 and reducing its difficulty level and that of "Nth Root" to *easy*.

If the difficulty level of these constructs was the same as in Figure 3, the constraints imposed by the parameters would be inconsistent. The requirement of medium global cumulative difficulty could not be satisfied. AGILMAT would give a warning, informing the user that it could not create exercises that satisfy the given parameters.

Alternative interfaces, where the users could tune several finer parameters, were tested with a focus group of six high-school teachers before we decided for the current version. In particular, they did some experiments with another interface where they could control finer subcategories of expressions, as in our former testbed generator Demomath [16]. They found it too complex, not very intuitive and somewhat bewildering. Hence, we decided to keep some parameters fixed through default configuration profiles.

The default profile fixes the mapping of the difficulty ranks (easy, medium and hard) to integer values, which may be distinct from basic function to basic function. By changing this encoding, we may tune AGILMAT to particular needs, although the underlying model for estimating the difficulty level is rather simplistic.

The predefined parameters include also the ranges of exponents (of radicals and powers) and of coefficients that may occur in the expressions. In order to keep the numbers that may arise in the computations small, the coefficients of the created expressions are relatively small also (e.g., integers ranging over $[-5,5]$).

As we see in the previous figures, the released prototype of AGILMAT, that is available in the World Wide Web, yields a one-line solution for each exercise. This may be very helpful to complement conventional class-based tuition, favoring retention of fundamental concepts or results.

It is important that students acquire or improve abstraction skills. Very often students do not really have to work out a solution with paper-and-pencil to grasp why the solution computed by AGILMAT is correct, as for example, when the problem is to "Find the set of solutions of $\frac{|-x-3|}{-x} \leq 0$", and AGILMAT output is $\{-3\} \cup]0, \infty[$. Students may be asked to justify why -3 is a solution and why x shall be positive otherwise.

The critical analysis of the one-line solutions output by AGILMAT may have a positive impact for the mastery of forms of reasoning. Although there is no formal user study, we exploited this feature during informal demos of AGILMAT to high school students and teachers. Their reactions were enough supportive and encouraging, although students' first reaction is usually to say that they are not especially keen on Mathematics.

As we can see in Figure 5, AGILMAT may be used to create more complex exercises. In this case, the solutions are not so immediate. To justify them, students need to work out the solutions steps using paper-and-pencil.

CHARACTERIZE THE MONOTONICITY OF

$$r(x) = -2 \left(\frac{-2x+1}{2x^2 - x + 1} \right) - 2$$

SOLUTION:
  r **is strictly increasing in**

$$]\frac{1}{2} - \frac{1}{2}\sqrt{2}, \frac{1}{2} + \frac{1}{2}\sqrt{2}[$$

r **is strictly decreasing in**

$$]-\infty, \frac{1}{2} - \frac{1}{2}\sqrt{2}[\cup]\frac{1}{2} + \frac{1}{2}\sqrt{2}, \infty[$$

Fig. 5. More complex exercises (grades 12)

3   Overview of AGILMAT's Architecture

The AGILMAT system is available to its users through a web interface. The AGILMAT system itself is a Constraint Logic Programing application, while its web interface is based on a web wizards framework developed as a Java web application. These two components are loosely coupled, thus providing a high degree of independence between them. The web wizards framework connects with the AGILMAT system through I/O streams, issuing Prolog queries and receiving its output. The web wizard generator uses XML files to configure the dependencies to the AGILMAT system. In particular, format conversions use

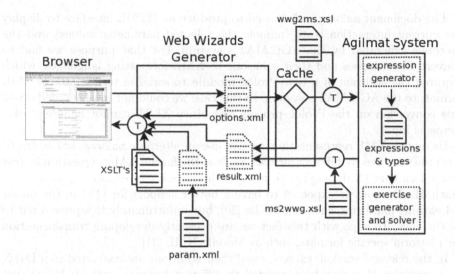

Fig. 6. AGILMAT system in the framework for developing web wizards

XSLT (W3C Recommendation, 1999). This setup is complemented by a cache system that avoids regenerating exercises in certain cases. Figure 6 contextualizes the AGILMAT system inside the framework for developing web wizards.

The web wizards generator, cache and AGILMAT system are represented as strong squares and rectangles, internal modules of the AGILMAT system are represented as dotted rectangles, points of transformation are represented as strong T labeled circles. A switcher is represented by strong rhombus. Physical files with XML documents are represented as strong file icons and XML documents in memory are represented as dotted file icons.

3.1 Web Wizards Generator

The state of the interaction with AGILMAT's web interface is managed by a set of *parameters* defined in the file `param.xml`, a valid document of a parameter definition language defined for this purpose. The parameter definition language includes such features as: composition of parameters, definition of default values as expression involving other parameters, dependencies between parameters, among others.

At each user request, parameters are converted into Prolog queries that are injected in the input stream to be interpreted and executed by Prolog engine. The document `wwg2ms.xsl` is used to map parameters into Prolog clauses that feed the AGILMAT's system. Although this conversion could be handled entirely on the framework's side, using XSLT transformations, we opted to keep this conversion fairly simple and develop a Prolog module on AGILMAT's system to process the parameters collected by the web interface.

The document `ms2wwg.xsl` is used to produce an HTML interface to display the current interaction state (namely the selected parameter values) and the exercises generated by the AGILMAT's system. For that purpose we had to convert the exercises and their solutions to XML formatting languages, which required the addition of a new Prolog module to serialize terms into an XML format, to the AGILMAT's system. In this case we could not have avoided doing this conversion on the Prolog process side since XLST cannot handle Prolog terms as input.

Using this XML representation, we can use an alternate `ms2wwg.xsl` to transform the exercises to different formats, such as the format XML - Question & Test Interoperability (XML - QTI) [9] with mathematical expressions represented in MathML. By now we expected to have a better support for QTI in the major E-Learning platforms, such as Moodle [20], but unfortunately this proved not to be the case. To cope with this fact we are presently developing transformation for platform specific formats, such as Moodle XML [21].

In the released version, exercises and their solutions are converted to a LaTeX representation that may be converted to different formats, such as: HyperText Markup Language (HTML), Portable Document Format (PDF) and PostScript (PS). The PDF file is embedded in the web interface. The released prototype is not yet using the document `ms2wwg.xsl` to convert exercises and their solutions to a XML representation. We hope to use this document in the next version of AGILMAT.

To improve the response time of the overall system with the web interface, we developed a cache system. When the cache is activated, the web wizards generator looks up for a system output previously generated with the same choice of parameters. Our experience showed that certain sets of choices, specially those selected in an early stage of the interaction, tend to be repeated since they are just default values of the initial screens. In these situations the cache system provides almost immediate feedback in these first attempts which encourages novice users to continue exploring the system's more complex features.

3.2   AGILMAT's Core System

In the AGILMAT system there are two main modules written in Prolog acting as filters: the *expression generator* processes the user constraints and produces an expressions and types file, the *exercise generator and solver* processes this file and produces exercises and theirs solutions. This last module is the control of the system and makes use of several libraries that handle arithmetic, set operations and symbolic constraints (to solve inequations, disequations and equations), along the lines of [16].

An interesting feature that distinguishes also AGILMAT from E-Learning tools that use pools of exercises [5] is the fact that its expression generator may potentially yield arbitrarily complex expressions. In the current release, these expressions are characterized by the grammar proposed in [16]. This grammar was written to describe a non-trivial set of expressions whose zeros and domains can be exactly computed by the algebraic procedures that students should master (up to the 12th grade). The constraints imposed by the selected profile and the user options restrict these generic forms further. The expression generator is a Prolog program that uses constraint programming to model such constraints as constraints on finite domain (integer) variables. Each generated expression belongs to some pattern (i.e., *type*). For instance, all the expressions of the following forms

$$\frac{a}{|by + c|} \quad \text{and} \quad \sqrt[n]{\frac{a}{(by + c)^m}}$$

would be of types k / abs o p1 o x and rad(n) o (k / pow(m) o p1 o x), respectively, where k, abs, p1, pow(m) and rad(n) represent a constant function, the absolute value function, a polynomial function of degree 1 and the mth-power and n^{th}-root functions, respectively. Further technical details may be found in [16].

The configuration parameters constrain these types. The constants arising in the expression – coefficients and exponents of radicals and powers – are also restricted by the values given in each configuration profile (defined in param.xml). The user cannot change their ranges directly in the interface, except by selecting a distinct default profile. As we mentioned already, a preliminary version of the interface, where users could tune several finer parameters, was tested with a focus group of high-school teachers. They found it too complex. Hence, we decided to keep parameters of this sort fixed through the default configuration profile.

The generator computes the type of the expressions and one (or more) expressions of each type. In this way, it is possible to produce several expressions with exactly the same type but distinct coefficients. This option is not yet available in web interface, although it is an interesting feature for applications in assessment, for instance.

All the modules supporting the solver are implemented in a Prolog-based constraint logic programming language. To guarantee the correctness of the computed answers and a consistent (safe) interaction with users, AGILMAT must have full control of the simplifications and rewritings performed. More often, web-based learning environments make use of available Computer Algebra Systems to reduce the effort of writing a solver, e.g., ActiveMath [7] and Wims [18], risking unexpected or wrong answers, as discussed in [1,4,11].

4 Some Ongoing Extensions and Discussion

We are addressing extensions of the core system to produce step-by-step solutions that resemble those worked out by human beings. Some initial results have been reported in [17]. This is a non-trivial design principle or goal common to some other mathematical tools for assisted learning, as MathXpert [1]. To understand and automate what people do when they do mathematics is a continuous research topic in Artificial Intelligence, Automated Reasoning, and Symbolic Computation [2,12].

When a student is using mathematical software for exploratory learning, it is reasonable that the system may output *don't know* or rather complicate formulas as an answer. This is not acceptable when the system is *asking* the student to solve a problem that it has automatically generated. Both the computer and the student (if he/she has learned the topic in assessment) must know how to solve the exercise. For instance, the system shall not produce an ad-hoc polynomial of degree greater than four and ask the student to find its roots. Indeed, it is known that there exist no generic algorithm to solve that. In contrast, there are algorithms to compute the *rational* roots of any polynomial with rational coefficients, which, nevertheless students may not have learned. For this reason, we try to understand how the algorithms learners should master condition the drills that may be created and solved automatically.

We are also considering extensions of the forms of expressions covered. In particular, we are investigating extensions of the types of numbers and sets supported. Supporting symbolic computation with generic real numbers raises theoretical difficulties. Many problems become undecidable. For instance, the computable real numbers represent a null measure set (within the real numbers) and there is no algorithm for deciding whether some real valued expression is zero. This means that from the computational point of view, there are some inherent difficulties that we have to circumvent. For educational purposes, we do not need to support full generality.

References

1. Beeson, M.: Design Principles of Mathpert: Software to support education in algebra and calculus. In: Kajler, N. (ed.) Computer-Human Interaction in Symbolic Computation, Texts and Monographs in Symbolic Computation, vol. XI, pp. 89–115. Springer, Heidelberg (1998)
2. Bundy, A.: The Computer Modelling of Mathematical Reasoning. Academic Press, London (1983)
3. Domingues, M.A., Leal, J.P.: Configuring Web Wizards in XML. In: Proc. of XATA2006, XML: Aplicações e Tecnologias Associadas, pp. 315–324 (2006)
4. Gottliebsen, H., Kelsey, T., Martin, U.: Hidden Verification for Computational Mathematics. J. Symbolic Computation 39, 539–567 (2005)
5. Isidro, R.O., Sousa Pinto, J., Batel Anjo, A.: SA3C - Platform of Evaluation System and Computer Assisted Learning. WEAS Transactions on Advances in Engineering Education 1:2, 1–6 (2005), http://pmate.ua.pt:8081/pmate/
6. Leal, J.P., Domingues, M.A.: Rapid development of web interfaces to heterogeneous systems. In: van Leeuwen, J., et al. (eds.) SOFSEM 2007. LNCS, vol. 4362, pp. 716–725. Springer, Heidelberg (2007)
7. Melis, E., et al.: ActiveMath: A Generic and Adaptive Web-Based Learning Environment. International Journal of Artificial Intelligence in Education 12:4, 385–407 (2001), http://www.activemath.org/
8. FP6-Project "LeActiveMath": Language Enhanced User Adaptive, Interactive eLearning for Mathematics (2004/2006) http://www.dfki.de/leactivemath/
9. IMS QTI Specifications. IMS Global Learning Consortium, Inc. www.imsglobal.org/question/index.html
10. Marriott, K., Stuckey, P.: Programming with Constraints – An Introduction. MIT Press, Cambridge (1998)

11. Ravaglia, R., Alper, T., Rozenfeld, M., Suppes, P.: Successful Pedagogical Applications of Symbolic Computation. In: Kajler, N. (ed.) Computer-Human Interaction in Symbolic Computation, pp. 61–88. Springer, Heidelberg (1999)
12. Robinson, A., Voronkoy, A. (eds.): Handbook of Automated Reasoning. Elsevier Science, Amsterdam (2001)
13. Rossi, F., van Beek, P., Walsh, T. (eds.): Handbook of Constraint Programming. Elsevier Science, Amsterdam (2006)
14. SICStus Prolog User Manual (Release 3.12.0), SICS, Sweden (2004) http://www.sics.se/isl/sicstuswww/site/index.html
15. Sierra, J., Moreno-Ger, P., Martínez-Ortiz, I., Fernández-Manjón, B.: A highly modular and extensible architecture for an integrated IMS-based authoring system: The <e-Aula> experience. Softw. Pract. Exper. 37:4, 441–461 (2007)
16. Tomás, A.P., Leal, J.P.: A CLP-Based Tool for Computer Aided Generation and Solving of Maths Exercises. In: Dahl, V., Wadler, P. (eds.) PADL 2003. LNCS, vol. 2562, pp. 223–240. Springer, Heidelberg (2003)
17. Tomás, A.P., Moreira, N., Pereira, N.: Designing a Solver for Arithmetic Constraints to Support Education in Mathematics. In: Proc. Artificial Intelligence Applications and Innovations (AIAI 2006). IFIP Series, vol. 204, pp. 433–441. Springer-Verlag, Heidelberg (2006)
18. Xiao, G.: On Public-Questions Tests, Univ. Nice Sophia-Antipolis, France (2004)
19. XSL Transformations (XSLT) W3C Recommendation (November 16, 1999), http://www.w3.org/TR/xslt
20. Moodle course management system. http://moodle.org/
21. Moodle XML. http://docs.moodle.org/en/Moodle_XML

An Improved Platform for Medical E-Learning

Liana Stanescu[1], Marian Cristian Mihaescu[1], Dumitru Dan Burdescu[1],
Eugen Georgescu[2], and Ligia Florea[2]

[1] University of Craiova, Bvd. Decebal, 107, Craiova, Romania
{stanescu, mihaescu, burdescu}@software.ucv.ro
[2] University of Medicine and Pharmacy, Bvd. 1 Mai no.66, Craiova, Romania
efgmed@yahoo.fr, ligiaflorea@yahoo.com

Abstract. The paper presents an improved E-Learning platform that is especially designed for medical education. There are presented users tasks, having the following roles: administrator, secretary and teacher. The facilities of the students are also presented: students have the possibility to download course materials, take tests or sustain final examinations and communicate with all parties involved. An element of originality for this platform is the image database that is permanently updated by the teachers. The students can use this database for simple text based queries, or content-based visual queries. The content-based visual query represents a modern possibility to query the image databases using characteristics that were automatically extracted from images: colour, texture or regions. Combining content-based visual query with other access methods (text-based, hierarchical methods) for a teaching image database, helps students to view images in the database in a simple and direct manner, stimulating learning by comparing the similar cases and their particularities, or comparing similar images that have different diagnostics.

Keywords: Medical E-Learning, teaching image database, content-based visual query, colour feature, texture feature, colour region.

1 Introduction

Today's medical educators are facing different challenges than their predecessors in teaching tomorrow's physicians. In the past few decades, changes in health care delivery and advances in medicine have increased demands in academic education, resulting in less time for teaching than has previously been the case [1]. Changes in sites of health care delivery, from acute care institutions to community-based settings for chronic care, have required adaptations in educational venues [2].

Finding time to teach "new" fields such as genomics, palliative care, geriatrics, and complementary medicine is difficult when medical school curricula are already challenged to cover conventional subjects [1]. Traditional instructor centred teaching is yielding to a student centred model that puts students in control of their own learning. A recent shift toward competency-based curricula emphasizes the learning's outcome not the process of education [3]. E-Learning refers to the use of Internet technologies to deliver a broad array of solutions that enhance knowledge and performance [4], [5].

H. Leung et al. (Eds.): ICWL 2007, LNCS 4823, pp. 392–403, 2008.

E-Learning can be used by medical educators to improve the efficiency and effectiveness of educational interventions to confront the social, scientific, and pedagogical challenges noted above. It has gained popularity in the past decade; however, its use is highly variable among medical schools and appears to be more common in basic science courses than in clinical clerkships [6], [7].

Innovations in medical education lay their mark on curriculum, technology, assessment and professionalism. The curriculum model of the future should be student-centred, problem- or task-based, integrated, interdisciplinary, inter-professional, community-based and elective-driven, with core and student-selected components. The goal is systematic outcome-based education [8]. But how is this ideal to be achieved? And how do we move ourselves beyond a list of motherhood statements? Curricula are already becoming blended, using different technologies that allow students to access learning opportunities for what they need to know and when they are ready to learn. Technology will continue to be an important aspect of future medical education, having simulation as a key feature [9]. To keep pace with curriculum changes, assessment must move beyond multiple-choice tests of knowledge and multi-station tests of "presupposed" clinical skills using simulated patients. There is an increasing need to assess aspects of professional behaviour and competence within the health system. Portfolio assessment may be one way to partially achieve this task, but we have a long way to go before we can be sure we are giving graduating diplomas to truly competent doctors with the necessary professional behaviour.

The traditional or electronic courses include a series of relevant images that enhance the text-based information. Generally, the number of images included is reduced. That is why a medical image database that includes a high number of images (hundreds, thousands) might bring high benefits for E-Learning. The medical images can also contain alphanumerical information added by the teacher: diagnostics, treatment and patient evolution.

The students can query this type of teaching image database in two different ways:

- Traditionally, by the text-based method; for example, the diagnostic is written and all the images associated to it are searched in the database.
- Content-based query; in this case keywords or other texts are not used. The query uses the characteristics extracted from images (for example colour or texture). This type of query is implemented taking into account the whole image, or only parts of it (regions). In the first case the name of the query is content-based image query. It will find in the database all the images that are significantly similar to the query image. In the second case, the name of the query is content-based region query. It needs to be selected one or several regions used as query regions and it searches in the database all the images that contain the selected regions. In this case it is necessary to have an automated region extraction algorithm for images, using certain characteristics (for example colour).

Medical learning is the most important direction for using content-based visual query, besides diagnostic aid and medical research.

Using content-based visual query with other access methods (text-based, hierarchical methods) to a teaching image database allows students to see images and associated information from database in a simple and direct manner. They only have to select a query image and find the similar ones; this method stimulates learning, by comparing similar cases along with their particularities, or by comparing cases that are visually similar, but with different diagnostics.

The paper presents an improved medical E-Learning platform. It has implemented both traditional functions with simple text based queries and content based retrieval for a teaching image database. This can enhance the level of teaching. These images are inserted in the database by teachers and are accompanied by a great variety of examples, diagnostics and special cases.

2   The Functions of the Medical Virtual Platform

The main goal of the application is to give students the possibility to download course materials, take tests or sustain final examinations and communicate with all parties involved. To accomplish this, four different roles were defined for the platform: sysadmin, secretary, professor and student.

2.1   Roles

The main task of sysadmin users is to manage secretaries. A sysadmin user may add or delete secretaries, or change their password. He may also view the actions performed by all other users of the platform. All actions performed by users are logged. This way the sysadmin may check the activity that takes place on the application. The logging facility has some benefits: an audit may be performed for the application with the logs as witness; security breaches may also be discovered.

A sysadmin user may block an IP so that no user will be able to access the application from that IP. Finally, the overall activity of users represents valuable data. This data may be off-line analyzed using machine learning or even data mining techniques so that important conclusions may be obtained regarding the quality of service for the application. The quality of service may have two indicators: the learning proficiency of students and the capability of the application to classify students according to their accumulated knowledge.

A sysadmin may post an instant message to any user and can view users that are active. For each of them, the sysadmin may obtain the list of executed actions.

A statistics page is also available. It displays the number of users that entered the application, the total number of students, and the number of students with and without activity, as well as other information that gives an overall view on the activity on the application.

Secretary users manage sections, professors, disciplines and students. These actions will finally set up the application so that professors and students may use it. The secretaries have also the task to set up the structure of study years for all sections. The structure of a study year is made of a list of periods. All periods that define the study year are disjunctive in time and are characterized by a name, start date and end date. For each period there is also specified the exams that may be taken and the grants needed. The secretaries have the possibility of searching students using different criteria like name, section, year of study or residence. The secretaries have a large set of available reports regarding the student's status.

The main task of a professor is to manage the assigned disciplines while the discipline is made up of chapters. The professor sets up chapters by specifying the name and the course documentation. Only students enrolled in a section in which a discipline is studied may download the course's document and take tests or examinations. Besides setting up the course's document for each chapter, the professor manages test and exam questions. For each chapter the professor has to define two pools of questions, one used for testing and one used for exams. He specifies the number of questions that will be randomly extracted to create a test or an exam. This way of generating tests and exams is intended to be flexible enough for the professor.

All tests and exams are taken under time constraints. For each chapter the professor sets up a number of seconds necessary to answer questions of that chapter. The professor has also flexibility for creating and editing questions. A question may contain pictures, and thus equations, formulas or other graphics may be imbedded in it. For each question the professor sets up the visible answers and the correct answers. There are two implemented formulas that may be used for calculating grades. For each discipline the professor chooses and sets any of the formulas such that it will be used for all tests and exams taken at that discipline.

Professors have also the possibility of searching students using different criteria and a large set of available reports that help them in working with students.

The application offers students the possibility to download course materials, take tests and exams and communicate with other parties involved, as professors and secretaries.

Students may download only course materials for the disciplines that belong to sections where they are enrolled. They can take tests and exams with constraints that were set up by the secretary through the year structure function.

Students have access to personal data and can modify them as needed. A feedback form is also available. It is composed of questions that check aspects regarding the usability, efficiency and productivity of the application with respect to the student's needs.

All users must authenticate through username and password. If the username and password are valid the role of the user is determined and the appropriate interface is presented. The platform assigns a set of actions that the user may perform. Each time a user initiates an action the system checks if that action is allowed. This approach ensures security at user's level and makes sure that a student may not perform actions that are assigned to professor, secretary or sysadmin users.

A record of sustained tests is kept for all students. In fact, the taken test or exams are saved in full for later use. That is why a student or a professor may view a previously taken test or exam if needed. For each question is presented what the student checked, which was the correct answer, which was the maximum score that could be obtained from that question and how many points did the student obtain. At the end it is presented the final formula used to compute the grade and the grade itself.

Besides these core functions for the on-line testing some other are implemented or currently under development. A message board is available for professors, secretaries and students to ensure peer-to-peer communication. This facility is implemented within the platform such that no other service (e.g. email server) may be necessary.

In order to enforce the year structure function that is set up by the secretary a grant/revoke system is implemented for students, secretaries and professors.

The logging facility that is mainly used by sysadmin is transparently implemented for all users (secretaries, professors and students). Whenever one of them performs an action (e.g. a student starts or finishes an exam) that action is recorded for later use.

2.2 Teaching Image Database

Further on, this paper presents the way in which a database with medical images is managed for educational purposes. This implies the insertion of images and the launch into execution of some pre-processing algorithms for extracting information related to colour and texture, as well as the significant colour regions. Thus the images are prepared for the next stage, which is that of content-based query by colour, texture or their combination.

For the **database management**, the system offers professors the possibility to insert new images in the database, together with their relevant information, namely: path and name of the image file, the diagnosis, as well as supplementary information that include specialists' observation regarding the disease and the way in which it is illustrated by image, treatment and evolution. The images are pre-processed, namely they are transformed from the RGB colour space to HSV colour space and quantized to 328 colours, being thus prepared for a future query. The HSV colour space is preferred, for its properties (compactness, completeness, naturalness and uniformity), which allow it to be proper for usage in the content-based visual retrieval [10].

For the quantization of the HSV colour space, the solution with 328 colours was chosen. The solution of quantization at 328 colours originated from the one proposed by Smith [10] and which assumed 166 colours. The researches conducted in [16] showed that in the case of HSV images quantized at 166 colours all the medically significant colour regions were not possible to be found. The solution to this problem consisted in the increase of the quantization degree to 328 colours. The quantization produces 36 hues, 3 saturations, 3 values and 4 greys, that means 328 distinct colours in the HSV colour space. The colour information from the image is represented by means of the colour histogram and by the binary colour set. The colour information is stored in the database and it is used furthermore in the content-based image query and content-based region query.

In order to realize the content-based region query on a database with medical images, an automated algorithm for detecting the colour regions, significant for the diagnosis, is necessary. The colour set back-projection algorithm was the one chosen. This was introduced initially by Swain and Ballard and then developed in research projects at Columbia University, in the content-based visual retrieval domain. This technique provides the automated extraction of regions and the representation of their colour content [10].

Together with colour, texture is a powerful characteristic of an image, which is present in nature and in medical images also. Thus a disease can be indicated by changes in the colour and texture of a tissue.

There are many techniques used for texture extraction, but there is not any certain method that can be considered the most appropriate, this depending on the application and the type of images taken into account. Among the most representatives methods of texture detection are the co-occurrence matrices and Gabor representations, presented here [11], [13] and [14]. These two reasons and the fact that studies have showed that the results of these two methods can complete one another, led us to the idea of using two methods in parallel in order to detect the colour texture.

In the case of Gabor filters, starting from the representation of the HSV colour space, the colour in complex can be represented. The affix of any point from the HSV cone base can be computed as [11], [13]: $z_M = S (\cos H + i \sin H)$. Therefore, the saturation is interpreted as the magnitude and the hue as the phase of the complex value b; the value channel is not included. The advantages of this representation of complex colour are: the simplicity due to the fact that the colour is now a scalar and not a vector and the combination between channels is done before filtering. So, the colour can be represented in complex [11],[13]:

$$b(x, y) = S(x, y) \cdot e^{iH(x, y)} . \tag{1}$$

The computation of the Gabor characteristics for the image represented in the HS-complex space is similar to the one for the monochromatic Gabor characteristics, because the combination of colour channels is done before filtering [11][13]:

$$C_{f, \varphi} = (\sum_{x, y} (FFT^{-1}\{P(u, v) \cdot M_{f, \varphi}(u, v)\}))^2 \tag{2}$$

The Gabor characteristics vector is created using the value $C_{f, \varphi}$ computed for 3 scales and 4 orientations [11], [13]:

$$f = (C_{0,0}, C_{0,1}, ..., C_{2,3}) \tag{3}$$

The similitude between the texture characteristics of the query image Q and the target image T is defined by the metric [11][13]:

$$D^2(Q,T) = \sum_f \sum_\varphi d_{f\varphi}(Q,T), where \; d_{f\varphi} = (f^Q - f^T)^2 \tag{4}$$

In the case of the co-occurrence matrices, for colour images, one matrix is computed for each of the three channels (R, G, B). For an image f(x, y), the co-occurrence matrix $h_{d\phi}(i, j)$ is defined so that each entry (i, j) is equal to the number of times for that $f(x_1, y_1)$ = i and $f(x_2, y_2) = j$, where $(x_2, y_2) = (x_1, y_1) + (d \cos \phi, d \sin \phi)$ [14].

This leads to three quadratic matrices of dimension equal to the number of the colour levels presented in an image (256 in our case) for each distance d and orientation ϕ.

The classification of texture is based on the characteristics extracted from the co-occurrence matrix: energy, entropy, maximum probability, contrast, inverse difference moment and correlation [14]. The three vectors of texture characteristics extracted from the three occurrence matrices are created using the 6 characteristics computed for d=1 and ϕ=0.

The texture similitude between the query image Q and target image T is computed by the Euclidian metric.

The students can retrieve the information from the medical teaching database in several ways. The **simple text-based query** is made at the level of the diagnostic. Such query has as a result the images that contain in diagnosis field the text completed by the user, using LIKE pattern operator. Detailed supplementary information is also displayed.

The **content-based image query on colour feature** requires the selection of an image as a query image and retrieval of all those images from database which best resemble it, taking into consideration the colour feature. Also, for every image detailed information is displayed. It should be mentioned that in this case three sets of result images are displayed, which correspond to calculation mode of the distances between query image and target image. There have been taken into consideration the intersection of histograms, square distance between histograms and Euclidian distance [10].

The reason why these three modalities for computing the images similitude were chosen is explained later in this work. The studies made and presented in [15] shown that the results of the content-based image retrieval were poorer in the case of medical images than in the case of the nature images. None of the distances mentioned above caused significantly better results than the others, so that to motivate it's choosing. In each case, relevant images for the query were retrieved with one of the distances and the others did not retrieve them. It could be observed that in most cases, all the results retrieved by computing the three distances may be useful for not loosing relevant images for the query, consequently they complement one another.

Figure 1 shows the window that displays the image query results. These results are organized in three sets. The first set contains the images retrieved using the histograms intersection, the second using the Euclidian distance and the last one computing the quadratic distance between histograms.

In the **content-based image query on colour texture feature** the query image has to be selected, the result being a set of images from the database that have a similar texture with it. The result will consist of two sets of images: the first one is retrieved using the co-occurrence matrices, while the second one is retrieved using the Gabor filters. It is recommended that the two methods be used in parallel, from the same reason, which is that of completeness in relevant results. Also, it gives students the possibility of visual interrogation using the colour and the texture as criteria, taking into consideration the fact that a sick tissue may present modifications of colour and texture. Moreover, studies have shown that the combination of the two features may produce a bigger set of relevant images [17].

In the **content-based region query on colour feature** is necessary to select an image and to display the colour regions detected with the colour set back-projection algorithm. The user must tick one or more colour regions for content-based region query. The result is a set of images from the database that contain the query region(s). The colour similitude between two regions is computed with the quadratic distance between colour sets [10].

If the content-based region query option is chosen a window like the one in figure 2 will be shown. The display of all colour regions detected for that particular image takes place. For each region there is a checkbox that allows the selection of one or more regions for the query. When pressing the button "Find Regions" the content-based query will be launched based on the query region(s).

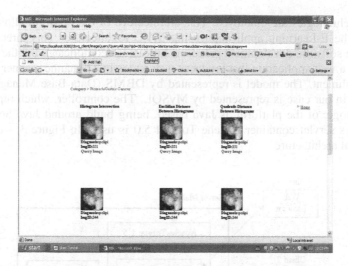

Fig. 1. The results of the content-based image query on colour feature

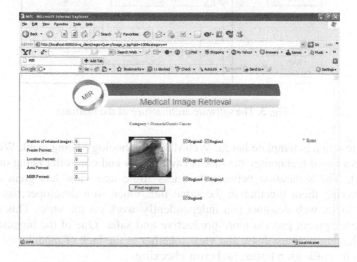

Fig. 2. The detected colour regions with colour set back-projection algorithm

3 The Platform's Architecture

Many issues appear when applications contain a mixture of data access code, business logic code, and presentation code. Such applications are difficult to maintain, because interdependencies between all of the components cause strong ripple effects whenever a change is made anywhere. The Model-View-Controller (MVC for short) design pattern solves these problems by decoupling data access, business logic, and data presentation and user interaction. The E-Learning platform consists of a framework on which a web application may be developed. On server side we choose only open source software that may run on almost all platforms. To achieve this goal Java related technologies are employed. This architecture of the platform allows development of the E-Learning application using MVC architecture. This three-tier model makes the software development process a little more complicated but the advantages of having a web application that produces web pages in a dynamic manner is a worthy accomplishment. The model is represented by DBMS (Data Base Management System) that in our case is represented by MySQL. The controller, which represents the business logic of the platform, is Java based, being build around Java Servlet Technology. As servlet container Apache Tomcat 5.0 is used. In Figure 3 it is presented the general architecture.

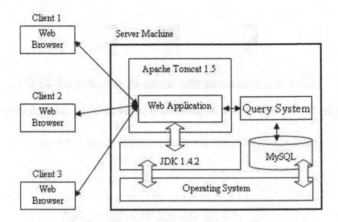

Fig. 3. The software architecture of the platform

The view tier is template based, WebMacro technology being used. WebMacro is also a Java based technology the link between view and controller being done at context level. The separation between business logic and view has great advantages against having them together in the same tier. Once web developer has set up the business logic, web designer can independently work on the view. This decoupling makes development process more productive and safer. One of the biggest disadvantages of having business logic and view together is the lack of modularity that brings problems in application testing and error checking.

The application is an implementation of platform to which new data sources, business logic, and data views may be added.

In Figure 4 the architecture of the content-based visual query module is presented. The module is made with JSP technology and uses a MySQL database. First time the professor inserts a new image in the teaching image database, the pre-processing module is activated and the following tasks are performed: the transformation of the image from RGB to HSV colour space; the quantization at 328 colours; the detecting of colour regions for which size is bigger than a threshold. All the information given by the user and those resulted after the pre-processing (colour histogram, the texture characteristics vectors, the binary colour set, the information for the colour regions detected) is stored in the database. Then, the student can query the database in three

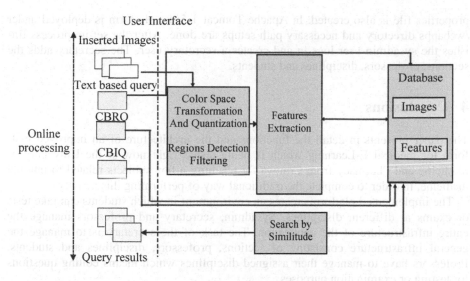

Fig. 4. Block diagram of the query system

ways: simple text-based query, content-based image query and content-based region query. These queries imply the access to the database, the use of information already stored in tables, the computing of distances presented above and the retrieval of the results to the user.

Another important part of software architecture regarding software development process is code and application testing. For this purpose JUnit is used. Unit tests are created for running the critical code like creating of a test, computing the result, saving the questions from the test, saving the test result, computing time for test. To accomplish this regressive testing is used. For each chain of actions a scenario is defined. If the computed result matches the expected result it means the test passed. Otherwise, it means something is wrong with the code because it does not behave as it is supposed to. Whenever a method is added, test cases are written trying to have a full coverage of the code. The code (either code itself or test code) is automatically nightly build and tests are automatically nightly run such that in the software development process many programmers can contribute.

Performance testing is also an important part of the development process. It is known that an E-Learning application may have hundreds or even thousands of registered users. We do not want to be in the situation when too many users slow down the platform or even make it crash due to a specific sequence of actions. To avoid this, performance tests scenarios were developed to see how the platform responds to different situations. Situations like twenty users trying to log in at the same time and taking a test are currently run. Whenever new functionalities are developed new scenarios for performance testing are created so that the platform shall run properly. The platform is currently in use on Windows 2003 Server machine. The setup process consists of two stages. After all needed software is installed (JDK 1.4.2, Apache Tomcat 1.5 and MySQL) the application is deployed. The database structure is created and a sysadmin user is added. A MySQL user that corresponds to values from a properties file is also created. In Apache Tomcat 1.5 the platform is deployed under /webapps directory and necessary path setups are done. After the set-up process finishes the sysadmin user logs in and creates a secretary user. The secretary adds the sections, professors, disciplines and students.

4 Conclusions

The paper presents in detail the functions and the architecture of an improved platform for medical E-Learning which is being tested right now at the University of Medicine and Pharmacy from Craiova for teaching a few subjects related to internal medicine, in order to complete the traditional way of performing this activity.

The implemented platform creates an environment in which students can take tests or exams at different disciplines. Sysadmin, secretary and professors manage the entire infrastructure of the application. The task of the secretary is to manage the general infrastructure consisting of sections, professors, disciplines and students. Professors have to manage their assigned disciplines which means editing questions for testing or examination purposes.

The final beneficiary is the student by having the possibility to take on-line tests within an E-Learning application that also puts at his disposal many other facilities. Among them there is peer-to-peer messaging between students, secretaries and professors, statistics and logs for the administrator, year structure for the secretary and many other. The implemented system offers students a multimedia medical teaching database that apart from the traditional information also contains medical images. The image database can be consulted in a modern way, image or region-based manner. These query facilities are implemented within the E-Learning platform by a separate module dedicated to this only purpose.

The E-Learning platform works in parallel with the classic way of teaching, as a method of to complete students' activity. Practically, the student is thus helped to classify different medical images according to certain criteria related especially to the clinical part of the subjects taught. We consider that learning and consolidating aspects relating to the identification of specific clinical situations is very much improved after the students use the facilities offered by the presented E-Learning platform.

References

1. Ozuah, P.O.: Undergraduate medical education: Thoughts on future challenges. BMC Med. Educ. 2, 8–10 (2002)
2. Nair, B.R., Finucane, P.M.: Reforming medical education to enhance the management of chronic disease. Med. J Aust. 179, 257–259 (2003)
3. Leung, W.C.: Competency based medical training: Review. BMJ 325, 693–696 (2002)
4. Rosenberg, M.: E-Learning: Strategies for Delivering Knowledge in the Digital Age. McGraw-Hill, New York (2001)
5. Wentling, T., Waight, C., Gallaher, J., La Fleur, J., Wang, C., Kanfer, A.: E-Learning: A Review of Literature. University of Illinois National Center for Supercomputer Applications, Urbana- Champaign, IL (2000) (accessed November 22, 2005), http://learning.ncsa.uiuc.edu/papers/elearnlit.pdf

6. Moberg, T.F., Whitcomb, M.E.: Educational technology to facilitate medical students' learning: Background. Acad. Med. 74, 1146–1150 (1999)
7. Ward, J.P., Gordon, J., Field, M.J., Lehmann, H.P.: Communication and information technology in medical education. Lancet 357, 792–796 (2001)
8. Harden, R.M., Sowden, S., Dunn, W.R.: Some educational strategies in curriculum development: The SPICES model. Med. Educ. 18, 284–297 (1984)
9. Issenberg, S.B., McGaghie, W.C., Petrusa, E.R.: Features and uses of high-fidelity medical simulations that lead to effective learning: A BEME systematic review. Med. Teach. 27, 10–28 (2005)
10. Smith, J.R.: Integrated Spatial and Feature Image Systems: Retrieval, Compression and Analysis. Ph.D. thesis, Graduate School of Arts and Sciences, Columbia University (1997)
11. Palm, C., Keysers, D., Lehmann, T., Spitzer, K.: Gabor Filtering of Complex Hue/Saturation Images For Color Texture Classification. In: Proceedings of JCIS2000, pp. 45–49 (2000)
12. Muller, H., Michoux, N., Bandon, D., Geissbuhler, A.: A Review of Content based Image Retrieval Systems in Medical Application – Clinical Benefits and Future Directions. Int J Med Inform 73(1), 1–23 (2004)
13. Zhang, D., Wong, A., Infrawan, M., Lu, G.: Content-Based Image Retrieval Using Gabor Texture Features. In: Proceedings of IEEE Pacific-Rim Conference on Multimedia, pp. 392–395 (2000)
14. Del Bimbo, A.: Visual Information Retrieval. Morgan Kaufmann Publishers, San Francisco (2001)
15. Stanescu, L., Burdescu, D., Ion, A.: A Comparative Study of Some Metrics used in Content-Based Image Retrieval. In: Proceedings of SYNASC, pp. 307–318 (2004)
16. Stanescu, L., Burdescu, D., Mocanu, M.: Detecting Color Regions and Content-Based Region Query in Databases with Medical Images. Buletinul Stiintific al Universitatii "Politehnica" Timisoara, Seria Automatica si Calculatoare 49(63), 117–122 (2004)
17. Stanescu, L., Burdescu, D., Ion, A., Brezovan, M.: Improving the Results of the Content-Based Image Query on Medical Imagery. In: Proceedings of ICINCO, pp. 432–437 (2006)

A 3D Geometry Search Engine in Support of Learning

Gary K.L. Tam[1,2], Rynson W.H. Lau[1,2], and Jianmin Zhao[2]

[1] Department of Computer Science, Durham University, United Kingdom
[2] College of Math., Physics and Info. Eng'g, Zhejiang Normal University, China
{g.k.l.tam, rynson.lau}@durham.ac.uk, zjm@zjnu.cn

Abstract. Due to the increasing popularity of 3D graphics in animation and games, the use of 3D geometry models increases dramatically. Despite its growth in importance, geometry models are in fact difficult and time consuming to build. A distance learning system for the construction of such models could greatly facilitate students from different places and times to learn and practice. In such a system, the most important component is the search engine, which serves as both the data source of teaching materials and also a sharing platform for students' portfolios. Though there are many search engines developed for text and for multimedia data, such as images and videos, search engines for geometry models are still in its infant stage. To design a search engine for a distance learning platform, there are still challenges to face. In this paper, we investigate two important issues, namely, feature analysis that affects the general usage of a system and the speed that affects the number of concurrent users. Our focus in this work is on deformable models (non-rigid models), which are most frequently used for animation and game design. Our method offers a mechanism to extract, match, index and fast retrieval of stable features from these models.

Keywords: Deformable geometry models, multimedia search engines, multimedia retrieval, geometry model retrieval.

1 Introduction

The Internet has become an important place for educational resources in recent years. Ranging from instructor-led learning to self-study, students are encouraged to actively learn from this free library. To find relevant information and learning materials from this huge knowledge collection, an effective search engine is typically needed, which means that the search engine may be considered as the entry point to the Internet. One notable search engine for text documents is Google. Taking a simple example of searching for a mathematic equation, a student may type in some descriptive keywords of the equation and the search engine will return its definition and usage. Hence, the search engine may also be considered as an important educational tool to help locate useful information from this huge information/knowledge/resource database of the Internet.

In the past, education was generally conducted through text books. With the advance in multimedia technology, we are beginning to see a lot of multimedia educational

H. Leung et al. (Eds.): ICWL 2007, LNCS 4823, pp. 404–415, 2008.

materials that include images, animation and videos. The use of multimedia in presentations not only promotes students' interests and interactivity but also helps prolong their memory on the subject materials [20]. Similar to text and documents, there is a growing demand for more effective search engines that support multimedia information too. 3D geometry models, being a type of multimedia information, are getting popularity recently due to their widespread use in animation and games. However, geometry models can also be used in many 3D applications for education too. For example, [14] discusses how to progressively transmit geometry models in a 3D training system or a 3D engine for educational games. Despite the advance in 3D modeling tools, geometry models are still difficult and time consuming to build. Students often need to spend a long time to learn and to construct geometry models because of the deep learning curve. Here, we can see that a learning system to guide the students in constructing geometry models may help reduce the learning time and encourage model sharing. To support this type of applications, an efficient geometry search engine that facilitates sharing and reuse of geometry models is essential. A typical scenario is that one may want to construct a model by combining parts coming from models made by others. This may require the retrieval desired objects [6]. Given a search engine, the user may first retrieve some related models, and then cut and past parts from them to form the new model.

As geometry models are becoming more popular, we are beginning to see geometry search engines that are developed for new applications which store 3D data in geometry form, e.g., medical data [12], protein molecules [9], cultural artifacts [18], and mechanical parts [1]. We can see that a search engine may help trainee doctors to search for similar organs, archaeology students to search for antiques, and mechanical students to search for mechanical parts from a geometry database. Hence, a geometry search engine is useful in many applications including education.

Currently, there is a substantial amount of work devoted to matching and retrieving rigid geometry models efficiently and accurately. For example, Princeton University has developed a search engine [5] where benchmarking is also available [21]. The method presented here, however, targets a more powerful type of models: the deformable models, i.e., models with similar skeletons but different postures. These models are very useful in designing and creating 3D applications for education and computer games. There are not many search engines designed for 3D deformable models, and they are generally slow because they apply graph matching techniques. In our recent work [24], we have presented an effective method for extracting and matching deformation-stable features. However, in order to build a search engine for web-based or distance learning systems, there are two challenges to overcome. First, it should be accurate in retrieval; second, it should be fast enough to support many users [8]. In this paper, we will focus our discussion on the necessary information for building a search engine that supports distance learning system.

The rest of this paper is organized as follows. Section 2 briefly surveys related work. Section 3 presents an overview of the whole matching framework. Section 4 discusses the representation and storage of features. Sections 5 and 6 discuss the algorithms for matching and indexing. These are the essential building blocks of a search engine. Section 7 provides some experimental results. Finally, Section 8 briefly concludes the work presented in this paper and discusses some possible future works.

2 Related Work

The earliest retrieval systems for multimedia content may date back several decades ago. Since we focus this paper on search engines that support geometry models, in particular deformable models, we would like to refer readers to [13] for a full survey of existing retrieval work for images, videos and audios. In this section, we briefly survey existing work on 3D geometry model retrieval. Classical 3D retrieval methods can be categorized into four approaches: geometry-based, transform-based, image-based, and topology-based. The first three methods can only handle non-deformable (i.e., rigid) models, whereas the fourth can handle deformable (i.e., non-rigid) models.

2.1 Non-deformable Geometry Models

Geometry, transform, and image-based approaches focus on retrieving non-deformable 3D models only. The geometry-based approach concerns properties related to the shape and size of a model. In general, methods of this approach can be classified into three types: methods based on extracting physical properties [11, 3], methods based on computing histograms or some distribution functions [17] and methods based on computing energy for morphing a model [25, 27]. The transform-based approach analyzes 3D models in a different feature domain. Transformation functions used include Fourier Transform [26] and Zernike Transform [15]. [5, 10, 15] propose Spherical Harmonic for extracting rotation-invariant features. The image-based approach captures features from 2D image views of a 3D model [2, 16].

2.2 Deformable Geometry Models

The topology-based approach is the only approach that supports matching of deformable models through analyzing the model with skeletal or topological information. As this approach is the focus of our work, we discuss these methods in more detail here. In [7], the Multiresolution Reeb Graph (MRG) is proposed. It first partitions a model into nodes using integral geodesic at different resolutions. Unlike Euclidean distance, geodesic measures distances on the surface and is not affected by model deformation. Thus, integral geodesic indicates how far a point is from the surface center. MRG then constructs an MRG tree by analyzing the adjacency of each node in the current and lower/higher resolutions. In each node, it uses area and length as geometric features. To match two MRG trees, a heuristic graph-matching algorithm is applied in a coarse-to-fine manner, starting from the root nodes of the two trees and traversing down the trees following the child nodes with maximum similarity. When all high-resolution nodes are exhausted, the matching process traces back to the lowest resolution nodes again. All similarity values computed are added up as the final similarity value. In [22], a voxel thinning method is proposed to extract the skeleton from a voxelized model. In each skeletal node, the radial distribution of edges is preserved for local shape matching. To speed up the query process, a topological feature vector is generated for each skeletal graph as an index to the database. Nearest neighbor search is then applied for model retrieval. To further verify the correctness of the retrieved models, an enhanced maximum cardinality minimum weight bipartite matching algorithm is used. Instead of using the skeletal graph, [23] analyzes models based on the component graph. A model is first split by mesh decomposition with each component node described by one primitive. An optimal error-correcting sub-graph isomorphism algorithm is then applied to match two component graphs.

In summary, topology-based methods handle deformable models using skeletal information. However, several research issues have still not been explored yet. First, although most of these methods work well in discriminating dissimilar-skeleton models, none of them consider the issue of discriminating similar-skeleton models as they use only local geometric features. Second, due to the large feature size or the use of slow graph matching techniques [23], these methods are generally slow in practice and do not scale well to large databases. Third, although [22] proposes an indexing scheme for large databases, it may still suffer from the accuracy problem when answering nearest neighbor queries as it separates topological matching and geometric matching into two processes. To improve the recall rate, it needs to return a large number of models in the first pass, causing a performance penalty to the indexing scheme.

3 Overview

The framework of a content-based 3D model retrieval system is shown in Fig 1. It is composed of several components: multimedia database, feature extraction, retrieval algorithm and the search engine interface. To build a multimedia database, 3D models are first converted into compact and representative features through the feature extraction process (Section 4). An indexing structure is then built to store the features in an efficient manner. A typical approach for content-based retrieval is called query by example. In 3D model retrieval, the user inputs a sample model. The system extracts the representative features from this model for matching with the features extracted from the models stored in the geometry database using a feature matching technique (Section 5). Models in the database with similar features will be returned to the user. To speed up the searching process, the system may employ the k-nearest neighbor search on the database index to find models that are most relevant to the given query, and return results through the search engine interface (Section 6).

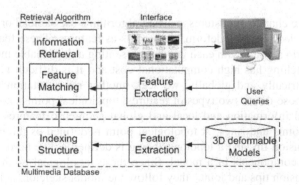

Fig. 1. A search engine for 3D geometry models

4   Feature Representation

The identification of compact and representative features is essential in content-based retrieval system for two main reasons. First, it is usually far more efficient to compare compact features than the raw data. For example, in the case of videos, there can be over several gigabytes of video data. If a search engine compares all the video data frame by frame, it would take a long time before it can return any results. This is certainly not a good searching experience for general users. Second, using representative features to represent the original data may allow certain kind of invariance analysis. For example, in the case of 3D models comparison, it is necessary that the system can handle rotation and scale invariance. Where scale invariance can be achieved by simple normalization, rotation invariance may not be trivial. To achieve rotation-invariant representation, Fourier analysis [26] and Spherical Harmonic analysis [5, 10] are proposed to convert rotation dependent features into rotation independent form by transforming them into another feature domain. Similarly, to handle 3D deformable models, we must obtain compact and representative features that are stable towards scaling, rotation and deformation. Considering the examples shown in Fig 2, it is impossible to compare the wolf and dog directly without taking care of their different postures.

Fig. 2. Compact and representative topological features (left: objects, right: features)

To handle the change of postures, existing algorithms use skeletal or topological information extracted from 3D deformable models as features. These features are interconnected to form a graph with each graph representing a deformable model. However, since graph matching has high computational cost and it is difficult to describe these features geometrically and globally, we seek another representation instead. In our system, we propose to use two types of features: topological points and rings to represent the skeletal information and local and global geometric features to characterize each of these points and rings. A topological point is defined as the salient point located at a protrusion tip, and a topological ring is defined as the border that separates two significant components in a model. Since these topological points and rings are located at protrusion tips and joints, they follow the model skeleton and thus are stable towards posture deformation. As an example, we color the components of three models (wolf and dog) in different colors as shown in Fig 2. The border of two color regions represents a topological ring. To further show the locations of topological points and rings, we have also presented them explicitly on the right of Fig 2. We can see that even though the two dogs have different poses, they have similar topological points and rings at similar locations.

Apart from topological features, it is also necessary to define geometric features to characterize each of the topological features so that the system can discriminate deformable models that may have similar topological points and rings (say, wolf and dog, or boy and baby). In our system, we consider two types of features, local (importance and spatial locations) and global features (three types of geodesic distribution data). The importance describes the weight of a topological feature. We note that the importance of a topological feature located in a finger should be smaller than that located in the leg. This is intuitive as removing a leg from a 3D model gives a larger perceptual impact than removing a finger. In our system, we use a scalar value which is equal to the surrounding area of a topological feature as importance. To specify where a topological feature is, we calculate a scalar value using normalized integral geodesic. The function of integral geodesic was proposed in [7] for partitioning a mesh into different sections. We apply this function because integral geodesic measures the centricity of a model surface [24]. Importance and spatial location are local features because they describe the topological features locally.

Apart from local features, we also consider three global geometric features: curvature, area and average distance. We construct three vectors from these features by first dividing the model into many bands according to their geodesic distances from a given topological feature. Since geodesic is calculated on the surface, the resulting feature vectors are stable towards mesh deformation. As an example, we divide two dog models shown in Fig 3 into geodesic bands relative to a topological ring located at one of the legs. Bands of the same color indicate that they are within the same geodesic interval from the ring. We can see that although the two dogs have different poses, the locations of the color bands are similar. In each of these bands, we capture three types of geometric information: curvature, area and average Distance. Curvature measures the local deformation of each band, area measures the size of each band, and average distance measures the thickness of each band. We can see that these bands and features are similar across similar models with similar skeleton. These features are global because they capture the overall global shape of a model.

Fig. 3. Geodesic distribution with respect to a topological ring in a leg

We summarize topological features and their geometric features in Fig 4. A_i and S_i represent the importance and spatial location, respectively. DC_i, DA_i and DT_i represent curvature, area and average distance (thickness) distribution, respectively. We store all these features in XML format, as it is convenient for debugging. A sample XML database is as follow:

```
<?xml version="1.0"?>
<!-- This is a model database -->
<ModelDB>
  <!-- This is a model -->
  <Model>
    <Name>Model File Name</Name>
    <Group>Model Grouping</Group>
    <Features>
      <!-- a feature -->
      <Feature>
        <ID>...</ID>
        <type>POINT</type> <!-- or RING -->
        <importance>...</ importance>
        <spatial>...</ spatial >
        <KgHist KgHistSize="..." kg01="..." ... kg20="..."/>
        <areaHist areaHistSize ="..." a01="..." ... a20="..."/>
        <ptDistHist ptDistHistSize="..." d01="..." ... d20="..."/>
      </Feature>
      <!-- another feature -->
      <Feature>.........
      </Feature>
    </Features>
  </Model>

  <!-- another model -->
  <Model>.........
  </Model>
</ModelDB>
```

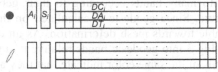

Fig. 4. Topological features and their corresponding geometric features

5   Feature Matching

When the representative features are available, we need a distance function to measure their similarity. If the distance between two sets of features is small, they are considered as similar. In general, it is not trivial to define an efficient distance function for a search engine as it must conform to the metric properties in order to apply an indexing technique. On the other hand, since we have different numbers of topological features for different models, direct application of the Euclidean distance is difficult.

In order to be able to compute a distance value efficiently while supporting indexing, we apply the Earth Mover Distance (EMD) approach. Given a predefined ground distance function, EMD calculates the similarity between two mass distributions in some features space. Supposing that one mass distribution is a collection of "earth" and the other mass distribution is a collection of holes, EMD measures the minimum amount of energy required to fill all holes with earths. The EMD approach computes its solution based on a transportation problem between supplier and consumer. Given some amount of goods and the cost of transporting one single unit of goods between each supplier and consumer, the transportation problem is to find the best flow of goods that is least-expensive. Similarly, computing the distance between two set of features can be modeled as a transportation problem by defining one set of features as the suppliers (earth) and the other as the consumers (holes), and let the cost function of transportation between suppliers and consumers be the predefined ground distance. Then, EMD computes the best flow (minimum energy) required. In our approach, we consider a topological feature as an EMD point and define importance (weight) as the amount of goods to transport. To describe the cost of transporting one unit of goods between two EMD points, we define a ground distance function Dist() based on geometric features as follows:

$$
\begin{aligned}
Dist(U_1, U_2) = \ & W_1 \times \mid G'_{norm}(U_1) - G'_{norm}(U_2) \mid \\
& + W_2 \times L_{2,norm}(K(U_1), K(U_2)) \\
& + W_3 \times L_{2,norm}(A(U_1), A(U_2)) \\
& + W_4 \times L_{2,norm}(H(U_1), H(U_2))
\end{aligned}
\tag{1}
$$

where G'_{norm} is the Normalized Integral Geodesic. K, A and H are the geometric vectors representing curvature, area and average distance (thickness), respectively, W_1, W_2, W_3, W_4 are ratios such that $W_1 + W_2 + W_3 + W_4 = 1$. We use these weights to adjust the relative importance of G'_{norm}, K, A and H. By using EMD, we can now avoid slow graph matching algorithms by converting the matching problem to a flow and transportation problem.

There are several advantages of using EMD. First, though EMD has a high computation complexity, it is very efficient practically as it is based on the simplex algorithm. Second, EMD can also be used to measure the distance between two multi-dimensional features. For example, it is intrinsically difficult in our case to define a distance between two models because our features are very complex: each model is described as a set of topological features with each of them characterized by local and global geometric features. Third, since our ground distance is a metric and we normalize all models to have equal weights, EMD becomes true metric naturally by definition [19].

6   Indexing and k-NN Search

A search engine should return results accurately and within an acceptable period of time. As most users are only interested in the first few tens of returned results, most search engines would employ an indexing structure so that relevant information can be retrieved without the need to traverse the whole database. For content-based retrieval systems, this is particularly important as the database is generally very large. One of the general approaches is to define features as k-dimensional points and apply existing spatial access indexing methods, like R-tree and KD-tree for fast retrieval. However, as explained in our previous section, our features are complex and it is difficult to transform them into k-dimensional points while preserving their distances. To support fast retrieval, we apply the vantage point (VP) tree [Chiueh94] to construct an indexing structure here.

The VP-tree is similar to the KD-tree in that both partition the metric space into separate spaces and build the search tree hierarchically on these spaces. While the KD-tree chooses the median as the separating point by projecting data to a dimension axis with maximum spread, the VP-tree partitions the space based on relative distances between data points and a particular vantage point. As shown in Fig 5a, the VP-tree algorithm chooses a vantage point (v) and partitions the feature space by a radius u. The space inside the circle represents features that are at most u distance away from v, whereas the space outside represents features that are at least u distance away from v. A VP-tree can then be constructed with the left branch storing features inside the circle (*Space₁*) and the right branch storing features outside the circle (*Space₂*). This partitioning process is applied recursively on all the features.

To apply the VP-tree in our 3D search engine, a distance function that satisfies the metric properties is required. Our method is based on the EMD approach, which can be proven a true metric. Therefore, our distance function is designed to fit into the VP-tree indexing structure. To search for the most relevant models with respect to an input query, it is equivalent to performing a k-Nearest Neighbor (kNN) search on the VP-tree. According to [4], kNN search on the VP-tree is like tree traversal while prune away unnecessary walk in the tree. Given a query q, as shown in Fig 5b, a kNN search is to find all neighbors within distance l, where l is dynamically adjusted to the distance of the kth nearest neighbor. Considering query q_1, since the query space does not overlap with *Space₁* of vantage point v, the traversal of left side of the tree can be avoided. Similarly for q_2, since there is no overlap between the query space and *Space₂*, the traversal of right side of the tree can be avoided. This kind of pruning can significantly reduce the computational and disk-IO costs. For query q_3, where the query space overlaps with both *Space₁* and *Space₂*, the search traverses both branches of the tree.

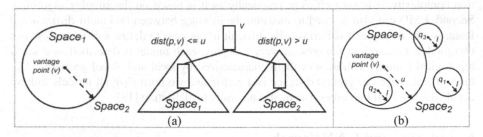

Fig. 5. Construction of a VP-tree & kNN search

7   Experimental Results

We have constructed a database of 600 deformable models, stored in XML format, which is easier for display and for debugging. In this section, we show some of the experimental results.

7.1   Feature Compactness

As seen in Table 1, sequential search is generally slow. It takes 0.88s for a full search of our database. This figure will scale up as the size of the database increases. After we apply indexing, however, the total speed is improved. This is particularly useful when the user just wants the first few relevant results. In the extreme case, if only the most relevant result is shown, it takes only 0.39s (43% of original full search time).

Table 1. Matching and retrieval times of a query

Average total time for matching one model	1ms
Average total time for one query (sequential search of whole database)	0.88s
VP-tree construction time from XML feature database	778.7s
Average time for 1-nearest neighbor search	0.39s
Average time for 2-nearest neighbor search	0.42s
Average time for 3-nearest neighbor search	0.47s
Average time for 4-nearest neighbor search	0.54s
Average time for 10-nearest neighbor search	0.77s

7.2 Matching Time

As seen in Table 2, after feature extraction, the total data size reduced from 487MB to 26.7MB, which is about 5% of the original data size. We expect that the storage size can be further reduced if we store the models in a binary format instead of XML.

Table 2. Storage size after feature extraction

Total size of all model files	487 MB
Average size of each model file	831 KB
Total size of the feature database (in XML)	26.7 MB
Average no. of topological features per model	30
Average size of the features per model (in XML)	45.6KB
Average memory space used for each model	16.2 KB
Size of the index file (VP-tree)	11 KB

7.3 Matching Accuracy

From our experiment, our feature representation is very efficient and effective. Fig 6 shows some of the experimental results and our web interface.

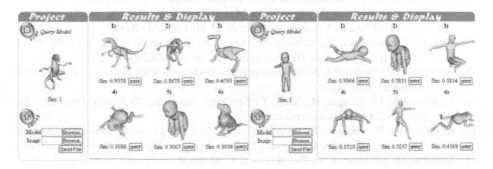

Fig. 6. The search engine interface and sample results

8 Conclusion

In this paper, we have proposed a search engine for 3D geometry (in particular deformable) models to support multimedia learning. Our method offers a mechanism for extracting, matching, indexing and efficient retrieval of deformation stable features. We have demonstrated the effectiveness of the proposed method with some experimental results. We have also shown that a geometry search engine can be useful in many learning-based systems. However, there is still much work to do in order to build a fully functional system. We summarize several future works here. From a user-centric point of view, a better interface is indeed needed. Currently, we allow users to upload a simple model or reuse an existing model as query input. Though it matches general use, it is not very user-friendly. One possible extension is to allow user to sketch and build their query models on the fly. Tools for cutting, copying, pasting or deforming may also be provided for the users to build their query models. From the technique-centric point of view, searching-by-parts (also called partial-matching) may be provided. This may allow, for example, a mechanical student who has an unknown part to query for all machineries in the database that contain the given part. Finally, from the application-centric point of view, an education platform should be customizable to different communities like teachers, students, doctors, animators. Profiling may be used to help improve the learning experiences.

References

1. Berchtold, S., Kriegel, H.: S3: Similarity search in CAD database systems. In: Proc. SIGMOD, pp. 564–567 (1997)
2. Chen, D., Tian, X., Shen, Y., Ouhyoung, M.: On Visual Similarity Based 3D Model Retrieval. In: Proc. Eurographics (2003)
3. Elad, M., Tal, A., Ar, S.: Content Based Retrieval of VRML Objects - An Iterative and Interactive Approach. In: Proc. EG Multimedia, pp. 97–108 (2001)
4. Fu, A., Chan, P., Cheung, Y., Moon, Y.: Dynamic VP-Tree Indexing for N-Nearest Neighbor Search Given Pair-Wise Distances. VLDB Journal (2000)
5. Funkhouser, T., Min, P., Kazhdan, M., Chen, J., Halderman, A., Dobkin, D., Jacobs, D.: A Search Engine for 3D Models. ACM Trans. on Graphics 22(1), 83–105 (2003)
6. Funkhouser, T., Kazhdan, M., Shilane, P., Min, P., Kiefer, W., Tal, A., Rusinkiewicz, S., Dobkin, D.: Modeling by Example. In: Proc. ACM SIGGRAPH (2004)
7. Hilaga, M., Shinagawa, Y., Kohmura, T., Kunii, T.: Topology Matching for Fully Automatic Similarity Estimation of 3D Shapes. In: Proc. ACM SIGGRAPH (2001)
8. Herremans, A.: Studies #02 New Training Technologies. UNESCO Paris and ILO International Training Centre (1995)
9. Kastenmüller, G., Kriegel, H., Seidl, T.: Similarity Search in 3D Protein Databases. In: Proc. German Conf. on Bioinformatics (1998)
10. Kazhdan, M., Funkhouser, T., Rusinkiewicz, S.: Rotation Invariant Spherical Harmonic Representation of 3D Shape Descriptors. In: Proc. Symp. on Geometry Processing (2003)
11. Kazhdan, M., Funkhouser, T., Rusinkiewicz, S.: Shape Matching and Anisotropy. In: Proc. ACM SIGGRAPH (2004)
12. Keim, D.: Efficient Geometry-based Similarity Search of 3D Spatial Databases. In: Proc. SIGMOD, pp. 419–430 (1999)

13. Lew, M., Sebe, N., Djeraba, C., Jain, R.: Content-based Multimedia Information Retrieval: State-of-the-art and Challenges. ACM Trans. on Multimedia Computing, Communication, and Applications 2(1), 1–19 (2006)
14. Li, F., Lau, R.: A Progressive Content Distribution Framework in Supporting Web-Based Learning. In: Proc. ICWL, pp. 75–82 (2004)
15. Novotni, M., Klein, R.: 3D Zernike Descriptors for Content Based Shape Retrieval. In: Proc. ACM Symp. on Solid Modeling and Applications (2003)
16. Ohbuchi, R., Nakazawa, M., Takei, T.: Retrieving 3D Shapes Based On Their Appearance. In: Proc. ACM SIGMM Workshop on Multimedia Information Retrieval (2003)
17. Osada, R., Funkhouser, T., Chazelle, B., Dobkin, D.: Matching 3D Models with Shape Distributions. In: Proc. Int'l Conf. on Shape Modeling and Applications, pp. 154–166 (2001)
18. Rowe, J., Razdan, A., Collins, D., Panchanathan, S.: A 3D Digital Library System: Capture, Analysis, Query, and Display. In: Proc. Int'l Conf. on Digital Libraries (2001)
19. Rubner, Y., Tomasi, C., Guibas, L.: The Earth Mover's Distance as a Metric for Image Retrieval. Int'l Journal of Computer Vision 40(2), 99–121 (2000)
20. Smith, S., Woody, P.: Interactive Effect of Multimedia Instruction and Learning Styles. Teaching of Psychology 27(3), 220–223 (2000)
21. Shilane, P., Min, P., Kazhdan, M., Funkhouser, T.: The Princeton Shape Benchmark. In: Proc. Int'l Conf. on Shape Modeling and Applications (2004)
22. Sundar, H., Silver, D., Gagvani, N., Dickinson, S.: Skeleton Based Shape Matching and Retrieval. In: Proc. Int'l Conf. on Shape Modeling and Applications (2003)
23. Tal, A., Zuckerberger, E.: Mesh Retrieval by Components. Technical Report, Faculty of Electrical Engineering, Technion, CCIT-475, EE-2004 (2004)
24. Tam, G., Lau, R.: Deformable Model Retrieval Based on Topological and Geometric Signatures. IEEE Trans. on Visualization and Computer Graphics 13(3), 470–482 (2007)
25. Tangelder, J., Veltkamp, R.: Polyhedral Model Retrieval Using Weighted Point Sets. In: Proc. Int'l Conf. on Shape Modeling and Applications, pp. 119–129 (2003)
26. Vranic, D., Saupe, D.: 3D Shape Descriptor Based on 3D Fourier Transform. In: Proc. ECMCS, pp. 271–274 (2001)
27. Yu, M., Atmosukarto, I., Leow, W., Huang, Z., Xu, R.: 3D Model Retrieval with Morphing-based Geometric and Topological Feature Maps. In: Proc. IEEE CVPR (2003)

A Piece-Wise Learning Approach to 3D Facial Animation*

Yushun Wang, Yueting Zhuang, Jun Xiao, and Fei Wu

College of Computer Science, Zhejiang University, China
{yswang, yzhuang, junx, wufei}@cs.zju.edu.cn

Abstract. Web-based 3D facial animation is an alternative of face to face communication. Animating 3D human faces is also a difficult task because of the substantive non-rigid facial motions and utmost human familiarity with facial expressions. This paper presents a novel piece-wise learning approach to 3D facial animation driven by facial motion capture data. The pipeline of our algorithm comprises three major parts: (1) data pre-processing, (2) facial region segmentation, and (3) facial deformation. We first present an effective preprocessing algorithm for non-rigid motion extraction and data alignment. Second, based on the statistical and kinematical analysis of motion capture data and the topological analysis of facial mesh, our system segments the facial regions by a two-layer clustering algorithm. The edges of segments are well considered using an adapted plane/space partition algorithm. During runtime, the stream of motion capture data and the 3D face model are efficiently fused by cluster-wise optimization. The experimental results show that our algorithm is not only realistic but also fast enough for real time applications.

Keywords: 3D facial animation, Clustering, Facial segmentation, Piece-wise learning.

1 Introduction

Students using a computer-based distant learning system are likely to study alone with less classmate support [1]. Online interaction with 3D facial animation is an alternative way of face-to-face communications. It is also highly difficult due to the substantive non-rigid facial motions coupled with rigid head movement and meanwhile the human familiarity with facial expressions.

The evaluation of facial animation techniques mainly derives from three practical requirements. First, the motion mechanism should be easily applied to animate new face models. Second, it should provide real-time user experience thus no exorbitant computation cost. Third, the results should be realistic in both spatial and temporal domains [2].

1.1 Related Work

The pioneering work of 3D facial animation was done by Parke in 1972 [3]. Currently, there are several main streams of available solutions.

---

* This work is supported by National Natural Science Foundation (NSF) of China (No.60525108, No.60533090), 973 Program (2002CB312101), Science and Technology Project (STP) of Zhejiang Province (2005C13032, 2005C11001-05).

H. Leung et al. (Eds.): ICWL 2007, LNCS 4823, pp. 416–427, 2008.

Physical model based methods: One of the approaches to facial animation is to approximate the anatomical structures of a face, i.e. skull, muscles and skin [4] [5] [6]. The animation from physical models reflects the underlying tissue stresses. Due to the complex topology of human faces, it requires tedious tuning to animate a new model.

3D reconstruction and playback: Guenter et al. [7] reconstructed both three-dimensional geometry and texture information in a video sequence for facial animations. Li et al [8] developed a real time structured light 3D scanning system to capture the 3D facial expressions. The generated head highly resembles the performer, which limits its applications.

Expression cloning: Noh and Neumann [9] proposed a retargeting method to map the displacements of vertices on source model to target meshes. The motion displacements are scaled and rotated with respect to the difference between local geometry of source and target meshes. This method only works in retargeting finished animation to similar target meshes.

Example based methods: Example based facial animation [10] [11] [12] relies upon a pre-defined set of example models with target expressions (morph targets) to span the space of possible facial expressions. Captured motion vectors are used to estimate the blending coefficients, by which new expression can be synthesized using a linear combination of the examples. These approaches may provide stable and accurate results. Nevertheless, the result animation is highly depending on the handcrafted 3D morph targets, which require a large amount of artistic work.

1.2 Our Approach

Instead of modeling all the complicated facial motions, data driven facial animation just exploits motion data captured in real scenes. The tracked feature points are then used to animate 3D face models to produce animation. Motion capture data usually performs as a trigger to activate animation mechanisms, e.g. physical muscle model [4] [6] or blending examples [11] [12], which also brings the drawbacks. In this paper, we propose a piece-wise learning approach to data driven facial animation. Besides 3D facial motion capture data, our system takes a single facial mesh as input. The only user manual work in our system is to assign several feature points on the facial mesh. Our system automatically pre-processes the data, segments kinematics and topology consistent facial regions and produces deformation results. Our solution efficiently fuses the temporal resolution of motion capture data and the spatial resolution of facial mesh.

Compared with the previous solutions, this paper has three points of novelties:

First, we propose a novel algorithm for automatically segmenting a facial mesh. Due to the complexity of facial structure, facial skin is deformed in a complex and non-rigid way. In traditional methods, it requires manual segmentation of facial functional regions [13] or extra information such as example expressions of the model [14] [15], to produce logical deformation. However, example expressions of the model are often unavailable and the manual segmentation is tedious and difficult for ordinary users. We solve this problem by a two-layer clustering algorithm.

Second, our system animates a facial mesh by using optimization within kinematics and topology consistent facial pieces. Driving facial animation with global optimization techniques will produce significant artifacts. As shown in Figure 1, using Radial Basis Function networks [16], a mouth opening deformation driven by sparse markers on both upper and lower lips will stretch the lips thicker but not open the mouth. The reason is that the motion characteristics and constraints in different regions i.e. the upper lip and the lower lip, are not well accounted for in global optimization. We use piece-wise optimization to obtain better results.

Third, the edges of facial segments are further fused using Voronoi-Cell algorithm, which is usually used in plane/space partition. In order to guarantee smooth deformation, the vertices on the edges of segmented regions should be properly considered. We adapted the Voronoi-Cell algorithm in the following aspects: (1) we use geodesic instead of Euclidean distance. (2) We weighted the vertex belonging to multiple cells in a fuzzy clustering way to ensure smooth deformation.

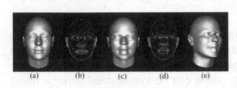

Fig. 1. Artifacts of opening mouth using global optimization techniques. (a) Face model with neutral expression. (b) Motion capture markers in neutral expression. (c) Face model with lips stretched instead of mouth opening. (d) Markers in opening mouth expression. (e) Side view of (c).

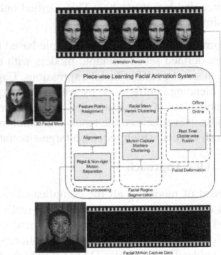

Fig. 2. System Overview

The rest of the paper is organized as follows. In Section 2, we give an overview of our algorithm. Section 3 describes the necessary pre-processing of facial motion capture data and 3D face models. Section 4 presents facial region segmentation based on the two-layer clustering algorithm. Section 5 discusses cluster-wise optimization techniques for facial deformation. Experiments are reported in Section 6. We conclude this paper and discuss some ideas for future work in Section 7.

2 System Overview

As shown in Figure 2, our system takes a facial polygonal mesh and 3D facial motion capture data as input, and outputs a sequence of 3D animation of the given mesh driven by the movement of the motion capture data. Our algorithm can be summarized into three major parts:

Data pre-processing: A user assigns a set of feature points on a facial mesh according to input motion capture markers. This is the only user manual work in our system. The motion capture data is separated into rigid head motion and non-rigid facial motion at each frame. The first frame of the motion capture data and the mesh are aligned automatically by estimating similarity transformation parameters.

Facial region segmentation: Our system determines the intrinsic grouping of motion capture markers based on statistical, kinematical and topological analysis. The facial mesh vertices are clustered using grouped markers as centroids. After clustering, the facial mesh is segmented into several regions.

Facial deformation: The fusion between the facial mesh and the movement of motion capture markers is calculated by cluster-wise optimization to provide animation results.

3 Data Preprocessing

After the user manually assigning the feature points on the 3D facial mesh according to the markers, our system pre-processes the data in two aspects. First, the motion capture data is separated into two parts: rigid transformation and non-rigid deformation. Second, the motion capture data is aligned with the facial mesh by measuring the first frame of the markers and the corresponding mesh feature points.

3.1 Rigid and Non-rigid Motion Separation

3D facial motion capture data is often coupled with both rigid and non-rigid motion, e.g. nodding head (rigid) with a smile (non-rigid). These two types of motion need to be separated first.

In facial motion capture, as shown in Figure 2 (bottom left), a performer wears several markers on top of one's head, where non-rigid deformation is absent. The trace of three rigid-motion markers will be enough to compute rigid transformation, which has six degrees of freedom (DOF): $(\theta_x, \theta_y, \theta_z)$ for rotation around x, y and z axes resulting in a matrix $R \in \mathbb{R}^{3 \times 3}$ and $t = (t_x, t_y, t_z)^T$ for translation along x, y and z axes.

The 3D position of rigid-motion marker j at frame i is represented by $v_j^{\ i}$, $1 \le i \le N_F$, $1 \le j \le N_j$. Here N_F is the number of frames and N_j is the number of rigid-motion markers. Therefore rigid transformation parameters R^i, t^i at frame i with respect to the start frame satisfy the equation below:

$$v_j^{\ i} = R^i v_j^{\ 1} + t^i, \quad 1 \le i \le N_F, 1 \le j \le N_j \tag{1}$$

Replacing $v_j^{\ i}$ and $v_j^{\ 1}$ with the 3D positions of the corresponding markers, we can solve the linear system to obtain R^i and t^i. The non-rigid motion of all markers at frame i can be calculated by an inverse rotation and translation:

$$v'^i_k = (R^i)^{-1}(v_k^{\ i} - t^i), \quad 1 \le k \le N_M \tag{2}$$

where N_M is the total number of markers.

3.2 Alignment of Motion Capture Data and 3D Face

Motion capture data and 3D face models can be acquired in different ways. Their facing directions, positions and size are usually different. In order to animate a face model using motion capture data, they should be aligned in a reference coordinate system. With support of the corresponding mesh feature points of the markers, our algorithm estimates similarity transformation, i.e. the parameters to be estimated are rotation R, translation t, and scaling s, from the motion capture data to the 3D face model. The alignment parameters are estimated once for the first frame of motion capture data and then applied to transform the entire motion capture data into the coordinate system of the 3D face model.

Our system chooses the feature points on eyes and mouth to estimate alignment parameters, as they are salient and indicative. Then the problem of pose estimation is transformed to the problem of similarity transformation parameters estimation between two point patterns. We use least squares estimation to minimize a cost function:

$$C(R,t,s) = \frac{1}{n}\sum_{i=1}^{n}\left\| p_i - (sRv_i + t)\right\|^2 \tag{3}$$

where $\{p_i = (x_i, y_i, z_i)\}$ is a set of feature points on 3D face model, $\{v_i = (x_i, y_i, z_i)\}$ is a set of 3D coordinates of motion capture markers, R : rotation, t: translation:, and s : scaling are the similarity transformation parameters, n is the number of feature points and vertices. Minimizing the cost function in Equation 3 will give the transformation parameters.

4 Facial Region Segmentation

In facial animation, the motion of markers needs to be propagated to the whole 3D facial mesh. Facial region segmentation is to decide the motion propagation boundaries of markers. Some methods have been reported to segment a 3D face in the scenario of example based facial animation [14] [15]. We propose an efficient solution for automatic facial segmentation, which consists of two layers. First, our system determines the intrinsic grouping of motion capture markers after a statistical data reduction. Second, the classified groups of markers are then used as centroids for mesh vertex clustering. Our system analyzes the topological properties from facial mesh and the kinematical properties from motion capture data. These two kinds of properties are adopted into our similarity measure during clustering.

4.1 Analysis of Facial Topology

Traditional techniques for facial deformation use the Euclidean distance to measure the similarity between two vertices. However, Euclidean distance metric does not take the connectivity of mesh into account. In recent years, nonlinear manifold modeling techniques have been developed in the research of subspace learning and face recognition [17] [18] [19]. A static face model can be regarded as a manifold, which is a local topological Euclidean space. The geodesic distance, or the shortest path, is a widely accepted concept in manifold learning to provide spatial understanding of nonlinear topology. Noticeably, as shown in Figure 3, points on different sides of lips are close in the Euclidean metric (straight line segment), but far away from each other in its actual topological properties, which can be better measured by geodesic distance (folding dot-line segments).

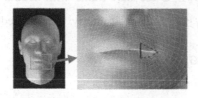

Fig. 3. Comparison between the Euclidean distance (straight line segment on the lower figure) and the geodesic distance (folding dot-line segments)

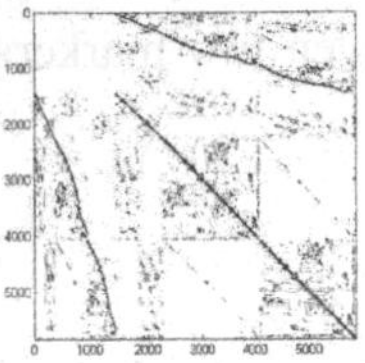

Fig. 4. Sparse matrix visualization of 3D face graph

In order to employ geodesic distance, we take facial mesh as an undirected graph, where mesh vertices and edges represent its nodes and arcs, respectively. As shown in Figure 4, the sparse matrix of the constructed graph (from the face model shown in Figure 3) is visualized, with only about 0.068% non-zero entries. The geodesic distances between facial mesh vertex v_i and feature point p_j are then computed as the shortest path:

$$G(v_i, p_j) = dijk(v_i, p_j), \ 1 \leq i \leq N_V, \ 1 \leq j \leq N_P \tag{4}$$

using Dijkstra algorithm. N_V is the number of mesh vertices and N_P is the num of feature points.

4.2 Layer 1: Clustering of Motion Capture Markers

After removing rigid transformation from the input motion capture data sequence as described in Section 3.1, our system extracts the most significant frames using principal component analysis (PCA).

Since the frame rate of motion capture is really high, often 60-120 fps, we employ PCA to reduce it. A frame of N_M markers can be represented as a $3N_M \times 1$ vector by concatenating $\{(x_i, y_i, z_i) \mid 1 \leq i \leq N_M\}$. Given N_F frames of motion capture data sequence, we first generate their component covariance matrix, which is a $3N_M \times 3N_M$ square matrix, to compute the eigenvalues and the corresponding eigenvectors. The most significant frames can be extracted by the most significant eigenvectors, which have large eigenvalues. We choose the number of eigenvectors $N_F{}'$ by preserving 95% of the variance of the data. After PCA, $N_F{}'$ significant frames, called *eigenframes*, are extracted out of the total N_F frames to analyze the kinematical similarities among markers.

In order to group the markers into clusters, we first establish similarity metric. Intuitively, nearby markers that coherently move with each other should be grouped into the same cluster. Our system measures the similarity by two normalized distances: geodesic distance G and cosine distance D.

In an *eigenframes* E^i, $0 \le i \le N_F{}'$, where E^0 is the start frame with neutral expression, given two markers m_k^i, m_j^i, $1 \le k, j \le N_M$, their similarity is measured as follows:

$$S(m_k^i, m_j^i) = G_{k,j}^i \cdot D_{k,j}^i,$$
$$1 \le i \le N_F{}', \ 1 \le k, j \le N_M \tag{5}$$

Where

$$G_{k,j}^i = 1 - \frac{G(p_k^i, p_j^i)}{\max_{a,b}\{G(p_a^i, p_b^i)\}}, \tag{6}$$

$$D_{k,j}^i = \begin{cases} \frac{1}{2}[\frac{(m_k^i - m_k^0)}{\|m_j^i - m_j^0\|} \cdot \frac{(m_j^i - m_j^0)}{\|m_k^i - m_k^0\|} + 1], \\ \quad \text{if } m_k^i - m_k^0 \ne 0 \text{ and } m_j^i - m_j^0 \ne 0 \\ 0, \ \textit{otherwise} \end{cases} \tag{7}$$

and p_k^i, p_j^i are the corresponding feature points of m_k^i, m_j^i on facial mesh.

We take the maximum of $S(m_k^i, m_j^i)$ over all the *eigenframes* to acquire the similarity function between m_k, m_j:

$$S(m_k, m_j) = \max_i(S(m_k^i, m_j^i)), \ 1 \le i \le N_F{}' \tag{8}$$

This similarity metric is sensitive to the motion similarity in any *eigenframe* by taking the maximum.

Based on the similarity metric above, the next step is to organize the similar markers into groups. Clustering considered as an important unsupervised learning technique has been studied for many years. Ordinary clustering algorithms like k-means or Mixture of Gaussians depend on an initialization of centroids, which reduces their efficiency. We use hierarchical clustering algorithm [20] starting with each marker in a cluster. We use our similarity function in the framework of a single-linkage hierarchical clustering algorithm as follows:

1. Start by assigning each marker to a cluster, so that if we have N_M markers, we now have N_M clusters, each containing just one marker. Let the similarities between the clusters the same as the similarities between the items they contain.

2. Find the closest (with the largest similarity) pair of clusters and merge them into a single cluster, so that now we have one cluster less.

3. Compute similarities between the new cluster and each of the old clusters. We consider the similarity between one cluster and another to be equal to the greatest similarity from any member of one cluster to any member of the other cluster.

4. Repeat steps 2 and 3 until the largest similarity between clusters is less than a threshold θ.

The threshold θ can be determined in a trial and error process. As shown in Figure 5, all markers except the 3 for rigid-motion estimation are divided into 13 clusters, represented by the transparent white shadows covering the markers. The 3D model in the top left corner is used to provide topological support for the segmentation. The threshold in this segmentation is 0.75.

4.3 Layer 2: Clustering of Mesh Vertices

In layer 1 of facial region segmentation the markers are clustered into different groups. The next step is to use the groups of markers as virtual centroids to classify the mesh vertices on facial mesh.

The distance used in our system between one marker group and a mesh vertex, is equal to the minimum geodesic distance from the members of the group to the mesh vertex.

$$Dist(C_i, v_j) = \min_k \{G(p_k, v_j) \mid p_k \in C_i\} \tag{9}$$

where v_j is the mesh vertex to be clustered, p_k is the corresponding feature point on facial mesh of marker m_k belonging to the group C_i.

The vertices on the edges of segmented regions should be properly considered to guarantee smooth deformation. Our vertex clustering is intuited by the Voronoi-Cell algorithm [21], which is a way to partition a plane/space therefore the points on bisectors will be properly weighted. We adapted the Voronoi-Cell algorithm in the following aspects: (1) we use geodesic instead of Euclidean distance. (2) We weighted the vertex belonging to multiple cells in a fuzzy clustering way to ensure smooth deformation. As indicated in Figure 6. The semi-transparent grey scale edge areas for each cell are partially owned by adjacent cells. The width of an edge is represented by a stiffness coefficient in our algorithm.

A stiffness coefficient for virtual centroid C_i is represented by:

$$s_i = \begin{cases} \min_{m \neq n}\{G(p_m, p_n)\}, \text{ if } N_i = 1 \\ \min_{j \neq k}\{G(p_j, p_k) \mid p_j, p_k \in C_i\}, \text{ otherwise} \end{cases} \tag{10}$$

Where N_i is the number of markers in C_i, p_k is the corresponding feature point on facial mesh of marker m_k.

The stiffness coefficient s_i is a representative for the minimum interval between the markers within C_i. When there is only one marker in a virtual centroid, the global minimum interval of all markers will take the place. The intuition is that a virtual centroid with sparse distribution of markers has more volume of influence (i.e. larger stiffness coefficient) than those with dense distributions.

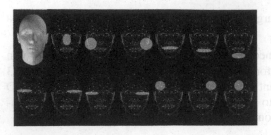

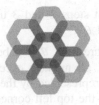

Fig. 6. Indicating diagram of our adapted Voronoi-Cell partition algorithm. The edge vertices are weighted among adjacent cells.

Fig. 5. Segmentation results of the facial motion capture markers

In order to judge the belonging of some vertex to a virtual centroid, our system first calculates the distance from this vertex to each of the centroids using the distance function described in Section 4.3.1. Meanwhile, we obtain the minimum bounding box of each group of markers by measuring the corresponding feature points on the facial mesh. Thereafter, we judge the belonging of a mesh vertex to one or more marker groups by using heuristic rules.

Condition 1: The vertex is inside the minimum bounding box of a marker group.

Condition 2: The path from the vertex to a group is the shortest compared with other groups measured by our distance function.

Heuristic rule 1: If the vertex and a group satisfy both the conditions simultaneously, the vertex belongs to this group.

Heuristic rule 2: If the vertex and a group can not satisfy the two conditions simultaneously, the vertex is considered to be an edge vertex and will be categorized to two or more groups which satisfy $Dist(C_i, v_j) \leq \alpha \cdot s_i$, where $\alpha > 0$ is an amplifying factor, which can used to adjust the width of cell edges. We simply use $\alpha = 1$ in our experiments.

Suppose $A = \{C_i \mid Dist(C_i, v_j) \leq \alpha \cdot s_i\}$ is a set with N adjacent groups for vertex v_j, we assign a set of terms to v_j respectively:

$$\{w_{i,j} = \frac{\sum\limits_{C_m \in A, C_m \neq C_i} Dist(C_m, v_j)}{(N-1)\sum\limits_{C_n \in A} Dist(C_n, v_j)}\} \tag{11}$$

representing the degree to which v_j is part of C_i.

5   Facial Deformation

Once the facial regions are segmented, optimization techniques can be used to get deformation results. The separated rigid motion can be applied to the facial mesh as a whole at each frame. The non-rigid motion, which is more difficult, will be discussed in this section.

5.1 Cluster-Wise Radial Basis Functions

For each vertex cluster, we construct a function that maps a set of 3D coordinates $V^0 = \{v^0_j\}$ (facial mesh vertices with neutral expression) to a set of new 3D coordinates $V^i = \{v^i_j\}$ (deformed facial mesh for animation frame i). The motion offsets of the motion capture markers within the cluster are used as examples to train the function. Constructing such a function can be regarded as an interpolation or approximation problem, which solves a problem of approximating a continuous multivariate function $f(\vec{x})$ by an approximate function $F(\vec{x}, \vec{c})$ with an appropriate choice of parameter set $\vec{c}$ where $\vec{x}$ and $\vec{c}$ are real vectors ($\vec{x} = x_1, x_2, ..., x_n$ and $\vec{c} = c_1, c_2, ..., c_k$).

The family of radial basis functions (RBF) is well known for its power to approximate high dimensional smooth surfaces and it is often used in model fitting. The network of RBF to infer the new position of a given vertex is:

$$v^i_j = \sum_{k=1}^{N} c_{j,k} \phi(\|v^0_j - p^0_k\|)) \tag{12}$$

where $\|v^0_j - p^0_k\|$ is the Euclidean distance between v^0_j and p^0_k, N is the number of training examples, $c_{j,k}$ denotes the parameters to be learned , j represents the jth component in the output vector, $\phi(r)$ is radially symmetric basis functions. Examples of basis functions are Gaussian functions $\phi(r) = e^{-(\frac{r}{c})^2}$, multi-quadrics $\phi(r) = \sqrt{(r^2 + c^2)}$ and thin plate splines $\phi(r^2) = r^2 \log r$ with a linear term added. Plugging the Hardy basis function into Equation 12 results in:

$$v^i_j = F_j(v^0_j) = \sum_{k=1}^{N} c_{j,k} \sqrt{\|v^0_j - p^0_k\|^2 + s_i^2} \tag{13}$$

where $s_i = \min_k \{\|v^0_j - p^0_k\|\}$ is the stiffness coefficient for balancing the scope of neighborhood.

Substituting the N pairs of training examples $\{(p^0_k, p^i_k) | 1 \leq k \leq N\}$ into Equation 13 will result in a linear system of N equations. Solving the linear system yields:

$$\vec{c} = H^{-1} \vec{p}^i \tag{14}$$

$$\vec{c} = (H + \lambda I)^{-1} \vec{p}^i \tag{15}$$

where $\lambda = 0.01$ is a small disturbing factor determined empirically to decrease the impact of noise and I is an identity matrix.

For those vertices belonging only to one cluster, their motion will be determined by the motion of the markers within the cluster. For those edge vertices, their deformation function will be a blending function as follows:

$$v^i_j = \sum_{m} w_{m,j} v^i_{m,j} \tag{16}$$

where $v^i_{m,j}$ is the coordinate vector of jth vertex derived from cluster C_m at frame i, and $w_{m,j}$ is the corresponding weight described in Equation 11.

6 Experiments

We used a commercial motion capture system from Motion Analysis Corporation. Four high speed cameras were employed to capture facial motion by a set of 42 markers.

Before capturing the pre-designed facial motion sequence, the actor performed some range motion for tens of seconds. Range motion is for the performer to stretch the facial muscles to their extremes and is commonly used at the beginning of the capture scenario in order to verify the setup. Our system employed the range motion sequence as the input data of facial region segmentation for it is representative for deformable possibilities.

The online part of our algorithm is to separate the rigid and non-rigid motion of markers and to deform the facial model using cluster-wise optimization. The time complexity of the online calculations is polynomial, which can be achieved in real time and has good scalability. In our experiments on a Dell Precision workstation 670 with Xeon 3.2G Hertz CPU, 2.0G RAM, our system produces a frame of animation of Mona Lisa, which has about 6K triangles, in 18 milliseconds. A frame rate of more than 50 frames per second, i.e. high quality of interactive animation, can be achieved.

7 Conclusions

This paper proposes a novel piece-wise fusion approach to 3D facial animation. In this algorithm, after pre-processing a sequence of motion capture data and an input 3D face model, the facial regions are segmented by a two-layer vertex clustering algorithm automatically. In facial deformation, our system efficiently fuses the stream of motion capture data and the 3D facial mesh by cluster-wise optimization. It requires less user intervention and provides robust and realistic results. It is efficient for many applications, such as teleconference and digital entertainment and video encoding.

References

1. Ou, K.-L., Chen, G.-D., Liu, C.-C., Liu, B.-J.: Instructional instruments for web group learning systems : The grouping, intervention, and strategy. In: Proc. of the Fifth annual SIGCSE/SIGCUE ITiCSE conference on Innovation and technology in computer science education, Helsinki, Finland, pp. 69–72 (2000)
2. Noh, J.-y., Neumann, U.: A Survey of facial modeling and Animation Techniques, USC Technical Report 99-705 (1998)
3. Parke, F.: Computer generated animation of faces. In: ACM National Conference, pp. 451–457 (1972)
4. Choe, B., Lee, H., Ko, H.: Performance-Driven Muscle-Based Facial Animation. The Journal of Visualization and Computer Animation 12(2), 67–79 (2001)

5. Sifakis, E., Neverov, I., Fedkiw, R.: Automatic Determination of Facial Muscle Activations from Sparse Motion Capture Marker Data. SIGGRAPH 2005, ACM TOG 24, 417–425 (2005)
6. Kalra, P., Mangili, A., Thalmann, N.M., Thalmann, D.: Simulation of Facial Muscle Actions Based on Rational Free From Deformations. Eurographics 11(3), 59–69 (1992)
7. Guenter, B., Grimm, C., Wood, D., Malvar H., Pighin, F.: Making Faces. In: SIGGRAPH 1998 Proceedings, pp. 55–66 (1998)
8. Zhang, L., Snavely, N., Curless, B., Seitz, S. M.: Spacetime faces: High-resolution capture for modeling and animation. In: ACM SIGGRAPH Proceedings, Los Angeles, CA, pp. 548–558 (2004)
9. Noh, J., Neumann, U.: Expression cloning. In: Proceeding of SIGGRAPH 2001, pp. 271–288 (2001)
10. Zhang, Q., Liu, Z., Guo, B., Terzopoulos, D., Shum, H.: Geometry-Driven Photorealistic Facial Expression Synthesis. IEEE Transactions on Visualization and Computer Graphics 12(1), 48–60 (2006)
11. Chuang, E., Bregler, C.: Moodswings: Expressive Speech Animation. ACM Transactions on Graphics 24(2) (April 2005)
12. Chai, J., Xiao, J., Hodgins, J.K.: Vision-based Control of 3D Facial Animation. In: Proceedings of the ACM SIGGRAPH/Eurographics Symposium on Computer Animation (July 2003)
13. Sánchez Lorenzo, M.A., Edge, J.D., King, S.A., Maddock, S.C.: Use and Re-use of Facial Motion Capture Data. In: Vision, Video and Graphics, VVG 2003, University of Bath, UK, pp. 135–142 (2003)
14. Joshi, P., Tien, W.C.: Learning Controls for Blend Shape Based Realistic Facial Animation. In: Proceedings of EUROGRAPHICS 2003, pp. 187–192 (2003)
15. Park, B., Chung, H., Nishita, T., Shin, S.Y.: A feature-based approach to facial expression cloning. Computer Animation and Virtual Worlds 6(3-4), 291–303 (2005)
16. Poggio, T., Giros, F.: A theory of networks for approximation and learning. Technical Report A.I. Memo No. 1140, Artificial Intelligence Lab, MIT, Cambridge, MA (July 1989)
17. Tenenbaum, J.B., de Silva, V., Langford, J.C.: A global geometric framework for nonlinear dimensionality reduction. Science 290, 2319–2323 (2000)
18. Roweis, S., Saul, L.: Nonlinear dimensionality reduction by locally linear embedding. Science 5500, 2323–2326 (2000)
19. Niyogi, P., Belkin, M.: Laplacian eigenmaps for dimensionality reduction and data representation, Technical Report, University of Chicago (January 2002)
20. Johnson, S.C.: Hierarchical Clustering Schemes. Psychometrika 2, 241–254 (1967)
21. Blum, H.: A transformation for extracting new descriptors of shape. In: Proceedings of the Symposium on Models for Perception of Speech and Visual Form, pp. 362–380. MIT Press, Cambridge, MA (1967)

Open Smart Classroom: Extensible and Scalable Smart Space Using Web Service Technology[*]

Yue Suo[1], Naoki Miyata[2], Toru Ishida[2], and Yuanchun Shi[1]

[1] Department of Computer Science and Technology, Tsinghua University, Beijing, China
[2] Department of Social Informatics, Kyoto University, Kyoto, Japan
suoy@mails.tsinghua.edu.cn, shiyc@tsinghua.edu.cn
miyata@ai.soc.i.kyoto-u.ac.jp, ishida@i.kyoto-u.ac.jp

Abstract. Real-time interactive virtual classroom with tele-education experience is an important type of distance learning, while the current available systems are not able to connect different classrooms in open network for intercontinental and intercultural learning. Open Smart Classroom, which is an upgrade learning system based on Smart Classroom using Web Service technology, provides more extensible and scalable features to tackle the new requirements and challenges of distance learning. Open Smart Classroom is developed based on Open Smart Platform, the software computing infrastructure for Smart Space, which provide three new features: 1) open and standard interface for better mobile devices connection and communication without any prior configuration; 2) open services invocation channel between inside modules and outside systems 3) open network in which multiple Smart Spaces can connect and communicate with each other. Making use of these new features, Open Smart Classroom shows a novel and interesting experience to both of the teachers and students for intercultural and intercontinental distant learning, which also gives a significant research perspective of future distance blended learning system.

Keywords: Pervasive Computing, Smart Space, Web Service.

1 Introduction

With the rise of a new generation of web-based learning system, traditional learning mode, where teachers and students are face to face with each other in the same classroom, however, still has its unrivaled advantages. Therefore, how to use the new methods and technologies raised by pervasive computing and Smart Space to enhance the effectiveness and experience becomes a very important topic of learning system. Many works have been done to address this problem, such as Tsinghua University's Smart Classroom [17], ActiveClass [11], Class Talk [3], which are all seeking for

[*] This research is funded by National High-Tech Research and Development Plan of China under Grant (No. 2006AA01Z198) and Specialized Research Fund for the Doctorial Program of Higher Education (No.20050003048). This work is also supported by International Collaborative Research Grants from National Institute of Information and Communications Technology (NICT), and International Communications Foundation (ICF).

H. Leung et al. (Eds.): ICWL 2007, LNCS 4823, pp. 428–439, 2008.
© Springer-Verlag Berlin Heidelberg 2008

better teaching and learning mode based on traditional face to face classroom learning. Especially, Smart Classroom adopts the blended learning way, implementing multiple modalities and human-computer interfaces to provide a tele-education experience similar to real classroom experience, which gives both of the remote and local students more natural experience on learning.

Smart Classroom is a Smart Space [19] on tele-education, which beyond the traditional classroom, working on pervasive/ubiquitous computing mode. Enabling the remote students to participate the traditional classroom education makes Smart Classroom an open classroom. However, as the trend of pervasive computing developing requires Smart Space to be more and more open, Smart Classroom is facing new requirements and challenges.

– Open interface for mobile devices to communicate better.

To support mobile devices communications is one of the requirements of learning system. Researchers in [5][12] emphasize that mobile devices play an important role in computer-supported collaborative learning. For example, the teacher uses his Smart Phone to bring the presentation file and control the slide show, while the students can use Laptop to discuss some problems with others. Several projects have partially taken into account of this issue. Active Class enables the students to use mobile devices to give feedback to the teacher, while the students cannot use it to invoke other classroom interfaces, such as PPT control interface, to control the devices and applications of the class. Smart Classroom supports mobile devices joining in and interacting with existing applications and devices [4], but it requires mobile devices to install the mobile driver program of Smart Platform (the software infrastructure for Smart Classroom) and pre-developed applications. With the mobile device developing, it is unfriendly and inconveniently to ask the users to install the specific driver program when they bring their device into Smart Classroom. Also, building those driver programs is complex and labored work because there are so many different system of mobile devices, such as Windows CE, Palm, Symbian OS, Linux and so on. Therefore, it shows the necessity that standard and open mobile devices communication interface should be built, which enables mobile devices to join in, control and interact with class without any prior configuration.

– Open services invocation channel between inside and outside.

How to enable services invocation between inside modules and outside system of Smart Space (maybe another system of Smart Space) while keeping it easy and standard is the second challenge. Smart Space is becoming more and more open, which gives the chance for the blended learning system to be more open. There are abundant services resources in the open network for the learning system to use, while some outside system may require of invoking inside services of the learning system. For example, the mobile company or Smart Classroom A want to dynamically find out whether the student attends the Class B, which is a service provided by Smart Classroom B. Current Smart Space related project, such as iRoom [2] and Smart Classroom, the services provided by modules can be invoked very easy by other modules inside of the Smart Space. However, it is not so easy to invoke outside services which do not belong to Smart Space. Neither of the outside system invokes the services inside of Smart Space. Therefore, creating well service invocation channel between inside and outside of Smart Space is very important and also useful to elevate the function of the class.

– Open network in which multiple classrooms connect.

The third challenge is to support multiple classrooms to connect with each other through intercontinental WAN and have classes together. As the increasing requirement of intercultural and intercontinental communication and learning, enabling remote students to participate in class of Smart Classroom and easily communicate with teacher and local students is not enough. Addressing two or several real-time interactive classrooms to connect with each other should be one of the aims of future distance learning systems. Moreover, because of the evitable difference among these connected classrooms, necessary transformation is needed. For example, the classroom in Kyoto University may use Japanese while the one in Tsinghua University may use Chinese. Simply connecting these two classrooms will cause misunderstanding because of different languages. Therefore, the robust translation service with highly accuracy, or other involved mechanism for intercultural communication should be taken to make the people in these classrooms understood. This simultaneously synchronous intercultural teaching mode, that multiple classrooms having one class with automatically translation features, has long-term significance for the research of intercultural learning and communication.

According to the three challenges showed above, based on Smart Classroom, we present Open Smart Classroom which not only well supports personal mobile device interactions but also implements the mechanism enabling multiple classrooms to connect with each other in the open network. Moreover, since the established service invocation channel between inside and outside of Smart Classroom, Open Smart Classroom provides its own services ontologies and utilizes the abundant web services. The service ontologies are used by outside system for better extensibility and workflow design modules for better scalability. The machine translation web service is used to transform the texts content in the classrooms for better intercultural and intercontinental understanding.

To implement Open Smart Classroom, we design and develop the software infrastructure Open Smart Platform, which greatly extends the function and ability of Smart Platform [15]. To adapt the challenges given by Open Smart Classroom, Open Smart Platform adds new modules and involves new criterion, so as to give better software infrastructure support for Open Smart Classroom and other future projects in Smart Space.

In this paper, we explore three successive phases of Smart Space and several related learning systems and software infrastructure in Section 2. Section 3 introduces the architecture, new features and implementation of Open Smart Platform. Section 4 explains the design of Open Smart Classroom and validation scenarios. Section 5 draws the conclusion and presents future work.

2 Background and Related Work

With the development of Smart Space, we propose three successive phases of Smart Space: *Individual Smart space, Open Smart Space* and *Smart Community*, as Figure 1.

The three phases are listed in logical order rather than temporal order, where new problems added continuously from the left to the right. Modulate symbol connecting each phase represents that new problems added on previous phase make it much more complex.

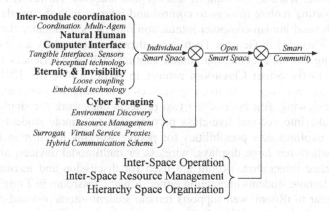

Inter-module coordination
Coordination Multi-Agent
Natural Human
Computer Interface
Tangible Interfaces Sensors
Perceptual technology
Eternity & Invisibility
Loose coupling
Embedded technology

Individual Smart Space ⊗ *Open Smart Space* ⊗ *Smart Community*

Cyber Foraging
Environment Discovery
Resource Management
Surrogate Virtual Service Proxies
Hybrid Communication Scheme

Inter-Space Operation
Inter-Space Resource Management
Hierarchy Space Organization

Fig. 1. The three successive phases of Smart Space

Individual Smart Space. In first phase, the research focuses on building a smart human-computer interactive space. It emphasizes the communication and the coordination mechanism among the software modules in a relatively close smart space. To support the coordination between modules, coordination models and multi-agent system have been studied. Also, lots of tangible UIs [10], such as sensors and awareness modules, have been applied to achieve friendly human computing interaction. Modules in Smart Space are loose-coupled in order to maintain system robust and embedded technologies are involved to remove the computing device from people sight. The Smart Classroom project is mainly in this phase.

Open Smart Space. In the second phase, the mobile and handheld devices become more and more popular in pervasive computing environment. These devices, roaming with users, can discover the existence of smart space environment and spontaneously take use of the resources and the services in the space to perform tasks of users in an enhanced fusion.

Smart Community. In the third phases, as researchers in [6] refers that it is almost impossible to establish an union pervasive computing environment all over the world in the near future, while great plenty of self-governed Smart Spaces exist by their own. Smart Community, which consists of multiple Smart Spaces, is considered as the research object of Smart Spaces. Inter-space operation and inter-space resource management mechanism among multiple Smart Spaces are needed to be studied on in this phase.

Note that the Open Smart Classroom mainly focuses on the second phase with primary work in the third phase. Besides studying cyber foraging, it also tries to establish well services invocation channels among inside and outside of Smart Space. Moreover, it tends to build the communication connection among Smart Spaces and does a primary study on inter-space resource management and communication.

There are several projects working on improving the experience of traditional classroom-based learning using Smart Space technologies. Active Class [11] is an application for encouraging in-class participation using personal wireless devices. The students give feedback of the class by their own wireless devices, improving the effect of traditional learning for both of teacher and students. However, Active Class lacks of supporting mobile devices to control and interact with the whole classroom, and has few natural human-computer interaction interfaces to enhance the experience of learning. eClass [1] in Georgia Tech is another project to study a general ubiquitous computing research theme, automated capture of live experiences for later access. Similar to the Smart Classroom project in Kyoto University [20], they both mainly study on capturing of the live experiences of the class for better understanding and further reviewing. But both of the two projects only work for single classroom and do not take into account live-class participation to remote students. iRoom in Stanford [2], explores new possibilities for people working together in technology-rich spaces, where has large displays, wireless or multimodal devices, and seamless mobile appliance integration. iRoom are used for discussion and learning, while it cannot allow remote students interaction either. Smart Classroom in Tsinghua University [17], similar to iRoom, well supports remote student interaction and communication, however, lacks of mobile devices communication mechanism without any pre-installed modules and is limited to utilize useful outside services. All these projects lack of supporting multiple classrooms working together, which is one of the important features that need to be emphasized in the future learning system.

Many software infrastructures for Smart Space exist with similar but a little different key features. Smart Platform [16] developed by Tsinghua University addresses the issue of performance and usability, which has three different communication schemes and loose-coupled multi-agent encapsulation architecture. However, Smart Platform has little implementation on the terms of services and multiple Smart Platforms communication. Similar to Smart Platform, iRos [2] by Stanford is meta-OS that ties devices together that each has their own low-level OS. As the extension of iRos, iCrafter [10] allows users of interactive workspaces to flexibly interact with the services in the workspace. Unfortunately, even with iCrafter, the software infrastructure does not consider the problem of multiple Smart Spaces communication. Hyperglue [8], which is a complement system of Metaglue [9] in MIT, involves the multiple Smart Spaces resource management. Meanwhile, both Hyperglue and Metaglue use Java RMI technology and their extended solution for direct coordination among different modules, which takes greater expenses because of the highly dynamic feature of Smart Space. Gaia [7] is a middle infrastructure with resource management and provides the user-oriented interfaces for such physical spaces populated with network-enabled computing resources. Gaia enables data and applications of users to be abstracted, that can be moved across and mapping to different the Smart Spaces. Gaia support services quite well, however, lacks of emphasizing on multiple Smart Spaces communications mechanism either.

3 Open Smart Platform

In this section, we are going to deeply introduce the details of its software infrastructure, Open Smart Platform.

3.1 Architecture

Single Smart Space. From single Smart Space view, the Open Smart Platform is described as Figure 2. Similar to Smart Platform, Open Smart Platform has a central DS, several container running on each of the host, each of which lots of agents running on. The reason why we inherit the multi-agent architecture of Smart Platform is because it has been well-developed and validated by several projects and also compatibility with previous work on Smart Platform concerns. The key improvement is that there are two system modules added: Web-Service-Wrapper-Agent (WSWA) and Smart-Platform-Agent-Webservice (SPAW).

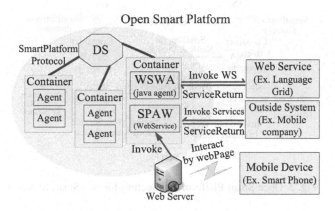

Fig. 2. Open Smart Platform architecture for single Smart Space

- WSWA is an agent, which invokes an outside web service based on the message received from other agents and returns the reply from the web service to the agents. Agents in Smart Platform can invoke outside web services by sending messages to this agent.
- SPAW is a web service deployed on Axis [21]. It receives messages from outside systems, transforms the messages to the protocol used in Smart Platform, creates a SPAW-agent to dispatch the message, and returns the reply from the agent to outside systems. Through this mechanism, outside systems can interact with agents in Smart Platform as web services. It also allows us to make and deploy workflows using agents in Smart Platform and web services, such as BPEL [13], has been involved, which makes the developer more easily customize their tasks. Moreover, as a web service, SPAW can be easily invoked by a web page server, where almost all current mobile devices can browse web pages and thus interact with modules inside of Smart Platform through SPAW.

In short, Open Smart Platform for single Smart Space is a multi-agent system with WSWA and SPAW as access point of communication between the inside and outside of Smart Space. From the inside view, communications are all based on Smart Platform Protocol, which is familiar with by previous Smart Platform developer. From the outside view, functions are all web services, which is the best for web service developer to build their tasks. Using WSWA and SPAW, we construct a communication bridge between the Smart Space and outside systems, which opens Smart Platform to outside systems.

Smart Community. For Smart Community, where several Smart Spaces communicate and coordinate with each other, we establish the communication channel for them suitable for open network among them. Take two Smart Spaces for the simplest Smart Community as example, the architecture is shown in Figure 3.

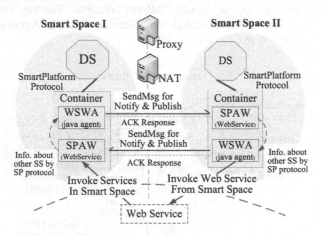

Fig. 3. Open Smart Platform architecture for two Smart Spaces

As mentioned above, WSWA and SPAW is the access point between inside the outside of Smart Space. Therefore, we take them for granted to exchange messages between Smart Spaces. Establishing the communication channel between every two access points is the ideal way for exchanging message, and using Web Service technology with HTTP protocol is the best way for the open network, where lots of routers, proxies, and NAT may exist along the message packet routing path.

In single Smart Space, agents publish messages to specific message group, and agents who have subscribed this message group will receive them. This Publish-Subscribe mechanism well supports the loose-coupled modules in Smart Space. And we believe it is also a good solution for message exchanging in Smart Community.

Therefore, we extend WSWA to be not only a delegation for agent in Smart Space to invoke outside web services, but also notify other Smart Spaces about message subscription and publication events. When SPAW receives one message of other Smart Spaces, it will first create a SPAW-Agent, by which publish the message content to the message group which is given in the message. So that all of the Smart Spaces can share their message group to each other, which makes the message exchanging just the same as what is in one Smart Space. It also alleviates the workload to update previous projects in single Smart Space to Smart Community environment.

Hence, the Open Smart Platform for Smart Community is still a multi-agent system which supports the Publish-Subscribe message exchanging method apparent to agents in each Smart Space.

3.2 New Features

Three new features of Open Smart Platform will be elaborated below:
- Extensibility for mobile devices.

Previous Smart Platform enables mobile devices roaming with users to connect into Smart Space by pre-installed modules (eContainer and eADK-based agent of Smart Platform), however, it lacks of convenience for the users, especially for those who first come into Smart Space to use their mobile devices. Open Smart Platform applies new mechanism named web-based-mobile-interface for mobile devices interaction in Smart Space. Open Smart Platform makes the required mobile interfaces, such as PPT upload or Turn-to-Next-Page, on web-based-mobile-interface as a website. Since almost all the mobile devices, such as Laptop, PDA, Smart Phone, or even normal cell phone have integrated web browser, the only thing that user need to do is to browse that website and click the corresponding link. The link is connected to SPAW, which will create a temporary SPAW-Agent to finish the whole task. If there is any reply information for that interface, for example, 'Check the schedule for Smart Classroom', the SPAW-Agent will return the result to SPAW and then got by the web browser of the mobile devices.

Note that new mechanism is not suitable for real-time streaming application (e.g. real-time multimedia streaming) because of the limitation of HTTP protocol new mechanism adopts. Therefore if the mobile users only use non-streaming function, such as controlling the PPT, he can use the web-based-mobile-interface to finish the task; otherwise, he can still utilize eContainer and eADK-based agent to help him to do that.
- Extensibility and scalability by services communication channel.

Thanks to WSWA and SPAW, invoking web services from outside and by outside systems (including other Smart Space systems) are possible, standard and easy. With WSWA delegation, it is unnecessary for each agent to deal with the problem of invoking web services, such as managing the life cycle of the web service stub. All is simple and easy by sending a web-service-request-message to WSWA and waiting for the result. Also, since all the services descriptions are shown on SPAW, it is very easy for the outside system to use services in Smart Space by simply invoking the corresponding services on SPAW. The services communication channel fills the gaps between the isolated services in Smart Space and outside services and systems, which makes the Smart Space more open.

Moreover, customization of tasks in Smart Space is easier. For example, the system should decide whether using machine translation or not according to the mother-tongue of users. As agents can easily create services in Open Smart Platform, and from the outside view, those services are all web services, therefore we are able to use mature workflow design tools to ease our customization work. We involve Active-BPEL [18] designer into our system, which really enhances the project developing efficiency by its visual interface and allows us to simulate our workflow to find bugs.
- Connection of multiple Smart Platforms in open network.

The most novel feature given by Open Smart Platform is enabling multiple Smart Platforms to connect with each other in open network. In the architecture, we place each Smart Space in equal hierarchy, which is primary work that just suitable for small scale Smart Community. Open Smart Platform focuses on building the communication channel among multiple Smart Spaces, which gives each Smart Space a single message access point (WSWA & SPAW), and extends the previous successful Publish-Subscribe mechanism to Smart Community communication.

In previous Smart Platform, three communication schemes are presented that concern three aspects: size of transferred data, sensitive to data drop, sensitive to real time [15]. In Open Smart Platform, there are similar three communication schemes correspond to three different QoS requirements, which are suitable to multiple Smart Spaces communication. The message scheme has been extended for multiple Smart Spaces, while the stream scheme and bulk scheme keep the same as in previous Smart Platform. In Open Smart Platform, WSWA and SPAW help the agent in one Smart Space to send query message to another agent in another Smart Space and transfer the response message back. Then the two agents in two Smart Spaces build their connection by themselves, using the stream or bulk scheme interface to communicate with each other.

Using SPAW and WSWA for the single access is more convenient for message management and system safety consideration. It also simplifies the agents developing process that the programmer does not need to think about how to get through frustrating NAT, Proxy or Firewall in the open network. Additionally, as all messages between one Smart Space and the other are transferred through the link between two pairs of SPAW and WSWA, we can choose the best network link for them to get best efficiency for messages transfer between the two Smart Spaces.

Open Smart Platform provides the necessary basis for the connection of multiple Smart Spaces in open network, thus makes the application of multiple Smart Spaces, such as Open Smart Classrooms, possible and easy to build.

To sum up, Open Smart Platform successfully addresses the issues raised by developing pervasive computing. It supports multiple Smart Spaces connections, easy mobile device interaction and services communication channel between inside and outside of Smart Space. These new features provide a well software infrastructure basis for building Open Smart Classroom and other Smart Space and Smart Community related projects.

4   Open Smart Classroom

Open Smart Classroom is an extension of previous Smart Classroom project. Besides the features such as real time interactive virtual classroom and blended learning mode, Open Smart Classroom mainly focuses on the following two issues, which make it an open classroom compared to other related works.

– Enabling multiple classrooms to connect with each other in the open network.

Involving multiple classrooms to have class together, especially for classrooms in different countries, has great significance to intercultural and intercontinental learning. Open Smart Classroom tries to combine several Smart Classrooms together to give novel experience for the teachers and students in the class. Also, considering the differences of classrooms, such as the different using language, the different infrastructures and devices, necessary transformation is needed in order to gain better connection effect. In the recent Open Smart Classroom, we primarily take different languages into account by involving Language Grid [14][16] translation engine for better understanding.

– Open the classroom interface and makes the classroom open to outside services.

Open concept is also for single Smart Classroom. The ease of using mobile device in the classroom to communicate and interact shows the open of the classroom. Moreover, the classroom easily taking use of the abundant resources, such as Language Grid translation service, presents the powerful extensibility of the classroom, which thus also embodies the open feature.

We build two scenarios to validate the Open Smart Classroom system, and also to present the open feature of our system.

Scenario I. Professor Shi enters smart classroom with a PPT, which is in Chinese, in her smart phone. She wants to give a presentation of that. Unfortunately, there are some students in smart classroom cannot understand Chinese but only English. The professor uploads her PPT file through the smart-classroom-ppt-support-website (SCPSW) by the web browser on smart phone. When the file is uploaded successfully, the website redirects to a link that invoking the workflow of this scenario: the PPT file is translated from Chinese to English automatically using Language grid web service of Kyoto university, then the translated version is shared to another machine which has another projector to show on. After that, the two versions of PPT will be started and synchronized on two projectors at the same time. As the class goes on, professor Shi uses her smart phone to control the presentation, such as turn to next page, by clicking the link given on the SCPSW.

Scenario II. Two Smart Classrooms are deployed in Tsinghua Univ. and Kyoto Univ. to have class together. Yue is giving a presentation in Tsinghua Univ, speaking English with an English PPT. The live video and PPT are shown in both of the two classrooms. And also, the translated PPTs, which are in Chinese and Japanese, show in Kyoto and Tsinghua respectively. However, Miyata, in Kyoto Univ. has some questions about this presentation. Avoiding interrupting the presentation, he raises his question in Japanese using Multi-language Chat Agent. Weijun, in China, who sees the question that has been translated in Chinese, answers his question in Chinese.

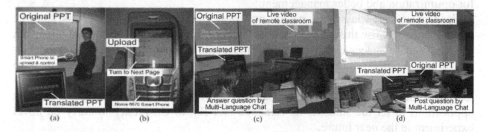

Fig. 4. Snapshots of Scenario. (a) Teacher using smart phone to control the PPT slideshow (b) The snapshot of PPT upload website on smart phone (c) The demo classroom in Tsinghua University (d) The demo classroom in Kyoto University.

The two scenarios of Open Smart Classroom were developed and tested successfully in Kyoto and Tsinghua Univ. from September in 2006 to February in 2007, which also validated our Open Smart Platform (see Figure 4). Most students reported that it was very interesting and useful to see the original and translated PPT at the same time, which help them a lot in understanding. The teacher also reported that to upload and control the PPT by Smart phone without any prior configuration is excellent and convenient, except the uploading process is a little delay, but it is tolerable. The little delay is because the speed of uploading PPT is limited by GPRS connection, which will surely be improved by 3G or 802.11n standard deployed pervasively in the near future.

We also evaluate the performance of message transfer between two Smart Spaces. In Scenario II the PPT file is transferred from Tsinghua University to Kyoto University. And students in two Smart Classrooms use Multi-language Chat Agent to send questions and answers to each other. In the experiment the message exchanging speed is well enough according to the students' comments.

5 Conclusion and Future Work

New requirements raised by the development of pervasive computing have been pointed out, and to meet them, we make Open Smart Classroom, which is based on Open Smart Platform to enable the teacher and students to have intercontinental and intercultural class with better mobile device cooperation experience. Open Smart Classroom envisions the future learning system, where classrooms are connecting and collaborating with each other in open network while the students and teachers with different cultural background in different countries are having class together.

Open Smart Platform, as an upgrade of Smart Platform, is still a multi-agent system integrated with several extensions, serving as the generic software infrastructure for Smart Space. It enables better support in three aspects: 1) Successful connection multiple Smart Platforms together in open network; 2) Service invocation channel between inside of Smart Spaces and outside systems; 3) Easy interaction for mobile device roaming with users.

Currently we place each Smart Space in equal hierarchy. However, as the emergence of more and more Smart Spaces, it is necessary to involve multi-layer hierarchy for optimization and better management.

For Open Smart Classroom, we are now developing a new project to study on the effect that people use this environment for intercultural learning, where participants in different Smart Spaces can listen to the presentation in formal communication language (e.g. English), and communicate with each other in their native language to understand the new word or new concepts which are not well explained in the presentation. At the same time, we also consider to build more web services and interesting applications to let the students in Tsinghua and Kyoto University to carry on novel experiment in the near future.

Reference

1. Abowd, G.: Classroom 2000: An Experiment with the instrumentation of a living educational environment. IBM Systems Journal 38(4), 508–530 (1999)
2. Johanson, B., Fox, A., Winograd, T.: The Interactive Workspaces Project: Experiences with Ubiquitous Computing Rooms. IEEE Pervasive Computing 1(2), 67–74 (2002)

3. Dufresne, R.J., Gerace, W.J., Leonard, W.J., Mestre, J.P., Wenk, L.: Classtalk: A classroom communication system for active learning. Journal of Computing in Higher Education 7, 3–47 (1996)
4. Chen, E., Shi, Y., Zhang, D., et al.: Intelligent meeting room: Facilitating collaboration for multi mobile devices on contextual information. In: The 8th International Conference on Computer Supported Cooperative Work in Design Proceedings, vol. 1, pp. 82–87 (2004)
5. Nakahara, J., Hisamatsu, S., Yaegashi, K., et al.: iTree: does the mobile phone encourage learners to be more involved in collaborative learning? In: Proceedings of CSCL 2005, pp. 470–478 (2005)
6. Kindberg, T., Fox, A.: System software for ubiquitous computing. IEEE Pervasive Computing 1(1), 70–81 (2002)
7. Román, M., Hess, C.K., Cerqueira, R., et al.: Gaia: A Middleware Infrastructure to Enable Active Spaces. In: IEEE Pervasive Computing, pp. 74–83 (October-December 2002)
8. Peters, S., Look, G., Quigley, K., Shrobe, H., Gajos, K.: Hyperglue: Designing High-Level Agent Communication for Distributed Applications. In: Alonso, E., Kudenko, D., Kazakov, D. (eds.) AAMAS 2000 and AAMAS 2002. LNCS (LNAI), vol. 2636, Springer, Heidelberg (2003)
9. Phillips, B.: Metaglue: A Programming Language for Multi-Agent Systems: [M.Eng Thesis]. Massachusetts, USA: Massachusetts Institute of Techonlogy (1999)
10. Ponekanti, S.R., Lee, B., Fox, A., et al.: ICrafter: A Service Framework for Ubiquitous Computing Environments. In: Proceedings of the 3rd International Conference on Ubiquitous Computing, Atlanta, pp. 56–75 (2001)
11. Ratto, M., Shapiro, R.B., Truong, T.M. Griswold, W.G.: The ActiveClass project: Experiments in encouraging classroom participation. In: Proceedings of CSCL 2003, pp. 477–486 (2003)
12. Kong, S.C., Lam, S.Y., Kwok, L.F.: A cognitive tool in handheld devices for collaborative learning: comprehending procedural knowledge of the addition of common fractions. In: Proceedings of CSCL 2005, pp. 341–345 (2005)
13. Andrews, T., Curbera, F., Dolakia, H., et al.: Business Process Execution Language for Web Services (2003)
14. Ishida, T.: Language Grid: An Infrastructure for Intercultural Collaboration. In: IEEE/IPSJ Symposium on Applications and the Internet (SAINT 2006), pp. 96–100 (2006)
15. Xie, W., Shi, Y., Xu, G., et al.: Smart Platform - A Software Infrastructure for Smart Space (SISS). In: Proc 4th IEEE International Conference on Multimodal Interfaces, pp. 429–434 (2002)
16. Murakami, Y., Ishida, T., Nakaguchi, T.: Language Infrastructure for Language Service Composition. In: International Conference on Semantics, Knowledge and Grid (SKG 2006) (2006)
17. Shi, Y., Xie, W., Xu, G., et al.: The smart classroom: merging technologies for seamless tele-education. IEEE Pervasive Computing 2(2), 47–55 (2003)
18. Active-BPEL, http://www.active-endpoints.com/active-bpel-engine-overview.htm
19. NIST Smart Space Laboratory, http://www.nist.gov/smartspace/
20. Smart Classroom in Minoh Lab, http://www.imell.kuis.kyoto-u.ac.jp/en/research/sclass.html
21. Web Services Axis, http://ws.apache.org/axis/

An Instructor's Guide to Design Web-Based Algorithm Animations

J. Ángel Velázquez-Iturbide[1], David Redondo-Martín[1], Cristóbal Pareja-Flores[2], and Jaime Urquiza-Fuentes[1]

[1] Departamento de Lenguajes y Sistemas Informáticos I,
Universidad Rey Juan Carlos,
C/ Tulipán s/n, 28933 Móstoles, Madrid, Spain
{angel.velazquez,jaime.urquiza}@urjc.es
[2] Departamento de Sistemas Informáticos y Computación,
Escuela Universitaria de Estadística, Universidad Complutense de Madrid,
Avda. Puerta de Hierro s/n, 28040 Madrid, Spain
cpareja@sip.ucm.es

Abstract. Much research effort was directed in last years to address two key issues in Web-based algorithm animations: lack of evidence of their educational benefit, and the considerable effort put on the part of instructors to construct animations. Consequently, there is a valuable corpus of lessons learnt to design effective algorithm animations, but these recommendations are very general. The designer of an animation has no guide for fine-grain decisions, which often are the basis of a successful animation. The goal of this study is to deepen in these issues by identifying good choices for the number of animations, structure and size of an animation, and size and value of input data. We describe the problem, our hypothesis and our findings, written as an instructor's guide for the design of educationally effective animations.

Keywords: Web-based algorithm animations, animation design, testing, instructor's guide, animation structure, input data.

1 Introduction

There is consensus among instructors about the potential of visualization and animation for computer science education. However, animations have not come to the mainstream of web-based courseware. Research efforts in past years mostly addressed two key issues: lack of evidence of their educational benefits [1], and the considerable effort put on the part of instructors to construct animations [2]. Attention was also devoted to develop use cases of animations in educational settings [3].

Consequently, there is a corpus of lessons learnt to design effective algorithm animations, but these recommendations are very general [3]. The designer of an animation has no guide for fine-grain decisions: it is a craft. However, these fine-grain decisions often are the basis of a successful or unsuccessful animation. Some issues a designer must address are: graphical design of visualizations, number of animations for an algorithm, size and structure of an animation, and size and values of input data of

H. Leung et al. (Eds.): ICWL 2007, LNCS 4823, pp. 440–451, 2008.
© Springer-Verlag Berlin Heidelberg 2008

the algorithm. Most of these issues determine the behaviour displayed and therefore are a key in understanding the algorithm.

The importance of these issues is implicitly acknowledged in the literature. With respect to input data, there is consensus since the first experiences using the Balsa system [4] about using small examples for novices and more challenging examples for advanced students.

Another issue is the number of animations created to illustrate an algorithm. The HalVis system [5] provides three animations for each algorithm. A first animation gives a conceptual view of the algorithm, typically to solve an everyday problem. A second animation allows watching an animation containing the algorithm pseudocode and several coordinated views. Finally, a more comprehensive animation with input data of large size is given. However, neither HalVis nor other systems allow several animations of the same algorithm placed at the same abstraction level.

A third key element of the structure of an animation is the set of important steps displayed in an animation. Systems use different approaches to identify them, depending on the specification technique used. In some cases, important steps are explicitly identified (e.g. as code actions in the "interesting events" approach [4] or as interactive actions to generate and customize program animations [6]). In other cases, selected operations are implicitly used to produce changes in the display of an automatically generated animation (e.g. operations on "self-animating" types [7]). Both approaches recognize the importance of identifying important steps. In the first case, they remain undocumented but embedded into the animation itself. In the second case, important steps are selected in a homogeneous but inflexible way.

Some authors acknowledge that more flexibility must be given to interact with the different steps of an animation. The HalVis system [5] allows the user to customize both the level of granularity of the operations displayed and the values of input data for the animation. Operations can be individual statements or "logical" operations (meaningful to the programmer). Input data is limited by the system to about 10 elements. The "Algorithms in Action" system [8] allows the user to interactively switch between different levels of detail in pseudocode. The animation window and others consistently update to display the required level of detail. The authors give some pieces of advice to designers: use a maximum of 3 levels and make pseudocode fit in a window. However, both systems fail in providing a clear and flexible support to instructors about the important steps to display. HalVis is even more rigid, since the user must fix visualization options before launching an animation.

The goal of this paper is to deepen in the study of these issues and to ultimately provide the instructor with a guide for the design of educationally effective animations. We consider that it is important to make explicit decisions on the issues discussed above. These decisions will form a body of knowledge to be used to either automatically or manually construct animations.

The paper is structured as follows. The following section summarizes the features of animations generated by the WinHIPE system; our findings are general, but we introduce WinHIPE to make the animations included in the paper understandable. Section 3 states the problem and explains the methodology used. The fourth section contains two sample animations. Section 5 describes our findings, in the form of an instructor's guide. Finally, we summarize our conclusions and describe future work.

2 Animations in the WinHIPE IDE

WinHIPE is an integrated programming environment for the functional paradigm that provides an interactive tracer [9], as well as a visualization and animation system [6] [10]. The former is based on the rewriting model of evaluation. The latter provides support to customize visualizations, to maintain and export animations to the Web, and to cope with large-scale visualizations and animations. Its main advantage over other visualization systems is an effortless approach to animation creation and maintenance. This approach is based on the automatic generation of visualizations as a side effect of program execution, and on a metaphor of animations as documents.

The evaluation model underlying functional programming is term rewriting. In this model, running a program consists in rewriting an initial expression, step by step, until a value is obtained. An evaluation is typically represented as a sequence of expressions separated by arrows. At each step, a subexpression, called the redex, is identified as the next subexpression to rewrite. For instance,

```
length ("ICWL")
↓
1 + length ("CWL")
↓
1 + (1 + length ("WL"))
↓
1 + (1 + (1 + length ("L")))
↓
1 + (1 + (1 + (1 + length (""))))
↓
1 + (1 + (1 + (1 + 0)))
↓
1 + (1 + (1 + 1))
↓
1 + (1 + 2)
↓
1 + 3
↓
4
```

In addition to a rewriting step, WinHIPE provides with the following actions:

- Performing *n* rewriting steps:

```
1 + length ("CWL")
↓4
1 + (1 + (1 + (1 + 0)))
```

- Performing the evaluation of the redex:

```
1 + length ("CWL")
↓r
1 + 3
```

- Rewriting until a breakpoint is reached (i.e. applying a user-selected function):

```
1 + length ("CWL")
↓p
1 + (1 + length ("WL"))
```

- Performing the evaluation of the complete expression.

Notice that in these examples we highlighted redexes with underlining. In addition, the arrow notation was augmented to represent an action. For instance, an arrow labelled with 'p' represents progress to a breakpoint. The environment allows the programmer to successively select actions until the evaluation is complete or it is abandoned. After each action, a new expression is displayed.

Any expression can be pretty-printed, i.e. displayed in textual format. In addition, WinHIPE provides an alternative, graphical representation for lists and binary trees, thereby avoiding the disadvantage of textual representations of data structures, which are frequently unreadable. The result is a mixed display.

WinHIPE provides discrete animations of a sequence of visualizations. The animation can be controlled using a VCR-like interface. Animations can be stored in and loaded from disk. In addition, the user can either play an animation within the programming environment or within a dynamic web page.

WinHIPE allows the friendly creation and maintenance of web animations [11] by means of simple dialogs. Web animations can be enriched with different textual contents: statement of the problem, algorithm that solves it, and source code of the program. It uses an XML representation that is transformed into a web page on demand. Four different formats of presentation were developed. They are inspired by general principles of web pages usability requirements [12].

In summary, we use for our study an animation system, the WinHIPE programming environment, which is aimed at the generation of discrete animations of functional programs. However, it can be used for our study without loss of generality given that particular features of WinHIPE have counterparts in most programming paradigms or languages. For instance, recursion is similar to iteration, and redex rewriting is analogous to stepping over a subroutine.

3 The Problem, Hypothesis and Methodology

Our aim is to develop an instructor's guide to give advice and hints on several, key elements in the design of an algorithm animation: number of animations, size and structure of each animation (including important steps of the animation and level of detail in different stages of an animation), and size and value of input data.

We want to call your attention to the similarity of two tasks: designing input data for an animation and designing input data for testing. In effect, in both cases the designer must decide what parts of the algorithm to deal with. The only difference is one of emphasis: the animation constructor is trying to display selected parts of an animation, while a testing designer is trying to execute selected parts of a program.

From our previous experience, we addressed our work according to the hypothesis that design of algorithm animations is in the border of two independent disciplines:

- Computer Science. Animating an algorithm is an operation very similar to testing and debugging. Therefore, techniques from these fields can be applied to the design of animations. In particular, black-box testing techniques can be used to identify different classes of input data from the problem specification. In addition, white-box testing techniques can be used to identify additional partitioning of input data, based on the particular algorithm solving the problem.
- Human Factors. Similar stages in an algorithm animation require different level of detail depending on their relative order. In effect, an animation is delivered to a student who does not know its behaviour. Consequently, initial stages must be displayed in detail, probably at the statement level. Subsequent stages often are similar, so they can be summarized into more abstract operations.

We scheduled the following methodology:

1. Review existing animations to analyze their (implicit) design decisions. We used a set of 39 web animations developed before by our research group using the facilities provided by the WinHIPE IDE [6][11]. They can be found at the system web site (http://vido.escet.urjc.es/winhipe).
2. Make an initial proposal of the instructor's guide. We based it on our previous experience as animation developers and on our hypothesis (read above) on being on the border of two disciplines.
3. Design animations for a set of well-known algorithms, based on the initial proposal of instructor's guide. According to our experience with these animations, the proposal was refined.
   For this study, we selected 18 algorithms of low or medium complexity. One or two animations were created for each algorithm. They fit the following categories:
   - Number algorithms: mcd (subtraction and module versions of Euclid's algorithm), checking primality and computing prime numbers, real and integer square root (Newton-Raphson method), Fibonacci numbers (2 versions), power (2 versions).
   - List algorithms: sorting (selectsort, insertsort, mergesort and quicksort).
   - Binary tree algorithms: tree traversal algorithms (preorder, inorder, postorder and breadth).
   In order to make a systematic analysis of these animations, a table was filled for each category. Each row in the table corresponded to a different algorithm. For each algorithm, the following columns were filled: name, parameters, equivalence classes (black-box testing), cases (white-box testing), parameters and result, number of steps in the evaluation, number of steps in the animation, and number of recursive steps. For most algorithms, it was interesting to develop two animations. In this case, each of the last four features was split into as many columns as animations.
4. Evaluation by other colleagues of the animations developed. Consequently, further refinements were made and the final version of the guide was delivered.

4   Two Sample Animations

The instructor's guide will probably be better appreciated if we first include and briefly comment two animations. They are simple but non-trivial algorithms that allow us illustrating many of the guidelines given in section 5. More complex or graphically appealing animations can be found elsewhere [6][10] and at the WinHIPE web site (http://vido.escet.urjc.es/winhipe). In particular, computing a binary tree from its pre- and in-order traversals can be found at the top of the main page.

4.1   Power of Two Numbers

We present here an animation with textual representation for a numeric algorithm. Fig. 1 contains the sequence of visualizations that are the material for the animation.

Consider the problem of computing the power of two integers:

$$b^0 = 1$$

$$b^{e+1} = b \cdot b^e$$

The specification suggests a direct algorithm based on multiplications. However, consider an alternative, more efficient algorithm that halves the exponent in each recursive call. Its implementation follows:

```
dec pow : num # num -> num;
--- pow (b,e) <=
    if e=0 then 1 else
    if e mod 2=0 then pow(b*b, e div 2)
    else b*pow(b*b, e div 2);
```

Some interesting elements of the animation are:

- Black-box testing techniques identify two classes of equivalence: $e=0$ and $e>0$.
- White-box testing techniques identify three cases: $e=0$, $e>0$ even and $e>0$ odd.
- A single animation can be generated integrating the three cases. Notice that $pow(3,4)$ corresponds to the case of e even. It calls $pow(9,2)$, $pow(81,1)$ and $pow(6561,0)$. The third and fourth calls correspond to different cases, but the call $pow(9,2)$ is maintained in order to keep the animation not too short.
- The complete evaluation consists of 29 rewriting steps, but the animation consists of only 11 steps.
- The first call was unfolded in detail, while the remaining ones are visualized more compactly.

4.2   Insertsort

Insersort is a direct, classical algorithm for sorting a sequence. Fig. 2 contains an excerpt of its animation; given the restrictions of space we omit two steps. The lowest part of the Figure should be read left to right.

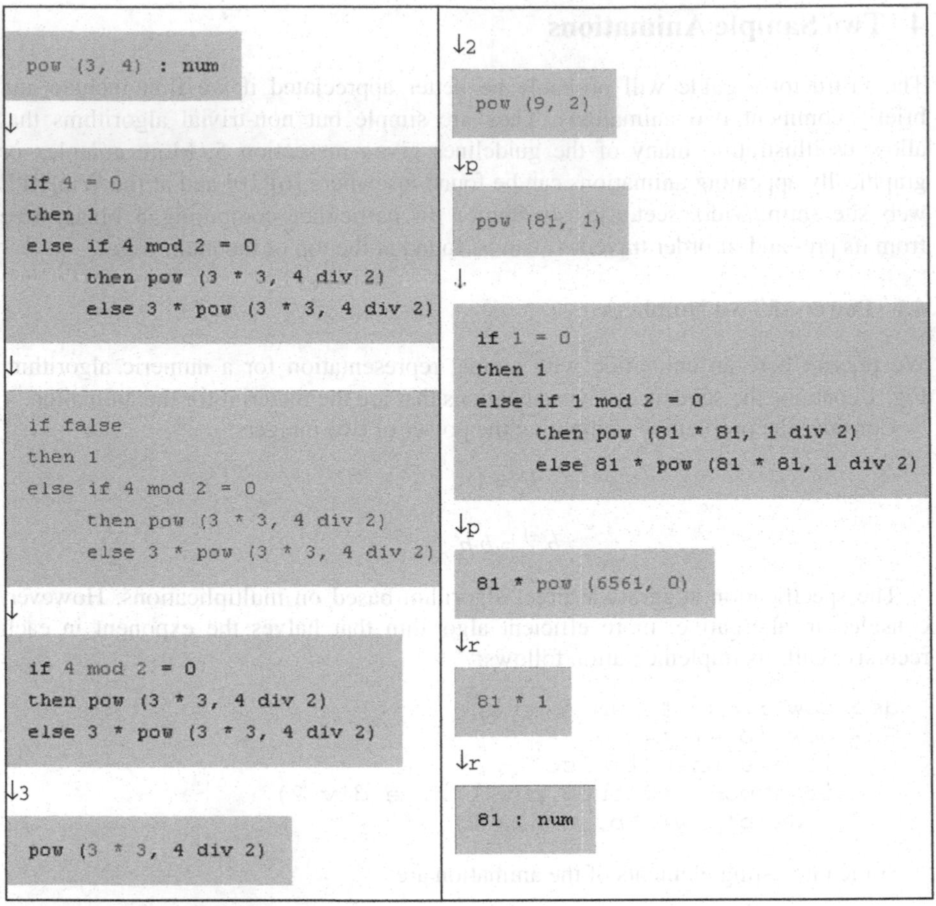

```
pow (3, 4) : num

↓

if 4 = 0
then 1
else if 4 mod 2 = 0
        then pow (3 * 3, 4 div 2)
        else 3 * pow (3 * 3, 4 div 2)

↓

if false
then 1
else if 4 mod 2 = 0
        then pow (3 * 3, 4 div 2)
        else 3 * pow (3 * 3, 4 div 2)

↓

if 4 mod 2 = 0
then pow (3 * 3, 4 div 2)
else 3 * pow (3 * 3, 4 div 2)

↓3

pow (3 * 3, 4 div 2)
```

```
↓2

pow (9, 2)

↓p

pow (81, 1)

↓

if 1 = 0
then 1
else if 1 mod 2 = 0
        then pow (81 * 81, 1 div 2)
        else 81 * pow (81 * 81, 1 div 2)

↓p

81 * pow (6561, 0)

↓r

81 * 1

↓r

81 : num
```

Fig. 1. An animation of the power of two numbers

An implementation of *insertsort* using lists follows:

```
dec insert : (alpha#list(alpha)) -> list(alpha);
--- insert (x, nil)
    <= x::nil ;
--- insert (x, y :: l)
    <= if x < y
        then x :: y :: l
        else y :: insert (x, l) ;
dec insertsort : list(alpha) -> list(alpha) ;
--- insertsort (nil)
    <= nil ;
--- insertsort (x :: l)
    <= insert (x, insertsort l) ;
```

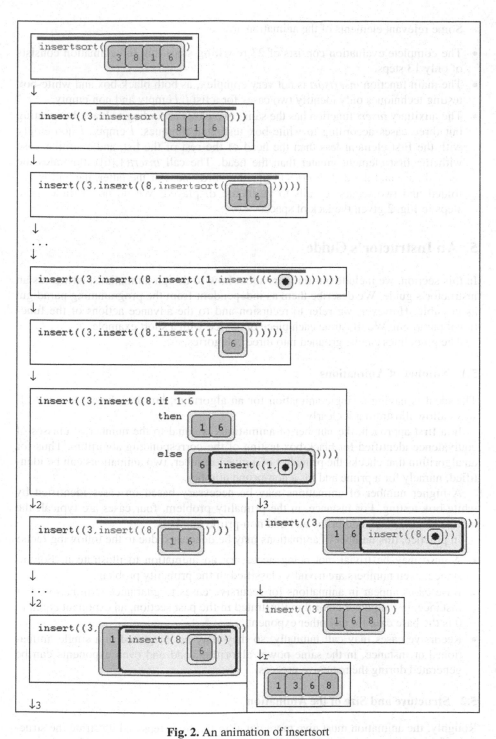

Fig. 2. An animation of insertsort

Some relevant elements of the animation are:

- The complete evaluation consists of 23 rewriting steps, but the animation consists of only 13 steps.
- The main function *insertsort* is not very complex, as both black-box and white-box testing techniques only identify two cases for a list *l*: *l* empty and non-empty.
- The auxiliary *insert* function has the same two cases according to black-box testing but three cases according to white-box testing techniques: *l* empty, *l* non-empty with the first element less than the head of the rest of the list, and a similar case with the first element greater than the head. The call *insert*(1,[6]) illustrates the second case and the call *insert*(8,[1,6]), the third one. For the latter, the call is unfolded and two recursive calls to insert are displayed. We do not include these steps in Fig. 2 given the lack of space.

5 An Instructor's Guide

In this section, we include our findings about how to design animations, written as an instructor's guide. We describe them as independent from the programming paradigm as possible. However, we refer to recursion and to the advance actions of the functional paradigm. We illustrate each piece of advice with a short example.

The guidelines can be grouped into three categories.

5.1 Number of Animations

The ideal is having a single animation for an algorithm, but this choice does not always allow illustrating it clearly.

In a first approach, the number of animations is equal to the number of classes of equivalence identified for black-box testing of the corresponding algorithm. Thus for an algorithm that checks the primality of a given number, two animations can be identified, namely for a prime and for a non-prime number.

A higher number of animations may be necessary based on cases identified by white-box testing. For instance, in the primality problem, four cases are typical: the number 2, and even, odd prime and odd non-prime numbers.

In practice, this number of animations may be decreased due to the following facts:

- A case may be trivial, not being necessary an animation to illustrate it. For instance, even numbers are trivially classified in the primality problem.
- Base cases appear in animations for recursive cases to guarantee termination. For instance, in the power algorithm illustrated in the past section, an exponent equal to 0 is the base case for any other exponent.
- Recursive cases may call mutually, so they may be integrated in a single animation. For instance, in the same power algorithm, odd and even exponents can be generated during the recursive process.

5.2 Structure and Size of the Animation

Roughly, the animation must give more detail in the first steps and illustrate the structure of the computing process in the following ones. Let us be more specific.

Start the animation unfolding completely the first call. For instance, look at the call *pow*(3,4) in the sample animation of the power algorithm included in Fig. 1.

If the first call contains several conditional branches:

- The first branch must be unfolded in detail. The atomicity of the operations displayed may depend on the expertise of students with the language. For instance, in the power animation, the evaluation of the outer condition and the simplification of the conditional expression are shown. However, for more advanced students, the third visualization can be removed without loss of information.
- The following branches will be unfolded with less detail. Again, the expertise of students will determine the amount of intermediate operations displayed.

For other recursive calls, we can distinguish three cases:

- If the function exhibits lineal recursion and a call corresponds to the same white-box case, it is not unfolded. In this case, advance to the next recursive call. This is the case of the call *pow*(9,2).
- If the function exhibits lineal recursion and a call corresponds to a different case, unfold it with less detail than the first call. This is the case of *pow*(81,1).
- If the function exhibits multiple recursion, give the result of any call that is not made in the first place. For instance, *Fibonacci* or *quicksort*.

As calls corresponding to different cases are displayed in detail, it is better having them early in an animation.

Recursive calls in non-final recursion leave a trail of pending operations. Perform them (in reverse order by redex) so that a trace-like structure of calls is shown, formed by pairs call-result. This can be easy illustrated with the computation of factorial, where the pending operations are multiplications.

For the base case, show directly its result (by redex advance). For instance, this is the case in the power algorithm for the call *pow*(6561,0).

If the function has an auxiliary function:

- If it is a simple operation, it must be ignored.
- If it is an important operation and it is invoked for the first time, unfold it in detail following similar guidelines as given above for recursive calls. For instance, an animation for *insertsort* uses an auxiliary function to insert a number into a sorted list.
- If it is an important operation and it is not invoked for the first time, the same rules apply as for other recursive calls of the main function. At the extreme, show just the call and its result (by redex advance).

Too long animations can be obscure but too short animations do not adequately explain an algorithm. Empirically, we observed that the size of the animation should be in a range of 15±5 visualizations. For instance, the animation of the power algorithm included above consists of 11 visualizations. Also, the number is recursive calls displayed should be in the range 5±2. In the same example, 4 calls are invoked.

5.3 Size and Value of Input Data

Some factors influence the size of input data. For simplicity, the smallest representatives of classes of equivalence or code cases should be chosen. However, they typically produce too short animations, so higher values are preferred. For instance, it is more clarifying to check the primality of 13 than of 3.

Another reason to have small input values is to make animations more understandable. However, values vary depending on whether they control the execution of the algorithm or they play an auxiliary role (for instance, contents of data structures). In the first case, typical values are below 10 whereas in the second case, they are below 100. For instance, we will animate the factorial of 5 but we will sort the list [12,5,35,9,40].

Some scheduling of arguments must be made to guarantee a given number of recursive calls. It may be tuned to the idiosyncrasies of each algorithm. For instance:

- To assure a result different enough from the parameters. For instance, avoid computing the third Fibonacci number because it is 3.
- To avoid a too large result.

With respect to size of and values in data structures, they also depend on the data type and the scheme of recursion:

- For instance, *selectsort* requires a shorter list than *quicksort*, as it is lineally vs. multiply recursive. In effect, the former requires a list of 5±2 elements (e.g. [6,2,5,11,8]), while the latter requires a list of at least 8 elements (e.g. [26,5,77,1,61,11,59,15,48,19]) to be able to split the list into at least 3 levels in a relatively balanced way.
- In the case of binary trees, 3-4 levels are adequate.

Additional scheduling also is necessary to have different cases early during execution, as shown in the *insertsort* animation.

6 Conclusion and Future Works

We have studied fine-grain decisions behind educational-ly effective animations. We described problem, hypothesis and findings, written as an instructor's guide.

We make here three remarks. Firstly, the guidelines are general for small- and medium-size animations. Secondly, they are specified in terms of functional programming, but adapting them to a different paradigm should not be problematic. Thirdly, they are applicable to any kind of animation. However, web-based animations, at least as generated by WinHIPE [11], have an advantage over other kinds of animations: they always display a view of code. Reading code facilitates tracking the behaviour of recursive calls displayed with little or no detail. For instance, this happened with *pow*(9,2) and *pow*(81,1).

In the near future, we plan to construct two collections of "canned" animations, following our instructor's guide, for two courses on constructs of programming languages and on algorithms, respectively.

Acknowledgments. This work was supported by project grants TIN2004-07568 and TIN2006-15578-C02-01 of MEC and S-0505/DPI/0235 of CAM.

References

1. Naps, T., Roessling, G., Almstrum, V., Dann, W., Fleischer, R., Hundhausen, C., Korhonen, A., Malmi, L., McNally, M., Rodger, S., Velázquez-Iturbide, J.Á.: Exploring the role of visualization and engagement in computer science education. ACM SIGCSE Bulletin 35 35(2), 131–152 (2003)
2. Naps, T., Roessling, G., Cooper, S., Koldehofe, B., Leska, C., Dann, W., Korhonen, A., Malmi, L., Rantakokko, J., Ross, R.J., Anderson, J., Fleischer, R., Kuittinen, M., McNally, M.: Evaluating the educational impact of visualization. ACM SIGCSE Bulletin 35(4), 124–136 (2003)
3. Pareja-Flores, C., Velázquez-Iturbide, J.Á.: Program execution and visualization on the Web. In: Aggarwal, A. (ed.) Web-Based Learning and Teaching Technologies, pp. 236–259. Idea-Group (2003)
4. Brown, M.H., Sedgewick, R.: A system for algorithm animation. ACM SIGGRAPH 18(3), 177–183 (1984)
5. Hansen, S., Schrimpsher, D., Narayanan, N.H.: Designing educationally effective algorithm animations. Journal of Visual Languages and Computing 13, 291–317 (2002)
6. Velázquez-Iturbide, J.Á., Pareja-Flores, C., Urquiza-Fuentes, J.: An approach to effortless construction of program animations. Computers & Education (in press)
7. Sutinen, E., Tarhio, J., Teräsvirta, T.: Easy algorithm animation on the Web. Multimedia Tools and Applications 19, 179–194 (2003)
8. Stern, L., Sondergaard, H., Naish, L.: A strategy for managing content complexity in algorithm animation. In: 4th Annual Conference on Innovation and Technology in Computer Science Education, pp. 127–130. ACM Press, New York (1999)
9. Velázquez-Iturbide, J.Á.: Improving functional programming environments for education. In: Brouwer-Janse, M.D., Harrington, T.L. (eds.) Man-Machine Communication for Educational Systems Design, pp. 325–332. Springer, Heidelberg (1994)
10. Pareja-Flores, C., Urquiza-Fuentes, J., Velázquez-Iturbide, J.Á.: WinHIPE: An IDE for functional programming based on rewriting and visualization. ACM SIGPLAN Notices 42(3), 14–23 (2007)
11. Urquiza-Fuentes, J., Velázquez-Iturbide, J.Á.: Effortless construction and management of program animations on the Web. In: Lau, R.W.H., et al. (eds.) ICWL 2005. LNCS, vol. 3583, pp. 163–173. Springer, Heidelberg (2005)
12. Nielsen, J.: Designing Web Usability. New Riders (1999)

Logging and Visualization of Learner Behaviour in Web-Based E-Testing

Gennaro Costagliola, Vittorio Fuccella, Massimiliano Giordano,
and Giuseppe Polese

Salerno University, 84084 Fisciano SA, Italy
{gencos,vfuccella,mgiordano,gpolese}@unisa.it

Abstract. In this paper we present a system for the logging and the visualization of the learners' behavior during the execution of structured tests based on *Multiple Choice* question type. The system is composed of two main components: a logging framework which, instantiated in *e-testing* systems, produces an XML formatted log of learners' interactions with the system during tests and a stand-alone application which visualizes charts containing a chronological review of the tests. By analyzing the charts obtained through an experiment led in our department, we have defined several typical strategies used by the learners to execute tests. The effectiveness of these strategies has been inferred by correlating the strategies with the obtained scores. Further useful applications of our system allow us to detect correlations among questions and cheating attempts by the learners.

1 Introduction

E-testing systems are more and more widely adopted in academic environments combined with other assessment means. Through these systems, tests composed of several question types can be presented to the learners in order to assess their knowledge. *Multiple Choice* question type is extremely popular, since, among other advantages, a large number of its outcomes can be easily corrected automatically. Among the disadvantages of structured tests, a low acceptance of the exam type by the learners is rather frequently noticed: many learners are afraid of not being able to best express their capacity, due to the characteristic of *multiple choice* questions of being closed. Even many examiners wonder if structured tests are effective in assessing the learners' knowledge and if some learners are conditioned more by the question type than by the actual question difficulty.

In order to teach to the learners how to better perform on *structured* tests, several experiments aimed at tracking learners' behavior have been carried out in the past using the think out loud method: the learners were informed of the experiment and had to speak during the test to explain what they were thinking, while an operator was storing their words using a tape recorder. This technique can result quite invasive, since it requires that the learners must modify their behavior in order to record the information to analyze [1,2,3,4,5].

H. Leung et al. (Eds.): ICWL 2007, LNCS 4823, pp. 452–463, 2008.
© Springer-Verlag Berlin Heidelberg 2008

In this paper we discuss a complete system that allows us to record and to analyze information about learners habits during on-line tests without informing them of the experiment and, consequently, without asking them to modify their behavior thus obtaining more realistic results. We use information visualization in order to define several typical strategies used by the learners to execute tests. When exploring data, humans look for structures, patterns and relationships between data elements. Such analysis is easier if the data are presented in a graphical form in a visualization. Information visualization is defined as the use of interactive visual representation of abstract data to amplify cognition [6]. In the past, information visualization has successfully used in an E-Learning application to measure the participation of the learners to on-line activities [7].

Our technique consists of logging all the interactions of the learners with the *e-testing* system interface. To elaborate, we capture the occurrence of question browsing and answering events by the learners. These data are used to visualize charts containing a chronological review of the tests. Besides identifying the most employed strategies, we try to determine their effectiveness by correlating their use with the scores obtained on the tests. Another useful application of our system allows us to detect correlations among questions: if a question contains a suggestion to solve other questions, this is easily visible in the charts. Lastly, unethical behaviors from the learners, such as cheating by watching on others' screens and *gaming the system* [8] attempts can be detected.

The proposed system is web based and adopts the *AJAX* [9] technology in order to capture all of the *learners* interactions with the *e-testing* system interface (running in the Web browser). The system is composed of a logging framework which can be instantiated in any *e-testing* systems and of a stand-alone application which analyzes the obtained logs in order to extract information from them and to produce graphical representation.

In order to demonstrate the effectiveness of our system, it has been used in the ambit of a university course at our department: the framework has been instantiated in an existing *e-testing* system, *eWorkbook* [10], which has been used to administer on-line tests to learners. The grade obtained on the tests has concurred to determine the final grade of the course exam.

The rest of the paper is organized as follows: Sect.2 gives the knowledge background necessary to understand some concepts on which the system is based. The logging framework and its integration in *eWorkbook* is presented in Sect.3. Lastly, in Sect.4, we discuss the techniques employed and the results obtained through the experiments. Several final remarks and a brief discussion on future work conclude the paper.

2   Background: The *AJAX* Technologies

AJAX is a style of web application development that uses a mix of modern web technologies to provide a more interactive user experience. *AJAX* is not a technology it is an approach to web applications that includes a couple of technologies. These are *JavaScript, HTML, Cascading Style Sheets (CSS), Document*

Object Model (DOM), *XML*, *XSLT* and *XMLHttpRequest* as a messaging protocol. These core technologies are mature, well-known and widely used in web applications. *AJAX* became so popular because it has a couple of advantages for the browser based web applications developers. It eliminates the stop-start nature of interactions, user interactions with the server happen asynchronously, data can be manipulated without having to render the entire page again and again in the web browser, and requests and responses over the *XMLHttpRequest* protocol are structured *XML* documents. This enables developers easily integrate *AJAX* applications into Web Services.

AJAX drew some attention in the public after *Google* started developing some new interesting applications. Some of the major products *Google* has introduced over the last year by using the *AJAX Model* are *Google* Groups, *Google* Suggests, *GMail*, and *Google* Maps. Besides the *Google* products *Amazon* also has used the *AJAX* approach in its search engine application. A developer can use *AJAX* in his/her web applications by just writing his/her own custom *JavaScript* code that directly uses the *XMLHttpRequest* protocol's API. However, the developer must take into consideration the implementation differences among the web browsers. Instead of using pure *AJAX* and dealing with the browser differences, the developers can use some newly developed libraries which provide higher level *AJAX* services and hide the differences between browsers. Among these are *DWR*, *Prototype*, *Sajax*, and *AJAX.NET*.

3   The Logging Framework

The purpose of the Logging Framework is to gather all of the *learner* actions during the browsing of the Web pages of the test and to store raw information in a set of log files in *XML* format.

The framework is composed of a server-side and a client-side module. The client-side module is responsible for "being aware" of the behavior of the *learner* while he/she is browsing the test pages. The server-side module receives the data from the client and creates and stores log files on the disk.

Despite the required interactivity level, due to the availability of *AJAX*, it has been possible to implement the client-side module of our framework without developing plug-in or external modules for Web browsers. *JavaScript* has been used on the client to capture *learner* interactions and the text-based communication between the client and the server has been implemented through *AJAX* method calls. The client-side scripts are added to the *e-testing* system pages with a light effort by the programmer.

The events captured by the framework are the following:

- Actions undertaken on the browser window (open, close, resize, load, unload)
- Actions undertaken in the browser client area (key pressing, scrolling, mouse movements and clicks)

The event data is gathered on the browser and sent to the server at regular intervals. It is worth noting that the event capture does not prevent other scripts present in the page to run properly.

The server-side module has been implemented as a Java servlet which receives the data from the client and prepares an *XML* document in memory. At the end of the test session the *XML* document is written to the disk. The logger can be instantiated and then enabled through the configuration.

The information *Model* used for the log data is quite simple and is shown in Fig.1. The information is organized per *learner* test session. At this level, the user name (if available), the IP of the *learner* and session identifier are logged as well as agent information (browser type, version and operating system). Inside a session, a list of event elements is present. The data about the user interactions are the following:

- Event type
- *HTML* source object involved in the event (if present)
- Mouse information (pressed button, coordinates)
- Timing information (timestamp of the event)
- More information specific of the event. I.e. for a response type event (a response given to a question), the question and option identifiers and the indication whether the response was right or wrong are recorded.

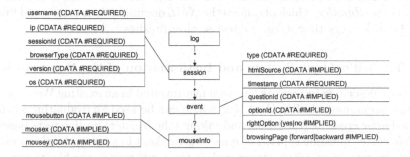

Fig. 1. The information *Model* for log data

An important concern in logging is log size. If an experiment is done involving a large set of learners and the test is composed of many questions, log files can reach big sizes. A configuration system, including the following configuration settings, has been conceived in order to reduce log sizes:

- List of events to capture
- Sub-set of attributes to store in the log for each event
- *sections* of the Web pages (*divs* or table cells) to monitor as sources of the events
- Time interval between two data transmissions from the client to the server
- Sensitivity for mouse movements (short movements are not captured)

The configuration is read by the server-side module but affects the generation of the *JavaScript* modules running on the client-side. The architecture of the framework is graphically represented in Fig.2.

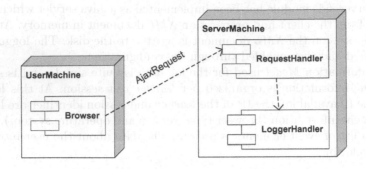

Fig. 2. The Logging Framework Architecture

On the client machine, everything can be done in the web Browser. The *JavaScript* modules for event capturing, *dynamic*ally generated on the server according to the configuration settings, are downloaded and run in the browser interpreter. Data is sent to the server through an *AJAX* request. On the server-side, a module called *RequestHandler* receives the data and sends it to a module called *LoggerHandler*, which organizes the *XML* document in memory and flushes it to the disk every time a *learner* test session finishes.

3.1   The *eWorkbook* System and Instantiation of the Framework

The above described framework has been instantiated in an existing Web-based *e-testing* system, named *eWorkbook* [10], which can be used for evaluating learner's knowledge by creating (the tutor) and taking (the *learner*) on-line tests based on *multiple choice* question types. The questions are kept in a *hierarchical* repository, that is, the repository is tree-structured, in the same way as the file system of an operating system. In this structure, the files can be thought of as questions, while the directories can be thought of as *macroareas*, which are containers of questions usually dealing with the same subject. The tests are composed of one or more *sections*. This structure facilitates the selection of the questions from the database, but it is still useful for the assessment, where it can be important to establish if one section is more important than another to determine the final grade for the test. There are two kinds of *sections*: *static* and *dynamic*. The difference between them is in the way they allow question selection: for a *static* section, the questions are chosen by the tutor. For a *dynamic* section, some selection parameters must be specified, such as the difficulty, leaving the system to choose the questions randomly whenever a *learner* takes a test. In this way, it is possible with *eWorkbook* to make a test with banks of items of different difficulties, thus balancing test difficulty, in order to better assess a heterogeneous set of learners.

eWorkbook adopts the classical three-tier architecture of the most common J2EE Web-applications. The *Jakarta* Struts framework has been used to support the *Model* 2 design paradigm, a variation of the classic *Model View Controller* (MVC) approach. Struts provides its own *Controller* component and integrates with other technologies to provide the *Model* and the *View*. In our design choice, Struts works with *JSP*, for the *View*, while it interacts with Hibernate [11], a powerful framework for *object/relational persistence* and query service for Java, for the *Model*. The application is fully accessible with a Web Browser. No browser plug-in installations are needed, since its pages are composed of standard *HTML* and *EC-MAScript* [12] code. The integration of the server-side component in the *eWorkbook* system has been rather simple: the JAR (Java ARchive) file containing the framework classes has been imported as a library in the system. A modification to the system's deployment descriptor has been necessary in order to deploy the server-side module (servlet) which receives the events from the client.

The integration of the client-side component of the *framework*, composed of several *JavaScript* files, has been slightly more complicated, due to the structure of the *eWorkbook* interface: the test is launched in a child browser window of the main system Web page. This window displays a timer to inform the learner of the remaining time to complete the test and contains the controls to flow among the questions (*forward* and *backward* buttons) and the button to submit the test. The *stem* and the form containing the *options* are loaded in an *iframe* window present in the centre of the page.

4   Test Visualization

The system has been experimented by using it across a test session in a university course: *eWorkbook* has been used to administer on-line tests to learners. The learners were not informed of the experiment; they just knew that the grade obtained on the tests concurred to determine the final grade of the course exam. The test, containing a set of 25 items to complete in a maximum time of 20 minutes, was administered to 71 learners, who took the test concurrently in the same lab. The assessment strategy did not foresee any penalty for incorrect responses and the *learner* were aware of that. The logger was enabled and an approximately 4Mb sized *XML* log file has been obtained. The logging activity produced no visible system performance degrading.

The next sub-section shows the chart production *phase*, while the subsequent sub-*sections* describe the experiments performed using log data.

4.1   Chart Production

A chronological review of the test has been made available through a chart, obtained by showing the salient points of a test execution, synthesized in the interactions recorded in the log file. This chart shows, at any time, the item browsed by the *learner*, the mouse position (intended as the presence of the mouse pointer on the stem or on one of the options) and the presence of response type interactions, correct or incorrect. The chart is bi-dimensional. The horizontal axis reports a continuous measure, the time, while the vertical axis displays categories, the progressive number of the item currently viewed by the *learner*.

The test execution is represented through a broken line. The *View* of an item for a determined duration, is shown through a segment drawn from the point corresponding to the start time of the *View* to the one corresponding to its end. Consequently, the length of the segment is proportional to the duration of the visualization of the corresponding item. A vertical segment represents a browsing event. A segment oriented towards the bottom of the chart represents a backward event, that is, the *learner* has pressed the button to *View* the previous item. A segment oriented towards the top is a forward event. Using the logger with *eWorkbook*, we will only see one unit long segments (except for the transition from the last to the first question), since *eWorkbook* only allows to browse items sequentially. The responses given by a *learner* on an item are represented through circles. The progressive number of the chosen option is printed inside the circle. The indication of correct/incorrect response is given by the filling color of the circle: a blue circle represents a correct response, while an incorrect response is represented through a red circle. The color is used also for representing the position of the mouse pointer during the item *View*. The position of the mouse pointer can be a significant indicator of the part of the item analyzed by the *learner*, since it has been demonstrated to be correlated to the position of the gaze of the user [13]. The presence of the mouse pointer in the stem area is represented through a black color for the line. As for the options areas, the red, yellow, green, blue and purple colors have been used, respectively, for 1 to 5 numbered options. More options are not supported. At last, grey is used to report the presence of the mouse pointer in a neutral zone.

The graphical chronological review of a sample test is shown in Fig.3. The test is composed of 25 items and the maximum duration foreseen is 20 minutes, even if the *learner* has completed and submitted the test in 17 minutes approximately. The whole *View* of the chart in the figure shows the strategy adopted by the *learner* in the test: the test execution is visibly composed of two successive *phases*. In the first one (nearly 9 minutes), the *learner* has completed the *View* of all the items from 1 to 25. Responses to 19 questions have been given in this *phase*. Several items present more than one response, maybe due to learner's reflection, while a few items have been skipped. The mouse position for each item *View* is visible through a zoom, performed by using a suitable zoom tool of the analyzer.

4.2   Strategies for Executing Tests

From the analysis of the charts obtained through our experiment the following strategies, with a few exceptions, have been adopted by the students to execute the tests:

- **Single Phase.** This strategy is composed of just one *phase*. The time available to complete the test is organized by the *learner* in order to browse all the questions just once. The *learner* tries to reason upon a question for an adequate time and then gives a response in almost all cases, since he/she knows that there will not be a revision for the questions. Eventual *phases* subsequent to the first one have a negligible duration and no responses. A sample of this strategy is shown in Fig.4a.

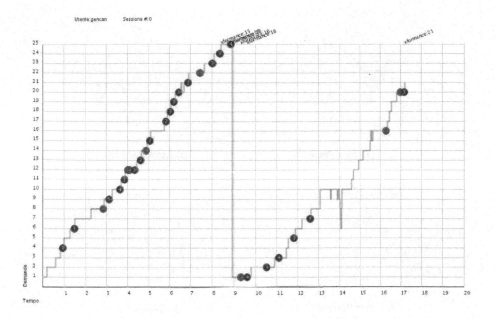

Fig. 3. Graphical Chronological Review of a Sample Test

- **Active Revising.** This strategy is composed of two or more *phases*. The *learner* intentionally browses all the questions in a shorter time than the time available, in order to leave some time for revising *phases*. The questions whose answer is uncertain are skipped and the response is left to subsequent *phases*. As a general rule, the first *phase* lasts a longer time and the subsequent *phases* have decreasing durations. A sample of this strategy is shown in Fig.4b.
- **Passive Revising.** This strategy is composed of two or more *phases*. The *learner* browses and answers all the questions as fast as possible. The remaining time is used for one or more revising *phases*. As a general rule, the first *phase* lasts a longer time and the subsequent *phases* have decreasing durations. A sample of this strategy is shown in Fig.4c.

For both the definition of the strategies and the classification of test instances, the charts have been visually analyzed by a human operator. The above tasks are rather difficult to perform automatically, while a trained human operator can establish the strategy used by the *learner* from a visual inspection of the charts of the test instances and giving advice to the learners on how to perform better next time. According to the data of our experiment, the most frequently adopted strategy is the Active Revising, used by 40 learners over 71 (56,5%), followed by the *Passive Revising* strategy (20 learners over 71, 28,2%) and by the Single *Phase* one, used only in 9 cases over 71 (12,7%). Only two learners have adopted an atypical strategy (see Fig.4d) which cannot be classified in any of the previously described patterns. The best results have been obtained by the

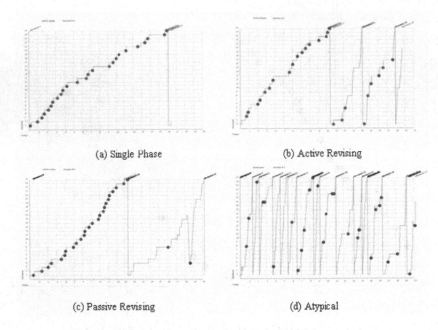

(a) Single Phase

(b) Active Revising

(c) Passive Revising

(d) Atypical

Fig. 4. Samples of Test Execution Strategies

learners who adopted the *Passive Revising* strategy, with an average score of 17.6 exact responses on the 25 questions test. With the *Active Revising*, instead, an average score of 16.4 has been obtained. Lastly, the Single *Phase* strategy reveals itself as the worse one, showing an average score of 15.1.

Then, a winning strategy foresees more than one *phase* and this is confirmed by the lightly positive linear correlation (0.14) observed between the number of *phases* and the score obtained on the test. For both the strategies that foresee more than one *phase*, the score is often improved through the execution of a new *phase*. The improvement is evident in the early *phases* and tends to be negligible on the growing of the *phase* number: starting from a value of 14.3 obtained after the first *phase*, the average score increases to 16.2 after the second *phase*. The presence of further *phases* brings the final score to an average value of 16.5. The average duration of the first *phase* of the *Passive strategy* (14'50") is longer than the one registered for the Active strategy (11'51"). This result was predictable, since, by definition, the Active strategy foresees the skipping (= less reasoning) of the questions whose answer is more uncertain for the learners. Another predictable result, due to the above arguments, is that the Passive strategy has less *phases* than the Active one, on average (2.55 and 3.2, respectively).

4.3 Detection of Cheating

As proven by several studies in the education field, many learners cheat at exams, when they can [14,15]. Cheating detection in assessment tests is not an easy task:

most of the techniques employed so far have been based on the comparison of the results obtained in the tests [16]. These techniques cannot give the certainty of the guilt, since a high similarity of two tests can be due to coincidence.

Furthermore, as in all fraud detection systems, the task is complicated by several technological and methodological problems [17]. It could be useful to gain information on the learners' behavior during the test. Analysis on these data can be integrated to results comparison in order to have a more comprehensive data set as input for a data mining technique to detect cheating. For example, let's consider the following situation: during the test, *learner* A answers *true* to a question and *learner* B, who is seated behind the former, answers the same few instants later. The tracking of this information, available through the charts of our system, could be useful to prove that the *learner* has cheated, looking on the screen of his classmate.

Copying from the colleague set in front of someone is not the only one frequently encountered cheating exploit: in some cases several attempts of *gaming the system* [8] have been reported. This exploit consists of executing a large number of tests with the only scope of having from the *e-testing* feedback system as much correct responses as possible. When some suspect cases are detected from the frequency of self-assessment test access and the strange scores obtained, our system can confirm the cheating attempts, by revealing atypical patterns of test execution.

4.4   Detection of Correlation Among Questions

By visually inspecting learner's behavior we can also be assisted in the detection of correlated questions. In some cases, a visual pattern similar to a *stalactite* occurs in the chart, as shown in Fig.5. The occurrence of such a pattern tells that, while the *learner* was browsing the current question, he/she could deduce

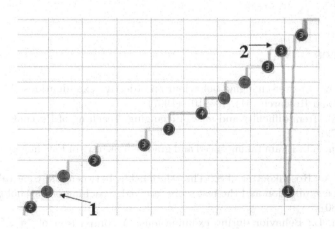

Fig. 5. A *Stalactite* in the Chart Shows the Correlation Between Two Questions

the right answer to a previous question. In the example shown in the figure, the *learner* who was browsing the question "2", understood that he/she had given a wrong response to the question "1", and came back to change the response, from option 5 to option 1.

5 Conclusion

In this paper we have presented a system for capturing and visualizing the behavior of the learners during *e-testing* sessions based on structured tests. The system is composed of a logging framework which can be instantiated in *e-testing* systems and of a stand-alone application which produces the charts. A chart produced with our system shows the chronological review of a test executed by a *learner*.

The use of information visualization in this context has been proven to be useful for various applications, such as analysis of the strategies used by the learners during the execution of a structured test; cheating detection and detection of correlation among questions. We are confident that more interesting applications can be discovered. Furthermore, our system allows experimenters to perform realistic experiments, since learners are not informed of the experiment and are not forced to modify their behavior.

The system has been used for an experiment under determinate circumstances (established number of options per item, time to complete the test adequate to the number of questions, assessment strategy known by the learners and with no penalty factors). Future work is aimed at performing new experiments in more general conditions. Further studies will also be devoted to understand if valuable information can be obtained by observing the mouse pointer position during test browsing, which is at present recorded by the log and displayed with different line colors in the chart, but has not yet been linked to any concrete application.

References

1. Bath, J.A.: Answer-changing behaviour on objective examinations. The Journal of Educational Research (61), 105–107 (1967)
2. Best, J.B.: Item difficulty and answer changing. Teaching of Psychology 6(4), 228–240 (1979)
3. Johnston, J.J.: Exam taking speed and grades. Teaching of Psychology (4), 148–149 (1977)
4. Paul, C.A., Rosenkoetter, J.S.: The relationship between the time taken to complete an examination and the test score received. Teaching of Psychology (7), 108–109 (1980)
5. McClain, L.: Behavior during examinations: A comparison of "a", "c," and "f" students. Teaching of Psychology 10(2), 69–71 (1983)
6. Plaisant, C., Shneiderman, B.: Show me! guidelines for producing recorded demonstrations. vlhcc 00, 171–178 (2005)

7. Mazza, R., Dimitrova, V.: Student tracking and personalization: Visualising student tracking data to support instructors in web-based distance education. In: Proceedings of the 13th International World Wide Web conference on Alternate Track papers & posters, pp. 154–161 (2004)
8. Baker, R.S., Corbett, A.T., Koedinger, K.R., Wagner, A.Z.: Off-task behavior in the cognitive tutor classroom: when students "game the system". In: CHI 2004: Proceedings of the SIGCHI conference on Human factors in computing systems, pp. 383–390. ACM Press, New York (2004)
9. (SDN), S.D.N.: Asynchronous javascript technology and xml (ajax) with the java platform (2007)
10. Costagliola, G., Ferrucci, F., Fuccella, V., Gioviale, F.: A web based tool for assessment and self-assessment. In: Proceedings of ITRE, pp. 131–135 (2004)
11. Hibernate: Hibernate framework (2007)
12. ECMAScript: Ecmascript language specification
13. Chen, M.C., Anderson, J.R., Sohn, M.H.: What can a mouse cursor tell us more?: correlation of eye/mouse movements on web browsing. In: CHI 2001 extended abstracts on Human factors in computing systems, pp. 281–282. ACM Press, New York (2001)
14. Dick, M., Sheard, J., Bareiss, C., Carter, J., Joyce, D., Harding, T., Laxer, C.: Addressing student cheating: definitions and solutions. SIGCSE Bull. 35(2), 172–184 (2003)
15. Harding, T.S., Carpenter, D.D., Montgomery, S.M., Steneck, N.: The current state of research on academic dishonesty among engineering students. In: Proceedings of FIE 2001, vol. 3, pp. 13–18 (2001)
16. Mulvenon, S.V., Turner, R.C., Thomas, S.: Techniques for detection of cheating on standardized tests using sas. In: Proceedings of the Twenty-Sixth Annual SAS Users Group International Conference, pp. 1–6 (2001)
17. Shao, H., Zhao, H., Chang, G.R.: Applying data mining to detect fraud behavior in customs declaration. In: Proceedings of International Conference on Machine Learning and Cybernetics, vol. 3, pp. 1241–1244 (2002)

Tracking and Visualisation of Student Use of Online Learning Materials in a Large Undergraduate Course

Judy Hardy[1], Simon Bates[2], Jon Hill[1], and Mario Antonioletti[1]

[1] EPCC and [2] The School of Physics
The University of Edinburgh
James Clerk Maxwell Building, Mayfield Road, Edinburgh EH9 3JZ
{j.hardy, s.p.bates, Jon.Hill, Mario.Antonioletti}@ed.ac.uk

Abstract. This paper presents a detailed study that tracks the use of online supplementary material used by 250 students enrolled on an introductory University course in Physics. We describe the software tools used for tracking, which provide a richer and far greater level of detail than tools included as standard within Virtual Learning Environments. We also describe how the recorded data can be visualised in order to illuminate spatial and temporal routes taken by students through the material. The recorded styles of use are analysed in terms of students' level of achievement, as measured by their performance in the end-of-course examination, and how this changes for students failing the course and resitting the exam six months later.

Keywords: tracking, blended learning, Physics, visualisation.

1 Introduction

E-Learning has touched almost all disciplines at all levels of education, ranging from the ubiquitous "putting slides on the web" in support of traditional face-to-face teaching, to the provision of sophisticated courses blending the best of both traditional approaches and online resources. At the end of this spectrum falls distance learning, where online materials provide the main (or even sole) learning activity. Regardless of the approach taken, valuable information about how E-Learning resources are used in practice may be obtained by tracking the way students interact with, and make use of, online material. For example, the online activity of campus-based undergraduate students has been investigated through analysis of Web server logs [1] while the impact of online discussion boards has been studied by tracking student use [1]. Students' "behaviour" online has also been investigated by direct observation (see for example [3]).

The integrated monitoring of the student experience is considered an essential component of the "minimum standards" of requirements for online learning provision [4]. There are many different pathways to learning; "the complexity of coming to know" as it has been termed [5], and it is interesting to speculate whether it follows from this that there are different yet equally valid pathways in the way that E-Learning materials are used. If this is the case, then how much is determined – or constrained - by the aspirations and practices of the student cohort and/or the way in which the underlying course design philosophy utilises the E-Learning material?

H. Leung et al. (Eds.): ICWL 2007, LNCS 4823, pp. 464–474, 2008.

The production of E-Learning material, regardless of whether it plays a core or supplementary role in a teaching strategy, is a time-consuming and laborious process; it can take many hours to generate the online equivalent of a single lecture [5]. However, despite this large investment in time and effort, there is often a tendency to regard the production of the materials as an end in itself and not evaluate how the online content produced is used in practice, and how this relates to the originally envisaged mode of utilisation. In addition, the provision of on-line content, whether this is done through sophisticated delivery agents offering integrated solutions, such as WebCT or Blackboard, or through little more than a stand alone web server, allows twenty-four hour, seven days a week availability. This means that students will be able to access the material at all hours of the day and not necessarily with the same software as that available in the class room environment for which the content may have originally been designed. In order to determine usage patterns, there is a wealth of data that could be captured and used to provide valuable feedback as to how an electronic course is actually being used and whether this indeed matches the originally envisaged goals. This information, together with direct feedback from students and assessments, may be used to modify the course materials accordingly to match the actual usage patterns.

There already is some provision for tooling that allows usage patterns to be captured, henceforth referred to as student tracking. Some of this is already bundled in with integrated delivery agents, such as WebCT, or, at worst, one can data mine the web server logs but this is tedious and onerous, requires specialised knowledge and one may not even have direct access to these logs. Moreover, the tracking capabilities of commercial delivery agents usually offer a granularity that is fixed, generally either too coarse or too fine grained to allow relevant questions to be answered. This paper describes a possible solution that can be used to track course material, that works independently of the delivery agent and that can be used to track a course served from one or more sites at a single network point. Here, we outline the mechanics of the student tracking tool and visualisation of the data generated by such a tool. A companion paper describes the analysis and conclusions derived from actual course data, using these tools, obtained for an introductory level undergraduate physics course run at the University of Edinburgh [6]; another companion paper describes the design, delivery and underlying pedagogical motivation of this physics course [6]. A third recent paper has investigated some of the broad aspects of material usage over a spectrum of different academic disciplines, different course levels and different functions of online resources. That study included four courses from the Schools of Physics, Divinity and Psychology at the University of Edinburgh, comprising over 700 students in total [8].

In this paper, we focus on a more in-depth presentation of the technical aspects of the tracking procedure. Additionally, we present details of how the vast quantity of tracked data may be visualised to gain insight into the complex spatial and temporal routes taken by students through the material. We then apply this method of analysis to study two specific aspects of student use of online material on the introductory level Physics course, going beyond broad brush overviews. These are an investigation into correlations between style of use and performance in the end-of-course exam, and changes in style of use for students failing the course and resitting the exam six months later.

2 Setting the Scene: The Course and Its Delivery

Physics 1A: Foundations is a first-year, first Semester course taken by students at the University of Edinburgh. The student cohort is large and diverse; approximately one half of the ~250 students taking the course are studying for degrees in subjects other than Physics. The course is an introduction to the classical (Newtonian) physics of space and time. Despite its simplicity, this material is well-documented to be fraught with pitfalls to conceptual understanding [9]. Over the last eight years or so, the course team has developed a large amount of rich and interactive online material to supplement the face to face teaching on the course. Specific details are reported elsewhere [6] but here we simply reiterate some of the salient features.

Course materials are presented to students in both paper and electronic format, with electronic course content made interactive via the use of on-page elements we call "inlines" and "popups". The former open up in the main frame of the page, allowing students more detail or explanation on a topic; they typically contain, explanations, commentaries, worked examples etc. Popups are deliberately different; they open up in a separate window (as the name suggests) and provide additional material off the beaten track of the course. This is for information only, and often includes complementary material, links to external web material, applets, videos or additional mathematical details. Both these constructs accommodate a diverse student cohort, by facilitating differentiated routes through material in terms of both breadth and depth. The interactive on-page elements are supplemented by embedded links within content, to relevant course questions and "self-tests" (formative, interactive MCQs). A screenshot of the online content, deployed via the University's VLE (WebCT Vista 4), is illustrated in Fig. 1. The course content is also supplemented with additional material used in formal class sessions ("workshops").

One final point to note is that the online content utilises MathML for display of mathematics [10]. This is supported natively in the Firefox browser, and a free plug-in for Internet Explorer is available (MathPlayer [11]).

3 Software Tools for Tracking and Visualisation

3.1 Tracking Tools

The tracking tools were designed to be non-invasive, whilst providing information not available in standard web server logs. The tools also allow the tracking of non-standard page elements, such as inlines and allowed a great measure of control over what information is recorded.

The tracking tools were based on a set of tools originally developed at the Meteorology Department of the University of Edinburgh for the EuroMet project[1]. The design was completely "stand-alone": if the tracking server became unavailable the course would still be served. However, in order to enable tracking some modification of the course web pages was necessary: an image URL had to be embedded and a line of JavaScript added to the page. In addition, the tracking scripts (written in PHP) had to be set at the tracking server.

---

[1] For background on this project see: www.euromet.org

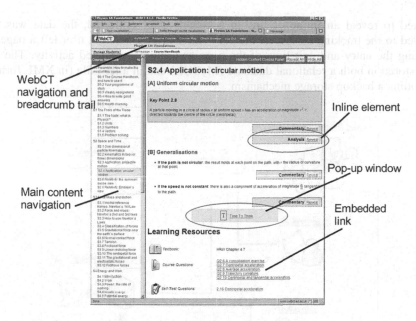

Fig. 1. Screenshot of WebCT course page. The navigation, breadcrumb trail and embedded links provide non-linear access around the site. Inline elements and pop-up windows add extra information to the pages.

In order to fulfill the main requirement of a non-invasive tracking mechanism, two servers were used. The first was the course web server responsible for serving the online course pages (at the University of Edinburgh this is done via WebCT). Tracking was carried out by a second server, the tracking server, which was independent of the course server. In order to send data from the course server to the tracking server, JavaScript was used to dynamically annotate client side information into an image URL already embedded in the course page. This image was then served by a PHP script located at the tracking server. The script collected the data encoded in the image name and, together with additional server side information, logged it to a file and a relational database. It then returned a one pixel image to the client which used the no-caching instruction in the HTTP header, thus avoiding page-caching issues. Page caching could, potentially, result in page hits being under sampled when viewed in the web server log. The tracking mechanism may therefore result in a more accurate access page count. The general flow of data is summarised as shown in Fig. 2. Course pages were served from the course server, step 1 in the diagram, to students, for example located in a computer lab or working remotely at a laptop. Every time a page was loaded into their browser a dynamic component was triggered, step 2. This caused an image to be annotated with client side information and for it to be pulled from the tracking server, step 3. The tracking server returned a one pixel image to the client while logging the tracking information directly to a database, step 5, and a back-up file, step 4. Further details of the tracking tools are available online [12].

The use of JavaScript in the tracking mechanism allowed the use of JavaScript events to add information to the tracking image, such as page loading, a link being clicked to reveal an inline or fire up a popup. Once collected, the data was then handed to the tracking server via the PHP tracking page when a user left a page, recording the entry and exit time of the page and any page-related activity. The data was stored in both a relational database (MySQL) and in a text file (in XML format), providing a backup storage mechanism.

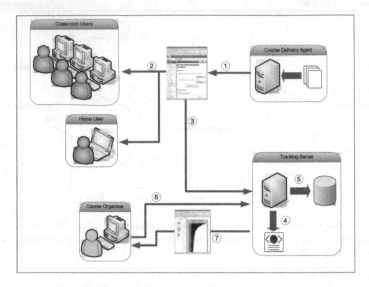

Fig. 2. Overview of the tracking mechanism

The tracking process could thus be divided into two main phases largely independent of each other: data collection and data analysis. The data captured was for three main types of event: page accesses, the viewing or hiding of inlines and the firing-up of popups, each event storing relevant information on the tracking server. Each event had a common data set. User and session identifiers were captured from a WebCT cookie. Information such as the client machine information was captured using JavaScript commands and client IP and domain information via the HTTP header. An internal page identifier for the page accessed was also recorded as well as the URL used to access the given page.

In addition to the information detailed above, page access data was also recorded; the referrer URL which could be used to determine the path a student used to navigate through the course; a start and an end time for a page access – this time was measured at the client. This provided temporal information as to when the course was being viewed. Interestingly, anomalies did arise, presumably through students not setting their local clocks correctly thus giving erroneous access times. The difference between the start and end time could be used to determine the amount of time spent on each page although, of course, this could be skewed by students leaving themselves logged on whilst engaged in other activities. In practice an upper bound was used to truncate times and thus compensate for this. Information was also stored on he client IP address and the corresponding domain, allowing identification of where the students were viewing pages from. The type of browser used provided information about the actual browsers students viewed content with and also supplied information about the underlying operating systems that the browsers were running on. Additional information about the local hardware characteristics at the client end was captured.

Inline events were also recorded: an internal inline identifier unique to a given page; the event time at which the inline was revealed or hidden together the even type, which could be one of: reveal, hide, reveal all and hide all. This would provide feedback as to how inlines were used by students. Finally, popups also recorded an internal identifier and the event time at which the popup was fired-off. It was not possible to record the end time for viewing popups. In addition to on-page interactive elements (inlines and popups) and links to related sections (e.g. MCQs, self-tests), the course also included links to a number of external web sites. However, it was not possible to record accesses to these external sites using the tracking tools.

3.2 Visualisation Tools

As the tracking tools record the URL of both the page and the referring page together with the start and end times, it was possible to construct the route taken through the online course material by individual students during a single "session of work" (referred to as a session in the following discussion). A range of graphical representations were developed as an aid to interpretation and visualisation of this data. The visualisations used were:

Path taken: The path taken through the session, including all pages, inline accesses and pop-up windows. Path visualisations take in the form of a directed graph. Each page is represented by a node, which is colour coded by the section of course being viewed. There are three node shapes which depict the type of page being viewed (see Table 1). The nodes are linked by an arrow with a number indicating the order of access, starting from zero. The visualisation also includes the student ID (or staff user name) and the times of the first and last accesses (Fig. 3A.).

Page accesses: The length of time on each page. No inline or pop-ups are included. These visualisations are also in the form of a directed graph, with nodes representing pages and edges representing access between pages (Fig. 3B). No inline or pop-up windows are shown so node shape is not relevant and all nodes are circular. The size of the circle depicts the length of time spent on that page, derived from the start and end times recorded in the database. The node size is not linearly related to the time spent on the page and the relationship between node-size and time spent is logarithmic, such that the difference in node size between 5 and 10 seconds is approximately the same as the difference between 2 and 10 minutes. There is a minimum time limit of around 2.5 second s and a maximum of 600 seconds (10 minutes).

Access time: The time of page accesses. No inline or pop-ups are included. These are 2D graphs with a vertical line representing a page access. Lines that are close together show rapid access, while lines further apart show slow access times, for example see Fig. 3C.

The graphical representations were produced using either gnuplot [13] or GraphViz [14]; the input data files were constructed from the information in the MySQL tracking database using a set of short Perl scripts. These scripts were used mainly from the command line, however a web interface was developed that enabled the user to generate Path visualisations for sessions based on the userid and date range.

Table 1. Key to shapes and shading used in path visualizations

Node	Shape
Page	Ellipse: tutorials:intro:thinking
Inline	Rectangle: thinking:solution
Pop-up	Pentagon: contents:intro:onedowns:senses
Content	**Shading**
MCQ	Medium Grey, Black Text: mcqs:intro:units
Tutorial	Medium Grey, White Text: tutorials:intro:thinking
Contents	Dark Grey, White Text: contents:preamble
Workshop	Light Grey, Black Text Workshops:WS1:Startup

Interpretation and Analysis of Visualisation Data

There are a large number of sessions (of the order of thousands) that could be visualised and rather than attempt to provide some kind of overarching conclusions from these, we shall highlight some interesting examples. Navigation through the site is fundamentally dictated by the available links on any given page together with the available browser controls. A single page can have three type of links displayed. The main navigation links occupy a space to the left of the page (see Fig. 1). These can be used to move around the current content type. Secondly, there are breadcrumb trails and general links on the top of the page. These include the last few sections visited as well as links to the homepage and general WebCT navigation. Finally, there are links embedded on the page itself, as in any other webpage. Access to the inline elements and pop-up windows is through this type of link. The complex navigations structure outlined above leads to complex pathways through the course material. An example of such a pathway is shown in Fig. 3A. This example displays highly "non-linear" usage – the student did not simply click down the list of a single type of content (as displayed in the navigation bar), but journeyed between different online lecture notes and related tutorial questions. This is not to say that they navigated in a random or haphazard way, instead they kept within the same area of the course (oscillatory motion), but used different types of material. From the path visualisation alone, it is not entirely clear what the student was doing. Did they stop and read every page in detail? Were pages simply used as a reference point to gain access to other materials?

Using the page access visualisation more detail can be added and a clearer picture of the session can be constructed to give a "story" of the session. The student spent a long time on the first two nodes even though the first node ("thinking") is not in the same subject area as the rest of the pages, but may have been used as a stepping point for content. The student then read the tutorial page on the mass on a spring experiment. They did not use any of the supplementary material on that page, which includes inlines, pop-ups and links to other parts of the course. They then went back to the homepage and looked through the course handbook (content nodes) until settling on the simple harmonic motion context page (from link 7 to 8). They then went back to the original tutorial page via another which is linked on the bottom of the simple

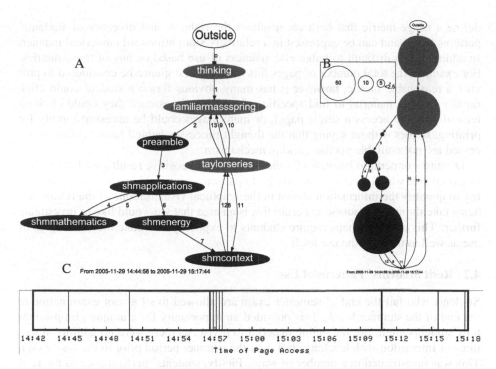

Fig. 3. Examples of visualisations. A) *Path taken*. The numbers on each node are the order of each request, starting from 0. The arrow indicates the direction taken through the course. B) *Page accesses*. The path taken through the pages (nodes) and the length of time spent at each page (size of node). Shading represents the type of page accessed. C) *Access time*. Each page access is represented as a vertical line at the time access.

harmonic motion context page. They then flicked back and forth between the tutorial section and the contents page, spending some amount of time on each. In other sessions, students have used the full range of materials available on a page, including inline elements and pop-up windows and show repeated visits to the same pages.

4 Student Perspectives

4.1 Comparison with Exam Performance

Anecdotal evidence suggests that the use of online material as part of a blended-learning strategy offers real benefits to students. However, these benefits are very difficult to quantify objectively. One possible approach is to compare patterns of use of online material with objective benchmarks of scholastic success. We compared students' performance in the end-of-course examination with range of simple "usage metrics". These included: number of page hits, number of distinct sessions, average session length, the total time spent, and, number of hits within a particular section of the online material. There was no significant correlation between any of these metrics and exam performance. This is perhaps not surprising; it is not straightforward to define a usage metric that both encapsulates the richness and diversity of students' patterns of use and can be expressed in a relatively straightforward numerical manner. In addition, it is difficult to judge effectiveness of use based on any of these metrics. For example, the total number of pages hits might at first glance be considered to provide a reasonable metric, however it has many obvious flaws: a student could click rapidly through material to find specific information (in essence they could click on tens of pages to access a single page), or many pages could be accessed rapidly for printing. It goes without saying that the thought processes behind how a course is accessed are not available via the tracking mechanism.

Despite – or perhaps because of – the lack of initial positive results, we believe that this is an area which merits further study. In particular, it would be extremely interesting to quantify the information shown in the graphical visualisations of the routes students take through the course material; this is an area that we would like to investigate further. This would perhaps require students to explicitly articulate their strategies of use as well as tracking the use itself.

4.2 Resit Students' Patterns of Use

Students who fail the end-of-semester exam are allowed to sit a resit examination at the end of the summer break. This provided an opportunity for a unique glimpse into how students might use the online material to revise, as there were no additional lectures or interaction with teaching staff over the summer period prior to the resit exam. This was investigated in a number of ways. Firstly, students' performance in the resit exam was compared to their access of the online material using the metrics described earlier. As with the end-of-semester exam, no significant correlation was observed.

Another approach taken was to plot the change in marks for each student against the number of accesses to the online course from the end of the course to the resit exam, see Fig. 4.

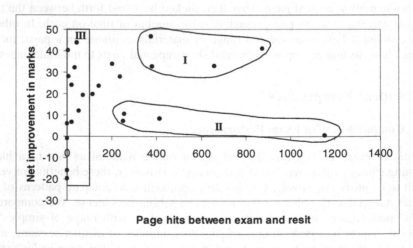

Fig. 4. Improvement in mark against number of hits for summer resit students. (I = many hits +improvement in marks; II = some to many hits +little improvement in marks; III = very few hits + range of improvements in marks.)

From this, it can be seen that the students may be broadly classified into three groups. The first group (I) achieved a substantial increase in their mark and made significant use of the online course. The second group (II) did not show a significant improvement in their mark, but still used the online material. The final group (III) only used the online material briefly. Of this group three students failed to improve their mark and the majority gained at least 10 additional marks. In addition, the range of content (in terms of both type of material and breadth of use) that was accessed in the period before the resit exam was compared to the usage before the end-of-semester examination. Most students showed some change, in terms of both the type and breadth of content accessed and their behaviour in accessing the material. An example is shown in Fig. 5.

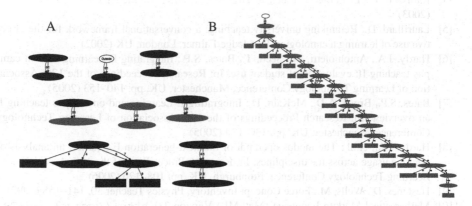

Fig. 5. Examples of the change of behaviour using the path visualisation from the semester 1 access patterns (all page hits shown) (A) and the summer access patterns (one from nine sessions shown) (B) of a student from group II. Each shape denotes a page access with the shading showing type of content accessed (see Table 1). Due to the number of pages accessed in the summer session the page title has been removed.

5 Conclusions

In this paper we have presented a relatively straightforward way of tracking and visualising use of online course material. The tracking mechanism works independently of the course delivery agent; the extra framework required to activate tracking is minimal and tracking operates in a non-invasive manner. This has been used to capture a representative amount of online student activity for a large mainstream undergraduate course, providing a significant volume of rich and detailed data. A novel method of visualising this data has been developed which offers detailed views of the pathways that students take through the course material. The extent of students' use of the online course has been compared with their performance in both the end of semester and resit exam.

Acknowledgments

This work was partially supported by the University of Edinburgh Principal's E-Learning Project Fund.

References

[1] Crook, C., Barrowcliff, D.: Ubiquitous Computing on Campus: Patterns of Engagement by University Students. International Journal of Human Computer Interaction 13(2), 245–256 (2002)

[2] De la Varre, C., Ellaway, R., Dewhurst, D.: Analysis of the large scale use of online discussion boards in a blended learning environment. In: Research Proceedings of the 12th Association of Learning Technology Conference, Manchester, UK, pp. 86–97 (2005)

[3] Crook, C.: Deferring to resources: collaborations around traditional vs. computer-based notes. Journal of Computer Assisted Learning 18(1), 64–76 (2002)

[4] Ramsden, P.: Learning to Teach in Higher Education. Routledge/Falmer, London, UK (2003)

[5] Laurillard, D.: Rethinking university teaching: a conversational framework for the effective use of learning technologies. Routledge/Falmer, London, UK (2002)

[6] Hardy, J.A., Antonioletti, M., Seed, T., Bates, S.P.: Integrating E-Learning and on campus teaching II: evaluation of student use. In: Research Proceedings of the 12th Association of Learning Technology Conference, Manchester, UK, pp. 140–153 (2005)

[7] Bates, S.P., Bruce, A.D., McKain, D.: Integrating E-Learning and on campus teaching I: an overview. In: Research Proceedings of the 12th Association of Learning Technology Conference, Manchester, UK, pp. 130–139 (2005)

[8] Hardy, J.A., et al.: The modus operandi of the next-generation E-Learner: an analysis of tracking usage across the disciplines. In: Research Proceedings of the 13th Association of Learning Technology Conference, Edinburgh, UK, pp. 108–120 (2006)

[9] Hestenes, D., Wells, M.: Force Concept Inventory. Physics Teacher 30, 141–158 (1992)

[10] Mathematical Markup Language (MathML) Version 2.0, http://www.w3.org/TR/MathML2/

[11] Design Science MathPlayer™, http://www.dessci.com/mathplayer

[12] Antonioletti, M., et al.: Integrating E-Learning and on-campus teaching II: technical implementation of usage, http://www.epcc.ed.ac.uk/~steer/reports/antonioletti-II-2005.pdf

[13] gnuplot home page, http://www.gnuplot.info/

[14] Graphviz home page, http://www.graphviz.org/

Web-Based Outcome-Based Teaching and Learning – An Experience Report

Yu Mong, Mangtang Chan, and Francis Kar Ho Chan

[1] Department of Computer Science, City University of Hong Kong,
83 Tat Chee Avenue, Hong Kong
{csymong, csmtchan}@cityu.edu.hk, francisc@cs.cityu.edu.hk

Abstract. Outcome-based education (OBE) is being implemented in many institutions despite controversies and debates about issues concerning whether learning outcomes could be clearly defined. The concept of learning outcomes has been used in a lot of education research work. However the measurement of learning outcomes is usually done in a simple way using one metric. Report of experience about deployment of OBE in real-life situation using different learning outcomes in different curricula has not been commonly seen. In this paper, Achieved Learning Outcome Indicator (ALOI) was proposed to refine the modeling of assessment quantification in terms of hierarchical learning outcomes and many-to-many mapping between learning outcomes and assessment activities. A Web-based Learning Outcome Tracking System was designed to implement the ALOI. The system could also provide of analysis to give different levels of visualization of learning outcomes achievement of students. The system had been tested with course data collected over a period of three years. Experience of implementation in City University of Hong Kong and lessons learned were reported in this paper.

Keywords: Learning Outcome, Outcome-Based Education, Achieved Learning Outcome Indicator, Assessment.

1 Introduction

There has been a lasting development over the past four decades that outcome-based education (OBE) has come to its current form. OBE can be characterized by [1]:

- development of clearly defined and published learning outcomes that must be achieved before further progression;
- design of a curriculum and learning to ensure the achievement of the learning outcomes;
- design of an assessment process matched to the learning outcomes for individual students to ensure that they achieve the outcomes;
- provision of remediation and enrichment for students as appropriate

Proponents of OBE believe that it promotes authentic forms of assessments and consequently encourages higher expectations and greater learning of students. It also favours the decision making of teaching methods, curriculum design and academic

H. Leung et al. (Eds.): ICWL 2007, LNCS 4823, pp. 475–483, 2008.
© Springer-Verlag Berlin Heidelberg 2008

structure and management [2]. On the other hand, OBE has been also criticized as not able to specify exactly what is to be achieved as a result of learning and because the designers and teachers control the product-orientated curricula, leading to student disempowerment [3].

USA has embraced the concept of OBE and implemented it in many states, with ample experience and arguments for the pros and cons. Manno [4] reported a detail analysis of the implementation experience in various states, and in particular Minnesota. In United Kingdom, the Quality Assurance Agency in the year 2000 made OBE a key component in the academic review [1]. Despite the debate of OBE would go on, it is inevitably that more and more education commissioners and universities are endorsing the introduction of OBE. In our University, we are launching a campaign to implement OBE. The learning management system (LMS) we are using at the moment however does not provide any feature in supporting OBE. One of the objectives of our work is to explore the use of web-based systems in running OBE courses within the context of an existing LMS. The experience gained would provide directions to the full scale implementation in the near future.

2   Related Work

While there is extensive work on outcome-based learning, there has been limited discussion of educational technology to support OBE. One of the examples is integrated outcome assessment application [5], for example the design of a database to accumulate learner performance output by outcome assessment application and stored as learner profiles. These profiles could then serve as valuable input to produce customized learning content or to conduct overall performance evaluation.

From Jenkins and Unwin [6], one of the benefits of OBE is to allow instructor become aware of weaknesses of students in a specific area through reviewing their achievements in the learning outcome. As a result, the instructors could focus on learning outcomes that require improvement and hence adjust their teaching methods and styles accordingly. This is a significant aspect in defining learning outcomes as it is part of the process for implementing successful OBE. Very often the instructor wants to know if the change in their pedagogy is effective and the curriculum designer has to regularly review and evaluate academic decision made over an extensive period of time. This has initiated a need to have a web-based system proposed in this paper to facilitate work flow management and provide appropriate statistical and data visualization tools to be made available to teachers and curriculum designer.

Charlotte [3] argued learning outcomes cannot specify exactly what is to be achieved as a result of learning and examples from medical students were cited. This provides good arguments for the need of quantification of learning outcomes. To judge whether a learning outcome is achieved by students is more than just a yes or no. The question of how well is often needed to be asked. As reported by Manno [4], a main reason of clash between stakeholders in the implementation of OBE in many states of USA was the promotion of vague outcomes emphasizing values, attitudes and behaviors by some of the education bureaucrats so as to make accountability impossible. It is therefore crucial to establish quantification of learning outcomes that can be used across different curricula and disciplines. In our university, various learning outcome indicators have been used, ranging from the most standard ones such as examination and course work assessment to the more high-level ones such as graduate survey and employment statistics. We defined a normalised student performance indicator to allow better view of student progress and peer comparison.

3 The Achieved Learning Outcome Indicator

There have been different approaches in using OBE. In our University, the framework of Constructive Alignment developed by Biggs [7] was adopted and the term Outcome-based Teaching and Learning (OBTL) has been used. This approach identifies three essential concepts: intended learning outcome (ILO), teaching and learning activities (TLA) and assessment tasks. Constructive alignment spells out their relations that learning is being achieved by having the students carrying the TLA and articulated clearly by the ILO. Assessment tasks are then used to see how well the TLA has been conducted. ILOs are also aligned in a hierarchical way with ILO of a graduate at the top, followed by that of a curriculum and then individual courses within the curriculum. Detail implementation of this framework from a technology perspective has not been described in Biggs's work nor in the University's proposal. We found that a systematic way to record student achievements in assessment tasks which could ultimately related back to the graduate learning outcomes is far from simple.

An Achieved Learning Outcome Indicator (ALOI) had been defined to quantify student achievement. It is basically a measure of how well a student has achieved a learning outcome which is obtained from one or more assessment activities (AA). Meanwhile, an assessment activity may test students on more than one skills or abilities characterized by one or more ILO in a course. Hence, there could be a many-to-many relationship between AAs and ILOs. The course teacher or curriculum designer has to set up these mappings so that evidences could be collected systematically to keep track both specific details and overall picture of student performance.

We proposed to calculate ALOI using a weighted factor approach. A teacher decides on the weightings of each AAs of an assignment or a test contributing to the ILOs defined for a course. A matrix of weightings would be set up to represent the many AAs to many ILOs mapping. Table 1 shows an example mapping for a course with one assignment and a project each with two AAs and an exam contributing to four ILOs

Table 1. Matrix of weightings for a course

	AA \ ILO	Lo_1	Lo_2	Lo_3	Lo_4
Asg 1	AA_1	w_{11}	w_{12}	w_{13}	w_{14}
	AA_2	w_{21}	w_{22}	w_{23}	w_{24}
Project	AA_3	w_{31}	w_{32}	w_{33}	w_{34}
	AA_4	w_{41}	w_{42}	w_{43}	w_{44}
Exam	AA_5	w_{51}	w_{52}	w_{53}	w_{54}

ALOI of the learning outcome lo1 is calculated from the scores S1 to S5 of a student in all the assessment activities AA1¬ to AA5 respectively by applying the following formula, ALOILo1 = where wi1 for all i must have a sum of 1 to normalize the ALOI for the each ILO. Note that on the other hand, the sum of weightings of an AA to all the ILOs is not necessarily normalized because the ILOs are independently defined. The weighting factor approach provides a logical way for teachers to design assessments, as well as to calculate the ALOI.he online version of the volume will be available in LNCS Online. Members of institutes subscribing to the Lecture Notes in Computer Science series have access to all the pdfs of all the online publications. Non-subscribers can only read as far as the abstracts. If they try to go beyond this point, they are automatically asked, whether they would like to order the pdf, and are given instructions as to how to do so.

4   Learning Outcome Tracking System

To try out the model of ALOI and its integration with our existing LMS environment, The Learning Outcome Tracking System (LOTS) has been designed as a web-based application with features to address some of the issues related to the technological aspect of using OBTL. It is an outcome assessment application with embedded tracking function, integrated with other student and academic information systems to form a web-based infrastructure to support OBTL. It provides overall management of learning outcomes and accesses to both teachers and students. Availability of the learning outcomes information for stakeholders other than teachers is important as it fulfils one of the characteristics of OBTL – learning outcomes have to be clearly defined and published [1]. Other detail features of LOTS also include the assistance to instructor in measuring teaching effectiveness using the weighing factor technique based on ALOI.

4.1   Components

In brief, the system consists of six components, namely, group, metric, learning outcome, incident, correlation and analysis. The former four provide management functions of those entities while the latter two allow users, mainly teachers to perform correlation between and analysis for entities. Figure 1 illustrates the relationship among the components for a single group instance. Group includes student and group administration, where users can manage students and groups in the database. A group can be a course, degree program, or a subset of students. This allows the flexibility of performing comparisons in different situations, which is discussed below.

Metric represents the assessment management, where users can create a metric and associate it with a course. Metric data is introduced as an instance of a metric to prevent redundancy of assessments given to students frequently. In addition, each metric is associated with multiple learning outcomes and weightings. Figure 2 shows a screenshot of setting the weightings for a learning outcome in the system.

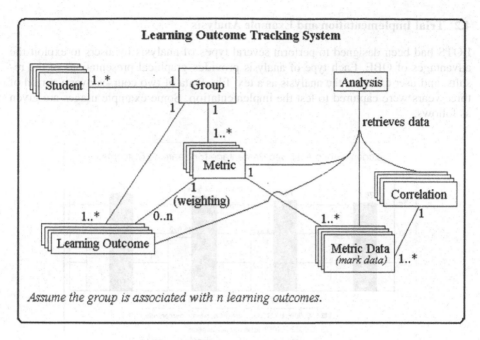

Fig. 1. LOTS component relationship

Incident is an event such as teaching methods, training sessions or lab sessions. It is to provide reference for user on how different incidents may affect student's ALOI. On the other hand, correlation enables user flexibility in combining several metric data written in mathematical formula, and subsequently to perform analysis on them.

Learning Outcome	Apply principles and techniques of object-oriented programming to devise software solutions to problems
Total Percentage	100

Finish assignments

Metric Name	Percentage
Course Test	10
Exam	20
Homework	10
Project1	30
Project2	20
Test	10

Fig. 2. Screenshot of setting weightings for a learning outcome in LOTS

Analysis is a component that enables user to perform analysis upon inputting all the data for the components discussed above. There are several types of analysis implemented in LOTS and will be discussed in the next sub section.

4.2 Trial Implementation and Example Analysis

LOTS had been designed to perform several types of analysis for users to exploit the advantages of OBE. Each type of analysis provides graphical presentations of the results, and user can save the analysis as a text file. Data of two courses over a period of three years were captured to test the implementation. Some example usages are given as follows.

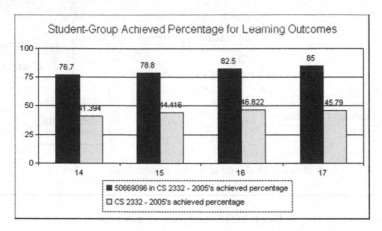

Fig. 3. An analysis of a student's performance in a course in LOTS

A single student analysis is available to track an individual student's performance in a group. This provides evidence of the student's weaknesses for improvement. Furthermore, the analysis illustrates the ALOI based on the average marks for the assessments in the group. This enables users to view how the performance of the student compared to the students in the course. Figure 3 shows a bar chart when analyzing a student, with ID 50669096, in course CS2332. The x-axis indicates the learning outcome IDs, while the y-axis is the ALOI of the corresponding learning outcome. The bar on the left (blue) and right (yellow) represents the student's ALOI and the course average's ALOI respectively.

A group analysis is available to compare performance of students in two groups. The ALOI of each intended learning outcome is calculated based on the averaged assessment marks. The objective of this analysis is to enable user to compare, initially, the students' performance in two different years. User can then analyze the reasons of the performance with respect to the students' standard, teaching methods, or change in the curriculum. Figure 4 illustrates the group analysis output by comparing two groups taught at course level using different methods, which is similar to the previous analysis. Each group is associated with an incident of its teaching method, which is using the LEGO (blue) and the Visual Studio (yellow) respectively. LOTS can also facilitate user to perform analysis at programme level, for example, comparing the Computer Science degree programmes of the 2001 and 2002 cohorts.

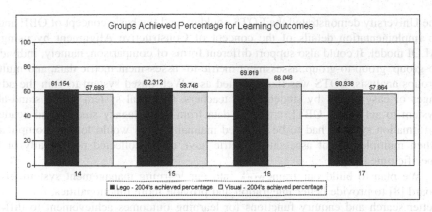

Fig. 4. A graphical analysis of two groups with different teaching methods

Analysis to compare two sets of learning outcome metric is also available. The main objective of this analysis is to view the same metric data in different instances of time, e.g. different years or incidents.

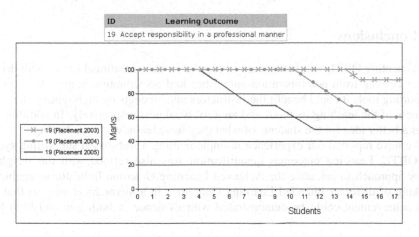

Fig. 5. A graphical analysis of a course in three years

Figure 5 shows the ALOI (shown in the small box on top as number 19 – Accept responsibility in a professional manner) of a specific learning outcome in a Placement course over a period of three years. In this analysis, individual students' ALOI are listed in descending order, hence user can compare the performance easily.

5 Discussions

The proposed model of ALOI and its implementation as the LOTS to support OBTL worked well in the environment of our university. Issues raised by the critics of OBE have been addressed. Trial use of the LOTS with actual courses and student data in the University demonstrated the LOTS could extend the basic concept of OBE and fill in implementation details of the concept of Constructive Alignment by using the ALOI model. It could also support different forms of comparison, namely, individual-to-group, group-to-group, assessment metric-to- assessment metric data, and multiple groups analysis. LOTS was implemented as a Web-based system to gain the advantages of easy access by students and teachers. Our trial system was a stand-alone system to act as the OBTL core and data from other legacy student and academic information systems had to be obtained manually. This would lead to complication when multiple sets of assessment metric have to be collected periodically or in a specific time line.

We plan to build our framework into our learning management system, Blackboard [8] to provide better integration and provide more functionalities, for example, better search and enquiry functions for learning outcomes achievement to different users, especially students. In our trial runs, we encountered a privacy issue which is important but seldom discussed in the literature. There were situations where access rights to learning outcomes have to be granted but not the detail assessment information, and in particular, individual students should not be identified by unauthorized users. In our current implementation, a random pseudonym was generated for each student to mask the real identity. This issue would be further investigated.

6 Conclusions

Implementing OBTL will become more popular in the educational sector with driving forces coming from administration authorities and accreditation bodies. With proper supporting tools it could benefit the instructors and students by highlighting the effectiveness of the teaching methods and areas of weakness respectively. In addition, this gives a better idea for the students of what they have learnt when graduating.

We have reported our experience in implementing a web-based supporting system for OBTL. Learning outcomes quantification was also refined with the weighting factor approach to calculate the Achieved Learning Outcome Indicator to enable the tracking of different Intended Learning Outcomes in a hierarchical way so that student achievement could be demonstrated with evidence in both low and high level ways.

Acknowledgments. The work in this paper was supported by the Teaching Development Fund (Project Number 6980061), City University of Hong Kong.

References

1. Harden, R.M.: Developments in outcome-based education. Medical Teacher 24(2), 117–120 (2002)
2. North Central Regional Educational Laboratory. "Outcome-Based" Education: An Overview (accessed February 2007),
   http://www.ncrel.org/sdrs/areas/issues/envrnmnt/go/go4outcm.htm
3. Rees, C.E.: Outcomes-based teaching – The problem with outcomes-based curricula in medical education: insights from educational theory. Medical Education 38(6), 593 (2004)

4. Manno, B.V.: Outcome-Based Education: Has It Become More Affliction Than Cure? Center of the American Experiment (1994) (accessed February 2007), http://www.americanexperiment.org/publications/1994/199408manno.php
5. Huang, A.H.: A framework of educational technology applications and development opportunities. Journal of Computer Information Systems, 08874417 41(3) (2001)
6. Jerkins, D.U.: How to write learning outcomes (accessed February 2007), http://www.americanexperiment.org/publications/1994/199408manno.php
7. Biggs, J.: Teaching for Quality Learning at. University, Buckingham: The Society for Research into Higher Education and Open University Press (2003), ISBN 0-335-21168-2
8. Blackboard Inc. http://www.blackboard.com/us/index.Bb

Evaluating Asynchronous Message Boards to Support Cross-Cultural Communities of High-School Students

Caterina Poggi and Nicoletta Di Blas

Department of Electronics and Information – Politecnico di Milano, piazza Leonardo da Vinci 32, 20133 Milano, Italy
{Caterina.Poggi, Nicoletta.Diblas}@polimi.it

Abstract. Can online forums effectively support collaboration, discussion, and cultural exchange among high-school students from different countries? We present results from the analysis of a set of asynchronous message boards within Learning@Europe, a project where students meet in real time in shared 3D virtual environments, and keep in touch through online forums. Between March 2005 and December 2006 about 5000 students and 250 teachers from 17 European countries took part in Learning@Europe, posting on a total of 194 forums. Focusing on a detailed analysis of the first L@E implementation (involving about 1000 students and 50 teachers from 6 European countries), we show how forums can support more or less effectively collaboration and discussion tools, what challenges must be faced, and how the tool's evaluation must take into account the components and set of goals of the entire learning experience.

Keywords: Forum, Message Board, Cross-Cultural, Learning Community, Evaluation, Asynchronous Discussion.

1 Introduction and Related Research

Web-based communication, with its ability to overcome time and space constraints, offers exciting opportunities to education. This paper focuses on one in particular: can online forums be used for supporting a collaborative learning experience across different countries and cultures? Previous research, described in the remainder of this section, has underlined the potential educational benefits of a similar activity, along with its risks. We propose a tentative answer to this question, basing on the analysis of a series of asynchronous message boards used within Learning@Europe, a project by Politecnico di Milano where students meet in real time in shared 3D virtual environments, and keep in touch between meetings through online forums. Between March and May 2005, about 1000 students and 50 teachers from 6 European countries took part in Learning@Europe, posting over 2,400 messages on 41 different forums. A detailed analysis has been performed on these data. Preliminary results from the following implementations, involving about 4000 users from 17 countries, will also be presented. After briefly describing the forums and their role within the learning experience (details can be found in [3] and [7]), we present the data collected, the analysis techniques and the main results. In the conclusions we draw a few lessons. Learning how to collaborate asynchronously with remote partners, mastering virtual communication and expression are important skills for the 21st Century workplace,

H. Leung et al. (Eds.): ICWL 2007, LNCS 4823, pp. 484–495, 2008.
© Springer-Verlag Berlin Heidelberg 2008

and schools and governmental policies are starting to recognize them as such, also in an international perspective. Collaboration is also a potentially very rich opportunity in educational terms. Collaborating with remote peers from different cultures can help the development of the students' identity. Identities "must be worked out in practice" [13]: students who work together with foreign peers are involved in a community of practice; it provides exposure to different habits and lifestyles, so that students learn more about who they are also by realizing what they are not: "Non-participation is, in a reverse kind of fashion, as much a source of identity as participation" [13]. On the other hand, collaboration is essential in a Constructivist perspective to provide opportunities for the social negotiation of meaning. According to Vygotsky [11], meaning is a social construct and learning is a social, collaborative process. Learners need a social environment providing alternative views that they can use "to test the viability of their understanding and in building the body of propositions that constitute 'knowledge'" [1]. Learning happens also through spontaneous group interaction; Daniel et al. [2] for instance classify sociability, sharing experience, peer support, and others as discourse variables typical of "incidental learning", whereas inquiry, argumentation, elaboration, clarification, etc., belong to the "intentional learning" cluster. It is important to note that collaborating online is different from face to face collaboration, for instance in terms of interpersonal skills required: interlocutors cannot rely, as in face to face communications, on visual and auditory cues such as physical appearance, facial expressions, gesturing, intonation, etc. [12]. On one hand, people who are shy, or likely to incur in prejudices based on their appearance, can find in a forum a powerful self-expression means. On the other hand, it is more difficult to understand the tone of a message: is the author joking, or serious, or angry? Misunderstandings are frequent, also because - in an asynchronous forum - what seems obvious to the sender at the moment of writing may not be equally clear to the reader a few days later. Students therefore must learn to explicit what they are referring to, and need to practice how to argue a point or disagree with someone without sounding aggressive. All of these are valuable skills to learn, and some educators regard the forum as even more effective than face-to-face interaction for supporting this kind of higher-level learning, in that students have the time to reflect upon one's point of view (recorded in a written post), carefully construct and revise their answer [8]. How can online forums be used effectively for learning, and for creating a thriving community of learners? Setting up an online message board and allowing people to post on it does not make a community. According to Preece [10], designing an online virtual community involves thinking about the people to be reached, the purposes of the community, and the policies regulating interaction, so that everyone's goals can be achieved. It requires a usable infrastructure, supporting sociability: trust needs to be built among users, and the critical mass must be reached, i.e. the number of users that make the community interesting and attractive, without giving the impression of being "lost in the crowd".

2 Learning@Europe: An Educational Experience Involving a European Online Community

L@E is structured upon a 6-7 weeks experience: four classes of high school students from different European countries take part in a cultural competition (2 classes against 2). Students meet together on a shared online 3D environment accessible over the Internet, for four times: four cooperative sessions (of one hour each) distributed across two months. 2 students per class are represented in the 3D world by "avatars" (i.e. graphical human-shaped representations, see Fig. 1). Meetings are devoted to cooperative activities, such as discussions and games. All games are based on cultural riddles requiring an accurate knowledge of the subject matter, i.e. the formation of nation-states in European modern history.

Fig. 1. Avatars presenting their towns and countries

Students interact via chat in the 3D world and asynchronously through online forums during the intervals between sessions. The language of all interactions is English. Every online cooperative session lasts approximately 1 hour; 10 avatars move around in the virtual world: 8 students (2 per school), plus 2 on-line tutors (a Guide and a Helper). While two students in each class control an avatar in the 3D world, two more interact with remote peers via the "2D chat", a chat panel separated from the 3D graphics); the rest of the class groups around them or follows from a projection screen, taking turns and helping them to answer questions. In the intervals between a session in the virtual world and the following, students are asked to study a set of

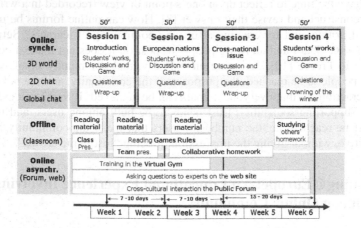

Fig. 2. Schema of the educational experience

contents – in the format of interviews to international experts – and to prepare a homework in collaboration with their team members, by doing some research. Every class can keep in touch with other participants between the sessions thanks to a set of online forums: the Common Forum is reserved to the 4 classes involved in an Experience, the Team Forum is accessible only to the 2 classes composing a Team, and the Public Forums are visible to everyone: there students and teachers can meet participants in other Experiences, and ask questions about history to the Experts of the Scientific Committee in the Meet the Experts Forum. Below is a schema of the virtual educational experience's structure (Fig. 2).

In Session 1 students meet each other and are introduced to the experience. Before Session 2 they have to study material about the history of the four countries involved: the discussion and games of Session 2 are based on this material. They also have to prepare a html team presentation about their national symbols and everyday life, collaborating with their remote partners on the Team Forum. During Session 2 they present their teams, discuss the contents studied, and play a game. They receive a second set of study material for Session 3, which also hosts a discussion and a game. By Session 4, they need to have completed the research homework in collaboration (on the forum) with their team partners; they will present these works during the last online meeting. Guides post on the Common Forum dates and times of online meetings, tasks, instructions and materials, partial scores and announcements. When one or both classes in a team have difficulties accessing the forum, they exchange materials for common assignments via the teachers' emails. Common Forums are moderated by the Guides, Team Forums by the students themselves. Moderators received a short Forum Moderator Manual with instructions and tips on how to perform their role.

3   Data Collection and Analysis

Between March 1st 2005 and December 19th 2006, a total of 250 teachers and 5,000 students aged 14 to 19 took part in Learning@Europe, in various phases and in 3 different school years: 2004-05, 2005-06, and 2006-07. They came from 149 high schools in 17 European countries: Belgium, Bulgaria, Czech Republic, Estonia, France, Germany, Greece, Hungary, Italy, Latvia, Lithuania, Norway, Poland, Romania, Spain, Sweden, and UK. In addition to surveys to teachers and students before, during and after the experience, and to a large amount of qualitative data (including the chat logs of every session, all the works produced by students, and videos shot in the classrooms or screen-captured from the Guide's monitor), we collected and archived all the messages posted on the online forums supporting the experience.

In the first implementation, L@E 2004-05, a supervisor monitored all the forums for the duration of the project, periodically reporting about online activity. 11 reports were produced, recording the numbers of threads, posts, views, and describing online collaboration. In addition, Guides were asked to rate with a 10-points scale the quality and quantity of messages in their forums according to 7 parameters: Socialization, Collaboration, Discussion of Contents, Discussion on L@E, Other Discussions,

Table 1. Learning@Europe: the forums

	2004-05 March - May 05	2005-06 Nov 05 – Jun 06	2006-07 phase 1: Nov-Dec 06	Total
Total forums	41	126	27	194
Public forums (open 3-5 months)	5	6	3	14
Experience forums (open 8 weeks)	36	120	24	180
Total messages posted	2178	7215	3536	12929
Forum users	222	529	174	925
Average posts per forum	53.12	57.26	130.96	80.45
Average posts per user	9.81	13.64	20.32	14.59
Average views per post	17.25	160.07	154.52	110.61
% active users	21.14%	14.78%	27.58%	21.16%

Moderator, and Problems. They evaluated the forums at 4 different times. After the end of the project, all forum posts were saved in archives for quantitative analysis: the forum database records – with each forum post – the author, the date and time of posting, the forum, the thread, the number of times it was edited, etc. In addition, a more in-depth qualitative analysis was performed on Forum Xp207_TeamB: the most successful Team Forum, not only for the relatively high number of posts (341, an average of 20 posts per user), but for the quality of the interaction and collaboration processes in it. Each message was coded according to the behaviours expressed in the text, categorized in a list adapted from [9]. Additional analysis were performed on various aspects, including communication flows between individuals and various groups: the team, the town, the country, etc. Due to the number of participants in L@E 2005-06, it was impossible for one supervisor to report about all the 126 forums. Guides completed online weekly reports on each of the Experience forums they moderated, and a final forum report after the conclusion of each experience. L@E staff monitored the Public forums and reported about them. All forum messages were archived in a database, on which quantitative analysis were performed. 343 weekly forum reports and 123 final forum reports were collected. The same approach was followed in L@E 2006-07: so far we collected 143 weekly forum reports and 24 final forum reports.

4   Results of the First Forum Implementation: L@E 2004-05

At a first glance, participation in the forums seems rather low, considering that the average number of people enabled to access each forum is about 80 students: 78% of forums count less than 50 posts, with an average of 22.78 posts each (2.64 posts a week, and an average of 408.71 views per forum). The remaining 22% however have an average of 167.87 posts each (18.91 posts a week, and an average of 1753.75 views per forum).

4.1 What Did Not Work Well...

Is lack of participation related to problems of usability of the interface? The participants' computer literacy is generally low, and hardly any of them has ever posted in a
forum before. According to a preliminary survey, almost half of respondents use
computers less than 3 hours a week (N=588), and about 44% do not use email; 20%
of teachers use computers less than 3 hours a week. Various messages are clearly experiments of users who wished to see how the interface works, e.g.: *"Just wanted to
try"*. Two usability problems may have negatively affected interaction: a malfunction-
ing in the "add attachment" button and complicated login names: in at least 5 forums
students logged in with the account of their teachers, and in a few forums they did not
log in at all until the staff checked all their accounts. Login problems were mostly due
to students' typing errors; yet, if the login interface is not fault-tolerant, usernames
should be kept simple. Simple errors perhaps due to lack of expertise, such as posting
the same message twice, or requiring students to edit their message, are quite frequent
among the first posts of each forum. However, they decrease considerably with time:
this suggests that inexperienced users learn how to use the forums with practice –
which in terms of educational goals is certainly a benefit. In many cases problems
have been a spur for the students, who searched for alternative solutions, or got help
from their partners. A possible reason for low participation might be limited access to
Internet facilities. An analysis of the Teachers' Surveys responses concerning usage
of the forum, cross-checked with the times of posting in Team forums (we assumed
that messages posted between 8 a.m. and 1 p.m. had been sent from school, and after
5 p.m. at home), reveals that the majority of students can access the forums from
school. Yet, the ideal scenario of use – the class in the computer lab every week, plus
students connecting more frequently from home – occurred only in 12.5% of classes.
In addition, in 2 classes students accessed their Team Forum only from home, and 4
classes never managed to access the forum at all (Fig. 3).

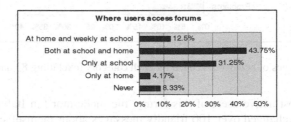

Fig. 3. Percentages of classes accessing Team Forums from school and from home

While in the majority of cases students did have access to forums both from school
and from home, most did so neither regularly nor frequently. In 68.7% of classes,
teachers did not supervise them – with a perceivable impact in terms of quality and
quantity of participation. One reason may be lack of time; a teacher writes: *"because
lately they have had a difficult period at school (tests and quizzes) they wrote on the
forums from their homes."* A factor decreasing motivation is the lack of messages
from the partner class. A teacher reports: *"students were asked to check the forum and*

take part in it ... but were disappointed of their peer absence." When your remote partners are missing, posting forum messages to the classmate sitting next to you appears rather pointless. An analysis of the forum reports shows that in less than 40% of Team Forums, both classes managed to complete their two collaborative tasks together, and in 19.1% of forums there was no real collaboration.

4.2 What was Achieved!

The forums were designed to allow users to keep in contact with remote participants in the intervals between sessions, a need emerged in the testing of SEE, a previous version of this educational experience [3-5]. As additional educational benefits, the forum offered a platform for students to collaborate with their team partners (in SEE all exchanges of ideas and materials passed through the teachers' emails), an extra channel for organization and support, and above all a place were cultural discussions started via chat could be resumed in a less hectic environment, allowing time for reflection. Finally, practicing English in authentic contexts and learning how to use this communication technology would be benefits in their own right for many users. Data suggest that, for students who used the forums, most of these benefits were achieved. Analysis of Forum Xp207_B (Fig. 4) shows that 34.13% of posts were related to collaborative tasks: asking and giving information on work progress, attaching documents and proposing ideas, arranging online meetings, etc.

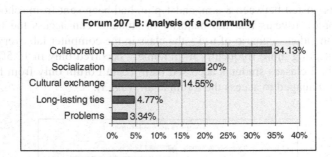

Fig. 4. Percentages of behaviours coded for each category (excluding 83 anomalous posts)

The three most active users of this forum, the moderator (an Italian girl) and two Belgian girls, exchanged over 100 friendly messages about themselves and their everyday life, such as: *"this morning I went for a ride by bike with a friend, we followed all the wonderful seashore!"*; *"S. you are so active in your free time!"*. This off-task informal chatting helped building social ties that smoothened collaboration and lasted beyond the end of the project: toward the end of the experience, users sent at least 20 messages proposing to meet in real life, and exchanging email and instant messaging accounts; messages posted weeks after the last session show evidence that the Belgian and Italian girls did remain in touch even after the end of the school year. Relatively few students and classes took advantage of the possibility of asking questions to a history scholar. However, the quality of the questions posted on the Experts Forum show that students took ownership of what they studied, were curious, and saw the forum as an opportunity to find out more. In 4 questions students re-elaborated some concepts in the study materials and asked the expert if their interpretation was correct. In 6 questions, they identified contradictions in historical phenomena and asked the expert to explain more in depth, e.g. *"What if the king (or queen) of England [who is also head of the Church] is a non-believer????"*). 2 students asked comprehension questions. Finally, 3 questions were unrelated to the study material. but showed the students' interest for their own past and their reliance on the Experts Forum for fast and accurate historical information. Students learnt much about each other's countries, lifestyles and traditions just through social interaction. Some very interesting cross-cultural exchanges took place, especially on the Public Forums – where students of all 6 participating countries could meet. Discussion topics in one of the Public Forums ranged from summer holidays (16 posts) to world news, such as Pope John Paul II's funerals (19 posts) to foreign languages in Europe (51 posts). Students had a chance to see how differently people faced the same issue in various countries, for example comparing the different reactions to the Pope's death in different countries (crowds of mourners in Rome, memorial ceremonies everywhere in Poland, nothing at all in France). Students had a chance of being exposed to "other ways of doing things, other enterprises, other practices, and other communities" [13], of seeing what is different and what is "the same" for all.

4.3 A Glance at the Experience as a Whole

When asked to evaluate the forums, the Guides gave rather low ratings: the average global score is 2.92 on a 5-points scale, where 1=very poor, 3=acceptable and 5=very good. Teachers seem to have a better opinion of the forums: they rated them in average 3.82 on a 5-points scale. The forums are most active before Session 2 and Session 4, when students are requested to use them for team tasks. Those who express low satisfaction, mainly complain about lack of participation from their partners. A teacher commented: *"These forums don't work well because the participation of the Italian class is very poor. They can only go online once a week on Thursday for 1 hour!"*. When comparing Learning@Europe's overall educational impact to the teachers' ratings of the forums, online sessions, and study materials, it is interesting to note that most teachers rated the overall impact significantly higher than each of L@E features: for example, the 15 teachers who rated the forum 3, gave in average more than 4 to the educational impact. The students' improvements as reported by teachers are also much higher than the ratings assigned to project's components: about 60% of teachers rate their students' improvements in the understanding of history "high" or "very high". Above-average improvements rise to 75% for functional English skills, 88% for the use of technologies in learning, and 95% for group work (N=44). In addition, 79% of students are reported to have shown a high or very high increase of respect and curiosity for other cultures: interacting and making friends with people from different countries is an effective way of improving respect and curiosity for these people and their nations. Since teachers evaluate the educational impact of the experience as a whole, it is difficult to determine the specific role of the forums in terms of learning. However, they certainly helped those who used them to achieve the educational benefits described above.

5   Results of 2005-06 and 2006-07 Implementations

Data from the two following implementations of Learning@Europe seem to confirm
the results outlined in the previous paragraphs.

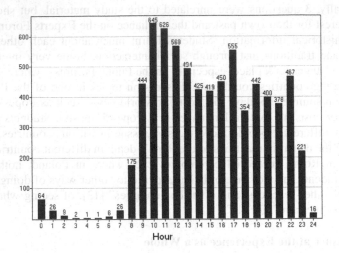

Fig. 5. Hours of usage of all 126 forums in L@E 2005-06. The height of the bars represents the
number of messages posted in each hour of the day.

While only a minority of students takes advantage of the forum, their activity is often sufficient to guarantee a good amount of learning for those who write, and also to
some extent for those (many more) who read. With respect to L@E 2004-05, access
to the forums seems in general less of a problem. Fig. 5 shows peak hours of forum
activity between 10:00 and 12:00, therefore during school lessons, and between 18:00
and 19:00, probably from home. Although participation in the public forums was
quite active, collaboration in Team forums – where users of two classes are expected
to collaborate for the homework – was much more difficult to achieve. Only 17% of
teams managed to collaborate for the homework, and 64% failed to deliver a complete
assignment (N=112). This is probably among the main reasons why the guides rated
the overall forum experience in L@E 2005-06 low: in average 2.02 on a 5-points
scale (N=112). The teachers, as usual, were more positive: their average rating is 3.35
(N=108). In L@E 2006-07, with less participants at a time and a refined organizational workflow, it was easier to offer support to everyone and send reminders whenever needed. Collaboration was successful in 34.8% of teams, and only in 18.75% of
teams one class did not do its part (N=23). Guides wrote more frequently reports such
as "*A very good cooperation in homework: they shared the drafts, added comments,
asked for integrations or agreement about pictures!*", and rated the overall forum experience in average 3.38 on a 5-points scale (N=24). Teachers' average rating again
was higher: 3.41 (N=29). While students did not always manage to use the forums for
completing assignments, nor for discussing history, they certainly enjoyed using them

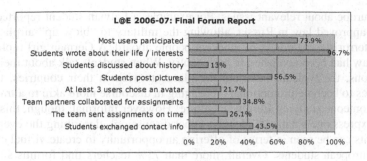

L@E 2006-07: Final Forum Report

Most users participated	73.9%
Students wrote about their life / interests	96.7%
Students discussed about history	13%
Students post pictures	56.5%
At least 3 users chose an avatar	21.7%
Team partners collaborated for assignments	34.8%
The team sent assignments on time	26.1%
Students exchanged contact info	43.5%

Fig. 6. Results from the guides' reports on L@E experience forums 2006-07. (23 respondents).

for social purposes (see Fig. 6). Discussion topics include: self-presentations, free time, past session, next session, each other's cultures, how they are, where they are from, what are their interests, their zodiac signs, music, homework, what they did during the weekend, school, their habits, TV series, school exchange programs, and so on.

Team spirit grows stronger through forum interaction. Also, students appointed as managers of the Team Forum generally did a very good job. A guide-moderator reported: "*Both team asked about the scores and posted messages to cheer or to boost the enthusiasm for next session 3 and will to win. After session 3 team manager A (polish) wrote as usual students' immediate feedback saying the class enjoyed very much the session*". The guide observes that "*he noticed that everyone is proud of national heroes and that this is the main thing in common among different countries.*" As for the Experts Forum, in L@E 2005-06, with over 3000 potential users and low moderation, 20 questions were posted in 4 months. In L@E 2004-05, with a more active moderator and about 1000 potential users, only 15 questions were posted over 7 months. In L@E 2006-07, with about 600 users and a relatively responsive moderator, 20 questions were posted in the first 3 months. Data suggest that the number of questions to be expected is rather low. However, the level of questions is generally quite good, and the experts' answers are interesting. The kinds of questions asked indicate that students rely on the experts for asking not just about facts or additional information, but especially about causal relationships, and seem quite interested in the expert's opinion about their own interpretation of historical events. The limited number of questions should not be intended as a sign of low interest; instead, it is important to underline the questions' quality: a result of the students' reflections. Finally, 1871 messages were posted in the main Public Forum of L@E 2005-06. The "L@E online community" public forum of L@E 2006-07 counts already 1868 messages at the time of writing (March 2007), and it will stay open for another 3 months. One reason for the highly intense activity of L@E 2006-07 might be the active participation in the very first phases of the forum's opening. Differently from the previous years, when students only accessed the forums after Session 1, they received access to the forums one week before the first online meeting; they were strongly encouraged by guides (who were in direct contact with teachers) to send self-introductory messages; the forum was actively moderated. As the moderator of the public forum commented, "*The topics about history are never the most popular among students, but someone is willing to talk about it!*". Many interesting discussions show the opinions of students across Europe about relevant issues. For example, a Latvian student reported about a recently approved law in Russia, allowing the military to "blow up" airplanes taken over by terrorists, regardless of innocent people aboard. A German girl replied that a similar law had been abolished in her country. When students talk about their holiday destinations, the typical foods and the places to visit in their countries, they tend sometimes to become promotional – engaging in discourse more akin to a travel agent than to someone studying European culture! However informal, though, this is also a way to express one's national identity. Other discussions, describing the everyday life of students can be seen in terms of offering an opportunity to create virtual communities of European students. Overall, more than 75% teachers find forums sufficiently effective, good, or very good (Fig. 7).

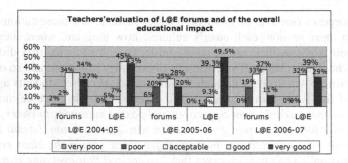

Fig. 7. Teachers' evaluation of the forums and of L@E's overall educational impact in L@E 2004-05 (44 respondents), 2005-06 (108 respondents) and 2006-07 (30 respondents)

6 Discussion and Conclusions

Although participation was generally low, when forums are considered within the entire learning experience, they result to offer a significant contribution to the overall educational impact. A few general lessons can thus be drawn, referring to "blended-learning experiences" in which forums are but one of the components. Our main observation is that although collaboration (in the sense of performing a task together – e.g. a homework) is very difficult to achieve, forums do serve other purposes that strongly contribute to the achievement of educational benefits. Therefore they are a very recommendable feature, because they allow an in-depth collective reflection on cultural issues, they support intercultural exchanges and direct contact between learners, tutors and experts, they encourage the creation of social bonds and motivate involvement in learning activities. In order to achieve an educationally effective use of forums, we recommend to monitor them closely (even those directly moderated by the users), for 2 reasons: first, since collaboration is crucial, it is very important to discover whether some of the parties are not active and immediately solicit their participation; second, it is important to check the moderator's work and replace non-motivated moderators. Also, we suggest allowing time (more than in face-to-face situations; see [9]) and opportunities for socialization, which is fundamental for building trust and creating bonds. It is essential to give clear tasks, so that users do not waste time figuring out what to do, but are immediately challenged by attractive topics. If deemed convenient, an official recognition to forum's participation (like for example scores) can be a further incentive to active participation.

Acknowledgments

The authors wish to thank Jenny Preece for her precious help with the analysis of online communities and all the people and institutions that cooperated to create Learning@Europe: Accenture International Foundation, Fondazione Italiana Accenture, and our wonderful staff (their names are at www.learningateurope.net).

References

[1] Barab, S., Thomas, M., Dodge, T., Carteaux, R., Tuzun, H.: Making learning fun: Quest Atlantis, a game without guns. Educational Technology R&D 53(1), 86–107 (2005)
[2] Daniel, B., Schwier, R., Ross, H.: Intentional and Incidental Discourse Variables in a Virtual Learning Community. In: Proc. e-Learn,1953–1965, AACE, Chesapeake, VA (2005)
[3] Di Blas, N., Gobbo, E., Paolini, P.: 3D Worlds and Cultural Heritage: Realism vs. Virtual Presence. In: Proc. Museums & Web, Vancouver, Canada (2005)
[4] Di Blas, N., Paolini, P., Poggi, C.: SEE (Shrine Educational Experience): an Online Cooperative 3D Environment Supporting Innovative Educational Activities. In: Proc. ED-MEDIA, Honolulu, Hawaii, USA (2003)
[5] Di Blas, N., Paolini, P., Poggi, C.: Educational benefits: testing and evaluation of a collaborative 3D world. In: Proc. ED-MEDIA 2005, AACE, Montreal, Canada (2005)
[6] Preece, J., Nonnecke, B., Andrews, D.: The top five reasons for lurking: improving community experiences for everyone. Computers in Human Behavior 20(2), 201–223 (2004)
[7] Gobbo, E., Poggi, C., Torrebruno, A.: Measuring Educational Benefits of ICT-mediated Cultural Heritage Experiences. In: Proc. of Heritage Impact, Brighton, UK (2005)
[8] Hiltz, S.: Teaching in a Virtual ClassroomTM. International Journal of Educational Telecommunications 1(2/3), 185–198 (1995)
[9] Maloney-Krichmar, D., Preece, J.: A multilevel analysis of sociability, usability and community dynamics in an online health community. Transactions on Human-Computer Interaction (special issue on Social Issues and HCI) 12(2), 201–232 (2005)
[10] Preece, J.: Online Communities: Designing Usability, Supporting Sociability. John Wiley & Sons, Chichester (2000)
[11] Vygotsky, L.S.: Mind in society. Harvard University Press, Cambridge (1978)
[12] Walther, J.B.: Interpersonal effects in computer-mediated interaction: A relational perspective. Communication Research 19(1), 52–90 (1992)
[13] Wenger, E.: Communities of Practice. Learning, Meaning, and Identity. Cambridge University Press, Cambridge, UK (1998)

From Learning Objects to Educational Itineraries: Helping Teachers to Exploit Repositories

Emanuela Busetti[1], Giuliana Dettori[2], Paola Forcheri[1], and Maria Grazia Ierardi[1]

[1] Istituto di Matematica Applicata e Tecnologie Informatiche del CNR,
Genova – Italy
{emma, forcheri, marygz}@ge.imati.cnr.it
[2] Istituto per le Tecnologie Didattiche del CNR, Genova – Italy
dettori@itd.cnr.it

Abstract. In this paper we describe an experience with the construction of educational itineraries based on Learning Objects (LOs). The experience was carried out with a group of 130 trainee teachers of secondary school using LODE, a collaboration environment associated with a repository of LOs, aiming to facilitate teachers' work with LOs and the exchange of pedagogical experience. From the discussion of this activity we derive some suggestions to improve the LODE environment and to increase teachers' opportunities to make the sharing of LOs an occasion of professional growth.

Keywords: Learning object, Collaborative environments, Educational itinerary.

1 Introduction

Repositories of Learning Objects (LOs) can be a source of knowledge for teachers and a valid help to speed up and facilitate class preparation. By means of LOs, teachers can share not only materials to be re-used as such, but also interesting ideas of activities to carry out with the students. This holds true not only for online professional courses, whose efficient production at limited costs is at the basis of many studies on LOs [7], but also for regular high school teaching, provided that repositories are organized so as to allow the transmission not only of content knowledge but also of pedagogical ideas and application experience [2]. Standard metadata [1] are useful to communicate applicability and technical requirements of LOs, but are too schematic to express in a meaningful way the educational intention underlying them, and miss information on application experience. For this reason, we designed and implemented a communication environment connected with a LO repository (LODE, i.e., Learning Objects Discussion Environment) aiming to facilitate teachers' collaborative work on LOs by giving its users the possibility to share comments on LOs and descriptions of use experiences [5]. A first application of it in a teacher training course resulted satisfactory as concerns both ease of use and trainees' appreciation as a powerful tool for professional growth [3].

The first prototype realized, however, did not address a problem that contributes to determine the current limited use of LOs by school teachers, that is, the fragmentation of the material provided in the form of LOs. Being atomic materials, i.e. self-contained and addressing a single topic [6], is an essential feature of LOs, which determines their possibility to be re-used across different learning situations and to be adapted to a variety of educational needs. In school teaching, however, it is extremely important to construct knowledge as a connected whole, since only in this condition students can become effective problem solvers. It is not by chance that teachers often plan their activity in the form of itineraries rather than of single lessons.

Building articulated paths by extracting LOs from a repository is not always easy, since detecting LOs which are related and consistent as concerns both topic and pedagogical approach is often a complex task. Without suitable cues, teachers may end up to limit their choice to some materials and build other modules on their own, in order not to spend much time looking for suitable contributions.

Studies analyzing the practical difficulties of teachers in using a repository for the construction of learning itineraries are still limited. Some indications in this respect may be obtained by a few studies on what characteristics of a repository support teachers to integrate LOs in their educational plans. For instance, Recker et al. [8], through the analysis of the behaviour of a group of teachers dealing with a repository, try to detect teachers' motivation in using online resources, what barriers they perceive, what strategies of search and selection they use, how they adapt the resources at disposal for teaching and for autonomous training, what functions they expect to find in digital resources. This study suggests that guaranty of quality, peers' positive opinion and a materials' organization that responds to educational needs are key points for teachers' satisfactory use of a repository. Christiansen & Anderson [4], on the other hand, focus on benefits and issues associated with the creation of courses entirely from available LOs, by analyzing the results of three case studies. The outcomes of their experience show that quantity and quality of material is an essential condition, while heterogeneity of material constitutes a difficulty.

Quantity and quality are very important features, but, in our opinion, are not sufficient. In order to give further support, we endowed the LODE environment with the possibility to share experiences of use in the form of comments. Based on the experience we gained by observing trainee teachers using the environment, we now think that yet more support should be provided by suggesting conceptual connections among LOs. In the first prototype of LODE, teachers had the possibility to specify connections of their proposals with other LOs present in the repository, pointing out if their material was somehow derived from some other(s). These links, however, mainly aimed to show the evolution of objects due to teachers' work on the repository, helping to detect the competence of all teachers working on a given LO [5]. Therefore, they did not give information on possible relations of other kinds, such as interdisciplinary or multidisciplinary. It appeared therefore necessary to check if the kinds of links provided in the first prototype of LODE could be sufficient to support teachers in the creation of rich and articulated educational itineraries, taking fully advantage of the wealth of ideas offered by a repository. In order to answer this question, we needed further investigation.

For this sake, we planned an activity on LODE with trainee teachers, focused on creating educational itineraries by detecting LOs that they considered convenient for some educational purpose. The results of this experience showed that the support provided for the creation of itineraries needed to be improved by allowing a more flexible use of the connections between LOs and by providing meaningful examples worked out by other teachers. This led us to design some changes to LODE, in order to overcome the spotted problems.

This paper describes the experience carried out and the consequent modifications made to LODE. In particular, Section 2 presents the context of the experience and the tasks assigned. Section 3 illustrates its outcomes, pointing out what kinds of itineraries were developed and the influence of this activity on the production of new LOs. Section 4 describes the features of the first prototype of LODE aiming to support the creation of educational itineraries and the modifications made to improve such support. Finally, some considerations on the positive influence that building itineraries can have on teachers' activity with LOs conclude the paper.

2   An Experience with Educational Itineraries

We carried out the mentioned experience within the Course "Multimedia in Education" of the Teacher Training School (SISS) of the University of Genoa (Italy) in the winter semester 2006. This course for trainee teachers of secondary school in all subjects was attended by around 130 people. The trainees had different backgrounds as concerns both the school subjects of their interest and the amount of teaching experience, which ranged from none to short periods in public schools and up to several years in private schools. Most of them had very limited or none experience with online learning, and in particular with communities of practice.

2.1   Materials at Disposal

A choice of educational modules worked out by the trainees of the previous years had been uploaded in the environment, revised in order to offer good quality materials. These LOs were different as regards typology, pedagogical orientation and prospective users.

As for content, most LOs focused on subjects that are central in the Italian secondary school, like history, literature, mathematics, physics, natural and earth science, English, French or German as second languages, informatics and information technology, philosophy, Latin, art. Some of the LOs covered more general topics, like health, road education, sport. There was some difference in the number of LOs per school subject, due to the higher number of trainees in the humanistic area with respect to the scientific and linguistic ones.

As for typology, the materials included multimedia presentations, simulations, educational games, exercises, guides for activities to carry out with the computer or in the lab, or a combination of them.

As for pedagogical orientation, there were proposals of problem solving activities and individual reflections, lessons to be given by a teacher and mixed approaches.

As for the prospective users, most LOs were directed to students between low and upper secondary school (13-15 years old); a number of them were to be applied in the last years of upper secondary school (16-19 years old students); only a few were addressed to 11-12 years old students. Finally, some LOs were made to work with students with learning difficulties.

2.2 Assigned Tasks

The activity was preceded by a lesson on LOs and a guided tour of the environment. An overall description of the activities to be carried out and their meaning completed the introduction. Our trainees where requested to carry out four different tasks:

- To explore in depth the LODE environment. This task could be carried out in the lab or at a distance, in both cases with our support. This activity aimed to let the trainees understand the opportunities offered by the environment and to have an idea of its content and features.
- To select a LO in LODE and analyse its content, organization, technical aspects, pedagogical approach and target population, suggesting possible educational uses and a classification according to LODE's metadata. This activity aimed to give our trainees guidelines, by means of an active approach, on the main aspects they had to focus on when building a LO.
- To outline an educational itinerary by means of the materials of LODE and, if necessary, of other sources, formulated so as to be used by teachers as a basis for classroom activity. We asked to describe the itinerary by specifying objective, focus, educational approach, work outline, student and teacher roles, activities and materials to be used. Since the number of LOs in LODE was still not very high, we allowed the trainees to include in their itineraries also some new LOs to be developed, by sketching their main features. The trainees were also asked to report on: 1) how difficult it had been for them to detect the material they wanted; 2) if they found the links between LOs more or less useful; 3) if the environment organization and materials' connections were apt to give ideas of interesting learning itineraries; 4) what suggestions they had to improve the process. This activity had a twofold aim, i.e., to encourage the trainees to avail themselves of the work of their peers, and to give us hints on their capability to figure out different uses of LOs to build an articulated educational path. We also wanted to obtain information on the usefulness of the links between objects to support teachers in developing their educational ideas.
- To produce a LO of their choice, and upload it in LODE (after our approval), specifying any link(s) with LOs already present in the repository. This activity aimed to stimulate trainees' creativity and increase their competence in building educational material. It also aimed to give us cues on the possible influence of the work made with educational itineraries on the production of new LOs.

3 Outcomes of the Experience

3.1 What Kinds of Itineraries Were Produced

Despite the limited amount of materials at disposal in LODE, and the diversity of their forms and approaches, our trainees managed to suggest a variety of meaningful and articulated itineraries. These included many different activities (field experiences and work in the lab, games, exercises, reflections, group activities, discussions) and proposed to use materials of different kinds (digital presentations, web sites, movies, books, lab equipments etc.). As concerns the pedagogical approaches underlying the proposals, most itineraries integrated teacher's intervention and students' activities.

Not all LOs in the repository were used in some itinerary, while a few LOs were used in more than one, with different educational aims. The trainees showed a preference for LOs that included not only the presentation of some content knowledge but also the description of some activity. Several itineraries made reference also to some module external to the repository (mainly on the web) or to be created on purpose.

The itineraries showed a variety of pedagogical orientations, as described below.

Multidisciplinary itineraries entailed the development of a same theme from the point of view of two or more topics.

Example: An itinerary to teach English and French as second language, aiming to introduce students of lower secondary school to the culture of the second language and to linguistic production through typical phrases and expressions. This itinerary starts with the LO "Animal Idioms", which presents in a playful way English phrases related to animals, and with an analogous one on French expressions. The plan is to use these LOs in a classroom conversation where students compare the English and French expressions with the corresponding Italian ones, and analyse the possibilities of misunderstanding. After this activity, the students are requested to find a suitable translation in English and French of other Italian expressions.

Interdisciplinary itineraries aimed to develop a topic from the point of view of several school subjects, highlighting connections, peculiarities, similarities. They mostly made use of LOs in the form of presentations as a starting point to analyse a problem situation.

Example: An itinerary on the evolution of the house in ancient times, aiming to spot differences and similarities between Greek and Roman cultures through the analysis of their different ways of living. It integrates visits to archaeological sites and classroom reflections supported by two LOs: "The domus: evolution of the house in ancient Rome", and "The Greek house".

Itineraries to tackle a broad topic by deepening related themes entailed the parallel use of LOs examining aspects that contribute to give a global picture of the considered topic.

Example: An itinerary on "Italian painting of the XV century", starting from the LOs Italian art in the '400 (a general presentation), and "Bellini" (an introduction to the work of this artist, including some games to learn to recognize his work) and proposing the development of other two LOs, analogous to Bellini, on "Botticelli" and "Mantegna".

Itineraries deepening a topic by analysing it at increasingly finer levels include LOs to analyse particular aspects of the considered topic.

Example: An itinerary on astronomy, making use of "Introduction to the Solar system" (a presentation of the currently widely accepted theory on the formation of the Solar system) and "Heavenly bodies" (which discusses the nature and possible formation of heavenly bodies), and requiring the development of a new LO on the most recent theories on the development of the solar system. This itinerary is based on an active approach to learning, with lab activities guided by the teacher by means of the mentioned LOs, a field observation and a phase of reflection.

It appears from the above examples, that LOs were used in the developed itineraries with a variety of different roles, in particular as:

- enriching elements within an articulated experience;
- introductory elements of a proposal that develops in different directions;
- support for reflection and starting point for shared discussions;
- occasion to focus on a basic concept underlying different LOs that tackle parallel topics;
- support to deepen a given topic;
- proposal of practical activities or assessment exercises.

A few itineraries entailed the use of only some parts of the selected LOs, suggesting that it would be useful to have at disposal simplified or shorter versions of the considered proposals.

3.2 Influence of the Activity on Itineraries on the Production of New LOs

The LOs produced by our trainees in the last of the tasks assigned resulted more thoughtful and fancy than those produced by the trainees of the previous years. In particular the materials produced:

- resulted more easily adaptable to different educational situations, in that they show more clearly the articulation of their different components; this was probably influenced by the wish, expressed by several trainees in their itineraries, to use only part of some LO, and of the consequent observation of how difficult it can result to extract some material from a LO, if its overall organization is not well articulated;
- proposed pedagogical variants of existing materials, for instance complementing a theoretical approach with a problem-based one, or viceversa;
- constructed prerequisite modules for the use of some complex LOs, so as to make it easier to use in actual classroom work;
- provided examples of general phenomena close to students' life, so as to encourage students' interest and support motivation;
- included some LOs conceived as cohesive framework for other LOs on somehow related topics, so as to provide a kind of narrative guidance for a better use of those LOs.

It is easy to see in many of these new proposals an influence of the reflection entailed by the construction of itineraries, that appears to give the trainees a better awareness of the problems teachers have to solve to actually re-use LOs.

The production of the new LOs, however, was mostly not directly targeted to completing the proposed itineraries, even though several of them were referring to LOs yet to be constructed. This, in our opinion, was mainly due to the fact that the produced LO contributed to the final evaluation of the work carried out in the course. Hence, the trainees preferred to focus on some topic that they were more able to express in a creative and appealing way. It is reasonable to expect that, without the constraint of the evaluation for credits, teachers would rather concentrate on the production of LOs completing their itineraries, since this would turn out to their advantage. Moreover, in the context of an in-service community, the requests of LOs completing proposed itineraries could be shared within the community, contributing to enrich the repository's educational offer in a meaningful way.

The above considerations suggest that the itinerary construction resulted to be a formative activity for the trainees, and a simple but effective way to lead them to a more thoughtful construction of LOs.

3.3 Appreciation of the Experience

Trainees' comments on the experience highlight that they considered the use of their peers' materials a good occasion to improve their work.

They appreciated several aspects of LODE that helped them in selecting the material they needed to shape their own teaching itinerary:

- the fact that these LOs are the product of ideas of their colleagues, and hence likely suitable to actual classroom use;
- the fact that they are focused on disciplinary topics, hence suitable to be used in actual teaching;
- the possibility given by LODE to associate to LOs the report of use experiences; this allows teachers interested in re-using some LO to take advantage of the experience of their peers.
- the connection between the LOs, to easily find LOs with conceptual similarities;
- the guaranty of quality, that they assumed was offered by the fact that we had allowed those LOs in the environment.

The trainees also pointed out some difficulties they found in making use of more than one LO retrieved from LODE in their itineraries:

- the fact that the material available in LODE was in limited amount (due to our decision to include in it only good material produced by previous years trainees, and the environment had been in use only for a couple of years);
- the fact that LOs may result very heterogeneous as concerns presentation choices, language used and proposed pedagogical approach;
- the fact that in some cases the LOs they had selected were too big or detailed for the use they wanted to make in their itineraries.

Scarcity of material is a problem often pointed out in the literature [10], that can be solved only by stimulating the activity and cohesion of a community of teachers working on a repository. In the case of our course for trainee teachers, we expect it to become less and less important over the years, since each year we add to the repository the trainees' products at the end of the course.

The heterogeneity of approaches is in part not avoidable, since the materials collected in a repository reflect the pedagogical intentions of a variety of different people. This problem would likely result even more evident in a community formed by in-service teachers, since years of teaching practice obviously consolidates personal tendencies. The solution worked out by our trainees to attribute a mediating role to the teacher in their learning itineraries appears very practical and constructive, and worth including in a training program to the use of LOs.

Finally, the excessive size or detail of some LOs are likely avoided when teachers become more experienced in the construction of LOs. Some help in this respect can also derive from the suggestion given by several trainees to add a link pointing to simplified versions of LOs, when available.

4 Supporting the Construction of Itineraries

4.1 Facilities in the LODE Prototype

Building an itinerary with the LOs included in a repository entails having at disposal some tools to select the materials of interest. In LODE, these are provided by the pedagogical metadata and by the links among LOs.

As concerns metadata, we point out that we decided not to use standard metadata since they add a level of unwanted complexity from the pedagogical point of view, and interoperability issues are outside the scope of our research. Hence, we defined our own metadata, and kept them limited to the information strictly necessary to characterize a LO for the educational practice. Our metadata, include: author, language, date, key words, pedagogical approach, technical requirements, school topics, school level, producer's intention, educational role, links with other objects [5]. The choice not to use standard metadata should not appear as a deficiency of our environment, since the limited pedagogical interest of the current standards is widely recognized and makes the definition of useful metadata a still open issue [9].

Our trainees (obviously!) considered very useful for searching the item Topic, but observed that a finer classification of the content would be preferable, especially for articulated topics including very different aspects (e.g. not simply Latin, but Latin literature, Latin authors, Latin grammar, etc.). Moreover, materials which do not strictly belong to any school subject but could be used in several of them (e.g. a study on the properties of colours can be of interest for art or physics, but strictly speaking does nor belong to any of them) are difficult to be retrieved when searching by metadata since such materials are currently classified in generic way.

Also the current classification of the school level resulted not completely satisfactory, in that the different kinds of high school currently available in Italy often show a rather different orientation, ranging from the very theoretical to the highly practical, which can make the use of a LO suitable for one kind of high school but not for another, even though the students addressed have the same age.

Another problem that emerged from this experience is the fact that the short description given for the LO content was often made in different ways; a template to uniform them would speed up the work of prospective users who could get a better idea of the material's features without needing to examine its content. Also LOs' titles were criticized for not always giving a clear idea of the actual content. The trainees overcame these problems by browsing through the repository, thanks to the limited amount of material currently present, but this solution is certainly not feasible with a bigger repository. This problem will also be addressed in the future, but its solution does not appear urgent in the current situation.

As concerns links among LOs, they were appreciated by almost all trainees (91%), for various reasons, as shown in Table 1, which reports the answers to an open question,

Table 1. Why links among LOs were appreciated by our trainees (more than one reason could be given; 105 respondents)

I found the links useful because ...	% of respondents
they speed up search	39,06
they stimulate inter-disciplinary work	32,57
they give hints yet leaving one free to choose	22,89
they facilitate multi-disciplinary work	21,98
they help educational planning	19,98
they help to understand the main possible aims of a LO	16,49
they give ideas to make itineraries I had not thought of	15,89
they help in planning new LOs	8,29

grouped by similarity. The link's names (derives from, substitutes, specializes, complementary to), however, were often seen as not representing correctly their meaning; this sometimes led the trainees to criticize one or the other of them as not useful or meaningful.

Problems with the use of links probably depended on the fact that the implemented ones had been designed to point out "historical" relations among the LOs of LODE, that is, in order to record which LOs had influenced the creation of a new one. Hence they mainly aimed to keep track of the evolution of the knowledge stored in a repository due to the work made on it by its users [5]. We still consider this function important, but the experience carried out highlighted that also semantic links are necessary to guide teachers in the selection of LOs. The aim of semantic links is to let a LO's author point out conceptual similarities with other LOs he/she sees, even though the new LO is not directly derived from them. Due to the importance of links to facilitate the construction of itineraries, we therefore decided to plan a modification of them.

4.2   Improving LODE to Support the Creation of Itineraries

Itineraries produced are not mere lists of LOs, but include pedagogical ideas to help shaping a whole from several disjoint pieces. They are actually a way to share pedagogical ideas and experience connected with the use of LOs, as much valuable as other discussion forms provided by LODE. We therefore decided they should play in LODE a role similar to comments, which can be used by teachers to communicate observations and outcomes of use experiences.

To this end, we added in each LO's home page a list of the available itineraries that make reference to that LO, together with a command to insert new ones (see the list is on the left hand side, after the list of available comments in Fig. 1). They are realized in the same way as comments, that is, by exploiting the possibility offered by ATutor (the open-source Learning Management System used to implement LODE; see

Fig. 1. A LO's home page, showing on the left hand side the lists of comments and itineraries available for this LO

www.atutor.ca) to associate lists of materials to a course (which is the ATutor feature used to realize LOs).

An itinerary is described by specifying information of several kinds, namely objectives, content, target population, LOs used, time required, development, necessary tools, pedagogical approach. The names of the LOs of an itinerary are clickable (see Fig. 2), to facilitate their retrieval. When a user adds an itinerary for a LO, the same itinerary is automatically associated to all LOs mentioned in it. Any user can add itineraries even if he/she is not the author of any of the LOs included.

As concerns links among LOs, we reformulated their names as follows: deepens, variant of, inspired by, related to. Moreover we added a link "simplifies", following the suggestion of several trainees, to indicate a LO simpler than the connected one, hence more suitable to be used in a lower school grade or with students with learning difficulties. When a link to a LO is inserted, the system automatically adds in the page of the connected LO a symmetrical one, in order to show that it is mentioned by another LO. Links associated to a LO can be specified only by the author; if other users want to communicate their ideas of semantic connections among LOs, they can make it by means of itineraries involving them.

These modifications improve LODE in that they provide a new means to help teachers make explicit and share their pedagogical knowledge, consistently with the other communication tools provided by the environment. Itineraries, together with comments, forums and links, allow teachers' competence to play a reciprocal scaffolding role within the community, helping to transfer it from the individual production level to the sharing one. This interplay between individual and shared competence is aimed at producing richer and more thoughtful LOs; these belong to both the production

Fig. 2. An itinerary's page, showing the LOs used in it; on the left hand side, a list of all information available for this itinerary

and the sharing levels, in that they have their roots in teachers' individual knowledge and are transformed and enriched by the joint activity on them.

5   Concluding Remarks

The described experience aimed at improving teachers' actual work on LOs by providing tools to facilitate the construction of educational itineraries based on suitable materials retrieved from LODE's repository. The study carried out with a group of 130 trainee teachers can be considered successful, for at least two reasons.

Firstly, it allowed us to gain understanding of what elements can effectively support the creation of itineraries, and to modify the LODE environment accordingly.

Moreover, it was interesting to find that the activity on itineraries led our trainee teachers to produce better LOs, likely because this practical experience induced a reflection on what characterizes easily re-usable educational material. Devising educational itineraries helped them understand, from an operative point of view, the pedagogical competence necessary to successfully deal with LOs, namely: 1) to find a balance between different presentation styles and objectives of the selected materials; 2) to give cohesion to articulated itineraries 3) to adapt the material presentation to the students' needs and context's constraints. This understanding emerges from the fact that our trainees, in their itineraries, attributed a mediating role to the teachers. As pointed out in the literature [4], this is crucial to overcome integration problems determined by the possible heterogeneity of the re-used materials.

Sharing meaningful examples of itineraries, therefore, appears particularly useful and important during teacher training. It can result advantageous also for in-service teachers, however, not only because it is a way to share pedagogical experience, but also because it calls attention on the need to enrich a repository with LOs on some topics. This can contribute to increase a repository size and to create that critical mass of high quality, easily accessible material which is as an essential point for the success of sharing activities.

References

1. Anido, L.E., Fernandez, M.J., Caeiro, M., Santos, J.M., Rodriguez, J.S., Llamas, M.: Educational metadata and brokerage for learning resources. Computers & Education 38(4), 351–374 (2002)
2. Busetti, E., Forcheri, P., Ierardi, M.G., Molfino, M.T.: Repositories of Learning Objects as Learning Environments for Teachers. In: Proceedings of ICALT 2004, pp. 450–454. IEEE Comp. Soc. Press, New York (2004)
3. Forcheri, P., Busetti, E., Dettori, G., Ierardi, M.G.: Promoting Teachers' Collaborative Reuse of Educational Materials. In: Nejdl, W., Tochtermann, K. (eds.) EC-TEL 2006. LNCS, vol. 4227, pp. 61–73. Springer, Heidelberg (2006)
4. Christiansen, J., Anderson, T.: Feasibility of Course Development based on learning objects: research analysis of three case studies. Int. Journal of Instructional Technology and Distance Learning 1(2) (2004)
5. Forcheri, P., Dettori, G., Ierardi, M.G.: Endowing LOs with a Social Dimension. In: Liu, W., Li, Q., Lau, R.W.H. (eds.) ICWL 2006. LNCS, vol. 4181, pp. 189–202. Springer, Heidelberg (2006)
6. Littlejohn, A. (ed.): Reusing on line resources: a sustainable approach to E-Learning. Kogan Page, London (2003)
7. Malcolm, M.: The exercise of the object: issues in resource reusability and reuse. BJET 36(1), 33–42 (2005)
8. Recker, M.M., Dorward, J., Miller Nelson, L.: Discovery and use of Online Resources: Case Study Findings. Educational Technology and Society 7(2), 10–93 (2004)
9. Sinitsa, K. (ed.): Learning objects metadata: implementations and open issues, Special section of Learning Technology Newsletter 5 (1). Learning Technology Task Force (LTTF). IEEE Computer Society (2003), http://lttf.ieee.org/learn_tech/
10. Ternier, S., Duval, E., Neven, F.: Using a P2P architecture to provide interoperability between Learning Objects. In: EdMedia 2003 - World Conference on Educational Multimedia, Hypermedia & Telecommunications, June 26, 2003, Honolulu, Hawaii, USA (2003)

Adult Distance Learning Using a Web-Based Learning Management System: Methodology and Results

Konstantinos Antonis, Petros Lampsas, and Jim Prentzas

Technological Educational Institute of Lamia
Department of Informatics and Computer Technology
Lamia GR-35100, Greece
{k_antonis, plam, dprentzas}@teilam.gr

Abstract. In this paper, we present the methodology and results derived from a distance learning programme offered by a higher education institute to adults. Computer Science and interdisciplinary courses are offered through a Web-based Learning Management System (LMS). Administrative, technical and pedagogical issues are considered systemically and a methodology is developed taking into consideration the group of learners, appropriate learning methods, assessment methods, social and economical aspects concerning distance learning and the technological infrastructure in place. An assessment procedure is reached and carried out thoroughly involving all components of the programme. Results depict success in certain aspects of the overall programme, as well as suggestions for enhancement of the distance learning setting.

1 Introduction

Distance learning is becoming an increasingly important part of lower and higher education. This type of education can take place over the Internet, in which occasion instruction and educational content are delivered via the Internet. The North American Council for Online Learning (NACOL) surveyed over thirty countries aiming to highlight international trends in distance learning for K-12 students mainly, identify distance learning initiatives and projects in individual countries, and promote international dialogue for future collaboration [13]. Survey results showed continuous growth in use of distance learning programmes in all countries.

Nowadays, there is a growing interest in higher education institutes to offer lifelong learning programmes. In [1] the results of a set of surveys and interviews conducted in twenty-one higher education institutes of various types are summarized. Results showed that the usage of distance learning is considered successful mainly for undergraduate students. Additionally, some potential insights into the common success factors for successful adoption of Internet-supported learning are provided.

In order to support distance learning and collaborative work, various Web-based Learning Management Systems (LMSs) have been developed, such as the Web Course Tools (WebCT), the Web Course Homepage System (WebCH), the Blackboard Learning System and the System for Multimedia Integrated Learning (Smile). LMSs have become popular since they incorporate a suite of functionalities addressed

H. Leung et al. (Eds.): ICWL 2007, LNCS 4823, pp. 508–519, 2008.

to learners, tutors and system administrators. These functionalities are designed, among other services, to create, deliver and manage learning content, track and report on learner activity and progress, enable synchronous and asynchronous collaboration/ communication and provide centralized control and administration to tutors and system administrators. All such services are integrated within a robust, web-based environment effectively supporting many simultaneous users.

Various LMSs have been used for distance learning programmes offered by higher education institutes. To name a few, in [5] a curriculum in nuclear medicine and radiotherapy was designed. It consisted of self-directed learning, an online discussion forum and discussion rounds. Online courses were delivered via Netlearn LMS. Exams and evaluation of the curriculum were taken online. In [15], distance learning critical success factors (CSFs) are specified as perceived by university students. A survey involving 538 university students revealed eight categories of distance learning CSFs, each including several critical acceptance and success measures. In [12] the Technology Acceptance Model is extended to include technical support as a precursor and then the role of the extended model in user acceptance of WebCT is investigated. In [7] effects of message constraints and labels on collaborative argumentation in asynchronous discussions via Blackboard LMS are examined.

Technological Educational Institutes (T.E.I.) in Greece comprise the technological sector of higher education. T.E.I. of Lamia provides distance learning opportunities to adults, who are Computer Science graduates, or graduates that use computers as a tool in their work, via the Blackboard LMS. This paper presents the methodology, distance learning setting and derived results.

The curriculum contains 37 online courses mainly in Computer Science, but there are also some interdisciplinary courses. So far, three semesters have been completed, with totally over 500 participations in courses. The assessment procedure considers both the overall distance learning setting and knowledge acquired by learners. Assessment results assisted the enhancement of the educational process from semester to semester and depict satisfaction of all participants from the activity as a whole.

Although many organizations nowadays provide distance learning through use of an LMS, to the best of our knowledge the approach presented in this paper concerns aspects of a distance learning setting not usually dealt with in other similar approaches. Firstly, this paper presents a systemic treatment of administrative, technical and pedagogical issues taking into consideration the group of learners, appropriate learning methods, assessment methods, social and economical aspects concerning distance learning and technological infrastructure in place [9]. Secondly, it involves a curriculum of courses offered online whereas other approaches usually involve a specific course or a group of courses. Thirdly, learners are graduates/professionals living and working in geographically dispersed areas. Fourthly, each course is conducted exclusively through the use of LMS and does not involve traditional classroom instruction.

The paper is organized as follows. Section 2 discusses the overall design of the distance learning setting. Section 3 presents assessment methodology and results. Section 4 demonstrates aspects of the setting that can be improved. Finally, section 5 concludes and points out aspects for future work.

2 Design of Distance Learning Environment

2.1 Overview

In this section, we present the overall design of the distance learning setting, encompassing learning model, human resources (teaching, technical and administrative personnel) and available technology. This design caters for effectively providing a setting for distance learning through a web-based LMS.

37 distance learning courses are provided involving various Computer Science and interdisciplinary fields (e.g. Bioinformatics, GIS, Computers in Education). Tutors are experienced in teaching the same or quite similar courses at higher education institutes. A fraction of them have experience as tutors in distance learning courses. Courses have been organized into three categories (i.e., introductory, fundamental and advanced-specialized) to attract learners with different background and interests.

To facilitate the learning process, learners attending a course are limited to twenty at most. The learning content of each course is organized into units and consists of theory, examples, self-rating tests, unit tests, mid-term and final tests. For the creation of the learning content, LMS tools as well as other software tools have been used. The learning content includes presentations, documents, animations, audio/video and SMIL files. Synchronous and asynchronous communication among tutors and learners is performed by employing LMS's collaboration tools (such as shared workspace, virtual classroom, chat, discussion forum, bulletin board, email) and/or the use of the media server. Media server has been found very useful for synchronous interaction among tutors and learners and streaming. The learning content of courses is accessible online at http://blackboard.teilam.gr.

We adopted two learning models: (a) a directed learning approach, namely learner-oriented model and (b) a more constructivist learning model, namely a hybrid one integrating problem-based with collaborative learning. The former has been applied to the majority of courses whereas the latter to selected courses.

Apart from the learning model, other crucial factors affect success of a distance learning course as well. In [14], some of these factors are identified, namely degree of interaction, support during course and administrative/ technical issues. In the following sections, our efforts to address these factors are integrated within the learning environment. In our design considerations, we took into account that, as far as web-based courses and programs are concerned, characteristics of successful online courses include among others well-designed and structured courses, engaging collaborative activities and an interactive learning community [14].

2.2 Learner-Oriented Model

In a course carried out according to a learner-oriented scenario, availability of learning content is combined with tests, projects and (both synchronous and asynchronous) interaction among tutors and learners. The scenario is implemented in a weekly or fortnightly basis.

At predetermined intervals the tutor makes available the learning content of each course unit in the LMS and sufficient amount of time is given to learners to study it.

Learners interact with the tutor synchronously in online sessions and asynchronously by using LMS tools and/or media server functionalities. The main purpose of interaction among learners and tutor is for the tutor to scaffold and facilitate learners in mastering course units. In most courses, synchronous interaction is mainly accomplished with virtual classroom and chat tools of LMS. In certain courses, real-time audio transmission functionalities of the media server have also been employed in online sessions. Asynchronous interaction is mainly performed through messages posted on the discussion forum and bulletin board. Tutors interact synchronously with learners, during online sessions, at an agreed upon schedule on a weekly basis.

To avoid coordination problems among tutors and learners during online sessions, learners are organized into groups of at most ten members. The organization of learners into groups takes place prior to the beginning of the course. The tutor interacts with each group at different time schedules. Furthermore, certain arbitration rules are applied during online sessions of the tutor with each learner group. For instance, learners pose questions according to a predetermined (round robin) order. This means that each learner asks the tutor a question only when it is his/her turn (unless previously ordered learners do not have a question to pose). The learners' order in posing questions is determined prior to the beginning of the online session. Learners are advised to post questions to the discussion forum rather than sending e-mails to tutors so that the interaction is available to all learners. Recorded audio and/or video lectures may also be stored as streaming media in the media server.

2.3 Hybrid Learning Model

The hybrid learning method combines problem-based with collaborative learning. We first briefly present the two combined pedagogical methods and then the hybrid one.

2.3.1 Problem Based Learning
Problem Based Learning (PBL) is a pedagogical method focusing on learners [4]. It is primarily a 'learning-by-doing' procedure. A typical course structured according to PBL starts with presentation of a complex and (preferably) applied problem that cannot be dealt with by learners based on current knowledge status. Further on, the learning process focuses on two main aspects involving learners: (a) how to determine lacking knowledge skills contributing in problem handling and (b) to learn how to acquire these skills. That is, learners learn 'to know what they do not know'.

The primary characteristics/advantages of the method are the following: (a) learners actively participate in the learning process, (b) learners learn to handle problems with initially unknown parameters, (c) learners learn how to effectively exploit various information sources (i.e., books, papers, technical reports, the Web, etc.) when searching for specific knowledge items determined by them, and (d) the tutor's role is to guide, supervise and encourage learners [6]. In certain (extreme) cases, learners may have to find the answers to their questions by themselves.

2.3.2 Collaborative Learning
Collaborative Learning (CL) in general adopts a socialized view to learning by considering that learners cooperate in order to achieve their common learning goals [17]. CL aims to enhance individualized learning through cooperation of individuals in working

groups when fulfilling a learning task. There may also be 'group goals' requiring team-work to be achieved. CL acknowledges that every person should play an active role for the formation of his/her knowledge. CL is applied to a 'class' encompassing the follow-ing characteristics: (a) knowledge is shared among learners and also among tutors and learners, (b) tutors act as mediators of knowledge and (c) there may be heterogeneous groups of learners.

The tutor acts as knowledge mediator through discussion and cooperation. Media-tion can be defined as scaffolding, coaching, modeling and facilitating learners throughout the learning process. Ideally, tutors should train learners to the point they have matured enough to learn by interacting with other group members [16].

2.3.3 The Hybrid Learning Model

Research has shown difficulties in applying PBL and CL in early stages of a learning process. In fact, PBL resembles (to a large degree) the research process during post-graduate studies. More specifically, the roles of postgraduate students and supervising teaching staff resemble the roles of learners and tutors in PBL [2].

A hybrid pedagogical method was applied integrating PBL and CL methods. The instructional process consists of two main phases: an initial phase resembling (to a large degree) the learner-oriented method and a subsequent phase based on the inte-gration of PBL and CL methods. A more constructivist approach seems reasonable in an adult distance learning setting, taking into account that adults pursuing lifelong learning are generally exposing motivation in achieving learning objectives and will-ingness to cooperate in learning communities [18].

In the initial phase, the teaching scenario resembles the learner-oriented method. In-dividual and group projects are frequently assigned to learners. The purpose of these projects is threefold. Firstly, the learners' response is used to evaluate their perform-ance. Secondly, they contribute in acquainting each learner with the other group mem-bers. Thirdly, learners within groups get used to collaborating. During the initial phase, the tutor creates groups of learners based on their knowledge level, place of residence and maturity to pass on to the next phase of the learning process. By and large, the purpose of the initial phase is twofold. On the one hand, it introduces learners into the learning process by providing the essential knowledge background. On the other hand, it points out possible problems within learners' groups and primary aspects of each learner's performance [8], [11], [19].

In the second phase, a PBL approach is employed. The tutor assigns each group a specific problem that is part of a larger problem to be dealt with. Thus, special care should be given to organizing the task each group has to fulfill. Some amount of time should be initially given to learners to ponder over the posed problem. Meanwhile, group members can use LMS communication tools to discuss problem issues. Re-cording of these discussions enables the tutor to observe the thinking process within each group, as well as commitment and contribution to shared objective.

After the initial 'pondering' phase, a 'seek' phase should follow. The tutor should provide additional tips or teaching material regarding the problem. The main purpose of this phase is to assist the coordination between group members in order to figure out by themselves how to proceed. Learners employ available communication tools to

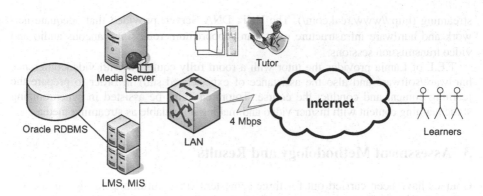

Fig. 1. An abstraction of the overall distance learning setting

communicate with each other and with the tutor. This interaction also assists learning process coordination, an issue dealt with within each group, with tutor's guidance.

2.4 Tutors

In [3] it is argued that distance learning tutors need different skills than instructors teaching traditional courses. Distance learning tutors can rarely possess such skills unless they have experience as instructors in distance learning settings. To overcome this shortcoming, prior to courses' beginning, tutors with no previous experience in distance learning became learners in at least one online course offered by another tutor, using the distance learning setting of our institute [14].

The role that the tutor must perform and the skills he/she should possess are: (a) preparation of learning content and creation of course environment in the LMS, (b) assessment of learners' performance, (c) synchronous and asynchronous scaffolding and facilitation of learning process, and (d) assessment of distance learning setting.

2.5 Available Technology

Figure 1 depicts an abstraction of the overall distance learning environment. The primary software platform is the Blackboard LMS. The LMS communicates with an Oracle RDBMS storing data concerning learners, tutors and offered courses.

The application server also hosts the project's Web site (http://esp.inf.teilam.gr) and the management information system (MIS) supporting the overall process. The project's Web site provides information regarding the project such as course outlines, tutors and prerequisites. The MIS consists of an RDBMS and a Web-based user interface. It provides administrative services (e.g. submission and management of candidate learners' applications, submission and management of learner and tutor questionnaires etc.) and learning process services (e.g. statistics regarding learners' performance and learning process).

Audio and video transmission can be done either synchronously or asynchronously. This is achieved with the operation of the Media Server (i.e., the Helix DNA Server), which in cooperation with the Helix DNA Producer enables webcasts and video streaming (http://www.real.com/). The Helix DNA Server, provided that adequate network and hardware infrastructure exist, can support numerous simultaneous audio and video transmission sessions.

T.E.I. of Lamia provides the tutor with a room fully equipped with videoconference hardware/software and also the assistance of experienced staff in order to prepare the learning content and conduct the course. Tutors can also be assisted in synchronizing static learning content with his/her video and making it available as streaming media.

3   Assessment Methodology and Results

Courses have been carried out for three semesters since autumn 2005. More specifically, 10, 22 and 11 courses were available in the first, second and third semester respectively. In total, the registrations for course participation were over 500. It should be mentioned that a learner is allowed to enrol to two courses at most.

3.1   Assessment Methodology

Apart from typical LMS assessment options, we adapted and applied an assessment methodology tailored to the specific needs of our web-based courses. Among the forms of assessment applying to online learning [14], we selected to use the portfolio assessment in which students create a collection of their work throughout the learning process best determining their efforts and achievements. A pass/fail mark for learners in a course is determined as a combination of all these factors.

Evaluation of learner achievement in a course, when learner-oriented approach is used, is based on the following factors: test results, assignments and participation in the discussion forum and online sessions. Learners take the following types of tests:

- A pretest prior to course beginning. This test assists tutors in obtaining an indication of learners' knowledge level regarding the course. By comparing pretest and posttest results, an indication of learner's progress is obtained.
- Unit tests upon completion of a course unit.
- A midterm test (optional) and a final test or project.

Learner's degree of interaction with the LMS is an essential component of his/her portfolio, because it demonstrates commitment in the course. This parameter involves aspects such as learner's recorded activity in the shared resources of the LMS.

In the hybrid learning method, assessment of individual and group achievement is accomplished using the portfolio approach. Another dimension of assessment is that learners and tutors assess the distance learning setting by completing questionnaires, preparing reports and conducting face-to-face meetings.

For assessment purposes, all interactions among learners using communication tools of the LMS are recorded [10]. In this way, the tutor will be able to observe how the learning process progresses. Progress will be assessed not only based on the final outcome but also on the recorded interactions among group members, among group members and tutor and among whole groups. Therefore, the tutor will be able to obtain a thorough view to individual and group progress. Moreover, useful conclusions could be reached concerning actions required in order to improve the learning outcome. Such actions could involve group support and encouragement of group members to collaborate among themselves and with learners of other groups.

3.2 Questionnaire Results

Tutors and learners completed questionnaires to evaluate the overall process, point out aspects requiring improvement and propose their suggestions. Learners were asked to complete three questionnaires: prior to course beginning, at midterm and right after the end of courses. The questionnaire prior to course beginning includes general questions regarding the interests of each learner and reasons for choosing to participate in the distance learning process. The other two questionnaires involve the following: (a) learning content evaluation, (b) evaluation of the overall process, (c) LMS evaluation, (d) problems encountered during learning process, (e) suggestions for improvement of overall process. Tutors were asked to complete questionnaires at midterm and right after the end of courses. Tutors were asked to make remarks about their interaction with learners and learners' response to overall process.

Learner and tutor questionnaires (in Greek) are available online at the project's Web site (http://esp.inf.teilam.gr). Tutors and learners have completed questionnaires during the first three semesters that courses have been carried out. Useful conclusions have been reached from completed questionnaires.

3.2.1 Learner Questionnaire Results

The vast majority of learners had negligible previous experience in distance learning while several learners had experience in using stand-alone educational software. Assessment results and administrative statistics revealed that 44% of enrolled learners dropped lessons 2-3 weeks after lessons commenced. 40% of enrolled learners succeeded, while the remaining 16% attended lessons without managing to succeed.

Learners' motivation in acquiring knowledge was the primary reason for attending distance learning courses (34%). Main reasons for learners' participation are also flexibility in controlling learning pace and learning content in certain courses.

Learners have generally expressed positive opinions about the learning process. Table 1 depicts learners' evaluation results corresponding to midterm and final questionnaires respectively. An interesting result is that right after the completion of the course, for 5% of learners the learning process did not come up to their expectations, while in the middle of courses the same figure was 0%. In midterm questionnaires, 61% of learners expressed a very positive opinion about the learning process whereas in final questionnaires the corresponding portion reached 70%.

Table 1. Learners' evaluation of learning process

	less ←					→ more
midterm questionnaires	0%	0%	4%	35%	48%	13%
final questionnaires	0%	5%	0%	25%	40%	30%

Learners classified the advantages of a distance learning setting as the ability to learn at home, the inexistence of alternative ways of learning and the ability to communicate synchronously and asynchronously with tutors and learners. A general disadvantage is the impersonal communication among learners and tutors.

Moreover, learners exposed positive attitude towards the learning process. Primary reasons for learners' positive opinions were considered the tutors (29%), learning content (30%), the LMS (13%) and interaction with other learners (13%). Working with other learners in team projects does not seem to add up significantly to overall positive views. Certain learners stressed out other learners' lack of interest in the learning process. At the end of the semester, about 95% of learners expressed willingness to enrol to other courses and would also suggest to other interested learners to enrol to courses.

Table 2. Learners' satisfaction in interaction with other learners

Less ←					→ more
8%	5%	15%	34%	23%	15%

Learners were not very satisfied by their interaction with other learners (Table 2). Only 38% of learners deemed the interaction with other learners very satisfactory, while 13% deemed the interaction unsatisfactory.

Table 3. Frequency of learners' participation in online sessions

Always	Once every fortnight	Less Often	Never
57%	23%	15%	5%

Over 90% of learners accessed the LMS very often (i.e., everyday or several days a week). Furthermore, online sessions are popular among learners (Table 3). Only 20% of learners reported not to take part in online sessions frequently. However, learners did not use frequently enough the discussion forum for asynchronous communication (Table 4), a result that could be attributed to lack of collaboration mentality. Roughly 50% of learners reported to use the discussion forum at least once a week.

3.2.2   Results from Tutors' Questionnaires and Reports

Overall, tutors expressed positive opinions about the learning process. Nevertheless, only 30% of tutors reported to have been very satisfied by learners' participation in the learning process. It turned out that learners enrolling to more than two semester courses had difficulties in keeping up with the pace of the learning process. Furthermore, certain learners had not realized certain distance learning requirements.

Over 95% of tutors expressed positive opinions concerning the following: (a) they would like to continue teaching distance learning courses in the following semesters,

Table 4. LMS and discussion forum access frequency

	LMS access frequency	forum access frequency
Everyday	29%	3%
Several days per week	62%	24%
Once a week	2%	25%
A few times per fortnight	2%	24%
Less often	5%	21%
Never	0%	3%

(b) they would suggest to other learners to enrol to the courses, (c) they would suggest to other colleagues to teach courses in a similar way and (d) they would suggest to other higher education institutes to teach courses in a similar way.

4   Issues of Distance Learning Setting Requiring Improvement

Learners and tutors pointed out issues and proposals that could improve learning process. Such issues were discussed during meetings involving tutors, learners and project managers. Some deficiencies pointed out during the first semester, have already been dealt with in the second and third semester.

The following administrative issues needing improvement have been pointed out:

- Provision of a successful applicant's profile description to potential applicants in the call for applications period: This would enable applicants to consider more thoroughly if they meet certain programme requirements and could therefore lead to reduced drop rates.
- Availability of sample learning content to candidate learners.

The following aspects have been pointed out regarding learning content:

- Learning content enrichment to encompass multiple knowledge representations.
- All teaching material was electronically available through the LMS and certain learners expressed desire for availability of printed teaching material as well.
- Though an effort was made to adjust the learning content to distance learning requirements, steps need to be taken to enhance this adjustment.

The following issues concerning the learning process have been pointed out:

- Voice transmission during online sessions: During the second semester, tutor's voice transmission was made available by employing the media server. This facility proved to be effective in the following semesters as it fosters community formation and helps sustaining the "classroom".
- Encouragement of learners to use the discussion forum.
- Greater emphasis on hybrid learning model: The hybrid learning model has not been extensively employed and tested during the first three semesters. However,

during the fourth semester, four appropriate courses have been selected as pilot case for application and assessment of the learning model. Results and feedback will guide hybrid model's adaptation and application to all appropriate courses.

- A mini tutorial for the effective distance learner addressing issues that could maximize learner's benefits from the distance learning experience.

5 Conclusions and Future Work

In this work, we present an adult distance education approach supported by the use of a web-based LMS and a media server. A curriculum consisting of Computer Science and interdisciplinary courses was conducted and assessed. We developed a systemic methodology to carry out the programme based on state-of-art research in education and psychology concerning adult distance education and learning theories as well as taking into account available information and communication technologies.

A specific for the programme assessment method was applied, encompassing all aspects of the learning environment. Results are positive and depict that, although considerable issues must be taken into account for such approaches to be efficient, there is a growing interest for the potential learning outcomes of such a method.

The findings demonstrated that the key to success is the systemic treatment of all issues involving a distance learning setting. The approach could provide guidelines to organizations interested in offering distance learning facilities to graduates with support of an LMS. Feedback has shown an increasing interest from graduates to enhance the knowledge in their field by exploiting distance learning facilities.

As part of our future work we plan to incorporate SCORM compliant methods and practices in the learning process and further apply and evaluate the hybrid learning model.

Acknowledgement. This work was partially supported by the European Social Fund and National Resources - (EPEAEK-II).

References

1. Abel, R.: Achieving Success in Internet-Supported learning in Higher Education: Case Studies Illuminate Success Factors, Challenges, and Future Directions (2005), http://www.a-hec.org/IsL_orig_study.html
2. Albanese, M., Mitchell, S.: Problem-Based Learning: a Review of Literature on its Outcomes and Implementation Issues. Academic Medicine 68, 52–81 (1993)
3. Cyrs, T.E.: Competence in Teaching at a Distance. In: Cyrs, T.E. (ed.) Teaching and Learning at a Distance: What it Takes to Effectively Design, Deliver and Evaluate Programs, Jossey-Bass, San Francisco (1997)
4. Ertmer, P., Newby, T.: Behaviorism, Cognitivism, Constructivism: Comparing Critical Features from an Instructional Design Perspective. Performance Improvement Quarterly 6, 50–72 (1993)

5. Gotthardt, M., Siegert, M., Schlieck, A., Schneider, S., Kohnert, A., Grob, M., Schäfer, C., Wagner, R., Hörmann, S., Behr, T., Engenhart, R., Klose, K., Jungclas, H., Glowalla, U.: How to Successfully Implement E-Learning for Both Students and Teachers. Academic Radiology 13, 379–390 (2006)
6. Hoffman, B., Ritchie, D.: Using Multimedia to Overcome the Problems with Problem-Based Learning. Instructional Science 25, 97–115 (1997)
7. Jeong, Joung, S.: Scaffolding Collaborative Argumentation in Asynchronous Discussions with Message Constraints and Message Labels. Computers & Education 48, 427–445 (2007)
8. Jonassen, D.H., Peck, K.L., Wilson, B.G.: Learning with Technology: A Constructivist Perspective. Prentice-Hall, Upper Saddle River, New Jersey (1999)
9. Lampsas, P., Triantafylloy, V., Antonis, K.: On the Systemic Overview of the Introduction of Information and Communication Technologies in Learning Environments. Open Education Journal 2, 36–50 (2006)
10. Lave, J., Wenger, E.: Situated Learning: Legitimate Peripheral Participation. Cambridge University Press, Cambridge (1991)
11. Miao, Y., Fleschutz, J.M., Zentel, P.: Enriching Learning Contexts to Support Communities of Practice. In: Proceedings of the 1999 conference on Computer support for collaborative learning, Integrated Publication and Information Systems Institute (1999)
12. Ngai, E.W.T., Poon, J.K.L., Chan, Y.H.C.: Empirical Examination of the Adoption of WebCT using TAM. Computers & Education 48, 250–267 (2007)
13. Powell, A., Patrick, S.: An International Perspective of K-12 Online Learning. A Summary of the 2006 NACOL International E-Learning Survey (2006)
14. Roblyer, M.D.: Integrating Educational Technology into Teaching, 4th edn. Prentice-Hall, Upper Saddle River, NJ (2005)
15. Selim, H.: Critical Success Factors for E-Learning Acceptance: Confirmatory Factor Models. Computers and Education 49, 396–413 (2007)
16. Vygotsky, L.S.: Mind in Society. Harvard University Press, Harvard (1978)
17. Wenger, E.: Communities of Practice: Learning, Meaning, and Identity. Cambridge University Press, Cambridge (1999)
18. Slavin, R.E.: Cooperative Learning: Theory, Research and Practice. Prentice Hall, Upper Saddle River, NJ (1990)
19. Wilson, B.G.: Metaphors for Instruction: Why we Talk about Learning Environments. Educational Technology 35, 25–30 (1996)

Language-Driven Development of Web-Based Learning Applications

José-Luis Sierra, Baltasar Fernández-Manjón, and Alfredo Fernández-Valmayor

Dpto. Ingeniería del Software e Inteligencia Artificial. Fac. Informática. Universidad Complutense de Madrid
C/ Profesor José García Santesmases s/n. 28040 Madrid. Spain
{jlsierra,balta,valmayor}@fdi.ucm.es

Abstract. In this paper we propose a language-driven approach for the high-level design of web-based learning applications. In our approach we define a domain-specific language that characterizes the key application aspects. Then we assign a suitable operational semantics to this language, and we keep it independent of low-level implementation details such as interaction / presentation or database updating. The resulting design can be easily implemented using the model-view-controller pattern that is very well supported by standard implementation technologies. In addition, these language-driven designs also allow for rapid prototyping, exploration and early discovery of application features, as well as for rational collaboration processes between instructors and developers. We exemplify our approach with a Socratic Tutoring System.

Keywords: Development of web-based learning applications, language-driven development, domain-specific languages document-oriented approach, Socratic tutors.

1 Introduction

As a result of our previous experiences in the development of several web-based E-Learning applications for various purposes [11,18,19,21] we have realized the importance of adopting a well-principled and rigorous approach for modeling the key application aspects (e.g. structure, behavior, interaction) in the very first stages of development. For this purpose, we have adopted a *language-driven approach* [12]. In this approach, we start by defining the *domain specific language* (DSL) that characterizes the key application aspects. Then we assign operational semantics suitable to such a DSL in order to achieve a high-level behavioral characterization of the application. Finally we isolate these semantics of the low-level implementation details regarding the basic interaction, presentation and updating operations. The resulting high-level designs can be easily implemented using the well-known model-view-controller (MVC) pattern [10], which is typically used for organizing almost all modern web-based applications. In addition, this linguistic approach also facilitates rational collaboration processes between instructors and developers. The DSL is near the knowledge and the expertise of the instructors. Therefore they can understand and use the language (provided that a user-friendly notation be available). In this paper we present this language-driven approach.

H. Leung et al. (Eds.): ICWL 2007, LNCS 4823, pp. 520–531, 2008.
© Springer-Verlag Berlin Heidelberg 2008

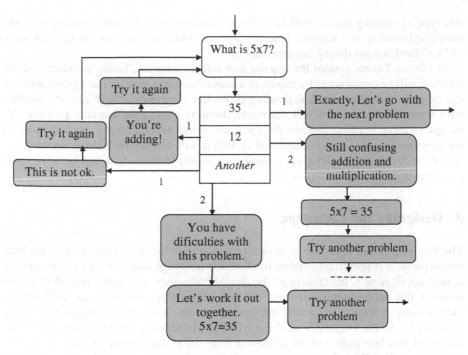

Fig. 1. Graphic representation of a tutorial fragment for a Socratic tutoring system (example adapted from [8])

The structure of the paper is as follows. In section 2 we present a simplified example of the E-Learning application that we will use to illustrate the different aspects of our approach. Section 3 deals with the structural aspects of the design. Section 4 addresses the specification of behavior. Section 5 provides some implementation guidelines. Finally, section 6 presents the conclusions and some lines of future work.

2 An Example of Application

In this paper we will use a simple tutoring system to illustrate the main aspects of our approach. The system is called <e-Tutor>, and it is the web-based version of a previous desktop system developed to explore some concerns in our *document-oriented approach* to the production and maintenance of content-intensive applications [17].

Tutoring systems were popularized during the eighties and nineties of the past century [22]. Although their pedagogical adequacy as mechanisms to support sophisticated learning processes has been heavily questioned, today there is a very active community working in this field, as well as relevant initiatives (see, for instance, [23]). However, our reason for choosing this kind of systems for exemplifying our approach is not so much pedagogical as technological, since the goal of our work is not to criticize or to defend a particular learning approach, but to provide guidelines that can be effectively used to produce and maintain E-Learning applications. For this purpose, we need a language simple enough to be fully addressed in this paper, and this type of tutoring system will let us do so. Indeed, our <e-Tutor> system is a very simplified version of a Socratic Tutoring System, which is based on the seminal work of Prof. Bork's team during the eighties [2,8].

In our <e-Tutor> system the learner will follow tutorials, facing problems whose solution will be constructed by means of a master-disciple dialog. The system will ask questions to the learner and, depending of his/her responses, it will provide him/her with some feedback and it will determine the next step in the learning process. Although in more realistic systems the feedback could depend on the whole history of the previous answers, in our simplified version it will depend exclusively on the number of times that the learner gives a particular answer to a question. In Fig. 1 we show a simple example of this kind of organization for the tutorials.

3 Designing the Language

The first step in our approach is to design a language for describing the key application aspects. It is important to point out that this language does not try to represent the *actual* application's features (e.g. the actual messages and hints provided to the learner), but only to represent their structure. Therefore, this language will include mechanisms to refer to the actual information. In this sense, the language is in some way similar to the languages used for marking documents up [5]. Furthermore, the design of this language will be addressed from an abstract point of view. Thus, the language itself will be characterized as an *information model*, instead of as a grammar for a concrete textual or visual language. This information model can be provided using standard data modeling techniques (e.g. entity-relationship diagrams, or UML class diagrams), and it can be further formalized in terms of a first-order signature (i.e. a set of function and predicate symbols) with the aim of subsequently enabling the formal definition of the operational semantics.

In the case of <e-Tutor>, the abstract structure of the Socratic dialog in the previous section is a weighted directed graph whose nodes contain different types of information, and which is oriented to represent the type of dialog between master and disciple on which this kind of tutorials is based. In Fig. 2a we sketch the information model for the <e-Tutor> language. In Fig. 2b we further formalize this model in terms of predicate symbols. We also document them with their intended meanings.

Notice that our approach follows the current practice in E-Learning specifications, where each specification is usually accompanied by its corresponding information model. Concrete notations can then be subsequently provided as appropriate *bindings* (e.g. as XML-based markup languages). Notice that it is also a common practice in the design of conventional computer (usually programming) languages, where abstract and concrete syntaxes are clearly identified. Abstract syntaxes let language designers capture the features of the language that are essential for further specifying the meaning of their constructs, while concrete syntaxes provide notations for the final language's users [7]. In our approach concrete syntaxes (*bindings*, following the more widely accepted terminology in E-Learning) will be very important in order to involve instructors in the production and maintenance of the learning contents and other pedagogical aspects. Indeed, we will promote the provision of bindings as

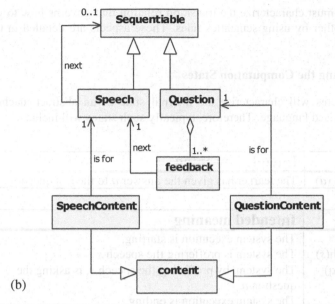

(b)

Predicate	Intended meaning
speech(*s*,*n*)	The speech *s* is followed by *n*. In this item, *n* can be another speech, a question point, or the end of the learning process. Besides, *s* is a unique identifier.
question(*q*)	A question point identified with the unique identifier *q*.
feedback(*q*,*a*,*n*,*s*)	A feedback for the answer *a* (a unique identifier) collected in a question point *q*. Besides, *n* is the number of times that the answer has been collected. The feedback itself will start with speech *s*.
content(*i*,*c*)	The content of the question / speech *i* is *c*.

Fig. 2. (a) Information model for the <e-Tutor> language; (b) predicates used to formalize the model in (a)

domain-specific descriptive markup languages (i.e. we promote DSLs with XML bindings) for the application's contents and complementary aspects, as proposed in our work on the aforementioned document-oriented approach.

4 Specifying the Operational Semantics

Once the language for structuring the application is available, developers must model the runtime behavior of such a language by assigning to it suitable *operational semantics*, which model such a behavior as transitions between computation states [14]. Therefore, we firstly need to decide on a suitable representation for the computation states. Next we must characterize the transition relation that governs how to go from one state to another by using semantics rules. These aspects are detailed in the next sections.

4.1 Representing the Computation States

Computation states will characterize the internal state of an abstract machine that executes the devised language. Therefore, typically such states will include:

(a)

Term	Intended meaning
answered (a)	The learner has given the answer a to the last question.

(b)

Term	Intended meaning
do-start	The system execution is starting.
do-speech(s)	The system is proffering the speech s
do-ask(s,q)	The system, by proffering the speech s, is asking the question q.
do-end	The system execution is ending.

Fig. 3. (a) Terms in the *view2controller* stream; (b) Terms in the *controller2view* stream

- The application description, in terms of the language provided. This description will play the role of the *program* stored in the machine's memory. Alternatively, sometimes it will be possible to drop this description from the computation states themselves, and to assume that it is globally available.
- A *control term*, which will usually coincide with the predicate definition in the application description currently under consideration. This term will be used to decide the next step to take in the execution.
- A *context*, which contains additional information used to perform the transitions and which expresses the dependence of the actions on previous responses or states.
- Three different streams. The *view2controller* stream will contain suitable representations of the user's interactions. In the *controller2view* stream the controller will write appropriate commands to govern the view's update. Finally, in the *controller2model* stream the controller will write appropriate update commands for the information model (for those applications where the model is not updated, but only queried, this last stream can be safely omitted). These streams are very useful for isolating the behavioral details from the presentation / interaction / updating aspects. Also this organization naturally leads to an MVC architecture for the final implementation, as previously mentioned.

In <e-Tutor>, computation states will be associated with the states of the master-disciple dialog and the evolution of this dialog. Therefore we will represent these computation states as 5-tuples of the form $<\theta,T,\rho,in,out>$, where:

- θ is the control term and T is the structure of the tutorial represented as a set of ground (i.e. variable-free) facts using the signature described in the previous section.
- ρ is the context, which in this example will be constituted by a set of counters associated with the answers. With ρ_c we will denote the value of the c counter in ρ, while with $\rho_c := v$ we will denote the new set of counters resulting from updating the value of c in ρ with v. Also, if a counter is not set, its value will be considered 1, since it will be the first time that the learner proffers the associated answer.
- *in* and *out* are the *view2controller* and the *controller2view* streams respectively. Since in this example the model is not updated, the *controller2model* stream is not required, and it can be dropped from the computation state. In Fig. 3a we characterize the possible terms in the *view2controller* stream, which will simply contain the learner's answers. In Fig. 3b we show the possible terms in the *controller2view* one, which will contain the commands for presenting the system's speeches and questions, as well as for announcing the init and the end of the system's execution.

Besides this kind of states, we will also introduce a special format for initial and final states. Initial states will be represented as $<s,T,in,out>$, with s the starting speech. Final states will be represented simply as $<\rho,out>$.

4.2 Describing the Semantic Rules

Once we agree on the structure of the computation states, we can formalize the language's runtime behavior. For this purpose we propose using the *structural style* of operational semantics [14,16]. In this style the semantics will be described by a set of *semantic rules* that will resemble the rules of formal *calculi* in logic. These rules characterize the transitions between computation states. With $\sigma \rightarrow \sigma'$ we will denote the transition from the state σ to the state σ'. In these rules we also can use additional constraints expressed with logic and set-theoretic notations. For this purpose, we will use $\vdash \Phi$ to denote a logical / set-theoretical formula Φ that must be true. At the top of the rules we put the applicability conditions, using such logical notations, while at the bottom we describe the resulting transitions. In addition, we encourage the use of a *small-step* style of specifying the semantics [14]. This style concentrates on characterizing transitions between consecutive states, and will ease the move to a subsequent implementation.

In Fig. 4 we show the semantic rules for our example. Thus, these rules formally state the informal behavior outlined in section 2. In these rules stream manipulation is abstracted using the *in* and the *out* operations, whose behavior is left unspecified. The rules themselves read as follows:

- The *starting* rule models the execution's init. For this purpose, the starting speech is queried in the tutorial. Besides, the first speech is picked from such a tutorial and it is set as the control term. Also notice that the context with the answers' counters is initialized to the empty set (i.e. as indicated above, the counter for every answer will be 1). Finally, a suitable command announcing the beginning of the execution is written in the *controller2view* stream.

- The *speaking* rule models how the system proffers a speech which is followed by another speech: a command to proffer the speech is written in the *controller2view* stream, and the next speech is set as the control term.
- The *asking* rule models the proffering of a speech when it is followed by a question point. This time the system announces the question asked with the speech to be proffered.
- The *evaluating* rule models what happens at a question point. The learner's answer is read from the *view2controller* stream, a suitable feedback is picked from the tutorial, and its associated speech is retrieved and set as the control term. Besides, the counter associated with the answer is incremented.
- Finally, the *ending* rule models how the system finishes the execution. It holds when there is not such a thing as a following question or speech in the learning flow. Hence the final speech is proffered, and a command announcing the end is written in the resulting output stream.

$$\frac{\vdash \text{speech}(s,ns) \in T}{\langle s,T,In,Out \rangle \to \langle \text{speech}(s,ns),T,\varnothing,In,\text{out}(Out,\text{do-start}) \rangle} \quad \textbf{starting}$$

$$\frac{\vdash \text{speech}(ns,nns) \in T}{\langle \text{speech}(s,ns),T,\rho,In,Out \rangle \to} \quad \textbf{speaking}$$
$$\langle \text{speech}(ns,nns),T,\rho,In,\text{out}(Out,\text{do-speech}(s)) \rangle$$

$$\frac{\vdash \text{question}(q) \in T}{\langle \text{speech}(s,q),T,\rho,In,Out \rangle \to \langle \text{question}(q),T,\rho,In,\text{out}(Out,\text{do-ask}(s,q)) \rangle} \quad \textbf{asking}$$

$$\frac{\vdash \text{feedback}(q,a,\rho_a,s) \in T \;;; \; \vdash \text{speech}(s,n) \in T \;;; \vdash \text{in}(In) = \langle \text{answered}(a),In' \rangle}{\langle \text{question}(q),T,\rho,In,Out \rangle \to} \quad \textbf{evaluating}$$
$$\langle \text{speech}(s,n),T,\rho_a := \rho_a + 1,In',Out \rangle$$

$$\frac{\vdash \text{speech}(n,\_) \notin T \;;; \; \vdash \text{question}(n) \notin T}{\langle \text{speech}(s,n),T,\rho,\_,Out \rangle \to \langle \rho,\text{out}(\text{out}(Out,\text{do-speech}(s)),\text{do-end}) \rangle} \quad \textbf{ending}$$

Fig. 4. Semantic rules for the <e-Tutor> language

```
transition([S,In,Out]->[speech(S,Ns),[],In,NOut]) :-
    out(Out,do_start,NOut),
    speech(S,Ns).

transition([speech(S,Ns),Cs,In,Out]->
            [speech(Ns,NNs),Cs,In,NOut]) :-
    speech(Ns,NNs),
    out(Out,do_speech(S),NOut).

transition([speech(S,Q),Cs,In,Out]->
            [question(Q),Cs,In,NOut]) :-
    question(Q),
    out(Out,do_ask(S,Q),NOut).
    ...
```

Fig. 5. Encoding of the *starting*, *speaking* and *asking* rules in a Prolog prototype for the <e-Tutor> language

We have realized how the effort employed in this kind of specifications pays out, since these specifications are very valuable in anticipating the more obscure aspects of the application's dynamic behavior without being obfuscated by technological and/or implementation details. Indeed, based on these specifications it is possible to perform rapid prototyping of the applications using, for instance, approaches similar to those described in [6]. As an example, in Fig. 5 we show a fragment of a Prolog prototype for the semantics of Fig. 4 (see [20] for more details). Finally, the formal flavor of the specifications provides the opportunity to apply optimizations and refinements in very early stages of the development process.

5 Implementation

In this section we examine how to organize the final applications from their designs in the terms stated in this paper. While the particular implementation strategies depend on the particular technologies and platforms chosen, we can still abstract some general implementation guidelines that can be useful in most of the cases. As indicated above, the resulting applications are amenable to being architected following the MVC pattern. Semantic rules in the language's operational semantics are useful in order to structure the application's controller. The language's structural characterization is in turn useful to structure the application's model. Finally, the structure of the different streams involved in the semantics is useful to identify the basic presentation commands, user actions and updating operations.

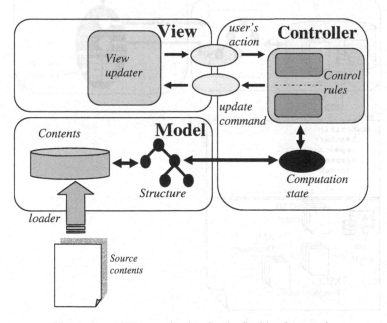

Fig. 6. A possible organization for the final implementations

In Fig. 6 we sketch the resulting organization. Notice how the computation state is configured as a global structure that in turn makes reference to information elements in the model (the implementation counterparts to the ground facts used to control the language's runtime behavior in the operational semantics). Also notice how the stream-based communication between the controller and the view is refined using call-back mechanisms. For this purpose, the controller is activated as response to the user's events. As a consequence, the view is updated. This updating is centralized using a *view updater* component. Communication itself is carried out using appropriate *user's actions* and *update commands*, which are transferred between the controller and the view. Finally, also notice how contents are encapsulated in the model. The updating of these contents is performed by invoking the appropriate operations on the model's structure, which in turn will act on the actual contents. Also notice that this structure can be referenced in the user's actions and in the update commands, therefore making the relevant parts of the model accessible for the view. Finally, notice how a *loader* is explicitly identified. It lets us load bodies of author-oriented contents in the application's model.

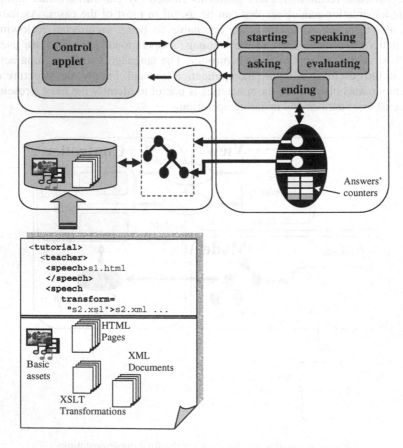

Fig. 7. High-level organization of the web-based version of <e-Tutor>

These contents will be structured according to a suitable binding of the application DSL. In our experiences we have performed such bindings in terms of appropriate descriptive markup DSLs, letting authors provide the contents as documents structured according to such languages [17].

The structure of the web-based version of <e-Tutor> is sketched in Fig. 7. The controller is organized in terms of the semantic rules sketched in the previous section. Since communication with the view is managed in terms of an observer-observable base, the streams are dropped from the computation state. This state maintains a reference to the overall model's structure, another reference to the current control term, and a table with the answers' counters.

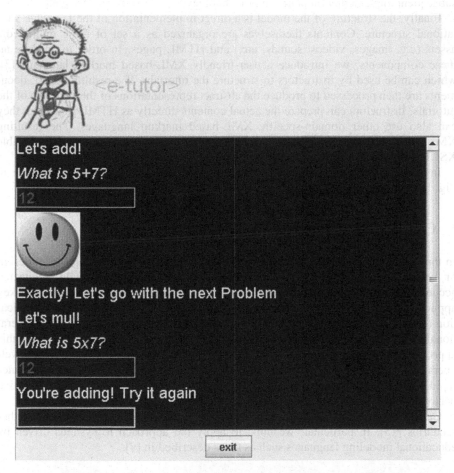

Fig. 8. Snapshot for a run of the simple tutorial of Figure 1 in <e-Tutor>

We use a java applet to implement the *view updater*. Indeed, by inspecting the operational semantics we can discover the proactive nature of the controller in a very early stage of the development process. It means that once the controller has read a user's action, it can communicate to the view several update commands, since the tutoring system can proffer several speeches before asking a new question. Since this behavior is not directly supported in HTTP, we need an active component on the client side (in this case, the control applet) taking care of it. Indeed, this type of internet-rich applications is very common in web-based learning, where similar solutions have also been adopted (e.g. the runtime in the SCORM – Shareable Content Object Reference Model – specification [1]) and the rigorous design of the application can help to anticipate it. Currently we are re-factoring this implementation in terms of AJAX technology [15]. Regardless of the migration of the controller aspect to the client side, the implementation is being substantially facilitated by the earlier effort made in the formal design, which has been shown to be pretty independent of the subsequent implementation platform or technology.

Finally, the structure of the model is a direct implementation of the language's relational structure. Contents themselves are organized as a set of basic multimedia assets (e.g. images, videos, sounds, etc.) and HTML pages. In order to produce all these components, we introduce a user-friendly XML-based markup language [3], which can be used by instructors to structure the tutorials. The resulting XML documents are then processed to produce the abstract representations of the structure of the tutorials. Instructors can prepare the actual contents directly as HTML pages, but they can also use other domain-specific XML-based markup languages. The resulting XML documents can be transformed into final HTML presentations using suitable XSLT transformations [4].

In Fig. 8 we show a snapshot of the tutorial corresponding to the example in Fig. 1.

6 Conclusions and Future Work

In this paper we have presented a language-driven approach to the high-level design of web-based learning applications. The resulting applications are easily architected according to the MVC pattern. The approach is focused on characterizing the key application aspects with a language specifically designed for such a kind of application (i.e. a DSL). Then the interactive behavior is described with appropriate operational semantics for this language. As it has been tested in several developments, this approach promotes an innovative way of collaboration between instructors and developers during the design and development of E-Learning applications. It also facilitates rapid prototyping, as well as the discovering of relevant features of the interactive behavior of the final applications in very early stages of the development.

Currently we are systematizing the approach and further testing it in many other scenarios [13]. In particular, we hope to apply the approach to systems driven by educational modeling languages such as those described in [9].

Acknowledgements

The Spanish Committee of Education and Science (Projects TIN2004-08367-C02-02 and TIN2005-08788-C04-01) and the Regional Government / Complutense University of Madrid (research group 910494) have partially supported this work.

References

1. Advanced Distributed Learning - Shareable Content Object Reference Model (ADL-SCORM), Faulkner Information Services (2003)
2. Bork, A.: Personal Computers for Education. Harper & Rows, New York (1985)
3. Bray, T., et al. (eds.): Extensible Markup Language (XML) 1.0 (Second Edition). W3C Recommendation (2000)
4. Clark, J. (ed.): XSL Transformations (XSLT) Version 1.0. W3C Recommendation (1999)
5. Coombs, J.H., Renear, A.H., DeRose, S.J.: Markup Systems and the Future of Scholarly Text Processing. Communications of the ACM 30(11), 933–947 (1987)
6. Clément, D., et al.: Natural Semantics on the Computer. Tech. Rep. 416. INRIA (1985)
7. Friedman, D., Wand, M., Hayes, C.T.: Essentials of Programming Languages, 2nd edn. MIT Press, Cambridge (2001)
8. Ibrahim, B.: Software Engineering Techniques for CAL. Education & Computers 5, 215–222 (1989)
9. Koper, R., Tatersall, C. (eds.): Learning Design: A Handbook on Modeling and Delivering Networked Education and Training. Springer, Heidelberg (2005)
10. Krasner, G.E., Pope, T.S.: A Description of the Model-View-Controller User Interface Paradigm in the Smalltalk 80 System. Journal of Object Oriented Programming 1(3), 26–49 (1988)
11. Martínez-Ortíz, I., Moreno-Ger, P., Sierra, J.L., Fernández-Manjón, B.: <e-QTI>: A Reusable Assessment Engine. In: Liu, W., Li, Q., Lau, R.W.H. (eds.) ICWL 2006. LNCS, vol. 4181, pp. 134–145. Springer, Heidelberg (2006)
12. Mauw, S., Wiersma, W.T., Willemse, T.A.C.: Language-driven System Design. International Journal of Software Engineering and Knowledge Engineering 14(6), 625–664 (2004)
13. Moreno-Ger, P., Sierra, J.L., Martínez-Ortiz, I., Fernández-Manjón, B.: A Documental Approach to Adventure Game Development. Science of Computer Programming 67(1), 3–31 (2007)
14. Mosses, P.D.: Formal Semantics of Programming Languages: An Overview. Electronic Notes in Theoretical Computer Science 148(1), 41–73 (2006)
15. Paulson, L.D.: Building Rich Web Applications with AJAX. IEEE Computer 38(10), 14–17 (2005)
16. Plotkin, G.D.: An Structural Approach to Operational Semantics. Technical Report DAIMI FN-19. Computer Science Dept. Aarhus University (1981)
17. Sierra, J.L., Fernández-Valmayor, A., Fernández-Manjón, B.: A Document-Oriented Paradigm for the Construction of Content-Intensive Applications. Computer Journal 49(5), 562–584 (2006)
18. Sierra, J.L., et al.: From Research Resources to Virtual Objects: Process model and Virtualization Experiences. Journal of Educational Technology & Society 9(3), 56–68 (2006)
19. Sierra, J.L., et al.: A Highly Modular and Extensible Architecture for an Integrated IMS based Authoring System: The <e Aula> Experience. Software-Practice & Experience 37(4), 441–461 (2007)
20. Sierra, J.L., Fernández-Valmayor, A., Fernández-Manjón, B.: How to Prototype an Educational Modeling Language. In: Proc. of the IX International Simposium on Computers in Education SIIE 2007, November 14–16, 2007, Porto, Portugal (2007)
21. Sierra, J.L., Moreno Ger, P., Martínez Ortiz, I., López Moratalla, J., Fernández-Manjón, B.: Building Learning Management Systems Using IMS Standards: Architecture of a Manifest Driven Approach. In: Lau, R.W.H., Li, Q., Cheung, R., Liu, W. (eds.) ICWL 2005. LNCS, vol. 3583, pp. 144–156. Springer, Heidelberg (2005)
22. Sleeman, D., Brown, J.S. (eds.): Intelligent Tutoring Systems. Academic Press, London (1982)
23. XTutor web site. http://icampus.mit.edu/xtutor (last visited June 8, 2007)

System Control Through the Internet and a Remote Access Laboratory Implementation

Barış Doğan[1] and Hasan Erdal[2]

[1] (M.Sc.) Research Assistant in Department of Mechatronics Education
[2] (Phd.) Assistant Professor in Department of Computer and Control Education,
University of Marmara, Göztepe Campus 34722, Kadıköy, İstanbul, Turkey
{baris, herdal}@marmara.edu.tr

Abstract. Nowadays, remote access laboratories are getting popular in technical education. This paper illustrates a Remotely Access Control Laboratory (RACL) implementation in which students can make control experiments on a real plant through the Internet. Process Level Trainer is used as a plant, which is a practice environment for the fundamentals of the process control education. A Data Acquisition Card (DAQ Card) installed computer, as a control unit, is connected to the plant. A pan-tilt movable, CCD, IP Camera is preferred to transmit the look of the plant during the experiment. In order to control the plant through the Internet, special control software is developed using Delphi programming language and web pages including PHP scripts are designed. A Flash object is also developed for displaying the result graphics of experiments online. A user, after login from any computer that has an Internet connection, can easily study basic control algorithms, such as Open Loop, On-Off, PID with changing their parameters as well.

Keywords: Web Based Control, Remote Laboratory, Remote Access Laboratory, Remote Access Control Laboratory.

1 Introduction

The history of remote education goes back many years. The first examples of remote education had been by post and as the developing technology; Radio/TV Broadcasts were used for sending education environment to the users. Open education can be an example for this kind of education. Nowadays, the Internet is a very common communication platform offering an interactive media to the millions of people. Because of its time and place independent properties, the Internet is widely used for remote education with different implementations like Virtual and Remote Laboratories.

Although both remote education types use the Internet as a medium, there are great differences between them and the real laboratories.[1] In [2], a coupled tank apparatus was used as a plant, a DAQ card was used for data-acquisition, LabView and Java were preferred to create the software part of the remote laboratory. The view of the experiment was sent to the user by a camera and a multimedia server. In [3], a remote plant in the campus was controlled via a DSP control unit; name ARCS, by 22 computers in the computer lab. One person acts as an instructor while the others only

H. Leung et al. (Eds.): ICWL 2007, LNCS 4823, pp. 532–541, 2008.
© Springer-Verlag Berlin Heidelberg 2008

watch the experiment. MATLAB and Simulink were used to create the control software and user interfaces. The view of the experiment was sent to the user by an IP Camera. In [4], there are seven different experiments; which distinguishes this study from the others explained before. A user can even select one of the experiments, change the control algorithm, define the parameters and watch the experiment. MATLAB was used to create the control software and for this reason, user can load his own control algorithm created with using Simulink environment as well. Java was chosen to design remote user interfaces. In [5], an inverted pendulum is used to demonstrate a Java/Matlab based remote control system laboratory. Experiment graphical interface is pure Java applet and control software is designed by using Matlab. Client-server connection is established with TCP sockets. A camera and a hardware video server are used for transmitting the experiment environment. In [6], a dc motor control module is used as an example to illustrate their design. Their system composed of a DAQ installed computer, web server, video server and an application created by using LabView. They focus more on the system security, database technique enhancement and stability of operating system. In [7], they allow multiple remote users control multiple robots at the same time with minimum number of PCs. Visual C++ is used to create the control software and remote user interfaces are designed with Java in order to have full platform independence. In [8], there are useful case studies about web based control applications which may be helpful to understand the developments in energy information and control systems.

Most of the remote access laboratory implementations utilize MATLAB and Lab-View web server. Although these particular software really reduce the effort for creating the platform of remote laboratories, we preferred to develop a control software by using a common structured programming language. While establishing the Remotely Access Control Laboratory (RACL), our purpose is to create our own strategy for controlling systems through the Internet. [9] Programming the data acquisition and control system can be accomplished in the following three ways: hardware-level programming, driver-level programming and package level programming. [10][11] Our control software is an example of driver-level programming.

2 Hardware Infrastructure

Hardware of the RACL consists of four main components which are plant, server computer, data acquisition card (DAQ) and IP Camera. Fig.1 shows the general hardware component scheme of the RACL.

2.1 Plant (RT512)

While designing the RACL, we prefer to use a ready-made plant, which we made modifications on, as an experiment environment rather than building a new plant. Our purpose is to minimize possible errors derived by the plant architecture. A plant, RT512, which is present at the Robotic Laboratory in the Technical Education Faculty of University of Marmara, and manufactured by GUNT Company [12], is used in the RACL in order to let the users make remote experiments.

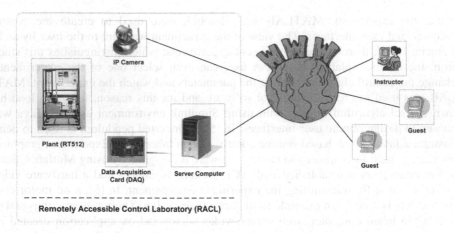

Fig. 1. The general hardware component scheme of the RACL

RT512 Process Level Trainer is a closed loop control system that offers an experiment environment for the fundamentals of control technology education. Level control is based on this trainer as an example. The main purpose of the experiment is to keep the water level at a desired point.

2.2 Server Computer

The heart of the RACL is the server computer. All necessary applications for the RACL run on this computer. It is the main controller of the RACL and responsible for managing the plant, serving the web pages and storing the data that were obtained during experiments.

The operating system on this server computer is Windows XP Professional Edition with Service Pack 2 upgrade installed. Since the server computer is located in our campus network, the computer is under the protection of campus security rules against attacks originated from the Internet and virus treatments.

2.3 Data Acquisition Card (DAQ)

In computer based control applications, data acquisition is an essential task. Units in plants generally use electrical signals to communicate with each other, while computers understand only digital zeros and ones. The conversion between these electrical signals and digital data is generally performed by using data acquisition cards. In the RACL, water level value has to be read from the plant and after calculating the output, the generated control signal has to be sent to the electro-pneumatic valve. For these reasons, a DAQ PCI-1711, manufactured by Advantech Company [13], is installed into a PCI slot of the server computer.

2.4 IP Camera

In remotely access laboratory implementations, users interact with real systems. In order to give the user feeling of a real laboratory, the view of the experiment environment is sent to the user interface simultaneously. We use IP Camera manufactured by Dlink Company [14], DCS-5300G, for transferring the view of the experiment environment.

IP Cameras differ from usual web cameras as they are sending the media stream directly to the client via their own network connections. They do not need any multimedia stream server or video server applications like Real Server or Windows Media Encoder to broadcast the camera view.

3   Plant and Server Connection

Before using RT512 in the RACL, first of all, we made some modifications on the hardware in order to make the plant be fully computer manageable. Then, it would be possible to control the plant through the Internet.

An electronic circuit was designed and installed into the plant. This circuit provides the signal coherence between the plant and the DAQ and it enables the water pump control too. The general signalization and software scheme between the plant and the server computer is in Fig.2.

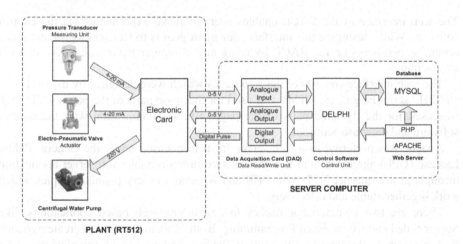

Fig. 2. The general signalization and software scheme

4   Software Architecture

The software part of the RACL can be divided into two main groups. One is the control software which is running on the server computer, controlling the plant by managing the data acquisition process and enabling the remote access to the RACL. The other one is the web pages which enable the user to login the RACL, make remote experiments through the Internet and watch the view of the experiment. Applications like database, web server, adobe flash object can be put into the last group.

4.1 Control Software

Control Software is responsible for starting/stopping the experiment, data acquisition, managing the plant by using desired control algorithm/parameters and recording experiment data to the database or a text file.

In the RACL, no popular proprietary commercial software, like MATLAB and LabView, is used for designing the control software. Instead, we have preferred to create our remote control software platform. Borland Delphi programming language was preferred to design the control software because it has stable high performance working properties and it can easily reach the hardware layer.

The control software enables the user to make experiments on RT512 for the education of basic control algorithms. Manuel Control (Open Loop), On-Off Control and PID Control are the control algorithms supported by the RACL. A user can make experiments with changing the control algorithm and parameters, see the online experiment graphics through the Internet. Also, user can save the experiment results on his computer as a csv[1] text file.

4.2 Web Interface

The web interface of the RACL enables users to make experiments via the control software. While designing this interface, our main goal is to let users log in and make remote experiments on the RACL by using any computer having an active Internet connection.

The web interface consists of the web pages which were designed by using HTML and PHP script languages. HTML was used for the static parts of the pages while PHP was used for the dynamic parts of the pages like communication with the control software and database activities.

Apache was preferred as a web server for it is licensed under the General Public License (GPL) agreement and it is the most common reliable web server application throughout the Internet [15]. Also PHP and Apache are very popular couples which work together stable and effectively.

There are two common approaches in developing web based applications, like Server Sided and Client Sided Programming. Both of them are used to create dynamic Web pages that offer interactivity between the user and connected web platform. As it is clear form their names, server-sided scripts run, as a module or service in coordination with web server software, in the server computer. Java Server Pages (JSP), Active Server Pages (ASP) and Hypertext Pre-processor (PHP) are the examples for server sided scripts. These scripts are invisible to the client and executed before sending the web pages to the clients web browser. Client sided scripts like Java Scripts, Activex, Flash Action Scripts operate on the client computer and script codes are visible to the client.

In the RACL, both server sided and client sided scripts are used together for drawing online web based graphics which represent the experiment values. In the server side, a PHP script is used for reading the values from database and a Flash Object draws online graphics. Because these graphics read values that has already been written to the

---

[1] csv is a text file and the short name of comma-separated values.

database by the control software, a negligible delay occurs between the real experiment values and the shown values in graphics.

For showing the view of the experiment environment on the web interface, an ActiveX object was used which is a part of the IP Camera.

Fig.3 represents the software connection scheme between the client and the RACL.

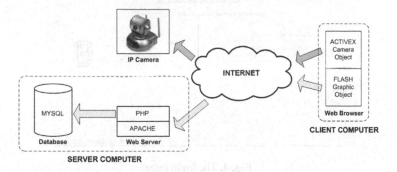

Fig. 3. The general software connection scheme

4.3 Database

Database is one of the important units in web based applications where user interaction occurs. In the RACL, a database was used for storing user data and experiment values. While considering the database, our main goal is to select the best suitable database for the software we use in the RACL. As we are using Apache Web Server and PHP for remote access, we prefer to use MySQL open source relational-database, which is freely distributed under the GPL license and a good companion with Apache and PHP. Also Delphi can easily work with MySQL by adding just a few extra dll functions into the software.

MySQL is a relational database and stores data into tables. Tables are consist of fields, where similar data are grouped together, and rows representing each record. MySQL is a structured query language (SQL) database which allows users to create and execute complex questions. MySQL has low connection overhead so it operates very fast and efficiently.

5   An Example Experiment on Remote Access Laboratory

The RACL offers a physically independent experiment environment to the users and it can be reached from any computer just having an Internet connection and web browser software[2] installed. When connected to the RACL, the first page that welcomes the users is the login page. Fig.4 shows the login page. This page can be divided into two parts. On the left side, there are links to the relevant web pages that are introducing the Faculty, the Department, the RACL and how it works. On the

---

[2] Microsoft Internet Explorer 6.0 + SP2 or higher version is needed.

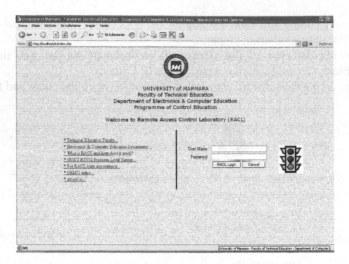

Fig. 4. The login page

right side, there are fields for username and password which are needed for the RACL log-in. The "traffic light" shows the status of the RACL, whether it is busy or not.

After the log-in, the RACL introduces the experiment page through which users can make control experiments by changing the control algorithm and parameters as well. Every user has time periods for making experiments in the RACL and the re-maining time is viewed to the users on the experiment page. When the time expires, users are directed to the log-out page, where their opinions on the RACL are asked. As it is shown in Fig.5, the experiment page is divided into three frames.

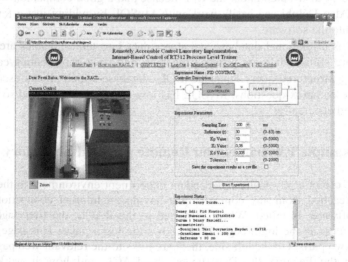

Fig. 5. The experiment page

On the top frame, there are navigation links to different pages through the RACL. Users can change the control algorithm by using these links. On the left frame, the activex component shows the appearance of the experiment environment via the IP Camera, adjacent to the plant. Also the remaining appointment time is shown at the bottom of this frame. The right frame of the page changes by the selected control algorithm for each algorithm needs different parameters. Users can define the parameters, start / stop the experiments, view the online experiment graphics and save the experiment results into their computer by using the objects in the page. There are two graphics on the experiment page; one is showing the water level and the reference values together while the other graphic shows only the output signal of the controller. Fig.6 shows an example of experiment results page.

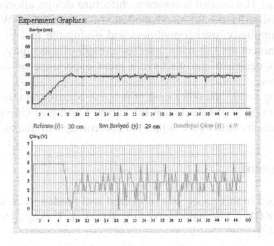

Fig. 6. The experiment graphics

6 Evaluation

So far, the RACL has worked only in the university Intranet because of our campus network security restrictions. For this reason, the RACL has been used during "Automatic Control" and "Digital Control" lessons as an education material. During these lessons in the classroom, it is very useful to demonstrate students the response of the plant, by the changing control algorithm and control parameters. This really reduces the difficulty of understanding the control theory for the students and the effort for teaching these subjects. We can see the good effects of this practical environment form the examination results of the students when compared with previous ones.

In the near future, students will be able to reach the RACL from outside the university. This will let them use the RACL as a complimentary laboratory work of their study. When they meet the real plant in the lab, they will have less difficulty on understanding the plant's behaviors and reactions, also which will shorten their preparation time at the lab.

7 Conclusion

This paper illustrates a web-based remotely accessible control laboratory implementation which is an example of practical E-Learning platforms and tools. There are many techniques in online system control through the Internet and remote laboratory applications. When the example studies related to this subject were examined, generally, MATLAB and LabView were used as the base of control software. This really reduces the required effort for developing the control software and minimizes possible errors that may derived by the software architecture.

In this study, we have preferred to create our own control software by using a common programming language, which works stable, effective and can easily reach the hardware layer. The control software architecture design allows adding new control algorithms easily, for the future developments of the RACL. While designing the user interfaces, simplicity, user-friendliness and giving the feel of presence in a real laboratory environment are our main aim. As a result of this study, a remotely accessible laboratory is designed and we have a great experience on controlling systems through the Internet.

We are planning to add the other kind of process control trainers that are present at the Robotic Laboratory in the Technical Education Faculty of University of Marmara, into this study while increasing the supported control algorithms, as a future work.

Acknowledgement

The study described in this paper was supported and funded by Scientific Researches Committee (BAPKO) of Marmara University, Istanbul, Turkey. [Project Serial: FEN-YLS–201205–0242].

References

1. Nedic, Z., Machotka, J., Nafalski, A.: Remote Laboratories Versus Virtual and Real Laboratories. In: 33rd ASEE/IEEE Frontiers in Education Conference T3E-1 (2003)
2. Ko, C.C., Chen, B.M., Chen, J., Zhuang, Y., Tan, K.C.: Development of a Web-Based Laboratory for Control Experiments on a Coupled Tank Apparatus. IEEE Transactions on Education 44(1) (2001)
3. Miele, D.A., Potsaid, B., Wen, J.T.: An Internet-Based Remote Laboratory for Control Education. In: Proceedings of the American Control Conference, Arlington, VA (2001)
4. Casini, M., Prattichizzo, D., Vicino, A.: The Automatic Control Telelab: A User-Friendly Interface for Distance Learning. IEEE Transactions on Education 46 (2003)
5. Sánchez, J., Dormido, S., Pastor, R., Morilla, F.: A Java/Matlab-Based Environment for Remote Control System Laboratories: Illustrated Withan Inverted Pendulum. IEEE Transactions On Education 47(3) (2004)
6. Yeung, K., Huang, J.: Development of a remote-access laboratory: a dc motor control experiment. Computers in Industry 52, 305–311 (2003)
7. Sozbilir, C.O., Sabanovic, A., Goktug, G., Onat, A.: A Proposed Architecture for Remote Mechatronics Laboratory. IEEE, Los Alamitos (2002)

8. Capehart, B.L., Capehart, L.C.: Web Based Energy Information and Control Systems: Case Studies and Applications. The Fairmont Press (2005)
9. Doğan, B.: Web Based System Control and Development of Remote Access Laboratory. Institute of Pure and Applied Sciences, Msc Thesis in Computer and Control Education Dept., University of Marmara (2007)
10. Korkmaz, H., Can, B.: Real Time Thermal Expansion Measurement System and The Data Acquisition and Control Application Software – User Interface. In: IEEE International Symposium on Virtual Environments, Human - Computer Interfaces and Measurement System, Lugano, Switzerland (2003)
11. Total Solutions for PC-Based Industrial Automation, Solution Guide vol. 61, ADVAN-TECH Co.
12. GUNT RT512 Process Level Trainer, http://www.gunt.de/static/s3588_1.php?p1=&p2=&pN=
13. Advantech PCI 1711 DAQ, http://www.advantech.eu.com/products/Model_Detail.asp?model_id=1-23I1JT
14. DLink 5300G IP Camera, http://www.dlink.com/products/?sec=1&pid=342
15. Netcraft: Web Server Survey Archives, http://news.netcraft.com/archives/web_server_survey.html

Secure and Efficient Information Sharing in Multi-university E-Learning Environments

Hua Wang[1] and Qing Li[2]

[1] Department of Maths & Computing
University of Southern Queensland
Toowoomba QLD 4350 Australia
wang@usq.edu.au
[2] Department of Computer Science
City University of Hong Kong
Kowloon, Hong Kong, China
itqli@cityu.edu.hk

Abstract. Digital information sharing of multi-university environments usually occurs in broad, highly dynamic network-based environments, and formally accessing the resources in a secure manner poses a difficult and vital challenge. This paper aims to build a new rule-based framework to identify and address issues of sharing in multi-university environments through role-based access control management (*RBAC*). The framework includes a role-based group delegation granting model, group delegation revocation model, authorization granting and authorization revocation. Finally, the current proposal is compared with other related work.

Keywords: Information sharing, E-Learning, security.

1 Introduction

Delegation is recognised as vital in a secure distributed computing environment [1,2]. The most common delegation types include user-to-machine, user-to-user, and machine-to-machine delegation. They all have the same consequence, namely the propagation of access permission. Propagation of access rights in decentralized collaborative systems presents challenges for traditional access mechanisms because authorization decisions are made based on the identity of the resource requester. Unfortunately, access control based on identity may be ineffective when the requester is unknown to the resource owner [22]. Recently some distributed access control mechanisms have been proposed in distributed E-Learning environments [13,14,1,15]. For example, Lu [14] introduced a mediator-based architecture to build open multi-agent applications for E-Learning. An agent services description language was presented to enable services advertising and collaboration. The language provided flexible access management for developers in any suitably constrainted languages.

The National Institute of Standards and Technology developed a role-based access control (*RBAC*) prototype [5] and published a formal model [7]. In *RBAC*

H. Leung et al. (Eds.): ICWL 2007, LNCS 4823, pp. 542–553, 2008.

models, permissions are associated with roles, users are assigned to appropriate roles, and users acquire permissions through roles. Users can be easily reassigned from one role to another. Roles can be granted additional permissions and permissions can be easily revoked from roles as needed. Therefore, *RBAC* provides a means for empowering individual users through role-based delegation in distributed multi-university collaboration environments. The importance of delegation in E-Learning has been recognized for a long time [18,3], but the concept has not been supported in *RBAC* models [6,8]. This paper provides a bridge of the gap between delegation techniques and *RBAC* models in distributed E-Learning environments.

The remainder of this paper is organized as follows: Section 2 presents the related work associated with delegation models and *RBAC*. As a result of this section, we find that both group-based delegation within *RBAC* and its implementation with *XML* have not been presented and analysed in the literature. Section 3 proposes a delegation framework which includes the structures of role-based delegation, role-based group delegation and revocation models. Section 4 provides delegation authorizations. Granting authorization with pre-requisite conditions and revocation authorization are discussed in this section. Definitions of *Can_delegate*, *Can_revoke*, *role range* are introduced. Section 5 compares the work in this paper to related previous work. Finally, the conclusion of the paper is in Section 6.

2   Motivation

Delegation is an important feature in collaborative E-Learning applications. For example, imagine that the University of Southern Queensland (USQ) is developing partnerships between the Victoria University of Technology (VUT) and La trobe University (LaU) to address possible problems. The three universities are able to prevent illegal resource access and unavailable study materials if they efficiently collaborate with the people in other universities. The problem-oriented collaboration system (*POCS*) is proposed to improve the service to students as a part of the multi-university's ongoing community efforts including identifying potential problems and resolving them before they become significant. With efficient delegation, staff members respond quickly to urgent messages and increase the time spent confronting problems.

The concept of delegation is not new in authorizations [4,24], role-based delegation has received attention only recently [23,25,26]. Zhang et al [25,26] proposed a rule-based framework for role-based delegation including the *RDM2000* model. The *RDM2000* model was based on *RBDM0* model which was a simple delegation model supporting only flat roles (i.e. no role hierarchy) and single step delegation. Furthermore, as a delegation model, it does not support group-based delegation. The model does not analyse how original role assignment changes impact on delegations or implement with XML-based language.

We have analysed these issues in the current paper and implement them with XML-based language. Jajodia et al. [11] proposed a logical language for the specification of authorizations. The language allows users to specify, together with the authorizations, the policy according to which access control decisions are to be made. Although the language supports multiple access control policies, it is not a role-oriented framework. It cannot specify authorizations in role hierarchies. In addition, their framework does not address delegation authorization. All these previous works were not successful in addressing the requirements of role-based delegation in E-Learning environments.

This paper focuses exclusively on a role-based delegation model which supports group-based delegation in multi-university E-Learning environments and its implementation with *XML* technology. We propose a delegation framework including delegation granting and revocation models, and group-based delegation. To provide sufficient functions with the framework, this paper analyses how changes to original role assignment impact upon delegation results. This kind of role-based group delegation and its implementation with *XML* have not been studied before.

3   The Role-Based Delegation and Revocation Framework

In this section we propose a role-based group delegation framework called *RBGDF* which supports role hierarchy and group delegation by introducing the delegation relation.

3.1   Role-Based Delegation Model

An important concept within *RBAC* is a session, which involves a mapping between a user and possibly many roles. For example, a user may establish a session by activating some subset of assigned roles. A session is always associated with a single user and each user may establish zero or more sessions. There may be hierarchies within roles. Senior roles are shown at the top of the hierarchies. Senior roles inherit permissions from junior roles. Let $x > y$ denote x is senior to y with obvious extension to $x \geq y$. Role hierarchies provide a powerful and convenient means to enforce the principle of least privilege since only required permissions to perform a task are assigned to the role.

Although the concept of a user can be extended to include intelligent autonomous agents, machines and even networks, for simplicity we limit a user to a human being in our model of multi-university collaborative system. Figure 1 shows the role hierarchy structure of *RBAC* in *POCS*. The following Table 1 expresses an example of user-role assignment in *POCS*. There are two sets of users associated with a role r: *Original users* are those users who are assigned to r; *Delegated users* are those users who are delegated to r.

The same user can be an original user of one role and a delegated user of another role. Also it is possible for a user to be both an original user and a delegated user of the same role. For example, if Christine delegates her role *HO1*

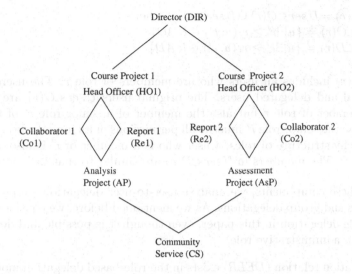

Fig. 1. Role hierarchy in *POCS*

Table 1. User-Role relationship

RoleName	UserName
DIR	Tony
HO1	Christine
HO2	Mike
Co1	Richard
Re1	John
CS	Ahn

to Richard, then Richard is both an original user (explicitly) and a delegated user (implicitly) of role *Co1* because the role *HO1* is senior to the role *Co1*. The original user assignment (*UAO*) is a many-to-many user assignment relation between original users and roles. The delegated user assignment (*UAD*) is also a many-to-many user assignment relation between delegated users and roles.

We have the following components for role-based delegation model in multi-university E-Learning environments:

U, R, P and S are sets of users (e.g. lecturers, professors), roles (e.g. course coordinator, course developer), permissions (e.g. read gradebook, update gradebook), and sessions, respectively.

1. $UAO \subseteq U \times R$ is a many-to-many original user to role assignment relation.
2. $UAD \subseteq U \times R$ is a many-to-many delegated user to role assignment relation.
3. $UA = UAO \cup UAD$.
4. Users: $R \Rightarrow 2^U$ is a function mapping of roles to sets of users.
   $Users(r) = \{u|(u,r) \in UA\}$ where UA is user-role assignment.

5. $Users(r) = Users\_O(r) \cup Users\_D(r)$ where
   $Users\_O(r) = \{u | \exists r' \geq r, (u, r') \in UAO\}$
   $Users\_D(r) = \{u | \exists r' \geq r, (u, r') \in UAD\}$

$Users(r)$ includes all users who are members of role r. The users may be original and delegated users. The original users $Users\_O(r)$ are not only the member of role r but also the member of a senior role r' of r. This is because the senior role r' inherits all permissions of its junior role r. With the hierarchy structure of roles, a user who is a member of r' is also a member of role r. The members in $Users\_D(r)$ are similar to that in $Users\_O(r)$.

With these components, we analyse user-to-user delegation supporting role hierarchies and group delegations. As we mentioned before, we consider only the regular role delegation in this paper, even though it is possible and desirable to delegate an administrative role.

A delegation relation ($DELR$) exists in the role-based delegation model which includes three elements: original user assignments UAO, delegated user assignment UAD, and constraints. The motivation behind this relation is to address the relationships among different components involved in a delegation. In a user-to-user delegation, there are five components: a delegating user, a delegating role, a delegated user, a delegated role, and associated constraints. For example, (*(Tony, DIR), (Christine, DIR), Friday)* means Tony acting in role *DIR* delegates role *DIR* to Christine on Friday. We assume each delegation is associated with zero or more constraints. The delegation relation supports partial delegation in a role hierarchies: a user who is authorized to delegate a role r can also delegate a role r' that is junior to r. For example, *((Tony, DIR), (Ahn, Rel), Friday)* means Tony acting in role *DIR* delegates a junior role *Rel* to Ahn on Friday. A delegation relation is one-to-many relationship on user assignments. It consists of original user delegation (*ORID*) and delegated user delegation (*DELD*). Figure 2 illustrates components and their relations in a role-based delegation model.

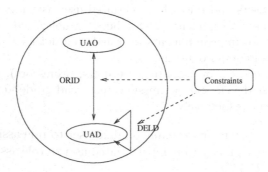

Fig. 2. Role-based delegation model

From the above discussions, the following components are formalized:

1. $DELR \subseteq UA \times UA \times Cons$ is one-to-many delegation relation. A delegation relation can be represented by
   $((u,r),(u',r'),Cons) \in DELR$, which means the delegating user u with role r delegated role r' to user u' when the constraint $Cons$ is satisfied. With the partial delegation requirement in our E-Learning environments, we emphasize that the user u can only delegate role r or its junior role r' to the user u'.
2. $ORID \subseteq UAO \times UAD \times Cons$ is an original user delegation relation.
3. $DELD \subseteq UAD \times UAD \times Cons$ is a delegated user delegation relation.
4. $DELR = ORID \cup DELD$.

The last equation shows that delegation relations consist of original and delegated user delegation relations. Based on the user - to user delegation, we now analyse group delegation in the remaining part of this section.

3.2   Role-Based Group Delegation and Revocation

The scope of our model is to address Role-based group delegation with role hierarchies and constraints that support multistep and partial delegations. There are two kinds of group delegation: user-group delegation and group-group delegation. We first discuss user-group delegations, which consist of original user-group and delegated user-group delegations. The new relation of user-group delegation is defined as delegation group relation ($DELUGR$) which includes: original user assignments UAO; delegated user assignments UAD; delegated group assignments GAD; and *constraints*. In a user-group delegation, there are five components: a delegating user (or a delegated user; a delegating role; a delegated group; a delegated role; and associated constraints. For example, $((Tony, DIR), (Project 1, DIR), 1:00pm-3:00pm Monday)$ means Tony acting in role DIR delegates role DIR to all people involved in Project 1 during 1:00pm–3:00pm on Monday. A user-group delegation relation is one-to-many relationship on user assignments. It consists of original user group delegation ($ORIUGD$) and delegated user group delegation ($DELUGD$). Figure 3 illustrates components and their relations in the role-based delegation model. Hence we have the following elements and functions for user-group delegation:

1. G is a set of users. GA is a set of group-role assignments.
2. $DELUGR \subseteq UA \times GA \times Cons$ is one-to-many delegation relation. A delegation relation can be represented by $((u,r),(G,r'),Cons) \in DELUGR$, which means the delegating user u with role r delegated role r' to group G if the constraint $Cons$ is satisfied. In multi-university E-Learning environments, $r' = r$ or r' is a junior role of role r.
3. $ORIUGD \subseteq UAO \times GAD \times Cons$ is a relation of an original user and a group with constraints.
4. $DELUGD \subseteq UAD \times GAD \times Cons$ is a relation of a delegated user and a group with constraints.
5. $DELUGR = ORIGD \cup DELGD$.

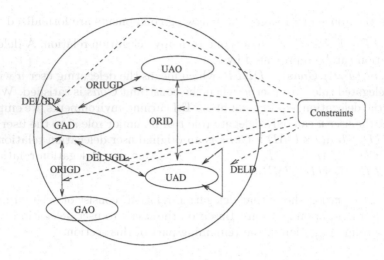

Fig. 3. Role-based group delegation model

Similar to user-group delegation, group-group delegation consists of original group assignment *GAO*, delegated group assignment *GAD* and constraints. As shown in Figure 3, there are the following elements and functions in group-group delegation:

1. *G* is a set of users. *GA* is a set of group-role assignments.
2. $DELGGR \subseteq GA \times GA \times Cons$ is one-to-many delegation relation. A delegation relation can be represented by $((G, r), (G', r'), Cons) \in DELUGR$, which means the delegating group *G* with role *r* delegated role *r'* to group *G'* if the constraint *Cons* is satisfied. Where $r' = r$ or r' is a junior role of role *r*.
3. $ORIGGD \subseteq GAO \times GAD \times Cons$ is a relation of a group and a group with constraints.
4. $DELGGD \subseteq GAD \times GAD \times Cons$ is a relation of a delegated group and a group with constraints.
5. $DELGGR = ORIGGD \cup DELGGD$.

Revocation is a significant function in role-based group delegations. For example, Tony delegated role *DIR* to Peter; if Peter moves to another company and does not work at the university, his delegated role *DIR* has to be revoked instantly. Several different semantics of user revocation exist [10]: global and local (propagation), strong and weak (dominance), deletion or negative (resilience), user grant-dependent and grant-independent revocation (grant-dependency). Propagation refers to the extent of the revocation to other delegated users. Dominance refers to the effect of a revocation on implicit/explicit role memberships of a user. Grant-dependency refers to the legitimacy of a user who can revoke a delegated role. For example, there are two types of revocation in dominance: weak and strong revocation [20]. A strong revocation of a user from a role requires that the user be removed not only from the explicit membership but also from the implicit memberships of the delegated role. A weak revocation only removes the user from the delegated role (explicit membership) and leaves other roles intact. Strong revocation is theoretically equivalent to a series of weak revocations. To perform strong revocation, the implied weak revocations are authorized based on revocation policies.

Based on the results of the structure with role-based group delegation, we discuss group delegation and revocation authorizations in the next section.

4   Delegation Authorization

We develop delegating and revocation models in this section. The notion of a *prerequisite condition*, *Can_delegate* and *Can_revoke* are key parts in group delegation process.

4.1   Authorization Models

The delegation authorization goal imposes restrictions on which roles can be delegated to whom. We partially adopt the notion of prerequisite condition from [21] to introduce delegation authorization in the delegation framework.

A *prerequisite condition* is an expression using Boolean operators '$\wedge$' and '$\vee$' on terms of the form r and $\bar{r}$ where r is a role and '$\wedge$' means "and", '$\vee$' means "or". A prerequisite condition is evaluated for a user u by interpreting r to be true if $(\exists r' \geq r), (u, r') \in UA$ and $\bar{r}$ to be true if $(\forall r' \geq r), (u, r') \notin UA$, where UA is a set of user-role assignments.   ◇

We say a group satisfies a prerequisite condition if all users in the group satisfy the prerequisite condition.

For a given set of roles R let CR denote all possible prerequisite conditions that can be formed using the roles in R, for example, $CR = r_1 \wedge r_2 \vee \bar{r}_3$. In some cases, we may need to define whether or not a user or a group can delegate a role to a group and for how many times, or up to the maximum delegation depth. Not every user can delegate a role to another user. The following relation provides what roles a user can delegate with prerequisite conditions.

Definition 1. *Can_delegate* is a relation of $R \times CR \times MDD$ where R, CR, MDD are sets of roles, prerequisite conditions, and maximum delegation depth, respectively.   ◇

The meaning of $(r, cr, mdd) \in$ *Can_delegate* is that a user who is a member of role r (or a role senior to r) can delegate role r (or a role junior to r) to any group whose current entitlements in roles satisfy the prerequisite condition cr without exceeding the maximum delegation depth mdd. To identify a role range within the role hierarchy, the closed and open interval notation is used [21].

Role-based group delegation is authorized by *Can_delegate*. Table 2 shows the *Can_delegate* relations with the prerequisite conditions in the *POCS* example. The meaning of *Can_delegate* $(DIR, [CS, HO1], 1)$ is that a member (a user or

Table 2. Can delegate relations in POCS

RoleName (R)	Prereq.Condition (CR)	Maximal Dele Depth (MDD)
DIR	[CS, HO1]	1
HO1	[AP, HO1)	2
AP	CS	1
CS	ϕ	2

group of role DIR can delegate role DIR and all roles in POCS (since all roles are junior to DIR) to a group whose current membership satisfies the prerequisite condition [CS, HO1] with one-step delegation. The second tuple authorizes that a user or a group of role HO1 can assign role HO1, and Col, Rel, AP and CS to a group in which users are members of either role AP, or Col, or Rel (since AP, Col and Rel are in the range of [AP, HO1)).

There are related subtleties that arise in RBGDF concerning the interaction between delegating and revocation of user-group delegation membership and the role hierarchy.

Definition 2. A role-based group delegation revocation is a relation $Can\_revoke \subseteq R \times 2^R$, where R is the set of roles.   ◇

The meaning of $Can\_revoke(x, Y)$ is that a member of role x (or a member of a role that is senior to x) can revoke the delegation relationship of a group from any role $y \in Y$, where Y defines the *range of revocation*. Table 3 gives the Can-revoke relation in Figure 1. The first tuple shows that a member of role HO1 can revoke a delegation relationship of a group from any role in [Col, CS].

Table 3. Example of can revoke relation

RoleName	Role Range
HO1	[Col, CS]
Rel	[Rel, AP]

We extend the definition of explicit and implicit members of a role from a user to a group, and then analyse weak revocation and strong revocation [21].

Definition 3. A group G is an explicit member of a role x if $(u, x) \in UA$, for all $u \in G$, and that G is an implicit member of role x if for some $x' > x, (u, x') \in UA$, for all $u \in G$.   ◇

Weak revocation only revokes explicit membership from a user and does not revoke implicit membership. On the other hand, strong revocation requires revocation of both explicit and implicit memberships. Strong revocation of $G's$ membership in x requires that G be removed not only from explicit membership in x, but also from explicit (implicit) membership in all roles senior to x. Strong revocation therefore has a cascading effect upwards in the role hierarchy. For example, suppose there are two delegations $((Tony, DIR), (Ahn, AP), Friday)$ and $((John, Re1), (Ahn, AP), Friday)$ and Tony wants to remove the membership of AP from Ahn on Friday. With weak revocation, the first delegation relationship is removed, but the second delegation has not yet removed. It means that Ahn is still a member of AP. With strong revocation two delegation relationships are removed and hence Ahn is not a member of AP.

5   Comparisons

The closest work to this paper is on an architecture for supporting vicarious learning in a distributed environment [17].

Neely et al [17] discussed that the existing software systems designed to support learning could not adequately provide for vicarious learning in a cross-institutional collaborative environment. The authors developed an architecture based on role-based access control, which provides the necessary security, robustness, flexibility, and explicit formulation of policy. They also planned to improve tool support for writing policies, in particular the development of the user interface and some validation procedures. However, a possible weakness of the system, without better tool support, is that users wishing to use a completely new policy need to be able to write XML files, or at least be able to customize existing ones. The paper did not analyse role-based delegation but instead discussed a case study in a distributed E-Learning environment of how to apply $RBAC$ on a particular project. The architecture could be viewed as an application of $RBAC$ in their work. However some important features and requirements in distributed E-Learning were not addressed such as group delegation, multistep delegation, partial delegation and delegation revocation. As such their work does not fully satisfy the requirements of multi-university E-Learning systems. By contrast, the work in this paper provides a rich variety of options that can deal with delegation authorization and revocation.

6   Conclusions

This paper has discussed a role-based delegation model for multi-university E-Learning environments and its implementation with XML. We have analysed a delegating framework including delegating authorization and revocation with constraints, and extended it to include group-based delegation. To provide a practical solution for role-based group delegations, we have analysed role hierarchies and the relationship of senior and junior roles. The theory in this paper was demonstrated by its implementation with XML. The work in this paper has significantly extended previous work in several aspects, for example group-based delegation, group delegation authorization with prerequisite conditions and revocation authorization.

References

1. Abadi, M., Burrows, M., Lampson, B., Plotkin, G.: A calculus for access control in distributed systems. ACM Trans. Program. Lang. Syst. 15(4), 706–734 (1993)
2. Barka, E., Sandhu, R.: Framework for role-based delegation models and some extensions. In: Proceedings of the 16 Annual Computer Security Applications Conference, New Orleans, pp. 168–177 (2000)
3. Edgar, R.W.: Security in E-Learning, vol. 16. Springer, Heidelberg (2005)
4. El-Khatib, K., Korba, L., Xu, Y., Yee, G.: Privacy and security in E-Learning. International Journal of Distance Education Technologies 1(4), 11–30 (2003)
5. Feinstein, H.L.: Final report: Nist small business innovative research (sbir) grant: role based access control: phase 1. technical report. In: SETA Corp. (1995)
6. Ferraiolo, D., Cugini, J., Kuhn, R.: Role-based access control (rbac): Features and motivations. In: The 11th Annual Computer Security Applications Conference, New Orleans, LA, pp. 241–248 (1995)
7. Ferraiolo, D.F., Kuhn, D.R.: Role based access control. In: 15th National Computer Security Conference, pp. 554–563 (1992)
8. Ferraiolo, D.F., Barkley, J.F., Kuhn, D.R.: Role-based access control model and reference implementation within a corporate intranet. In: TISSEC, vol. 2, pp. 34–64 (1999)
9. Frolik, J., Weller, T.M.: Wireless sensor systems: an approach for a multiuniversity design course. IEEE Transactions on Education 45(2), 135–141 (2002)
10. Hagstrom, A., Jajodia, S., Presicce, F., Wijesekera, D.: Revocations-a classification. In: Proceedings of 14th IEEE Computer Security Foundations Workshop, Nova Scotia, Canada, pp. 44–58 (2001)
11. Jajodia, S., Samarati, P., Subrahmanian, V., Bertino, E.: A unified framework for enforcing multiple access control policies. In: Proceedings of the 1997 ACM SIGMOD international conference on Management of data, pp. 474–485. ACM Press, New York (1997)
12. Li, Q., Atluri, V.: Concept-level access control for the semantic web. In: Proceedings of the 2003 ACM workshop on XML security, pp. 94–103. ACM Press, New York (2003)
13. Lowe, H., Wallis, A.M., Newman, J.: Role-based access control for vicarious learning. In: Proc. European Conference on E-Learning, pp. 43–50. Brunel University, Uxbridge (2002)
14. Lu, H.: Open multi-agent systems for collaborative web-based learning. International Journal of Distance Education Technologies 2(2), 36–45 (2004)
15. Mendling, J., Neumann, G., Pinterits, A., Simon, B., Wild, F.: Indirect revenue models for E-Learning at universities - the case of learn@wu. In: E-Learning Workshop Hannover - Einsatzkonzepte und Geschftsmodelle, Hannover, Germany (2004)
16. Michael, H.: XSLT Programmer's Reference. Wiley, Chichester (2001)
17. Neely, S., Lowe, H., Eyers, D., Bacon, J., Newman, J., Gong, X.: An architecture for supporting vicarious learning in a distributed environment. In: SAC 2004, pp. 963–970. ACM Press, New York (2004)
18. Seufert, S.: E-Learning business models: Framework and best practice examples. Idea Group, pp. 11–36 (2001)
19. Wang, H., Cao, J., Zhang, Y.: A consumer anonymity scalable payment scheme with role based access control. In: 2nd International Conference on Web Information Systems Engineering (WISE 2001), Kyoto, Japan, pp. 53–62 (2001)

20. Wang, H., Cao, J., Zhang, Y.: Formal authorization allocation approaches for role-based access control based on relational algebra operations. In: 3nd International Conference on Web Information Systems Engineering (WISE 2002), Singapore, pp. 301–312 (2002)
21. Wang, H., Cao, J., Zhang, Y.: Formal authorization allocation approaches for permission-role assignments using relational algebra operations. In: Proceedings of the 14th Australian Database Conference ADC 2003, Adelaide, Australia, pp. 125–133 (2003)
22. Wang, H., Cao, J., Zhang, Y.: An Electronic Payment Scheme and Its RBAC management. Concurrent Engineering: Research and Application 12(3), 247–275 (2004)
23. Wang, H., Sun, L., Zhang, Y., Cao, J.: Authorization Algorithms for the Mobility of User-Role Relationship. In: Proceedings of the 28th Australasian Computer Science Conference (ACSC 2005), Newcastle, Australia, pp. 167–176 (2005)
24. Wang, H., Zhang, Y., Cao, J., Varadharajan, V.: Achieving secure and flexible m-services through tickets. IEEE Transactions on Systems, Man, and Cybernetics, Part A, Special issue on M-Services, 697–708 (2003)
25. Zhang, L., Ahn, G., Chu, B.: A rule-based framework for role-based delegation. In: Proceedings of ACM Symposium on Access Control Models and Technologies, Chantilly, VA, pp. 153–162 (2001)
26. Zhang, L., Ahn, G., Chu, B.: A role-based delegation framework for healthcare information systems. In: Proceedings of ACM Symposium on Access Control Models and Technologies, Monterey, CA, pp. 125–134 (2002)

Protecting Disseminative Information in E-Learning

Lili Sun, Hua Wang, and Yan Li

Department of Maths & Computing
University of Southern Queensland
Toowoomba QLD 4350 Australia
{sun, wang, yanli}@usq.edu.au

Abstract. E-Learning organisers prefer to disseminate their message as widely as possible, and in the same time authorised people only can access some disseminative information. It becomes a challenge to protect the digital message from access such as reading and updating which has been disseminated out from the organisations.

The paper aims to substantially provide a foundation for developing appropriate security solutions for organizations' secure dissemination of digital information. An application-level secure architecture is developed based on the references on both of server-side and client-side. The architecture provides control and tracking capabilities for dissemination and usage of digital information while others provide only tracking capability. The outcomes of this paper can immediately apply to prevent unauthorized dissemination of digital content amongst agents of universities regardless of their intention or possession of the digital information and will contribute to higher security in E-Learning.

Keywords: Access control, dissemination, security.

1 Introduction

With recent advances in the Internet and information technologies, we find ourselves accustomed to the pervasive and convenient availability of digital information. The proliferation of inexpensive digital equipment and the Internet has expedited this availability to a scale imagined. E-Learning, as a product of current advanced technology, has bring great benefits to both of education organisers and students since students can access digital information provided by E-Learning organisers without space and time limits [3,7]. Such E-Learning strategies are required to satisfy the changes in a competitive and commercial industry market [19,13]. The new strategies will reshape the role of education and create enduring advantages for both students and universities. Digital information sent from the organisers to students or agents may not be further disseminated with some commercial reasons. Therefore unauthorized dissemination of digital content has emerged as one of the most problematic and challenging issues in information security on E-Learning. Digital information in E-Learning are divided into two types based on their purposes: Payment-Based Type (PBT) and Payment-Free

H. Leung et al. (Eds.): ICWL 2007, LNCS 4823, pp. 554–565, 2008.

Type (PFT). An example of PBT is the course information, students can access the study materials if they have paid the tuition fee; and the information of learning structure and major components are the example of PFT. In PBT, a payment is required in order to access digital information and security breaches of digital assets result directly in financial loss. In PFT, dissemination of digital information does not require payment, but as the PFT example mentioned, organisers could not happy to show competitors the learning plans and components which must be controlled nonetheless to satisfy confidentiality or other security requirements. Unlike the commercial distribution environment, there are situations in which payment function is not required and higher distribution security is the primary concern. In the intelligence community, for instance, digital information is often disseminated to organizations in various agents. For instance, the University of Southern Queensland (USQ) may wish to distribute a document in digital form to its education agents in such a manner that the received digital information is not revealed either intentionally or accidentally, to other malicious organizers. Similar situations can exist in the commercial sector. In recent business-to-business (B2B) e-commerce, it is common for a computer organization to distribute information digitally to its several partners. The challenge is to prevent further distribution of the digital information by the partners to others. For instance, IBM could disseminate technical descriptions in digital form to different suppliers who provide the specific parts of IBM computers. However, IBM would not like to disseminate the digital information amongst suppliers regardless of their intention or possession of the digital information. Digital content providers have put much effort into protecting digital information from unauthorized distribution [24]. However, no systematic study has been done for controlling digital information dissemination [2,4].

The most successful E-Learning models in the future will be hybrid E-Learning networks that are combinations of academic, professional and corporate content [18]. Human interaction administration, as a shortcoming of E-Learning, is a critical component of E-Learning market, especially in several organisers' collaborative environments. There are situations in which E-Learning strategies and plans are disclosed to other competitors due to insufficient protection management systems in E-Learning could not securely control the dissemination of the strategies and plans. It is still an open question how efficiently technical skills can be trained to protecting the disseminative information in distributed E-Learning environments [20,18].

The main objective of this paper is to develop a secure system for digital information dissemination by defining the security architectures that can provide control ability on the disseminated digital information. The security architectures should support tracking ability on the disseminated digital information. More specifically, proposed security architectures should make it difficult or useless for recipients to re-disseminate the received digital information if not authorized, regardless of their intention. In addition, they should make it difficult for new recipients to access the illegitimately re-disseminated digital information that they possess.

This paper presents authorization models which adopt usage control to manage access to digital information and secure architectures to protect against malicious dissemination. Traditional access control has analysed authorization decisions on a subject's access to target resources. "Obligations" are requirements that have to be followed by the subject for allowing access resources. "Conditions" are subject and object independent requirements that have to be passed. In today highly dynamic, distributed environment, obligations and conditions of new hosts are decision factors for the management of digital documents. Because of the complex environment of the Internet, users are required to obey obligations and satisfy conditions and ongoing control with different security policies. Usage control [16] has been recognized as the next generation access control to be efficient in security administration. Authorizations, obligations and conditions are used to build a secure architecture. The ongoing control provides dynamic access verification for digital documents.

The remainder of this paper is organized as follows: Section 2 presents the motivation of the paper including the background of disseminative digital information and section 3 introduces usage control which is a new and efficient access management approach. Three decision factors *Authorization, Obligation, Conditions* and Continuity properties *pre* and *ongoing* are introduced in this section. Section 4 shows our proposed authorization models for usage control. It includes *pre-Authorizations, ongoing-Authorizations, pre-Obligations, ongoing-Obligations, pre-Conditions* and *ongoing-Conditions*. Section 5 discusses how to build secure architectures for digital information by using reference monitors in details. Section 6 compares our work with the previous work on digital document security. The difference between this work from others is presented. Finally section 7 concludes the paper and outlines our future work.

2   Motivation

Many documents including study books and course specification are in digital form in E-Learning. These documents are usually disseminated to other organisations such as education agents and collaborative offices due to the efficient response, and they should be securely protected from accidental or malicious attacks, even the digital information has been delivered to other organisations. The digital information of PFT is different from that of PBT. In PBT situation, digital information leakage is acceptable and desired [2] while this may be rejected for PFT message. The objective of a PBT message is to distribute as many copies as possible for attracting payment of each copy. On the other hand, the dissemination of PFT information should be limited. The number of copies with PBT is larger than the copies of PFT. Therefore, the solutions on the information dissemination of PFT differ from the solutions on PBT.

Recently, dissemination of digital information has obtained increasing attentions from both commercial and non-commercial views. The disseminative digital information should be managed by a distributor who can limits recipients' access to the information. The recipients of the digital information need an access permission to the information, and additionally some restrictions such as the recipients are not able to modify and copy the information. There may be some undesirable leakage of digital information in E-Learning, a secure protocol is required to control the recipients access to a digital message but also to trace the further behaviours on the message such as who has re-disseminated and what occurred. For instance, the distance eduction office (*DEO*) at USQ sent out a new study plan to its collaborative organisers at HK with a confidential level. The *DEO* does not like the organisers resend out the new plan as well as any changes. Hence, several protection requirements are necessary:

1. Access control management. There are many access approaches in traditional access control, we should chose an efficient one for the E-Learning since most of students are not happy to buy a high cost equipments.
2. Trace what happened on the digital information. A application level secure architecture is needed for the track which should not have too much work on both of server side and client side.
3. Revocation schemes are an important feature of E-Learning systems. They take away the access permissions. There are different revoking schemes; among them are strong and weak revocations, cascading and noncascading revocations, as well as grant-dependent and grant-independent revocations [22].
4. Constraints are an important factor in E-Learning for laying out higher-level organizational policies [21]. They define whether or not the access permission or revocation process is valid.

To achieve these requirements, we introduce usage control first at the next section.

3   Usage Control

There are eight components: subjects, subject attributes, objects, object attributes, rights, authorizations, obligations, and conditions in usage control model [16] (see Figure 1). Subjects and objects are familiar concepts from the past thirty years of access control, and are used in their familiar sense in this paper. A right represents access of a subject to an object, such as read or write. The existence of the right is determined when the access is attempted by the subject. The usage decision functions indicated in Figure 1 make this determination based on subject attributes, object attributes, authorizations, obligations and conditions at the time of usage requests.

Subject and object attributes can be used during the access decision process. Examples of subject attributes are identities, group names, roles, memberships, credits, etc. Examples of object attributes are security labels, ownerships, classes, access control lists, etc. In an on-line shop a price could be an object attribute, for instance, the book Harry Potter is priced at $20 for a read right and priced at $1000 price for a resell right.

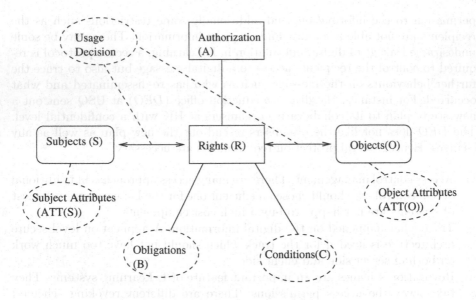

Fig. 1. Components of Model

Authorizations, obligations and conditions are decision factors used by decision functions to determine whether a subject should be allowed to access an object. Authorizations are based on subject and object attributes and the specific right. Authorization is usually required prior to the access, but in addition it is possible to require ongoing authorization during the access, e.g., a certificate revocation list (CRL) may be periodically checked while the access is in progress. An access is immediately revoked if the relevant certificate appears on the CRL. Authorizations may require updates on subject and object attributes. These updates can be either 'pre', 'ongoing', or 'post' that are called continuity properties shown in Figure 2.

For example, pre-paid mobile phone requires update of the subjects (users) clearance prior to access and also requires periodic updates of the remaining credits while usage is in progress, with possible termination in case of overuse. Fixed phone payment system requires updates after the usage has ended to

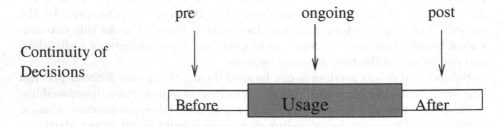

Fig. 2. Continuity Properties

calculate current usage time. Obligations are requirements that a subject must perform before (pre) or during (ongoing) access. An example of a pre-obligation is the requirement that a user must provide some contact and personal information before accessing IEEE digital library. The requirement that a user has to keep certain advertising windows open while he is accessing some service, is an example of an ongoing obligation. Subject and object attributes can be used to decide what kind of obligations are required for access approval.

Conditions are decision factors that depend on environmental and system-oriented requirements. For example, IEEE member can access full papers in the IEEE digital library. They can also include the security status of the system, such as low level, normal, high alert, etc.

As discussed above, continuity is another decision factor as shown in Figure 2. In traditional access control, authorization is assumed to be done before access is allowed (pre). However, it is quite reasonable to extend this for continuous enforcement by evaluating usage requirements throughout usages (ongoing).

4   Authorization Models

We now discuss authorization models for digital documents adopting usage control in this section. Based on three decision factors: authorizations, obligations, and conditions, we develop a family of core models for usage control. By core models, we mean that they focus on the enforcement process and do not include administrative issues. We assume there exists a usage request on an digital information object. Decision-making can be done either before (pre) or during (ongoing) exercise of the requested right. Decision-making after the usage has no influence on the decision of current usage. Based on these criteria, we have 6 possible cases spaces as a core model for usage control: pre-Authorizations, ongoing-Authorizations, pre-Obligations, ongoing-Obligations, pre-Conditions and ongoing-Conditions. Depending on the access requirements on digital documents in real world, it is possible to utilize more than one case.

For simplicity we consider only the pure cases consisting of *Authorizations*, *Obligations* or *Conditions* alone with *pre* or *ongoing* decisions only. We focus on developing comprehensive usage control models for digital documents. Next we present usage control models (UCM) with different pure cases.

A. UCM_{preA}:pre-Authorizations Model
In an UCM_{preA} model, the decision process is performed before access is allowed. The UCM_{preA} model has the following components:

1. *Sub, DiM, R, ATT(Sub), ATT(DiM)* and usage decision Boolean functions *preA* on *DiM*, where *Sub, DiM, R* represent Subject, digital message and Rights required on digital document (e.g. read, write) respectively. *ATT(Sub), ATT(DiM)* represent attributes of subjects, digital document respectively. *preA* is predicate about authorization functions. Fox example,

when users log in USQ website, $preA$ is a function on users' account and
password (subject attributes), digital documents and rights (read, write or
resell) that is used to check whether users can access the documents with
the right or not,

2. $allowed(Sub, DiM, r) \Rightarrow preA(ATT(Sub), ATT(DiM), r)$,
   where $A \Rightarrow B$ means B is a necessary condition for A. This predicate indicates that if subject Sub is allowed to access digital document DiM with
   right r then the indicated condition $preA$ must be true.

The UCM_{preA} model provides an authorization method on whether a subject
can access digital document or not. At this stage, digital information in E-
Learning environments is restricted.

B. UCM_{onA}:ongoing-Authorizations Model

An UCM_{onA} model is used to check ongoing authorizations during access
processes. The UCM_{onA} model has the following components:

1. $Sub, DiM, R, ATT(Sub), ATT(DiM)$ as before, and ongoing usage decision
   functions onA on DiM (digital document), onA is used to check whether
   Sub can continue to access or not.
2. $allowed(Sub, DiM, r) \Rightarrow true$,
   This is a prerequisite for ongoing authorization on DiM.
3. $stopped(Sub, DiM, r) \Leftarrow \neg onA(ATT(Sub), ATT(DiM), r)$,
   The access of subject Sub to DiM is terminated if the ongoing authorization
   onA is failed.

UCM_{onA} introduces the onA predicate instead of $preA$.
$allowed(Sub, DiM, r)$ is required to be $true$, otherwise ongoing authorization
should not be initiated. Ongoing authorization is active throughout the usage of
the requested right, and the onA predicate is repeatedly checked for continuation access. These checks are performed periodically based on time or event. The
model does not specify exactly how this should be done. When attributes are
changed and requirements are no longer satisfied, $stopped$ procedures are performed. We use $stopped(Sub, DiM, r)$ to indicate that rights r of subject Sub on
the digital object are revoked and the ongoing access terminated. For example,
suppose only one user can access the exam papers of a course simultaneously. If
another user requests access and passed the pre-authorization, the user with the
earlier time access is terminated. While this is a case of ongoing authorizations,
it is important that the certificate should be evaluated in a pre decision.

We do not detail other four models dues to the length limits of the paper.

5   Security Architecture

In this section, we discuss architecture solutions for digital access control based on
reference monitors. Reference monitors have been discussed extensively in access

control community. Subjects can access digital objects only through the reference monitor since it provides control mechanisms on access digital document.

5.1 Structure of Reference Monitor

ISO has published a standard for access control framework by using reference monitors [9]. Based on the standard, dissemination reference monitor consists of Usage Decision Facility (UDF) and Usage Enforcement Facility (UEF) as shown in Figure 3. Each facility includes several functional modules.

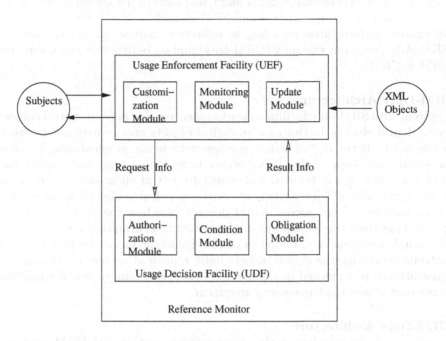

Fig. 3. XML Reference Monitor

UEF includes *Customization, Monitor and Update modules* and UDF includes *authorization, conditions and obligations decision modules*. When a subject sends an access request through *Customization module* to *Authorization module*, *Authorization module* verifies authorization process and checks whether the request is allowed or not. It may return yes or no or metadata information of the authorization result. This metadata information can be used for approved access on digital objects by *Customization module* in UEF. *Condition module* is used to make a decision for whether the conditional requirements are satisfied or not. *Obligation module* is applied to verify whether obligations have been performed or not before or during the requested usage. When any obligation is changed, it must be monitored by *monitor module* and the result has to be resolved by *Update module* in UEF. Applications of these modules rely on object systems requirements.

5.2   Architectures

There are two kinds of reference monitors: Server-side Reference Monitor (SRM), and Client-side Reference Monitor (CRM). Servers provide digital document and clients require access to the digital message. Like a traditional reference monitor, an SRM works in server system environment and manages access to digital information in the server. On the other hand, a CRM works in the client environment and controls access to digital message when it works as a server for other clients. For example, the client acts as a server when the digital document is disseminated to other users. SRM and CRM can coexist within a system. For real implementations, both CRM and SRM should be used for better security. We analyse architectures according to reference monitors on server side only (SRM-only), on client side only (CRM-only) and on both server and client sides (SRM & CRM).

SRM-Only Architecture

A system with SRM-only facilitates works on server side only to control subjects access digital objects. In this case an digital objects may or may not be stored in client-side. If the digital object is allowed to reside in client-side, it means the saved client copy of the digital object is no longer valid and doesn't have to be controlled. It can be used and changed freely at client-side. For example, an student payment bank statement can be saved at a client's local machine for his records and the server (bank) doesn't care how the copy will be used by the client since the bank keeps original account information safe. However if the digital document or some parts of the document has to be protected and controlled centrally, the digital objects must remain at server-side storage and is not allowed to be stored in client-side. This is the main topics of traditional access control and trust management system.

CRM-Only Architecture

No reference monitor exists on the server-side in a system with CRM-only environment. Rather, a reference monitor exists at the client system for controlling usage of disseminated digital documents. In this environment digital objects can be stored either centrally or locally. The usage of digital objects saved at the client-side on behalf of a server is still under the control of CRM. Distributed digital document are associated with certain usage rules and users may need to prove they have sufficient credentials to access the document.

SRM and CRM Architecture

With both SRM to CRM, this architecture can provide a comprehensive access control. SRM may be used for distribution related control while CRM can be used for digital document dissemination. For instance, in SRM, digital objects can be pre-customized for distribution. The pre-customized digital objects can be further controlled and customized by CRM. As a result, server can restrict or eliminate unnecessary exposure of digital objects that do not have to be distributed. If a user requests certain digital document that includes some secret information, SRM can pre-customize the requested objects before distribution such that the distributed version of the objects doesn't include any secret information. If the document cannot be disseminated, the CRM at client side can do this work.

The SRM & CRM architecture provides a solution for restricting access to digital documents and protecting digital documents from malicious dissemination.

6   Comparisons

Related work has been done on secure and selective dissemination of XML documents [1] securing XML Web services [5].

Elisa and Elena [1] proposed an access control system supporting selective distribution of XML document among possible large user communities by using a range of key distribution methods. They demonstrate a formal model of access control policies for XML documents. Policies defined in the model take into account both user profiles, and document contents and structures. An approach based on cryptograph is designed to allow sending the same document to all users, and to enforce the stated access control policies. The approach consists of encrypting different portions of the same document according to different encryption keys, and selectively distributing these keys to the various users. This proposal is different from ours in two aspects. First, it focuses on key distribution methods to protect XML document. Therefore, it only discussed the management in server side and without any management about how to control the XML document when users get keys. By contrast, our work provides a rich variety of options that can deal with digital documents in both server and user sides. Second, users can access digital documents with their keys at any time, even as their properties are updated. It means there is no ongoing authorization for users. In our scheme, users have to satisfy pre-Authorizations, pre-Obligations and pre-Conditions as well as ongoing-Authorizations, ongoing-Obligations, and ongoing-Conditions.

Securing XML Web services is described by Damiani, Vimercati and Samarati in 2002 [5]. Two experiments are discussed. One is that restricting access to an XML Web service to authorized users. Another one is that protecting the integrity and confidentiality of XML messages exchanged in a Web service environment. The authors introduce SOAP highlights, how to use SOAP headers for credential transfer and access control. The main difference between our scheme and the work in [5] is that we focus on a systematic level for digital documents by using usage control model and consider a solution for different kinds of authorizations, whereas the latter is a discussion of providing a secure infrastructure to XML Web services.

7   Conclusions

This paper has analysed the dissemination of payment-free-type digital information in E-Learning, and discussed access models and architectures by using usage control. We have analysed not only decision factors in usage control such as authorizations, obligations and conditions, but also the continuity. Different kinds of models are built for digital documents. To protect digital documents from malicious dissemination, we have analysed reference monitors on both server and client sides and obtained several secure architecture solutions. The work in this paper has significantly extended previous work in several aspects, for example, the ongoing continuity for authorizations, obligations and conditions. These methods can be used to control digital documents in E-Learning environment since they provide a robust access control for digital information and can protect sensitive messages from dissemination. It also begins a new application with usage control.

The future work includes develop algorithms based on the models and architectures proposed in this paper and application of the algorithms in real implementation.

References

1. Bertino, E., Ferrari, E.: Secure and selective dissemination of xml documents. ACM Trans. Inf. Syst. Secur. 5(3), 290–331 (2002)
2. Brad, C.: Superdistribution. Addiso Wesley, MA (1996)
3. Cisco Systems: E-Learning. Partner E-Learning Connection (2004)
4. Cynthia, D.: Copyright? protection?, the mathematics of information coding, extraction, and distribution. The IMA Volumes in Mathematics and its Applications 107, 31–47 (1999)
5. Damiani, E., Capitani, S., Samarati, P.: Towards securing xml web services. In: Proc. of the 2002 ACM Workshop on XML Security, Washington, DC, USA, pp. 90–96 (2002)
6. El-Khatib, K., Korba, L., Xu, Y., Yee, G.: Privacy and security in E-Learning. International Journal of Distance Education Technologies 1(4), 11–30 (2003)
7. White, G.: The changing landscape: E-Learning in schools. Technical Report at education.au limited (2003),
   www.education.edu.au/papers/changing_landscape_gw.pdf
8. Goldschlag, D., Reed, M., Syverson, P.: Onion routing for anonymous and private Internet connections. Communications of the ACM 24(2), 39–41 (1999)
9. ISO: Security frameworks for open systems: Access control framework. Iso/iec 10181-3 (1996)
10. Jajodia, S., Samarati, P., Subrahmanian, V., Bertino, E.: A unified framework for enforcing multiple access control policies. In: Proceedings of the 1997 ACM SIGMOD international conference on Management of data, pp. 474–485. ACM Press, New York (1997)
11. Li, Q., Atluri, V.: Concept-level access control for the semantic web. In: Proceedings of the 2003 ACM workshop on XML security, pp. 94–103. ACM Press, New York (2003)

12. Lowe, H., Wallis, A., Newman, J.: Role-based access control for vicarious learning. In: Proc European Conference on E-Learning, Brunel University, Uxbridge, pp. 43–50 (2002)

13. Lytras, M.: E-learn is about business: A business model for the digital economy. In: Proceedings of World Conference on E-Learning in Corporate, Government, Healthcare, and Higher Education, Montreal, Canada, pp. 2658–2659 (2002)

14. Mendling, J., Neumann, G., Pinterits, A., Simon, B., Wild, F.: Indirect revenue models for E-Learning at universities - the case of learn@wu. In: E-Learning Workshop, Hannover, Germany (2004)

15. Neely, S., Lowe, H., Eyers, D., Bacon, J., Newman, J., Gong, X.: An architecture for supporting vicarious learning in a distributed environment. In: SAC 2004, pp. 963–970. ACM Press, New York (2004)

16. Park, J., Sandhu, R.: Towards usage control models: beyond traditional access control. In: Proceedings of the seventh ACM symposium on Access control models and technologies, pp. 57–64. ACM Press, New York (2002)

17. Schmidt, K., Wippel, T., Furst, K.: Security system for distributed business applications. International Journal of Web Services Research 2(1), 77–88 (2005)

18. Seufert, S.: E-Learning business models: Framework and best practice examples. Idea Group, pp. 11–36 (2001)

19. Seufert, S., Lechner, U., Stanoevska, K.: A reference model for online learning communities. International Journal on E-Learning 1(1), 43–54 (2002)

20. Stafford, T.F.: Understanding motivations for internet use in distance education. IEEE Transactions on Education 48(2), 301–306 (2005)

21. Wang, H., Cao, J., Zhang, Y.: A consumer anonymity scalable payment scheme with role based access control. In: 2nd International Conference on Web Information Systems Engineering (WISE 2001), Kyoto, Japan, pp. 53–62 (2001)

22. Wang, H., Cao, J., Zhang, Y.: Formal authorization allocation approaches for permission-role assignments using relational algebra operations. In: Proceedings of the 14th Australian Database Conference ADC 2003, Adelaide, Australia, pp. 125–133 (2003)

23. Wang, H., Cao, J., Zhang, Y.: An Electronic Payment Scheme and Its RBAC management. Concurrent Engineering: Research and Application 12(3), 247–275 (2004)

24. Wang, H., Cao, J., Zhang, Y.: A flexible payment scheme and its role based access control. IEEE Transactions on Knowledge and Data Engineering 17(3), 425–436 (2005)

25. Wang, H., Zhang, Y., Cao, J., Varadharajan, V.: Achieving secure and flexible m-services through tickets. IEEE Transactions on Systems, Man, and Cybernetics, Part A, Special issue on M-Services, 697–708 (2003)

Mobile Learning Support with Statistical Inference-Based Cache Management

Qing Li, Jianmin Zhao, and Xinzhong Zhu

College of Mathematics, Physics and Information Engineering, Zhejiang Normal University,
688 Yingbin Avenue, Jinhua, Zhejiang, China
{ql,zjm,zxz}@zjnu.cn

Abstract. Supporting efficient data access in the mobile learning environment is becoming a hot research problem in recent years, and the problem becomes tougher when the clients are light-weight mobile devices such as cell phones whose limited storage space prevents the clients from holding a large cache. A practical solution is to store the cache data at some proxies nearby, so that mobile devices can access the data from these proxies instead of data servers in order to reduce the latency time. However, when mobile devices move freely, the cache data may not enhance the overall performance because it may become too far away for the clients to access. In this paper, we propose a statistical caching mechanism which makes use of prior knowledge (statistical data) to predict the pattern of user movement and then replicates/migrates the cache objects among different proxies. We propose a statistical inference based heuristic search algorithm to accommodate dynamic mobile data access in the mobile learning environment. Experimental studies show that, with an acceptable complexity, our algorithm can obtain good performance on caching mobile data.

Keywords: Mobile learning, mobile data management, mobile devices, data caching, statistical caching, cache management.

1 Introduction

Mobile data management has been an increasingly hot research problem over the past few years, as it is crucial to the successful deployment into a number of applications including mobile learning. An important topic (sub-problem) there is efficient data access in a mobile learning system, especially from the perspective of data caching and quality of services (QoS). Generally speaking, a local memory space is necessary for a mobile device to cache, in advance, some data objects since the data server on the Internet may need to handle tens of thousands of requests simultaneously. But it becomes unpractical to cache a lot of data on the so-called light-weight mobile devices (particularly, cell phones) due to their very limited capability. Instead, data caching over the proxies becomes a viable approach in order to enable the mobile clients to access the learning objects (data) efficiently. The proxies may serve as a secondary levelcache if a mobile device can maintain a small local cache, or serve as a direct cache if the mobile device cannot hold a local cache at all. However, how to

H. Leung et al. (Eds.): ICWL 2007, LNCS 4823, pp. 566–583, 2008.

dynamically maintain the cache data across the multiple proxies in order to enhance the overall performance of a mobile learning system is a challenging problem.

There are two main difficult problems for maintaining the cache data on the proxies. First of all, a proxy is limited by its hardware capability, which may prevent it from caching all the required data for the mobile clients. When a mobile device needs to access some data from a location whose proxy does not have the data cached, the proxy must decide if it should replicate/migrate the data from other proxies, depending on the actual situations and constraints. Because an earlier decision may impact the subsequent performance, it is very complex and costly to find a global optimal replication/migration algorithm. Secondly, global knowledge on mobile clients' movement and data access patterns is hard to obtain accurately, if not impossible. Yet even a rough approximation of such global knowledge will surely be useful for making sensible decisions.

In this paper, we propose to develop an efficient mobile learning system through devising a statistical caching mechanism, in which each proxy makes use of prior knowledge (statistical data) to decide whether any cache objects should be replicated, migrated or deleted. Our method is different from the traditional approaches, e.g., Markov Chain-based models. Such kinds of models typically have an assumption which may not simulate real-life user movement accurately, and some of them even incur a very high computational cost. In contrast, our mechanism converts the distributed caching problem into a heuristic search problem and uses statistical inference to supervise the decision.

The rest of the paper is organized as follows. We give a brief review of related work in section 2. Our system architecture including the performance metrics is introduced in section 3. Section 4 discusses the statistical caching mechanism in detail. Section 5 gives our experiment results and section 6 summarizes our work and offers a few future research topics.

2 Related Work

In this section, we review some earlier research works related to our research. Such relevant works can be divided into three categories: mobility model (movement prediction), data migration and data caching.

2.1 Mobility Model

Several user mobility models can be found in previous research papers for modelling the user movement. The fluid flow model in [1] is one of the early models widely used, in which mobile users are assumed to be uniformly populated and the users carrying terminals are moving at an average velocity with uniformly distributed moving-direction over $[0, 2\pi]$. During the last fifteen years, other mobility models have been suggested, such as random way point model, city model, highway model etc. Most of these models assumed that user behaviour is absolutely random. [2] introduced a new mobility model based on HSMM process and used it to facilitate resource allocation in wireless networks. To study and predict the movement of mobile users, [3] takes another approach in which modelling the behaviour of individual mobile user is composed of two parts: a random movement component and regular movement component. In turn, the regular movement consists of identical movement patterns of each mobile user, which represents the special behaviour of the movement of the user within a defined period of time; the MT/MC model is proposed to model the regular movement of mobile users. [4] has presented a novel scheme which takes full advantage of the correlation between a mobile's current velocity and location and its future velocity and location based on Gauss-Markov random process. In [5], an adaptive fuzzy inference system is developed to predict the probabilities that a mobile user will be active in the nearby cells at future moments using the real-time measurement data of the pilot signal powers received by the mobile user..

2.2 Data Migration

Data migration in distributed database systems has been a classical problem of research, and there are a good number of papers published in this area. In [6], S. Khuller et al. studied a particular kind of data migration problem, namely: given several data items, find a migration schedule using the minimum number of rounds to migrate these items from their source disks to the destination disks. Each disk can transfer, either as a sender or receiver, only one data item. The underlying network is assumed to be fully connected and data items are all of the same size. This problem is NP-hard and the authors suggested a polynomial-time approximation algorithm.

Research has also been conducted on how to find the optimal solution to satisfying a sequence of requests in a distributed environment [7][8]. Page replication and migration problems arise in a multi-processor system where each processor has its own local memory. For a writable page, only one page copy can be kept; for a read-only page, many copies can be kept in the network. There are two kinds of algorithms proposed: online and offline ones. The former works under an uncertain future and the latter assumes to have knowledge of the future request sequence. An online algorithm for a given problem is said to be c-competitive when the cost incurred by the algorithm is at most c times the cost incurred by the optimal offline algorithm. However, these algorithms did not consider the space constraint of a server, which may not work when the data volume involved becomes large.

H. M. Gladney, in [9], suggested a method to replicate copies in different locations but these replicas are not synchronized with the source data "eagerly" when an update occurs. An algorithm is proposed by the author to record the used portion of the source database, as a way to identify obsolete replicas. This approach performs well in a large scale, weakly connected network.

2.3 Data Caching

The third category of related work is on traditional database caching systems. We review such (non-mobile) data caching systems briefly through some representative works.

R. P. Klemm described the WebCompanion in [10] as a friendly client-side Web prefetching agent. It pursues a prefetching strategy based on estimated round-trip times for Web resources that are referenced. The longer the estimated round-trip time for a resource is, the more likely it will be prefetched. Of special interest to us is that, the solution was guided by the design goal of avoiding a penalty to the user for accessing the Web through WebCompanion, and to prefetch as many resources as possible while limiting network and server overhead as well as local resource consumption.

D. Kossmann et al. studied the problems of query optimization and distributed data placement together [11]. By integrating query optimization and data placement, the performance looks beyond the one of a single query. M. Altinel et al. introduced a new database object called "cache table" that enables persistent caching of the full or partial content of a remote database table [12]. The content of a cache table is either defined declaratively and populated in advance at setup time, or determined dynamically and populated on demand at query execution time. Both [11] and [12] have a common characteristic that they consider query and data placement together in order to get higher performance.

A. Ailamaki et al. in their work "weaving relations for cache performance" [13] demonstrate that in-page data placement is the key to high cache performance. A natural extension of that work into a distributed caching environment can thus reconfirm the importance of a well organized distributed cache structure for such applications as stream media data access.

3 System Model and Evaluation Metrics

Our mobile learning system architecture assumes a three-tier hierarchy model for cellular systems, as depicted in Fig. 1.

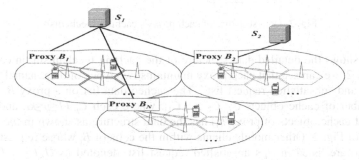

Fig. 1. Architecture of data access model for mobile learning

A data server S_j in Fig. 1 provides multimedia courseware access services over the Internet, which may handle tens of thousands of requests simultaneously. There are N proxies, numbered as $B_1, B_2,..., B_N$, respectively, that can serve as data cache for mobile users. Several cells compose a Location Area (LA). A single proxy is assigned to a LA to ensure that the proxy can detect user location update conveniently, and all users' requests from a LA will be processed by the corresponding proxy. Each B_i is responsible for forwarding a user's request (including server IP, port, user name, password, and starting time) to a designated data server S_j, the latter handles the request and returns the requested content via B_i.

In our model, the cache mechanism of a mobile device is implemented on the proxies. In this way, if a data item is cached already, future users who want to access the same data item need not go through the process of downloading the data from a data server. As we stated before, there can be many requests at the same time but the hardware capability may prevent a data server from handling all of them instantly, thus user requests may end up with being queued up on the data server for a long time. While there have been a good number of research results obtained on reducing the wireless channel/bandwidth, the communication delay between a proxy and a data server has been largely overlooked, which nevertheless contributes to the total effect of quality of services (QoS) substantially. In this paper, we aim at reducing the communication delay by devising an efficient caching mechanism on the proxies.

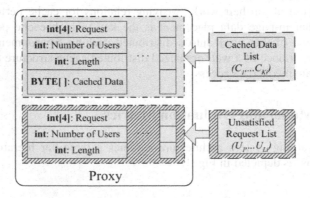

Fig. 2. Data structure of each proxy's caching mechanism

Fig. 2 shows the detailed data structure of the caching mechanism on each proxy. From Fig. 2, we can see that each proxy maintains two types of data, namely, "cached data list" and "unsatisfied request list". The cached data list on a proxy B_i is formed by a number of cache objects $C_1, C_2, ..., C_{Ki}$, where each C_p ($1 \leq p \leq Ki$, and Ki is the number of cache objects of proxy B_i) has the data structure as shown in the upper left gray box of Fig. 2. Other mobile clients within the cells of B_i whose requested data is not cached are listed in B_i's unsatisfied request list, denoted as $U_1, U_2, ..., U_{Li}$, where each U_q ($1 \leq q \leq Li$, and Li is the number of unsatisfied objects of B_i) has the data structure as shown in the lower left box.

The two lists are implemented by using two hash tables for fast access. Notice that with a large number of requests from a LA, there is a concern of how many records can be held in these two lists. In our model, we assume a proxy has enough space to store the two lists because the size of each record is very small. In the case that a cached data list gets overflowed, some cached data will have to be removed from the proxy – a sub-problem to be addressed in the next section. Table 1 gives a detailed explanation of the elements appeared in C_p and U_q.

In addition, a data object is allowed to be cached in multiple proxies simultaneously. If a proxy B_i is determined (cf. section 0) to be necessary to cache a data object, it calculates the corresponding *Req* using MD5 sum and broadcasts it to its nearby proxies, each of which compares the *Req* with its local records upon receiving the broadcast. If a proxy B_j has a $B_j.C_p.Req$ equal to Req, it replies a confirmation to allow B_i to copy the data object from B_j, thereby saving the waiting time for B_i to fetch the data from a server. In the case that B_i does not get any reply, it has to contact the corresponding data server for the data object to cache.

Table 1. Data types appeared on the proxy

Name	Type	Explanation
Req	int[4]	The ID of the data
N	int	The number of users within Bi whose request has the same value as *Bi.Req*
Len	int	The length of the data
Data	BYTE[]	The data object

To enable pertinent / objective evaluation of our overall system performance, particularly the caching mechanism to be described in next section, two popular metrics called *BHR* and *ASD* are incorporated and utilized, as described below.

Byte Hit Ratio

Byte Hit Ratio (*BHR*) is widely used as a metric which takes into account the differences among different cache objects [14]. In particular, *BHR* is defined as the ratio of total bytes satisfied by the cache to the total bytes transferred to the client. Because we have maintained cached data list and unsatisfied request list, the total bytes from cached objects and the total bytes requested by mobile users can be easily calculated. Therefore, one of the design aims of our caching mechanism is, according to the data structure in Fig. 2, to maximize *BHR* under the following constraint:

$$\sum_{p=1}^{K_i}(B_i.C_p.Len+6)+6L_i < Q_i, \forall i=1,...,N \tag{1}$$

This objective can be achieved by replicating / migrating cache data blocks among the proxies, a problem we term as "cache data scheduling" (cf. section 0). Note that in the expression Q_i stands for the storage quota of data cache blocks for proxy B_i.

There are other performance metrics introduced in the related fields, e.g. Backbone Traffic Reduction Ratio (*BTRR*) [22]. However, metrics such as *BTRR* can be calculated using the same formula as *BHR*, since *BTRR* is defined as the fraction of the total bytes that are served by a cache. So for simplicity, we only use *BHR* in our work to measure the benefit brought up by using the data caching mechanism.

Average Service Delay

In addition to *BHR*, we adopt another metric named Average Service Delay (*ASD*) since to reduce the waiting time spent on the data transferring is another major objective of our caching mechanism.

A request from a mobile device A_x to a proxy B_i has to be forwarded to a data server if none of the nearby proxies has the requested data in its cache, in which case B_i puts the request into an unsatisfied request list. Therefore A_x would wait for a longer time for the desired data. Adapted from [22], the ASD of A_x is mathematically calculated by formula   (2).

$$ASD\ (A_x) = \frac{1}{R} \sum_{x=1}^{R} \left[\frac{\overline{B}(A_x, T)}{b(A_x, T)} - T \right]^+ \tag{2}$$

In formula   (2), b(A_x, T) stands for the bandwidth that a requested server reserves to a mobile device A_x, and $\overline{B}(A_x, T)$ equals to the number of bytes the mobile device A_x requests during time window T if the requested data is not cached in any proxy; otherwise, it equals to zero. Also, function u=[v]+ means that if v<0, then u=0; otherwise, u=v.

We re-iterate that ASD, as defined above, is not the same as BHR. In particular, ASD serves as another important yardstick for assessing the performance of data cache mechanism from the user's perspective.

4 Statistical Caching

In this section, we detail our statistical caching mechanism for efficient data access in mobile learning systems. Since the problem of finding an optimal solution is NP-complete [29], a statistical inference based approach is targeted at which can provide a good performance with an acceptable complexity.

4.1 Cache Block Scheduling

As mentioned previously, our approach to maximize the BHR metric is to replicate / migrate the cached data among the proxies dynamically. **Fig. 3** outlines our approach to addressing this cache scheduling problem for two cases: (1) a mobile device A_x accesses a cache block from proxy B_n and, (2) a mobile accesses a cache block from proxy B_n and, (2) a mobile device A_x stops its access to or leaves from proxy B_m.

Specifically, *Algorithm_access(A_x, B_n)* in **Fig. 3** can be executed on proxy B_n and *Algorithm_stop_access (A_x, B_m)* on proxy B_m, respectively.

Algorithm_stop_access (A_x, B_m) in our system is relatively simple. As shown in lines 1' to 2', if B_m has a cached object serving for A_x, its recorded number of users (N) is decreased by 1 after A_x stops its access; the cached object will be destroyed and the space released if no more mobile device uses it, as lines 3' to 4' indicate. On the other hand, lines 5' through 9' cope with the situation when A_x does not find the data cached on B_m, in which case proper bookkeeping is done accordingly based on the data structure of Fig. 2.

For *Algorithm_access(A_x, B_n)*, the situation is more complicated due to the fact that there are three possible cases to be dealt with. Specifically, lines 1 to 2 correspond to the simplest case that there is already a cached object in B_n which is identical to A_x's request, so A_x can access it directly. Lines 3 to 4 depict the second case where B_n does not have the required object cached but still has sufficient space for caching new data. In this case, a cached object $B_m.C_p$ from a nearby proxy B_m is copied to B_n using the broadcasting method as mentioned before. The third case, captured by lines 5 and 6, is the most complex one. In this circumstance, the data object requested by A_x is not cached on proxy B_n, and there is no enough space in B_n to cache it. There are two possible choices for B_n: the first one is to put A_x's request into the unsatisfied request list; the second choice is to remove one or more existing cached objects and use the freed space to accommodate the data requested by A_x. Because B_n does not have the whole picture to predict the consequence of the choices on the overall performance, in line 6, B_n puts together all such messages (from the same time window) for strategic consideration in order to maximize the global *BHR*; the detailed algorithm is discussed in the next subsection.

```
Algorithm_access(Ax, Bn)
1. if ∃p∈[1,Kn], Ax.req = Bn.Cp.req
2.    increase Bn.Cp.N by 1;
3. else if enough space to cache Ax
4.    create cache data for Ax;
5. else
6.    make a decision based on
      statistical data
```

```
Algorithm_stop_access(Ax, Bm)
1'. if ∃p∈[1,Km], Ax.req = Bm.Cp.req
2'.    decrease Bm.Cp.N by 1;
3'.    if Bm.Cp.N=0
4'.       destroy Bm.Cp and free its
          memory;
5'.    else
6'.       find ∃p∈[1,Lm] so that Ax.req =
          Bm.Up.req;
7'.       decrease Bm.Up.N by 1;
8'.       if Bm.Up.N=0
9'.          destroy Bm.Up and free its
             memory.
```

```
Algorithm_findreplace()
1. for p = 1 to Kn
2.    Mp = Bn.Cp.Len • Bn.Cp.N ;
3. let M'1 < M'2 <...< M'Kn be
   the ascending order of
   {M1,...,MKn};
4. let sum = 0, p = 1;
5. while sum < Len.Ax
6.    sum = sum + Mp';
7. return M1,...,Mp.
```

Fig. 3. Pseudo-code for cache scheduling   **Fig. 4.** Pseudo-code for finding C_g in B_n

Note that the messages are considered together by the proxy B_n based on the same time window $T=[t_1, t_2]$, which can in principle lead to a better result than by handling each message one by one [16]. But a problem may occur when there are a large number of messages sent within the same time window to the proxy for handling. In particular, a large number of messages would lead to an expensive decision-making process by the proxy with an exponential complexity. In section 4.3, we will address this problem by using a statistical inference based algorithm. But first, we detail in the following the two choices faced by an individual proxy (with a view on their consequences over *BHR* value change).

4.2   Effect of the Two Choices

We now describe, for the two choices depicted in lines 5 and 6 of Fig. 3 in section 4.1, the calculation of the new *BHR* after A_x's access.

Note that in the second choice, it would cost a lot to find a proper set of cached blocks to remove and cache the new data block brought in by A_x. The best solution is to find such a set $C_g = \{C_{p'} \mid p'=1,...,Y\}$ from $\{B_n.C_p \mid p=1,...,K_n\}$ under the constraint:

$$\sum_{p'=1}^{Y} B_n.C_{p'}.Len > A_x.Len$$

(where $A_x.Len$ means the size of the data requested by A_x), so as to minimize

$$\sum_{p'=1}^{Y} (B_n.C_{p'}.N \bullet B_n.C_{p'}.Len)$$

. To find this best solution is, however, a fractional knapsack problem without taking partial items, which is known as NP-complete [23]. In order to avoid the expensive calculation, we devise a heuristic approach as depicted in Fig. 4. Intuitively, the algorithm in Fig. 4 is to find an optimized C_g to remove *if* proxy B_n decides to go for data replacement (this decision is however supervised by the SIB*heus* algorithm to be presented in next section), so that a relatively large value of *BHR* can be obtained. The computational complexity of *Algorithm_findreplace()* depends on the 3rd step, which yields a computational cost of $O(K_n log_2 K_n)$.

4.3   SIB*heus* Algorithm

As stated in section 4.1, when a data object requested by A_x is not cached on proxy B_n, and there is no enough space in B_n to cache it, we have two possible choices for B_n: put A_x's request into the unsatisfied request list or remove one or more existing cache objects and use the freed space to accommodate the new data. However, B_n does not know which decision would be better to maximize the global *BHR*. To this end, we transform the decision-making process into a search problem over a complete binary tree G, in which the cost function between a node and its direct subnode (denoted as an edge e of G) can be defined as the change of *BHR* value by each decision. In this context, the immediate problem of our caching mechanism is to find the shortest path from the root (s) to one of the leaves in G. As mentioned, a large number of messages within a time window T would lead to an expensive decision-making process by a proxy with an exponential complexity, hence it must be addressed realistically for practical applications.

As studied in [3], user movement in cellular systems is regular to a great extent, and each user has his/her mobility pattern. However, it is difficult to mathematically model this pattern in an accurate way. Previous prediction algorithms as mentioned in section 2 are incapable of finding a mathematically accurate pattern. In addition, even if we can sometimes find the pattern and predict a user's location, it would be difficult and costly to update / inform the information for every proxy promptly. Generally speaking, a distributed decision making mechanism without assuming the availability of a mathematically accurate moving pattern is needed instead. Our proposed method is enlightened from SA search [26] based on statistical inference, which assumes every branch of the search tree follows a specific statistical distribution. In particular, *SA* search consists of a statistical inference method and *Best-First (BF)* heuristic search, which can be treated as a two-phased loop operation. In the first phase, it identifies quickly the most promising subtree using $a(n)$ (global statistics or subtree statistics). In the case of a binary tree, in particular, the two search directions, i.e., the subtrees $T(n_{11})$ and $T(n_{12})$ rooted at nodes n_{11} and n_{12}, are examined for possible rejection if it does not satisfy the null hypothesis [24]. *SA* takes the nodes of each subtree in the next level as its input (called "observed samples"). The subtrees which contain the "goal" g (a leaf node with maximum *BHR*) with a low probability are rejected / pruned. The one which is not pruned by the above steps is the most promising subtree to be accepted for phase two's further processing. During phase two, *SA* expands nodes within the accepted subtree using a node evaluation function $b(n)$ (local statistics or node statistics). This constitutes a complete round of *SA* search, and the next round is started recursively until the goal is found.

Knowing that *SA* can employ different statistical inference methods which may result in different search results, we use asymptotic efficient sequential fixed-width confidence intervals for the mean, or ASM [26] for short, as a testing hypothesis. The advantage of our algorithm is that it is not necessary to know the distribution of the subtree evaluation function $a(n)$, which is hard to obtain in a distributed caching system anyway. Our caching algorithm uses ASM as the statistical inference method. Assume that $\{x_i\}$ ($i=1,\ldots,n$) are identically and independently distributed variables, which have a common distribution function F with a finite fourth moment [25]. Given $\delta>0$ and $0<\gamma<1$, the stopping variable $R(\delta)$, adopted from ASM, is defined as the minimal integer which satisfies formula   (3):

$$R \geq \frac{a^2}{\delta^2} \left\{ \frac{1}{R} \left[1 + \sum_{i=1}^{R} (x_i - \overline{x}_R)^2 \right] \right\} \tag{3}$$

where $\overline{x}_R = \frac{1}{R}\sum_{i=1}^{R} x_i$, $\phi(x) = \frac{1}{\sqrt{2\pi}} \int_{-\infty}^{\infty} e^{-t^2/2} dt$, and $a = \phi^{-1}(\frac{1+\gamma}{2})$.

Let μ be the mean of $\{x_i\}$, formula   (3) has the property that $\forall F$, the probability of $\mu \in (\overline{x}_R - \delta, \overline{x}_R + \delta)$ is greater than γ, where $(\overline{x}_R - \delta, \overline{x}_R + \delta)$ is a fixed-width confidence interval denoted by $I(\overline{x}_{R(\delta)}, \delta)$. Consequently, the smaller δ is, the more precise our prediction of μ will be.

The whole search procedure begins with the root. First, given $R=1$, formula (3) is tested. If formula (3) holds, interval $I(\Gamma, \delta)$ is computed (where Γ is a wild card); otherwise, newly observed samples are tested against formula (3).

However, if a statistical inference method is directly used here, it may impose a rejection (hence "service failure") problem. In particular, it is possible that all subtrees at a certain level are rejected by the algorithm. This is not a desirable property, since such a failure would stop our cache mechanism from providing continuous services. So, we make some modifications to the search procedure. The basic idea is as follows: Given an arbitrary constant δ_1, confidence intervals $I(p_i, \delta_1)$ ($i=1, 2$) are obtained according to the definition, where p_i is the ith subnode at current level. If $I(p_1, \delta_1)$

intersects with $I(p_2, \delta_1)$, a new constant δ_2 ($<\delta_1$) is tried in place of δ_1, and the whole process gets repeated until we find a δ_n, so that $I(p_1, \delta_n)$ does not intersect with $I(p_2, \delta_n)$. So, finally, the algorithm consists of two parts. The first part is the statistical learning procedure (Proc1), and the second part is the SIB*heus* search procedure (Proc2).

```
Algorithm_stat()
1.  let i = 0, left = right = 0;
2.  find goal g by Branch-and-
    Bound search;
3.  while g ≠ s
4.     m = the parent node of g
5.     if g is the left subnode
       of m
          left=left+Subroutine_sum(g);
6.     else
          right=right+Subroutine_sum(g);
7.     g=m;
8.     increase i by 1;
9.  return c=(left−right)/i.

Subroutine_sum(N)
1'. sum = 0;
2'. for i = 1 to N
3'.    sum = sum+e_l(i)+e_r(i);
4'. return sum.
```

```
Algorithm_search()
1.  given α_0;
2.  for i = 0 to D
3.     let γ=1- α_0 and δ=c/4;
4.     let x_1=e_l(i) and x_2=e_r(i);
5.     for j = 1 to 2
6.        calculate  x̄_R(δ)  using
          formula 4;
7.        let I(p_j, δ) = I(x̄_R(δ), δ);
8.        if  I(p_1, δ)  does  not
          intersect I(p_2, δ)
9.           increase i by 1;
10.          if p_1<p_2
11.             prune the right branch
12.          else
13.             prune the left branch;
14.          break;
15.       else
16.          δ= δ/2;
17.    decrease i by 1.
```

Fig. 5. Statistical learning in SIB*heus* (Proc1)   **Fig. 6.** SIB*heus* algorithm (Proc2)

In Fig. 6, $e_l(i)$ stands for the cost function from node i to its left subnode, while $e_r(i)$ stands for the cost function from node i to its right subnode. Also, D is the depth of the search tree G. The variable α_0, which is given at the top, is called the significance level in statistical inference. (A brief discussion on α_0 and its usage is given in Appendix A.) Practically, the smaller the value of α_0 has, the more accurate result we can obtain. However, if α_0 is too small, the possibility that $I(p_1, \delta)$ does not intersect with $I(p_2, \delta)$ will be high, which can make the "if" condition false in line 8 and increase the number of loops. This suggests that a trade off between accuracy and efficiency is inevitable for the real world applications.

With Proc1 and Proc2, the entire search algorithm runs as follows: The proxy B_n does the initialization work by calling Proc1 to get the value of c, which will be used in Proc2. Proc2 is executed once per time window T to get the near-best solutions. Note that the computational cost of Proc1 in Fig. 5 is $O(2^D)$ which is a little bit high, as it takes several time windows to run line 3 to find the optimal goal g. So, in comparison with Proc 2, Proc1 is called much less frequently to refresh c as the (latest) estimation of the distribution pattern of the search tree G.

Theoretically, our proposed statistical searching algorithm has a complexity of an upper bound $O(Dln^2D)$ and the error probability $2\alpha_0$, the proofs of which are given in Appendices B and C.

4.4 Discussion

Traditional caching algorithms based on LRU (Least Recently Used), LFU (Least Frequently Used), and FIFO (Fist In First Out) are all essentially of depth-first search nature if we treat the decision procedure as a binary tree search problem. However, depth-first search cannot find the best result in most cases. In contrast, our SIBheus algorithm is a more accurate approach to find a near-optimal solution. It consists of a periodical learning procedure (viz., Proc1) and a searching procedure (Proc2) with an acceptable complexity $O(Dln^2D)$.

Our algorithm is characterized by applying statistical inference into the heuristic search, so that the searching procedure is guided by the statistic knowledge. During the searching procedure, only one branch is kept and the other is pruned at each level, which resembles the same behaviour as depth-first search. But our method deviates from depth-first search in that the decision it makes is not simply dependent on the cost function between a node and its subnodes. Instead, it uses statistical inference to choose a branch to prune, which is more accurate than that of the depth-first search. More specifically, the probability that the searching algorithm can find the optimal solution is $1-2\alpha_0$ (ref. the proof in appendix C).

5 Experiment

As part of this research, a simulation system has been developed to evaluate the effect and performance of our proposed caching mechanism. First, we give a brief description of the experiment set up as a necessary context for our subsequent discussions.

User distribution
The mobile user distribution simulation comes from a tilt data file [28], which includes more than 60,000 points. 8,000 of them are randomly selected, representing the initial user positions on the map, with each position being of (x, y) format where x and y range within [0, 10000].

User movement
Movement of each user is depicted by a state chain, where each state stands for the user location represented by the cell number. We use the user mobility models in [3] which assumes that user movement is of two parts: random part and regular part. In the regular part, a period T_p is defined and user movement will represent periodicity based on T_p. Intuitively, this situation is close to our daily life. In each T_p, a user chooses a random point as the destination and the **speed** of movement follows Zipf distribution in $[10/T, 20/T]$ (skewed towards 0). After reaching the destination, the user will randomly choose another point to move on. In the random part, some tiny Gaussian white noises are added over the regular part.

Access pattern

Each data object is randomly assigned with a value representing its popularity. The mobile users choose data objects based on such values. The larger a value is, the more possible that users may access that object. We assume the **time** of accessing each data object to be following Zipf in [60T, 600T] based on the result of [27], in which the distribution of client requests of data objects is observed to be Zipf-like (α around 0.5).

Proxy Allocation

We group several cells into one LA and assign a proxy to it. The number of cells per LA can be regarded as a parameter and we can adjust it dynamically. At first no data is cached on any proxy, and once users begin to move, each proxy starts to adopt our statistical caching algorithm to dynamically replicate / migrate data objects.

As mentioned in section 4, there is a trade off between efficiency and accuracy in the binary tree searching. We use "*product* = error rate * number of loops" as a measure on the effect of this trade off. The error rate is calculated as the mean square error of the costs from root s to g and g', where g is the leaf node with maximum BHR value (viz., the "goal" in section 4), and g' is the actual leaf node found by our algorithm.

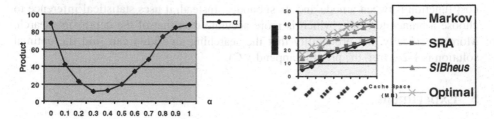

Fig. 7. Efficiency-accuracy trade off against α **Fig. 8.** Performance comparison with *BHR* against cache space

Fig. 7 plots the product curve against α based on the simulation data, from which we can see that when α is about 0.34, *product* has the smallest value.

To test the performance of our caching mechanism, we compare our SIB*heus* algorithm with two other caching policies, namely, *SRA* [29], and a Markov model-based prediction algorithm [4]. The comparisons are in terms of their *BHR* values against each proxy's cache space. As shown in Fig. 8, our algorithm outperforms the other two strategies under various cache spaces. We also see that the performance of our algorithm is not far from optimal replication/migration under the exhaustive search of the decision tree. Although for this test case, we set the time interval $T=1s$, cache block size = 40KB and the cell radius equal to 500, similar relationships among the three curves are obtained with different values on the parameters.

Fig. 9 shows the performance of our caching mechanism against time with the proxy's cache space equal to 600MB, and the parameter c being refreshed once every 80 time windows. Here we compare the three caching policies from another point of view. As depicted in Fig. 9, when time increases, *BHR* curves of *SRA* and *Markov based algorithm* are nearly a straight line with little change. However, *BHR* becomes a zigzag curve for our algorithm, which can be explained as follows: Each time when a proxy learns from the historic data and calculates a new value of c, *BHR* will have an abrupt jump because our algorithm also predicts the future requests. However, with the change of the user movement pattern over time, this prediction becomes less accurate, and the original c could no longer lead to a near-optimal solution. This explains the gradual decrease of BHR after each jump.

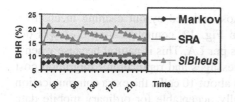

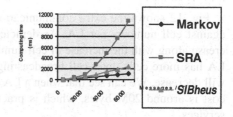

Fig. 9. Performance comparison with *BHR* against time

Fig. 10. Computing time comparison against message numbers per time window

Similarly, we can compare with *SRA* and *Markov based algorithm* from the perspective of *Average Service Delay (ASD)*. Not surprisingly, the *ASD* of our algorithm is also a zigzag curve against time, but is almost of an inverse shape to that of *BHR*.

The comparison of the computation time of these three algorithms is given in Fig. 10. We can see that due to statistical estimation, SIB*heus* (with complexity $O(Dln^2D)$) outperforms *SRA* (with complexity $O(D^2)$) in all cases. In fact, when there are a large number of accesses within a short time window, *SRA* becomes unpractical for realistic mobile applications. For the Markov-based model, the computing time is the best due to its linear algorithm, but the relatively poor performance on *BHR* (and *ASD*) against time and space still leaves it unfavorable and unacceptable from the perspective of real mobile users.

We further tested the practicality of our SIBHS caching mechanism from two aspects. Fig. 11 shows the performance of our caching mechanism against cell numbers

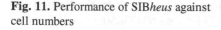

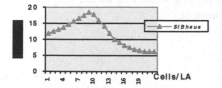

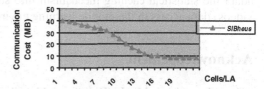

Fig. 11. Performance of SIB*heus* against cell numbers

Fig. 12. Extra Communication Cost of SIB*heus* against cell numbers

per LA. As depicted in Fig. 11, when cell numbers increases, *BHR* will increase at first, and then decrease after reaching a peak value. This can be explained as follows: When a LA has a small number of cells, each proxy cannot benefit much from statistical caching because user movement information is insufficient, which leads to a poor prediction. However, when a single LA has many cells, although a proxy can statistically learn much from historical data and decide more precisely, the storage quota of each proxy would prevent it from caching all the data objects that are already determined to cache. So for different situations, we may have different optimal cell numbers. As depicted in Fig. 11, the optimal cell number under our simulation conditions is about 11.

Fig. 12 shows the extra communication cost induced by our caching mechanism against cell numbers per LA. As depicted in Fig. 12, communication cost will decrease along with the increase of cell numbers per LA. This is natural because when a LA has more cells, inter-cell broadcasting messages and replication / migration cost will decrease. We can see that when a LA has about 10 cells, the extra communication cost is around 20M bytes, which is practically acceptable for ordinary mobile data services.

6   Conclusions

Mobile data management including mobile data access has become an increasingly hot research problem due to its applicability to practical mobile/wireless applications, particularly mobile learning. In this paper, we have presented a practical caching mechanism for data access in mobile learning systems. This caching mechanism makes use of prior knowledge (statistical data) to predict the user mobility pattern. Based on the statistical heuristic search, a statistical caching algorithm is developed. Experimental studies show that our caching mechanism can obtain good performance on caching courseware data for mobile learning systems, with a computational complexity of $O(Dln^2D)$, which is acceptable for most (if not all) mobile learning applications.

Admittedly, there are issues remaining to be addressed. We are currently studying some other testing hypothesis methods different from ASM [26], as well as the effect of the selection of a testing hypothesis method on the performance. While our cache mechanism described in this paper works for mobile learning systems, we also plan to adapt the statistical caching mechanism into supporting streaming media (eg, lecture videos) data access in the mobile learning environment.

Acknowledgement

The authors thank Mr. Li Xiang and Mr. Zhai Jian for their contribution to the experimental research of this project. The work has been supported by the Natural Science Foundation of China with the projects 60773197 and 60473050.

References

1. Thomas, R., Gilbert, H., Mazziotto, G.: Influence of the movement of mobile station on the performance of the radio cellular network. In: Proc. of 3rdNordic Seminar, Copenhagen (September 1988)
2. Kobayashi, H., Yu, S.Z., Mark, B.L.: An integrated mobility and traffic model for resource allocation in wireless networks. In: Proceedings of the Third ACM International Workshop on Wireless Mobile Multimedia, pp. 39–47 (2000)
3. Liu, G.Y., Maguire Jr, G.Q.: A class of mobile motion prediction algorithms for wireless mobile computing and communications. Mobile Networks and Applications 1, 113–121 (1996)
4. Ben, L., Haas, Z.J.: Predictive Distance-Based Mobility Management for Multidimensional PCS Networks. IEEE/ACM Transactions on Networking 11(5) (October 2003)
5. Shen, X., Mark, J.W., Ye, J.: User mobility profile prediction: An adaptive fuzzy inference approach. Wireless Networks 6(5), 363–374 (2000)
6. Khuller, S., Kim, Y.A., Wan, Y.C.: Algorithms for Data Migration with Cloning. In: Proceedings of PODS conference (2003)
7. Manasse, M.S., McGeoch, L.A., Sleator, D.D.: Competitive Algorithms for Server Problems. J. Algorithms 11(2), 208–230 (1990)
8. Chrobak, M., Larmore, L.L., Regingold, N., Westbrook, J.: Page Migration Algorithms Using Work Functions. J. Algorithms 24(1), 124–157 (1997)
9. Gladney, H.M.: Data Replicas in Distributed Information Services. ACM TODS 14(1), 75–97 (1989)
10. Klemm, R.P.: WebCompanion: A Friendly Client-Side Web Prefetching Agent. IEEE TKDE 11(4), 577–594 (1999)
11. Kossmann, D., Franklin, M.J., Drasch, G.: Cache Investment: Integrating Query Optimization and Distributed Data Placement. ACM TODS 25(4), 517–558 (2000)
12. Altınel, M., Bornhövd, C., Krishnamurthy, S., Mohan, C., Pirahesh, H., Reinwald, B.: Cache Tables: Paving the Way for an Adaptive Database Cache. In: Proceedings of VLDB conference (2003)
13. Ailamaki, A., DeWitt, D.J., Hill, M.D., Skounakis, M.: Weaving Relations for Cache Performance. In: Proceedings of VLDB conference (2001)
14. Paknikar, S., Kankanhalli, M., Ramakrishnan, K.R., Srinivasan, S.H., Ngoh, L.H.: A Caching and Streaming Framework for Multimedia. In: Proceedings of ACM MM conference (2000)
15. Wang, B., Sen, S., Adler, M., Towsley, D.: Optimal Proxy Cache Allocation for Efficient Streaming Media Distribution. In: Proceedings of INFOCOM conference (2002)
16. Wu, K.L., Yu, P.S., Wolf, J.L.: Segment-Based Proxy Caching of Multimedia Streams. In: Proceedings of WWW conference (2001)
17. Lim, E.J., Park, S.H., Hong, H.O., Chung, K.D.: A Proxy Caching Scheme for Continuous Media Streams on the Internet. In: Proceedings of ICIN conference (2001)
18. Das, S.K., Kumar, M., Wang, Z., Shen, H.: Investigation of Cache Maintenance Strategies for Multi-cell Environments. In: Chen, M.-S., Chrysanthis, P.K., Sloman, M., Zaslavsky, A. (eds.) MDM 2003. LNCS, vol. 2574, pp. 29–44. Springer, Heidelberg (2003)
19. RTSTP, http://www.rtsp.org/
20. IETF, http://www.ietf.org/rfc/rfc1321.txt
21. Shen, B., Lee, S.-J., Basu, S.: Performance Evaluation of Transcoding-Enabled Streaming Media Caching System. In: Chen, M.-S., et al. (eds.) MDM 2003. LNCS, vol. 2574, pp. 363–368. Springer, Heidelberg (2003)

22. Jin, S.D., Bestavros, A., Iyengar, A.: Accelerating Internet Streaming Media Delivery using Network-Aware Partial Caching. In: Proceedings of ICDCS conference (2002)
23. Papadimitriou, C.H.: Computational complexity. Addison-Wesley, Reading (1994)
24. Kiefer, J.C.: Introduction to statistical inference. Springer, Heidelberg (1987)
25. Rosenblatt, M.: Random processes. Springer, Heidelberg (1974)
26. Zhang, B., Zhang, L.: Theory and Applications of Problem Solving. North-Holland, Amsterdam (1992)
27. Chesire, M., Wolman, A., Voelker, G.M., Levy, H.M.: Measurement and Analysis of a Streaming-Media Workload. In: Proceedings of the USENIX Symposium on ITS (2001) (Best paper award)
28. Shladover, S.E.: The California PATH Program of IVHS Research and Its Approach to Vehicle-Highway Automation. In: Proceedings of the ACM Symposium on IV (1992)
29. Loukoupoulos, T., Ahmad, I.: Static and Adaptive Data Replication Algorithms for Fast Information Access in Large Distributed Systems. In: Proceedings of ICDCS conference (2000)
30. Gal, A., Eckstein, J.: Managing Periodically Updated Data in Relational Databases: A Stochastic Modeling Approach. Journal of the ACM 48(6), 1141–1183 (2001)
31. Kangasharju, J., Roberts, J., Ross, K.W.: Object replication strategies in content distribution networks. Computer Communications 25(5), 376–378 (2002)

Appendix A. Significance Level

In the theory of statistical inference, there are two types of judging errors, namely, type I error (if the alternate hypothesis H_1 is chosen when in fact the null hypothesis H_0 is true) and type II error (the opposite to type I error). The significance level α_0 controls the possibility of occurrence of type I error. In our model, we let H_0 be the negation of H_1 and let the possibility of occurrence of the type II error β_0 be the same as α_0 for simplicity.

Appendix B. The Computational Complexity of the SIB*heus* Search Algorithm

Claim: Assume that $\{\alpha_k(\Gamma)\}$ (where Γ is a wild card) satisfies the null hypothesis H_0 and has a finite fourth moment. Given (α_0, β_0), let $\alpha=\min(\alpha_0, \beta_0)$, $A = \sum_{i=1}^{\infty}(\frac{m}{i^2})$. The computational complexity of the statistical inference based binary tree search algorithm is of $O(D\ln^2 D)$.

Proof: Given the significant level (α_0, β_0), we use a significant level $\left(\alpha_i = \dfrac{\alpha}{(i+1)^2}, \beta_i = \dfrac{\alpha}{(m-1)(i+1)^2}\right)$ in *ASM*, where m is the number of subtrees within level i. If the number of observation surpasses a given threshold d_j,

$$d_j = 2b_2 \ln(j+1)\cdot \ln\frac{j+1}{\alpha}, b_2 = \frac{4m\sigma^2}{(\mu_1 - \mu_0)^2}$$

then, the hypothesis H_0 is rejected for $i=0, 1$. search pointer is under level $(\alpha, \frac{\alpha}{m-1})$.

In i-th depth, the threshold is:

$$d_j = 2b_2 \ln(j+1) \cdot \ln\frac{j+1}{\alpha} \sim C\ln^2(j+1)$$

So, the upper bound of the complexity is

$$\sum_{j=1}^{N} C\ln^2(j+1) \sim O(D \cdot \ln^2 D)$$

Appendix C. The Error Rate of the SIB*heus* Search Algorithm

Claim: Assume that $\{a_k(\Gamma)\}$ (where Γ is a wild card) satisfies the null hypothesis H_0 and has a finite fourth moment. Given (α_0, β_0), let $\alpha_0=\min(\alpha_0, \beta_0)$, $A = \sum_{i=1}^{\infty}(\frac{m}{i^2})$. The goal g can be found by the search under α with probability$\geq 1-b$, $b \leq \alpha_0+\beta_0$.

Proof: The probability of the occurrence of type I error in deciding on i-subtrees is $\leq \alpha/(i+1)^2$ and the probability of the occurrence of type II is $\leq (m-1)\alpha/(i+1)^2$, where m is number of subtrees within level i. Because the error probability in deciding on i-subtrees is $\alpha*m/(i+1)^2$, the total error probability P_e is therefore:

$$P_e \leq \sum_{i=1}^{N-1}\left(\frac{\alpha m}{(i+1)^2}\right) < \alpha\sum_{i=1}^{\infty}\left(\frac{m}{i^2}\right) = \alpha A = \min(\alpha_0, \beta_0) \leq \alpha_0+\beta_0$$

Design and Implementation of an Automated System for Assessment of Computer Programming Assignments[*]

Marian Choy, Sam Lam, Chung Keung Poon, Fu Lee Wang, Yuen Tak Yu,
and Leo Yuen

Department of Computer Science, City University of Hong Kong
{csmchoy, csckpoon, flwang, csytyu}@cityu.edu.hk
lamaslam@hotmail.com
leoyuen@leoyuen.idv.hk

Abstract. Learning computer programming is known to be difficult for many beginners. With the primary aim to improving the practice of teaching and learning of computer programming, we have developed a web-based automated system, known as PASS, for use in our courses. Since its first introduction a few years ago, PASS has proved to be a valuable tool for both students and instructors. PASS has now undergone significant revisions, with enhanced capabilities that have created opportunities for new pedagogy and innovative strategies for both teaching and learning. This paper describes the functionalities, design and implementation of PASS, how it can be used to enhance students' interest of learning and monitor their progress, and illustrates several approaches with which PASS can facilitate blended learning of good practices in computer programming.

Keywords: Computer programming, assessment, blended learning.

1 Introduction

Learning computer programming has been known to be difficult for many beginners [3]. Programming skill has to be acquired through lots of practice [4]. When teaching programming, the instructor typically gives many programming exercises and assignments to students, hoping that they will gain enough hands-on practice. However, assessment of programming exercises and assignments by manual inspection of code on paper is notoriously inefficient and error-prone [10]. More importantly, such a practice is educationally undesirable because students generally have to wait for a long time before they can receive feedback from the instructors to help them improve their work.

With the primary aim to improving the practice of teaching and learning of computer programming, we have developed a web-based automated *Programming Assignment aSsessment System*, better known as *PASS*, for use in our courses [5]. PASS

[*] The work described in this paper was substantially supported by grants from City University of Hong Kong (Project No.: 600143, 600144, and 6000145). This paper is an extended version of [7].

H. Leung et al. (Eds.): ICWL 2007, LNCS 4823, pp. 584–596, 2008.
© Springer-Verlag Berlin Heidelberg 2008

automates the process of collecting and assessing programming assignments. It has been proved to be a valuable and indispensable tool for the users [6, 12], by reducing the feedback waiting period for students, and easing the programming assessment procedure for instructors.

In order to be prepared for future extensibility, a critical revamp is made on PASS recently. With enhanced capabilities, PASS has created opportunities for new pedagogy and innovative strategies for both teaching and learning. This paper describes the functionalities, design and implementation of PASS, how it can be used to enhance students' interest of learning and monitor their progress, and illustrates several approaches with which PASS can facilitate blended learning of good practices in computer programming.

2 Functionalities of PASS

PASS was first developed in our university in 2004 as an executable prototype for demonstration [5], but it was soon re-engineered to a working system for production use [10]. Although the first version of PASS contained the core functionalities which were already very helpful to students, it nevertheless carried its built-in design limitations that significantly hindered its enhancement.

The basic function of the system is to allow the student to submit their program code, automatically execute the program with predefined test cases (determined by the instructor beforehand), and return the execution results to the student. In this way, the student gets instant feedback from PASS as to whether his/her program is correct with respect to the selected test cases. When the submitted program is incorrect, PASS will also indicate to the student exactly at which position the actual output differs from the correct (expected) output. For assignment submissions, the instructor can execute students' programs with a much larger set of hidden test cases in a single batch so that a more comprehensive assessment of the submissions can be performed efficiently. Afterwards, all the execution results can be released to the students so that they know exactly which test cases their programs fail, if any. This kind of prompt feedback to students in the whole class was rarely possible before PASS was developed [6].

PASS has been deployed for use for three years, having served more than a thousand students in various courses, ranging from introductory programming to data structures and data mining. It has recently been upgraded to its third version (PASS3), with many enhanced capabilities to facilitate not only fast feedback and detailed performance statistics, but also the adoption of new approaches and pedagogy towards the design of teaching and learning activities to benefit from web learning.

PASS has recorded all the program submission activities of students. All the submitted files and the execution results are stored. Students can retrieve their own submission, and download any files that they had submitted before. This design allows the user to keep track of all the versions of programs he/she had created, and understand when and what difficulties they had encountered in the past. An instructor has the privilege to access all the submission history related to the course. This gives the instructor a very detailed log on the activities of his/her students in PASS. He/she can also give feedback to a student based on a specific submission. The system also gives comprehensive information based on the raw information of test/submit history (Fig. 1). PASS provides these statistics to help the instructor understand the performance of the class. For example, the instructor can see the students' performance in individual programming problems in the course. The system allows the instructor to closely monitor each individual student's learning progress.

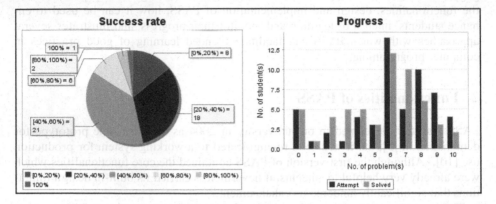

Fig. 1. Statistics of Students' Performance

We have recently done a survey on PASS3. Among the comments from students who had used both PASS3 and previous versions of PASS, 2 of them find that the previous version of PASS is better, 5 of them do not find any outstanding differences, while 16 of them think that PASS3 is better than the previous one: *"Now it becomes more useful by adding some functions"*, *"It is [more] faster."*, *"The current version is easier to use and very [user] friendly."*.

In the next section, we shall describe various aspects of the design and implementation of the latest version of PASS. Section 4 illustrates some new approaches and pedagogy towards blended learning facilitated by PASS. Section 5 concludes this paper.

3 Design and Implementation of PASS

A critical difference between PASS and its earlier versions is the employment of J2EE application server. The sophisticated functions, *e.g.* Remote Method Invocation, Message-Driven Bean, *etc.*, provided by J2EE allow PASS to handle the technical issues in an efficient and platform-independent way. Besides, PASS now employs standard frameworks in all the layers in the Model-View-Control model. Moreover, the architecture of PASS is designed deliberately to ensure its modularity, configurability and extensibility. Other than the technical differences, PASS has a number of new functionalities, *e.g.* plagiarism detection, graphical statistics, submission history, problem repository, *etc.*, making PASS a multi-functional tool that takes care of many more aspects in a computer programming course.

System Flow

Fig. 2 shows the system architecture of PASS. Any actions caught at the user web pages will be passed to the Web Controllers which control the page flows and are dispatched to the corresponding back-end logic. Web Controllers are built based on Struts, a well-known view framework for Java web applications. The Web Controllers then pass the actions to the corresponding Application Controllers by means of remote method invocation (RMI), for instance, to invoke Program Management Session Bean (PMSB) to complete the program submission process. By decoupling web control and application control, PASS can be flexibly plugged to any other view framework or interface if necessary in the future. When an Application Controller gets the action orders, which could come from PASS itself or from an external system, it calls the relevant internal logic to complete the required actions.

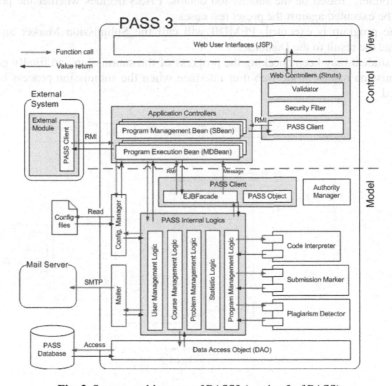

Fig. 2. System architecture of PASS3 (version 3 of PASS)

To illustrate the system flow, we shall use the program submission process as an example (Fig. 3). The sequence of actions for such a process is as follows:

1. The student selects a problem, uploads the program code file and clicks the submit button on the web interface.
2. A corresponding Web Controller packages the web form data to a submission bean object and calls the Program Management Session Bean (PMSB) with the façade in PASS client.

3. After the Authority Manager in PMSB checks the user's authority of program submission, it will call the Program Management Logic (PML) to proceed with the program submission process.
4. PML stores the submission details in the Database via the Data Access Object (DAO), and the submission file(s) in a specific folder designated for the user.
5. PML sends the program execute message to the queue of Program Execution Message Driven Bean (PEMDB) and then returns the submission result via RMI to PASS Client and finally to the web user interface.
6. If PEMDB is free, it picks the message from the program execution message queue, and then calls the Program Execution Session Bean (PESB) to execute the program.
7. The submitted program is then compiled by PESB using a corresponding Code Interpreter. Based on the submission details, PASS decides whether the program will be executed against the preset test cases.
8. If the program is executed, PEMDB will call the Submission Marker and then update the result to the Database.
9. The student may keep checking the progress of the submission and finally gets the submission results at the web user interface when the submission process is completed.

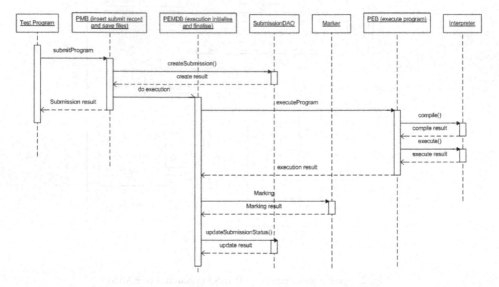

Fig. 3. Sequence of actions for a typical program submission

The process of handling other actions, such as creating a user, is more or less similar (but usually less complicated).

Session Bean and Message Driven Bean
Session Bean (SB) and Message Driven Bean (MDB) technology is used to allow remote access to the internal logics of PASS. SB is used to handle internal logics that need immediate response or return value. The corresponding modules, such as data

management, problem submission and statistics retrieval, are all put in SB. MDB is used to handle internal logics that do not need immediate attention, so that the client does not need to wait in case the process needs a long time to complete.

For example, a complicated program with a large number of test cases may require a long computational time when students test their programs in PASS. Such actions will be handled by MDB. Furthermore, more than one program execution server can be set up to share the work load and avoid overwhelming the program execution services. The main server will then select the available program execution servers to execute students' programs. In this way, the reliability and scalability of the system can be greatly improved.

The usage of EJB also enables the access of PASS by an external system with PASS client package. In our implementation, we have connected PASS with Blackboard, the E-Learning portal of the University. A Bb2PASS module is developed based on PASS client package to allow users to login PASS directly from Blackboard. In due course, Blackboard can remotely import the student assignment scores from PASS and record them in its Gradebook database.

Security of Program Execution
Submitted program codes can be in any form and may contain improper or harmful instructions, either innocently or due to malicious intention. To validate a submitted program by restricting the use of harmful keywords would be ineffective, as the user can manipulate the value of variables in any possible way. To handle such security threats, a guest account with limited privilege is used to establish a J2EE server. A submitted program will be handed to the session bean of this J2EE server for execution. Since the guest account only has access rights to its own folder, any unauthorised operation such as deleting files or reading files in other folders will be forbidden at the operating system level. Moreover, the separation of the execution server and the main server can also help to protect the system files and data from corruption due to the execution.

Queuing of Program Execution
PASS maintains a queue to handle requests of program execution. When too many users submit and run their programs at the same time, the resources of the system will eventually be exhausted. To prevent such an adverse impact to the system, MDB is used. Every program execution request is first sent to the message queue and then waits for a free server. This ensures the fairness of execution and also prevents the exhaustion of the system resources.

Configurability
Most of the system properties, such as, the user authority, are kept in a configuration file. All the authorities for the actions against user roles can be defined individually. For example, a course leader can browse or make change to all submission records for his/her course, while students in a course can only retrieve their own submissions. Other properties like compiler settings, database settings and system log settings are all configurable by editing the configuration file. Putting all properties separately from codes makes it easier to maintain the system setup. Besides, PASS allows

dynamic loading of the properties so that changes of the configuration file will take effect without restarting its services.

Extensibility

PASS has been designed to leave room for future feature extensions and enhancements. By implementing the appropriate interfaces, a system developer can create new modules without the need for extensive modifications to the current logics. Extensible components in PASS include the code interpreter, test marker and plagiarism detector. These components can be replaced easily by other components that implement the same programme interfaces.

Flexibility in View Layer

Apache Struts is employed in the View and Control layers of the Model-View-Controller (MVC) architecture. This framework allows a tidy and flexible implementation for Java web applications. For the control layer, flows of logic or JavaServer Pages (JSPs) are maintained within XML (eXtensible Markup Language) files. Validation of user inputs can also be done by defining validation rules within XML files. These XML configuration files integrate important logics and flows, which permit an easy way of maintaining the web application. At the view layer, Struts provides several sets of tag libraries to reduce the size of the JSP codes, making them cleaner and clearer.

Besides using Struts, PASS makes good use of servlet filters. Logics like front end security controls and HTTP request marshalling are implemented into servlet filters to reduce duplicate codes.

Message resources, such as labels or wordings in the JSPs, are maintained within properties files. It unifies the messages displayed among different pages, and makes them easy to modify. Besides, internationalization is also enabled by preparing different properties files that can then be loaded based on the locale setting within the user's operating system.

User-friendliness of the Interface

Various APIs are used in PASS for better presentation of information. For example, DisplayTag is used for most of the table presentations in the JSPs. With the built-in functions like page break, sorting and data export, the system developer can focus on the system design and implementation. Also, JFreeChart is used for generating various kinds of professional quality charts for statistics display (Fig. 1).

Timely hints are generally useful for users to make decisions when they are trying different options before committing to their decisions. PASS uses the technique of Asynchronous JavaScript and XML (AJAX) [7], an advanced usage of JavaScript, as a solution to avoid massive information to be fetched for each page. In brief, finely-grained HTTP requests are made when users interact with the controls within a JSP. Instant responses can then be given to the user, without reloading the whole page.

This technique can be used when user types in some IDs. In the traditional way, the user will be prompted whether their input ID is valid or not only after they have submitted their form to the server. By using AJAX, the system can give an interactive hint to tell if the ID being input by the user is valid or not (Fig. 4).

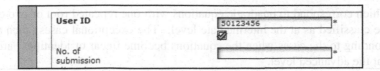

Fig. 4. AJAX application example

Plagiarism Detection

PASS includes a plagiarism detector that calculates similarity scores among the submitted program codes. Pairs of program codes are considered to be excessively similar if their similarity score exceed a certain threshold, which may be adjusted by the instructor. To help instructors identify groups of students who might have shared the same source code, PASS can cluster the submitted program codes with similarity scores greater than the threshold. The current version of PASS calculates the similarity score based on the longest common subsequence between two program codes. Provisions have been made in PASS to facilitate the incorporation of new or more powerful algorithms for the purpose so that in the future, different plagiarism detectors may be used together or separately by different instructors.

4 Approaches to Blended Learning Using PASS

The teaching and learning of computer programming is a challenging job. A well-designed pedagogy can make the instruction most effective. However, the traditional mode of education imposes a lot of constraints to the design of pedagogy. Certain types of teaching and learning activities are extremely difficult to conduct within a standard classroom setting. Students often find it difficult to master those advanced programming paradigms without adequate practice. Blended learning combines different media and methods to maximise students' learning. PASS enables us to blend our courses to render the teaching and learning of programming more effective.

It is believed that effective instruction involves working the content to provide stepwise learning experiences with checks along the way to assure that each step is learned [11]. It is important to ensure that students are well-trained in the fundamentals to the extent that they can eventually consider some problems with high-level complexity. We pay extra care to design the teaching and learning activities to incorporate stepwise learning. Students taking computer programming courses very often come with diverse backgrounds and ability levels. PASS allows us to design exercises with various levels of difficulty to fulfil the differing needs of students with diverse backgrounds and ability levels. Also, we can create a series of test cases with different levels of difficulty for the same programming problem (see Fig. 5 and 6).

To illustrate the idea, we take the programming exercise of solving a quadratic equation as a running example (Fig. 5). We may group the test cases into three levels of difficulty, namely, the beginner level, intermediate level and advanced level. The equations which have two distinct real roots are considered relatively easier; and therefore we classify the corresponding test cases as at the beginner level. The test cases which correspond to quadratic equations with one repeated root or two complex roots are classified as at the intermediate level. The exceptional cases (such as those corresponding to the cases when the equations become linear or identities) are classified as at the advanced level.

A Programming Exercise of Solving a Quadratic Equation

Write a program to solve a quadratic equation. The general form of a quadratic equation is $ax^2 + bx + c = 0$, where a, b, c are real numbers. When $a \neq 0$, the solution of the equation is given by the quadratic formula $x = \dfrac{-b \pm \sqrt{b^2 - 4ac}}{2a}$.

Assume all inputs are integers, and the outputs are to be displayed in descending order.

Test Cases at the Beginner Level of Difficulty

Input	Expected Output
$a = 1, b = -5, c = 6$	$x = 3, 2$
$a = 2, b = -7, c = -15$	$x = 5, -1.5$
$a = 1, b = 6, c = 8$	$x = -2, -4$

Test Cases at the Intermediate Level of Difficulty

Input	Expected Output
$a = 1, b = -2, c = 1$	$x = 1$
$a = 1, b = 2, c = 5$	$x = -1+2i, -1-2i$
$a = 2, b = 12, c = 18$	$x = -3$

Test Cases at the Advanced Level of Difficulty

Input	Expected Output
$a = 0, b = 2, c = 4$	$x = -2$
$a = 0, b = 0, c = 0$	x = any real numbers
$a = 0, b = 0, c = -4$	No solution

Fig. 5. Description of a programming exercise at different levels of difficulty

Unit	Prob. No.	Problem difficulty	Prob. Type
Quadratic Equation	Beginner Level	☆☆	Practice
Quadratic Equation	Intermediate Level	☆☆☆☆	Practice
Quadratic Equation	Advanced Level	☆☆☆☆☆ ☆☆	Practice

Fig. 6. Exercises at different levels of difficulty and sample runs of submissions in PASS

PASS allows us to inform the students the level of difficulty of each exercise (Fig. 6). For the same problem, students can attempt the exercises based on their capability. For example, the less talented students may design a simple program to solve the problem at the beginner level of difficulty. They must enhance their programs in order to solve the problem at the intermediate level of difficulty. However, the talented students may work directly to solve the problem at the intermediate level of difficulty. They can even try to challenge the exceptional test cases by submitting their programs to solve the problem at the advanced level of difficulty. Eventually, they should come up with a single program which can solve the problem up to a certain level of difficulty. This approach allows the students to regulate their own learning pace. Additionally, we require students to study the given test cases at different difficulty levels for each exercise to figure out how we select the test cases so that they can learn how to test their programs on their own.

Furthermore, a programming course typically has a large class size. It is difficult to closely monitor individual student's learning progress in the traditional teaching mode. PASS provides very useful information of students' performance. The summary of student performance supports fast decision making as well. We can identify the slow learners quickly and offer corresponding help. At the same time, we encourage the talented students to offer peer assistance to other students. Moreover, we find that the talented students put in additional efforts to study all related materials before they offer help. Besides, they can further enhance their understanding by explaining the programs to others. This approach improves the learning of both groups of students.

As instructors of computer programming courses, we not only have to teach students how to write programs, but also need to develop our students with good programming practices, such as modularity, reusability and information hiding. With the support of PASS, we have incorporated and promoted these good programming practices in designing our teaching and learning activities.

When we design a programming activity, we break the program into smaller modules in the form of functions and classes. The students are required to implement their individual modules in separate files. The files are then uploaded to PASS for testing by using the test driver which is pre-loaded to PASS by the instructor. This approach highlights the modularity of computer programs. The students are exposed to programs that are built from modules so that they learn the concept of modularity of program by implicit learning [2].

Moreover, we require the students to archive all the files developed in their activities. When designing a programming activity, we intentionally require the students to make use of some modules developed in previous activities by importing the corresponding files. For example, we may require students to develop a program to solve a quadratic inequality (Fig. 7) based on the module developed earlier in the programming exercise of solving a quadratic equation (Fig. 5). In this way, students will naturally acquire the concept of code reuse through their own experience of reusing the previously developed code, as concrete experience is important in the learning cycle [9]. On the other hand, we sometimes ask students to exchange files and develop their applications based on modules written by other students. For different exercises of the same programming problem, we sometimes provide different implementations of the same module as separate exercises in PASS. Students are required to submit their solutions to all exercises of the problem. In order to pass all the exercises, the students need to write the code purely based on the module interface. By doing these exercises, students will gradually recognise the importance of information hiding.

Finally, traditional pedagogy focuses on the development of small applications. Without the support of related technology, students usually develop small applications by writing the code solely on their individual effort. The student may become an analyst programmer in the future and may be involved in some large scale projects. Students often find it difficult to manage large software development jobs when they work in the industry. It is very important to provide students with experiences of software development in large scale applications while they are studying. However, there are practical difficulties to require students to develop a large application. First of all, students' learning motivation drops very fast as the time they have to spend on study increases. If we require the student to code a large application, they are usually unable to see their results before the completion of the whole application. They will lose their interests in programming soon after they started. Lack of motivation is one of the major resistances to learning [1]. As we foresee the need, we consider large application development as an essential part of an advanced programming course. Some special arrangements have to be made to keep the students' learning motivation. When we design a large application, we may divide the application into several modules. After the student has completed one module of the application, he/she can submit the modules to PASS. Some stubs or test drivers can be provided for testing their individual modules. It is important to reinforce the student's success upon his/her completion of one module. This approach also increases the student's confidence in learning. The intermediate results can keep students' learning motivation constantly high. The students will develop the application in a progressive manner. After the students have completed the entire application, they can submit it to PASS, which will test all the modules together as a single integrated application.

A Programming Exercise of Solving a Quadratic Inequality

Write a program to solve a quadratic inequality based on the module developed earlier in the programming exercise of quadratic equation. In general, a quadratic inequality can be written in one of the following standard forms, where a, b, c are real numbers:

$$ax^2 + bx + c \geq 0$$
$$ax^2 + bx + c > 0$$
$$ax^2 + bx + c \leq 0$$
$$ax^2 + bx + c < 0$$

Suppose that the equation $ax^2 + bx + c = 0$ has two real roots x_1 and x_2, where $x_1 < x_2$. If $a > 0$, the solution sets of the inequalities are, respectively, as follows.

Inequality: $ax^2 + bx + c \geq 0$. Solution: $(-\infty, x_1] \cup [x_2, +\infty)$

Inequality: $ax^2 + bx + c > 0$. Solution: $(-\infty, x_1) \cup (x_2, +\infty)$

Inequality: $ax^2 + bx + c \leq 0$. Solution: $[x_1, x_2]$

Fig. 7. A programming exercise based on a previously completed module

5 Conclusion

This paper has described the design and functionalities of the latest version of PASS. PASS now allows the instructor to effectively locate the slow learners and identify the high achievers by the statistical data it collects while students are using it to test their own programs. We have also explained, with concrete illustrative examples, how classroom teaching and learning activities may be blended with practice exercises that are supported and monitored by PASS. By designing exercises at different levels of difficulty, PASS can provide stepwise learning experiences to students, such that they can solve problems pertaining to their corresponding ability levels. Instructors can also define problems in various ways in PASS so as to make students familiar with modules programming and be prepared for large projects.

We have demonstrated just a few ideas on how PASS can be used to support blended learning. PASS is still under active development and enhancement. We anticipate that PASS will continue to evolve in various ways to support more types of web teaching and learning activities, ultimately aiming towards the goal of improving students' learning of computer programming.

References

1. Atherton, J.S.: Resistance to learning: A discussion based on participants in in-service professional training programmes. Journal of Vocational Education and Training 51(1), 77–90 (1999)
2. Berry, D.C. (ed.): How implicit is implicit learning. Oxford University Press, Oxford (1997)
3. du Boulay, B.: Some difficulties of learning to program. In: Soloway, E., Spohrer, J.C. (eds.) Studying the novice programmer, L. Erlbaum Associates, Hillsdale, NJ (1989)
4. Cheang, B., Kurnia, A., Lim, A., Oon, W.C.: On automated grading of programming assignments in an academic institution. Computers & Education 41(2), 121–131 (2003)
5. Chong, S.L., Choy, M.: Towards a progressive learning environment for programming courses. In: Liu, W., Shi, Y., Li, Q. (eds.) ICWL 2004. LNCS, vol. 3143, pp. 200–205. Springer, Heidelberg (2004)
6. Choy, M., Nazir, U., Poon, C.K., Yu, Y.T.: Experiences in using an automated system for improving students' learning of computer programming. In: Lau, R.W.H., Li, Q., Cheung, R., Liu, W. (eds.) ICWL 2005. LNCS, vol. 3583, pp. 267–272. Springer, Heidelberg (2005)
7. Choy, M., Lam, S., Poon, C.K., Wang, F.L., Yu, Y.T., Yuen, L.: Towards blended learning of computer programming supported by an automated system. In: Fong, J., Wang, F.L. (eds.) Blended Learning, Person, pp. 9–18 (2007)
8. Garret, J.J.: Ajax: A new approach to web applications (2005) (last access April 4, 2007), http://www.adaptivepath.com/publications/essays/archives/000385.php
9. Graham, C.R.: Blended learning systems: definition, current trends, and future directions. In: Bonk, C.J., Graham, C.R. (eds.) Handbook of blended learning: global perspectives, local designs, Pfeiffer Publishing, San Franciso, CA (2006)
10. Kolb, D.A.: Experiential learning: experience as the source of learning and development. Prentice-Hall, New Jersey (1984)

11. Nazir, U., Poon, C.K., Yu, Y.T., Choy, M.: Automated assessment for improving the learning of computer programming: Potentials and challenges. In: Proc. 9th Global Chinese Conference on Computers in Education (GCCCE 2005), pp. 634–639 (2005)
12. Schulman, M.: Basic understandings for developing learning media for the classroom and beyond. Learning Technology Newsletter 3(1) (2001)
13. Yu, Y.T., Poon, C.K., Choy, M.: Experiences with PASS: Developing and using a programming assignment assessment system. In: Proc. 6th International Conference on Quality Software (QSIC 2006), pp. 360–365. IEEE Computer Society Press, Los Alamitos (2006)

Web-Based Logging of Classroom Teaching Activities for Blended Learning

Joseph Fong

Department of Computer Science, City University of Hong Kong, Hong Kong
csjfong@cityu.edu.hk

Abstract. Nowadays, eLearning has been adapted in all educational institutes, starting from kindergartens, primary schools, high schools, to the universities. Teachers are encouraged to use computer and Internet as a teaching medium in addition to the classroom teaching. The result is a blended learning which combines eLearning as a supplementary learning means to classroom learning. The issue becomes what is the best approach for blended learning for the effective and productive teaching methods. This paper suggests to record (log) all teaching activities into a web site for students to self study after classroom learning. The objective is to provide students more flexibility in learning with more facilities of eLearning, classroom learning and/or blended learning. A case study is illustrated in the paper for discussion.

Keywords: blended learning, teaching activities, classroom learning, eLearning, Education.

1 Introduction

Education in general are undergoing rapid transition from the traditional learning and teaching to the more self-motivated mode constructivism through the application of IT. Many education institutes have made a tremendous step forward in the setting up of EDO (education office) in the promotion of eLearning. Efforts have been made on the implementation of a university wide educational Extra/Internet with the aim of facilitating a better learning and teaching environment as well as improving the overall student administration. Products such as WebCT [1] and Blackboard [2] have been in use for the past few years with a degree of success. As a rule, these products all suffer on two counts:

1. They focus more on course management rather than learning process.
2. Little consideration is given to areas such as workshops and projects. There is a complete absence of semi-automatic assessment facilities with performance tracking for facilitating an understanding of the strength and weakness of students.

Basically, eLearning can be categorized into different areas as follows:

eLearning for adaptive learning –In order to speed up the learning curve of learners, we aim to supplement classroom learning with eLearning. The students can do

H. Leung et al. (Eds.): ICWL 2007, LNCS 4823, pp. 597–605, 2008.
© Springer-Verlag Berlin Heidelberg 2008

self learning from web-based learning exercises on the Internet, which will assess the students' academic level and provide them with suitable online exercises to work on. As a result, the students can learn everywhere, any time through Internet.

eLearning for teacher helpers –In order to reduce teachers' workloads in authoring exercises for their students, in getting student feedback and in communicating with students more effectively, many eLearning systems facilitate these functionalities for teachers as their helpers. For example, eLearning authoring tools can help teachers to prepare exercises, and BLOG journal files can help teachers get student feedback on a particular learning problem or subject.

eLearning for distance learning –Besides traditional classroom learning, students can also access learning facilities remotely. For example, a virtual cyber laboratory can help students to perform their laboratory exercises at home through the Internet. An online tutorial session can help students access their tutors through their notebook computers. Consequently, students can learn in a very comfortable environment without incurring traveling time, cost and hassle.

eLearning technology infrastructure –In order to make eLearning a success, technology infrastructure is a must. In fact, eLearning is more cost effective whenever it can be accessed by mass learners, because individual costs will be less with increased numbers of learners for eLearning while the eLearning development time and effort is fixed. In other words, once an eLearning package has been produced, it can be reused many times with minimal operating cost. However, such mass learner operations need the support of technology. Thus, research on eLearning technology infrastructure is another important area for researchers to explore.

On the educational side, Blended Learning provides educators with the opportunity to showcase best practice by reporting the match between learning or outcome objectives and the development and implementation of this hybrid (blended) learning strategies and material to engage students in achieving those objectives. Ideally underpinned by learning theory, we should also attempt to demonstrate the value added to learning by using the blended approach. Both components of hybrid learning — the classroom and the eLearning contributions — should be presented to the students..

2 Related Work

A definition of Blended Learning [3] is the combination of multiple approaches to learning, such as self-paced, collaborative or inquiry-based study. Blended learning can be accomplished through the use of 'blended' virtual and physical resources. Examples include combinations of technology-based materials, face-to-face sessions and print materials.

Another definition of Blended learning [4] is a powerful training solution that combines E-Learning with a variety of other delivery methods for a superior learning experience.

A third definition of Blended learning [5] combines face-to-face and computer mediated instruction.

Some educators [6] give their experience of implemented of Outcome-based learning as blended learning in University of Sydney. As standards for the use of Information and Communication Technology in teaching and learning are a relatively new aspect of the blended learning, their adoptions by the academics are still in its early stage.

Other educators [7] valuated blended learning as a mixture of online and fact-to-face learning using a variety of learning resources and communications options available to students and lecturers. In so doing a learning environment is created that is richer than either a traditional face-to-face environment or a fully online environment.

ICWL2006 keynote [8] states that Learning theory, collaborative learning, and deep consideration of the technologies that may be leveraged should all be pulled together in defining techniques and guidelines for the creation of great Web-based contents and blended curricula.

The objective of this paper is to implement the idea in the keynote.

3 Classroom Teaching Activities Logging

In general, classroom activities include lectures, tutorial session, laboratory, project, review, questions and answers, open forum and presentation etc. Each course focuses in certain aspect of activities due to its syllabus requirements. To the students, they are mainly interested in two issues: how much do they learn and what is their grade for the course. If the lecturer can log these activities into a web site for student's reference, it will be easier for students to know the priority importance of each teaching activity as follows:

- Lectures: - We can video record lectures for students to review them at home. However, this involves facilities management and operations. Many long distance education institutes provide such services for remote learning. Also, sometimes students complain about spending too much time copying the written notes from the blackboard. In this case, lecturer may consider storing the images of the written notes into the web site for students to download after the lecture. Furthermore, references can also be put into the web site for students to enhance their knowledge in the subject.
- Tutorial sessions – Students come to tutorial sessions for small group learning. They can ask more questions in the sessions for peer-to-peer learning, with more in-depth discussion of the subject. An effective approach is for teachers assess the students' knowledge by giving tutorial exercises in the sessions. After marking the answers from students, the lecturers can discuss the answers with the students. Thus, the questions and answers are logged into the web site for students to review them. In this way, the students can learn even if the students are absent in the sessions.
- Laboratory exercises – Students use laboratory for their hands-on exercises. However, they may not have enough time to finish them in the laboratory. An alternative is to do the exercises on the Internet at home. Sometimes, for long distance education institutes, they allow students access laboratory facilities through remote logging. Both techniques can serve the students well.

- Open forum – It is important for students discuss questions about the lecture among themselves. An open forum in the classroom and in a web site can be very helpful. A BLOG system is good to log these open forum conversation. Students can refer them even though they were not involved at the beginning of the discussion. This open forum is managed by the lecturer just in case incorrect message or information is passed among students.
- Mind set diagram – A course in general covers many subjects. It is important for students to know the learning sequence of these subjects. A mind set diagram of the course can help students realize the position of each subject in the course. In other words, how the subjects are related to each other. Students should also be allowed to put their comments in the subjects which are the syllabus of the course. A picture is worth thousands words. The diagram is very helpful for the students' understanding of the course.
- Grading system – A computerized grading report system can assess students knowledge effectively and make them realize their understanding of the course materials immediately. The lecturers post the students' grade of each assignment online along with the model answers so that the students can correct their mistakes at once. This will trigger students ask more questions in the class.
- Project management – Lecturers act as project supervisors to student's projects. They define the project requirements and monitor student's progress through face-to-face interview during the duration of the project. Furthermore, an eLearning system allows students to ftp their work to a departmental server on a regular basis. A test log of submitted work and simple version control tracks students' performance. A particular server allows students to install software in pre-specified folders. This reduces the chance of hard coding, which is a bad practice normally committed by most students. Video conferencing facilities can be in place to allow formal communication between students and supervisor at pre-defined interval, such as once a week, and a log on students' progress and supervisors can be maintained.
- Assessment – The assessment system usually composes of two elements: quiz and test. Quiz provides immediate feedback to enhance the learning process whereas tests are for evaluation of students progress with the following functions:
  ✓ Calculate marks automatically
  ✓ Generate reports on the performance for quiz as well as test for the individual, the class and for different cohorts.
  ✓ Students can learn at their own pace and are free to choose the time and level for their quiz with summary feedback on the performance indicating weakness in certain areas.
  ✓ Students' learning pattern rules can be derived through statistical analysis of their learning results be the course web site using data mining approach.
- Course Work Management – Students can submit coursework with specific instructions and assigned readings. The collection of assignments is based on a predetermined schedule and at the pace of students' progress.
  ✓ Create lockers with unlimited number and level
  ✓ Edit the lockers

✓ Remove the lockers
✓ Submit homework to the locker through the web browser
✓ Acknowledgement on receipts to avoid disputes

- Scheduling – This acts as a communication channel between lectures and students. Course assignments, submission deadlines and requirements can be broadcasted to students by lecturers. The lecturers can also mark down project meetings and agreed work schedule with students. Shareware can be modified for this purpose.

4   A Case Study

To illustrate the teaching techniques of blended learning, we choose teaching a course on "Data warehousing and Data mining" as a case study. The subject is rich in content, and each syllabus can be taught in depth for several lectures. The course aims to focus on the practical application of the data warehousing and data mining.

The whole course web site hierarchy is designed as simple as possible. It is done according to Hick's law [9]. It has predicting for a web site which consumes the user lesser time to browser if the hierarchy is small. In turns, the user will get the appropriate data easily with less short-term memory load.

The home page covers the course teaching plan, scheduling, and outcome based teaching and learning objectives. The coursework consists of the project assignment, review and tutorial questions, hands-on and eLearning exercises, and references etc. The Grade web page is to list out students' grades for each submitted assignment. The Open forum is for students communicating with each other and the lecturers for general discussion on the lecture. The Mind Mapping web page describe the learning sequence of syllabuses in the course.

In the whole web sites, every web page contains a header and a navigation bar, the consistency layout let the user easily browse the web site without getting lost. Furthermore, there is no table in the layout. It is good for both search engine optimization as well as the accessibility of the users who use the screen readers as shown in Fig. 1.

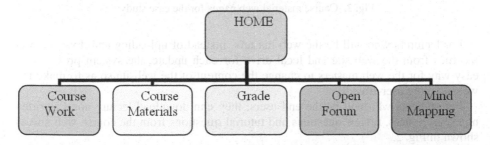

Fig. 1. System Architecture of a course web site

In each lecture, lecture notes, written notes, references, review questions, tutorial questions, hands-on and eLearning exercises are all put into the course web for students to review and comprehend.

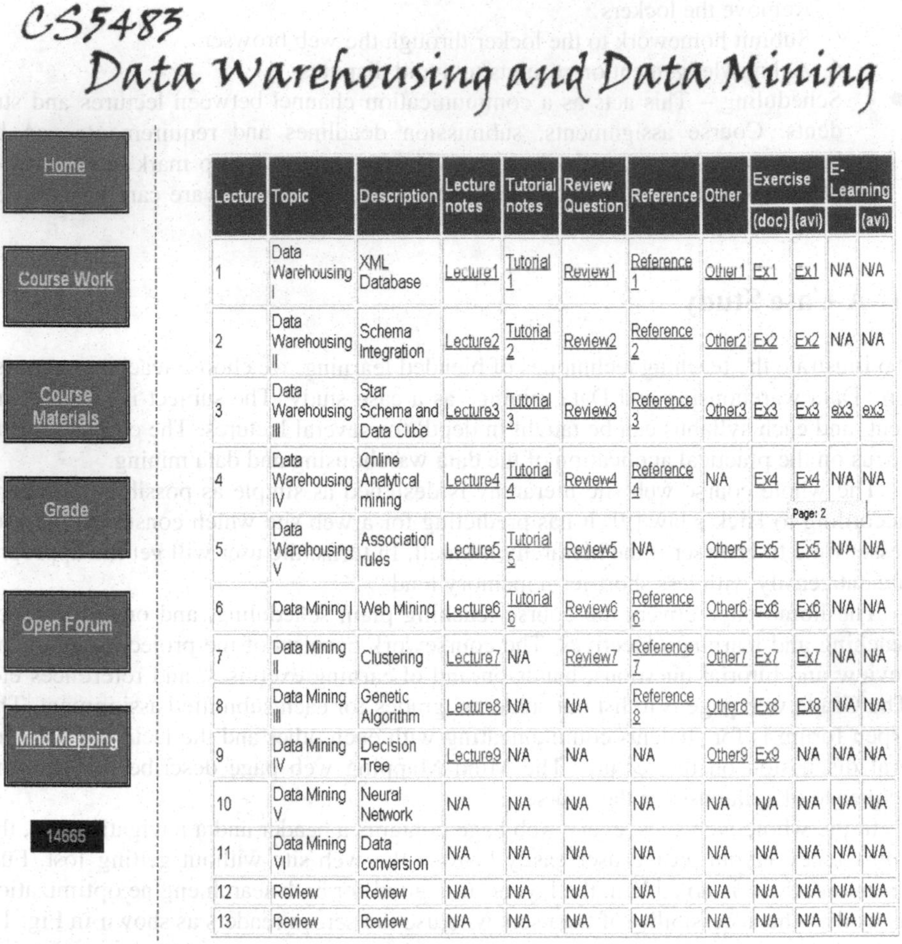

CS5483
Data Warehousing and Data Mining

Lecture	Topic	Description	Lecture notes	Tutorial notes	Review Question	Reference	Other	Exercise (doc)	Exercise (avi)	E-Learning (avi)	E-Learning (avi)
1	Data Warehousing I	XML Database	Lecture1	Tutorial1	Review1	Reference1	Other1	Ex1	Ex1	N/A	N/A
2	Data Warehousing II	Schema Integration	Lecture2	Tutorial2	Review2	Reference2	Other2	Ex2	Ex2	N/A	N/A
3	Data Warehousing III	Star Schema and Data Cube	Lecture3	Tutorial3	Review3	Reference3	Other3	Ex3	Ex3	ex3	ex3
4	Data Warehousing IV	Online Analytical mining	Lecture4	Tutorial4	Review4	Reference4	N/A	Ex4	Ex4	N/A	N/A
5	Data Warehousing V	Association rules	Lecture5	Tutorial5	Review5	N/A	Other5	Ex5	Ex5	N/A	N/A
6	Data Mining I	Web Mining	Lecture6	Tutorial6	Review6	Reference6	Other6	Ex6	Ex6	N/A	N/A
7	Data Mining II	Clustering	Lecture7	N/A	Review7	Reference7	Other7	Ex7	Ex7	N/A	N/A
8	Data Mining III	Genetic Algorithm	Lecture8	N/A	N/A	Reference8	Other8	Ex8	Ex8	N/A	N/A
9	Data Mining IV	Decision Tree	Lecture9	N/A	N/A	N/A	Other9	Ex9	N/A	N/A	N/A
10	Data Mining V	Neural Network	N/A	N/A	N/A	N/A	N/A	N/A	N/A	N/A	N/A
11	Data Mining VI	Data conversion	N/A	N/A	N/A	N/A	N/A	N/A	N/A	N/A	N/A
12	Review	Review	N/A	N/A	N/A	N/A	N/A	N/A	N/A	N/A	N/A
13	Review	Review	N/A	N/A	N/A	N/A	N/A	N/A	N/A	N/A	N/A

Navigation buttons: Home, Course Work, Course Materials, Grade, Open Forum, Mind Mapping, 14665

Page: 2

Fig. 2. Course material web pages for the case study

For lecturers who will be the web masters, instead of uploading and downloading the files from the web site and local drive for each update, the system provides an easy way for the web masters to change the content of the website so as to make the website more user-friendly.

For students who will be the end users, they can download lecture notes, written notes, references, review questions and tutorial questions from the course web site as shown in Fig. 2.

In order to help students learn effectively, a mind set diagram is set up on the course web site for the students to know the learning sequence of the course. They are the syllabuses of data cleaning, data integration, star schema design, data cube loading, followed by different data mining techniques of Association Rules, Clustering, Decision Tree, Neural Network, Web Mining and Genetic Algorithm. XML technology

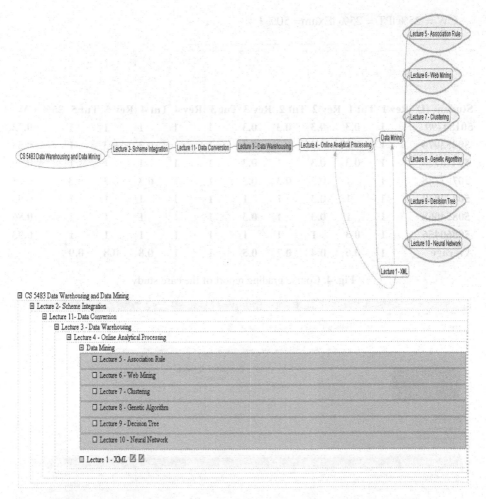

Fig. 3. Mind Set diagram for course on Data Warehousing and Data Mining

is introduced in the course for report generation and transmission on the Internet. The arrows signs show the sequence of learning syllabus in the course.

For students, there is a mind-map learning page provided for them as end users. They can give out their opinion about the structure of the course with fully understanding the basic structure of the web site as shown in Fig. 3.

Instead of uploading and downloading of excel file to update the grades of students, the system can provide dynamically function for the web master to record the grade with the address [10].

After marking the review and tutorial questions, the grades are put on the course web site. The score ranges from-0 (no score) to 1 (full score). The review questions are on theories and the tutorial questions are on the application of the theories taught in the class. Students are encouraged for peer-to-peer learning through discussion to each other before submitting their answers as shown in Fig. 4.

CW = 25% |PT = 25% |Exam= 50% |

Student ID	Rev 1	Tut 1	Rev 2	Tut 2	Rev 3	Tut 3	Rev 4	Tut 4	Rev 5	Tut 5	25% CW
50184799	1	0.3	0.3	0.3	0.3	1	1	1	1	1	0.72
50453076	1	0.3	0.3	0.3	0.3	1	1	0.3	0.3	1	0.58
50478728	1	0.3	0.3	1	0.3	1	1	1	1	1	0.79
50797788	1	1	0.3	0.3	0.3	1	1	0.3	0.3	0.3	0.58
50832039	1	1	0.3	1	1	1	1	1	1	1	0.93
50854068	1	1	0.3	1	0.3	1	1	1	1	1	0.86
50860456	1	0.3	1	1	1	1	1	1	1	1	0.93
Average	1	0.6	0.4	0.7	0.5	1	1	0.8	0.8	0.9	

Fig. 4. Course grading report of the case study

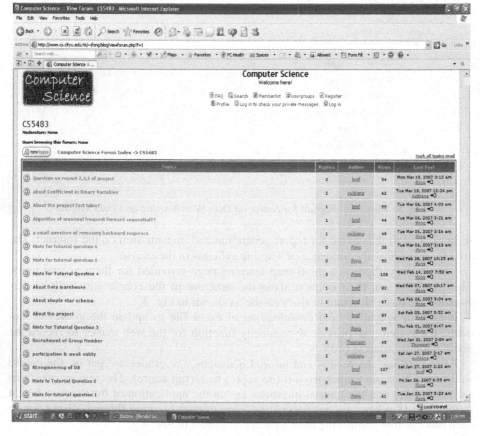

Fig. 5. Open forum for the course web site

In order to encourage peer-to-peer learning, an open forum is put on the course web site for students discuss problems and solution among themselves. They can also ask lecturers on the lectures. The open forum applies blogging system such that students are free to append their comments to each particular subject that they are interested in. Security need to be implemented to block non-students intruders erase the blog messages as shown in Fig. 5.

5 Conclusion

Ever since IT has been widely used in teaching, blended learning is the trend of teaching method for all levels of educational institutes. Combined with eLearning as supplementary learning avenue to class room learning, this paper introduces many ways of logging teaching activities into the web site which can help students learn more effectively inside and outside of the classroom. The result will be a very close partnership between teachers and students in teaching and learning.

Reference

1. http://www.WebCT.com
2. http://www.Blackboard.com
3. http://en.wikipedia.org/wiki/Blended_learning
4. http://www.E-Learningcentre.co.uk/eclipse/Resources/blended.htm
5. Charles, G.: Blended Learning Systems. In: Bonk, C.J., Graham, C.R. (eds.) Handbook of blended learning: Global Perspectives, local designs, Pfeiffer Publishing, San Francisco, CA (2003) (An Imprint of Wiley)
6. Applebee, A., Elis, R., Sheely, S.: Developing a blended learning community at the U of Sydney. In: Atkinson, R., et al. (eds.) Beyond the Comfort Zone. Proceedings of the 21st ASCILITE Conference, pp. 58–66 (2004)
7. Harding, A., Kaczynski, D., Wood, L.: Evaluation of blended learning analysis of qualitative data. In: Proceedings of UniServe Science Blended Learning Symposium, pp. 56–61 (2005)
8. Kim, W.: Directions for Web-Based Learning. In: Liu, W., Li, Q., Lau, R.W.H. (eds.) ICWL 2006. LNCS, vol. 4181, pp. 1–9. Springer, Heidelberg (2006)
9. http://www.hockscqc.com/articles/hickslaw.htm
10. http://www.cs.cityu.edu.hk/~jfong/grade/CS5483

Blended Teaching and Learning of Computer Programming*

Fu Lee Wang[1], Joseph Fong[1], Marian Choy[1], and Tak-Lam Wong[2]

[1] Department of Computer Science, City University of Hong Kong,
Kowloon Tong, Hong Kong
{flwang, csjfong, csmchoy}@cityu.edu.hk
[2] Department of Computer Science and Engineering,
The Chinese University of Hong Kong,
Shatin, Hong Kong
wongtl@cse.cuhk.edu.hk

Abstract. Teaching of computer programming has created significant difficulties to both teachers and students. Blended teaching and learning combines face-to-face instruction and computer-assisted instruction to maximize students' learning. This paper will share our experiences in City University of Hong Kong (CityU) as we teach computer programming courses by blended model. Evaluation has showed that blended teaching and learning provide great flexibilities to both teaching and learning of computer programming. The students' academic results have been greatly improved in computer programming courses.

Keywords: Blended Learning, Computer Programming, Outcome Based Teaching & Learning.

1 Introduction

Computer programming is an essential fundamental skill required in many curriculums for higher education nowadays. It is commonly believed that the students would develop their general problem-solving skills through learning computer programming. However, learning of computer programming has created significant difficulties for high-school and university students, and has failed to catalyze the development of higher order thinking skills [9]. A number of challenges have been identified for both teaching and learning computer programming [9]. Related research has showed that intelligent computer-assisted instruction (ICAI) technology can be a more effective way of teaching introductory computer programming courses - for certain populations [1].

Blended teaching and learning is to combine face-to-face instruction with computer-assisted instruction [5, 7]. Blended model is the convergence of two representative learning environments. The traditional face-to-face learning environment has been used for centuries. On the other hand, the rapid development of technologies provides distributed learning environment as an alternative. In the past, these two environments are separated

---

* The work described in this paper was substantially supported by a grant from City University of Hong Kong (Project No.: 6000144). This paper is an extended version of [12].

H. Leung et al. (Eds.): ICWL 2007, LNCS 4823, pp. 606–617, 2008.

because they use different media/method combinations. Therefore, they are used to address the needs of different audiences [5]. Traditionally, distributed learning is used as an expansion to the face-to-face learning.

Taking the university education as an example, the face-to-face learning environment is used in a teach-directed synchronous environment where the interpersonal interaction is a key component. On the other hand, the distributed learning environment is usually used in distanced learning, which focus on asynchronous self-paced learning and learning-material is the key component [7]. The rapid development of technology has a significant impact on the learning environment. In fact, there is an increasing trend to integrate the two learning environments as a single system. Nowadays, more and more universities conduct the learning activities under both environments.

As there is an increasing need for blended learning systems, efforts have been continuously devoted into the research of blended learning [5]. A number of blended learning platforms have been developed in real world. Blackboard Academic Suite (Bb) is a well-developed learning platform [12] which has been widely used in educational institutes. WebCT is used to be a competitor of Blackboard [14]. At this moment, two leading companies co-operate to provide services to the education industry.

The City University of Hong Kong (CityU) has put a lot of effort in development E-Learning. The university has deployed the Blackboard Academic Suite [12] as its unified campus-wide E-Learning platform. Many E-Learning activities are currently conducted in this platform. The Department of Computer Science is one of the departments who are devoted in E-Learning development.

Last year, the department underwent a major restructure in the course design in order to incorporate the implementation of Outcome Based Teaching & Learning (OBTL). We have successfully implemented blended model to teach computer programming courses. This paper is going to share our experiences of blended teaching and learning. We have combined the advantages of both learning environments to deliver computer programming courses. The statistics has shown that students are greatly benefited with this mode of study.

2 Teaching and Learning Programming Courses at CityU

City University of Hong Kong (CityU) is one of the eight institutions of higher education which are financially supported by the government of Hong Kong. It is strong in the field of engineering, technology and computer science. The Department of Computer Science is one of the funding departments under the Faculty of Science and Engineering. In addition to the courses offered to the students who are majored in Computer Science, the department also offers a lot of service courses to the students from other departments. Computer programming is one of the common courses offered to students from various departments. We have implemented a blended model of teaching and learning computer programming courses.

2.1 Blended Teaching and Learning with OBTL

As a strategic plan, the City University of Hong Kong focuses on enhancement of teaching and learning qualities. The University has implemented Outcomes Based Teaching and Learning (OBTL) [12], which is a student-centered approach for education. The curriculum topics in a program and the courses contained in it are expressed as the intended learning outcomes for the students to learn. Teaching is designed to directly encourage the students to learn those outcomes and assessments will then be done to confirm that.

The OBTL is developed based on the concept of constructive alignment [2]. The key elements of a course, such as learning activities and assessment tasks, must be aligned to each other so that the intended learning outcomes may best be achieved. Teaching and learning activities are designed such that the students are required to enact the learning activities and therefore they will most likely to achieve the intended learning outcomes. The activities can be teacher, peer, or self-initiated. The students actively gain knowledge through engaging in appropriate learning activities.

In OBTL, the teaching and learning activities must be coherently aligned with the intended learning outcomes. However, the traditional classroom education does not meet the requirements of OBTL. Traditionally, the learning activities are limited inside the classrooms and assessment tasks are usually in the form of examinations. In order to enhance the qualities of teaching and learning, blended teaching and learning is introduced to the computer programming courses in CityU to implement OBTL.

Blended teaching and learning combines classroom education with E-Learning technology. It provides a large degree of flexibilities to the teachers for course design. With the support of technologies, the teachers at CityU are able to deliver the course materials in multiple channels. In the following sub-sections, we will explain more details how program courses are delivered in mixed channels. Activities in different formats can be provided to the students with time and geographical constraints. This approach not only promotes active learning, it also challenges the students to take control of their own learning.

On the other hand, assessments play an important part in OBTL. Assessments are designed to align with the intended learning outcomes of the corresponding course to provide evidences on how well each student has achieved the outcomes. Moreover, assessments must be able to measure students in multiple dimensions. The students are evaluated by their performances in each intended learning outcome. Such evidence could be provided by project work, case studies, assignments, examinations, practicum, presentation, laboratory work and reports, etc.

2.2   Computer Programming Courses at CityU

In the past, computer programming courses at CityU are taught in a traditional mode. The courses ware delivered in a mixture of large-sized face-to-face lectures and small-sized face-to-face tutorials (which might be in the form of laboratory sections). The students were evaluated by coursework and final examinations. The coursework was usually in the format of programming assignment or written quiz, and the final examination was in the format of paper-based written examinations.

After implementation of blended teaching and learning, the computer programming courses are delivered in multiple channels:

- The teachers present the primary course materials in the large-sized face-to-face lectures.
- Small-sized face-to-face tutorials are conducted by the tutors to allow students to do some programming practices.
- Supplementary course materials are delivered in Internet through the university E-Learning platform. For example, extensive examples are provided to help students to appreciate the good programming skills.
- Online intelligent computer-assisted instruction system (subsection 2.3) has been developed to provide a programming practice platform to the students.
- Computer programming clinic scheme (subsection 2.4) has been setup to provide consultations to students.

There is one major difference between the OBTL and traditional teaching. The intended learning outcomes are clearly stated at the beginning of the courses. Each learning activity is aligned with the learning outcome. It provides a high level of transparency to the students. The students have a clear picture about the course structure. They know what learning activities they must enact in order to achieve the intended learning outcomes.

On the other hand, the students are assessed by how well they have achieved the intended learning outcomes. The assessments are usually measured in multiple dimensions. In CityU, the assessments of computer programming courses include the followings:

- Both online and offline short quizzes will be conducted to evaluate the student's performances during the semester.
- Students are required to do some programming assignments to demonstrate their programming capabilities. The E-Learning platform allows a great flexibility in assignment design. For example, we provide some testing modules in the E-Learning platform. This allows the student to complete the assignments stepwisely [11].
- The data collected in the intelligent computer-assisted instruction system may also be used to evaluate the students.
- The E-Learning environment in blended teaching and learning makes it feasible to conduct online programming quizzes.

2.3 Online Intelligent Computer-Assisted Instruction System for Programming

Instant support to the student is a critical factor to the success of teaching and learning of computer programming. However, it introduces a huge pressure in the resources, and it may not be affordable by some universities. It has been showed that intelligent computer-assisted instruction technology can be a more effective way of teaching introductory computer programming courses [1]. We have implemented a computer-assisted instruction system to support our teaching of computer programming courses. The detail functionalities, design and implementation can be found in [4, 5].

Fig. 1 shows the Programming Assignment aSsessment System (PASS). PASS is a web-based computer-assisted instruction system for computer programming developed at CityU [4]. PASS is a fully automated system to help students to study computer programming.

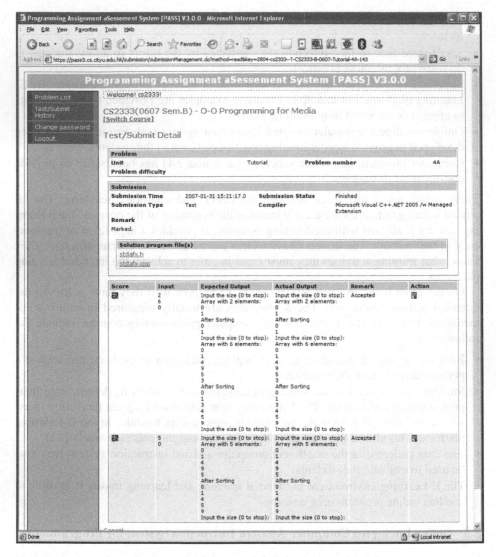

Fig. 1. Programming Assignment aSsessment System (PASS)

PASS allows the teachers to setup some tutorial problems. The teachers provide the input and the corresponding output to each test case. The students then submit their program for testing. The system automatically complies and executes the program submitted. By comparing the output generated by the students' program and the expected output provided by the teacher, the system will then provide feedbacks to the students. For example, if the student gets wrong in certain type of inputs, the system will show the attached annotation provided by the teacher to give some hints of possible mistakes to the student. The instant feedback provided by the system provides concrete assistances to students to revise their programs, and debugging will become more interesting.

On the other hand, some teaching strategies are incorporated with the intelligent computer-assisted instruction system:

- In OBTL, a student need to demonstrate their skills in each intended learning outcome in order to pass the computer programming course. When the teachers design the programming activities in PASS, they will associate each activity with specified outcome. This approach helps the teachers to review the effectiveness of their programming activates to each intended learning outcome.

- PASS has a powerful statistical function of students' performance in each programming problems. It can tell individual student's performance in each outcome. Therefore, the system allows the teacher to measure students in multiple dimensions. Moreover, teachers have a close monitoring of the students' learning progress.

- The system allows the teachers to give test cases in different difficulty levels. For example, some normal cases will be tested as warm-up exercises to the students. Later on, some boundary cases will be used to test the robustness of the students' programs. The students may even try some exceptional cases. This mechanism allows the students to control their paces of learning. On the other hand, we can cater the needs of students with various learning capabilities.

- Traditionally, the students are required to complete a program before they can do some testing. Our system allows the teachers to provide the main body of the program, and students to submit their implementation of functions to the system, or vice versa. Then, the system will integrate the source codes together as a single program. This type of exercise is welcomed by the students, as they can speedily see the outcomes of their program without writing many lines of code. It significantly improves student's incentive of learning. Moreover, it makes the students understand more about the concept of modular programming and also implementation hiding.

- The system allows the students to submit components of a program as separate files. The components files may be developed by individual student. The system will integrate the source files together as a single project. This team-work style exercise makes the students understand the paradigm of software development.

- Finally, the system provides comprehensive statistical information of students' performance. It helps the teacher to identified slower learners and talented students. We encourage the talented students to offer peer assistance to other students. The talented students put in additional efforts to study all related materials before they offer help. Besides, they can further enhance their understanding by explaining the programs to others. This approach improves the learning of both groups of students.

PASS allows a tailor-made learning pace and style for individual student. It has provided a quick and convenient channel for students to test their work without manual involvement. Instant feedback to students encourages them to enhance their programming skills. The introduction of PASS has made the learning of computer programming more rewarding than before.

2.4 Computer Programming Clinic Scheme at CityU

For effective learning, it is important to provide the students with a good learning environment of computer programming. A pilot scheme of Computer Programming Clinic has been setup in CityU with the support of the Department of Computer Science.

The clinic recruits students of senior years who are good at computer programming as programming consultants. The consultants will share their programming experiences with students of junior years. The senior students have similar backgrounds as the junior students. They understand clearly what problems the junior students are currently facing, and therefore be the most suitable persons to offer helps. This clinic is developed based on the idea of "help desk" system. We have setup a face-to-face clinic in the Computer Laboratory of Department of Computer Science. The junior students can visit the clinic for consultations during school hours. The consultants will perform the following tasks:

- answer students' questions related to general computer programming,
- help students to identify the bugs in their program at high levels,
- help students to formulate high-level pesudocode before programming,
- suggest some appropriate readings for the students if necessary,
- demonstrate a small segment of programming code to the students to help them to understand their program if necessary,
- assign some simple tutorial problems to the students to help them to understand the programming concepts.

Another obstacle for the students to learn computer programming is that they do not know where to seek help when they have encountered problems. Usually, the students encounter problems when they are doing some programming work after they returned home. Most students will put the problems aside and forget to solve their problems when they return to school. It greatly reduces their enthusiasm to study computer programming, if they lack of instant supports.

In order to provide instant supports to the students beyond normal school hours, we have setup a virtual extension of the Computer Programming Clinic in Internet. CityU has deployed the Blackboard Academic Suite (Bb) as its unified E-Learning platform [12]. To align with the E-Learning strategic development of the University and to eliminate the development cost, we have implemented online clinic based on the Blackboard (Fig. 2). During school hours and after school hours, consultants will be on duty to offer help to the junior students.

We devote actively in monitoring the students' learning. In addition to face-to-face and on-line consultations, the consultants will analyze the coursework submitted in the computer programming courses and data in the electronic systems to identify the slow learners. Moreover, the teachers of the computer programming courses will also refer the students who have difficulties in computer programming to our clinic. Corresponding personalized learning program will be provided to the students. This project will greatly enhance the learning environment of computer programming.

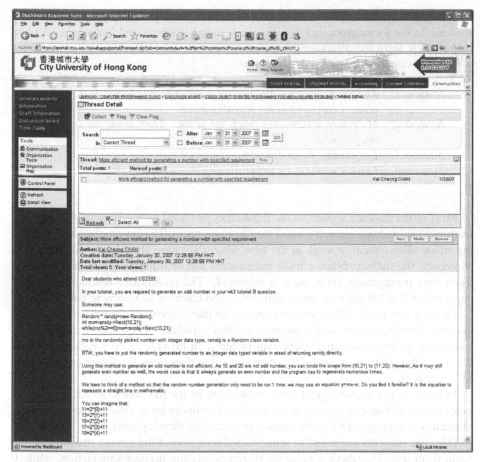

Fig. 2. Computer Programming Clinic – Online Clinic

3   Evaluation and Discussion

A number of extensive evaluations have been conducted to measure the effectiveness of our teaching model. Evaluation results have shown that the blended teaching and learning model is a promising approach in teaching and learning of computer programming.

3.1   Evaluation of Course Structure

It is suggested that the blended learning can be measured by interviews and questionnaires [8]. We have conducted both evaluations to measure the effectiveness of the blended teaching and learning.

A focus group session has been held with students who enrolled for any blended courses of computer programming in the Department. A set of interview questions are designed by professionals in education development. The students are interviewed by an independent interviewer and none of the course lecturers were presented. All the students in the focus group believe that the blended teaching and learning model can help them to learn the computer programming courses more effectively.

Few responses are extracted as examples:

Student 1:   The programming assignment with different levels is a fresh idea. I can control my learning pace.

Student 2:   My fellow classmates teach me a lot. They know clearly of my problem.

Student 3:   Eventually, I can develop a computer game by myself.

Student 4:   I enjoy working on programming during midnight.

...

Most of the students appreciate the flexibilities provided by the blended teaching and learning. The students can self-control their learning paces. The anytime/anywhere studying mode allows them to work at the time when they have the highest productivities. Moreover, the students become more independent and self-disciplined in their learning. Their time management skills are also enhanced. The preliminary results of interview suggest that blended teaching and learning is a good teaching and learning model.

On the other hand, all the students appreciate interactivity of the online assessment system. However, some of the students are less satisfied. They hope that the online intelligent computer-assisted instruction system can provide more feedbacks to help them to debug their programs. This provides some directions for future enhancement of the system.

In order to get a more quantitative measurement for the course structure of computer programming courses, we have conducted a survey by questionnaires. The questionnaires are designed by professionals in education development in the similar way as [8]. The students are asked to score each dimension of the course structure on the scale from 0 to 10, where a score of 10 represents the highest satisfaction, while 0 represents the least satisfaction. 250 students have participated in the survey. The results are summarized as Fig. 3.

In Fig. 3, we can clearly see that the students are highly satisfied with the course structure. The students are happy with the flexibilities provided by the blended teaching and learning. They most believe that the mixture of teaching channels, such as mixture of tutorial, assignment, supplementary web and online assessment system, can effectively teach them about computer programming. They help the students to identify their weakness and control their own learning paces. Therefore, the students can achieve the intended learning outcomes effectively (Fig. 3).

An ideal blended teaching and learning is a mixture of classroom learning and electronic learning. Self-paced learning is one of the major advantages of electronic learning [5, 7]. However, the students are generally less satisfied with the effectiveness of self-paced learning (Fig. 3). As a result, there is potential to further blend our courses. In the future, we will investigate on how to improve the self-pace learning in computer programming courses.

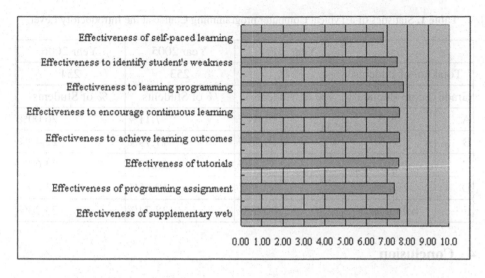

Effectiveness of self-paced learning

Effectiveness to identify student's weakness

Effectiveness to learning programming

Effectiveness to encourage continuous learning

Effectiveness to achieve learning outcomes

Effectiveness of tutorials

Effectiveness of programming assignment

Effectiveness of supplementary web

0.00 1.00 2.00 3.00 4.00 5.00 6.00 7.00 8.00 9.00 10.0

Fig. 3. Result of Questionnaires about the Course Structure

3.2 Evaluation of Students' Performances

In the past, the students taking computer programming courses in CityU are assessed by coursework and final examinations. The coursework was usually in the format of programming assignments, and the final examination was in the format of written examinations. After implementation of OBTL, the students are assessed in multiple dimensions. We have compared the results of the students before and after the implementation of OBTL.

We have selected a typical computer programming course at the introductory level as an example. Because the class size of this course is very large, the statistical information of this course is worthy trusted. On the other hand, the materials of assessment are moderated by peer review to ensure the standard of assessment. No scaling of score has been conducted in this course. The score boundary for each grade has been fixed by the department. As a result, this graded distribution of students is a very important indicator to show the performances of teaching and learning.

In years 2004 and 2005, the computer programming courses were taught in traditional mode. Only a small percentage of students got grade "A", while a large percentage of students failed the course in these two years (Table 1). These students who failed the course may retake the course in the next year. After the blended teaching and learning was implemented in year 2006, the percentage of grade "A" students increased dramatically from 7~8% to 26% (Table 1). At the same time, the percentage of failure decreased significantly. As shown in the table, the students' performance in the computer programming course increases significantly after the implementation of the blended teaching and learning. This is a strong evidence to show the success of the blended model.

Table 1. Statistics of a Typical Computer programming Course at the Introductory Level

		Year 2004	Year 2005	Year 2006
Total no. of students		277	253	251
Grade	Score Boundary	% of Students	% of Students	% of Students
A	69.5	7.94%	7.11%	26.00%
B	54.5	16.25%	17.79%	22.40%
C	39.5	35.38%	23.72%	23.60%
D	34.5	9.75%	12.65%	4.80%
F	below 34.5	30.69%	38.74%	23.20%

4 Conclusion

This paper has shared our experiences in implementing blended learning in teaching computer programming in City University of Hong Kong. The traditional teaching model imposes a lot of constraints in implementing teaching and learning activities. In contrary, blended teaching and learning provides great flexibilities to both the teachers and the students. At the same time, it can cater students with different learning paces. The interviews and questionnaires have shown that blended teaching and learning is very effective in teaching and learning of computer programming. The students' performances in the assessments have further confirmed our findings. We believe that the blended teaching and learning can be applied to other courses in the future as well.

Acknowledgement

PASS is a system developed by C.K. Poon, Y.T. Yu, Marian Choy, Fu Lee Wang, Celine Chong, Usman Nazir, P. F. Tam, Isaac Yeung, Sam Lam and Leo Yuen at Department of Computer Science, City University of Hong Kong. The projected was substantially supported by a grant from City University of Hong Kong (Project No. 6000118). The Computer Programming Clinic is a project lead by Fu Lee Wang, Kenneth Lee and Jiying Wang at Department of Computer Science, City University of Hong Kong. We would like to thank individuals for their significant contributions to the paper.

References

1. Anderson, J.R., Skwarecki, E.: The automated tutoring of introductory computer programming. Communications of the ACM 29(9), 842–849 (1986)
2. Biggs, J.: Teaching for Quality Learning at University, 2nd edn. McGraw-Hill Education, Open University Press (2003)

3. Bok, D.: Our Underachieving Colleges: A Candid Look at How Much Students Learn and Why They Should Be Learning More. Princeton University Press, Princeton (2005)
4. Choy, M., Nazir, U., Poon, C.K., Yu, Y.T.: Experiences in using an automated system for improving students learning of computer programming. In: Lau, R.W.H., Li, Q., Cheung, R., Liu, W. (eds.) ICWL 2005. LNCS, vol. 3583, pp. 267–272. Springer, Heidelberg (2005)
5. Choy, M., Lam, S., Poon, C.K., Wang, F.L., Yu, Y.T., Yuen, L.: Towards blended learning of computer programming supported by an automated system. In: Fong, J., Wang, F.L. (eds.) Blended Learning, Person, pp. 9–18 (2007)
6. Graham, C.R.: Blended learning system: definition, current trends, and future directions. In: Bonk, C.J., Graham, C.R. (eds.) Handbook of blended learning: Global Perspectives, local designs. Graham, C.R, pp. 3–21. Pfeiffer Publishing, San Francisco, CA (2005)
7. Graham, C.R., Allen, S.: Blended learning: An emerging trend in education. In: Howard, C., et al. (eds.) Encyclopedia of Distance Learning, p. 99, pp. 172–179. Idea Group Inc., Hershey, PA (2005)
8. Harding, A., Kaczynski, D., Wood, L.N.: Evaluation of blended learning: analysis of qualitative data. In: Proceedings of the Symposium of Blended Learning in Science Teaching & Learning, The University of Sydney, Australia, September 28–30, 2005, pp. 56–62 (2005)
9. Sleeman, D.: The Challenges of teaching computer programming. Communication of the ACM 29(9), 840–841 (1986)
10. Soloway, E.: Learning to program = learning to construct mechanisms and explanations. Communications of the ACM 29(9), 850–858 (1986)
11. Wang, F.L., Wong, T.L.: Effective teaching and learning of computer programming with large class size. In: Fong, J., Liu, L.C., Wang, F.L. (eds.) Hybrid Learning, City University of Hong Kong, pp. 55–65 (2007)
12. Wang, F.L., Fong, J., Choy, M.: Blended learning for programming course: a case study of outcome based teaching & learning. In: Fong, J., Wang, F.L. (eds.) Blended Learning, Person, pp. 30–41 (2007)
13. Blackboard Academic Suite, http://www.blackboard.com/us/index.Bb
14. WebCT, http://www.blackboard.com/webct

Discovery of Educational Objective on E-Learning Resource: A Competency Approach

Shi-Ming Huang, Hsiang-Yuan Hsueh, and Jing-Shiuan Hua

National Chung Cheng University, Chia-Yi, Taiwan
{smhuang, hyhsueh, jshua}@mis.ccu.edu.tw

Abstract. It is indeed important to implement E-Learning platforms for education and training purposes in a variety of domains. However, facing the enormous amount of learning resources, guidance on E-Learning platform for meeting the educational objectives is still a neglected issue. The learning experiences cannot be optimized and personalized. In this study, a semantic and systematic mechanism is proposed to discover the educational objectives of learning resources with competency information on E-Learning platform. To verify the feasibility of mechanism proposed in this study, the design and implementation of prototype system for the assessment of E-Learning effectiveness using the proposed mechanism are also discussed and demonstrated. By feasibility verification with system implementation for practical requirement, the effectiveness of the proposed mechanism can be basically certified.

Keywords: E-Learning; Bloom taxonomy; Competency; O*Net competence database.

1 Introduction

It is indeed for importance of E-Learning implementations and platforms for education and training purposes in a variety of domains, including educational purposes in organizations or individuals and human resource development facilities in enterprises. It is indicated that the notion of E-Learning has widely been adopted as a proper solution for human resource development in enterprises. The related investment of IT for E-Learning and web-based training programs is therefore expected to increase human resources and talents with better quality [3].

With the adoption of E-Learning platform, E-Learning mechanisms and strategies are expected to be dramatically switched from traditional advisor-lead instructions to learner-oriented paradigms [4]. It emphasizes the interaction among actors on E-Learning platforms including learners, instructors, developers, and managers. Users' requirement and behavior played dominant roles during the development and refinement phases of E-Learning experiences [4]. However, facing enormous amount of learning resources on E-Learning platform, guidance on E-Learning platform for educational objectives is still a neglected issue. The learning experiences cannot be optimized and personalized, since learners cannot be guided to use learning resources to satisfy their personal learning objectives, particularly the overflowing learning

H. Leung et al. (Eds.): ICWL 2007, LNCS 4823, pp. 618–629, 2008.

resources on E-Learning platform. It is easy to retrieve any categories of learning contents from a computer-based E-Learning platform, but it is still necessary to look for additional solutions to determine the educational objectives for optimization. In such assumption, the importance rank of learning resource is needed to be established in a personalized manner in order to fit learners' requirement.

In this study, the authors argued that additional information for educational objectives of learning resources should be systematically generated and appended on E-Learning platform. As for the standard of such additional information, one potential solution is the competency information specifications proposed as the O*Net competence database, which is the common standard for taxonomy, collection, description, evaluation, and publication of competency information with the form of dimensional factors. Several factors including a set of characteristics of employees, occupational opportunities, skills, and abilities are included in the standard. With an open descriptive meta-data and language, it is easy to express, identify, and clarify the competency of job searchers and competency requirements for one job opportunity in an enterprise with quantitative approaches. Information system solutions for competency management are also possible to implement with the aim of such underlying notion and open description language.

In this article, a semantic and systematic mechanism is proposed to discover educational objectives, which is formulated by well-known Bloom taxonomy for educational objectives in this study, of learning resources on E-Learning platform. Strategically, the required educational objectives for competency information specified in O*Net metadata should first be determined. Educational objectives of learning resources in E-Learning platform, which reflect a set of competency information, can then be determined in a systematic and semantic manner. In order to verify the feasibility of mechanism proposed in this study, the design and implementation of a prototype system for the assessment of E-Learning effectiveness using the proposed mechanism are also discussed and demonstrated. By feasibility verification with system implementation for practical requirement, the effectiveness of the proposed mechanism can therefore be basically certified.

2 Theoretical Foundations

2.1 Computer-Based Learning Platforms

Information Technology has played an important role in modern learning program, which is one of key enablers for individually tailored learning experience. As for the technical E-Learning platform, it is widely accepted that the advent of World Wide Web dramatically changed traditional computer-based technology. It provided a widely accessible communication topology based on open and common standards to access information and knowledge with unified manners [1]. The specification of Shareable Content Object Reference Model (SCORM) therefore provided a set of referential guideline to support the development of web-based E-Learning platform and collaboration of learning resources and contents. With the view of Learning Management Systems (LMS), SCORM specification covers technical details in each layer of such information system. By definitions of technical foundations for web-based learning environment, it is possible to construct and deploy E-Learning platform that assumed the presence of strong, server-side, LMS-based learning content distribution [1].

2.2 Competency Information for Characterizing Occupational Profiles

The notion of competency management is important for human resource management and optimization in enterprises. The term competency can be defined as the measurable corresponding knowledge, skill, ability, and other behavioral characteristics (KSAOs), which always come out in reference to a given context, for the determination of efficiency and effectiveness of certain missions or tasks. It is therefore applicable to determine distinguished talents in a systematical manner. Competency management therefore concerns the way in which competencies are properly organized and controlled [5]. It is responsible for the management of intangible assets of human resources, such as knowledge, know-how, and behavior, for competency either required by system or acquired by individuals.

A variety of studies and standards are presented currently. One main category is the modeling and assessment of competency from the available competency information with the view of human resource management. For example, Linder investigated the status of competency assessment and human resource management performance as an empirical case study for the maturity measurement of competency information utilization [6]. An important standard of competency information is the O*Net, the Occupational Information Network, which is a comprehensive database for the occupational information of employee properties and job characteristics. It also provides a unified language for defining and describing the corresponding occupations. Its flexible design also captures various job requirements with the aim of information technologies. In this article, the authors attempted to apply such complete competency information schema for expression and further analysis on competency management processes.

2.3 Bloom Taxonomy for Educational Objectives

The term "educational objective" of learning resources or activities can be referred to as the educational goal which should be identified during the design phases of learning or tutoring activities. Educational objectives should also be reviewed after learning activities in order to determine the effectiveness of learning activities.

The most well-known taxonomy of educational objectives is originated by Bloom. In the taxonomy, educational objectives can be categorized in six levels including knowledge, comprehension, application, analysis, synthesis, and evaluation phases. In this study, the authors recommended to formulate educational objectives by extended Bloom taxonomy of educational objectives, which is the refinement to the original taxonomy, proposed by Anderson [2]. Rather than one-dimension approach, the extended taxonomy involves two dimensions, including knowledge dimension and cognitive dimensions. The cognitive process dimensions can be categorized as:

- *Remember:* Exhibit the memory of previous-learned materials by recognizing or recalling facts, terms, basic concepts and answers.
- *Understand:* Understanding of facts and ideas by interpreting, exemplifying, classifying, summarizing, inferring, comparing, and explaining main ideas.
- *Apply:* Using the available knowledge to execute and implement solutions in different ways.
- *Analyze:* Differentiating, organizing, and attributing knowledge by manipulating information using certain criteria.
- *Evaluate:* Checking and Judgments about information, validity of proposed ideas, or quality of work by certain criteria.
- *Create:* Generating, planning, and producing information or knowledge together and proposing new solutions.

On the other hand, the knowledge dimension can be categorized as:

- *Factual Knowledge:* Knowledge about terminology and specification details.
- *Conceptual Knowledge:* Knowledge about generation, classification, and structural modeling of certain concept.
- *Procedural Knowledge:* Knowledge about workflows, algorithms, methods, procedures, and events.
- *Meta-Cognitive Knowledge:* Knowledge about strategies and decisional conditions.

Strategically, the authors attempted to apply taxonomy as a tool to discover the characteristic of competency information and learning resources with the form of location in the taxonomy matrix. For example, the learning resources about "*Normalization forms in relational data models*" can be inferred as (*Apply, Procedural*). That is, its educational objective is to provide *procedural knowledge* to learners so that they can *apply* learned algorithms to improve the quality of database design.

3 Discovery of Educational Objectives Using Bloom Taxonomy

In this study, feature mapping involves the discovery of potential keyword from competency information specified in O*Net metadata and identification of educational objective for learning resources inferring from competency information. Figure 1 illustrates the mechanism.

3.1 Specification of Competency Information in Competency Reservoir

In this study, the competency reservoir is required to store and retrieve competency information. According to competency definition from O*Net, training program or occupation requirement can be measured by 17 dimensions. In the simulation experience, with the view of learning facilities, 4 dimensions (tools, technologies, knowledge, and skills required by training programs or occupation requirement) are selected, as shown in Figure 2. In specifying O*Net metadata, the competency information can be categorized by occupational requirement. For example, the competency information of *Computer Programmer* (No. 15-1021.00) defined in O*Net specification can be expressed by the following metadata.

Table 1. Partial competency information for sample occupational requirement

Tools required	Computer Servers, Desktop Computers, and Mainframe Computers, etc.
Technologies required	Analytical or Scientific Software, Application Server Software, and Compiler and de-compiler software, etc.
Knowledge required	Computers and Electronics, English Language, and Mathematics, etc.
Skills required	Programming, Critical Thinking, and Complex Problem Solving, etc.

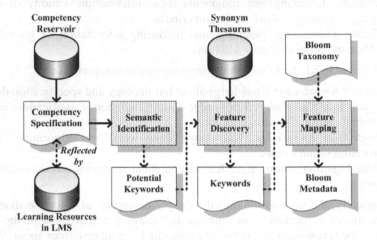

Fig. 1. Feature discovery and mapping on competency information

Fig. 2. Taxonomy of competency information

3.2 Specification of Educational Objectives with Bloom Taxonomy

On the other hand, the educational objectives of learning resources, which should be discovered by extended Bloom taxonomy, can be systematically identified by synonym thesaurus is provided in this study. Table 2 shows partial contents of synonym thesaurus for cognitive process dimensions [2]. On the other hand, synonym of knowledge dimensions should be manually defined, since knowledge is domain specific. Sample contents of synonym thesaurus used for Computer Programmers are shown in Table 3.

Table 2. Synonym thesaurus for cognitive process dimensions to discover educational objectives

Cognitive Process Dimension	Partial Potential Synonyms (3 synonyms are selected)
Remember	Recognizing, Recalling, Retrieving
Understand	Interpreting, Clarifying, Representing
Apply	Executing, Implementing, Carrying out
Analyze	Distinguishing, Discriminating, Organizing
Evaluate	Critiquing, Testing, Monitoring
Create	Planning, Designing, Constructing

Table 3. Synonym thesaurus for knowledge dimension to discover educational objectives

Knowledge Dimension	Partial Potential Synonyms (3 synonyms are selected)
Factual	Computers, Servers, Mail
Conceptual	Markup Languages, Data Models, Programming Languages
Procedural	Problem-Solving, Decision-Making, Troubleshooting
Meta-Cognitive	Deductive Reasoning, Active Learning, Active Listening

3.3 Semantic Identification

The first step of educational objectives discovery is the potential semantic identification from competence information, which is responsible to extract potential keywords which have more likelihood to reflect the educational objective defined in Bloom taxonomy. For example, considering the skill competency information defined in O*Net metadata for Computer Programmers: {*Active Learning — Understanding the implications of new information for both current and future problem-solving and decision-making.*}, potential keywords reflecting cognitive processes include *Potential_ Cognitive_Keywords = {Learning, Understanding, Problem-Solving, Decision-Making}*. On the other hand, in the sentence, a set of potential knowledge keyword *Potential_Knowledge_Keyowrds = {Learning, Understanding, Problem-Solving, Decision-Making, Implementation, Information}* can also be extracted.

3.4 Feature Discovery

The second step of educational objectives discovery is the feature discovery by filtering the potential keyword lists using predefined synonym thesaurus. For example, the keyword lists generated in the last section can be pruned as *Cognitive_Keywords = {Understanding}* and *Knowledge_Keyowrds = {Problem-Solving, Decision-Making}*.

3.5 Semantic Mapping

The last step of educational objectives discovery involves the mapping of competency information into educational objectives with Bloom taxonomy. In the example discussed in previous sections, it can be interpreted that the skill competency information "*Active Learning*" involves the "*understanding*" of "*procedural knowledge*" including "*Problem-Solving and Decision-Making*". It should be noticed that for any competence information, it is possible to reflect a set of educational objectives. For example, the competency information "*Active Learning*" also involves the interpretation for "*understanding*" of "*meta-cognitive knowledge*" about "*implication*". The following Figure 3 shows the corresponding matrix of the sample skill competency information "*Active Learning*" and "*Complex Problem Solving*".

Knowledge Dimension	Cognitive Process Dimension					
	Remember	Understand	Apply	Analyze	Evaluate	Create
Factual						
Conceptual			Complex Problem Solving	Complex Problem Solving		
Procedural		Active Learning				
Meta-cognitive		Active Learning				

Fig. 3. Interpretation of educational objective for competence information

3.6 Discovery of Educational Objective on E-Learning Resource

As the educational objectives of competency information are discovered, the educational objective of learning resources reflected a set of competencies can therefore be identified. For example, learning resource {*R: Understanding Case Based Reasoning*} reflects a set of competency information defined in O*Net metadata including {"*Complex Problem Solving*", "*Active Learning*"}, the educational objectives can be inferred as shown in the following Figure 4.

Knowledge Dimension	Cognitive Process Dimension					
	Remember	Understand	Apply	Analyze	Evaluate	Create
Factual						
Conceptual			R	R		
Procedural	R					
Meta-cognitive	R					

Fig. 4. Interpretation of educational objective for learning resource

4 Application: Assessment of E-Learning Effectiveness

In this section, the authors attempted to discuss the practical application applying the proposed mechanism to evaluate the effectiveness of E-Learning on users using competency information and Bloom taxonomy in order to demonstrate the feasibility and practicality of proposed mechanism. The application of the proposed mechanism for the assessment of E-Learning effectiveness is based on the belief that:

■ Effectiveness of users' E-Learning experience can be measured by the status of educational objectives owned by learners.
■ Users attempted to access learning resources for certain learning purposes which can be reflected by occupational requirements.

- ■ Assessment of Learning experiences involves quizzing with questions reflected a set of competency information.
- ■ Quiz, which reflects a set of competency requirements can also measure the status of educational objectives owned by learners.

Figure 5 illustrates such belief.

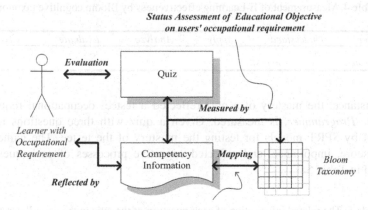

Identification of Educational Objective for Competency Specification

Fig. 5. Belief of proposed mechanism applying on assessment of E-Learning experience

4.1 Assessment of E-Learning Effectiveness with Bloom Taxonomy

In this study, the assessment of E-Learning effectiveness can be performed as in the following. A quiz is given with a set of questions randomly generated by Sequential Probability Ratio Test (SPRT) model. Each question can be reflected by a set of competency information, and each competency can be reflected by a set of cognitive processes. That is, each question (q_i) can be properly reflected by a set of cognitive processes as:

$$q_i = \coprod_T C_{iT} , \ \forall i \in N .$$

(1)

where C_{iT} denotes the presence of cognitive process T on q_i. For example, a question of a quiz may be reflected by a set of cognitive processes including "*Apply, Analyze*" of "*Conceptual knowledge*" for the competency "*Complex Problem Solving*".

The mastery of a quiz reflected user-specified occupational requirement can be evaluated by the union of score of each cognitive process dimension that user obtained in the quiz:

$$S_T = \coprod_{q_i \in T} G(q_i) \times P(q_i) .$$

(2)

where the function $G(q_i)$ means the score of question i gained by a testee and the function $P(q_i)$ denotes the importance of question i. The effectiveness of E-Learning can be measured by the mastery matrix with cognitive process dimensions, as shown in Table 4.

Table 4. Measurement of E-Learning effectiveness by Bloom cognitive taxonomy

Remember	Understand	Apply	Analyze	Evaluate	Create
$S_{t='REMEMBER'}$	$S_{t='UNDERSTAND'}$	$S_{t='APPLY'}$	$S_{t='ANALYZE'}$	$S_{t='EVALUATE'}$	$S_{t='CREATE'}$

For instance, the mastery of a quiz reflected a testee' occupational requirement, *Computer Programmer*, is measured. Given a quiz with three questions randomly generated by SPRT models for testing the mastery of the testee. The gained score, allotted score, importance, and reflected cognitive processes of each question are displayed in Table 5.

Table 5. The related information of each question of the quiz in the case illustration

Question number	Gained score	Allotted score	Importance	Reflected cognitive processes
1	7	10	5	"*Apply, Analyze*" of "*Conceptual knowledge*" for the competency "*Complex Problem Solving*"
2	0	15	10	"*Apply*" of "*Factual knowledge*" for the competency "*Analytic and scientific software*"
3	0	10	5	"*Analyze, Create*" of "*Procedural knowledge*" for the competency "*Programming*"

The gained score which presented mastery for cognitive processes are shown in Table 6. It can be inferred from Table 6 that the effectiveness of learning on the testee is poor in the case illustration.

Table 6. Summarized the estimated mastery of cognitive processes in the case illustration

Gained score / Full marks	Cognitive processes dimension					
	Remember	Understand	Apply	Analyze	Evaluate	Create
Question 1			35/50	35/50		
Question 2			0/150			
Question 3				0/50		0/50
Total	N/A	N/A	35/200	35/100	N/A	0/50

4.2 Prototype System Architecture

In this study, the authors have developed a web-based prototype system for assessment of E-Learning effectiveness using the proposed mechanism. Figure 6 shows the architecture.

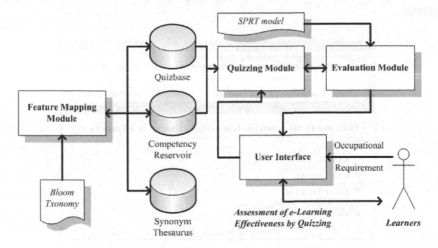

Fig. 6. Architecture of the prototype system

The prototype, which was developed for "Project of Personnel Training of Electronic Business" executed by the Ministry of Economic Affairs in Taiwan, has been deployed on Microsoft Windows server platform with Microsoft SQL Server and Internet Information Service (IIS). Some important features of the implementation include:

- *Feature Mapping Module:* This is the core module that implements the proposed mechanism. It is responsible for the systematic and semi-automatic discovery educational objectives of quizzes and competency information.
- *User Interface:* The interface is used for retrieving users' learning requirements with the form of occupational requirements defined by O*Net metadata.
- *Quizzing Module and Evaluation Module:* These two modules are responsible for assessing the E-Learning effectiveness of users by applying SPRT based on user-specified occupational requirement.

Figure 7 shows the screenshot of sample questions in the user interface generated by the quizzing module. Figure 8 shows the screenshot of mastery matrix with cognitive process dimensions after quizzing. Practically in the prototype system, the matrix can be visualized by the radar diagram for better interpretation by users. It should be noted that it is not necessary for all cognitive process dimensions to appear in the radar diagram. Dimensions involved are highly depended on the nature of questions in the quiz.

To test the preliminary feasibility of the proposed mechanism embedded in the prototype system, an internal test is performed by surveying twenty-two internal users and adopting T-test for statistical inference. The calculated t value is 8.57 > $t_{0.95}(21) = 1.721$ under significance level $\alpha = 0.05$, and therefore information satisfaction of users is significant. It means that the proposed mechanism in this paper is potential.

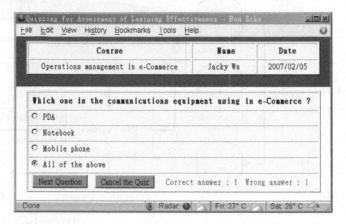

Fig. 7. Screenshot of sample questions in user interface

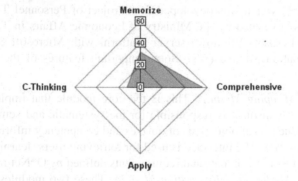

Fig. 8. Visualized result of E-Learning effectiveness by Bloom cognitive taxonomy

5 Conclusion Remarks

In this article, a semantic and systematic mechanism is proposed to discover the educational objectives, which is formulated by well-known extended Bloom taxonomy, of learning resources on E-Learning platform. In the first phase, the required educational objectives for competency information specified in O*Net metadata should be determined. The educational objectives of competency information can be visualized with a two-dimensional matrix. Educational objectives of learning resources in

E-Learning platform, which reflect a set of competency information, can therefore be inferred in a systematic and semantic manner. In order to verify the feasibility of mechanism proposed in this study, the authors selected the assessment of E-Learning effectiveness as potential practical application using the proposed mechanism. A prototype system is designed and implemented for assessment of E-Learning effectiveness using the proposed mechanism in order to demonstrate the feasibility of the application using the proposed mechanism. By feasibility verification with system implementation for practical requirement, the effectiveness of the proposed mechanism can therefore be basically certified.

As for future research with respect to the mechanisms of educational objective discovery and management, the authors recommended that the proposed mechanism could be widely adopted in individual or distributed learning facilities on E-Learning platform. With automatic discovery or retrieval of learning resources with user-specified educational objectives or competency requirements, it is possible for educational objectives as a behavioral guidance of learning resources to satisfy users learning requirement, since the characteristics and profiles of learning resource can be predicted by information provided by proposed mechanism.

Acknowledgments. The work presented in this paper has been supported by National Science Council, Taiwan, R.O.C, under Grant No. 95-2524-S-194-004-. The authors deeply appreciate their financial support and encouragement.

References

1. ADL: SCORM 2004, 2nd (edn.) Overview (2004),
   http://www.adlnet.org/downloads/70.cfm
2. Anderson, W., Krathwohl, D.: A Taxonomy for Learning, Teaching, and Assessing: A Revision of Bloom's Educational Objectives. Longman, New York (2001)
3. Chang, K., Sung, Y., Lee, C.: Web-based Collaborative Inquiry Learning. J. Computer Assisted Learning 19(1), 56–69 (2003)
4. Friedman, R., Deek, F.: Innovation and Education in the Digital Age: Reconciling the Roles of Prdagogy, Technology, and the Business of Learning. J. IEEE Transactions on Engineering Management 50(4), 403–412 (2003)
5. Harzallah, M., Berio, G., Vernadat, F.: Analysis and Modeling of Individual Competencies: Toward Better Management of Human Resources. J. IEEE Transactions on Systems, Man, and Cybernetics 6(1), 187–207 (2006)
6. Linder, J.: Competency Assessment and Human Resource Management Performance of County Extension Chairs in Ohio. J. Agricultural Education 42(4), 21–31 (2001)

Structured Blended Learning Implementation for an Open Learning Environment

Jason K.Y. Chan and Ken C.K. Law

Department of Computer Science, City University of Hong Kong,
Tat chee Ave., Kowloon, Hong Kong
jasonchan@cml3.mit.edu, cskckl@cityu.edu.hk

Abstract. This paper proposes a structured blended learning for providing E-Learning strategies adopted by the Open University of Hong Kong (OUHK). The paper identified the factors that are likely to impact on the use of learning technologies in future. By introducing the structured blended learning with the concept of learning cycle, the problem of being lost in hypermedia environment can then be solved. Knowledge can be delivered more effectively and efficiently to meet student learning needs. A scenario example on the use of E-Learning technologies and user interface are illustrated. The implications of the learning strategy adopted at OUHK will also be discussed.

Keywords: blended learning, learning preference, Open Learning Environment (OLE), proactive planning, asynchronous and synchronous online learning.

1 Introduction

This paper proposes a structured blended learning mode for providing distance education by the Open University of Hong Kong (OUHK) in the few years. According to Iverson (1993), traditional methods of curriculum development usually require four-to-seven year cycle in the process from draft originals to final revised curriculum implementation. In the world of fast changing information technology and ever changing applications, this development cycle will encompass an enormous amount of changes. Such a period would also involve the assessment of current strengths and weaknesses of the learning environment and the identification of new educational trends. In Hong Kong, most higher education institution's strategic plan adopted a 5-year development cycle. (OUHK, 2002; HKU, 2002; CityU, 2002) In this paper, the factors that are likely to impact on the potential use of learning technologies in the OUHK over the next few years will be described. In the first section, we will provide a brief teaching and learning environment at the OUHK, reviewing the factors that are likely to impact on the potential use of learning technologies in the OUHK over the next few years. In the second section, we will introduce the proactive plan about what learning technologies will be likely to be employed at that time. In the third section, we will discuss the implications of this change, followed by a brief conclusion in the fourth section.

H. Leung et al. (Eds.): ICWL 2007, LNCS 4823, pp. 630–640, 2008.
© Springer-Verlag Berlin Heidelberg 2008

1.1 Blended Learning

The OUHK is a self-financing and non-profit making university to offer open and distance education in Hong Kong. The University has offered more than 130 postgraduate, degree, associate degree and sub-degree programs. (OUHK, 2005) The OUHK offers studies with flexible form of learning environment, for students to choose, where and when, and also provides them with carefully structured materials to guide them through the courses. The learning style offered by OUHK is a blended learning mode via printed materials, CD-Rom, non-classroom face-to-face tutorial sessions held in the evening and weekend and also online learning. Students can decide on their study path and pace, making use of a variety of print and interactive multimedia materials, tutorial support and also access to electronic library resources. The OUHK provides classroom sessions around Hong Kong for tutorial lessons through rental means. There are also trained tutors to conduct tutorial sessions, tutorial discussions and course work assessments, and also responded to students' queries by phone and e-mail. The adoption of *Online Learning Environment (OLE)*, students can access a comprehensive range of learning resources and personalized services to help them study more effectively without the constraints of time and place. (OUHK, 2005)

1.2 Readiness of Student with Information Technology

To use electronic means of communication, OUHK need to know if the students are familiar and be able to access the necessary facilities and equipment. The OUHK carried out surveys on students regarding their information technology readiness on a regular basis. One of the surveys revealed that an increasing trend of PCs ownership by students, access to the Internet, and willingness to use email for communication. (OUHK, 2005) Another recent survey in July 2003 (Chung, 2003) indicates that: 99.0% of students have PCs; 97.5% of students have access to the Internet; 78.5% use broadband, and 63.5% use email more than once a day; 78.0% of students prefer to use the Internet for communication with the university, tutors and other students (8.0% do not prefer to do so; the rest are neutral); and 84.0% of students prefer to receive information or materials from the University's Registry via email .

Table 1. I.T. Access of OUHK Applicants (Chung, 2003)

	1999	2001	2003
Access to PCs	96.6%	97.0%	99.0%
Access to Internet	80.7%	93.8%	97.5%
Broadband	4.2%	34.7%	78.5%
Usually use email	56.0%	66.3%	-
Use email > once a day	-	-	63.5%
Prefer to use email for communication with OUHK	78.8%	75.8%	78.0%
Prefer to receive info from OUHK thru email	87.5%	88.6%	84.0%

The results reveal that the majority of students are technologically prepared and have access to information technology equipment. Fewer than 10% of our students do not want to use electronic means as the primary form of communication with OUHK. (Yuen, 2004)

1.3 Student Learning Preferences

When the students have access to the related facilities, another thing we need to know is their willingness or preference to use learning technologies. Another OUHK survey (Vermeer and Murphy, 2004) revealed that there is a strong student preference for using multiple forms of media in learning.

Table 2. Student Preferences for Using Different Forms of Media in Learning (Vmeer and Murphy, 2004)

Medium	Highly ineffective	Ineffective	Neutral	Effective	Highly effective
Face-to-face tutorials	.9%	3.5%	15.9%	44.6%	35.1%
Course websites	2.8%	9.7%	31.7%	38.2%	17.6%
Online discussion boards	4.9%	13.0%	28.8%	32.9%	20.4%
CD-ROMs	6.9%	19.1%	37.6%	27.5%	8.8%
Audio tapes	12.6%	31.8%	33.5%	16.6%	5.5%
Television programs	12.3%	30.2%	38.1%	14.5%	4.8%

OUHK students' first preference is clearly face-to-face contact. Yet two forms of online learning support -- informational course websites, and online discussion boards -- still ranked very high, with over 50% of respondents considering them either 'effective' or 'highly effective'. Since other data, both research-based and anecdotal, show a highly variable commitment to the use of online learning tools in OUHK courses, these positive results are significant. Equally significant is students' disappointingly low opinion of course CD-ROMs: only 36% of respondents found them effective or highly effective, and 26% considered them ineffective or highly ineffective. (Vermeer and Murphy, 2004)

OUHK course studies still utilize two traditional forms of media, i.e. video and audio tapes, as many students suggested the OUHK to provide online, streamed versions of as Audio/Video content. Numerous respondents in fact suggested that the University provide 'video lectures', 'tutorial notes in PowerPoint' and 'highly interactive Flash notes'. Another significant theme in respondents' comments was repeated requests for multiple forms of access to course content. The OUHK students want a varied media mix, including overlapping provision of content using different media, and they want it delivered using the latest technologies. However, the University need to consider the key factors for the change involved in time, effectiveness and also financially viable. (Vermeer and Murphy, 2004)

1.4 Insufficient Interaction and Guidance in Existing OLE

Successful E-Learning environment involve interactivity between teachers and students, between students and the learning environment, and among students themselves, as well as active learning in the classroom (Sherry 1996). Multimedia equipment such as graphics, video, animation, and sound, can add richness in contents to materials, but they do not add interactions. An animation sequence or colorful graphical scene attracts the learners' attention, but does not engage them in making decisions or immerse them in the program. Interactions make learning active rather than passive, and they provide learners and the instructor with feedback. Interaction is a cyclic process in which two actors alternatively listen, think and speak (Crawford, 2000). It is important to develop teaching materials with a variety of interactive techniques.

Interactivity takes many forms; it is not just limited to audio and video, nor solely to teacher-student interactions. It also represents the connectivity the students feel with aides, facilitators and their peers. Garrison (1990) argued that the quality and integrity of the educational process depends upon sustained two-way communication. Without connectivity, E-Learning degenerates into the old correspondence course model of independent study. The student becomes autonomous and isolated, procrastinates, and eventually drops out. Effective distance education should approach Keegan's ideal of an authentic learning experience. However, the existing web-based learning does not provide sufficient interaction means.

Moreover, the existing OLE connects hypermedia such as text, graphics, animation, audio and video in a nonlinear manner. The major problem with hypermedia leads to feel lost in learning hyperspace. Learners may get lost in complex hypermedia connected webs. It is difficult for learners to find a way to organize the learning material as a guided learning in an orderly manner. Besides, there is the unpredictable nature of how readers link to hypermedia elements. If essential information is located in a hypermedia link that is not structured, the learner will not master the objectives in that lesson. Finally, a learning gap will exist between learners and teachers, teachers and knowledge delivery, knowledge delivery and learners. The interactions and communications between teachers and learners are not sufficient and efficient. (Chan, 2003)

2 Proactive Planning

University policy makers, nowadays are required to have proactive thinking of how the university will be lead, managed and structured the learning environment. They also need to face many important issues and decisions concerning the impacts of information technology on their institutions such as organization, governance, management, and its relationships to students, faculties, and staffs. All of them will require careful reevaluation, forecast and almost certain changes. (Duderstadt, Atkins and Houweling, 2002)

2.1 Scenarios of Information Technologies in OLE

The OUHK imitated an E-Learning project in January, 2004, which aimed to develop a **WEB-based Interactive Tutoring System (Webits)** that enabled teachers and students to interact effectively online, supported educational multimedia data transmission in real time such as video, audio, text, and enhanced white-board data, presentation of educational materials. The project was developed based on the following scenario imagination and assumptions. Assume that technology developments, that most people will have access to a wireless network with bandwidth of at least one gigabyte per second within a few years. Most computers will be equipped with webcam with face tracking technology as the basic standard device. The developments in mobile computing technologies, the university server will remind the students' course schedule via SMS or MMS messages. Some course introductions might be delivered in video and audio via cell phones. The new communication means will blur the distinction between traditional and distance education. The technologies have potential uses in both situations with little noticeable differences. The main pedagogical issue is to understand where the new technology will have real impact on learning effectiveness. Some of the technologies will ease the constraints of time and distance by bringing the possibilities of face-to-face tutoring to the students, in the home, on the street or anywhere, as long as the students have access to a Internet connected device.

2.2 Combination of Asynchronous and Synchronous Online Learning

The advantage of asynchronous OLE is flexible learning especially for global distance education, as it does not require the learners or instructors to be online at the same time. However, learners may get lost in complex hypermedia information webs. Learners may find it difficult to orient to find their way to the learning topics. (Chan and Law, 2004) It is concluded, apart from adapting the asynchronous OLE, interactive tutoring systems will be introduced to provide synchronous interaction for more efficient moderating of learners' discussion and immediate feedback from instructors.

The asynchronous and synchronous online learning platforms do not exclude each other but provide complimentary ways of communications and interactions for different teaching and learning purposes. The range of tools available in an interactive tutoring system makes complex topics manageable. Complex topics can be explained directly by using tools such as whiteboards, application sharing, text-chat, real-time audio, and video-conferencing. These synchronous tools will be combined with asynchronous tools such as video clips, text, images and animation. Instructors and learners will be able to illustrate their ideas in both directions interactively.

2.3 Learning Cycle in the OLE

The major challenge for distance education is to address the issues of dialogue across the response and psychological distance between teachers and students. (Uys, 1999)

Chizmar and Walbert (1999) argue that pedagogy must drive the choice of instructional technology. To provide successful teaching, teachers must be considerate and design a series of steps that make connections with the students' prior understanding, actively process new information or practice skills, and set the stage for demonstration of the learning outcomes. Teachers can adjust these steps in the light of the 'classroom' experience as it unfolds. (Chan, Yim and Chen, 2005) And hence, the blended learning model can be more structured by having a four-stage Learning Cycle in the OLE platform as illustrated in Figure 1. The four stages are: PrE-Learning; Lecturing; Tutoring; and Assessment. We can see the flow of user interfaces and how they are interrelated with the four learning stages to accomplish the learning cycle.

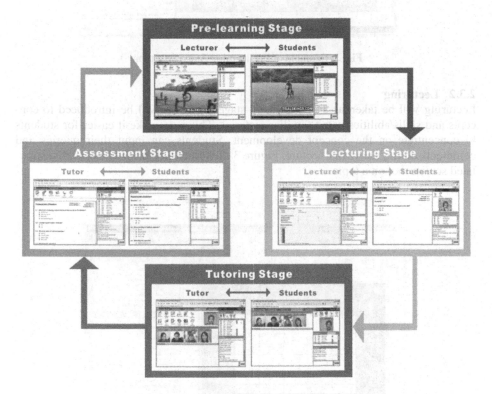

Fig. 1. Web-based Learning and Interactive Tutoring System with Learning Cycle. (Chan, 2003).

2.3.1 Pre-learning
The activities in Pre-learning stage will capture the student's attention, stimulate their thinking and help them access prior knowledge. The teaching materials at pre-learning stage can be asynchronous. Figure 2 illustrated Pre-lecturing Stage with a simulated screen shot on a topic.

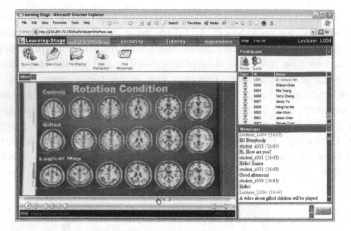

Fig. 2. Example of Pre-learning Stage on a topic

2.3.2 Lecturing

Lecturing will be taken as a one-to-many stage. Students will be introduced to concepts and skills/abilities using familiar material. This is to make it easier for students to concentrate on the concept development. Students can input their queries and comments during the virtual lecture. Figure 3 illustrated Lecturing Stage with a simulated screen shot on a topic.

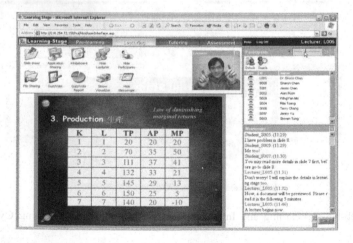

Fig. 3. Example of Lecturing Stage on a topic

2.3.3 Tutoring

Tutoring stage will be the most interactive stage and give students the opportunity to expand and solidify their understanding of the concept. Students will be involved in an analysis of their exploration. Their understanding will be clarified and modified because of reflection via synchronous interactive activities. In the tutoring stage, all participants connected by web-cams to their computers will show their video images to the system and all participants. Figure 4 illustrated Tutoring Stage with a simulated screen shot on a topic, noticed the video-conference feature (with web-cam devices) to enable discussions between tutor and students.

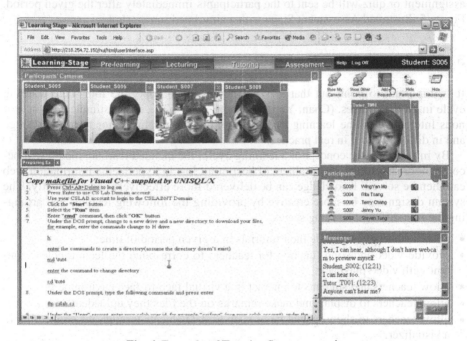

Fig. 4. Example of Tutoring Stage on a topic

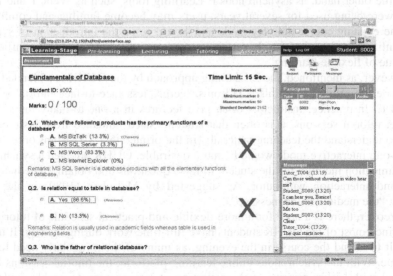

Fig. 5. Example of Assessment Stage on a topic

2.3.4 Assessment

Finally, the learning cycle will close with an assessment stage that answers the questions: "Was the instruction effective?", and "What is the next step for the learner?". In this stage, the instructor will deliver a prepared assignment in multiple-choice mode to the students to complete in a given period of time. The results and statistics of the assignment or quiz will be sent to the participants immediately after the given period. Figure 5 illustrated Assessment Stage with a simulated screen shot on a topic.

3 Meeting the Learning Needs

It is important to point out that it is not necessary to apply the four-stage learning cycle in all the courses. (Chan, Yim and Chen, 2005) The above stimulated synchronous interactive online learning system should allow the instructor to use any stage and in different order in real practice.

By introducing the concept of a learning cycle, the blended learning model will become more structured. The problem of becoming lost in hypermedia information web can then be solved. Knowledge can be delivered more effectively and efficiently. The system design may be more creative by providing the following features and arranging them in different learning stages:

- allow teachers to schedule their tutorials in a given period of time;
- provide video indexing function for teachers to correspond the lecture notes' content with video playback;
- allow teachers and students to interact in a virtual face-to-face environment;
- allow teachers to display and make remarks on the files they uploaded; and
- allow teachers to show special items such as 3-D objects through the connection to a visualizer.

On the other hand, as asynchronous E-Learning tools, such as WebCT and Blackboard were being used for several years, users may become familiar and comfortable with the existing course delivery mode and would resist the introduction of synchronous online learning platform. In certain cases, users may believe it will conflict with the value of flexible learning.

However, as mentioned, the E-Learning approach by the OUHK is a blended learning mode via printed materials, CD-Roms, lecture-less face-to-face tutorial sessions and OLE. In practice, instructors often give lectures in a one-to-many mode. However, in tutorial sessions, it is often that students need guidance from instructors in order to understand the teaching materials (in the printed text, CD-Roms or websites), one-to-one interactive mode would be more desirable. OUHK adopted a synchronous communication medium for the student to raise questions and obtain immediate feedback and interaction with tutor. As suggested by McLuhan (1989) in the work, quoted, "the medium is the message".

Moreover, there is a need for a more flexible and practical schedule of tutorial sessions since most of the OUHK students have full-time work during the day. It may be difficult to attend the course in the evening, as many of them regularly need to work overtime. With the synchronous online learning platform, the tutorial sessions can be arranged with higher priority, such as starting at late evening to enable students to cope with their overtime demand from employers. This is clearly more flexible for OUHK students and their work life style.

4 Conclusion

By using a more structured blended learning platform with learning cycle, students can gain the more guidance in learning and the University can provide more flexible E-Learning environment. However, "E-Learning is not a cheap alternative to face-to-face teaching" (Bates, 2002). But, for the OUHK, the combination of asynchronous and synchronous online learning platform will reduce the need to have classrooms around the city, (OUHK, 2005) with some cost saving in classroom rentals. This has direct impact on the tuition fee reduction, to attract more students and helps to increase enrolments. Although the "contact-hour course" is still labor-intensive (Graves, Henshaw, Oberlin and Parker, 1997), it is still acceptable to the OUHK which needs to provide mandatory face-to-face tutorial sessions. But the challenge is, as Bates describes, "to develop a system that encourages teaching units to be innovative and able to respond quickly to changes in subject matter, student needs, and technology. At the same time, redundancy and conflicting standards and policies across the institution must be avoided" (Bates, 2000). The University will need to provide additional resources for tutor training and briefing sessions to students for adoption of the new OLE, if the University is determined to have the full-scale phase in of using information technology in the learning environment.

References

Anderson, T.: Getting the Mix Right Again: An Updated and Theoretical Rationale for Interaction. In: International Review of Research in Open and Distance Learning, 4(2) (2003), Retrieved February 10, 2005, from http://www.irrodl.org/content/v4.2/anderson.html

Bates, A.W.: Theory and practice in the use of technology in distance education. In: Keegan, D (ed.) Theoretical principles of distance education. Routledge, London (1993)

Bates, A.W.: Managing Technological Change: Strategies for College and University Leaders. Jossey Bass, San Francisco (2000)

Bates, A.W.: National Strategies for E-Learning in Post-Secondary Education and Training. Paris: UNESCO/International Institute for Educational Planning (2002)

Chan, J.K.Y.: Web-based Learning and Interactive Tutoring System with Learning Cycle, Thesis of Master of Science in Computing, City University of Hong Kong (2003)

Chan, J.K.Y.: Experience in developing interactive conferencing tool (voice chat), Communications Technology Forum, Island Learning Centre, OUHK, January 15, 2005 (2005)

Chan, J.K.Y., Law, K.: A need for a fine tuned interactive online learning system with learning cycle. In: The conference of the 21st ICDE World Conference on Open Learning and Distance Education, Hong Kong, February 18-22, 2004 (2004)

Chan, J.K.Y., Yim, P.Y., Chen, L.: Web-based interactive learning system and learning cycle. China Educational Technology (3) (2005)

Chizmar, J.F., Walbert, M.S.: Web-Based Learning Environments Guided by Principles of Good Teaching Practice. The Journal of Economic Education 30, 248–259 (1999)

Chung, L.: Survey on OUHK students' use of IT – 2003, unpublished report, The Open University of Hong Kong, Hong Kong (2003)

City University of Hong Kong. Strategic Plan 2003 to 2008: Meeting the Challenge of Change (2002). Retrieved March 20, 2007, from http://www.cityu.edu.hk/op/plan/plan_2003-2008_01.htm

Crawford, C.: Understanding Interactivity. Self published, 2000. Republished 2002, by No Starch Press as The Art of Interactive Design (2000)

Duderstadt, J.J., Atkins, D.E., Houweling, D.V.: Higher education faces a brave new world. Higher Education in the Digital Age, pp. 3–22 (2002)

Graves, W., Henshaw, R., Oberlin, J., Parker, A.: Infusing information technology into the academic process. In: Peterson, M., Dill, D., Mets, L.A. and Associates (eds.) Planning and Management for a Changing Environment, pp. 432–452. Jossey Bass, San Francisco (1997)

Gunn, C.: Virtual technologies in higher education: vision or reality? In: Peters, M., Roberts, P. (eds.) Virtual technologies and tertiary education, pp. 134–145. Routledge, London (1998)

HKU. The University of Hong Kong Strategic Development 2003-2008, (2002) Retrieved March 20, 2007, from http://www.hku.hk/strategic-booklet/text/eng-html.htm

McLuhan, M., Fiore, Q.: The Medium is the Message. Touchstone, New York (1989)

OUHK. Business Plan 2003–2006, (2002) Retrieved November 30, 2005, from https://staff.intranet.ouhk.edu.hk/items/po/bp/index.htm

OUHK. The Open University of Hong Kong Staff Intranet. (2005) Retrieved February 13, 2005, http://www.ouhk.edu.hk

Raskin, J.: The Humane Interface. New Directions for Designing Interactive Systems. Addison-Wesley, Reading (2000)

Vermeer, R., Murphy, D.: What students want – students get?. In: Paper presented at the 18th Annual Conference of AAOU, Shanghai, November 28-30, 2004 (2004)

Uys, P.M.: Towards the Virtual Class: Technology Issues from a Fractal Management Perspective. In: Proceedings of the ED-MEDIA 99-World Conference on Educational Multimedia, Hypermedia & Telecommunications. AACE: Seattle (1999) Retrieved February 10, 2005, from http://www.globe-online.com/philip.uys/www.globe-online.com, philip.uys,edmedia1999.htm

Uys, P.M., Siverts, S.A.: Managing Technological Transformation in Higher Education: A Southern African Perspective. In: Proceedings of the 22nd World International Council for Distance Education Conference, Dusseldorf, Germany (2001)

Vermeer, R., Murphy, D.: What students want - students get?. Paper presented at the 18th Annual Conference of AAOU, Shanghai, November 28-30, 2004 (2004)

Wong, W.-m.: Electronic Library Services for Distance Learners - Its Developments in the Open University of Hong Kong. In: Proceedings of the ICDE Librarians Roundtable, 11-12, The Open University of Hong Kong, pp. 82–85. Open University of Hong Kong, Hong Kong (1999)

Yuen, K.S.: Replacing postal mail by electronic mail for communication in distance education: how is this achieved at the OUHK?. In: Paper presented at the 18th Annual Conference of AAOU, Shanghai, November 28-30, 2004 (2004)

The Marriage of Rousseau and Blended Learning: An Investigation of 3 Higher Educational Institutions' Praxis

Esyin Chew[1], Norah Jones[1], and David Turner[2]

[1] Centre for Excellence in Learning and Teaching (CELT),
[2] Education Department at Faculty of Humanities and Social Science,
University of Glamorgan, United Kingdom, CF37 1DL
{echew, njones2, dturner}@glam.ac.uk

Abstract. This paper sets out the central problem of current blended learning research that it does not have an appropriate focus on educational theory. The paper explains how the blended learning praxis in higher education can be understood in terms of Rousseau's educational theory. The research methods for collecting qualitative data from 28 academics in 3 universities are explained concisely. The analysis and discussion of institutional practices are used to identify best practice for blended learning. The role of the educator and student on holistic learning are examined. Overall, the authors urge that the focal point of blended learning research should not merely focus on the innovative technology and instructional design issues; educational theories remain the fundamental foundation for any educationalist as well as for any educational technologist.

Keywords: Blended learning, educational theory, educational technology, higher education.

1 Introduction

"...blended leaning could become one of the most significant developments of the 21st century." [26, p. 26]

Blended Learning is a phrase which is increasingly being used in higher education. However, Whitelock [27] claims that blended learning has not gained ground with theorists but is embraced by practitioners. Practitioners of technology and education show more interest in blended learning than educational theorists do. Boyle [6] further explains that the design and development of blended learning solutions should be pedagogically driven.

There has been an increasing number studies on blended learning programmes, which have examined such aspects as its effectiveness and its impact on learning in modern higher educational [22, 16, 21, 24] and how it promotes the innovative dialogues and practices in the learning environment [5]. The increasing interest shown by researchers in these topics has gone hand in hand with the development of technology, especially the emergence of the internet, rich media objects [26], mobile technology and artificial intelligence [7].

H. Leung et al. (Eds.): ICWL 2007, LNCS 4823, pp. 641–652, 2008.

Loveless [18] asserts that technological development is a cultural artifact in the experience of students and educators. Technology is a tool of cultural artifact to the educator or student who applies it. It is varying from one individual to another and one discipline to another. Dewey [11] argues that if the learner is not trained in the right use of the tools, there is grave danger that he may deprave himself and injure others. Croft [9] explains Dewey's idea in the following statement:

"...individuals inappropriately acquainted with the technologies in contemporary use risk deterioration of self and damage society itself..." (p. 302)

Otte [21] further emphasises that the tool, technology, should be thought of merely as a means, and that pedagogical ends should be paramount. Matthews [19] suggests an interesting metaphor, namely that an educator without the pedagogy end is like a sailor without a rudder - blown around by whatever fashions and technology which dominate the current educational direction.

In the blended learning context, the learning process may be insignificant if the technology adopted does not perform consistently or if it is not coherent with the educational considerations. This result in two critical questions: Are such pedagogical considerations underpinned by adequate educational theories or are they merely common sense but labeled as "learning theories"? Does such theory speak to the needs of educators or students from different disciplines?

Hence, there is a need to explore educational theory and its relationship with blended learning. The educational philosopher, Jean-Jacques Rousseau was chosen in this research because he is the earliest and influential educationalist who scattered the traditional educational ideas as to the replacement of banking concept by investigation and reason [10].

2 The Marriage of Rousseau and Blended Learning

The systematic integration of technology into education may only take place when the technologist is able to understand educational theories and embed them to meet the needs of educators and students [4]. Technologies and effective content development methods are the major concern in most of the blended learning practices, at the expense of the educational theories underneath. How blended learning practice is driven by educational theories is rarely considered.

In general, current blended learning practices in higher education underline Dewey's [12, 25] and Vygotsky's [8, 14] conceptions of social interaction, social constructivism and a guided learning environment. However, this paper uses the theoretical framework taken from Rousseau, who claimed that the goal of education should be to cultivate humanity's natural tendencies [23, 13]. This overarching philosophy can be linked to the development of holistic blended learning practice.

Rousseau's central idea is to reject the authority of the teacher and place an emphasis on individual reasoning and reflection. The student must be developed in the consciousness of complete freedom. The student must commit to the reasoning willingly. The learning process is not instilling by an authoritarian teacher but developing according to the dictates of human nature, not to the authoritative instructions from an educator. Rousseau also contended that the three great teachers of man were nature, man, and experience, and that the second and third tended to destroy the value of the first [10]. The challenge for the educator is to create such a free and natural learning environment, but with certain constraints, without learners recognising the constraint. The constraint is meant to protect the learner from disruption from "man and experience". This is the challenge for the educators.

This perception should be inevitably a major consideration in blended learning design and development. Student-led instruction using educational technologies can be used to create an open and free discussion space within a context. The collaborative tools such as online discussion boards and wikis allow participants to commit to open reasoning, open investigation and reflection on knowledge. The educator or the editorial board plays the role of facilitator to create the constraint, for instance to delete disruptive information or to suggest guidelines to the learner in such an e-environment in a non-authority manner. The learner is the decision maker and he or she can choose which information to agree with or to take issue with.

Rousseau's educational idea is to educate people to bring out their natural goodness, self-esteem, independence, compassion and equality [15]. This is a difficult aim and cannot be realised in the face-to-face classroom. The process of education is thoroughly developmental and it shall follow the growth of human 'nature'. Blogs and Wikis allow the learner to practice social interactions as well as to express their candid views and reflections. Through the reasoning and investigation process, learning is cultivated in a natural way. The learner will thus be fully developed not only in relation to their knowledge but also in relation to their ethical development because the education process is by internal nature and not by external forces. Whatever is posted on the web would always be there and open for review and criticism. The learner will be conscious of her/himself as an independent individual, responsible for her/his own thoughts and actions, completely independent from others, yet able to interact with others and direct her/his life by reason.

Before the time of Rousseau educationalists had opined that the education is a kind of top (educator) - down (learner) instilling concept. Rousseau enlightens the later educationists to "autonomy as an educational environment". Hence, the aim of this paper is to study Rousseau's pedagogical practice, and to consider how it might be developed in the context of blended learning. Based on this view of pedagogical practice, it will go on to investigate three current higher education institutions which are embedding blended learning into their teaching, both formally and informally.

3   Research Method

Anderson [2] defines education as a process and therefore a research method which is flexible and process-oriented is needed. According to Adelman [1], case study methodology can be used to evaluate the flexibility of reality especially in the variety and complexity of educational purposes and environments. With these boundaries, the present study incorporated case studies with qualitative-quantitative interactive continuum methodology [20] because such a method integrates the strengths of both qualitative and quantitative strategies. First, the arguments of Rousseau are studied. In order to study the practice in higher education institutions, three universities were visited and observed. 28 academic staffs and 6 students from varying disciplines were observed and interviewed. Interviews lasted between 40 minutes to 2.5 hours. Qualitative as well as quantitative data has been collected from their teaching and learning experiences. The names of the interviewees as well as the institutions are anonymous due to considerations of confidentiality and ethics.

The principal criterion in the selection of exemplary higher educational institutions was not "which HEI represent the totality?", but rather, "which group of HEIs can provide a better understanding of the research questions?" and "which group of HEIs reflect strong, positive and constructive examples of the research interest?" Given these criterions, a diverse group of HEIs and faculties were needed. For instance the traditional old universities and the new universities upgraded from polytechnics, and the contrasting nature of disciplines related to technology such as a Faculty of Computer Science and Faculty of Education; or the Faculty of Information and Communication Technology and the Faculty of Humanities and Social Sciences are proposed to meet the criteria stated above. To maximize the findings in a case study, a range of formal and informal data collection instruments such as recorded face-to-face interviews and site visits to the case study institutions were used. The responses have been analysed and discussed in the following section.

4   Discussion and Analysis

28 academic staffs were formally interviewed and their disciplines are summarized in the table below:

Table 1. The Disciplines of the Interviewees

University Category \ Disciplines	University A (Old university with 102 years of history)	University B (New university with 6 years of history)	University C (New university with 14 years of history)	Total
Science, Engineering, Computing and IT	6	8	3	17
Art, Language, Education, Business, Humanities and Social Sciences	4	3	4	11
Total	10	11	7	28

The major technologies and E-Learning system used in these three universities were investigated and observed. Overall, the effort on E-Learning development is mainly initiated at institutional level. However, awareness of, and commitment to, blended learning varies from one institution to another. The discussion on this section focuses on cross-institution comparison based on Rousseau's educational ideas. The data were used to identify and analyse institutional policies and pedagogical issues in three main areas: (1) Blended learning awareness and best practices which exemplify their institutional policies, together with actual implementation; (2) The role of lecturer after embedding blended learning (3) The value of blended learning in promoting holistic learning. Table 2 illustrates the overview and the preliminary observations from the four months of data collection.

Table 2. Overview of the Preliminary Data Collection

	University A	University B	University C
Blended Learning Awareness	Less awareness of blended learning as well as E-Learning.	Awareness on E-Learning space than blended learning.	Awareness of blended learning across the university.
Blended Learning Practices	Not an institutional-wide commitment. The blended learning practices are up to the faculty and individual academic interest.	Made a commitment to web-based mediated learning. Aimed to promote the use of ICT and IT-intensive learning through innovative courses and learning support systems. Support the web-based leaning space intensively with workshop and training.	Made a commitment to the adoption of Blended Learning across the institution. A three-year project to embed Blended Learning across the University's provision with high publicity. A clear model, named continuum of E-Learning is used.
VLE Implemented Across Institution	**Elearning**, an in-house built web-based learning management system but not well publicized to the academics and students. Many lecturers and students are not aware of the existence of such system.	**WEBLE**, an in-house built virtual learning space and courseware for the academics and students. Known by most of the lecturers and students.	**Blackboard**, Question*mark* Perception, in-house built rich media or web-based applications based on bidding process initiated by the academics. Known by most of the lecturers and students.
Technology or Pedagogy?	Emphasis on the traditional instructional methods.	Emphasis on the technological concerns.	Emphasis on both technological and pedagogical concerns.

4.1 Blended Learning Awareness and Best Practices

Figures 1 and 2 depict the awareness of blended learning in these three universities. From the interview, 63% of the interviewees were aware of the concept and definition of blended learning, although one interviewee out of the 63% has a misconception about the definition of blended learning:

Interviewee B3: In my opinion, blended learning is same as hybrid learning, I think they are similar.

Fig. 1. The Awareness of Blended Learning

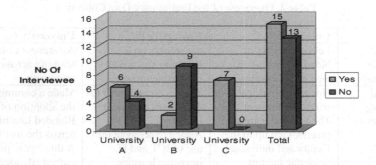

Fig. 2. The Awareness of Blended Learning by Institution

A large numbers of the academics in University B have never heard of the term "Blended Learning". Less concern was focused on the pedagogical issues, as the institutional ethos was shaped by the fact that the institution has a background as a vocational college. Most of the academics who understand and agree on the benefits of teaching mediated by technologies were from University A and C. The latter has obviously made a commitment to the adoption of blended learning across the institution's provision, driven by a three-year project with high publicity such as a well-design blended learning website with exemplars of case studies, monthly seminars and a road show. It has a clear institutional policy to embed blended learning across the campus compared with the other two universities. Such practice is inspired by a continuum of E-Learning model shown in the figure 3. This blended learning model shows the concise blend of an individual as well as institutional growing in blended

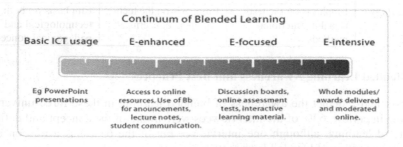

Fig. 3. Continuum of E-Learning [17]

learning. The self evaluation state and the direction ahead are well-defined for anyone who adopts this model.

The clear model embedding across the University C has raised the awareness of the academics as well as students on blended learning. Such awareness is the initial and substantive move for the changes. Few of the positive responses from the academics after using technology to complement the face-to-face classroom are clearly presented in the following:

> *Interviewee C3: I have used Blackboard as support material and engaging dialogue with students. I found that very helpful.*

> *Interviewee C2: I am quite excited about the prospect to be able to use Questionmark Perception...I would like to be able to use something like that to give students formative feedback and summative feedback as well...I am quite interested in the technology that can be interactive.*

> *Interviewee C6: Yes, I started to use Blackboard more this year compared with last year...at the moment it is easier for me to go through the lecture, it's all there...If there is something that I forgot, they are going to be there, I know all the information is there.*

However, sufficient resources such as technical and IT staff as well as educationalist, financial support from the management are the key factors for embedding blended learning across the institution after awareness rising. These are the major concerns raised from the academics:

> *Interviewee C3: I think you got to sort out this resource...there must be some sense of resources available; the university is either bite the bullets and pay for it, or forget all about this.*

> *Interview B8: ...depending on the implementation, depending on the management wanted the lecturer to be as a designer or executor. It would be a good thing if he is a designer and back-up by a group of technical team...For example **the lecturer is the director of a movie and back up by a team of people**, this is excellent. If he is the director and the cameraman, and also in charged of the lighting yet worrying about the sound effect, he will kill himself at the end.*

The idea of "director and support team" has precisely explained the successful mechanism in blended learning. Interestingly University A has no clear institutional-wide policy to embed blended learning however their awareness came from individual research interest, the culture and facilities at the faculty level, and above all, from the individual passion for enhancing the learning and teaching quality:

> *Interviewee A2: ...when you get your hands on the digital one such as computer, I think you can't go back anymore. I mean you just have to use it...it is a so effective!*

Most of the interviewees agree with the teaching and learning will be enhanced when they are mediated by technology. However it emphatically plays as a supplementary tool to compliment face-to-face rather than replacing it, technology can never replace the face-to-face instruction. This point is precisely stated by the following interviewees:

> *Interviewee B2: To me, there is always the main stream and supplementary in education. And the main stream will never change, from the very beginning till the end, the things which are changed are the supplementary and tools. Regardless the technologies, or chalks or paper, the main stream would never change.*

On the other hand, these two elements can be also seen as a symbiosis or conflating for better teaching and learning experience:

> *Interviewee A3: Blended Learning make use technology and also the humanity values, face-to-face... the technology alone is not enough, with the human alone is still also have certain constraint, as we are now in a technological world. So we need to combine both.*

University B aimed to offer the learning experiences that instill in students a consciousness of their role in a rapidly changing and technological oriented world with a strong sense of professional and social responsibility. This aligned with Rousseau's view on education is how to prepare a better individuals to construct a better society, not how to teach or learn effectively. However, such ideal is too theoretical and yet to be imparted to the academics and students practices. The current implementation of blended learning across the university is still in the "unawareness" and technological-focus stage.

4.2 The Role of the Lecturer After Embedding Blended Learning

One of the research questions is to obtain the interviewees' opinion on whether the role of lecturer will be or will not be changed by embedding educational technologies into the teaching and learning practices. The below table describes the quantitative findings:

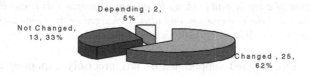

Fig. 4. Will the Role of the Lecturer be Changed after Embedding Blended Learning?

25 academics opine that their role would be changed after embedding blended learning, whereas 13 academics assert an opposite view. This is a debating issue from the pedagogical perspective. There is an essential view offered from academic discussed next:

> *Interviewee A5: With the advancement of the Internet, the information rich society, nobody claim that we know everything. We have students who are hardworking, they know more than us. The lecturers are no longer dictate, we merely facilitate.*

The role of the lecturer will be changed from merely knowledge deliverer to knowledge facilitator. In facts, Rousseau against this kind of "top-down" knowledge instilling process in education centuries ago and it should not have happened today. The academics who argue that the role will not be changed fall into the group of senior and experienced educator. They view technology-driven teaching as the different form of instruction method without changing the main role as an educator:

> *Interviewee B2: ... Before the time of white board and marker, people were using black board and chalk...You will use Power Point after such technology had been invented. In the future, you may use other new things when they are invented. However, these technologies are helping us to conduct our classes in a better way.... who is the one who organise and conduct the class? The lecturer is..*

The argument here is: what are the fundamental role(s) of a lecturer? According to Rousseau, the role of the educator is to create an autonomy and nature learning environment, not by any techniques to instill the knowledge to learner. The learner learns from self reflection and reasoning, not to the authoritative instructions or "knowledge transfer" from educator. Hence,

> *"It's depends on the role in the past. If your role is the "baby-sitter" to the students then you would change. But if your role isn't spoon feeding at the beginning then it would not be changed. To me, my role never change in the past ten plus years. I don't care there is Internet or no". ~ Interviewee A8.*

Relatively an experienced e-moderator concludes this with an insight view:

> *Interviewee C7: When we first started delivering e-moderating course, we have a very firmly view, that if you are a good tutor offline and you would be a good tutor online...you are a good tutor means you are a good tutor whatever the medium is.*

This view shows that good teaching is driven by pedagogy and it is not platform dependant. The technology as a means, and that pedagogical ends should be paramount.

4.3   The Values of Blended Learning in Promoting Holistic Learning

Blended learning does help in evaluating soft skills and promoting holistic learning in the sense of not only assess then task accomplishment but the hidden and high order thinking and communication skill. The following academics' explicate such perspective:

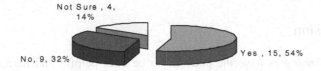

Fig. 5. Blended Learning help in Holistic Learning?

> *Interviewee C7: if I monitor their progress using some kind of online discussion forum or blog for their experiences, I can see who is participating and who is giving leadership and in which the leadership is being challenged and where the conflict is...so I think they are very powerful tools...not about the task but about the individual and powerful learning tools.*

This experience actually aligned with Rousseau's cultivation of human kind natural tendencies. It can be realised and enriched educational technologies such as blog and wiki in order to stimulate the natural tendencies such as social interaction, knowledge sharing, free and open discussion and etc. It is merely difficult to be realised in the face-to-face classroom with space and time constraint:

> *Interviewee A7: If the number of students is not very big. If you have a very big class you will not have the time to read through whatever the students' post.*

Rousseau's philosophy of education, therefore, is not related simply at particular techniques that best ensure that the students in a big class will absorb information and concepts. His goal was to produce an education that maximized individual human potential rather than restricted it. From such basis, the educator shall make sure of the current technologies such as blog and wiki to create an open and independent learning environment to reflect and to develop the human potential such as critical thinking and to throw out their ideas. Through the dialogues and ideas exchange, the relationship between educator and learner are brought closer:

> *Interviewee A3: To if you have the wiki or blog, they become more interactive in the sense, more creative and encourage students for throwing out their ideas...*

> *Interviewee B8: I join some of the students' blog from Journalism study. ...Sometimes I do give some comments and I feel my relationship with them is much closer. I think this is helpful as I know their life and what happening around them, as well as their views at political issues...This blog is unique as they really stimulate the critical thinking in life.*

Time constraint indeed is above all the critical considerations for the lecturer:

> *Interviewee B5: I am not sure how far such technologies can help but one thing I can sure is with such things the students would be 'troubling' me more than the past.*

Without the understanding of the educational theory and individual passion in education, such obstacles would lead to frustration and the most, drop out from blended learning.

5 Conclusion

The new technologies have the potential to be both helpful and harmful, as do the educational systems. Educators and educational technologist cannot merely geared by all sorts of E-Learning technologies but left behind the educational theory. Instead, quick responses and reasonably understanding of educational theories are required [3]. The heart of the blended learning praxis lays the need for a deep understanding of the trends and educational theories, only through that understanding can emerge initial interest and passion.

Rousseau's educational theory was chosen for this research. His central idea is to reject the authority of the teacher and emphasis on individual reasoning and reflection. The student must be committed to the reasoning willingly and in an autonomous environment. The learning process is not instilling by an authoritarian teacher but developing according to the dictates of human nature, not to the authoritative instructions from educator. Thus, this research investigated the current praxis of blended learning in higher education based on Rousseau's idea. The result reflected a clear institutional policy will promote the awareness across the university, follow up individual interest and passion on teaching and learning. Resources and support team in place is the critical successful factor. The role of the lecturer will be enhanced if the educator does not realise the values of "creating autonomy, not by any techniques to instill the knowledge to learner" initially. In addition to this, blended learning does help in holistic learning with bringing closer the relationship between educator and learner with autonomous communication, and to stimulate the natural tendencies without space and fixed-time constraint. In contrary, language barriers and the abuse usage may cause frustration and above all, time constraint is the major challenges for implementing blended learning.

In conclusion, it is asserted that the educational theories remain the fundamental foundation for any educationalist as well as educational technologist. With such understanding and passion would triumph over the challenges mentioned above. Blended learning researchers, therefore, are urged to shift the focal point from innovative technology and instructional design issues, to educational foundation.

References

1. Adelman, C., Kemimis, S., Jenkins, D.: Rethinking Case Study: Notes from the Second Cambridge Conference. In: H. (ed.) Towards a Science of The Singular, Centre for Applied Research in Education, University of East Anglia, pp. 45–61 (1980)
2. Anderson, G.: Fundamentals of educational Research, 2nd edn. RoutlegeFalmer London (2004)
3. Aspy, D.N., Aspy, C.B.: Toward Effective Advocacy for Humanistic Values. Journal of Humanistic Education and Development 37(2), 85–95 (1998)
4. Bailey, G., Pownell, D.: Tecnology Staff-Development and Support Programs: Applying Abraham Maslow's Hierarchy of Needs. Learning and Leading with Technology 26(3), 48–64 (2006)
5. Barker, T.: Computer Adaptive Assessment and Its Use in the Development of a Student Model for Blended Learning, Blended Learning – Promoting Dialogue in Innovation and Practice, University of Hertfordshire. In: First Annual Blended Learning Conference. Learning in Higher Education and Workplace Learning Settings' Hatfield (2006)
6. Boyle, T.: A Dynamic, Systematic Method for Developing Blended Learning, Education. Communication and Information 5(3), 221–232 (2005)

7. Chew, E., Jones, N.: Generic Model of Computation for Intelligent Computer-aided Assessment Progress (iCAP). In: Chew, E., Jones, N. (eds.) University of Loughborough: Tenth International Computer Assisted Assessment (CAA) Conference, Loughborough, pp. 107–124 (July4-5, 2006)
8. Cortazzi, M., Hall, B.: Vygotsky and learning. Education Libraries Journal 42, 17–21 (1999)
9. Croft, R.S.: What Is a Computer in the Classroom? A Deweyan Philosophy. Journal of Educational Technology Systems 22, 301 (1994)
10. Cubberley, E.P.: The History Of Education, Blackmask Online (2003)
11. Dewey, J.: Democracy and Education: An Introduction to the Philosophy of Education. The Macmillan Company, New York (1922)
12. Ehrlich, T.: Reinventing John Dewey's Pedagogy as a University Discipline. The Elementary School Journal, ProQuest Psychology Journals 98, 489 (1998)
13. James, J.D.: Jean-Jacques Rousseau. In: James, F., Bradley, D. (eds.) The Internet Encyclopaedia of Philosophy (2006), http://www.iep.utm.edu/[Accessed: 3.3.2007]
14. Jennifer, A.J.S., Monfries, M.: Motivation to Learn in University Students: Links with Vygotsky's Assisted Discovery. In: European Conference on Educational Research. Bath (1995)
15. Johnston, I.: Introduction to the Eighteenth Century and Rousseau's Emile. Media Relations & Publications Department, Malaspina University-College (1996)
16. Johnson, J., Tang, M.: Integration of e-Management, e-Development and E-Learning Technologies for Blended Course delivery. AACE Journal 13(2), 185–199 (2005)
17. Jones, N.: Chapter 13: E-College Wales, A Case Study of Blended Learning. In: Bonk, C.J., Graham, C.R. (eds.) Handbook of blended learning: Global Perspectives, local designs, Pfeiffer Publishing, CA (2006)
18. Loveless, A.M.: Where do You Stand to Get a Good View of Pedagogy? Journal of Technology and Teacher Education 8(4), 337–349 (2006)
19. Matthews, M.: Knowledge, Action and Power. In: MACKIE, R. (ed.) Literacy and Revolution: the Pedagogy of Paulo Freire, Pluto Press, London (1980)
20. Newman, I., Benz, C.R.: Qualitative-Quantitative Research Research Methodology: Exploring the Interactive Continuum. Southern Illinois University Press, IL (1998)
21. Otte, G.: Using Blended Learning to Drive Faculty Development (And Vice Versa). Sloan-C Series 6, 71–84 (2005)
22. Ross, B., Gage, K.: Global Perspective on Blended Learning: Insight from WebCT and Our Customers in higher Education. In: Bonk, C.J., Graham, C.R. (eds.) Handbook of blended learning: Global Perspectives, local designs, Pfeiffer Publishing, CA (2006)
23. Rousseau, J.-J.: Emile. The Project Gutenberg EBook (2004)
24. Salmon, G., Lawless, N.: Management Education for the Twenty-First Century. In: Bonk, C.J., Graham, C.R. (eds.) Handbook of blended learning: Global Perspectives, local designs Ch, 28, Pfeiffer Publishing, CA (2006)
25. Simpson, D.J.: John Dewey's Concept of the Student. Canadian Journal of Education 26 (2001)
26. Thorne, K.: Blended Learning: How to Integrate Online & Traditional Learning, Kogan Page London, p. 18 (2003)
27. Whitelock, D.: Blended Learning: Forget the Name But What About The Claims? In: Whitelock, D., Mason, R. (eds.) Bledned Learning. Special Issue of Education, Communication and Information (2004)

Author Index

Lecture Notes in Computer Science

Sublibrary 3: Information Systems and Application, incl. Internet/Web and HCI

For information about Vols. 1– 4563
please contact your bookseller or Springer

Vol. 4802: J.-L. Hainaut, E.A. Rundensteiner, M. Kirchberg, M. Bertolotto, M. Brochhausen, Y.-P.P. Chen, S.S.-S. Cherfi, M. Doerr, H. Han, S. Hartmann, J. Parsons, G. Poels, C. Rolland, J. Trujillo, E. Yu, E. Zimányie (Eds.), Advances in Conceptual Modeling – Foundations and Applications. XIX, 420 pages. 2007.

Vol. 4801: C. Parent, K.-D. Schewe, V.C. Storey, B. Thalheim (Eds.), Conceptual Modeling - ER 2007. XVI, 616 pages. 2007.

Vol. 4797: M. Arenas, M.I. Schwartzbach (Eds.), Database Programming Languages. VIII, 261 pages. 2007.

Vol. 4796: M. Lew, N. Sebe, T.S. Huang, E.M. Bakker (Eds.), Human–Computer Interaction. X, 157 pages. 2007.

Vol. 4794: B. Schiele, A.K. Dey, H. Gellersen, B. de Ruyter, M. Tscheligi, R. Wichert, E. Aarts, A. Buchmann (Eds.), Ambient Intelligence. XV, 375 pages. 2007.

Vol. 4777: S. Bhalla (Ed.), Databases in Networked Information Systems. X, 329 pages. 2007.

Vol. 4761: R. Obermaisser, Y. Nah, P. Puschner, F.J. Rammig (Eds.), Software Technologies for Embedded and Ubiquitous Systems. XIV, 563 pages. 2007.

Vol. 4747: S. Džeroski, J. Struyf (Eds.), Knowledge Discovery in Inductive Databases. X, 301 pages. 2007.

Vol. 4744: Y. de Kort, W. IJsselsteijn, C. Midden, B. Eggen, B.J. Fogg (Eds.), Persuasive Technology. XIV, 316 pages. 2007.

Vol. 4740: L. Ma, M. Rauterberg, R. Nakatsu (Eds.), Entertainment Computing – ICEC 2007. XXX, 480 pages. 2007.

Vol. 4730: C. Peters, P. Clough, F.C. Gey, J. Karlgren, B. Magnini, D.W. Oard, M. de Rijke, M. Stempfhuber (Eds.), Evaluation of Multilingual and Multi-modal Information Retrieval. XXIV, 998 pages. 2007.

Vol. 4723: M. R. Berthold, J. Shawe-Taylor, N. Lavrač (Eds.), Advances in Intelligent Data Analysis VII. XIV, 380 pages. 2007.

Vol. 4721: W. Jonker, M. Petković (Eds.), Secure Data Management. X, 213 pages. 2007.

Vol. 4718: J. Hightower, B. Schiele, T. Strang (Eds.), Location- and Context-Awareness. X, 297 pages. 2007.

Vol. 4717: J. Krumm, G.D. Abowd, A. Seneviratne, T. Strang (Eds.), UbiComp 2007: Ubiquitous Computing. XIX, 520 pages. 2007.

Vol. 4715: J.M. Haake, S.F. Ochoa, A. Cechich (Eds.), Groupware: Design, Implementation, and Use. XIII, 355 pages. 2007.

Vol. 4714: G. Alonso, P. Dadam, M. Rosemann (Eds.), Business Process Management. XIII, 418 pages. 2007.

Vol. 4704: D. Barbosa, A. Bonifati, Z. Bellahsène, E. Hunt, R. Unland (Eds.), Database and XML Technologies. X, 141 pages. 2007.

Vol. 4690: Y. Ioannidis, B. Novikov, B. Rachev (Eds.), Advances in Databases and Information Systems. XIII, 377 pages. 2007.

Vol. 4675: L. Kovács, N. Fuhr, C. Meghini (Eds.), Research and Advanced Technology for Digital Libraries. XVII, 585 pages. 2007.

Vol. 4674: Y. Luo (Ed.), Cooperative Design, Visualization, and Engineering. XIII, 431 pages. 2007.

Vol. 4663: C. Baranauskas, P. Palanque, J. Abascal, S.D.J. Barbosa (Eds.), Human-Computer Interaction – INTERACT 2007, Part II. XXXIII, 735 pages. 2007.

Vol. 4662: C. Baranauskas, P. Palanque, J. Abascal, S.D.J. Barbosa (Eds.), Human-Computer Interaction – INTERACT 2007, Part I. XXXIII, 637 pages. 2007.

Vol. 4658: T. Enokido, L. Barolli, M. Takizawa (Eds.), Network-Based Information Systems. XIII, 544 pages. 2007.

Vol. 4656: M.A. Wimmer, J. Scholl, Å. Grönlund (Eds.), Electronic Government. XIV, 450 pages. 2007.

Vol. 4655: G. Psaila, R. Wagner (Eds.), E-Commerce and Web Technologies. VII, 229 pages. 2007.

Vol. 4654: I.-Y. Song, J. Eder, T.M. Nguyen (Eds.), Data Warehousing and Knowledge Discovery. XVI, 482 pages. 2007.

Vol. 4653: R. Wagner, N. Revell, G. Pernul (Eds.), Database and Expert Systems Applications. XXII, 907 pages. 2007.

Vol. 4636: G. Antoniou, U. Aßmann, C. Baroglio, S. Decker, N. Henze, P.-L. Patranjan, R. Tolksdorf (Eds.), Reasoning Web. IX, 345 pages. 2007.

Vol. 4611: J. Indulska, J. Ma, L.T. Yang, T. Ungerer, J. Cao (Eds.), Ubiquitous Intelligence and Computing. XXIII, 1257 pages. 2007.

Vol. 4607: L. Baresi, P. Fraternali, G.-J. Houben (Eds.), Web Engineering. XVI, 576 pages. 2007.

Vol. 4606: A. Pras, M. van Sinderen (Eds.), Dependable and Adaptable Networks and Services. XIV, 149 pages. 2007.

Vol. 4605: D. Papadias, D. Zhang, G. Kollios (Eds.), Advances in Spatial and Temporal Databases. X, 479 pages. 2007.

Vol. 4602: S. Barker, G.-J. Ahn (Eds.), Data and Applications Security XXI. X, 291 pages. 2007.

Vol. 4601: S. Spaccapietra, P. Atzeni, F. Fages, M.-S. Hacid, M. Kifer, J. Mylopoulos, B. Pernici, P. Shvaiko, J. Trujillo, I. Zaihrayeu (Eds.), Journal on Data Semantics IX. XV, 197 pages. 2007.

Vol. 4592: Z. Kedad, N. Lammari, E. Métais, F. Meziane, Y. Rezgui (Eds.), Natural Language Processing and Information Systems. XIV, 442 pages. 2007.

Vol. 4587: R. Cooper, J. Kennedy (Eds.), Data Management. XIII, 259 pages. 2007.

Vol. 4577: N. Sebe, Y. Liu, Y.-t. Zhuang, T.S. Huang (Eds.), Multimedia Content Analysis and Mining. XIII, 513 pages. 2007.

Vol. 4568: T. Ishida, S. R. Fussell, P. T. J. M. Vossen (Eds.), Intercultural Collaboration. XIII, 395 pages. 2007.

Vol. 4566: M.J. Dainoff (Ed.), Ergonomics and Health Aspects of Work with Computers. XVIII, 390 pages. 2007.

Vol. 4564: D. Schuler (Ed.), Online Communities and Social Computing. XVII, 520 pages. 2007.